Essentials
of Marketing

Joel R. Evans   Barry Berman

Hofstra University   Hofstra University

Essentials of Marketing

Macmillan Publishing Company

NEW YORK

Collier Macmillan Publishers

LONDON

Macmillan Publishing Company
866 Third Avenue, New York, New York 10022

Collier Macmillan Canada, Inc.

LIBRARY OF CONGRESS CATALOGING IN PUBLICATION DATA
Evans, Joel R.
  The essentials of marketing.

  Includes bibliographical references and index.
  1. Marketing.   I. Berman, Barry.   II. Title.
HF5415.E859   1984   658.8   83-9866
ISBN 0-02-334590-X

Printing: 1 2 3 4 5 6 7 8   Year: 4 5 6 7 8 9 0 1 2
ISBN   0-02-334590-X

To: Linda, Jennifer, and Stacey

Linda, Glenna, and Lisa

Preface

Our major goal in researching and writing *Essentials of Marketing* has been to develop a text that is appealing to both professors and students. When we started this project, a set of guidelines were established to attain this objective. We wanted *Essentials of Marketing* to be comprehensive, complete, well integrated, of moderate length, readable, real, contemporary, lively, and a mix of theory and applications. Both traditional and emerging areas of marketing would be examined in great detail.

We began formulating an outline for *Essentials of Marketing* after a thorough and free-flowing focus group interview with professors from a variety of colleges. This was followed by in-depth probing of our own students and a nationwide mail survey of marketing professors. On the basis of this research, we wrote the manuscript for the book. More than twenty professors throughout the country reviewed the manuscript and offered additional analysis. Appropriate revisions were made.

The completed *Essentials of Marketing* consists of nineteen chapters divided into eight parts. Part One is an introduction to marketing and contains an overview of marketing, the environment of marketing, and information for marketing decisions. Part Two examines consumers, both final and organizational, and the methods for developing a target market. Part Three provides an overview of product planning and a discussion of product planning from new products to deletion. Part Four deals with distribution planning, physical distribution, wholesaling, and retailing. Part Five centers on promotion planning and the elements of promotion: advertising, publicity, personal selling, and sales promotion. Part Six presents an overview of price planning and how to develop a price strategy. Part Seven expands the scope of marketing by looking at international marketing, service and nonprofit marketing, and marketing and society. Part Eight concludes the text with a discussion of marketing management and future planning.

Since both professors and students stressed the value of pedagogy, *Essentials of Marketing* includes the following:

- *Part openers* that introduce the material covered in each section of the text.
- *Chapter previews* that outline the major topics to be covered in each chapter.
- *Chapter objectives* that note the three to five learning goals in each chapter.
- *Opening vignettes* that begin each chapter with a real-life situation.
- *Numerous examples*—in Chapter 1 alone, Safeway Stores, Parker Brothers, the Brooklyn Academy of Music, Whirlpool, Scripto, Lubrizoil, higher education, Pillsbury, General Foods, B. F. Goodrich, May Department Stores, and Chrysler are among the illustrations provided.
- *Bold face key terms* that highlight key terms and concepts.

- *Descriptive margin notes* that summarize information throughout each chapter.
- *Extensive artwork, figures, photos, and tables* that explain marketing concepts and provide up-to-date information.
- *Chapter summaries* that recap the material in each chapter.
- *Listings of key terms* at the end of each chapter that encourage self-examination.
- *Discussion questions* that vary in scope and depth from definitions to complex decisions.
- *Cases* that are based on organizations such as Mennen, Bausch & Lomb, General Foods, Minnetonka, Coca-Cola, Nike, Sensormatic, The Limited, Kellogg, Nissan, Kodak, Radio Shack, Dayton Hudson, General Motors, American Airlines, IBM,

Helene Curtis, Levi Strauss, Procter & Gamble, H&R Block, and Manville. In all, there are 36 cases.
- *Appendixes* that cover hints for solving cases, careers in marketing, marketing arithmetic, and a glossary.
- *Name and subject indexes.*

A strong and well-rounded package accompanies *Essentials of Marketing*. The student study guide incorporates chapter objectives, chapter overviews, key terms, short-answer questions, discussion questions, and exercises. Comprehensive teaching materials are available for professors.

J. R. E.
B. B.

Acknowledgments

A number of colleagues throughout the United States participated in focus-group interviews and provided detailed reviews for *Essentials of Marketing*. We would like to thank them for their vital contributions:

Al Berkowitz
Kingsborough Community College

James Brock
Montana State University

John Bunnell
Broome Community College

Benjamin J. Cutler
Bronx Community College

Peter T. Doukas
Westchester Community College

Stanley Garfunkel
Queensborough Community College

Donald Gordon
Illinois Central College

Blaine Greenfield
Bucks County Community College

Nathan Himmelstein
Essex County College

J. Steven Kelly
DePaul University

William Layden
Golden West College

Edward J. Moore
State University of New York College at Plattsburgh

Donald Nagourney
New York Institute of Technology

Kenneth Papenfuss
Ricks College

Dennis Pappas
Columbus Technical Institute

Gregory M. Snere
Ellsworth Community College

Ed Timmerman
Abilene Christian University

Mildred Whitted
Saint Louis Community College at Forest Park

Martin Wise
Harrisburg Area Community College

Joyce Wood
Northern Virginia Community College

Gene C. Wunder
Ball State University

Many other colleagues responded to a lengthy questionnaire; we would like to recognize their assistance:

Ray Attner, Brookhaven College; **James D. Barnes**, California State College, Bakersfield; **Kenneth W. Blair**, Northern Montana College; **Charlane Bomrad**, Onondaga Community College; **James L. Brock**, Montana State University; **Harvey S. Bronstein**, Oakland Community College-Orchard Ridge; **John R. Brooks**, West Texas State University; **Lawrence Chase**, Tompkins Cortland Community College; **Nancy J. Church**, State University of New York College at Plattsburgh; **C. Robert Clements**, University of

Massachusetts at Boston; **D. A. Cords,** California State University-Fresno; **Michael F. D'Amico,** University of Akron; **Arnold Di Silvestro,** Davis and Elkins College; **Jeffrey Doutt,** Sonoma State University; **John Ernest,** Los Angeles City College; **Leslie Falk,** Jefferson College; **Harold Fell,** Community College of Rhode Island; **Herman Floyd,** Catonsville Community College; **George N. Freedman,** Dutchess Community College; **Peggy Gilbert,** Southwest Missouri State University; **Susan C. Green,** Ohio University; **James L. Grimm,** Illinois State University; **Timothy P. Hartman,** Ohio University; **Ellis L. Hoffman,** Saint Louis Community College at Meramec; **Donald L. James,** Fort Lewis College; **Kenneth L. Jensen,** Bradley University; **Donald L. Knight,** Lansing Community College; **Michael V. LaRocco,** College of St. Francis; **Ed Laube,** Macomb Community College; **David Litchford,** Utah Technical College at Provo; **James R. Maggert,** Grand View College; **F. Maidment,** University of South Carolina; **Hugh McCabe,** Westchester Community College; **James M. McHugh,** Saint Louis Community College at Forest Park; **Charles J. Meehan,** Hudson Valley Community College; **Harry J. Moak,** Macomb Community College; **Thomas E. Moritz,** Hardin-Simmons University; **J. Nagel,** Bronx Community College; **Leonard L. Palumbo,** Northern Virginia Community College; **Roy B. Payne,** Purdue University; **Barbara A. Pendleton,** University of South Carolina; **William S. Penn,** San Jose State University; **Barbara L. Piasta,** Somerset County College; **Donna Qureshi,** California State Polytechnic University-Pomona; **Glenn Roach,** South Plains College; **Karole Rocke,** Richland Community College; **James M. Rovelstad,** University of Wisconsin-Parkside; **Carol Rowey,** Community College of Rhode Island; **Daniel Sarel,** University of Miami; **Elaine Schiff,** Jefferson Community College; **David Sewer,** Pierce College; **Leonard Sheffield,** Tri-State University; **David E. Shepard,** Virginia Western Community College; **Robert E. Stanley,** Indiana State University; **Verna Stoner,** Columbus Technical Institute; **Ely A. Tarplin,** Suffolk County Community College; **Harold N. Thompson,** El Paso Community College; **F. G. Titlow,** St. Petersburg Junior College; **Rich Van Ausdal,** Dixie College; **L. M. Vukelich,** Portland Community College; **Kent R. Waggoner,** Vincennes University; **A. J. Walter,** Suffolk County Community College; **James A. Wegge,** Grossmont College; **David R. Wheeler,** Suffolk University; **Sumner M. White,** Massachusetts Bay Community College; **Kitty Wilkinson,** Southwest Missouri State University; **Joyce Wood,** Northern Virginia Community College; **Morrie R. Yohai,** New York Institute of Technology; **Robert F. Witherspoon,** Triton College.

We also appreciate the continued support of the marketing students and faculty at Hofstra, as well as the encouragement of Dean Herman A. Berliner.

Several people at Macmillan have worked hard on this project and we thank them all, in particular Bill Oldsey, Bob Doran, Dave Horvath, Leo Malek, Ed Neve, Bob Pirrung, Chip Price, and Steve Vana-Paxhia.

Carol Bloom and Phyllis Knauf were invaluable typists, who worked hard and fast. Linda Berman prepared the name and subject indexes.

To our wives and children, words cannot express our gratitude—without you, our efforts would have little meaning.

JOEL R. EVANS
BARRY BERMAN
HOFSTRA UNIVERSITY

Brief Contents

Contents

6 *Developing a Target Market*   *130*

Part Three
Product Planning   159

7 *An Overview of Product Planning*   161

8 *Product Planning: From New Products to Product Deletion*   192

Part Four
Distribution Planning   221

9 *An Overview of Distribution Planning and Physical Distribution*   223

13 *Personal Selling and Sales Promotion* 338

Part Six
Price Planning 365

14 *An Overview of Price Planning* 367

15 *Developing a Pricing Strategy* 390

Part Seven
Expanding The Scope of Marketing 423

16 *International Marketing* 425

Part
One

An Introduction to Marketing

Introduction to Part One

Chapter 1, an overview of marketing, shows the dynamics of marketing. The chapter broadly defines marketing, traces its evolution, and explains the marketing concept. The turbulent history and marketing practices of Chrysler are traced.

Chapter 2 examines the total environment within which marketing operates. Particularly emphasized are the controllable and uncontrollable factors that are directed and adapted to by an organization and its marketers. Without adequate environmental analysis, a firm is likely to function in a haphazard manner. A short-sighted, narrow-minded view of marketing and its environment must be avoided.

Chapter 3 explains why marketing decisions should be based on sound information in order to direct and adapt to the marketing environment. Marketing research is defined and the marketing research process is detailed. Marketing research may involve surveys, experiments, observation, and other forms of data collection. The marketing information system coordinates marketing research, monitoring of the environment, and data storage. It thus provides the basis for decision making.

An Overview of Marketing

1

Chapter Preview

Chapter Objectives

1 To illustrate the dynamic, exciting, changing nature of marketing

2 To define marketing and detail its importance, scope, and functions in a modern society

3 To trace the evolution of marketing from a production to a sales to a marketing department to a marketing company orientation

4 To examine the marketing concept

5 To present and contrast successful and unsuccessful approaches to marketing

Tic Tac mints were introduced in the United States in 1972. By 1975, Tic Tac had a 12 per cent market share in the U.S. breath mint/hard candy business. It became the fourth most popular product in this category, trailing only Certs, Life Savers, and Dynamints. Initial success was due to the convenience and sanitary nature of Tic Tac's plastic package (which appealed to adults) and the fun aspect of the small mint (which appealed to children)—"Put a Tic Tac in your mouth and get a bang out of life." Children accounted for 60 per cent of sales. Figure 1-1 shows Tic Tac's unique packaging.

However, Tic Tac's sales quickly dropped, as many competitors heightened their emphasis on bubble gum for children. In particular, Bubble Yum took away sales from Tic Tac. Then, the adult market dropped as another competitor introduced Velamints, which was positioned as a strong breath refresher that was sugar-free. Despite added flavors and larger-sized packages, Tic Tac's market share fell to 2 per cent, number nine, in 1979.

At this point, Tic Tac decided to give up the children's market, since this segment was too "fickle" and the product was not really meant to be a fun item. Tic Tac was intended to be a breath mint, with convenient and modern packaging. As a result, ad-

Figure 1-1
The unique packaging of Tic Tac mints, which have only 1½ calories in each mint

vertising was now aimed exclusively at adults. Sales and distribution organizations were revised. Tic Tac pushed hard to overcome distributors' and retailers' resistance and re-established the brand as if it were new. A low-calorie theme was stressed and comparisons were made to Velamints in ads. Within two years, Tic Tac attained a 6 per cent market share, fifth place in the market. Full national advertising was planned for 1983, to spread the Tic Tac story and further increase sales.[1]

The Dynamics of Marketing

Marketing is stimulating, quick-paced, and influential.

Marketing is an exciting, dynamic, and contemporary field. It encompasses a wide range of activities such as environmental scanning and marketing research, consumer analysis, product and service planning, distribution planning, promotion planning, price planning, international marketing, and marketing management.

The picture portfolio following page 10 demonstrates the breadth of marketing and how it influences every aspect of our daily lives—yet is new in each situation. Through the next several examples, we will glimpse the varied nature of marketing and look for fundamental concepts.

The major U.S. automobile manufacturers are again offering extended service warranties, lasting from two to five years, that are broad in nature and part of the purchase price of a car. This is a return to a practice followed in the 1960s. The new programs are intended to satisfy customers, not make profits. The auto makers are responding to a soft market caused by a weak economy, strong foreign competition, and some unhappiness among car owners as models get smaller, lighter, and less powerful.

Safeway, the country's leading supermarket chain, is developing "superstores" to broaden its product lines and sell more-profitable merchandise. These outlets sell everything from Sony color televisions to small home appliances to 8,000 + different food items. The superstores require further decisions by the management of Safeway regarding credit, closing of small stores, and computerized inventory reports.

Parker Brothers had big plans for Riviton, a kit of plastic parts, rubber rivets, and a riveting tool with which children could put together anything from a windmill to an airplane. Its first year on the market, Riviton outsold all previous toys the company had introduced. After the sale of 450,000 Riviton sets, an eight year-old boy choked to death by swallowing one of its quarter-inch-long rubber rivets. Parker's president read the autopsy report and concluded the toy was safe. "After all, peanuts are the greatest cause of strangulation among children and nobody advocates banning the peanut." Ten months later, with Riviton's sales well on the way to an expected $8.5 million for the year, a second child strangled on a rivet. Despite costs that could be as high as $10 million, Parker Brothers' president halted production and sales and recalled the toy. As a result, the company turned to other product concepts and beefed up its new-product development process to regain the sales lost by the removal of Riviton. By 1981, through the use of Strawberry Shortcake and Star Wars characters and new video cartridges, Parker Brothers was able to obtain record profits.[2]

The Brooklyn Academy of Music (BAM) is a thriving cultural center that markets ballet and theater the way other firms market television sets. For example, to promote its first African dance series, BAM held a street fair with African crafts and an elephant ride for children. To boost ballet sales, it conducted a "dance lover's sweepstakes." Prizes included a trip to London, two treatments by a dancer's masseur, and a stage backdrop from Swan Lake complete with a giant plastic swan. Said a BAM official, "We're in the business of selling a perishable product. In supermarkets, lettuce wilts. In our case, the curtain goes up."[3]

Whirlpool recently unveiled a new long-term marketing plan centering on "quality, value, honesty, service to 'make your world a little easier.'" This plan is intended to enhance the firm's reputation and continue its commitment to customer service, without "exaggerated claims."[4] Figure 1-2 shows one of the advertisements Whirlpool began placing in 1982.

Throughout most of the 1970s, Scripto had sizable losses on its products. Then, the company overhauled its marketing management team and began to develop attractive new products that capitalized on its strengths. Important new products were the Scripto Erasable Pen, Ultra Lite disposable lighter, and Wilkinson Sword self-sharpening knife ("The built-in sharpener sharpens the stainless-steel blade."). Low prices and heavy advertising were used to support the new entries. In 1982, Scripto showed a large profit.[5]

Lubrizoil, a company in the oil additive market, has the widest

Figure 1-2
**Quality, Value, Honesty, and
Service at Whirlpool**

They come with a promise.

At Whirlpool, we build a promise into everything we make.

A promise of pride in our workmanship, to create good honest quality. Like a washer and a dryer with the ease and flexibility of solid state touch controls. And a dishwasher you can set to start washing hours after you turn it on.

The promise of a design that assures you your money's worth. Like a refrigerator that uses solid state technology to monitor itself and help you protect your food. And ranges and microwave ovens specially designed to be easy to clean.

And finally the promise of our entire company to stand behind each product with pride. With our trained and authorized Tech-Care® service representatives. And with our toll-free 24-hour Cool-Line® service to help you with problems or questions you might have.*

Every major home appliance that carries our name also carries our promise.

Whirlpool can't promise to solve all your problems. But we can make your world just a little bit easier.

*Call 800-253-1301. In Alaska and Hawaii call 800-253-1121. In Michigan call 800-632-2243.

Whirlpool
Home Appliances

Making your world a little easier.

Reprinted by permission.

product range of any firm in the market and does about twice the business of large oil companies. Additives account for 20 per cent of the content of a can of motor oil. The additives increase the oil's slipperiness, control its thickness, improve its durability, and enable it to perform for up to 12,000 miles between oil changes.

Education experts warn colleges and universities of potential problems resulting from a decrease in the number of eighteen-year-olds, apprehension about high tuition and other costs, and society's lowering value on a liberal arts education. Colleges and universities need to improve their offerings, appeal to different consumer groups, and upgrade their marketing skills if they are to hold their own in the 1980s.

In many companies, inventory managers are very much the people in the middle. Sales officials request more inventory on hand, while financial executives try to keep inventory investments down (as inventory managers try to buy ahead to stay ahead of inflation). The inventory manager attempts to balance the costs of inventory against the risks of stock-outs. The uncertainty of sales also complicates the role of the inventory manager in ordering merchandise.

The preceding illustrations show the involvement of marketing in nonprofit institutions (Brooklyn Academy of Music, colleges), the critical importance of marketing to an organization's success (the revitalization of Scripto), the broad range of marketing activities (such as customer service, industrial marketing, merchandise selection, inventory control, credit, pricing, warranties, and consumer protection), and that the role of marketing does not end when a sale is made (Parker Brothers, Whirlpool).

The formal study of marketing requires an understanding of its definition, importance, scope, and functions, as well as the evolution of marketing and the marketing concept. These principles are discussed in the next three sections.

Definition of Marketing

A broad, integrated definition of marketing will be used in this text:

> *Marketing* is the anticipation, management, and satisfaction of demand through the exchange process.

Marketing involves products (durable and nondurable), services, organizations, people, places, and ideas. See Figure 1-3.

Anticipation of demand requires a firm to do research on a regular basis in order to develop and introduce offerings that are desired by consumers. Management of demand includes stimulation, facilitation, and regulation. Stimulation is arousing consumers to want the firm's offering through attractive product design, intensive promotion, and other strategies. Facilitation is the process whereby the firm makes it easy to buy its offering through convenient locations, availability of credit, well-informed sales staff, and other strategies. Regulation is needed when there are peak periods for demand rather than balanced demand throughout the year or when demand is greater than the availability of the offering. Then, the goal is to spread demand throughout the year or to **demarket** a product or service (reduce overall demand). Satisfaction of demand involves actual product or service performance, safety, availability of options, aftersales service, and other factors. Consumer expectations must be satisfied through ownership or use of a product or service.

Marketing activities can be directed to consumers and to publics. **Consumer demand** refers to the characteristics and needs of final consumers, industrial consumers, channel members (such as wholesalers and retailers), government institutions, international markets, and nonprofit institutions. A firm may appeal to one or a combination of these. **Publics' demand** refers to the characteristics and needs of employees, unions, stockholders, consumer groups, the general public, government agencies, and other internal and external forces that affect company operations.

Marketing involves anticipation, requiring the firm to conduct research; management, which involves stimulating, facilitating, and regulating demand; and satisfaction, fulfilling expectations.

Demand is affected by the characteristics and needs of both consumers and outside publics.

Products

Television Sets

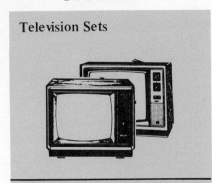

Cosmetics

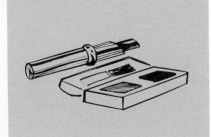

Services

Banking

Repairs

Organizations

Red Cross

"Support
our
blood
drive"

Unions

"Buy
union
products"

People

Political
Candidates

Entertainers

Places

"The
Vacation
State"

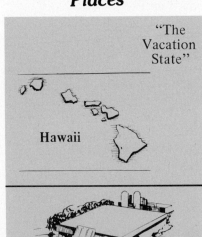

Hawaii

"Build your
plant in
Burlington,
N. C."

Ideas

"Buckle your seat
belt for safety."

"Smoking is a
matter of life
and breath."

**Figure 1-3
What Marketing Includes**

The marketing process is not complete until consumers and publics **exchange** their money, their promise to pay, or their support for the offering of the firm, institution, person, place, or idea.

Exchange completes the process.

Some examples of the broadened definition of marketing are a person voting for a presidential candidate or selecting a college after seeing a television commercial, a museum promoting art and art classes, a dairy trade association promoting the "Grade A Way" for milk, the change in a McDonald's storefront to accommodate area residents, product modifications to avoid recalls mandated by the government, the passage of Proposition 13 in California, and a retailer canceling a purchase because of dissatisfaction over the manufacturer's terms.

Evolution of Marketing

The origins of marketing can be traced to people's earliest use of the exchange process: barter (trading one resource for another—for example, food for animal pelts). To aid the exchange process, trading posts, traveling salesmen, general stores, and cities evolved along with a national monetary system.

During the latter 1800s the Industrial Revolution marked the beginning of the modern concept of marketing. Until this time, exchanges were limited because people did not have surplus items to trade. With the start of mass production, better transportation, and more efficient technology, products could be manufactured in greater quantities and sold at lower prices. People began to turn away from self-sufficiency (such as making all of their clothes) to purchases (such as buying a new suit or dress). Improved transportation, densely populated cities, and specialization also enabled more people to participate in the exchange process.

During the initial stages of the Industrial Revolution, output was limited and marketing was devoted to the physical distribution of products. Because demand was high and competition was low, companies did not have to conduct consumer research, modify products, or otherwise adapt to consumer needs. Their goal was to increase production to keep up with demand. This was known as the **production era** of marketing.

The *production era* occurred when businesses increased production to keep up with demand.

Once a company was able to maximize its production capabilities, it hired a sales force to sell its inventory. At first, while the company developed its products, consumer tastes or needs received little consideration. The role of advertising and the sales force was to make the desires of consumers fit the features of the products being manufactured. For example, a shoe manufacturer would produce brown wingtip shoes and use advertising and personal selling to convince consumers to buy them. The manufacturer would not determine consumer tastes before making shoes and adjust output to those tastes. This was known as the **sales era** of marketing.

In the *sales era* businesses manufactured and sold products without first determining consumers' desires.

As competition grew, supply began to exceed demand. A firm could not prosper without input from marketing. A marketing department was created. It conducted consumer research and advised management on how to design, price, distribute, and promote products. Unless the firm adapted to consumer needs, competitors might be better able to satisfy consumer demand and leave it with surplus inventory. Although the marketing department participated in company decisions, it remained in a lower or conflicting position to production, engineering, and sales departments during this period of evolution in marketing. This was known as the **marketing department era.**

In the past twenty years, the central role of marketing has been recognized by many firms; and the marketing department has become the equal of others in the company. At these firms, major decisions are made on the basis of thorough consumer analysis. Competition is intense and sophisticated. Consumers must be drawn and kept to the firm's brands. Company efforts are integrated and frequently re-evaluated. This is known as the **marketing company era.** Figure 1-4 details the evolution of marketing at Pillsbury, a consumer-oriented company.

The marketing concept and marketing philosophy are the underpinnings of the marketing company era. They are examined here.

Marketing Concept

The **marketing concept** is a consumer-oriented, integrated, goal-oriented philosophy for a firm, institution, or person.

One of the first formal statements on the marketing concept was made in 1957 by John B. McKitterick, then president of General Electric. McKitterick told a meeting of the American Marketing Association (AMA) that the marketing concept was a customer-oriented, integrated, and profit-oriented philosophy of business.[6]

During the past twenty-five years, many companies have acknowledged the value of marketing, as these illustrations show:

> Instead of trying to market what is easiest for us to make, we must find out much more about what the consumer is willing to buy. In other words, we must apply our creativeness more intelligently to *people* and their needs, rather than to *products.* (General Foods)

Marketing is:

> the process of defining, anticipating, and creating customer needs and wants and of organizing all the resources of the company to satisfy them at greater total profit to the company and to the customer. (B. F. Goodrich)

> Today, the thrust of our merchandising is more varied and complex, to meet the needs and desires of our customers. May [Department Stores] has diversified strategically to broaden and strengthen its position as a leading retailer, by growing through three distinct approaches to the market. Each of these operations serves the tastes, trends, and shopping patterns of significant segments of the consumer market. (May Department Stores)

AT&T has become, in its own words:

> a high technology business applying advanced marketing strategies to the satisfaction of highly sophisticated customer requirements.

The Essentials Of Marketing:

A Pictorial Essay

his pictorial essay presents an overview of marketing and shows its broad impact on our daily ves. The photos and their accompanying captions correspond to the eight parts of the book, and troduce some of the essential concepts in the field of marketing.

bserving the environment and undertaking marketing research are portant activities of marketing. At Radio Shack, a Store Operating stem uses microcomputers in 4,400 stores to transmit a steady ream of daily information to a mainframe computer at company adquarters in Fort Worth, Texas. As a result, the company can re-ond quickly to customer demand, to changes in the environment, to problems in a particular store.

oto reprinted with permission of Radio Shack, a Tandy company.

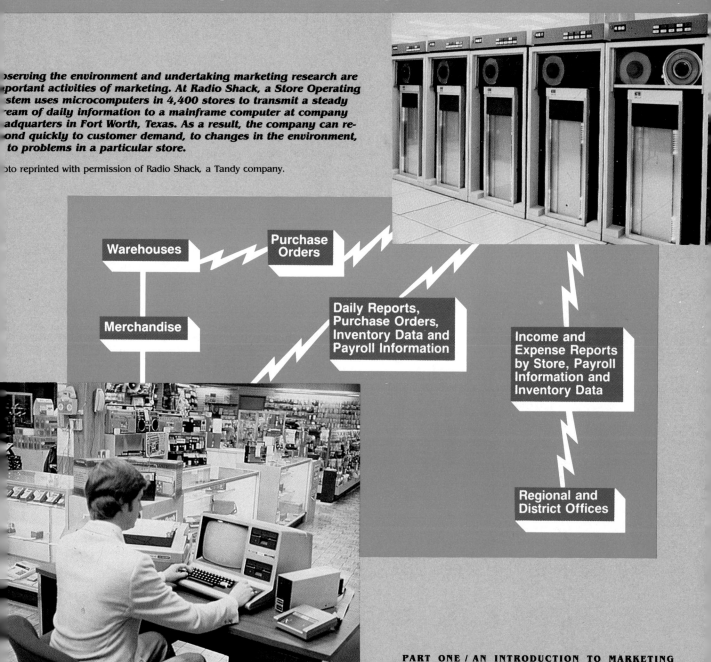

Warehouses

Purchase Orders

Merchandise

Daily Reports, Purchase Orders, Inventory Data and Payroll Information

Income and Expense Reports by Store, Payroll Information and Inventory Data

Regional and District Offices

His game is polo. His business is safaris. His watch is Rolex.

To say that Geoffrey Kent is a man of action is indeed a mild understatement. Imagine controlling a twelve hundred pound polo pony in a headlong gallop, pursuing a four-ounce bamboo ball, intent on driving it with a mallet through goal posts eight yards apart.

Then imagine that action combined with beauty and grace, skill and teamwork. A rare, powerful sport is polo.

The game comes naturally to Kent. As captain of the Abercrombie & Kent Team, he plays with the best. Among the Abercrombie & Kent victories are: U.S. Open Championship, 1978 and 1981; U.S. Gold Cup, 1978; Oak Brook International Open, 1979; Palm Beach Polo International Handicap, 1980.

But there's more to Kent than polo.

He is President of Abercrombie & Kent Safaris, perhaps the world's finest and most luxurious exotic travel corporation. Temples and tigers in India. Lions and champagne in Kenya. Civilized adventure from Tibet to Egypt. And no rifles, please; you hunt with your camera.

Geoffrey Kent is a singular man. And he wears a singular watch. Rolex. Nearly impregnable. The famous Oyster case is handcrafted step by step from a solid block of stainless steel. A unique combination of style and durability that says much about its wearer.

The game of polo combines strength, endurance and a certain savoir faire. Which gives it a lot in common with a Rolex.

ROLEX

Pictured: The Rolex Datejust Chronometer in stainless steel with matching bracelet. Also available in steel and 14 kt. yellow gold, and 18 kt. yellow gold.

Write for brochure. Rolex Watch, U.S.A., Inc., Dept. 200, Rolex Building, 665 Fifth Avenue, New York, N.Y. 10022-5383. World headquarters in Geneva. Other offices in Canada and major countries around the world.

Consumer analysis involves examining the characteristics, needs, and decision process of the market to which an organization appeals. On the basis of thorough consumer analysis, Rolex has targeted an expensive line of watches to affluent, upper-class consumers who have active life-styles and are conscious of social status. These consumers are willing to shop for a watch.

Photo reprinted with permission of Rolex.

(a)

Product (service) planning includes product line decisions, new-product development, branding, packaging, product deletion, and other activities. (a) Lever Brothers concentrates on a deep line of household products, some having multiple brands—such as Dove, Lux, and Shield soap. Unique package shapes are also important to Lever. (b) General Motors is continually involved in product testing for new and existing cars. At the GM Technical Center, the aerodynamics of the restyled Chevrolet Corvette were tested before its 1983 introduction.

Photos reprinted with permission of Lever Brothers and General Motors.

(b)

Distribution planning involves warehousing, physical distribution, wholesaling, and retailing. (a) As a national chain, J. C. Penney has its own warehouses for receiving merchandise from vendors and distributing items to branch stores. (b) Safeway supermarkets purchase much of their products, such as produce, from independent wholesalers and set up attractive in-store displays to ease customer shopping.

Photos reprinted with permission of J. C. Penney and Safeway.

Promotion planning deals with the mix of advertising, publicity, personal selling, and sales promotion; message content; media; timing; and cooperative efforts. Whirlpool has a comprehensive plan that incorporates all types of promotion. Annually, it publishes an advertising brochure that outlines goals and tactics. In 1983, Whirlpool advertised in 32 major magazines, from Architectural Digest to Yankee. It also used network television extensively.

Photos reprinted with permission of Whirlpool.

ARCHITECTURAL DIGEST

Better HOMES and Gardens

BUILDING IDEAS

THE SMALL HOUSE

Better Homes and Gardens: Remodeling Ideas
KITCHEN AND BATH IDEAS

Bon Appétit

Colonial Homes
Historic Holidays in southern manors

Country Living

Good Housekeeping

Gourmet

HOME

HOUSE BEAUTIFUL

Homeowners HOW TO

LIFE
REMAPPING THE HEAVENS

METROPOLITAN HOME

PERSONAL STYLE: Making a place your own

Money
FUN CARS COME BACK

THE **NEW YORKER**

People
E.T.

Smithsonian

Southern Living
Autumn at The South's Great Gardens

THE SATURDAY EVENING POST

TV GUIDE

WORKING MOTHER

SCOTT PAPER COMPANY
SCOTT ROLLS BACK PRICES!
"SIGNS"

COMM'L NO.: SPWC 2023

LENGTH: 30 SECONDS

ANN SCOTT: I'm Ann Scott with good news.

Scott has rolled back prices on your favorite products.

MANAGER: To help my customers' budgets.

ANN: Save on ScotTowels - 119 sheets on every roll.

Soft Family Scott Bathroom Tissue.

Scott Economy Pack Napkins - 300 per pack.

And soft, strong Scotties Facial Tissues.

MANAGER: All at rolled back prices.

SHOPPER: That's super news - a big sale!

MANAGER: Better than a sale - this price roll back will be in effect every day.

SHOPPER: Thanks, my budget needs help like that.

ANN: Scott quality at rolled back prices. Good news for your budget.

Price planning includes the level and range of prices, price flexibility, credit terms, markdowns, and the use of price as a major or secondary marketing factor. Scott Paper Company has recently adopted an aggressive pricing strategy, rolling back prices on a number of its products. Scott's goal is to increase sales by offering lower prices than competitors, such as Procter & Gamble.

Photo reprinted with permission of Scott Paper Company.

As the growth rate of the U.S. population has slowed down, many firms have entered into or expanded their involvement with international marketing. Many of these firms are focusing on rapidly increasing or relatively untapped foreign markets. Recently, Atari (a U.S. firm) was awarded a contract to supply more than 500 secondary schools in Hong Kong with home computers. Atari also has an exclusive agreement for its home computers to be used in vacationer workshops at several Club Med resorts around the world.

Photo reprinted with permission of Magnum Photos.

Successful marketing managers, such as those at Standard Rate & Data Service and National Register Publishing (shown here), meet regularly to carefully coordinate their efforts and plan for the future. Standard Rate & Data Service and National Register Publishing are two large business publishers who distribute the Standard Directory of Advertisers, a number of advertising rate books by medium, and other material. In response to changing technology and customer needs, these firms have spent several years and many millions of dollars developing computerized data base systems and other new products. The data base systems enable business clients to receive immediate electronic information, without waiting for printed matter.

Photo reprinted with permission of National Register Publishing Co.

Era		Characteristics and Goals
Product orientation **(1869-1930)**	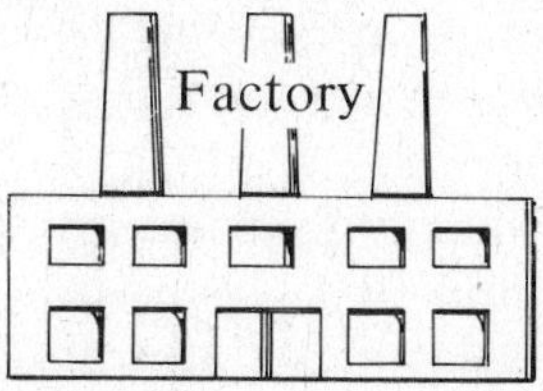 Factory	Professional flour miller interested in producing high–quality flour and disposing of by–products.
Sales orientation **(1930s-1950s)**	 Sales Personnel	Manufacturer of consumer products concerned about setting up a first–class sales force.
Marketing orientation **(1950s-1960s)**	 Marketing Department	Consumer goods manufacturer involved with selecting the best new products and maximizing sales. Marketing department first established.
Marketing control **(1960s-Present)**	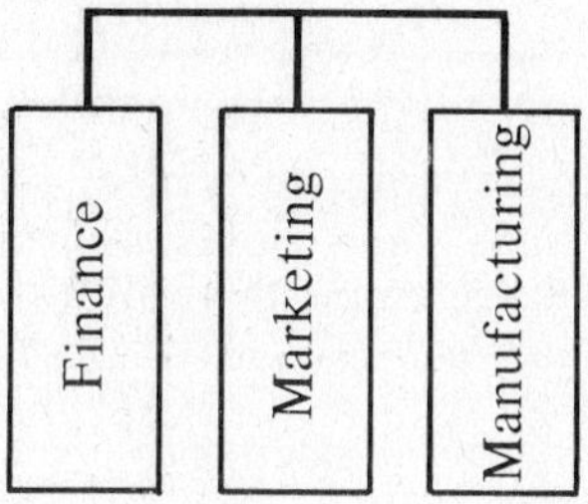 Finance / Marketing / Manufacturing	Integrated marketing company following the marketing concept and interested in long–term planning. Marketing directs a variety of areas from consumer research to advertising and sales.

Figure 1-4
Evolution of Marketing at Pillsbury

These statements demonstrate that, for a variety of firms, the marketing company era has arrived; marketing is now seen as the underlying philosophy of business, around which other decisions are made.

The elements of the marketing concept are critical to the ultimate success of a company, organization, or person. A customer orientation requires an examination of market needs, not production capability, and development of a plan to satisfy them. Products and services should be viewed as means to accomplish ends and not the ends themselves. Under an integrated marketing focus, all activities relating to products and services are coordinated, including finance, production, engineering, research and development, inventory control, and marketing. The

Marketing goals may be profit, a cure for a disease, or an improved corporate image.

firm, organization, or person should be goal oriented and employ marketing to achieve goals. The goals may be profit, a cure for a disease, increased tourism, the election of a political candidate, an improved corporate image, and so on. Marketing helps achieve goals by orienting the organization toward satisfying consumers and providing desirable products, services, or ideas.

While the marketing concept enables an organization to analyze, maximize, and satisfy consumer demand, it should realize that the concept is only a guide to planning. The organization must also consider its strengths and weaknesses in such functional areas as production, engineering, finance, and distribution. Marketing plans need to balance goals, customer needs, and resource capabilities. In addition, the impact of competition, government regulations, and other forces external to the firm must be evaluated. These factors are discussed in Chapter 2.

Selling Versus Marketing Philosophies

With a marketing orientation that stresses consumer satisfaction, selling is used to communicate with and understand consumers.

Table 1-1 focuses on the differences between selling and marketing philosophies. The benefits of a marketing, rather than a sales, orientation are many. Marketing stresses consumer analysis and satisfaction, directs the resources of the firm to making the products and services that consumers want, and adapts to changes in consumer characteristics and needs. Under a marketing philosophy, selling is used to communicate with and understand consumers; consumer dissatisfaction leads to changes in policy, not a stronger or different sales pitch. Marketing looks for real differences in consumer tastes and develops offerings to

Table 1-1

Contrasts in Thinking Between Sales and Marketing Executives

Sales executives tend to think in terms of:	Marketing executives tend to think in terms of:
sales volume rather than profits. They are not usually attentive to profit differences among products, services, or customer classes unless these differences are reflected in compensation.	*profit planning.* They plan customer, product, service, and marketing strategies to attain profitable sales volume and market share at acceptable levels of risk.
the short run. They concentrate on current customers, products, services, and strategies.	*long-run trends, opportunities, and threats.* They study how these will translate into new markets, products, services, and strategies that will assure long-term growth.
individual customers rather than groups of customers. They are knowledgeable about individual accounts and factors bearing on specific sales transactions.	*customer types and differences among groups of customers.* They attempt to appeal to profitable customer groups through superior value and distinctive offerings.
field work rather than desk work. They prefer to sell to customers instead of developing plans, strategies, and tactics.	*coordinated market analysis, planning, and control.* They compute the financial implications of marketing plans.

Source: Adapted from Philip Kotler, "From Sales Obsession to Marketing Effectiveness," *Harvard Business Review,* Vol. 55 (November–December 1977), pp. 68–69.

Figure 1-5
A Broadened View of Marketing

"You see buildings. I see a giant home-information market."

satisfy them. Marketing is oriented to the long run, and marketing goals reflect overall company goals and may be quite diverse in nature. Finally, marketing views customer needs in a broad (for example, transportation) rather than a narrow (for example, automobile) manner. See Figure 1-5.

The existence of a large marketing department and marketing plans does not necessarily mean an organization is properly applying the marketing concept. For example, the chief executive of one of the world's largest automobile companies commented that:

> I thought we were doing marketing. We have a corporate vice-president, a skilled advertising department, and elaborate market planning procedures. These fooled us. When the crunch came, I realized that we weren't producing the cars that people wanted. We weren't responding to new needs. Our marketing operation was nothing more than a glorified sales department.[7]

Importance and Scope of Marketing

It is important to study the field of marketing for several reasons. Marketing stimulates demand. A basic task of marketing is to generate consumer enthusiasm for goods and services. The Gross National Product

(GNP), the total market value of goods and services produced in a country during a year, in the United States is over $3 trillion.

A large amount of each sales dollar goes to cover marketing costs. Some estimates place the costs of marketing at 50 per cent or more of sales.[8] These costs should not be confused with marketing profits, nor should it be assumed that the elimination of marketing activities would lower prices. For example, could a consumer really save money by flying to Detroit to buy a new car directly from the manufacturer? Would a consumer buy clothing in bulk in order to save transportation and storage costs?

Between one fourth and one third of the civilian labor force in the United States is engaged in marketing activities. This includes people employed in the retailing, wholesaling, transportation, warehousing, and communications industries and those involved with marketing activities for financial, service, agricultural, mining, and other industries. For instance, more than 15 million people work in retailing, 5 million in wholesaling, and 5 million in transportation.

Marketing activities support entire industries, such as advertising and marketing research. Total annual advertising expenditures exceed $67 billion. In 1981, eleven agencies had worldwide billings of $1 billion or more, including Young & Rubicam, J. Walter Thompson, McCann-Erickson, and Ogilvy & Mather. The top 28 U.S. marketing research firms, including A. C. Nielsen, IMS International, SAMI, Market Facts, and Audits and Surveys, had total revenues of nearly $1 billion in 1981.

All people serve as consumers for various products and services. By understanding the role of marketing, consumers can become better informed, more selective, and more efficient. Effective channels of communication with organizations can also be established and complaints resolved more easily and favorably. Consumer groups have a major impact on firms.

Because resources are scarce, marketing programs and systems must function at their peak. For example, optimization of store hours, inventory movement, advertising expenditures, product assortments, and other areas of marketing will better coordinate resources. As mentioned earlier in the chapter, some industries may actually require demarketing (lowering the demand for products and services). The latter include oil and gasoline.

Marketing has a strong impact on people's beliefs and life-styles. In fact, marketing has been criticized as developing materialistic attitudes, fads, product obsolescence, a reliance on gadgets, conspicuous consumption (status consciousness), exaggerated product differences, and wasting resources. Marketers reply that they merely respond to the desires of people and make the best products and services they can at the prices people will pay.

Marketing has a role to play in improving the quality of life. For example, marketers encourage firms to make safer products, such as low-tar cigarettes and child-proof bottle caps. They create public service messages on energy conservation, cures for diseases, driver safety, abuses of alcohol, and other topics. They help new products, ideas, and services (for example, microwave ovens, improved nutrition, automated banking) to be accepted and used by people.

The scope of marketing is extremely wide. Among the areas in which marketing is involved are pricing, warehousing, packaging, branding, selling, sales force management, credit, transportation, social responsibility, retail site selection, consumer analysis, wholesaling, retailing, vendor appraisal and selection, advertising, public relations, marketing research, product planning, and warranties.

A knowledge of marketing is also valuable for those not directly involved with marketing. For example, marketing principles are important for doctors, lawyers, management consultants, financial analysts, research and development personnel, economists, statisticians, city planners, nonprofit institutions, and others. Each of these professions and organizations requires an understanding and satisfaction of patient, client, consumer, taxpayer, or contributor needs.

Marketing Functions and Performers

The basic **marketing functions** are customer analysis, buying, selling, product (service) planning, price planning, distribution, marketing research, opportunity analysis, and social responsibility. These are described in Table 1-2 and throughout the text. Although many transactions require the performance of similar marketing functions, such as buying, distribution, selling, pricing, and marketing research, there are a number of ways they can be carried out.

Marketing performers include manufacturers, wholesalers, retailers, marketing specialists, and final consumers. As shown in Table 1-3, each of these performers acts differently. It is important to note that while the responsibility for performing marketing functions can be shifted and shared in a variety of ways, the basic marketing functions must be performed by one party or another. They cannot be eliminated in most situations.

For a number of reasons, one party usually does not perform all marketing functions. Many producers do not have the financial resources to engage in direct marketing. As an illustration, even General Motors, one of the world's largest corporations, does not have the resources to undertake all the functions its dealers perform.

Direct marketing would often require producers to make complementary products or sell the complementary products of other manufacturers. For instance, there are about 200,000 grocery stores (comprised of supermarkets, superettes, small stores, and convenience stores), each carrying several thousand items. It would not be feasible for a producer of a limited line of foods to forego stores and sell directly to widely dispersed consumers.

A party may be unable or unwilling to perform certain functions and seek another party, with special competences, to fulfill them. For example, a firm may hire an advertising agency to develop its advertis-

> The basic *marketing functions* can be divided among parties but must be carried out by one or another *performer*.

> One party usually does not have the resources or ability to perform all marketing functions.

	Function	Description
Table 1-2		
Basic Marketing Functions	Customer analysis	Examination and evaluation of consumer characteristics and needs
	Buying	Procurement, vendor analysis and selection, terms of purchase, procedure for buying
	Selling	Advertising, sales promotion, sales force management, publicity, customer relations, dealer relations, warranties, public relations, displays, interaction with consumers
	Product (service) planning	New-product development, product management, assortments, brands, packaging, options, deletion of old products
	Price planning	Level and range of prices, credit availability and terms, cash flow, markdowns and sales, budgeting, flexibility, profits
	Distribution	Warehousing, physical distribution, inventory management, service levels, retail site locations, allocation, vendor control, method of transportation, wholesaling, retailing
	Marketing research	Data collection and analysis of information in all areas of marketing; basis for future decisions and planning
	Opportunity analysis	Appraisal of benefits and risks inherent in decision making
	Social responsibility	Obligation to offer safe, ethical, useful, and environmentally sound products, services, and ideas

ing campaign and create a desired company image; utilize a marketing research firm to design a questionnaire, collect data, and evaluate the results; or use a credit bureau to assess consumers' credit ratings.

Many parties are too small to perform certain functions. For example, consumers are unlikely to be able to buy in bulk and independent retailers cannot purchase full train loads of merchandise in order to minimize shipping costs; large wholesalers can. The overwhelming majority of retailers operate only one outlet.

For many products and services, established distribution methods are in force and it is difficult to circumvent them. A good illustration is the sale of packaged bakery products. Because of high delivery costs and the increase of one-stop shopping, these products must be sold in supermarkets (where it is sometimes difficult to gain shelf space). For similar reasons, items such as beer and soda also require distribution in supermarkets. High-volume sales almost always necessitate intensive, shared distribution.

Marketing in Action: The Chrysler Story[9]

During 1982, Chrysler earned a small profit for the first time in several years. This occurred despite a severely depressed United States automo-

Table 1-3 **Who Performs Marketing Functions**

Institution or Person	Definition	Typical Marketing Functions
Manufacturer	Firm or person that produces a product	A few manufacturers deal directly with final consumers and perform all marketing functions. Most employ wholesalers and retailers. The latter manufacturers analyze final consumers, buy raw materials, sell limited product assortments to wholesalers and retailers, advertise to final consumers, suggest prices, distribute to wholesalers or retailers, perform marketing research, analyze opportunities, and act responsibly.
Wholesaler	Establishment or person that buys items for resale to retailers and other merchants and/or to industrial, institutional, and commercial users. Significant amounts not sold to final consumers	A wholesaler may buy an item from the manufacturer and assume ownership or serve as a broker (agent) who receives a commission and does not assume ownership. A wholesaler analyzes final consumers, buys finished or semifinished items from manufacturers, sells in bulk to retailers, does not advertise to final consumers, has little impact on final prices, ships merchandise to the retailer, accepts credit, allocates inventory, does little marketing research, analyzes opportunities, and acts responsibly.
Retailer	Establishment or person whose business activities involve the sale of goods and services to the ultimate (final) consumer for personal, family, or household use	A retailer may buy from a manufacturer or a wholesaler. A retailer analyzes final consumers, buys finished items or creates services, interacts with final consumers, stores merchandise, gathers assortments, locates near consumers and sets convenient hours, promotes widely, usually accepts credit, handles complaints, sets final prices, researches its marketing strategy, analyzes opportunities, and acts responsibly.
Marketing specialist	Firm or person that performs one specific marketing function	A marketing specialist is hired by a manufacturer, wholesaler, or retailer to handle one function that the latter cannot undertake. Examples of specialists are advertising agency, warehouse, marketing research firm, delivery firm, credit bureau, marketing consultant, computer service bureau, common carrier, financial institution, and product testing laboratory.
Final consumer	Family or person who buys a product or service for personal, family, or household use	A consumer may visit the nearest store (or shop via telephone) and expect the retailer or manufacturer to perform all marketing functions or perform some functions him- or herself in order to save money. The latter may buy in bulk, purchase unfinished products or services, pick up merchandise, pay cash, use self-service outlets, and bargain with the retailer.

bile industry. The turnaround at Chrysler, from a company on the verge of bankruptcy in 1979–1980, was in large part due to revived marketing efforts sparked by Lee Iacocca, Chrysler's chief executive. The Chrysler story clearly indicates the central role of marketing in a firm's success or failure.

From 1967 to 1980, Chrysler's share of the domestic automobile market fell from 16 to less than 8 per cent. In 1980, the firm lost more than $1.7 billion, at that time the largest corporate loss in American history. Chrysler's decline was brought about by several marketing-related errors.

Chrysler never adequately defined the characteristics and needs of its customer market. For years engineering dominated product plan-

Chrysler's problems were caused by inadequate consumer analysis, lack of coordination, and improper planning.

ning. Although this approach resulted in many breakthroughs (such as power steering, the electronic ignition, and torsion-bar suspension), a clear marketing strategy was never delineated. Its competitors did specify their orientations: General Motors, "a car for every purse"; Ford, "a workingperson's car"; and American Motors, "innovative cars."

Changes in product design were radical, not continuous. Marketing efforts were disjointed and erratic. The firm was unable to establish any kind of public image beyond engineering. During the 1974–1975 recession, Chrysler laid off 30 per cent of its domestic work force. Most of the engineering staff were given three-month furloughs. This caused a delay in introducing the Volare and the Aspen. Whey they were introduced, they did not receive complete engineering checks. The cars were recalled a total of eight times, undermining the company's engineering reputation.

Chrysler's customers tended to be more conservative, older, blue-collar people than its competitors' customers. They were less inclined to buy cars loaded with high-profit options. These customers were the most likely to suffer in a recession. In addition, Chrysler was out of step with consumer tastes. As one past Chrysler president admitted, "half of the people buying a new automobile never even considered a Chrysler product." Frequently, successful General Motors designs were copied two and three years after their introduction. As recently as fall 1978, Chrysler continued to produce standard-sized St. Regis cars, when the market was unreceptive to them. By February 1979 the company had a 381-day supply of the St. Regis on hand.

Chrysler was the only big-three automaker to build cars for its own inventory. General Motors and Ford built products according to dealer orders. Although Chrysler could ship quickly, costly stockpiling also occurred. In mid-1979 there were 80,000 vehicles in inventory. Customer desires for mileage, horsepower, colors, and options had not been considered because management ordered cars to be built without input from dealers.

While Chrysler had an oversupply of full-sized cars and compacts with eight-cylinder engines, it had a critical shortage of Omnis and Horizons, which were in large demand. It relied on Volkswagen and Mitsubishi to make Omni and Horizon four-cylinder engines. Because they could not keep up with Chrysler's orders, Chrysler had to limit production and therefore sales. The cars remaining in inventory had per unit variable profit levels (excluding fixed overhead costs) of $1,500 to $5,400. The subcompacts, which were selling, contributed $700 per unit.

Chrysler was slow to recognize its declining position and adapt its marketing efforts accordingly. A number of industry experts questioned Chrysler's ability to be a full-line competitor of General Motors and Ford. They felt Chrysler needed to become a specialty manufacturer of small cars. For example, General Motors could make a car for $500 less than Chrysler could, because of General Motors' size and ownership of suppliers.

By September 1979 Chrysler had laid off 29,150 employees in the United States and Canada. During 1979, 320 dealers left Chrysler. Lee

Iacocca, former president of Ford Motor Co. and the new head of Chrysler, reduced his Chrysler salary from $360,000 plus benefits to a symbolic $1 per year. Iacocca would recoup his salary only if the company returned to profitability and stock prices rose. Other executives also reduced their immediate compensation.

In 1979 Chrysler applied for government aid in order to pay off creditors, avoid further layoffs, and save the company. After much debate, the Chrysler bailout plan was approved by Congress and was signed by President Carter on January 7, 1980. The legislation provided $1.5 billion in federal loan guarantees, contingent on wage concessions from workers and other forms of private assistance.

To sustain the company until its K cars were ready to be introduced Chrysler embarked on a very aggressive marketing campaign in 1980. It used Lee Iacocca in advertisements, gave cash discounts, concentrated on economy cars, pointed to many company improvements, and embarked on a risky, money-back guarantee plan. Under the plan, a car could be returned within thirty days or 1,000 miles. The full purchase price would be reimbursed, no questions asked.

Chrysler's turnaround was due to improved marketing practices, centering on advertising, product quality, pricing, warranties, etc.

In fall 1980, Chrysler introduced its long-awaited, fuel-efficient "K" cars, the Dodge Aries and Plymouth Reliant. These were Chrysler's first new cars since winter 1978. The "K" cars were an immediate hit with car buyers, because of their durability, price economy, roominess, and fuel mileage.

Since fall 1980, a number of major marketing strategies and tactics have allowed Chrysler to lift its share of the U.S. auto market to more than 12 per cent. Lee Iacocca has appeared in many ads, stressing Chrysler's quality ("If you can find a better car, buy it") and durability. This strategy is enhanced by Chrysler's unique 50,000 mile-5 year warranty. Chrysler also places great emphasis on its "Buy American" approach, appealing to consumers' patriotism.

New model Chrysler cars are now quite attractive in their styling. The LeBaron series has proven particularly popular; and the LeBaron convertible has led the way to a revival of convertibles made in the U.S. Figure 1-6 shows an advertisement for the first LeBaron convertible that was introduced in fall 1981. In 1982, Chrysler began expanding its product line in order to draw more families and upscale consumers.

Finally, Chrysler has corrected many of its earlier problems. For example, the company no longer builds cars for its own inventory; a younger customer mix is loyal to Chrysler products; and marketing and engineering efforts are better coordinated.

As Chrysler plans for the mid-1980s, it is aware that short- and long-run marketing efforts are essential and that labor, import, and other issues have to be resolved to ensure long-term profitability. Consumer orientation, integrated effort, and goal orientation are crucial.

Format of the Text

This book is divided into eight parts. The remainder of Part One concentrates on the environment of marketing and the information needed for

Figure 1-6
"The New Chrysler"

Reprinted by permission.

marketing decisions. These topics set the foundation for examining the specific components of marketing.

Part Two deals with the central orientation of marketing: understanding consumers. Consumer demographics, social and psychological factors, the decision process, organizational consumers, developing a target market, and sales forecasting are detailed.

Parts Three through Six describe the basic components of marketing (product, distribution, promotion, and price) and the decisions needed to carry out marketing plans.

Part Seven covers several topics that expand the scope of marketing, including international marketing, service and nonprofit marketing, and marketing and society.

Part Eight considers the implications of the topics raised throughout the text. Included are discussions of developing, integrating, and analyzing the marketing program as well as marketing in the future.

The text defines key terms, explains the significance of important concepts, studies the role of the marketing manager, and shows the scope of the field of marketing. In addition, numerous examples and illustrations of actual marketing practices by a variety of organizations are woven into the discussion of the framework of marketing and its components.

Summary

Marketing is an exciting and dynamic contemporary field that involves a wide variety of activities. It is defined as the anticipation, management, and satisfaction of demand through the exchange process. Marketing can involve products, services, organizations, people, places, and ideas.

The evolution of marketing can be traced to people's earliest use of the exchange process. Marketing has really developed since the Industrial Revolution, as mass production and improved transportation enabled more transactions to occur. For companies such as Pillsbury, marketing has evolved through four eras: production, sales, marketing department, and marketing company. The marketing concept requires a company to be consumer oriented, have an integrated marketing program, and be goal oriented.

When contrasting a marketing approach with a sales approach, marketing is found to be more involved with profit planning, analysis of trends, opportunities, and threats, assessments of customer types and differences, and coordinated decision making.

The field of marketing is important for several reasons: stimulation and regulation of demand, marketing costs, the number of people employed in marketing, its support of entire industries such as advertising agencies and marketing research firms, the recognition that all people are consumers in some situations, the necessity of the efficient use of scarce resources, its impact on people's beliefs and life-styles, and its input into the quality of life. The scope of marketing is quite broad and diversified.

The major classifications of marketing functions are customer analysis, buying, selling, product (service) planning, price planning, distribution, marketing research, opportunity analysis, and social responsibility. The responsibility for performing these functions can be shifted and shared in several ways among manufacturers, wholesalers, retailers, marketing specialists, and consumers. One party usually does not perform all the functions. This is due to costs, assortment requirements, specialized abilities, company size, and established methods of distribution.

Chrysler encountered large losses because it did not define consumer desires, copied competitors, did not adapt to changing conditions, lost many dealers, employed a costly inventory system, was oriented toward engineering, and never established a clear image. However, an aggressive marketing program, led by Lee Iacocca, has corrected many past mistakes and enabled Chrysler to regain market share and earn profits. Chrysler now follows the marketing concept.

After reading this chapter, you should understand these key terms: **KEY TERMS**

Marketing	**Sales era**
Demarket(ing)	**Marketing department era**
Consumer demand	**Marketing company era**
Publics' demand	**Marketing concept**
Exchange	**Marketing functions**
Production era	**Marketing performers**

QUESTIONS FOR DISCUSSION

1. If you were the product manager for Tic Tac, what would you do next? Why?
2. Explain the
   a. Anticipation of demand.
   b. Management of demand.
   c. Satisfaction of demand.
3. Give an example of a product, service, organization, person, place, and idea that may be marketed.
4. What is the exchange process?
5. Do marketing activities end when a sale is made? Explain.
6. Describe the four eras of marketing. Are any companies still able to operate in the production or sales era of marketing? Explain.
7. Define the marketing concept. How may it be applied to the Brooklyn Academy of Music?
8. Describe at least five benefits of a marketing over a sales orientation.
9. List at least five reasons for studying marketing.
10. What are the basic functions performed by marketing?
11. Why do most manufacturers not market their products directly to consumers?
12. Select a company that has recently had problems and present a marketing critique of the firm. Be sure to include recommendations to improve the situation. (Do not use Chrysler as your company.)

NOTES

1. Nancy Giges, "Daring Strategic Move Keys Tic Tac Turnaround," *Advertising Age* (April 19, 1982), pp. 4, 62.
2. Charles W. Stevens, "One Producer Finds Recall Is Best Policy for a Hazardous Toy," *Wall Street Journal* (March 2, 1979), pp. 1, 33; and "General Mills," *Advertising Age* (September 9, 1982), p. 90.
3. Roger Ricklefs, "High Class Hoopla: A Cultural Institution Succeeds by Marketing Its Wares Aggressively," *Wall Street Journal* (January 23, 1979), pp. 1, 35.
4. "Whirlpool Promises Quality, Value, Honesty, Service to 'Make Your World a Little Easier'," *Marketing News* (February 5, 1982), p. 10.
5. Gay Jervey, "Scripto Looks to Expand Now That Image 'Rebuilt,'" *Advertising Age* (October 25, 1982), pp. 4, 87.
6. John B. McKitterick, "What Is the Marketing Management Concept?" in Frank M. Bass (Editor), *The Frontiers of Marketing Thought and Action* (Chicago: American Marketing Association, 1957), pp. 71–82.
7. Philip Kotler, "From Sales Obsession to Marketing Effectiveness," *Harvard Business Review*, Vol. 55 (November–December 1977), p. 68.
8. See Reavis Cox. *Distribution in a High Level Economy* (Englewood Cliffs, N.J.: Prentice-Hall, 1965), p. 149; Paul W. Stewart and J. Frederick Dewhurst, *Does Distribution Cost Too Much?* (New York: Twentieth Century Fund, 1963), pp. 117–118; and Jules J. Schwartz, *Corporate Policy: A Casebook* (Englewood Cliffs, N.J.: Prentice-Hall, 1978), pp. 6–7.
9. Paul Blustein, "Another Chrysler Turnaround: But Is This One for Real?" *Forbes* (November 15, 1976), pp. 40–43; "Chrysler's Big Mistake," *Consumer Reports* (July 1978), pp. 376–377; "In the Driver's Seat: Lee Iacocca Dismissed by Ford, Will Become President of Chrysler," *Wall Street Journal* (November 2, 1978), pp. 1, 41; Andy Pasztor, "Deals on Wheels," *Wall Street Journal* (February 23, 1979), p. 38; Peter Schuyten, "Chrysler Goes for Broke," *Fortune* (July 19, 1978), pp. 54–58; "Talking with Kelmenson of Kenyon and Eckhardt: Switching to Chrysler," *New York Times* (March 8, 1979), p. D2; Irwin Ross, "Chrysler on the Brink," *Fortune* (February 9,

1981), pp. 38–42; "Chrysler Talks Back," *Fortune* (March 23, 1980), pp. 145–146; John Holusha, "Chrysler Rides High in Detroit," *New York Times* (August 29, 1982), Section 3, pp. 1, 8; Ralph Gray, "Chrysler to Tout Technology," *Advertising Age* (September 13, 1982), pp. 4, 73; Jerry Flint, "Wipe That Sneer," *Forbes* (June 7, 1982), pp. 38–41; Hal Lancaster and Sue Shellenbarger, "Corporate Clones," *Wall Street Journal* (January 28, 1983), pp. 1, 23; and "Can Chrysler Keep Its Comeback Rolling?" *Business Week* (February 14, 1983), pp. 132–136.

HINTS FOR SOLVING CASES

At the end of each chapter from 2 through 19, two cases are presented—a total of thirty-six. These cases are intended to build on the material in the text, improve reasoning skills, and stimulate class discussions.

The cases in *Essentials of Marketing* describe actual marketing situations faced by a variety of organizations. The facts, circumstances, and people are all real. The questions following each case are designed to help identify the key issues encountered by the organization, evaluate its responses to these issues, outline additional courses of action, and develop appropriate marketing strategies. The information necessary to answer the questions is contained within the case or the chapter to which the case relates.

These hints should be kept in mind when solving cases:

- Read the material carefully. Underline important data and statements.
- List the key issues, problems, and organizational responses.
- Read each question following the case. In outline form, write up tentative answers. Cover as many points as possible.
- Review the chapter. In particular, look for information pertaining to the case questions.
- Expand your tentative answers, substantiating them with data from the case and the chapter.
- Reread the case to be sure you have not omitted any important concepts in your answers.
- Integrate your answers. Consider their ramifications for the organization.
- Reread your solutions the next day. This ensures a more objective review of your work.
- Be sure your answers are not a summary of the case, but are analyses and recommendations.

The Environment of Marketing

2

Chapter Preview

Chapter Objectives

1   To examine the environment of marketing and show why it is necessary for marketers to understand the total environment in which they operate

2   To view the environment in a systematic and integrated manner

3   To study the controllable elements of a marketing plan and to differentiate between those elements controlled by top management and those controlled by marketers

4   To look at the uncontrollable elements that affect a marketing plan and how marketers may respond to them

5   To explain why feedback and adaptation to change are essential for marketers

Frito-Lay possesses a 40 per cent share of the $5+ billion per year salty-snack market. Frito-Lay originated in 1961 when two small regional companies merged. In 1965, it was acquired by PepsiCo. Frito-Lay now operates 43 plants; its brands include Lay's potato chips, Ruffles, Cheetos, and Doritos. Despite its success, Frito-Lay must carefully monitor and respond to its changing environment, particularly the rapid growth of competition and newer consumer life-styles.

Four major competitors are expanding their activity in the salty-snack market. Anheuser-Busch is marketing Eagle Snacks in bars, taverns, and airports throughout the United States. Eagle Snack products include corn curls, corn chips, potato snacks, and honey-roasted peanuts. They are distributed by beer wholesalers. Borden's, maker of Wise potato chips, Bravos corn chips, and Cheese Doodles, has expanded production capacity by 70 per cent during a three-year period and is developing grain-based snacks. Nabisco Brands, maker of Planters salted nuts, cheese balls, and corn chips, has an extensive distribution system and good product research facilities. Procter & Gamble markets three improved versions of Pringle's potato chips and is planning to enter other salty-snack markets.

Recently, consumer life-styles have begun to place greater emphasis on healthful, calorie-reduced foods. Traditional snacks

Figure 2-1
Frito-Lay Lights

are viewed by these consumers as too fattening and unhealthy. They have turned to fruit, yogurt, and natural food products.

As a progressive firm, Frito-Lay is addressing both of these environmental factors. To rebuff competitors, it has added plant capacity and is aggressively developing new products, such as Tostitos and Grandma's cookies. To appeal to health-conscious consumers, Frito-Lay has created "light" varieties of its corn-based products, revised packaging (to incorporate nutritional information), and reoriented advertising to reflect healthful themes.[1] Figure 2-1 shows one of the company's new light products.

Marketing and Its Environment

The environment within which marketing operates is shown in Figure 2-2. This figure divides the **marketing environment** into five parts: controllable factors, uncontrollable factors, organization's level of success or failure in reaching its objectives, feedback, and adaptation.

Controllable factors are those directed by the firm and its marketers. A number of basic interrelated decisions are made by top management. These include choice of a line of business, overall objectives, the role of marketing, and the role of other business functions. Next, marketing managers make a number of decisions based on these guidelines. Included are the selection of a consumer market, marketing objectives, marketing organization, marketing plans, and control. In combination,

The *marketing environment* consists of controllable factors, uncontrollable factors, organization's level of success or failure, feedback, and adaptation.

Figure 2-2
The Environment within which Marketing Operates

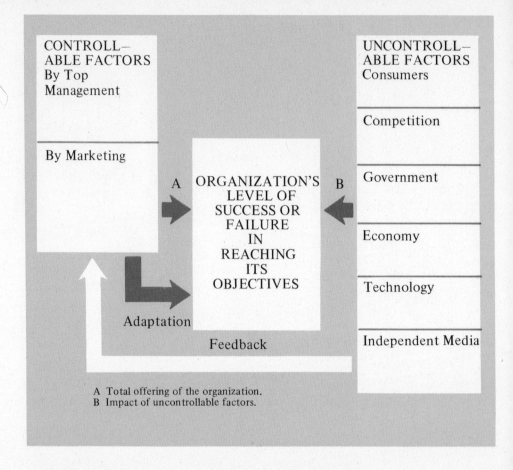

A Total offering of the organization.
B Impact of uncontrollable factors.

these factors result in an overall marketing strategy or offering. (A in Figure 2-2).

The major uncontrollable factors are consumers, competition, government, the economy, technology, and independent media. They have an impact on how well the organization and its offering are accepted. (B in Figure 2-2). For example, because of cultural influences, a product may not be popular. Competition may lower prices. The government may enact strict legislation. The inflation rate might slow down sales. Resource shortages might cause a necessary part to be unavailable. The media may present negative publicity about the firm.

Accordingly, the offering of the firm and the impact of the uncontrollable environment interact to determine the organization's level of success or failure in reaching its objectives. Feedback occurs when the firm makes an effort to monitor uncontrollable factors and review its areas of strength and weakness. Adaptation refers to the changes in its marketing plan than an organization makes in order to comply with the uncontrollable environment.

If a firm is unwilling to consider the entire environment (controllable and uncontrollable factors) in a systematic manner, it increases the likelihood that the organization will have a lack of direction and not attain proper results. Consumers may be inadequately analyzed, some

Failure to consider the entire environment systematically may result in the organization's lack of direction and poor results.

marketing functions may be omitted, departments may duplicate efforts, and interdepartment rivalries may occur. Opportunities may be missed and undesirable products or services retained. The organization may be excluded from distribution (such as supermarkets refusing to carry a new brand of toothpaste), and have disputes with distributors. The wrong image may be generated through an inefficient promotion mix and prices that are not reflective of quality.

Throughout this chapter, the various parts of Figure 2-2 are described and drawn together so that a marketer can understand and operate in the complex environment he or she faces.

Controllable Factors

Controllable factors are those elements that are directed by the organization and its marketers. Some of the controllable factors are directed by top management. These are not controllable by marketers, who must develop plans to satisfy organizational goals and work within the guidelines set by management. In situations involving small- or medium-sized institutions, broad policy and marketing decisions are made by one person, usually the owner. Even in these cases, broad policy should be stated first and marketing plans must adjust to it.

Controllable factors are directed by the organization and its marketers.

Factors Controlled by Top Management

Although management is responsible for numerous decisions, four basic ones are of extreme importance to marketers: line of business, overall objectives, the role of marketing, and the role of other business functions. See Figure 2-3. These decisions have an impact on all aspects of marketing.

The line of business refers to the general product/service category, functions, geographic coverage, type of ownership, and specific business of a company. By describing these factors, management is better able to plan and sustain its business.

The general product/service category is a broad definition of the kind of business a firm seeks to undertake. It may be energy, furniture, housing, education, or any number of others. The functions of the business outline a company's position in the marketing system, from supplier to manufacturer to wholesaler to retailer, and the tasks it seeks to undertake. It is important to note that a firm may want to undertake more than one of these functions. For example, Sherwin-Williams decided not only to perform production functions but also to market its paint products through its own retail outlets.

An organization must determine its span of geographic coverage. A firm can have a neighborhood, city, county, state, regional, national, or international focus. The type of ownership arrangement ranges from a sole proprietor or independent to a multiunit corporation. The specific business is a narrow definition of the firm, its functions, and its operations.

The overall objectives are the measurable goals set by management. The success or failure of the firm may be determined by comparing

The line of business outlines the general product/service category, functions, geographic coverage, type of ownership, and specific business of a company.

The overall objectives are those set by top management.

Figure 2-3
**Factors Controlled by
Top Management**

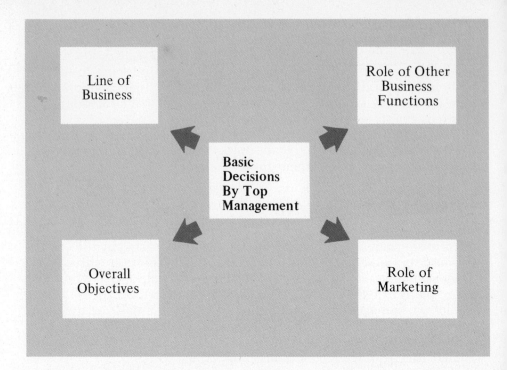

objectives with actual performance. Usually a combination of sales, profit, and other objectives is stated by management for short-run (one year or less) and long-run (more than one year) time periods.

**Management specifies
the role of marketing.**

Management determines the role of marketing by noting its importance, outlining its functions, and integrating it into the overall operation of the firm.

The importance of marketing in a firm is evident when marketing is given line (decision-making) authority, the rank of the chief marketing officer is equal to that of others (usually vice-president), and adequate resources are provided. Marketing is not considered important by a firm that gives marketing staff (advisory) status, places marketing in a subordinate position (such as reporting to the production vice-president), equates marketing with sales, and withholds the resources needed to research, advertise, and conduct other marketing activities.

The larger marketing's role, the greater the likelihood of the firm having an integrated marketing organization. The smaller the role of marketing, the greater the possibility that the firm operates its marketing activities on a project, crisis, and fragmented basis.

**The relationships of
marketing and other
business functions need
to be precise.**

The roles of other business functions and their interrelationships with marketing need to be laid out clearly in order to avoid overlaps, jealousy, and conflicts.[2] Table 2-1 shows the organizational emphasis and goals of marketing, production, finance, accounting, engineering, purchasing, and research and development.

After top management outlines the line of business, states overall company objectives, defines the role of marketing, and determines the role of other business functions, the marketing area begins to develop its controllable variables.

Table 2-1 **Departmental Objectives, Conflicts, and Compromises**

Departmental Objectives	Conflicts with Marketing	Compromises
Production seeks mass production, uniform products, limited options, long lead time (time from inception of idea until units are produced), standard parts, infrequent style changes.	*Marketing* seeks tailor-made products, great variety, many options, short lead time, unique-to-firm parts (to capture replacement demand), and frequent style changes (to foster quicker repurchases).	*Production* undertakes shorter production runs, accepts product diversity, and reduces lead time. *Marketing* undertakes adequate research, does not appeal to overly small segments, and gives production as much lead time as possible.
Finance seeks well-established budgets, spending limits, and detailed dollar analysis of project risks.	*Marketing* seeks flexible budgets, less restrictions on spending, and the opportunity to embark on projects showing potential.	*Finance* allows marketing input into budgeting. *Marketing* tries to work within a budget, understand the budget process, and fully detail new projects.
Accounting seeks standardized reporting, fully detailed costs, and routine transactions.	*Marketing* seeks frequent reports (keyed to specific products or services), considers marginal costs, and asks for unique expenditures.	*Accounting* works with *marketing* to develop standard terminology, key reports, cost data, and evaluate requests for unique expenditures.
Engineering seeks long lead time, exact specifications, limited models and options, and simple replacement parts.	*Marketing* seeks short time for design, flexible specifications, a variety of models, and unique-to-firm replacement parts (for captive replacement parts business). Product quality is dictated by the market.	*Engineering* and *marketing* conduct research together to reduce design lead time, have flexible specifications until close to production, and standardize replacement parts.
Purchasing seeks to acquire large, uniform orders at low prices. Small inventory levels are sought.	*Marketing* seeks tailor-made, frequent orders, regardless of the price. Large inventories are sought to ensure that demand can be fulfilled.	*Purchasing* acquires items desired by marketing at more frequent intervals. *Marketing* places orders as soon as possible to allow purchasing to shop around.
Research and development seeks technological breakthroughs, improvements in the quality of existing products, and recognition for innovations.	*Marketing* seeks new products and services that customers will demand and think are desirable enough to purchase.	*Research and development* and *marketing* work together to develop new products and improve old ones in ways that are attractive to consumers.

Factors Controlled by Marketing

The major elements under the direction of the marketer are the selection of a target market, marketing objectives, marketing organization, marketing mix, and control of the marketing plan. Table 2-2 shows some of the alternative choices available to marketers in each of these areas.

The selection of a **target market** (a defined customer group) involves two decisions, size and characteristics. A marketer can choose a very large target market, called mass marketing, or a small piece of the market, called market segmentation. In the latter instance, a marketing plan is geared to a specific group of people; with mass marketing, a general marketing plan is developed. The marketer must also define the characteristics of people in the target market—such as male or female,

The selection of a *target market* involves decisions regarding size and characteristics.

Table 2-2	*Factors*	*Examples of Alternatives*
Factors Controlled by Marketing	Selection of target market	
	Size	Mass market, market segment
	Characteristics	Male or female, young or old, conservative or liberal, married or single, east or west
	Marketing objectives	
	Image	Quality, economy, friendly, expert
	Sales	Brand loyalty, introduction of new products, appeal to untapped segments
	Profit	High profit per unit on status items, high total profit on mass-marketed items
	To create a differential advantage	Better product, availability, low price, extensive promotion
	Marketing organization	
	Types	Functional, product, market
	Marketing mix	
	Product (service)	One basic model versus many colors, styles, sizes, and options
	Distribution	Manufacturer-wholesaler-retailer-consumer, manufacturer-retailer-consumer, manufacturer-consumer
	Promotion	Advertising, publicity, personal selling, sales promotion
	Price	Low, high, at the market
	Control	
	Day-to-day	Analysis of internal data, monitoring of external environment
	Periodic	Marketing audit, in-depth research

married or single, and affluent or middle class—and key the marketing plan to these people.

Marketing objectives are more customer oriented than those set by top management. For example, marketers are extremely interested in the image consumers hold of the company and specific products. Sales objectives reflect a concern for brand loyalty (repeat purchase behavior), growth through new product introductions, and appeal to unsatisfied market segments. Profit objectives are set in per unit or total-profit terms. Last and most important, marketers seek to create a *differential advantage,* the set of unique features in a company's marketing program that causes consumers to patronize the company and not its competitors. Without a differential advantage, a company adopts a "me-too" philosophy and offers the consumer no reasons to select its offerings over a competitor's. A differential advantage can be achieved through a distinctive image, new products or features, product quality, availability, service, low prices, and other characteristics. See Figure 2-4.

A *marketing organization* is the structural arrangement for directing marketing functions. The organization outlines authority, responsibility, and tasks to be performed. Through the organization, functions are assigned and coordinated. An organization may be functional, with responsibility assigned on the basis of buying, selling, promotion, distribution, and other tasks; product oriented, with product managers for each product category and brand managers for each individual brand in

Marketing objectives are highly customer oriented.

A company's *differential advantage* consists of the unique features that attract consumers.

A *marketing organization* may be functional, product oriented, or market oriented.

Figure 2-4
Determining a Differential Advantage

"Gentlemen, we have to decide whether it's a miracle of space-age technology or lovingly fashioned by skilled craftsmen."

addition to functional categories; or market oriented, with managers assigned on the basis of geographic markets and customer types in addition to functional categories. A single company may use a mixture of these forms. See Figure 2-5 for illustrations of the three organizational forms.

The **marketing mix** describes the specific combination of marketing elements used to achieve objectives and satisfy the target market. The mix consists of four major factors: product or service, distribution, promotion, and price. The marketer must select the combination of factors that is best for the firm. The marketing mix requires a number of decisions.

Product or service decisions involve determining what to sell, the level of quality, the number of items to sell, the innovativeness of the company, packaging, features (such as options and warranties), the level and timing of research, and when to drop existing offerings. Distribution decisions include whether to sell through middlemen or directly to consumers, how many outlets to sell through, whether to control or cooperate with other channel members, what purchasing terms to negotiate, selecting suppliers, determining which functions to assign to others, and identifying competitors.

Promotion decisions include the selection of a mix of tools (advertising, publicity, personal selling, and sales promotion), whether to share promotions and their costs with others, how to measure effectiveness, the image to pursue, the level of customer service, the choice of media (such as newspaper, television, radio, magazine), the format of messages, and ad timing throughout the year or during peak periods. Price decisions include determining the overall level of prices (low, medium, or high), the range of prices (lowest to highest), the relation-

The *marketing mix* consists of product or service, distribution, promotion, and price factors.

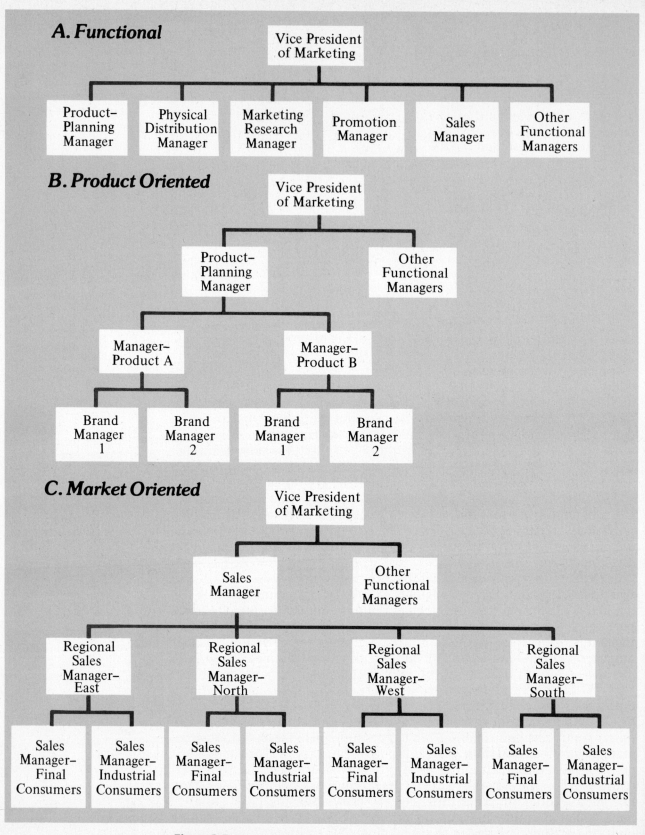

A. Functional

Vice President of Marketing

- Product–Planning Manager
- Physical Distribution Manager
- Marketing Research Manager
- Promotion Manager
- Sales Manager
- Other Functional Managers

B. Product Oriented

Vice President of Marketing

- Product–Planning Manager
  - Manager–Product A
    - Brand Manager 1
    - Brand Manager 2
  - Manager–Product B
    - Brand Manager 1
    - Brand Manager 2
- Other Functional Managers

C. Market Oriented

Vice President of Marketing

- Sales Manager
  - Regional Sales Manager–East
    - Sales Manager–Final Consumers
    - Sales Manager–Industrial Consumers
  - Regional Sales Manager–North
    - Sales Manager–Final Consumers
    - Sales Manager–Industrial Consumers
  - Regional Sales Manager–West
    - Sales Manager–Final Consumers
    - Sales Manager–Industrial Consumers
  - Regional Sales Manager–South
    - Sales Manager–Final Consumers
    - Sales Manager–Industrial Consumers
- Other Functional Managers

Figure 2-5
Marketing Organizations

ship between price and quality, the emphasis to place on price, how to react to competitors' prices, when to advertise prices, how prices are computed, and what billing terms to employ (such as a cash-only versus a credit policy).

In the development of a marketing mix, these four elements must be consistent with the selected target market and each other and be well integrated. For instance, neither a well-designed but poorly promoted product nor a well-promoted but overpriced product will be successful.

An example of an appropriate marketing mix is one used by a manufacturer of tennis equipment that appeals to advanced players. The firm produces a line of quality wooden and aluminum rackets, warm-up suits, and tennis shoes. The items are sold through tennis shops and sporting goods stores. Magazine ads appear in tennis publications. A lot of selling is conducted by pros in tennis shops. Tennis rackets are priced at $50 to $200, warm-up suits at $50 to $120, and tennis shoes at $40 to $80. The plan is keyed to the target market and integrates product, distribution, promotion, and price factors.

The last, and extremely important, aspect of planning by a marketer involves **control:** monitoring and reviewing overall and specific performance. Evaluations should be conducted at regular intervals. The external environment and internal company data should be reviewed continuously. In-depth research and analysis of performance (marketing audits) should be completed at least once or twice each year. Revisions need to be implemented when the external environment changes or the company encounters problems.

> *A marketer's control involves monitoring and evaluating overall as well as specific performance.*

Uncontrollable Factors

Uncontrollable factors are those elements affecting an organization's performance that cannot be directed by the organization and its marketers. It must be recognized that any marketing plan, no matter how well conceived, may fail if adversely influenced by uncontrollable factors. Therefore, the external environment must be continually monitored and its effects taken into account in any marketing plan. Furthermore, back-up plans relating to uncontrollable variables should be an important part of a marketing program. Uncontrollable variables that bear watching and anticipating are consumers, competition, government, the economy, technology, and independent media. See Figure 2-6.

> *Uncontrollable factors affect an organization's performance and cannot be directed by the organization and its marketers.*

Consumers

Although a marketer has control over the selection of a target market, he or she cannot control the characteristics of the population. Firms can react to but not control these consumer characteristics: age, income, marital status, occupation, race, education, and place and type of residence. For example, although Gerber could develop new baby foods, it could not stop the slowdown in births. To continue growing, Gerber has had to expand into other products and services, such as insurance.

A marketer must understand the cultural and social influences on consumer behavior. The purchases that consumers make are influenced

> *A marketer cannot control population characteristics.*

> *Cultural and social factors affect consumer purchases.*

Figure 2-6
Uncontrollable Factors

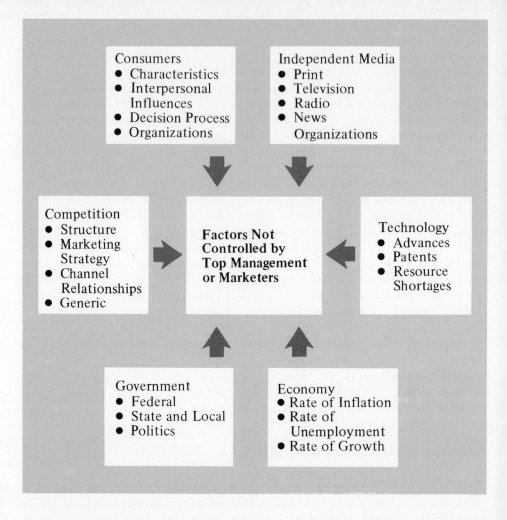

by family, friends, religion, level of education, standards for performance, taboos, customs, and other factors that shape a culture and society. For instance, in some parts of the United States, stores are not allowed to open on Sundays, liquor store sales are strictly regulated (as to prices, other goods that can be sold, days open, and who can buy alcoholic beverages), and movies are closely rated. In other parts of the United States, stores are regularly open seven days a week, liquor may be sold to eighteen-year-olds, and any movie can be shown uncut.

The decision process describes the actions a consumer takes when buying a product. Because consumers act differently in purchasing various types of products and services, a marketer needs to understand the consumer's decision process. The decision process explains the steps a consumer goes through when buying a product. In the case of an automobile, the consumer carefully searches for information about a number of cars, ranks several alternatives, selects a favorite, negotiates terms, and finally completes the purchase. With a hamburger, the consumer looks at his or her watch, sees that it is lunchtime, and goes to a nearby fast-food outlet.

Today, consumer groups and organizations speak out on behalf of consumers at public hearings, stockholder meetings, and before the media. To avoid negative consequences brought on by active consumer groups, a marketer must communicate with consumers, anticipate problems, respond to complaints, and make sure that his or her company operates properly.

Consumer groups and organizations are active.

Competition

A firm's competitors frequently affect its marketing strategy and its success in attracting a target market. Therefore, the competitive structure facing a firm needs to be defined and analyzed. The four possible competitive structures are monopoly, oligopoly, monopolistic competition, and pure competition. Table 2-3 shows the characteristics of each of these structures.

In a **monopoly,** one firm sells a particular product or service and has strict control over its marketing plan. With an **oligopoly,** there are a few large firms that account for most of an industry's sales and usually engage in nonprice competition. Under **monopolistic competition,** there are several firms, each of which tries to offer a unique marketing mix based on price or nonprice factors. In **pure competition,** many small firms sell identical products or services and are unable to create a differential advantage. Both domestic and foreign companies must be considered as part of the competitive structure. Monopolistic competition occurs most frequently, followed by oligopolistic industries.

Monopoly, oligopoly, monopolistic competition, or pure competition refers to the form of competitive structure within which a firm operates.

Table 2-3 **Competitive Structures**

Characteristics	Structures			
	Monopoly*	Oligopoly	Monopolistic Competition	Pure Competition
Number of firms	One	Few	Several	Many
Size of market for each firm	Small or large	Large	Small or large	Small
Control of marketing plan	Total control of price, distribution, promotion, and product	Some control of price, distribution, promotion, and product	Some control of price, distribution, promotion, and product	No control of price; ineffective control of distribution, promotion, and product
Ease of entry	Difficult	Difficult	Easy	Easy
Differential advantage	Only source of product	Nonprice marketing factors	Any marketing factors	None
Key marketing task	Maintain unique product status	Differentiate product on nonprice factors	Differentiate product on any factors	Ensure supply of product at low prices and widespread distribution

*Characteristics of a private sector monopolist (e.g., a firm with a patent for a product). A public-sector monopolist is more closely regulated.

After determining the characteristics of the market structure facing the firm, it must evaluate the marketing strategies of its competitors. Specifically, the firm must find out which markets are saturated and which are unfulfilled, the marketing plans and target markets of competitors, the images of competitors, the differential advantages of competitors, and the extent to which consumers are content with the level of service and quality provided by the competition.

Frequently, companies try to lessen competitors' impact by their own aggressive actions. For example, Clorox, the leading laundry bleach with well over half of all industry sales, adopted a heavy counterattack when Procter & Gamble began test marketing Vibrant bleach. Clorox introduced its own new brand, Wave, and stepped up advertising.[3]

The firm also needs to examine the existing channel relationships. In well-established industries, such as the supermarket industry, long-run relationships have been built up among manufacturers, wholesalers, and retailers. These relationships become assets as much as any raw materials or equipment. New firms may be unable to place products in channels like these, and existing firms may find it easy to place even the most innovative of products. For a firm such as Colgate-Palmolive, a great asset is its ability to place a new household product into virtually every supermarket across the United States.

Competition should be defined in generic terms—meaning as broadly as possible.

Finally, the firm should define its competition in generic terms, which means as broadly as possible. For instance, the competition for a movie theater is not just other movie theaters, but also television, sporting events, operas, plays, amusement parks, schools (continuing education programs), radio, reading materials, and parties. The theater owner needs to ask, "What can I do to compete with a whole variety of entertainment and recreation forms, in terms of movie selection, prices, hours, refreshments, parking, and the like?"

Government

Federal legislation deals with issues pertaining to interstate commerce. The *Federal Trade Commission (FTC)* is most responsible for enforcing this legislation.

For more than ninety years, the U.S. Congress has enacted a large amount of federal legislation that defines and controls the operations of business. During the early part of the twentieth century, this legislation was oriented toward protecting small businesses from large businesses. Laws involved antitrust, discriminatory pricing, and unfair trade practices. In the 1960s and 1970s, legislation was geared toward helping the consumer deal with deceptive and unsafe business practices. The late 1970s and early 1980s have seen a move toward greater deregulation of business.[4] Table 2-4 contains a listing of the main federal legislation affecting marketing. The **Federal Trade Commission (FTC)** is the major federal regulatory agency that monitors restraint of trade and enforces rules against unfair methods of competition.

Each state and local government has regulations for firms operating within its boundaries.

In addition to federal legislation and agencies, each state and local government has its own legal environment for firms operating within its boundaries. Laws regulate where a firm may locate, the hours it may be open, the types of items that may be sold, whether it may operate door-to-door, if unit pricing is required, and how merchandise must be labeled or dated.

State and local governments also provide incentives for companies

Table 2-4 **Key Federal Legislation Affecting Marketers**

A. Antitrust, Discriminatory Pricing, and Unfair Trade Practices

Year	Legislation	Major Purpose
1890	Sherman Act	To eliminate monopolies and sustain competition
1914	Clayton Act	To prohibit specific anticompetitive practices, such as tie-in sales, exclusive dealing, and price discrimination
1914	Federal Trade Commission (FTC) Act	To establish an independent regulatory agency to eliminate monopolies and restraint of trade and to enforce rules against unfair methods of competition
1936	Robinson-Patman Act	To prohibit price discrimination against channel members buying the same merchandise
1937	Miller-Tydings Act (repealed by Consumer Goods Pricing Act of 1975)	To permit retail price maintenance (price fixing) in order to protect small retailers against large chains and discounters
1938	Wheeler-Lea Amendment	To revise the FTC Act of 1914 to include unfair or deceptive practices
1946	Lanham Trademark Act	To protect and regulate trademarks and brand names
1950	Celler-Kefauver Antimerger Act	To limit or prohibit the acquisition of competitors or their assets if the effects of the acquisition would lessen competition

B. Consumer Protection

Year	Legislation	Major Purpose
1906	Food and Drug Act	To prohibit adulteration and misbranding of food and drugs, create the Food and Drug Administration, and regulate meat packing and shipping
1906	Meat Inspection Act	
1914	Federal Trade Commission Act	To establish an agency and provisions for protecting consumer rights
1938	Wheeler-Lea Amendment	
1939	Wool Products Labeling Act	To require wool products, fur products, and textile products to show contents and to prohibit sales of dangerous flammables
1951	Fur Products Labeling Act	
1953	Flammable Fabrics Act	
1958	Textile Fiber Identification Act	
1958	Food Additives Amendment	To prohibit food additives causing cancer, require the labeling of hazardous household products, and require drug manufacturers to demonstrate product effectiveness and safety
1960	Federal Hazardous Substances Labeling Act	
1962	Kefauver-Harris Drug Amendment	
1966	Fair Packaging and Labeling Act	To require packages to be labeled honestly and reduce package size proliferation
1966	National Traffic and Motor Vehicle Safety Act	To set safety standards for automobiles and tires
1966	Child Protection Act	To ban hazardous products used by children, create standards for child-resistant packages for hazardous products, and provide drug information
1969	Child Protection and Toy Safety Act	
1970	Poison Prevention Labeling Act	
1972	Drug Listing Act	
1966	Cigarette Labeling Act	To require health warnings on cigarette packages and ban cigarette advertising on radio and television
1970	Public Health Smoking Act	
1967	Wholesome Meat Act	To mandate federal inspection standards
1968	Wholesome Poultry Products Act	

Table 2-4 Key Federal Legislation Affecting Marketers (contd.)

B. Consumer Protection

Year	Legislation	Major Purpose
1968	Consumer Credit Protection Act	To have full disclosure of credit and loan terms and rates and regulate reporting and use of credit information
1970	Fair Credit Reporting Act	
1972	Consumer Product Safety Act	To create the Consumer Product Safety Commission and set safety standards
1975	Magnuson-Moss Consumer Product Warranty Act	To regulate warranties and set disclosure requirements
1975	Consumer Goods Pricing Act	To repeal the Miller-Tydings Act which permitted retail price maintenance
1980	Fair Debt Collection Act	To eliminate the harrassment of debtors and ban false statements to collect debts
1980	FTC Improvement Act	To reduce the power of the FTC to implement industry-wide trade regulations (This Act reversed the trend toward increased federal government protection of consumers)

C. Industry Deregulation

1978	Natural Gas Policy Act	To make the natural gas, airline, trucking, railroad, and banking industries more competitive
1978	Airline Deregulation Act	
1980	Motor Carrier Act	
1980	Staggers Rail Act	
1981	Depository Institutions Deregulatory Committee Act	
1982	Depository Institutions Act	

to operate. Recently, *Inc.* magazine rated each of the fifty states' attractiveness for small business on the basis of capital resources, energy costs, government commitment to small business, labor, taxes, and quality of life. Alabama, Arizona, California, Colorado, Idaho, Minnesota, Mississippi, North Carolina, North Dakota, and Texas were ranked highest.[5]

The political environment often signals legislation and government actions.

The political environment often affects legislation. Consumerism, nationalism, tax cuts, zoning, wage rates, unemployment, and other items are almost always discussed and debated through the political process before legislation is enacted. The issues of today frequently become the laws of tomorrow. A strength of the American political system is its continuity, which enables businesspeople to develop marketing strategies for long periods of time.

Economy

With high inflation, consumers may cut back on some purchases. *Real income* describes earnings after adjusting for inflation.

When the rate of inflation is high, the prices of some goods and services may go beyond the reach of many consumers; or consumers may be forced to alter their spending habits. For example, in 1981 the interest rate on mortgages reached 15 to 19 per cent, and the purchases of homes dropped dramatically. Likewise, as the price of meat goes up, many consumers switch to nonmeat substitutes.

Of importance to the marketer is what happens to *real income,* income adjusted for inflation, over time. For example, a marketer would not be concerned if a person's net income (after taxes) went from $15,000 to $20,000 per year while the price of food went from $100 to $120 per week. Income would have increased by 33⅓ per cent, while food prices rose 20 per cent. Therefore, real income would have increased, and there would be more money available for items other than food. On the other hand, if net income changed from $15,000 to $18,000 per year and food prices jumped from $100 to $150 per week, real income would decline (income up by 20 per cent; food up by 50 per cent) and there would be less money left for nonfood purchases.

A high rate of unemployment adversely affects some marketers, because people cut back on luxuries wherever possible. Low unemployment leads to increased sales of large-ticket items, as consumers are optimistic and willing to spend their earnings. In recent years, it has been extremely difficult for the U.S. economy to achieve low rates of inflation and low unemployment at the same time.

> High unemployment causes people to reduce purchases of luxuries.

The rate of economic growth is the annual increase in a region's or country's economy. The *Gross National Product (GNP)* measures the annual volume of goods and services produced in a country. When certain industries, such as automobile and housing, slow down, the effects are often felt in other areas, such as insurance and home furnishings. A high rate of growth means the economy in the region or country is usually good and marketing potential large.

> Economic growth is measured by annual changes in the *Gross National Product (GNP).*

During recessionary periods, firms usually alter their marketing strategies and place greater emphasis on the value and economy of their goods and services. For example, in 1982 commercials, A-1 Steak Sauce was shown on hamburgers, Michelin tires were called "surprisingly affordable," Ziploc food bags protected leftovers, and "The Citi never sleeps (Citibank)." At the same time, Xerox advertised the first sale in its history, made simple by a toll-free order number and easy-payment plan.[6]

Technology

Technology refers to the development and use of machinery, products, and processes. Many technological advances are beyond the control of individual firms, especially smaller ones. For example, no firm has been able to develop a cure for the common cold, and small retailers usually cannot afford the latest advances in physical distribution management.

> *Technology* includes machinery, products, and processes; and innovations may be beyond reach.

Patents (exclusive rights to sell new products or services for seventeen years) have limited lifespans. When a company loses patent protection, competition may increase sharply because other firms are able to use the original firm's techniques. In the late 1970s Kodak entered the self-developing camera market because Polaroid's early patents had expired.

As organizations head into the end of the twentieth century, they must realize the need for improved technology in order to remain competitive in foreign markets and to minimize the impact of resource shortages. Oil, clean air, clean water, and skilled craftspeople are among the declining resources that must be rechanneled.

> Organizations must plan to minimize the effect of resource shortages.

Independent Media

*Independent media help
shape perceptions of a
company's products and
overall image.*

The independent media can influence the government's, consumers', and publics' perceptions of a company's products and overall image. The media can provide positive or negative coverage of a company when it produces a new product, pollutes the air, mislabels merchandise, contributes to charity, or otherwise performs a newsworthy activity. This coverage may be by print media, television, radio, or news organizations. For these reasons, a good public relations department should distribute information to the independent media and always try to get the company's position written or spoken about.

It is important to note that, although public relations activities through independent media are uncontrollable, paid advertising is controllable by the marketer. Although media may reject advertising, if accepted it must be presented in the time interval and form stipulated by the firm.

Attainment of Objectives, Feedback, and Adaptation

*Together, controllable
and uncontrollable
factors affect success or
failure.*

The organization's level of success or failure in reaching its objectives depends on how well it directs and implements its controllable factors and the impact of uncontrollable factors on the marketing plan. As shown in Figure 2-2, it is the interaction of the organization's total offering with the uncontrollable environment that determines its success or failure.

*An organization needs
feedback to maximize its
efforts.*

In order to improve the marketing plan and ensure long-run attainment of objectives, the organization needs to acquire **feedback** (information about the uncontrollable environment, the organization's performance, and how well the marketing mix is received). Feedback is obtained by measuring consumer satisfaction, looking at competitive trends, evaluating the relationship with government agencies, monitoring the economy and potential resource shortages, reading or viewing the independent media, analyzing sales and profit trends, talking with channel members, and employing other methods of obtaining and assessing information.

*The firm needs to be
adaptive.*

After evaluating feedback, the firm needs to **adapt** its strategy to the surrounding environment, while continuing to utilize its differential advantage(s). To ensure long-term success, the firm must continually look for new opportunities that fit into its overall marketing plan and are attainable by the firm and respond to potential threats by revising marketing policies.

*Marketing myopia is an
inefficient, complacent
marketing approach.*

Marketing myopia, a short-sighted, narrow-minded view of marketing and its environment,[7] must be avoided at all costs:

> The duPonts and Cornings have succeeded not primarily because of their product or research orientation but because they have been thoroughly customer-oriented also. It is constant watchfulness for

opportunities to apply their technical know-how to the creation of
customer-satisfying uses which accounts for their prodigious output
of successful new products.[8]

Following are the adaptation approaches of three different organizations: Atari, Holiday Inn, and Southland Corporation. Each of these
companies has modified marketing strategy to maintain its strong position in the face of a dynamic environment.

Atari has dominated the home video game market. Nonetheless,
the firm has recently encountered serious problems in the wake of increased competition for both master components (Intellivision, Coleco,
etc.) and game cartridges (Activision, Parker Brothers, etc.), heavy price
cutting in the industry, overproduction of game cartridges, the personal
computer industry growing at the expense of the home video industry,
and the disappointing sales of the first Atari home computers. The company expected sluggish sales and poor profitability throughout 1983, as
it revised its strategy. Atari aggressively added new personal computers
and a sophisticated 5200 game system (shown in Figure 2-7), expanded
its advertising budget and employed Alan Alda as a spokesperson, sued
competitors for copyright infringement, cleared out overstocks of game
cartridges, and hired a new chief executive with a strong marketing
background. Atari hoped that these actions would restore it to its former
level of success.[9]

In the 1950s when Holiday Inn first developed the roadside signs
that were placed in front of its hotels, energy costs were low and the
"kitschy" green signs were used to attract customers, 95 per cent of

Figure 2-7
**The Atari 5200 Advanced
Game System**

Reprinted by permission.

(Left) The original basic
sign was forty-three feet
high and twenty-six feet
wide, with 426 incandes-
cent bulbs and 836 feet of
neon tubing. The marquee
had 128 feet of neon tubing.
Green, yellow, orange,
white, pink, blue, and red
colors were used.
(Right) The new basic sign
is shorter and narrower,
with only 32 fluorescent
tubes. The marquee uses little fluorescent tubing.
Green, orange, yellow, and
white colors are used; and
they are much brighter and
clearer than the old sign.
Reprinted by permission.

whom were vacationing families who drove up without reservations. By
1982, the energy costs of the signs had skyrocketed and less than 3 per
cent of customers checked in without prior reservations. In addition, a
survey showed that customers felt the signs made Holiday Inn appear
old-fashioned and cheap. As a result, Holiday Inn decided to spend $39
million to erect new signs at its 1,750 outlets in 56 countries. The new
signs are simple, sleek, and elegant. These signs will cut energy costs by
75 per cent and will be attractive to more sophisticated customers.[10]
Figure 2-8 shows the old and new Holiday Inn signs.

Southland Corporation owns and operates 7-Eleven, the largest
chain of convenience stores in the United States. Until the mid-1970s,
7-Eleven stores featured food, tobacco, and health and beauty aid items
and were located in midblock sites. Then, the stores' strategy was reviewed. The review showed that supermarkets were starting to stay
open longer hours and drawing some convenience store customers. In
addition, the 1973 oil embargo had caused service station gasoline
prices to rise substantially. In response to these factors, Southland increased the number of 7-Elevens carrying gasoline to 2,700 outlets (out
of 7,400) and began selling self-service gas at the lowest prices possible.
The company also expanded its use of corner store sites, closing many
mid-block stores. Both tactics have led to higher customer traffic and
sales. In 1975, 7-Eleven had total sales of under $2 billion and pumped
107 million gallons of gasoline. During 1982, total sales were more than
$6 billion and 1.15 billion gallons of gas were pumped.[11] See Figure 2-9.

Figure 2-9
7-Eleven Pumps Gasoline

Reprinted by permission of Southland.

Summary

The environment of marketing consists of all the controllable factors that are utilized by a firm and its marketers to achieve established objectives as well as the uncontrollable factors that influence the ability of a firm and its marketers to achieve these objectives.

Controllable variables are the elements of a strategy that are guided by the firm and its marketers. Top management decides on the line of business, overall objectives, the role of marketing, and the role of other business functions. Marketing directs the selection of a target market, the marketing mix (product or service, distribution, promotion, and price), and the control function. In addition, it is the responsibility of marketing to create a differential advantage, the set of unique factors in a company's marketing program that causes consumers to patronize the company and not its competitors.

Uncontrollable variables are the elements affecting an overall strategy that cannot be directed by the firm and its marketers. Among the most important uncontrollable variables are consumers, competition, government, the economy, technology, and the independent media.

An organization's level of success or failure is based on the interaction of controllable and uncontrollable factors. When implementing a marketing strategy, a marketer obtains feedback from the environment and adjusts the strategy to correct any deficiencies. Marketing myopia must be avoided.

KEY TERMS

After reading this chapter, you should understand these key terms:

Marketing environment	**Oligopoly**
Controllable factors	**Monopolistic competition**
Target market	**Pure competition**
Marketing objectives	**Federal Trade Commission (FTC)**
Differential advantage	**Real income**
Marketing organization	**Gross National Product (GNP)**
Marketing mix	**Technology**
Control	**Feedback**
Uncontrollable factors	**Adapt(ation)**
Monopoly	**Marketing myopia**

QUESTIONS FOR DISCUSSION

1. Explain the environment of marketing. Relate your answer to Frito-Lay.
2. What may occur if a firm does not analyze its entire environment in a systematic manner?
3. Which factors are controllable by top management? Why are these considered uncontrollable by marketers?
4. Describe the objectives, conflicts, and compromises among marketing and production, finance, accounting, engineering, purchasing, and research and development.
5. Which factors are controllable by marketing?
6. What are the two basic decisions to be made about the selection of a target market? Describe the target market for *Reader's Digest* magazine.
7. Give two real examples of differential advantage. Why is it so important for marketers?
8. Distinguish among functional, product-oriented, and market-oriented forms of marketing organizations.
9. What decisions must be made in developing a marketing mix?
10. Which factors are uncontrollable by the firm and its marketers?
11. What is meant by generic competition?
12. How can each of the following affect marketers?
    a. Rate of inflation
    b. Level of unemployment
    c. Changes in technology
    d. Resource shortages
13. If you worked for Intellivision, how would you respond to Atari's marketing strategy?
14. Why is 7-Eleven successfully able to sell gasoline while so many independent, full-service stations have gone out of business?

NOTES

1. "Frito-Lay May Find Itself in a Competition Crunch," *Business Week* (July 19, 1982), p. 186; and David P. Garino, "Anheuser-Busch Tests Eagle Brand Salted-Snack Foods," *Wall Street Journal* (February 14, 1983), p. 36.
2. See Philip Kotler, *Marketing Management: Analysis, Planning, and Control*, Fourth Edition (Englewood Cliffs, N.J.: Prentice-Hall, 1980), pp. 592–596; and Benson Shapiro, "Can Marketing and Manufacturing Coexist?" *Harvard Business Review*, Vol. 55 (October 1977), pp. 104–114.

3. Marilyn Chase, "P & G Wants to Market Bleach; Clorox Prepares for Big Fight," *Wall Street Journal* (June 24, 1982), p. 31.

4. See Ray O. Werner, "Marketing and the United States Supreme Court, 1975–1981," *Journal of Marketing*, Vol. 46 (Spring 1982), pp. 73–81; Edward Meadows, "Bold Departures in Antitrust," *Fortune* (October 5, 1981), pp. 180–188; Winston Williams, "Taking the Shackles Off Business," *New York Times* (March 1, 1981), Section 3, pp. 1, 15; and "Back to Cases at the FTC," *Business Week* (July 5, 1982), p. 90.

5. Kuldarshan Padda, "Report Card on the States," *Inc.* (October 1981), pp. 90–98.

6. Dennis Kneale, "Many Advertisers Alter Campaigns to Account for Recession Strategy," *Wall Street Journal* (August 10, 1982), pp. 1, 22.

7. Theodore Levitt, "Marketing Myopia," *Harvard Business Review*, Vol. 53 (September–October 1975), pp. 26–44, 173–181.

8. *Ibid.*, p. 27.

9. Neil Weinstock, "Atari's Video Game Invasion," *Marketing and Media Decisions* (Spring 1982, Special Edition), pp. 133–147; Laura Landro, "Atari Fiercely Tries to Protect Its Share of Video-Game Sales," *Wall Street Journal* (June 10, 1982), p. 33; and Bob Marich, "Cartridge Share Plummets; Can Atari Recover?" *Advertising Age* (February 7, 1983), pp. 3, 55.

10. Bill Abrams, "Holiday Inns Plans to Replace Its Kitschy Old Roadside Signs," *Wall Street Journal* (October 7, 1982), p. 35.

11. Shawn Tully, "Look Who's a Champ of Gasoline Marketing," *Fortune* (November 1, 1982), pp. 149–154.

MENNEN CO.: TURNING TO MARKETING FOR GROWTH* 1

CASES

Mennen Co. is a privately owned toiletries manufacturer that recently made the change from family to professional management of the firm. For the first time in Mennen's 100+ years, a nonfamily member now runs the company.

The shift to professional management was brought on by several factors. Internal management disputes were frequent, and personnel turnover was high. Despite being a pioneer in the marketing of products such as men's cologne and aftershave lotion, Mennen remained a small firm compared with its competitors. Annual sales were only $250 million per year. Said one observer, "Mennen is not a factor in any single market." In the shaving cream market that Mennen once dominated, it had a very small market share. This was also true of men's fragrances and deodorants.

Protein 21 women's shampoo provides a good illustration of Mennen's potential as well as its problems. The product was introduced in 1970 as a shampoo that would repair hair's split ends. Protein 21 quickly achieved 12 per cent of industry sales and had annual revenues of $50 million. Then, advertising and promotional support were cut back drastically. Today, Protein 21 has yearly sales of "a couple of million dollars."

Other past mistakes included:

- Rejecting a plan from Vidal Sassoon to sponsor a new brand of shampoos and hair conditioners. Currently, Vidal Sassoon has sales at about the same level as all of Mennen.
- Inadequate testing of Mennen E deodorant, which resulted in its removal from the market after consumers complained that it irritated their skin.
- Weak relations with retailers, brought on by inefficiency and poor promotion.

*The data in this case are drawn from "The Outsiders' Touch That's Shaking Up Mennen," *Business Week* (February 1, 1982), pp. 58–59.

To correct these errors, the new management at Mennen is taking a variety of actions. A team of marketing specialists has been hired. The advertising budget has been raised substantially. Attractive in-store product displays and innovative advertising campaigns are being implemented. Marginal items, such as Balm Barr skin care products for women, are being re-evaluated; and new product development efforts are being stepped up. The goal of the revised marketing strategy "is to broaden the corporate image from a marketer of toiletries aimed primarily at men to a supplier to the family—and particularly to the women's market."

QUESTIONS

1. Why did Mennen commit so many mistakes in the past?
2. How has the role of marketing changed at Mennen with the arrival of professional managers? What should the role of marketing be?
3. As a retailer, how would you react to Mennen's new strategy?
4. Will Mennen be able to succeed in the women's market? Explain your answer.

2 BAUSCH & LOMB: FACING STRONG COMPETITION IN THE CONTACT-LENS MARKET†

In 1971, Bausch & Lomb was given exclusive selling rights for soft contact lenses by the Food and Drug Administration. Three years later, other firms were allowed to enter this market. Now, almost 30 companies manufacture soft contact lenses, including Revlon, Johnson & Johnson, Ciba-Geigy, and Schering-Plough. And contact lens wearers are more loyal to their physicians or optometrists than to a brand of lenses.

When competition was first permitted, Bausch & Lomb reacted by changing its marketing strategy. It broadened the target market and aimed more promotion directly at consumers (rather than at physicians). Soft lenses were also distributed through boutiques staffed by opticians as well as through physicians' offices. Product quality was improved. Nonetheless, by 1982, competitors were able to lower Bausch & Lomb's share of industry sales to about 40 per cent of the total contact lens market. No individual competitor has more than 10 per cent of industry sales.

Bausch & Lomb's customers (physicians, opticians, retail stores) and competitors believe the firm lost market share because of arrogance toward clients and a lag in technological advances. One optometrist stated that Bausch & Lomb was "basically nasty to deal with. Now they realize, as lens fitting is getting more complex, they have to woo the professional practitioner."

To combat its competitors, who advertise heavily (Revlon "is peddling their lenses like perfume"), market many new products (such as extended-wear lenses), and offer gifts for volume purchases (such as a Mercedes-Benz for buying 15,000 lenses in a year or a Panasonic video recorder for 600 lenses), Bausch & Lomb has taken the offensive. It has a toll-free telephone service that enables doctors to receive lenses within 24 hours of an order. A marketing

†The data in this case are drawn from Ann Hughey, "Contact Lens Competition Gets Heated," *Wall Street Journal* (November 24, 1982), pp. 29, 39.

assistance program that takes care of all paperwork is available to doctors for $10 per patient. New lenses are being produced with greater regularity, such as toric lenses for astigmatism and bifocal lenses.

With falling profit margins, some competitors are abandoning contact lenses. One large firm, Warner Lambert, left the market since its research found that "even a substantial investment wouldn't guarantee anything more than a marginally profitable business."

QUESTIONS

1. Why would Bausch & Lomb have acted in a "nasty" manner toward the physicians and optometrists selling its products?
2. Could Bausch & Lomb have eliminated or limited competition by courting physicians and optometrists during the early 1970s?
3. What must Bausch & Lomb do now to protect or expand its share of the contact lens market?
4. Describe several environmental factors that Bausch & Lomb should consider as it plans for the future.

Information for Marketing Decisions

3

Chapter Preview

Chapter Objectives

1 To explain why marketing information is needed

2 To define marketing research and its components

3 To examine the scope of marketing research

4 To describe the marketing research process: problem definition, examination of secondary data, generation of primary data (when necessary), analysis of data, recommendations, and implementation of findings

5 To explain the role and importance of the marketing information system

The United States Census provides valuable information for all kinds of marketers. The 1980 *Census of Population*, released in 1981 and 1982, contains data collected from almost 100 million households. Other, more specialized censuses deal with manufacturers, wholesalers, and retailers and are conducted regularly. The Census Bureau processes more than 7,500 inquiries each month, forty per cent of which are from business.

Census data have many uses. They help companies in

- Specifying the size of a potential consumer market.
- Determining whether they should close due to a decline in the surrounding area.
- Identifying more affluent ZIP code areas for direct-marketing.
- Outlining industry sales and sales trends.
- Deciding when and where to buy advertising time and space.

- Monitoring environmental changes.
- Developing computer graphics of geographic areas.

In 1970, a complete copy of census data was sold to interested parties for $100,000. The entire 1980 census, more than 300,000 pages of printed statistics, is available on computer tape for about $10,000. Additionally, census materials are maintained in many libraries and summarized in the annual *Statistical Abstract of the United States*. The Census Bureau attends over 70 trade shows each year to describe its offerings.

The 1980 census incorporates four significant revisions over 1970. Head of household is defined as whoever holds the mortgage or pays the bills; previously, males were usually denoted as household heads. Better racial and ethnic data are available. Commuting patterns are traced. Small Area Income Data provide insights about very precise geographic areas.[1]

Why Information Is Needed

To operate properly in the marketing environment, it is necessary to obtain adequate information before and after making decisions. Relying on intuition, executive judgment, and past experience may not be sufficient, as Figure 3-1 indicates.

With good information, marketers can improve their decision-making abilities.

There are many reasons why relevant information should be collected when constructing, implementing, and revising a marketing plan or any of its elements. Risk is reduced, because potentially expensive failures can be avoided before cost outlays become too high and products or services that have a negative image can be modified or removed from the market before they hurt a company's overall image. Consumer attitudes, including likes and dislikes, are ascertained. The uncontrollable environment is monitored. The marketing strategy and each of its elements (product, distribution, promotion, and price) are coordinated; and the correct selection of one strategy alternative from among a number of choices is aided. Success or failure is measured by comparing actual performance with pre-established goals.

Marketing information is also helpful in selling a product because it can be used to enhance a firm's credibility. An advertisement or sales presentation that emphasizes factual information, such as the results of taste tests or the percentage of doctors recommending an item, has a higher level of customer acceptance than one that is merely entertain-

Figure 3-1
**A Problem Proper Marketing
Information Could Have
Avoided**

ROTHCO
ORIGINAL

Reprinted by permission of
Rothco.

"HERE'S THE PROBLEM: IT'S HOMOGENIZED, HYDROGENIZED,
ENRICHED, FORTIFIED AND POLYUNSATURATED - BUT IT STILL
TASTES TERRIBLE!"

ing. In addition, advertisements that make claims must be substantiated
by research findings and companies promoting price reductions on merchandise must prove that it was originally sold at higher prices.

Marketing and top management often need information to gain
support for a decision or to defend a decision already made. For example, a marketing manager may be better able to persuade top management to introduce a new product if a test market is favorable. After the
new product is introduced, top management may explain its decision to
stockholders by citing research results that indicate future success.

Finally, information is often gathered to verify intuition. In this
case, a marketer may have a feeling about some aspect of the marketing
plan or the overall plan itself but seek out further information to prove
or disprove that intuition before implementing a decision.

Marketing Research Defined

Marketing research is

> the systematic gathering, recording, and analyzing of data about
> problems relating to the marketing of goods and services. Such re-
> search may be undertaken by impartial agencies or by business firms
> or their agencies for the solution of their marketing problems.[2]

and:

> the inclusive term which embraces all research activities carried on
> in connection with the management of marketing work.[3]

Several points in these definitions need to be emphasized. First, to be effective, marketing research must be systematic and not haphazard or disjointed. Second, marketing research involves a series of steps or a process. It is not a one-step activity; it includes data collection, recording, and analysis. Third, data may be available from different sources: the company itself, an impartial agency, or a specialist in research working for the company. Fourth, marketing research may be applied to any aspect of marketing that requires information to aid decision making.

Marketing research involves a systematic approach that may be applied to any aspect of marketing requiring information.

When employing marketing research, the **scientific method** should be followed. The scientific method is based on objectivity, accuracy, and thoroughness.[4] Objectivity means that research is conducted in an unbiased, open-minded manner. Conclusions or opinions are not reached until after all data have been collected and analyzed. Accuracy refers to the use of research tools that are carefully constructed and utilized. Each aspect of research, such as the sample chosen, questionnaire format, interviewer selection and training, and tabulation of responses, needs to be well planned and implemented. For example, all questions in a survey should be pretested to ensure that each word is understood by prospective respondents. Thoroughness deals with the comprehensive nature of research. Mistaken conclusions may be reached if research does not probe deeply or widely enough.

The scientific method requires objectivity, accuracy, and thoroughness.

A company's decision to use marketing research does not mean that it must undertake extensive, expensive studies like test marketing and national consumer attitude surveys. The firm may achieve its objectives through an analysis of internal sales data or informal meetings with sales personnel.[5]

Marketing research may be formal or informal.

A recent study showed that many companies have some type of formal marketing research department and that large firms are more likely to have many researchers and higher budgets than small companies.[6]

Marketing Research Process

The **marketing research process** is comprised of a series of activities: the definition of the problem or issue to be studied; examination of secondary data (previously collected); generation of primary data (new), if necessary; analysis of information; recommendations; and implementation of findings.

The marketing research process consists of (1) problem definition, (2) secondary data, (3) primary data, (4) analysis, (5) recommendations, and (6) implementation of findings.

Figure 3-2 presents the complete marketing research process. Each step is undertaken in order. For example, secondary data are not examined until the firm has stated the problem or issue to be studied, and primary data are not generated until secondary data are thoroughly reviewed. The dotted line around primary data means that primary data do not always have to be collected. In many instances a firm is able to obtain sufficient information without gathering new data. Only when secondary data are inadequate should a firm collect primary data. The marketing research process is described next.

Figure 3-2
The Marketing Research
Process

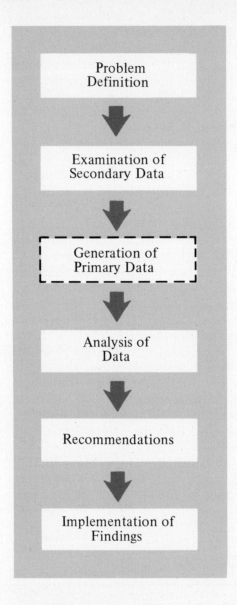

Problem Definition

**A *problem definition*
describes the marketing
research topic to be
investigated.**

Problem definition is a statement of the topic to be investigated in marketing research. Without a precise definition of the topic to be studied, a researcher may collect irrelevant and expensive data and confuse rather than clarify issues. Problem definition should direct the research process toward the collection and analysis of specific information for the purpose of decision making.

**Exploratory research is
used when the problem
definition is uncertain;
conclusive research is
used to solve a well-
defined study objective.**

When a researcher is uncertain about the precise topic to be investigated, **exploratory research** should be employed. The purpose of exploratory research is to develop a clear definition of the research problem by utilizing informal analysis. After the problem definition has been clarified, **conclusive research** should be used. Conclusive research is structured data collection and analysis for the solution of a specific problem or objective. Exploratory research techniques are not as structured as conclusive research. Table 3-1 shows how exploratory and conclusive research are used.

Secondary Data

Secondary data are those that have been previously gathered for purposes other than solving the current problem under investigation. Whether secondary data completely solve the research problem of the firm or not, their low cost and relatively fast availability require that primary data not be collected until a thorough search of secondary data is completed. To assess the overall value of secondary data, the researcher needs to weigh low costs, speed, and access against accuracy and relevance.

Secondary data have been previously gathered for purposes other than the current problem.

Many types of secondary data are inexpensive. Company records, trade publications, government publications, and general periodicals are each inexpensive to use. Data collection forms, interviewers, and experimental designs are unnecessary.

Advantages

The assembly of secondary data is normally quick. Company, industry, government, and library records can be gathered and analyzed almost immediately, whereas the generation of primary data may take up to several months.

There frequently are several sources of secondary data. These allow a company to obtain various perspectives and large amounts of information and to verify data. With a primary study, limited data and only one perspective are usually obtained.

The collection of secondary data is normally quick and inexpensive, and quite helpful in exploratory research.

A secondary data source may contain information that the firm would be unable to compile itself. For instance, the census data collected by the government could not be compiled by a private company.

When secondary data are assembled by an independent source such as *Fortune* or *Business Week*, the results are believable. Both of

Table 3-1 **Exploratory and Conclusive Research**

Vague Research Problem	Exploratory Research	Precise Research Problem	Conclusive Research
1. Why are sales declining?	1. Discussions among key personnel to identify major cause	1. Why is turnover of sales personnel so high?	1. Survey sales personnel, interview sales managers
2. Is advertising effective?	2. Discussions among key advertising personnel to define effectiveness	2. Do customers recall an advertisement the day after it appears?	2. Survey customers and noncustomers to gauge advertising recall
3. Will a reduction in price increase sales volume?	3. Discussions among key personnel to determine the level of a price reduction	3. Will a 10 per cent price reduction have a significant impact on sales?	3. Run an in-store experiment to determine effects
4. How can sales be increased?	4. Discussions among key personnel to determine alternatives	4. Should new product A or B be introduced?	4. Survey customers, collect and analyze marketing data

these sources have a high level of credibility and a reputation for thoroughness.

Secondary data are helpful in situations where exploratory research is needed. A search of secondary data often enables the researcher to develop a specific problem definition before collecting primary data. Furthermore, background information about a problem can be gathered from secondary data.

Disadvantages

Secondary data may not suit the purposes of current research, may be dated or imprecise, or may not be complete enough.

Available secondary data may not suit the purposes of current research because they were collected for other reasons. For example, the units of measurement may be different from what are needed. The firm might require regional or local data, while secondary information is broken down by state or country. In addition, secondary data may not be complete enough for the company—e.g., industry sales not collected by age group, income level, and occupation of customers.

Secondary data may be dated or obsolete. Because the information was obtained for other purposes, it may have outlived its usefulness. Conclusions and statistics of a few years before may no longer be valid. For instance, the *Census of Population* is conducted only once a decade and the *Census of Retail Trade* is undertaken only once each five years.

The precision with which secondary data were collected, analyzed, and reported may be lacking. The firm must determine for itself whether the data were compiled in an unbiased, objective manner. The purpose, data collection technique, and method of analysis of the original study should each be examined for bias. This is especially important when the source of the study had a special interest in the results. Supporting evidence (actual data) should be read as well as summary reports.

The source of secondary data may not present all of its findings in a public report, because it may be hurt if competitors gain too much information. Generalities and omissions should be noted by the researcher. It is also important to distinguish among sources and rely on the one with the best reputation. Conflicting results reported by equally accurate sources may require the researcher to collect fresh (primary) data.

The reliability of secondary data is not always known. Many research projects are not retested. Therefore, the user of secondary data hopes that the results from one limited prior study can be applied to a current research problem.

Sources

There are two major forms of secondary data, internal and external. Internal secondary data are available within the company. External secondary data are available from sources outside the firm.

Internal secondary data are available from a firm's records or its own past studies.

Internal Secondary Data. Before spending time and money searching for external secondary data or collecting primary data, the researcher should look at the information contained inside his or her company. Internal sources include budgets, sales figures, profit-and-loss statements, customer billings, inventory records, prior research reports, and written reports.[7]

External Secondary Data. If the research problem has not been solved through internal secondary data, a firm should utilize external secondary data sources. External data are available from both government and nongovernment sources.

The government collects and distributes a wide range of statistics and descriptive materials. *The Monthly Catalog of United States Government Publications* contains a listing of these items. When using government data, particularly census statistics, the date of the project must be considered.

There are three sources of nongovernment secondary data: regularly published periodicals; books, monographs, and other nonregular publications; and commercial research firms.

Regularly published periodicals contain articles on various aspects of marketing and are available in business libraries or via subscriptions. Some are quite broad in scope *(Business Week, Journal of Marketing)*; others are more specialized *(Journal of Advertising, Journal of Consumer Research)*.

Books, monographs, and other nonrecurring literature are published by a number of organizations. Some groups, such as the American Marketing Association, provide information to increase knowledge and professionalism. Others, such as the Better Business Bureau, are involved with self-regulation and public opinion. Yet another type, such as the National Retail Merchants Association, functions as a spokesperson for its industry as well as an information center. Each of these organizations distributes materials for a nominal fee or free of charge.

Commercial research firms conduct periodic and ongoing studies and make the results of the studies available to many clients for a fee. The fee can be quite low or range into the tens of thousands of dollars, depending on the extent of the data. This kind of research is secondary when a company acts as a subscriber and does not request specific studies pertaining only to itself. Several large commercial research firms specialize in selling secondary data and provide a number of services at lower costs than a company would incur if the data were collected for its sole use.

A. C. Nielsen, founded in 1923, is by far the largest commercial research firm in the U.S. with 1981 revenues of $411 million. Among the services offered by Nielsen are its retail store index, television viewing measurement, computerized grocery store product scanning, and a data bank containing 40 years of information.[8] Figure 3-3 shows Nielsen's newest meter for measuring television viewing.

Primary Data

Primary data are those collected to solve the specific problem or issue under investigation. Primary data are necessary when a thorough analysis of secondary data is unable to provide satisfactory information. To evaluate the overall value of primary data, the researcher must weigh precision, currentness, and reliability against high costs, time pressures, and limited access to materials.

Figure 3-3
The New Nielsen Television Meter

Nielsen's new meter box (right) and remote-control unit (left).

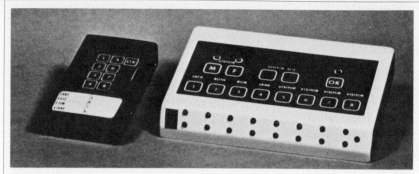

Here is how the new A.C. Nielsen push-button audience composition meter operates, according to Larry Fierk, Nielsen promotion director.

A Nielsen installer visits a household and places the meter box atop the family's TV set; if the household has four TV sets, four meter boxes are installed. The boxes come in two colors to match the decor of the viewing room and style of TV set. A wire is connected to the set so the meter box can monitor which channels are being viewed. The meter is calibrated with the number of channels available to the household. If the TV set is equipped with a remote-control channel selector, the homeowner is given a remote-control device to operate the meter. Homes without remote-control channel selectors are *not* given remote-control units for the meter boxes. This is done to maintain the viewer's normal channel-switching behavior. The black rectangle on the lower left side of the box is the sensor for the remote-control unit.

Another wire is run to an out-of-the-way location, where it is connected to a "multipurpose home unit," a small memory box which stores the viewing data and transmits them to Nielsen's central computer. A separate telephone line is used for this purpose, and allows Nielsen's computer to "communicate" with the meter boxes.

The top of the meter box has touch-sensitive panels which bear the names of each family member as well as "visitors" to the viewing room. Touch-sensitive panels also are included to record the sex of the visitor and his/her age. The age buttons are depressed until the proper numbers appear. Another panel labeled "OK" is pressed each time a channel is changed but the composition of the viewing audience stays the same (no one has entered or left the room). If the TV set is turned on, and the viewer fails to enter the appropriate information on the box, a red light (far right side of front panel) blinks until the data are entered.

If mom, dad, and son Joey sit down to watch TV, a family member will press the buttons marked mom, dad, and Joey. The front panel of the box has two rows of lights (red on top, green on bottom) corresponding to the touch-sensitive panels. The red lights indicate which individuals are not in the viewing room. The green lights indicate family members who are in the room while the set is on. If dad leaves the room for an hour, he must press the "dad" button to indicate he is not present. When dad returns to the room, he once again presses the "dad" button. A small pull-out drawer at the bottom of the box (not shown in photo) contains bilingual operating instructions (Spanish and English).

Source: Bernard Whalen, "How New Meter Works," *Marketing News* (January 21, 1983), Section 1, p.5; and A. C. Nielsen. Reprinted by permission.

Primary data are collected to fit the precise purposes of the current research problem. Units of measure and level of detail are matched to the objectives of the company. The data are current, because dated information is not used or collected. Attitudes, consumer characteristics, and other factors are up to date.

Data are collected by the firm itself or by an outside source carrying out a tailor-made research study for the firm. The source is known and controlled, and procedures are constructed for the specific study. There are no conflicting data from different sources, and the reliability of the research can be determined. Secrecy can be maintained if competitors do not see study results or know research is being conducted. This is not true with secondary data, which are more accessible.

When secondary data do not resolve all questions, the collection and analysis of primary data are the only way to acquire information.

The collection of primary data may be quite time consuming. For example, a test market may require six months for accurate results to occur. Primary data may be expensive to obtain. For instance, a consumer survey may cost several thousand dollars.

Some types of information cannot be collected. Usually, accurate census data can only be gathered by the government. In addition, some respondents may not answer questions or may not treat the study seriously.

The company's perspective may be limited, because only one data source is used. Finally, the organization may be unable to collect or analyze primary data and need understandable secondary data.

If the company decides that primary data are necessary, it must develop a research design. The ***research design*** is the "specified framework for controlling data collection"[9] and includes the following decisions.

Who Collects the Data? The company can collect the data itself or hire an outside research firm for a specific project. The advantages of an internal research department are knowledge of company operations, total access to company personnel, ongoing assembly and storage of data, and high loyalty or commitment. The disadvantages of an internal department are continuous costs, narrow perspective, and too much support for management. The strengths and weaknesses of an outside research firm are the opposite of those for the inside department.

What Information Should Be Collected? The kinds and amounts of information to be collected will be based on the problem definition formulated by the company. Exploratory research requires less data collection than conclusive research.

Who or What Should Be Studied? First, the researcher must stipulate the people or objects to be studied. This is known as the population. People studies generally involve customers (current, former, potential; light product users, heavy product users; customers categorized by demographic and life-style dimensions), company personnel (such as

Advantages

Primary data are precise, current, tailored to the company's needs, and private.

Disadvantages

The problems with primary data are collection time, expense, unavailability, and bias.

Research Design

The *research design* is an outline for data collection.

The company can use internal researchers or outside research personnel.

A population is the people or objects to be studied.

salespeople, sales managers), and/or channel members (wholesalers, retailers). Object studies usually center on company and/or product performance.

Second, the manner in which people or objects are selected for investigation must be determined. Large and dispersed populations frequently are examined by **sampling** procedures. Sampling requires the analysis of selected people or objects in the specified population, rather than all of them. Sampling saves time and money; when used properly, the accuracy and representativeness of sampling can be measured.

Third, the size of the sample to be investigated must be stated. Generally speaking, a large sample will yield greater accuracy and require higher costs than a small sample. There are statistical methods for assessing sample size in terms of costs and accuracy, but a description of them is beyond the scope of this text.

What Technique of Data Collection Should Be Used? There are four basic methods for primary data collection: survey, observation, experiment, and simulation.

A ***survey*** systematically gathers information from respondents by communicating with them. It can uncover data about attitudes, past purchases, and consumer characteristics. Yet, it is susceptible to incorrect or biased answers. With a survey, a questionnaire is used to record responses. A survey can be conducted in person, over the telephone, or by mail.

A survey may be nondisguised or disguised. In a nondisguised survey, the respondent is told the real purpose of the study. In a disguised survey, the respondent is not told the real purpose of the study. The latter is used to get honest attitudes or feelings and to avoid the respondent answering what he or she thinks the interviewer or researcher wants to hear or read.

The ***semantic differential*** is a list of bipolar (opposite) adjective scales. It is a survey technique that employs rating scales instead of, or in addition to, questions. It may be disguised or nondisguised, depending on whether the respondent is told the true reason for the study. Each adjective in the semantic differential is evaluated along a bipolar scale, and average ratings for all respondents are computed. An overall company or product profile is then developed. This profile may be compared with competitors' profiles and consumers' ideal ratings. An example of a completed semantic differential appears in Figure 3-4.

Multidimensional scaling is another popular survey research tool that may be disguised or nondisguised. With multidimensional scaling, respondents' attitudes are surveyed for many product and company attributes. Then, computer analysis enables the firm to develop a single product or company rating, rather than a profile of several individual characteristics. A statistical description of the technique is beyond the scope of this text, but Figure 3-5 shows how it can be used to construct single overall ratings. In the figure, consumer attitudes about six brands of facial tissue and the consumers' ideal rating of facial tissue are shown. Brand A most closely matches the consumer's ideal.

Sampling involves an examination of selected members of the population.

A *survey* gathers information from respondents by communicating with them.

The *semantic differential* is a survey technique that employs rating scales.

Multidimensional scaling analyzes respondents' attitudes in order to develop an overall product or company rating.

Figure 3-4
Semantic Differential for a Camera

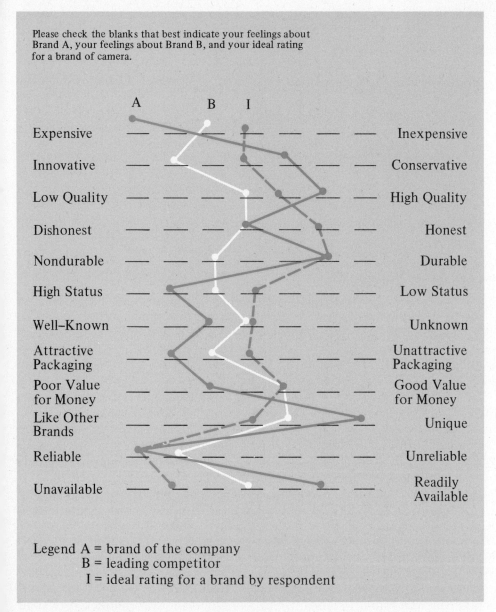

Please check the blanks that best indicate your feelings about Brand A, your feelings about Brand B, and your ideal rating for a brand of camera.

| A | B | I |

Expensive — — — — — — — Inexpensive
Innovative — — — — — — — Conservative
Low Quality — — — — — — — High Quality
Dishonest — — — — — — — Honest
Nondurable — — — — — — — Durable
High Status — — — — — — — Low Status
Well–Known — — — — — — — Unknown
Attractive Packaging — — — — — — — Unattractive Packaging
Poor Value for Money — — — — — — — Good Value for Money
Like Other Brands — — — — — — — Unique
Reliable — — — — — — — Unreliable
Unavailable — — — — — — — Readily Available

Legend A = brand of the company
          B = leading competitor
          I = ideal rating for a brand by respondent

Observation is a research technique in which present behavior or the results of past behavior are observed and recorded. People are not questioned, and their cooperation is not necessary. Interviewer and question bias are minimized. Frequently, observation is used in actual situations.[10] The major disadvantages are that attitudes cannot be determined and observers may misinterpret behavior.

In disguised observation, the consumer is not aware that he or she is being watched. A two-way mirror or hidden camera would be used. With nondisguised observation, the participant knows that he or she is being observed. Direct observation is the viewing of present behavior,

In *observation*, present behavior or the results of past behavior are observed and recorded.

Figure 3-5
Multidimensional Scaling—Ratings for Facial Tissues

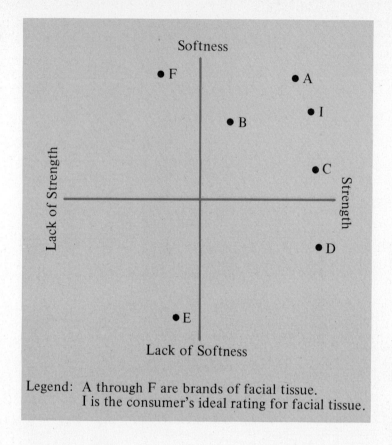

Legend: A through F are brands of facial tissue.
I is the consumer's ideal rating for facial tissue.

whereas indirect observation views past behavior. Litter in garbage dumps and food cans in consumer pantries are items that may be analyzed through indirect observation. Human observation is carried out by people; mechanical observation records behavior through electronic or other means, such as a movie camera filming in-store customer behavior.

In an *experiment,* one or more factors are manipulated by the researcher under controlled conditions.

An ***experiment*** is a type of research in which one or more marketing factors are manipulated under controlled conditions. A factor may be any element of marketing from package design to advertising media. In an experiment just the factor under investigation is manipulated; all other factors remain constant. For example, in order to evaluate a new package design for a product, the manufacturer could send new packages to five retail outlets and old packages to five similar retail outlets. All marketing factors other than packaging would remain the same. After one month, sales of the new package through the five test outlets would be compared with sales of the old package through the five similar outlets.

The major advantage of an experiment is that it is able to show cause and effect—for example, a new package design increases sales. It is also systematically structured and implemented. The major disadvantages are high costs, contrived settings, and the inability to control all factors in or affecting the marketing plan.

Simulation is a computer-based technique that manipulates mar-

Technique	Most Appropriate Uses	Table 3-2
1. Survey	Determination of consumer attitudes and motivations, evaluation of commercials, measurement of purchase intentions, relation of consumer characteristics to attitudes	**Uses of Primary Data-Collection Techniques**
Personal	Extensive, in-depth probing; open-ended responses determine direction of questions by interviewer; use of demonstrations and props; disguised study	
Telephone	Fast responses needed, short questionnaire, large sample	
Mail	Large sample, personal questions, funds limited, timing not important, lengthy questionnaire	
2. Observation	Examination under natural conditions, interest in behavior not attitudes	
Human	Traffic counts and flow, analysis of litter, employee behavior	
Mechanical	Tachistoscope (measures responses to changes in advertisement time), pupilometer (measures changes in the size of the pupil of the eye during advertisements in order to gauge emotional responses to messages), galvanic skin response (measures changes in perspiration during advertisements in order to gauge emotional responses to messages)	
3. Experiment	Control of the research environment essential, cause-and-effect relationship important to establish	
4. Simulation	Many interrelationships among variables to be derived and analyzed	

keting factors on paper rather than in a real setting. First, a model of the controllable and uncontrollable factors facing the firm is constructed. Then, the factors are manipulated via the computer to determine their effects on the overall marketing strategy. Simulation requires no consumer cooperation and is able to handle many interrelated factors. However, it is expensive and difficult to use.

    Table 3-2 shows the most appropriate uses for each technique of primary data collection.

Simulation involves complex computer analysis, based on marketer inputs.

How Much Will the Study Cost? The overall and specific costs of the study must be clearly outlined. These costs include executive time, researcher time, support staff time, computer usage, respondents' incentives (if any), interviewers, printing, pretesting, special equipment, and marketing costs (such as advertising). The costs of the study should be evaluated against the benefits to be derived from having better information.

The costs of research include everything from personnel time to marketing costs.

How Will the Data Be Collected? Data collection can be administered by others or self-administered. With administered questionnaires, interviewers are responsible for asking questions or observing behavior, noting responses or behavior, and explaining questions (if necessary) to a respondent. In self-administered questionnaires, respondents read the

With administered questionnaires, interviewers ask or observe; in self-administered questionnaires, respondents record their own answers.

questions and write their own answers. In the choice of these techniques, there is a trade-off between control and interviewer probing (administered) versus privacy and limited interviewer bias (self-administered).

How Long Will the Data Collection Period Be? The researcher must stipulate the time frame within which data will be collected, or else a study can drag on. Too long a time frame may cause inconsistent responses and violations of secrecy. Short time frames are easy to set for personal and telephone surveys. Mail surveys, observation, and experiments require substantially more time. Nonetheless, time limits must be defined.

When and Where Should Information Be Collected? The day and time of data collection must be specified. In addition, it must be decided whether the study is undertaken on the firm's premises or off them. The researcher has to weigh immediacy and convenience versus a desire to investigate hard-to-reach respondents at the proper time of the year.

Data Collection

After all aspects of the research design are thoroughly detailed, the data are actually collected. It is important that the personnel responsibile for data collection be adequately supervised and follow directions exactly. Responses or observations must be entered correctly.

Data Analysis

Data analysis consists of coding, tabulation, and analysis.

In *data analysis,* forms are first coded and tabulated and then analyzed. Coding is the process by which each completed data form is numbered and response categories are labeled. Tabulation is the calculation of summary data for each response category. Analysis is the evaluation of responses, usually by statistical techniques, as they pertain to the specific problem under investigation. The relationship of coding, tabulation, and analysis is shown in Figure 3-6.

Recommendations

Recommendations direct future actions.

Recommendations are suggestions for future actions by the company, based on the data collected by the researcher. They are generally presented in written (in some cases oral) form to management. The report must be written for the audience that will read it. For instance, terminology must be defined. Figure 3-6 shows recommendations flowing from completed research.

Implementation of Findings

Management must determine how to respond to research.

The research report represents feedback to management, which is responsible for utilizing findings. If management ignores weaknesses or company problems, research has little value. If management bases decisions on research results, then marketing research has great value and the organization benefits in the short and long run. Figure 3-6 contains an illustration of a company implementing research findings.

Partial Questionnaire

Total Responses

1. **Do you drink coffee?**

   ☐ Yes   01   375

   ☐ No   02   125

2. **Which of these brands have you heard of? Check all the answers that apply.**

   ☐ Brim   03   195

   ☐ Sanka   04   340

   ☐ Savarin   05   212

   ☐ None   06   63

3. **Compared to tea, coffee is (Check only <u>one</u> answer)**

   ☐ more bitter   07   140

   ☐ better for your health   08   12

   ☐ more energizing   09   240

   ☐ more expensive   10   108

Coding: Questionnaires numbered A001 to A500.
Each response labeled 01 to 10 (e.g., Sanka is 04, more energizing is 09).
Question 2 is a multiple–response question.

Tabulation: Total responses as shown above right.

Analysis: 75% drink coffee; Sanka is the most well–known brand; only 39% are familiar with Brim; coffee is viewed as energizing; yet compared to tea, it is not seen as better for health; high prices may be a problem.

Recommendations: The advertising of Brim must be increased and concentrate on stimulating brand awareness; emphasis should be placed on good taste, energizing qualities, and low price per serving.

Implementation of findings: A new advertising campaign will be developed and the annual media budget expanded. Other suggestions will be accepted as noted above.

Figure 3-6
Data Analysis, Recommendations, and Implementation of Findings for a Study on Brim Coffee

Marketing Information System

Companies should not approach marketing information collection as a haphazard, infrequent occurrence that is only necessary when the firm needs to generate data about a specific marketing topic. When marketing research alone is used, the company faces several risks:

When marketing information is seldom gathered, and only in the form of marketing research, the firm may encounter several risks.

1 Previous studies may not be stored in an easy-to-use format.
2 There may be a lack of awareness about environmental changes and competitors' actions.
3 Information collection may be disjointed.
4 Time lags may result whenever a new research study is required.
5 There may be no data to analyze over several comparable time periods.
6 Marketing plans and decisions may not be effectively reviewed.
7 Actions may be reactionary rather than anticipatory.

Marketing research should be considered as just one part of an ongoing, integrated information process. It is essential that a firm develop and utilize a system for scanning the environment in a continuous manner and for storing data, so that they may be reviewed in the future. A **marketing information system (MIS)** can be defined as

> a set of procedures and methods designed to generate, store, analyze, and disseminate anticipated marketing decision information on a regular, continuous basis.[11]

Figure 3-7 presents a basic marketing information system. In this system, the firm begins with a statement of company objectives. These objectives are influenced by environmental factors, such as competition, government, and the economy. The objectives provide broad guidelines that direct marketing planning. Marketing plans involve the controllable factors explained in Chapter 2: selection of a target market, marketing objectives, the type of marketing organization, the marketing mix (product or service, distribution, promotion, and price), and control.

The key part of a *marketing information system* is the *marketing intelligence network,* which involves *marketing research, continuous monitoring,* and *data storage.*

After the marketing plans are outlined, the total information needs of the marketing department can be specified and satisfied through a **marketing intelligence network,** which consists of marketing research, continuous monitoring, and data storage. **Marketing research** is used to obtain precise information to solve research problems. It may acquire information from storage (internal secondary data) or collect external secondary data and/or primary data. **Continuous monitoring** is the procedure by which the changing environment is regularly viewed. Continuous monitoring can include subscriptions to business and trade publications, observing news reports, regularly obtaining information from employees and customers, attending industry meetings, and watching competitors' actions. **Data storage** contains all the information previously collected through marketing research and continuous monitoring that is retained by the organization for future reference.

Figure 3-7
A Basic Marketing Information System

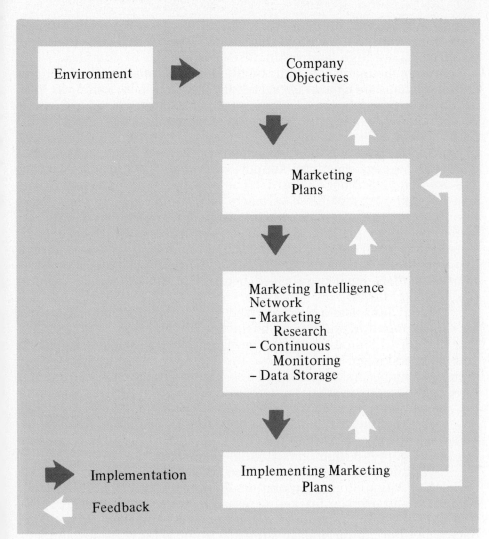

Depending on the resources of the firm and the complexity of information needs, the marketing intelligence network may or may not be computerized. Smaller firms can operate such systems very efficiently without computerization. The ingredients for the success of any system are consistency, thoroughness, and a good filing technique.

Marketing plans are implemented on the basis of information obtained from the intelligence network. For example, by continuous monitoring, the firm may determine that the costs of raw materials will be rising by 7 per cent during the following year. This would give the company time to explore its marketing options (e.g., switch to substitute materials, pass along costs, absorb costs) and select one alternative to be implemented. If monitoring was not in effect, the firm might be caught by surprise and forced to absorb costs, without any choice.

In general, a marketing information system offers many advantages: organized data collection, broad perspective, retention of important data, avoidance of crises, coordination of the marketing plan, speed, quantifiable results, and cost-benefit analysis. However, developing a marketing information system may not be easy. Initial time and manpower costs are high, and setting up a system can be complex.

Among the many companies with well-structured marketing information systems are Quaker Oats, Holiday Inns, and J. W. Robinson. Each devotes considerable time and resources to its system.

Quaker Oats has had a computerized marketing information system for more than a decade. This system "plays a significant role in tracking of new products, provides top management with summary statistics and charts for strategy meetings, supports brand and industry forecasting, and supports customer analyses." The MIS has data storage of 20 million numbers. Any of these numbers can be retrieved in less than a minute. Computer simulations can also be undertaken. At Quaker, the MIS relies on simple English language commands (such as GET for retrieve) rather than complex computer programming; this makes the system easy to use by marketing executives. The firm calculates that millions of dollars have been saved because of the information gained through the MIS.[12]

Holiday Inns uses a computerized marketing information system to anticipate, monitor, and review business opportunities. At first, its system developed simple models to measure lodging demand nationally and in several major markets. Now, the company is "building computer systems which combine internal and external data bases in order to have data bases on room supply, room-night sales, traveller characteristics, inspections, guest ratings, and prices." Some of the variables Holiday Inns examines are industry supply (rooms available), lodging demand as shown in consumer tracking studies, and industry occupancy ratios.[13] Figure 3-8 highlights Holiday Inns' MIS.

J. W. Robinson is a California-based department store chain that is a division of Allied Stores Corporation. Robinson's MIS includes frequent secondary and primary marketing research studies, monitoring population changes and competitors' offerings, projecting long-term trends, obtaining information from in-store electronic sales registers, and storing a variety of data. The goal of Robinson's system is to engage in a constant examination of consumer attitudes and sales (market-share) potential in order to "maintain a balance of our growth with the future growth of the 500-mile market" in which the chain operates. Robinson's computerized MIS has been unique among Allied divisions. It represents what the parent firm wants to accomplish in these other divisions.[14]

Summary

Marketing information is necessary to reduce risk, obtain consumer attitudes, assess the uncontrollable environment, integrate the marketing strategy, and evaluate success or failure. It also helps to enhance credibility and meet legal requirements, gain support or defend a decision, and validate intuition.

Marketing research is the systematic gathering, recording, and analyzing of data about problems related to marketing. The scientific

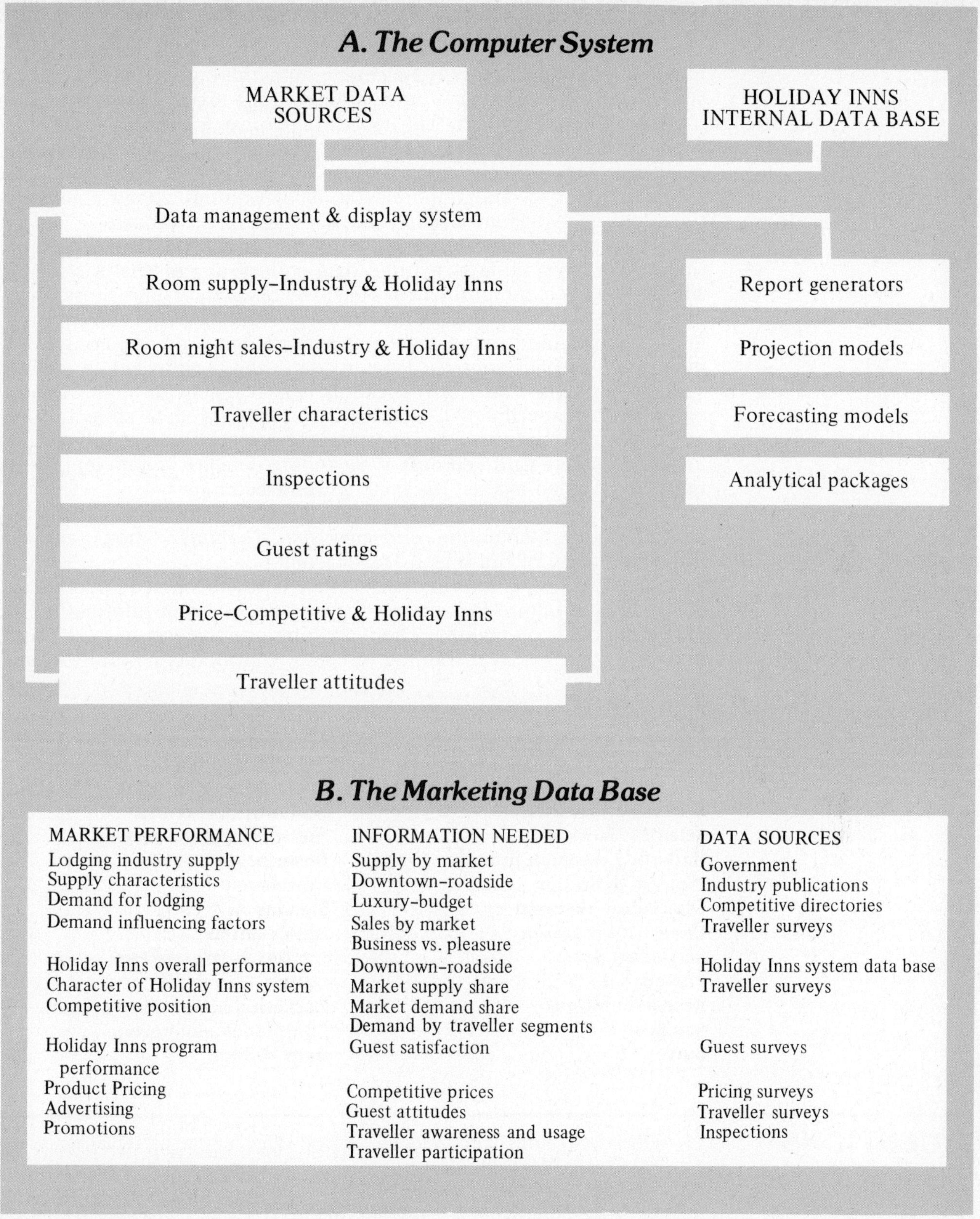

A. The Computer System

MARKET DATA SOURCES		HOLIDAY INNS INTERNAL DATA BASE

Data management & display system

Room supply–Industry & Holiday Inns

Room night sales–Industry & Holiday Inns

Traveller characteristics

Inspections

Guest ratings

Price–Competitive & Holiday Inns

Traveller attitudes

Report generators

Projection models

Forecasting models

Analytical packages

B. The Marketing Data Base

MARKET PERFORMANCE	INFORMATION NEEDED	DATA SOURCES
Lodging industry supply	Supply by market	Government
Supply characteristics	Downtown-roadside	Industry publications
Demand for lodging	Luxury-budget	Competitive directories
Demand influencing factors	Sales by market	Traveller surveys
	Business vs. pleasure	
Holiday Inns overall performance	Downtown-roadside	Holiday Inns system data base
Character of Holiday Inns system	Market supply share	Traveller surveys
Competitive position	Market demand share	
	Demand by traveller segments	
Holiday Inns program performance	Guest satisfaction	Guest surveys
Product Pricing	Competitive prices	Pricing surveys
Advertising	Guest attitudes	Traveller surveys
Promotions	Traveller awareness and usage	Inspections
	Traveller participation	

Figure 3-8
The Marketing Information System of Holiday Inns
Source: Thayer C. Taylor, "Computers That Plan," *Sales & Marketing Management* (December 7, 1981), special report. Reprinted by permission.

method requires objectivity, accuracy, and thoroughness. In a recent study, many of the firms surveyed reported the use of a formal marketing research department. The marketing research process involves a series of actions: problem definition, examination of secondary data, generation of primary data (when necessary), analysis of data, recommendations, and implementation of findings. Many considerations and decisions are needed in each stage of the process.

Exploratory research is used to develop a clear problem definition. Conclusive research is structured data collection and analysis for the solution of a specific problem or objective. Secondary data, those previously gathered for purposes other than the solution of the current problem, are available from internal and external (government, nongovernment, commercial) sources. Primary data, those collected to solve a specific problem under investigation, are available through surveys, observation, experiments, or simulation. Primary data collection requires a research design: the specified framework for controlling data. Primary data are gathered only if secondary data are insufficient. Costs must be weighed against the benefits of research.

The concluding stages of marketing research are data analysis (including coding, tabulation, and analysis), recommendations, and the implementation of findings by management.

The marketing information system is an organized, interacting, continuous structure that directs the flow and uses of information for marketing decision making. The marketing intelligence network phase of an MIS consists of marketing research, continuous monitoring, and data storage.

KEY TERMS

After reading this chapter, you should understand these key terms:

Marketing research	**Semantic differential**
Scientific method	**Multidimensional scaling**
Marketing research process	**Observation**
Problem definition	**Experiment**
Exploratory research	**Simulation**
Conclusive research	**Data analysis**
Secondary data	**Marketing information system**
Primary data	**(MIS)**
Research design	**Marketing intelligence network**
Sampling	**Continuous monitoring**
Survey	**Data storage**

QUESTIONS FOR DISCUSSION

1. Why is marketing information necessary? What may result if managers rely exclusively on intuition?
2. What is the scientific method? Give an example of how it can be used.
3. Under which circumstances would informal, inexpensive research be acceptable? Unacceptable?
4. What are the steps in the marketing research process?

5. How could *Time* magazine use census data?

6. When is primary data collection necessary?

7. Explain the concept of research design. Name the decisions included in a research design.

8. What is the major advantage of a survey? An experiment?

9. Why would General Motors use a disguised survey?

10. Why should a firm calculate the costs of marketing research before conducting it?

11. Explain the data analysis process of coding, tabulation, and analysis.

12. Many companies have not yet set up marketing information systems. Why do you think this has occurred?

NOTES

1. "Businesses Capitalize on Data from Census," *New York Times* (March 31, 1980), pp. D1–D2; "Computer Graphics of Census Data Aid Market Researchers," *Marketing News* (March 6, 1981), p. 8; and "Bargain Priced Census Data a Boon to Consumer, Market Researchers," *Marketing News* (May 15, 1981), Section 1, p. 14.

2. Ralph S. Alexander (Chairman), *Marketing Definitions: A Glossary of Marketing Terms* (Chicago, Ill.: American Marketing Association, 1960), pp. 16–17.

3. Ibid., p. 17.

4. Harper W. Boyd, Jr., Ralph Westfall, and Stanley F. Stasch, *Marketing Research: Text and Cases*, Fourth Edition (Homewood, Ill.: Richard D. Irwin, 1977), pp. 33–37.

5. See Arthur S. Katz, "Marketing Research Can 'Work' for Small Businesses, If They Ask the Right Questions," *Marketing News* (September 17, 1982), Section 1, p. 6.

6. Dik Warren Twedt, *1978 Survey of Marketing Research* (Chicago: American Marketing Association, 1978), p. 8.

7. See Louis Cohen, "There's Gold in Them Thar' Research Files: The Research Bank Technique," *Marketing Review* (November–December 1981), pp. 23–28.

8. Larry Marion, "Leader by Legacy," *Forbes* (May 25, 1981), pp. 110, 112; and Jack J. Honomichl, "Nation's 28 Top Market Research Companies See Revenues Jump 13.8% in 1981," *Advertising Age* (May 24, 1982), pp. M–7, M–10.

9. Boyd, Westfall, and Stasch, *Marketing Research*, p. 41.

10. See Steve Raddock, "Follow That Car!" *Marketing & Media Decisions* (January 1981), pp. 70–71, 103.

11. Robert Peterson, *Marketing Research* (Dallas: Business Publications, 1982), p. 16.

12. George A. Clowes, "Data Management Should Be No. 1 Priority in Developing On-Line MIS," *Marketing News* (December 12, 1980), pp. 1, 10.

13. Thayer C. Taylor, "Computers That Plan," *Sales & Marketing Management* (December 7, 1981), special report.

14. Isadore Barmash, "Research!" *Stores* (April 1981), pp. 23–24.

GENERAL FOODS: EXAMINING ITS COFFEE MARKETS* 1 **CASES**

General Foods is a large food manufacturer. Sales for the fiscal year ending April 3, 1982 were over $8.4 billion. Its major product lines are packaged con-

*The data in this case are drawn from "General Foods Corp.," *Advertising Age* (September 9, 1982), p. 89; Ann Mackay-Smith, "Both General Foods and P & G Look Like Coffee War Victors," *Wall Street Journal* (October 29, 1981), p. 33; and Gay Jervey, "Coffee Marketers Brew Generic Campaign," *Advertising Age* (August 16, 1982), p. 34.

venience foods, away-from-home foods, and grocery coffee. Among the well-known brands produced by General Foods are Jell-O, Kool-Aid, Maxwell House, Sanka, Shake 'n Bake, Oscar Mayer, Gaines dog food, and Tang.

The coffee line at General Foods has two components, regular and instant. Regular brands are Maxwell House, Sanka, Yuban, Max-Pax, Master Blend, Brim, and Mellow Roast. Instant brands are Maxwell House, Maxim, Sanka, Yuban, Freeze Dried Sanka, Brim, and Mellow Roast. In 1981, General Foods had a 32 per cent share of the regular coffee market; its leading competitor, Procter & Gamble, had 25 per cent. General Foods' market share for instant coffee was 46 per cent; the leading competitor, Nestlé, had about 26 per cent.

Despite its leadership position, General Foods' market share for both types of coffee fell between 1975 and 1981. In addition, the company is concerned about the drop in per capita coffee consumption, from 36 gallons in 1970 to 26 gallons in 1981.

During 1978, sales of regular Folger's (Procter & Gamble) exceeded those of regular Maxwell House for the first time. Instant Maxwell House, with a 22.3 per cent market share, continues to dominate the instant market. The competition between Maxwell House and Folger's has been intense, both in advertising and in price. In 1980, Procter & Gamble introduced High Point decaffinated coffee and spent $20 million on advertising. In 1981, General Foods countered with Master Blend coffee, backed by a similar advertising budget.

General Foods realizes that it must thoroughly research its regular and instant coffee markets, evaluate current attitudes toward its Maxwell House and other coffee brands, examine new product opportunities, and revise marketing strategies if it is to retain its leadership position in an industry with limited growth potential.

QUESTIONS

1. Present five problem definitions (study topics) for Maxwell House that General Foods might analyze through marketing research.
2. How can General Foods determine the difference in characteristics and desires between regular coffee customers and instant coffee customers?
3. Develop a semantic differential to determine the attributes of regular coffee customers' ideal coffee, their perceptions of Maxwell House, and their perceptions of Folger's.

2 MINNETONKA, INC.: USING MARKETING RESEARCH TO PLAN FOR THE FUTURE†

Between 1979 and 1982, Minnetonka, Inc. of Minneapolis increased its annual sales from $25 million to $100 million per year. While most consumers are still unfamiliar with the name Minnetonka, many are probably aware of the firm's major products—Softsoap and Shower Mate. For in 1979 and 1980, Minnetonka virtually created the liquid soap industry.

Softsoap was introduced in 1979 to eliminate the unsanitary nature of bar soap and to remove sloppy soap dishes from the bathroom sink. Softsoap came

†The data in this case are drawn from "Is the Bar of Soap Washed Up?" *Business Week* (January 12, 1981), pp. 109–116; Ellyn Spragins, "Update: Minnetonka Slip-Slidin' Away," *Forbes* (February 15, 1982), p. 100; and Steve Raddock, "Now He Sings in the Shower," *Marketing & Media Decisions* (Spring 1982, Special Edition), pp. 123–131.

in a plastic container with a pump dispenser. The initial response to Softsoap was so favorable that Minnetonka could not keep up with orders. Since the company believed an even larger market existed for soft soap that would be used in showers and bathtubs, it brought out Shower Mate in 1982. Shower Mate had all the advantages of Softsoap; and its plastic container had an attached hook that allowed it to be hung from a shower head or bathtub soap rack. Said Minnetonka's president, "In Europe, we know that the liquid soap market for the shower is equal to the bar soap business. So we have a feeling that the trend is a beginning with Shower Mate and will continue to grow (in the United States)."

Despite, or perhaps because of, its success with liquid soap, Minnetonka now faces competition from about 50 other brands, several of which are doing poorly. Some competitors sell their soap for one fourth to one sixth the price of Softsoap. As Minnetonka's president noted, "We just weren't able to accurately forecast the market size or the number of competitors."

Some observers wonder when Minnetonka's bubble will burst. They believe the soft soap market is nearly saturated, and see the firm confronted by billion-dollar competitors (with the smaller companies falling from the market). Minnetonka, on the other hand, has set a long-range sales goal of $500 million per year.

QUESTIONS

1. What internal secondary data can Minnetonka use to evaluate its past performance and plan for the future?
2. How might Minnetonka use government, nongovernment, and commercial data to evaluate its past performance and plan for the future?
3. Devise a brief questionnaire to determine the attitudes of retailers toward Softsoap and Shower Mate. How would a questionnaire aimed at consumer attitudes differ from the one geared to retailers?

Introduction to Part Two

Part Two provides an understanding of consumers and explains why consumer analysis is necessary. It discusses consumer profiles, characteristics, needs, and decision making and how companies can develop marketing programs that are responsive to consumers.

Chapter 4 is devoted to the demographics, life-styles, and decision making of final consumers. Demographics are the easily identifiable and measurable statistics used to describe the population. Consumer life-styles are based upon both social and psychological factors; they are useful in explaining how and why consumers act. The decision process involves the steps consumers move through when buying products and services. The interaction of demographics, life-styles, and decision making is shown. Marketing applications and limitations are noted.

Chapter 5 focuses on the organizational consumers that purchase products and services for further production, use in operations, or resale to other consumers. Organizational consumers are manufacturers, wholesalers, retailers, and government and nonprofit institutions. Organizational consumers are described on the basis of buying objectives, buying structure, use of the purchase, and constraints. The decision process for organizational consumers also is studied. Marketing implications are offered.

Chapter 6 examines the three alternative methods for developing a target market: mass marketing, market segmentation, and multiple segmentation. Segmentation on the basis of geographic demographic, personal demographic, social, and psychological factors is explained. A six-step procedure for planning a segmentation strategy is presented. The requirements for successful segmentation and the limitations of segmentation are listed. Finally, because the development of a target market depends on future projections of sales and a corresponding marketing program, sales forecasting is discussed.

Final Consumers

4

Chapter Preview

Chapter Objectives

1 To establish the importance and scope of consumer analysis

2 To define and describe important U.S. demographic and life-style factors and decision making for final consumers

3 To enumerate several applications of consumer demographics, life-styles, and decision making for final consumers, and to consider the limitations of these concepts

4 To show the interaction of consumer demographics, social concepts, psychological factors, and decision making for final consumers

It is estimated that there will be 20 per cent fewer teenagers in the United States in 1990 than in 1980, down to 23 million from 28.6 million. Accordingly, many firms are turning away from the teen market and aiming at growth markets, such as middle-age and senior-citizen consumers. Nonetheless, the youth market offers significant opportunities for insightful marketers, as shown in Figure 4-1.

Three out of five teenagers work at part-time or full-time jobs, generating $600 million in earnings each week. In addition, four of ten teens receive allowances, about $80 million a week. In total, the teen market has $35 billion a year to spend, nearly all on themselves.

Traditionally, marketers of acne products, cosmetics, record and tape albums, movies, electronic games, and other items used by teens have focused on the youth market. Other firms, such as food marketers, have ignored this market. Yet, the latter companies may be mistaken. A recent study found that 64 per cent of teenagers do some family food shopping; their grocery bill averages $24.20 per shopping trip. Teenagers also influence the selection of food brands and are more active in families where one parent works. There is little difference between the number of male and female teens who do food shopping.

A variety of companies are now heightening their efforts to capture the youth market, as these illustrations show:

- Castle & Cooke runs ads in *Seventeen* magazine featuring recipes and instructions for throwing parties, using its Dole pineapples and bananas and Bumble Bee tuna.
- Bausch & Lomb is using teens in its television and magazine commercials for contact lenses.
- U.S. Shoe Corp. purchased 116 Ups 'n Downs stores that carry apparel for teenage girls; this marked a return of the company to the twelve- to nineteen-year-old market after an absence of a decade.[1]

Consumer Analysis: Importance and Scope

As noted in Chapters 1 and 2, the central focus of marketing is the consumer. In order to develop appropriate marketing plans, it is necessary to determine the characteristics and needs of consumers, the social and psychological factors affecting consumers, and the process consumers go through when making a purchase.

In Chapters 4 through 6, the basic elements necessary for understanding and responding to consumers are detailed. Chapter 4 examines the demographic, social, and psychological characteristics and the decision process used by final consumers. *Final consumers* purchase products and services for personal, family, or household use. Chapter 5 centers on the characteristics and behavior of organizational consumers. *Organizational consumers* purchase products and services for further production, usage in operating the organization, or resale to other consumers. Chapter 6 explains how to develop a target market and the creation and uses of sales forecasts. By developing profiles of consumer characteristics, needs, and behavior patterns, an individual marketer is better able to satisfy the demands of consumers and remain ahead of the competition.

Final consumers purchase for personal, family, or household use; organizational consumers purchase for production, operations, or resale.

76

Figure 4-1
The Teenage Market

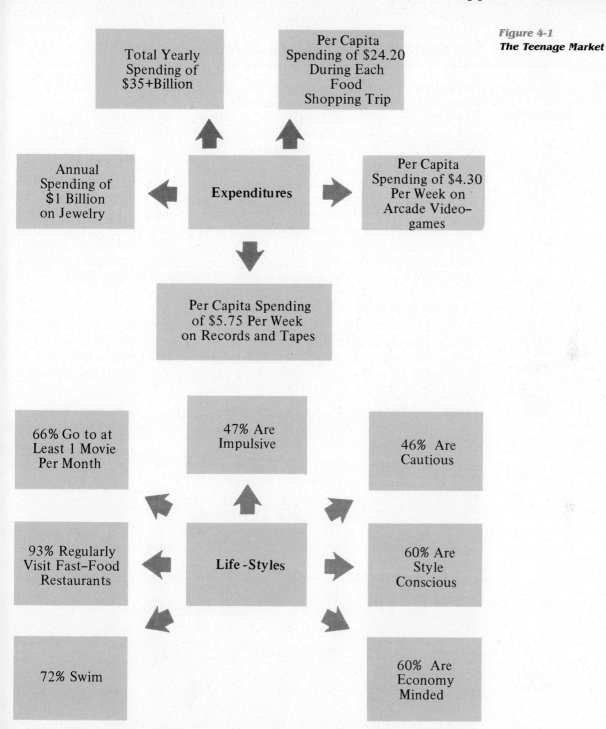

Total Yearly Spending of $35+Billion

Per Capita Spending of $24.20 During Each Food Shopping Trip

Annual Spending of $1 Billion on Jewelry

Expenditures

Per Capita Spending of $4.30 Per Week on Arcade Video–games

Per Capita Spending of $5.75 Per Week on Records and Tapes

66% Go to at Least 1 Movie Per Month

47% Are Impulsive

46% Are Cautious

93% Regularly Visit Fast–Food Restaurants

Life-Styles

60% Are Style Conscious

72% Swim

60% Are Economy Minded

Source: Mark N. Dodosh, "Widely Ignored Teen Market Has a lot of Spending Power," *Wall Street Journal* (June 17, 1982), p. 31; Sheila Jacobson, "Cashing in on the Youth Market Boom," *Zip* (April 1981), pp. 28–32ff; and B.G. Yovovich, "A Game of Hide-and-Seek," *Advertising Age* (August 2, 1982), pp. M-5–M-7.

Consumer Demographics[2]

Consumer demographics are statistics that are used to describe the population. They are easy to identify, collect, measure, and analyze. The demographics discussed in this chapter are population size, gender, and age; location and mobility; income and expenditures; occupations and education; and marital status.

Consumer demographics are statistics that describe the population.

In combination, demographics can establish consumer profiles that may present attractive market opportunities. For example, the potential market for a unisex hair salon may be composed of young, college-educated, urban single people. The potential market for instant soup may be comprised of young, white-collar working women in a northern climate. Figure 4-2 shows the separate factors that determine a demographic profile for a single consumer. By summing individual profiles, a firm can determine the total size of a potential consumer market.[3]

Consumer profiles combine demographics in ways that are useful to marketers.

Population Size, Gender, and Age

As of 1980, the population of the United States was more than 226 million people; this is projected to grow to 260 million by the year 2000. Despite the increase in the number of people, the rate of population growth has slowed considerably since the decade of the 1950s. Between

The United States has more than 226 million people, with a low population growth rate.

Figure 4-2

Factors Determining a Consumer's Demographic Profile

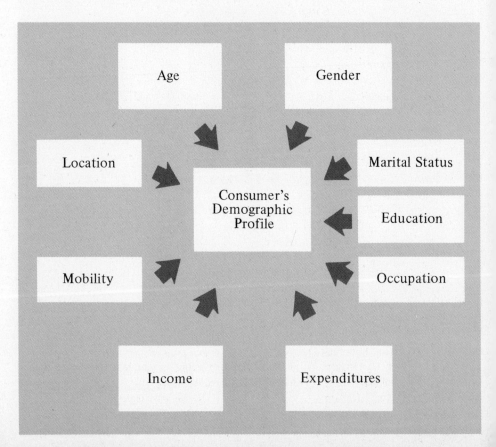

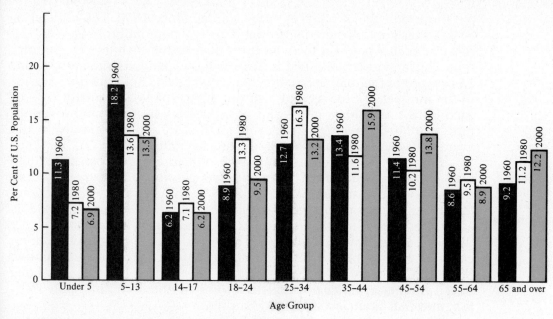

Figure 4-3
Age Distribution of U.S. Population, 1960–2000

Source: U.S. Bureau of the Census, *Current Population Reports*, Series P-25, Nos. 310, 311, 519, 704, 721.
Projections are based on Series II assumptions.

1980 and 2000, population will increase by less than 1 per cent each year. However, a large proportion of the births in the 1980s will be first-borns. During the 1960s, 25 per cent of all babies were first-born. In 1980, first-borns were estimated to be 40 per cent of all births.

In 1980, females comprised 51.4 per cent of the population, over 116 million people, and males represented 48.6 per cent of the population, almost 110 million people. The life expectancy for females born in 1980 is 77.3 years; for males born in 1980, it is 69.4 years. The median age of the population reached a low point of 27.9 years in 1970. The median age is expected to rise to 35.5 years by the year 2000. Figure 4-3 shows the changing age distribution in the population from 1960 to 2000.

> In the U.S., there are many first-borns, females outnumber males, and the population is becoming older.

Location and Mobility

During this century there has been a major movement of the U.S. population to large urban areas. The Bureau of the Census has defined these urban centers as **Standard Metropolitan Statistical Areas (SMSAs).** An SMSA is an integrated economic and social entity with a large population base and a central city with at least 50,000 people (or two contiguous cities with a total population of at least 50,000 people).

> *Standard Metropolitan Statistical Areas (SMSAs) are urban centers.*

Among the largest SMSAs are New York, Chicago, Los Angeles–Long Beach, Philadelphia, Detroit, San Francisco–Oakland, Washington, D.C., Boston, Cleveland, Baltimore, Dallas–Fort Worth, Houston, Minneapolis–St. Paul, Pittsburgh, St. Louis, and Atlanta.

Although urbanization has increased in the United States throughout the 1900s, major changes have occured since 1950. The number of SMSAs has grown from 169 to over 320. The population in SMSAs has risen from 56.1 per cent to about three quarters of the total U.S. population. The land area contained in SMSAs has expanded from 5.9 to about 15 per cent of the total U.S. land area. This reflects not only the increase in the number of SMSAs, but also the urban sprawl, or greater size, of each SMSA as central cities and suburbs have become more overlapping. In 1950 the average SMSA contained 1,225 square miles. Now, the average SMSA has more than 1,850 square miles.

*Standard Consolidated
Statistical Areas (SCSAs)
are made up of two or
more overlapping SMSAs.*

Recently the Bureau of the Census added a new urban classification known as **Standard Consolidated Statistical Areas (SCSAs)**. SCSAs are two or more continuous SMSAs with the size, urban character, integration, and contiguity set forth for single SMSAs. An SCSA is also called a megalopolis. As cities and their suburbs have drawn closer to neighboring cities and suburbs, the SCSA classification has taken on considerable importance. At present, seventeen SCSAs exist. The five largest SCSAs are New York-Newark-Jersey City, Los Angeles-Long Beach-Anaheim, Chicago-Gary (Ind.), Philadelphia- Wilmington-Trenton, and San Francisco-Oakland-San Jose.

**About 12 to 15 per cent
of the population moves
each year, most within
the same SMSA.**

The mobility of the U.S. population is quite high. According to the Bureau of the Census, about 12 to 15 per cent of the population moves each year. The greatest amount of mobility (about half) occurs for people moving within the same SMSA. The least mobility is for people moving from abroad. In addition, few people move from an SMSA to outside an SMSA or from outside an SMSA to an SMSA.

The mobility of the U.S. population varies by geographic region. Some regions are gaining in size, whereas others are declining. Figure 4-4 shows the regional distribution of the population for the period of 1970 to 2000. Major growth is occurring in the South Atlantic, West South Central, and Mountain regions. Moderate growth exists in the Pacific region. The New England and East South Central regions are stable. The relative sizes of the Middle Atlantic, East North Central, and West North Central regions are declining.

Income and Expenditures

**Real annual family
income grew 34 per cent
from 1960 to 1980, with
many U.S. families
having incomes of
$25,000 or more.**

From 1960 to 1980, average real annual family income rose from $15,637 to $21,023 (expressed in 1980 dollars). Most of this rise occurred in the 1960s and early 1970s. Real income has gone up slightly since then.

The number of families with annual incomes under $5,000 dropped from about one in nine in 1960 to one in sixteen in 1980. In 1960, 30.5 per cent of all families had incomes of less than $10,000 per year. For 1980, less than 20 per cent fit in this category. At the upper end of the income scale, 51.3 per cent of all families had annual incomes of $15,000 or higher in 1960. This rose to over 67 per cent of all families in 1980 and almost 40 per cent of all families had annual incomes of $25,000 and higher. Figure 4-5 shows the changing distribution of income in the United States.

Disposable income **is
used for spending and/or
savings;** *discretionary
income* **is used for
luxuries.**

Disposable income (aftertax income to be used for spending and/or savings) and **discretionary income** (earnings remaining for luxuries,

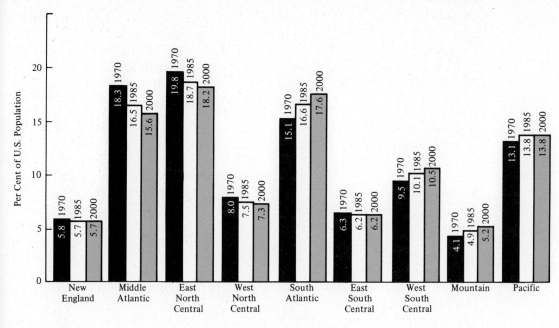

Geographic Region

KEY OF REGIONS

New England = Maine, New Hampshire, Vermont, Massachusetts, Rhode Island, Connecticut
Middle Atlantic = New York, New Jersey, Pennsylvania
East North Central = Ohio, Indiana, Illinois, Michigan, Wisconsin
West North Central = Minnesota, Iowa, Missouri, North Dakota, South Dakota, Nebraska, Kansas
South Atlantic = Delaware, Maryland, District of Columbia, Virginia, West Virginia, North Carolina, South Carolina, Georgia, Florida
East South Central = Kentucky, Tennessee, Alabama, Mississippi
West South Central = Arkansas, Louisiana, Oklahoma, Texas
Mountain = Montana, Idaho, Wyoming, Colorado, New Mexico, Arizona, Utah, Nevada
Pacific = Washington, Oregon, California, Alaska, Hawaii

Figure 4-4
Distribution of U.S. Population by Geographic Regions, 1970–2000

Source: U.S. Bureau of the Census, *Current Population Reports*, Series P-25, No. 460 and Series P-20, No. 324. Projections based on Series II assumptions.

such as a vacation or dining out, after necessities such as food, clothing, and shelter are bought) have grown as the result of increases in family income.

As income levels have changed, so have consumption patterns, The per cent of income spent on food, beverages, tobacco, and on clothing, accessories, and jewelry has declined substantially. The per cent spent on housing, medical care, personal business, recreation, and, recently, transportation has increased substantially. Since 1950 total annual consumption expenditures have risen from $192 billion to about $2 trillion.

By 1990, even more families will have annual incomes of $25,000 and higher. Families with incomes over $50,000 will more than double, from 1.8 to 3.9 million. Although incomes will rise between 1980 and 1990, the real growth rate will be relatively low. Because of inflation

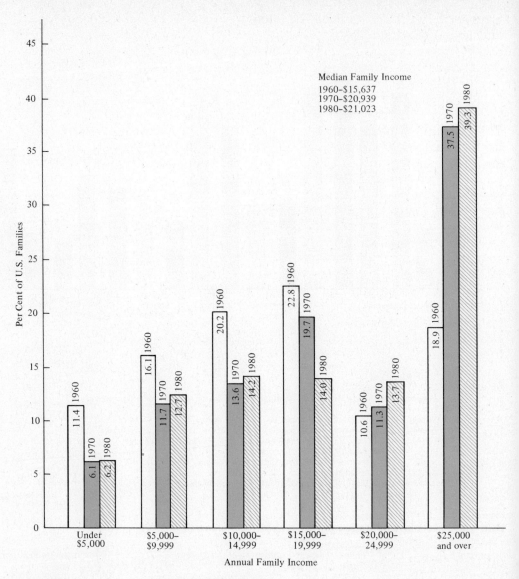

Figure 4-5
Distribution of U.S. Population by Annual Family Income, 1960–1980*

Source: U.S. Bureau of the Census, *Current Population Reports*, Series P-60 and other Bureau of the Census data.

The *Consumer Price Index (CPI)* measures changes in prices over time.

and periods of high unemployment, real income growth will not approach that of the 1950s and 1960s.

The federal government monitors the cost of living, the prices consumers pay for goods and services, through the **Consumer Price Index (CPI).** The CPI measures the monthly and yearly changes in the prices of selected consumer items in different product categories, expressing the changes in terms of a base year. Over the past fifteen years, the greatest price increases have occurred in medical services, food, housing, and transportation. The smallest price increases have taken place for apparel and upkeep and reading and recreation. Among major cities, Houston, San Francisco, and Minneapolis have incurred higher prices; New York, Anchorage, and Honolulu have seen smaller increases.

Occupations and Education

The labor force in the United States is continuing its steady movement toward white-collar and service occupations and away from blue-collar and farm occupations. In 1980 the total labor force was over 100 million people. From 1960 to 1980, the per cent of those employed in professional, technical, and clerical white-collar jobs rose substantially. The per cent of managers, administrators, and sales workers remained relatively constant. Over the same period, the per cent of people employed as operatives (nonskilled workers) and nonfarm laborers declined substantially, while craft and kindred workers were fairly constant. By 1980, less than 2.7 million people were employed as farm workers.

There is a continuing trend toward white-collar and service occupations.

Another important change in the U.S. labor force has been the increase in the number and per cent of working women. In 1960, 22.5 million women comprised 31.2 per cent of the employed labor force. By 1980, 44.6 million women accounted for 42.6 per cent of the total labor force, and 51.1 per cent of all adult women were in the labor force.

Women represent a large and growing percentage of the U.S. labor force.

The growth in the number and per cent of married women in the labor force has been substantial. In 1960, 12.3 million married women, 30.5 per cent of all married women, were employed. As of 1980, 23.2 million married women, 50.2 per cent of all married women, were in the labor force. The per cent of married women with children under six in the labor force jumped from 18.6 per cent in 1960 to 46.6 per cent in 1980.

During 1981 and 1982, the U.S. labor force suffered the highest unemployment rates since the depression of 1932. At the end of 1982, the unemployment rate reached about 11 per cent, meaning that around one in nine people were out of work. Some of the unemployment was temporary, due to domestic and worldwide economic conditions. But in other industries, such as automobile and steel, many job losses were permanent. Overall, this meant severe cutbacks in discretionary purchases until the unemployment rate was reduced.

The educational attainment of Americans continued its upward trend in the 1960s and 1970s. As of 1960, 58.8 per cent of all adults twenty-five years old and older had not graduated from high school. This figure dropped to 31.4 per cent in 1980. As of 1960 only 16.5 per cent of all adults twenty-five years old and older had received some college education. This rose to 31.9 per cent in 1980. Of those adults aged twenty-five to thirty-four in 1980, 85.4 per cent had graduated high school, 45.8 per cent had received some college education, and 24.4 per cent were college graduates. See Figure 4-6.

Over 85 per cent of young adults have graduated from high school; 46 per cent have gone to college.

The sharp increase in working wives and the increased educational attainment have contributed to the growing number of people in the upper-income brackets, while the relatively high unemployment rate and stagnant economy have caused other families to have low incomes.

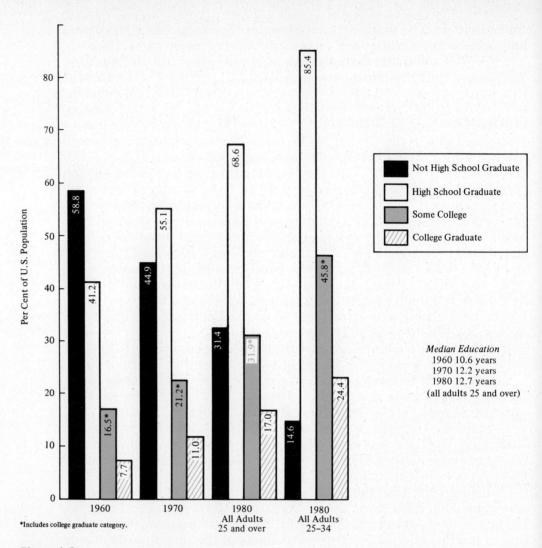

*Includes college graduate category.

Figure 4-6

Distribution of U.S. Population by Educational Level, 1960–1980 (For persons 25 years old and over)

Source: U.S. Bureau of the Census, *U.S. Census of Populations: 1960, 1970, and 1980;* and *Current Population Reports,* Series P-20, Nos. 207, 295, 314.

Marital Status

Despite some publicity to the contrary, the data indicate that marriage and family remain important in the United States. Well over two million couples get married each year. The per cent of the population 18 and older which was married remained relatively stable between 1950 and 1980 at about two thirds of this population group. In 1950 the median age at first marriage was 22.8 years for males and 20.3 years for females. For 1980 these figures were 24.6 and 22.1, respectively. Therefore, in recent years adults have been waiting somewhat longer to be married.

As a result, the size of the average family has declined slightly, from 3.5 members in 1950 to 3.3 in 1980.

A ***family*** is defined as a group of two or more persons residing together who are related by blood, marriage, or adoption. A ***household*** is defined as a housing unit with one or more people. Figure 4-7 compares families and households. There have been two important changes in family and marital status. First, the number of single-person house-

A *family* is a group of two or more persons residing together who are related; a *household* is a housing unit with one or more people.

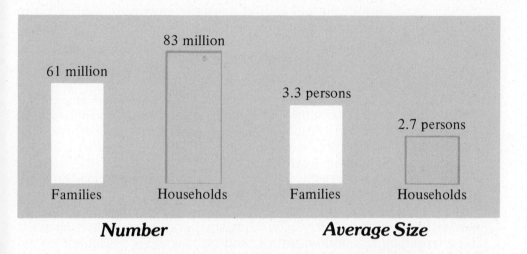

Number   **Average Size**

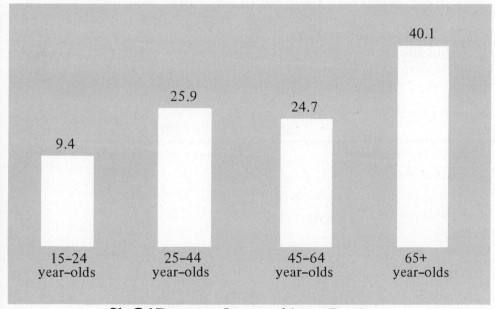

% Of Persons Living Alone By Age

Figure 4-7
Families Versus Households, 1980

Source: U.S. Bureau of the Census, *Current Population Reports.*

holds has gone from 4.7 million in 1950 to 17.8 million in 1980. More than 20 per cent of all American households are now comprised of one-person units. Singles account for roughly one eighth of total consumer spending for goods and services.

Second, the size of the average household dropped from 3.4 in 1950 to 2.7 in 1980, because fewer single adults now live with their parents and divorces have risen substantially. From 1950 to 1980 the number of divorces jumped from 385,000 to 1.2 million annually. During the same period, the per cent of adults widowed went from 8.3 to 8.1. However, the number of widowed adults rose considerably because of the greater number of adults in the overall population.

Marketing Applications of Demographic Profiles

After examining each of the preceding demographic factors separately, the marketer should develop a consumer demographic profile based on a composite of the most important demographics. In this section, some examples of demographic profiles are shown.

Due to high interest rates and rapidly rising prices, the housing market has changed drastically in recent years. Home buyers now are older, more likely to be unmarried, earn higher incomes, and are more apt to purchase condominiums. See Table 4-1. In response to consumer needs, the housing industry is building smaller homes, converting existing apartments to condominiums, and gearing sales presentations toward people buying homes for the second time.[4]

The increase in working women has greatly expanded the number of "two-earner" families. In 1980, half of all married couples fit into this category. Two-earner families have after-tax income that is 20 to 25 per cent higher than single-earner families. Unemployment has less impact on two-earner families, since one of the earners is usually able to maintain his or her position during weak economic times. In comparison to

Table 4-1		*1977*	*1981*
A Demographic Profile of U.S. Home Buyers, 1977 and 1981	Median age (in years)	32	34
	Unmarried (%)	17	30
	One- and two-person households (%)	46	57
	Median household income ($)	22,700	39,200
	First-time buyers (%)	36	14
	New condominiums (% purchasing)	Not available	22
	New houses (% purchasing)	25	26
	Houses 25 years and older (% purchasing)	24	30
	Median purchase price of home ($)	44,000	72,000
	Median down payment for home ($)	9,000	16,100
	Median monthly housing expenses ($)	400	800

Source: U.S. League of Savings Associations.

	Maturity Market	Young Adult Market	
			Table 4-2
Age	45 to 64	25 to 44	**The Maturity and Young Adult Markets in the U.S., 1980**
Per cent of total U.S. households	30.8	40.9	
Persons per household	2.79	3.25	
Average household income ($)	25,837	23,010	
Discretionary income as per cent of average household income	20	13	

Source: U.S. Bureau of the Census.

single-earner families, two-earner families spend substantially more on transportation, dry cleaning, clothing, home furnishings, and appliances.[5]

The maturity market consists of people between the ages of 45 and 64, "for the most part, beyond the child-rearing years, but still extremely active as wage earners." In the U.S., this market is very large and growing. About half of total discretionary income is possessed by the maturity market. In fact, mature consumers have average discretionary income equal to 20 per cent of their earnings, while consumers 25 to 44 years of age have discretionary income of 13 per cent. See Table 4-2. As a result, the mature market makes above-average purchases of vacation travel, personal care products and services, gifts, food, drug and related products, magazines, and transportation.[6]

B. Dalton Bookseller, a nationwide bookstore chain, uses demographic studies of 36,000 cities with information broken down by census tract. It defines heavy readers as those between twenty-one and forty-nine years of age, some college, high income, female, and employed in a management or professional position.[7]

Advertisers frequently collect and update demographic data about consumers in order to set advertising rates and attract clients. For instance, television, newspaper, and other advertising rates are set on the basis of audience size, age, income, location, occupation, and other statistics.

Limitations of Demographics

When using demographic data, these limitations should be noted. One, demographic information may be dated. The national census is conducted only once every ten years. Regular statistical updates normally have time lags—for example, 1984 data will not be widely available until mid-1986. Two, summary data and trends may hide opportunities and risks in small markets or specialized product categories.

Three, single demographic statistics are often not very useful. A consumer demographic profile is needed. Four, demographic data do not consider the psychological or the social factors influencing consumers. They do not explain the decision process consumers utilize when making purchases. Most importantly, demographics do not delve into the reasons why consumers make particular decisions; demographics are descriptive in nature.

Demographic data may be dated, may hide opportunities and risks, may require profile analysis, and may not consider consumer behavior.

A selected list of the marketing questions unanswered by demographic data follows:

Why do consumers act as they do?

Why do consumers with similar demographic characteristics act differently?

Why do consumers become brand loyal or regularly switch brands?

Why do some consumers act as innovators and buy products before others?

Under what situations do families employ joint decision making?

How do consumers behave when shopping for a product?

Why does status play a large role in the purchase of some goods and a small role in the purchase of others?

How does risk affect consumer decisions?

How do motives affect consumer decisions?

How important is a puchase decision to a consumer?

How long will it take for a consumer to reach a purchase decision?

To whom does a consumer look for advice prior to purchasing a product or service?

The Value of Consumer Life-Style and Decision-Making Analysis

To better understand consumers, marketers combine demographic, social, and psychological data and study consumer decision making. These dimensions help explain consumer *life-styles*, which are the ways people live.

In an attempt to answer these and other questions, marketers, in growing numbers, are using demographic data in conjunction with and as part of social, psychological, and consumer decision-making analysis.

Social and psychological factors comprise a consumer's **life-style,** which is the pattern in which a person lives and spends time and money. A life-style combines the influences of personality and social values that have been internalized by an individual.[8] A person's demographic background has a strong influence on the life-style, or way of living, adopted.

The social aspects of life-style include culture, social class, performance, reference groups, family life cycle, and time expenditures (activities). Psychological aspects of life-style include personality, attitudes, level of class consciousness, motivation, perceived risk, innovativeness, opinion leadership, and importance of purchase. Social and psychological analysis overlap and complement each other; they are not independent or exclusive of one another.

The consumer's decision process involves the steps a consumer goes through in purchasing a product or service: stimulus, problem awareness, information search, evaluation of alternatives, purchase, and postpurchase behavior. Demographics, social factors, and psychological factors affect the consumer's decision-making process.

By understanding and employing demographic, social, psychological, and decision-making analysis, a marketer can develop descriptive consumer profiles, answer each of the questions raised in the previous section, and create consumer-oriented marketing plans.

Consumer Life-Styles

The social and psychological characteristics that form consumer life-styles are described next.

Social Characteristics

The social characteristics of a consumer are a combination of culture, social class, performance, reference groups, family life cycle, and time expenditures (activities). See Figure 4-8.

A **culture** is a group of people sharing a distinctive heritage, such as Americans or Japanese. American culture has placed importance on achievement and success, activity, efficiency and practicality, progress, material comfort, individualism, freedom, external comfort, humanitarianism, and youthfulness.[9] Resource shortages, the power of foreign countries, and a maturing population may signal changes in these values. In Chapter 16, "International Marketing," the American culture is contrasted with other cultures.

A **social class system** is the ranking of people within a culture. Social classes are based on income, occupation, education, and type of dwelling. Social class systems separate society into divisions, grouping people with similar values and life-styles. Each social class may represent a distinct target market for a company. See Table 4-3.

The American culture *emphasizes success, material possessions, freedom, and youthfulness.*

A social class system *ranks people within a culture.*

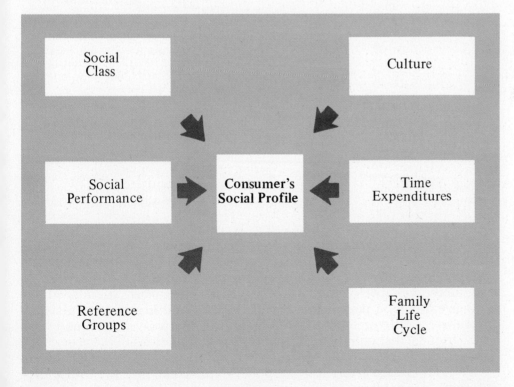

Figure 4-8
Factors Determining a Consumer's Social Profile

Table 4-3	*Class*	*Size*	*Characteristics*
The Social Class Structure in the United States	Upper-upper	Less than 1%	Social elite; inherited wealth; exclusive neighborhood; summer home; children attend best schools; money not important in purchases; secure in status
	Lower-upper	Combined with upper-upper equals 3%	Highest income level; earned wealth; often professionals; socially mobile; "nouveaux riche"; college-educated but not at the best schools; seek the best for children; active in social affairs; value material possessions; not secure in position; "conspicuous consumption"; money not important in purchases
	Upper-middle	12%	Career oriented; successful professionals and business people; earnings over $30,000; status based on occupation and earnings; education important; most educated in society; not from prestige schools; demanding of children; careful but conspicuous; attractive home; nice clothing; "gracious living"
	Lower-middle	35%	"Typical American"; respectable; conscientious; obedient; church going; conservative; home ownership sought; do-it-yourselfers; neat; work at shopping; price sensitive; variety of low-level white-collar occupations; incomes from $10,000–$25,000; purchases related to income and occupation; college for children
	Upper-lower	40%	Routine existence; blue-collar occupations; limited education; seek job security; income can overlap with lower-middle; life of wife monotonous; child oriented; impulsive for new purchases; brand loyal for regular items and "national brands"; little social contact; not status oriented; protective against lower-lower
	Lower-lower	10%	Present oriented; impulsive; overpay; use credit; poor education; limited information; unemployed or work at most menial jobs; large market for foods; poor housing

Source: This figure is derived, in part, from James F. Engel and Roger D. Blackwell, *Consumer Behavior*, Fourth Edition (Hinsdale, Ill: Dryden Press, 1982), pp. 128–129; and Terrell G. Williams, *Consumer Behavior: Fundamentals and Strategies* (St. Paul: West Publishing, 1982), pp. 194–196.

Social performance describes how a person carries out his/her social roles.

Social performance is how a person carries out his or her roles as a worker, family member, citizen, and friend. At one extreme, a person may become a vice-president in a company, have a happy family life, be an active member of the community, and have many friends. At the other extreme, a person may never be promoted higher than assistant manager, be divorced, not participate in community affairs, and have few friends. It should be clear that many combinations of these performance criteria are possible—for example, vice-president and divorced.

Reference groups influence a person.

A **reference group** is a group that influences a person's thoughts or actions. For many products and services, reference groups have an important impact on purchase behavior. Those reference groups that are face-to-face, such as family or fraternity, have the most influence on a person. Other, more general, reference groups also influence behavior and these are most frequently appealed to by marketers. For example, commercials that show products and services being used by college students, working women, and pet owners often ask viewers to join the "group" in making a similar purchase.

The *family life cycle,* shown in Table 4-4, describes how a typical family evolves from bachelorhood to marriage to children to solitary retirement. At each stage in the cycle, needs, experience, income, and family composition change. In addition, the use of *joint decision making*—the process whereby two or more family members have input into purchases—changes throughout the cycle. The family life cycle is an excellent tool for market segmentation and for developing marketing campaigns. The number of people in different stages in the cycle can be obtained through a study of demographic data.

When utilizing family life cycle analysis, marketers should take note of the growing numbers of people who do not marry, do not have

The *family life cycle* describes how a typical family evolves. Families often use *joint decision making.*

Table 4-4   **The Traditional Family Life Cycle**

Stage in Cycle	Characteristics	Relevance for Marketing
Bachelor, male or female	Independent; young; early stage of career; low earnings, low discretionary income	Clothing; automobile; stereo; travel; restaurants; entertainment; appeal to status
Newly married	Two incomes; relative independence; present and future oriented	Furnishing apartment; travel; clothing; durables; appeal to enjoyment and togetherness
Full nest I	Youngest child under 6; one income; limited independence; future oriented	Products and services geared to child; family-use items; practicality of items; durability; safety; pharmaceuticals; appeal to economy
Full nest II	Youngest child over 6; one-and-a-half incomes; husband established in career; limited independence; future oriented	Savings; home; education; family vacations; child-oriented products; some interest in luxuries; appeal to comfort and long-range enjoyment
Full nest III	Youngest child living at home, but self-reliant; highest income level; independent; thoughts of retirement	Education; expensive durables for children; replacement and improvement of parents' durables; appeal to comfort and luxury
Empty nest I	No children at home; independent; good incomes; thoughts of self and retirement	Retirement home; travel; clothing; entertainment; luxuries; appeal to self-gratification
Empty nest II	Retirement; limited income and expenses; present oriented	Travel; recreation; living in new home; pharmaceuticals and health items; little interest in luxuries; appeal to comfort at a low price
Sole survivior I	Only one spouse alive; actively employed; present oriented; good income	Immersion in job and friends leading to opportunities in travel, clothing, health, and recreation areas; appeal to productive citizen
Sole survivor II	Only one person alive; retired; feeling of futility; poor income	Travel; recreation; pharmaceuticals; security; appeal to economy and social activity

Figure 4-9
Factors Determining a Consumer's Psychological Profile

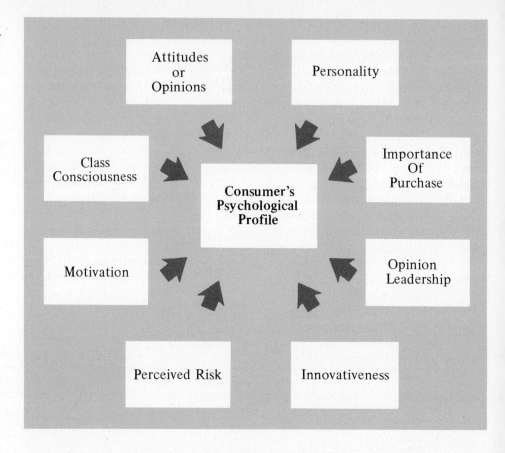

children, or become divorced. These people are not reflected in Table 4-4 but may represent good marketing opportunities.[10]

Time expenditures (activities) **have changed because the work week has declined, less time is spent in family care, and leisure activities have risen.**

Time expenditures (activities) involve the types of activities in which a person participates and the amount of time allocated to them. Since 1950 the average work week has declined by about five hours per week, from roughly 40 hours per week to 35. Two other trends are worth noting: urban Americans are spending significantly less time in family care and leisure-time activities are increasing substantially. Americans are quite active in picnicking, driving for pleasure, swimming, sightseeing, walking and jogging activities, attending outdoor spectator events, and playing outdoor games and sports.

Psychological Characteristics

The psychological characteristics of a consumer combine personality, attitudes, class consciousness, motivation, perceived risk, innovativeness, opinion leadership, and importance of purchase. See Figure 4-9.

Personality **describes an individual's traits that make him or her unique.**

A **personality** is the sum total of an individual's traits that make that individual unique. Self-confidence, dominance, sociability, defensiveness, and order are selected personality traits. Personality has a strong impact on an individual's behavior. For example, a self-confident and sociable person will not purchase the same products and services as an inhibited and aloof person. It is necessary to remember that a personality is made up of many traits operating in conjunction with one another.

Attitudes (opinions) are a person's positive, neutral, or negative feelings about products, services, companies, issues, and/or institutions. Attitudes are shaped by demographics, social factors, and personality. One role of marketing is to generate favorable attitudes toward a company's products or services. Given the intensive competition in many industries, a firm cannot normally succeed without positive consumer attitudes. When using attitude research, two concepts must be measured: the attitude itself and the purchase intent toward a company's brand.

Class consciousness is the extent to which social status is desired and pursued by a person. Class consciousness helps determine a consumer's use of reference groups, a person's concern about social class mobility, and the importance of prestige purchases. An *inner-directed person* is interested in pleasing him- or herself. This type of person is generally attracted by do-it-yourself products, products that perform well functionally, and products or services that are challenging and can be used when the person is alone. The inner-directed person relies on his or her own judgment, is not involved with social mobility, and does not value prestige items. An *outer-directed person* is interested in pleasing the people around him or her. Approval by reference groups, upward social mobility, and the ownership of prestige items are sought. An outer-directed person is generally attracted by products or services that provide social visibility, well-known brands, competition with others, and uniqueness. Functional performance may be less important.

Motivation is

> the driving force within an individual which impels him [or her] to action. This driving force is produced by a state of tension, which exists as the result of an unfulfilled need.[11]

By identifying and appealing to a consumer's *motives,* the reasons for behavior, a marketer can generate motivation. For example:

Motive	*Marketer Actions that Motivate*
Hunger	Television and radio commercials just before mealtime
Safety	Demonstration of a smoke detector
Sociability	Toothpaste and perfume commercials showing social success due to products
Achievement	Demonstration of knowledge obtained via a home computer
Economy	Newspaper coupons advertising sales

Each person has different motives for buying, and these change by situation and over time. Most consumers combine economic (price, durability) and emotional (status, self-esteem) motives when making a purchase.

Perceived risk is the level of risk the consumer believes exists; this belief may or may not be correct. Marketers must deal with perceived risk in either case, because a high degree of perceived risk may dampen

Attitudes or *opinions* are feelings about products, services, companies, issues, and institutions.

Class consciousness explains the value of status to a person. *Outer-directed persons* are most influenced by others, while *inner-directed persons* are not.

To obtain purchases, marketers need to *motivate* consumers.

Perceived risk is the degree of uncertainty felt by the consumer. It is important for marketers to minimize this risk.

motivation. In situations where perceived risk is high (for example, side effects of a drug product), the marketer must remove the disputed ingredient if it is really harmful and inform consumers of this change. If the disputed ingredient is not really harmful, this fact must be communicated to the consumer to reduce perceived risk. Communications are vital in lowering perceived risk.

Perceived risk can be divided into five major types:

1. Functional: the risk that the product will not perform adequately
2. Physical: the risk that the product will be harmful
3. Financial: the risk that the product will not be worth its cost or time commitment
4. Social: the risk that the product will cause embarrassment before others
5. Psychological: the risk that one's ego will be bruised[12]

Innovativeness **is willingness to try a new product or service that others perceive as risky.**

A consumer who is willing to try a new product or service that others perceive as having a high degree of risk is said to exhibit *innovativeness.* An innovator is likely to be well educated, literate, and have a high income and standard of living. This person is also apt to be knowledgeable, interested in change, achievement motivated, business oriented, open-minded, status conscious, mobile, venturesome, and have aspirations for his or her children.[13] It is essential for marketers to identify and appeal to innovators when introducing a new product or service.

Opinion leaders **influence other consumers through face-to-face interaction.**

Marketers are most interested in determining which innovators are *opinion leaders.* Opinion leaders are people who influence the purchase behavior of other consumers through face-to-face interaction. Opinion leaders tend to be expert about a product or service category, socially accepted, longstanding members of the community, outgoing, active, and trusted, and tend to seek approval from others. Opinion leaders normally have an impact over a narrow range of products; they are believed to be more credible than commercial sources of information.

The *importance of a purchase* **determines the time, effort, and money a consumer will spend.**

The *importance of a purchase* has a major impact on the time and effort a consumer will spend shopping for a product or service and on the amount of money allocated. An important purchase will involve careful decision making, high perceived risk, and probably a large amount of money. An unimportant purchase will receive little decision-making time (the product or service may be avoided altogether), have little perceived risk, and probably be inexpensive.

Marketing Applications of Social and Psychological Profiles

Several new products have done well recently because of their appeal to the social and psychological characteristics of consumers. Among them are bottled water, "light" food, and home computers.

In the late 1970s bottled water became very popular in the United States. In 1979 sales were $200 million; by 1983, sales were projected to be $500 million. Consumers were identified as those who were interested in health, diet, physical fitness, natural products, and purity. Companies like Perrier ensured their success by promoting extensively, distributing in supermarkets and other convenience stores, and setting fair prices, while retaining the features consumers wanted.[14]

Starting in the 1970s, "light" products became popular for food, cigarettes, beer, and soda. These products are low in calories (or in the case of cigarettes, tar and nicotine), while avoiding a diet connotation. Instead, the emphasis is on health or appearance. For example, Miller Lite is able to maintain a masculine image because of its heavy use of former athletes in commercials. Earlier attempts at low-calorie beer, such as Gablinger, failed because the wrong life-style connotation—nonmasculine—was projected. Current light products also appeal to taste-conscious consumers, unlike prior products. Figure 4-10 shows Stouffer's entry into the light food market.

As American society has become more convenience, knowledge,

Figure 4-10
Tasty, Low-Calorie Foods from Stouffer's

Reprinted by permission.

and leisure oriented, the market for home computers has grown. In 1978 the first mass-produced home computer was introduced by Radio Shack for $600. In 1982, the total sales of home computers were over $750 million.[15] Research indicates that

> consumers think the home computer will help simplify the complexities of their life-styles in areas related to personal finances, investments, taxes, household management. . . . The consumer also perceives the home computer not as a toy, but for game playing of a complexity found in only a few of today's video games—strategy games based on the stock market, investments, bridge, chess, etc.[16]

The social and psychological characteristics of consumers can also hold down sales, as well as increase them. For example, the U.S. automobile industry has gone through a major slowdown for many reasons. Among them are several consumer life-style factors. First, owning an older car is no longer socially unacceptable. As one consumer stated, "Instead of an ugly sight, it's a badge of honor." Second, consumers are becoming more concerned about durability and economy and less interested in minor model changes and styling. Third, people have reduced their driving mileage as a result of higher gasoline prices. Four, new automobile prices encourage consumers to invest in repairs for their existing cars. Five, consumers have shifted spending to other items, such as housing, energy, food, and personal computers (which now provide more status than autos). Six, as an American Motors executive commented, "In efforts to meet safety and fuel economy standards we all gravitated toward similar designs and styles." Another observer added that purchasing a car "is like buying a household appliance—you've got to have one, but you'll buy it only when you need it."[17]

Limitations of Social and Psychological Analysis

Many social and psychological factors are difficult to measure.

Unlike demographics, many social and psychological factors are difficult to measure, somewhat subjective, usually based on the self-reports of consumers, and sometimes hidden from view (to avoid embarrassment, protect privacy, convey an image, and other reasons). In addition, there are still ongoing disputes over terminology, misuse of data, and reliability.

Consumer Decision Making

The consumer's decision process consists of a series of stages from stimulus to postpurchase behavior. It is affected by demographic, social, and psychological factors.

The **consumer's decision process** is comprised of two parts: the process itself and factors affecting the process. The decision process consists of six basic stages: stimulus, problem awareness, information search, evaluation of alternatives, purchase, and postpurchase behavior. Factors that affect the process are a consumer's demographic, social, and psychological characteristics. The total consumer decision-making process is shown in Figure 4-11.

When a consumer buys a product or service, he or she goes through this decision process. In some situations all six stages in the process are

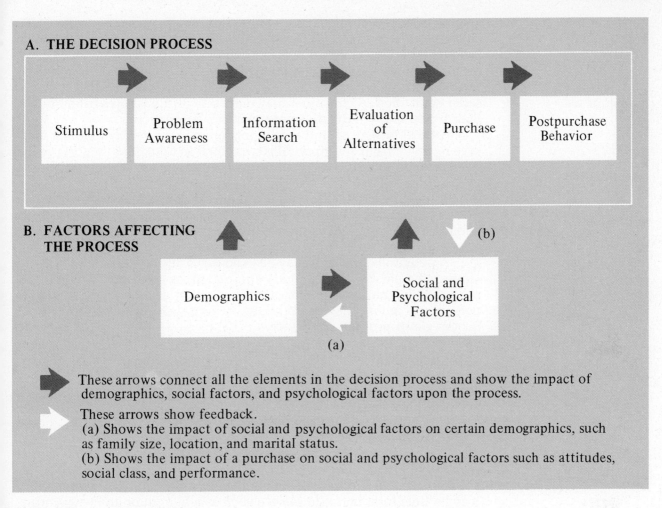

Figure 4-11
The Consumer's Decision-Making Process

used; in others, only a few of the steps are utilized. For example, the purchase of an expensive stereo requires more decision making than the purchase of a new tie.

The decision process outlined in Figure 4-11 assumes that the end result is the purchase of a good or service by the consumer. However, it is important to realize that at *any* point in the process a potential consumer may decide not to buy and terminate the process. The product or service may turn out to be unnecessary, unsatisfactory, or too expensive.

Stimulus

A *stimulus* is a cue (social, commercial, or noncommercial) or a drive (physical) meant to motivate or arouse a person to act. When one talks with friends, fellow employees, family members, and others, social cues are received. The distinguishing attribute of a social cue is that it comes from an interpersonal source not affiliated with the seller.

A second type of stimulus is a commercial cue, which is a message

A *stimulus* is a cue intended to motivate a person to act. A stimulus may be social, commercial, noncommercial, or an inner drive.

sponsored by a manufacturer, wholesaler, retailer, or other seller. The objective of a commercial cue is to interest a consumer in a particular product, service, or store. Advertisements, personal selling, and sales promotions are forms of commercial stimuli. These cues may not be regarded as highly as social cues, because consumers realize they are seller controlled. A consumer may react differently when a friend rather than a newspaper advertisement makes a suggestion.

A third type of stimulus is a noncommercial cue, which is a message received from an impartial source such as *Consumer Reports* or the government. This cue has credibility because it is not affiliated with the seller.

A fourth type of stimulus is a physical drive. This occurs when a person's physical senses are affected. Thirst, cold, heat, pain, hunger, and fear cause physical drives. If the drive is weak, it may be ignored. A strong drive requires further action.

A potential consumer may be exposed to any or all of these types of stimuli. If a person is sufficiently stimulated, he or she will go on to the next step in the decision process. If stimulation does not occur, the person will ignore the cue and delay or terminate the decision process for the given product or service.

Problem Awareness

During *problem awareness,* the consumer recognizes a problem of shortage or unfulfilled desire. He or she will act only if the problem is perceived as worth solving.

At the **problem awareness stage,** the consumer recognizes that the product or service under consideration may solve a problem of shortage or unfulfilled desire.

Recognition of shortage occurs when a consumer becomes alerted to the fact that a product or service needs to be repurchased. A product such as a suit, clock radio, or television may wear out. The consumer may run out of an item such as razor blades, coffee, or gasoline. Service may be necessary for a product such as an automobile or telephone. It may be time for a periodic service such as a haircut or an eye examination. In each of these examples, the consumer recognizes a need to replenish a product or service.

Recognition of unfulfilled desire occurs when a consumer becomes aware of a product or service that has not been purchased before. The product or service may improve a person's self-image, status, appearance, or knowledge in a manner that has not been tried before (cosmetic surgery, designer clothing, hair transplant, encyclopedia, luxury automobile), or it may offer new performance characteristics, not previously available (videotape camera, talking magazine, tobacco-free cigarettes, outer-space travel). In either case the consumer is aroused by a desire to improve him- or herself and evaluates the utility of fulfilling this desire.

Many consumers are more hesitant to react to unfulfilled desires than to shortages because there are more risks, and the benefits may be hard to judge. There is less experience with new items than with the replacement of a product or service whose characteristics are well known. Whether the consumer becomes aware of a problem of shortage or a problem of unfulfilled desire, he or she will act only if the problem is perceived as worth solving. A strong stimulus does not mean the presence of a worthy problem. An unworthy problem will not be acted on, and the decision process is delayed or terminated at this point.

Information Search

After the consumer decides that the shortage or unfulfilled desire is worth further consideration, information is gathered. The **information search** requires the assembly of a list of alternative products or services that will solve the problem at hand and a determination of the characteristics of each alternative.

The list of alternatives does not have to be very formal or even written. It can simply be a group of items the consumer thinks about. The key is that the consumer amasses a list of the products or services that are most likely to solve his or her problem. Normally, once the consumer has generated a list of alternatives, items (brands) not on the list do not receive further consideration.

This aspect of information search may be internal or external. Internal search takes place when the consumer has a lot of purchasing experience in the area under consideration and uses a search of his or her memory to determine the list of products or services that should be considered. A consumer with minimal purchasing experience will usually undertake external search to develop a list of alternatives. This type of search can involve commercial sources, noncommercial sources, and/or social sources. The consumer seeks information outside his or her memory.

The second type of information a consumer seeks deals with the characteristics of each alternative, as the attributes of each alternative under consideration are determined. This kind of information is gathered in the same manner as the list of alternatives was generated, internally or externally, depending on the expertise of the consumer and the level of perceived risk. As risk increases, the amount of information sought also increases.

Once the information search is completed, it must be determined whether the shortage or unfulfilled desire can be satisfied by any of the alternatives. If one or more alternatives are satisfactory, the consumer moves on to the next step in the decision process. The process is delayed or discontinued when no alternative provides minimal satisfaction.

Information search involves listing alternatives and their characteristics. Search may be internal or external.

Evaluation of Alternatives

At this point, the consumer has enough information to select one product or service alternative from the list of choices. Sometimes this is easy to do, when one alternative is clearly superior to the others across all characteristics. A product or service with excellent quality and a low price will be an automatic choice over an average quality, expensive one. Often the choice is not that simple, and the consumer must carefully **evaluate the alternatives** before making a decision. If two or more alternatives are attractive, the consumer needs to determine what criteria (attributes) to evaluate and their relative importance. Then the alternatives are ranked and a choice made.

The consumer evaluates alternatives by determining relevant product features and their importance, and then ranking alternatives.

Criteria for a decision are those product or service features that the consumer considers relevant. These may include price, color, style, options, quality, safety, durability, status, and warranty. The consumer sets performance standards for the features and evaluates (develops an attitude toward) each alternative according to its ability to meet the standards. In addition, the importance of each criterion is determined, because the multiple attributes of the product or service are usually of varying importance to the consumer. For example, a consumer may consider the price of a pair of shoes to be more important than style and act accordingly during a purchase by selecting inexpensive, nondistinctive shoes.

Next, the consumer ranks the alternatives from most desirable to least desirable and selects one product or service from among the alternatives. For some products or services, ranking is difficult because the items may be technical, poorly labeled, or new (the consumer has no experience with the brand or product type). These items are frequently ranked on the basis of brand name or price, which is used to indicate overall quality.

In situations where no alternative proves to be satisfactory, a decision to delay or not make a purchase is made.

Purchase

Following the selection of the best product or service from the list of alternatives, the consumer is ready for the **purchase act:** an exchange of money or a promise to pay for the acquisition of a product or service. Three important decisions remain: place of purchase, terms, and availability.

The place of purchase (where the product or service is bought) may be a store or nonstore location. The great majority of items (food, automobiles, clothing, drugs, beauty services) are bought at stores (discount, department, boutique). Some items are purchased at school (books, stationery), work (health insurance), and home (mail, telephone, and door-to-door sales). The place of purchase is evaluated in the same manner as the product or service itself. Alternatives are listed, characteristics defined, and a ranking compiled. The most desirable place of purchase is then chosen.

The terms of purchase are the price and the method of payment. Price is the total dollar amount (including interest, tax, and other charges) a consumer pays to achieve ownership or use of a product or service. The method of payment is the manner in which the price is paid (cash, short-term credit, or long-term credit).

Availability refers to stock-on-hand and delivery. Stock-on-hand is the quantity of an item that the place of purchase has in its inventory. Delivery is the length of time from when an order is placed by the consumer until it is received and the ease with which an item is transported to its place of use.

The consumer will buy a product or service if these three elements of the purchase act are acceptable. However, dissatisfaction with the place of purchase, terms, and/or availability may cause a consumer to delay or not buy the product or service, even though there is contentment with the product or service itself.

Postpurchase Behavior

After the purchase of a product or service, the consumer frequently is involved with ***postpurchase behavior***—either further purchases or re-evaluation. In many cases buying one product or service leads to further purchases. For example, the purchase of a house leads to the acquisition of fire insurance. The purchase of a suit leads to the purchase of a matching tie. The purchase of a home videotape system leads to the acquisition of blank and movie cassettes. In these and other situations, the purchase of one product or service stimulates other purchases, and the decision process continues for these items until the last purchase is made.

Postpurchase behavior frequently leads to further purchasing or re-evaluation.

The consumer may also re-evaluate the purchase of a product or service. Does the item perform as promised? Are the expectations of the consumer matched by actual product or service attributes? Satisfaction usually results in repurchase when the product or service runs out and there has been positive communication with other consumers interested in the same product or service. Dissatisfaction frequently results in brand switching and negative communications with other consumers.

Dissatisfaction with a purchase is often the result of ***cognitive dissonance,*** doubt that the correct decision has been made. The consumer may regret that the purchase was made at all or wish that another alternative had been chosen. To overcome cognitive dissonance and dissatisfaction, the firm must realize that the purchase process does not end with the purchase. Aftercare (follow-up telephone and service calls, advertisements aimed at purchasers as well as potential purchasers) is extremely important to reassure consumers, particularly for important and expensive decisions with many alternatives.

Cognitive dissonance is doubt that the correct purchase has been made. Firms can overcome it by proper consumer aftercare.

The coupling of a realistic promotion campaign, so that expectations are not raised too high, with consumer aftercare should reduce or eliminate cognitive dissonance and dissatisfaction.

Factors Affecting Consumer Decision Making

Demographic, social, and psychological factors have an important impact on the way consumers utilize the decision process. These factors are not only helpful for marketers in developing consumer profiles and adapting marketing strategies to them, but they also aid the firm in understanding how consumers use the decision process.

For example, a young male who participates in social activities and is outgoing would use the decision process differently than a middle-aged male who is a homebody and inner-directed. The former would place heavy emphasis on social sources of information, whereas the latter would not. An affluent consumer would move through the process more quickly than a middle-income consumer because the financial risk would be less. A person under tight time pressure would also move through the process more quickly than one who had sufficient time for shopping. An insecure consumer would spend more time making a decision than one who is secure.

By knowing how these factors affect the decision process, a company can fine tune its marketing strategies to cater to the target market and its purchase behavior; in addition, the company can answer these two questions: Why do two or more consumers use the decision process in the same way? Why do two or more people use the decision process in quite different ways?

Types of Decision Processes

Each time a consumer buys a product or service, he or she uses the decision process. Often, it is used subconsciously and the consumer is not even aware of its use. The decision process also is used differently in various situations. One situation may require the thorough use of each step in the process; another may allow the consumer to de-emphasize or skip certain steps. The three types of decision processes are extended, limited, and routine decision making.

Extended consumer decision making occurs when a consumer makes full use of the decision process shown in Figure 4-11. Considerable time is spent on information search and evaluation of alternatives before a purchase is made. Expensive, complex products or services with which the consumer has had little or no experience require this form of decision making. Perceived risk of all kinds is generally high. Examples of products or services requiring extended decision making are college, a house, a first car, and a location for a wedding.

At any stage of the purchase process, a consumer can delay or terminate activity; this often occurs for expensive, complex items. The factors affecting the process have their greatest impact on extended decision making. Demographic, social, and psychological factors (age, income, education, activities, stage in family life cycle, experience, personality, and others) have a major influence on the use of extended decision making. High levels of risk and uncertainty lead to increased information search, evaluation, and re-evaluation.

Limited consumer decision making takes place when a consumer uses each of the steps in the purchase process but does not need to spend a great deal of time on any of them. This type of decision making normally requires less time than extended decision making, because the consumer has some past experience with the product or service under consideration. In this category are items the consumer has purchased, but not regularly. Risk is moderate, and the consumer is willing to spend some time shopping. The thoroughness with which the process is used depends on the prior experience of the consumer and the importance of the purchase. Emphasis is usually on an evaluation of a list of known alternatives, based on desires or standards. An information search is important for some consumers. A second car, clothing, gifts, home furnishings, and a vacation are examples of items typically utilizing limited decision making.

The factors affecting the decision process have some impact on limited decision making. However, this impact lessens as experience increases and risk decreases. Income, education, the importance of the

---

Side notes (left margin):

Fine-tuned marketing strategies respond to the target market.

Extended consumer decision making involves full use of the decision process and is used for expensive, unique items.

Limited consumer decision making involves the use of every step of the purchase process but not much time on any of them. It is used for items purchased infrequently.

purchase, motives, and the time available for shopping play strong roles in the uses of limited decision making.

   Routine consumer decision making occurs when the consumer buys out of habit and skips steps in the decision process. The consumer tries to spend no time shopping and usually repurchases the same brands. In this category are items that are purchased regularly. These products have little or no perceived risk for the consumer because of the regular nature of their purchase (substantial experience by the consumer) and low purchase price. The key step for this form of decision making is problem awareness. Once the consumer realizes a product or service is depleted, a repurchase is made. Information search, evaluation of alternatives, and postpurchase behavior are normally omitted as long as the consumer is satisfied. Examples of routine purchases are the daily newspaper, a haircut by a regular barber, and weekly grocery items.

   Factors affecting the process have little impact on routine behavior. Problem awareness almost always leads to a purchase.

   Because consumers like to reduce risk, the time spent shopping, and the use of detailed decision making, most purchases are made through routine or limited decision making. ***Brand loyalty*** is the consistent repurchase of and preference for a brand. Through brand loyalty, consumers attempt to minimize risk, time, and thought. One study showed that in the U.S. about 60 per cent of consumers consider themselves likely to "try to stick to well-known brand names."[18] Where possible, consumers seek to avoid extended decision making.

> *Routine consumer decision making* **involves buying out of habit and skips many steps in the decision process. It is used for regularly purchased items.**

> *Brand loyalty* **is the consistent repurchase of and preference for a brand in order to reduce risk, time, and thought.**

Marketing Applications of Consumer's Decision Process

The consumer's decision process has been applied to a variety of marketing situations, as these two illustrations show.

   Drugstore shoppers make almost 60 per cent of final purchase decisions after entering the store. The items for which specific buying plans are made in advance include prescriptions, photographic equipment, tobacco and alcohol, and nonprescription drugs. However, personal care items, magazines, snack foods, hardware, cosmetics, accessories, nonalcoholic beverages, jewelry, and automotive supplies are largely unplanned purchases that are greatly affected by store displays, advertisements, and coupons.[19]

   Husbands and wives usually share purchase decisions for wine, fast food, film, and cigarettes. Husbands often play a greater role in the selection of beer, gasoline, Scotch, shaving cream, and cigars—wives generally play a greater role in the choice of baby food, soft drinks, headache remedies, shampoo, deodorant, and ice cream.[20]

Limitations of Consumer's Decision Process

The limitations of the consumer's decision process for marketers lie in the hidden (unexpressed) nature of many elements of the process, the consumer's subconscious performance of the process or a number of its components, and the impact of demographic, social, and psychological factors on the process.

> **Elements are hidden; actions may be subconscious; many variables affect decisions.**

Summary

By understanding consumers, a firm is able to determine the most appropriate audience to which to appeal and the combination of marketing factors that will satisfy this audience. This chapter examined the demographic, social, and psychological factors affecting behavior and the decision process of final consumers. Chapters 5 and 6 center on organizational consumers, the development of a target market, and sales forecasting.

Demographics are easily identifiable and measurable statistics that are used to describe the population. In combination, demographics can establish consumer profiles that may present attractive market opportunities. Important demographics are population size, gender, and age; location and mobility; income and expenditures; occupations and education; and marital status.

These potential limitations of demographics are noted: obsolete data, hidden trends or implications, limited use of single demographic statistics, and lack of explanation of the factors affecting behavior, consumer decision making, and motivation.

Because demographic data alone are often inadequate for making marketing decisions, many firms analyze consumer social, psychological, and decision-making information in conjunction with demographics and then develop descriptive consumer profiles.

Social and psychological factors comprise a consumer's life-style, the pattern in which a person lives and spends time and money. A consumer's social profile is made up of several elements, including culture, social class, performance, reference groups, family life cycle, and time expenditures. A psychological profile is based on a combination of these attributes: personality, attitudes, level of class consciousness, motivation, perceived risk, innovativeness, opinion leadership, and importance of purchase.

Even though social and psychological profiles have many marketing applications, they can be difficult to measure, somewhat subjective, based on self-reports by consumers, and sometimes hidden from view. There are disputes over terms, misuse of data, and reliability.

The consumer's decision process is composed of the process itself and the factors affecting it (demographics, social factors, and psychological factors). It can be delayed or terminated by the consumer at any point. The process consists of six steps: stimulus, problem awareness, information search, evaluation of alternatives, purchase, and postpurchase behavior. There are three types of consumer decision making: extended, limited, and routine. Brand loyalty, the consistent repurchase of and preference for a brand, is the consumer's attempt to minimize risk, time, and thought.

The limitations of the decision process for marketers lie in the unexpressed nature of many parts of the process, the subconscious nature of many actions by consumers, and the impact of demographic, social, and psychological factors.

After reading this chapter you should understand these key terms:

Final consumers
Organizational consumers
Consumer demographics
Standard Metropolitan Statistical Areas (SMSAs)
Standard Consolidated Statistical Areas (SCSAs)
Disposable income
Discretionary income
Consumer Price Index (CPI)
Family
Household
Life-style
Culture
Social class system
Social performance
Reference group
Family life cycle
Joint decision making
Time expenditures (activities)
Personality
Attitudes (opinions)

Class consciousness
Inner-directed person
Outer-directed person
Motivation
Motives
Perceived risk
Innovativeness
Opinion leaders
Importance of a purchase
Consumer's decision process
Stimulus
Problem awareness
Information search
Evaluation of alternatives
Purchase act
Postpurchase behavior
Cognitive dissonance
Extended consumer decision making
Limited consumer decision making
Routine consumer decision making
Brand loyalty

1. Name several potential product and service opportunities in the senior-citizen market.
2. Few families have annual incomes under $5,000 per year. What does this signify for marketers?
3. Distinguish between disposable income and discretionary income. During inflationary times, what occurs to the level of each?
4. Nearly all homes have radios, refrigerators, and televisions. What does this signify for marketers?
5. Explain the concept of the Consumer Price Index (CPI). What does it measure?
6. Distinguish between *family* and *household*.
7. Explain the consumer demographic profile.
8. Why are demographic data alone frequently insufficient for marketing decisions?
9. How do culture and social class affect a person's life-style and purchases?
10. Explain the family life cycle. What are the marketing implications at each stage?
11. Develop a five-question survey to determine the attitudes of consumers toward automobile air bags (in place of seat belts). What question must be included?
12. Define perceived risk. How may a firm reduce it?
13. Describe the consumer's decision process and each of its stages.
14. Why might a consumer not purchase an item after selecting a preferred alternative?
15. Define brand loyalty and explain its use by consumers.

NOTES

1. Mark N. Dodosh, "Widely Ignored Teen Market Has a lot of Spending Power," *Wall Street Journal* (June 17, 1982), p. 31; Sheila Jacobson, "Cashing in on the Youth Market Boom," *Zip* (April 1981), pp. 28–32ff; and B.G. Yovovich, "A Game of Hide-and-Seek," *Advertising Age* (August 2, 1982), pp. M-5–M-7.

2. The data in this section are drawn primarily from *Current Population Reports* and *Census of Population* (Washington, D.C.: U.S. Bureau of Census, Series P-20, P-25, and P-60).

3. For a good overview of demographics, see George J. Stolnitz, "Our Main Population Patterns: Radical Shifts, Cloudy Prospects," *Business Horizons,* Vol. 25 (July–August 1982), pp. 92–99.

4. U.S. League of Savings Associations; and Alan S. Oser, "America's 'Dream Adrift,' " *New York Times* (June 20, 1982), Section 8, pp. 7, 14.

5. "The Lasting Changes Brought by Women Workers," *Business Week* (March 15, 1982), pp. 61–64; Ronald D. Michman, "The Double Income Family: A New Market Target," *Business Horizons,* Vol. 23 (August 1980), pp. 31–37; and Lori Kesler, "Behind the Wheel of a Quiet Revolution," *Advertising Age* (July 26, 1982), pp. M-11–M-13.

6. Sheila Even-Tov, "Golden Mail-Order Years: Reaching the Over-45 Market," *Zip* (June 1982), pp. 22–29.

7. John Mutter, "B. Dalton Bookseller: A Novel Approach to Retailing," *Sales & Marketing Management* (May 14, 1979), pp. 49–51.

8. James F. Engel and Roger D. Blackwell, *Consumer Behavior,* Fourth Edition (Hinsdale, Illinois: Dryden Press, 1982), p. 188.

9. Leon G. Schiffman and Leslie Lazar Kanuk, *Consumer Behavior,* Second Edition (Englewood Cliffs, N.J.: Prentice-Hall, 1983), pp. 406–420.

10. See for example, Patrick E. Murphy and William A. Staples, "A Modernized Family Life Cycle," *Journal of Consumer Research,* Vol. 6 (June 1979), pp. 12–22.

11. Schiffman and Kanuk, *Consumer Behavior,* p. 49.

12. Ibid., p. 161.

13. Engel and Blackwell, *Consumer Behavior,* pp. 390–394.

14. Bernice Finkelman, "Perrier Pours into U.S. Market, Spurs Water Bottle Battle," *Marketing News* (September 7, 1979), pp. 1, 9.

15. Bryan Burrough, "Home-Computer Sales Take Off as Prices Drop Sharply and Video Games Catch On," *Wall Street Journal* (June 11, 1982), p. 27.

16. "Home Computer on Brink of Creating Life-Style Revolution, Says Bally's Wiles," *Marketing News* (January 26, 1979), p. 9.

17. Charles W. Stevens, "People Are Keeping Cars Longer as Costs Rise and Attitudes Change," *Wall Street Journal* (January 7, 1982), p. 23.

18. Bill Abrams, "Brand Loyalty Rises Slightly, But Increase Could Be Fluke," *Wall Street Journal* (January 7, 1982), p. 23.

19. "Pilot Study Finds Final Product Choice Usually Made in Store," *Marketing News* (August 6, 1982), p. 5.

20. *Purchase Influence: Measures of Husband/Wife Influence on Buying Decisions* (New Canaan, Ct.: Haley, Overholser & Associates, Inc.), pp. 13–23.

CASES

1   COCA-COLA: DEMOGRAPHICS FOR THE WINE MARKET*

With 26% of the domestic soft-drink market, Coca-Cola has vintage appeal for Americans. But as the nation's demographics change, shrinking the size of the teenage soda-drinking population, Coca-

*The data in this case are drawn from "Coca-Cola: A Spurt into Wine That Is Altering the Industry," *Business Week* (October 15, 1979), pp. 126–131; "Creating a Mass Market for Wine," *Business Week* (March 15, 1982), pp. 108–118; and Mitchell J. Shields, "Coke and Wine Is It," *Advertising Age* (January 10,1983), pp. M-16–M-18.

Cola Co. is seeking to apply the same marketing and production know-how that made Coke No. 1 in the frantically competitive soft-drink industry to a faster-growing but still tradition-bound market—wine.

Beginning in 1977, Coca-Cola spent about $110 million to enter the wine industry. It acquired New York-based Taylor Wine, maker of Great Western Champagne, because of its brand recognition (second only to Gallo). Coke then purchased two California wineries and labeled them Taylor California. A new group of wines was introduced in October 1978, using Taylor's existing distribution system. The new wines were geared to the largest-growing table wine market, midpriced wines selling for $2 to $5 per fifth. In 1980, a $15 to $20 million expansion of the Monterey production and storage facilities was begun.

By 1981, Coke had allocated a yearly advertising budget of $30 million for wine. During 1981, the wine division ranked fourth in the industry, and sales were over 27 million gallons (double those of 1978). For the end of the 1980s, Coke targeted annual sales at $1 billion, based in large part on the growth of the twenty-five to forty age group. (a significant market for table wine).

Other wine makers have become quite aggressive in response to Coke. Almadén turned out a new advertising campaign. Paul Masson tripled its promotional budget. Gallo planned the introduction of nine new low-priced wines and extensive advertising.

The U.S. wine market has great potential, despite the rise in competition. Annual wine drinking is expanding at a rate of 6 per cent, yet per capita consumption is only 40th on a worldwide basis.

QUESTIONS

1. Coca-Cola has shown a great interest in the age of its market. What other demographics of the wine market should it study?
2. The heaviest soda drinkers have been those ages ten to twenty-four. Because Coke projects a 13 per cent decline in this age group, should it cut back on its marketing efforts for soda? Explain.
3. Develop consumer demographic profiles for champagne and table wine.
4. For champagne and table wine, explain what, why, how, when, where, and how often consumers purchase.
5. Based on the demographic data contained in this chapter, are there any other beverage opportunities for Coca-Cola to pursue?

NIKE: INCREASING SALES AFTER THE JOGGING BOOM ENDS† 2

In 1964, Philip Knight became the U.S. distributor for Japan's Tiger running shoes. When Tiger ended Knight's exclusive selling rights in the U.S., Knight formed his own company—Nike (named after the Greek goddess of victory)—in 1972. By 1981, sales totaled $700 million annually.

Throughout the 1970s, Nike capitalized on the jogging boom in the U.S., where the total number of runners reached 20 million. Nike captured 50 per cent of the running-shoe market by offering quality products, celebrity endorse-

†The data in this case are drawn from Victor F. Zonana, "Jogging's Fade Fails to Push Nike Off Track," *Wall Street Journal* (March 5, 1981), p. 27; and Myron Magnet, "Nike Starts the Second Mile," *Fortune* (November 1, 1982), pp. 158–166.

ments, a full line of shoes, and aggressive marketing. A strong appeal was made to "self-involved" and brand-conscious consumers.

Wisely, Nike foresaw a leveling off of jogging in the U.S. by the early 1980s and broadened its product lines. Its U.S. sales are broken down as follows:

Running shoes	43%
Basketball shoes	24%
Racquetball shoes	18%
Children's shoes	8%
Apparel	3%
Other	4%
Total	100%

In addition, Nike has become active in the European running shoe market where Adidas and others are particularly strong. So far, consumer response in Europe has been limited. And, as one analyst observed, jogging is "not a national phenomenon. The English don't have the mad, ambitious striving . . . that it takes to make a whole country run. It's really a religion, this quest for self-perfection. People don't have that here." To this, replies Knight, "You are going to see guys jogging around Westminister Palace. It's happening."

QUESTIONS

1. In terms of American life-styles,
   a. Why did jogging become so popular?
   b. Why has the interest in jogging peaked?
2. Why has Nike been able to sell $60 running shoes and $75 warmup suits?
3. Evaluate Nike's U.S. sales breakdown, as shown in the case. Which product areas have the best and worst growth potential in the U.S.? Explain your answer.
4. What will Nike have to do to succeed in Europe?

Organizational Consumers

5

Chapter Preview

Chapter Objectives

1. To define the characteristics of organizational consumers and how they differ from final consumers

2. To describe the different types of organizational consumers and their buying objectives, buying structure, use of purchases, and purchase constraints

3. To explain the organizational consumer's decision process

4. To consider the marketing implications of organizational buyer types, characteristics, and behavior

In 1978, Boeing began a $3+ billion program to develop and market two new aircraft, the single-aisle 757 and the wide-body 767. But after a large sale of 757s to Delta in 1980, orders for the new jets fell drastically; during 1982, no 767s were purchased. Said one Boeing executive, "I feel like a basketball coach whose team is running hard, shooting well, and rebounding beautifully. But the auditorium is on fire."

Boeing produced the 757 and 767 jets with specific objectives in mind: to greatly improve fuel consumption, to reduce cockpit personnel from three to two, to share interchangeable parts, and to service different capacity needs of airlines (the 757 seats 186 people; the 767 seats 211 to 289 people).

Despite success in achieving these goals, a number of factors have caused Boeing's customers to avoid or postpone purchases of the 757 and 767. The entire airline passenger market in the U.S. has performed poorly; and because passenger travel has been down, airlines have been reluctant to purchase new planes. During 1982, the U.S. airline industry lost about $2 billion. Those airlines not canceling orders are letting them "slide," industry slang for postponing delivery dates.

Airlines are less concerned about fuel consumption, since costs dropped from $1.10 to $1.00 a gallon and stabilized at that level, and more concerned about aircraft costs ($35 million for a 757 and $50 million for a 767).

In a poor passenger market, the 186-seat 757 has proven to be too large for many airlines; a competitor offers a 150-passenger plane. Also, a number of airlines are buying used aircraft, for as little as 10 per cent of the price of new aircraft. Finally, airlines have seen some traditional lenders retreat, drying up funds for aircraft purchases.

Boeing believes its 757 and 767 jets will succeed in the long run, after the airlines improve their profitability and passenger travel takes an upturn. As a financially strong company, it has the resources to ride out the current situation. After all, the 727 had limited sales for more than two years. Then, the 727 became the best-selling and most profitable plane ever.[1] Figure 5-1 shows the 757 and 767.

Organizational Consumers Defined

Firms dealing with organizational consumers are involved with industrial marketing.

Organizational consumers are formal entities that purchase products and services for further production, usage in operating the organization, or resale to other consumers. In contrast, final consumers purchase products and services for personal, family, or household use. Organizational consumers are manufacturers, wholesalers, retailers, and government and other nonprofit institutions. When firms deal with organizational consumers, they are engaged in **industrial marketing.**

Organizational consumers differ from final consumers in several important ways. These differences are due to the nature of products and services purchased and the nature of the market. See Table 5-1 and the discussion in the following subsections.

Differences from Final Consumers Due to the Nature of Purchases

Organizational and final consumers vary in the way they use products and services and in the types of products and services they purchase. Organizational consumers use products and services in further production, operations, or for resale to other consumers. They purchase capital

Figure 5-1
Boeing's Fuel-Efficient New Aircraft

Reprinted by permission.

equipment, raw materials, semifinished goods, and other products and services. Final consumers acquire products and services for personal, family, or household use. They usually buy finished items and are not involved with million-dollar purchases of plant and equipment.

Because of the nature of the products and services purchased by organizational consumers, such consumers are more likely to use specifications, multiple-buying decisions, value and vendor analysis, leased equipment, and competitive bidding and negotiation than are final consumers.

Many organizational consumers rely on **product specifications** in purchase decisions. Products are not considered unless they satisfy minimum specifications, such as engineering and architectural guidelines, purity and grade standards, horsepower, voltage, type of construction, and materials employed in construction. Final consumers often purchase on the basis of description, style, and color.

Product specifications must be met to satisfy organizational consumers.

Table 5-1

Differences in Purchases

Major Differences Between Organizational and Final Consumers

1. Organizational consumers acquire for further production, use in operations, or resale to other consumers. Final consumers acquire only for personal, family, or household use.

2. Organizational consumers commonly purchase installations, raw materials, and semifinished materials. Final consumers rarely purchase these goods.

3. Organizational consumers purchase on the basis of specifications and technical data. Final consumers frequently purchase on the basis of description, fashion, and style.

4. Organizational consumers utilize multiple-buying and team-based decisions more often than final consumers.

5. Organizational consumers are more likely to apply value and vendor analysis.

6. Organizational consumers more commonly lease equipment.

7. Organizational consumers more frequently employ competitive bidding and negotiation.

Differences in the Market

1. The demand of organizational consumers is derived from the demand of final consumers.

2. The demand of organizational consumers is more subject to cyclical fluctuations than final-consumer demand.

3. Organizational consumers are fewer in number and more geographically concentrated than final consumers.

4. Organizational consumers often employ buying specialists.

5. The distribution channel for organizational consumers is shorter than for final consumers.

6. Organizational consumers may require special services.

7. Organizational consumers are more likely than final consumers to be able to make products and services as alternatives to purchasing them.

Multiple-buying responsibility is shared by two or more employees who coordinate complex or expensive purchases.

Organizational consumers often utilize **multiple-buying responsibility,** in which two or more employees participate in a decision for complex or expensive purchases. This procedure is formal, with duties fully outlined. For example, the decision to buy computer-based cash registers would involve input from computer personnel, marketing personnel, the operations manager, a systems consultant, and the controller. The firm's president would make the final choice about the characteristics of the system and the supplier. Although final consumers might use multiple-buying responsibility, they use it less frequently and less formally.

Value analysis eliminates unnecessary costs; vendor analysis rates specific suppliers.

In their well-defined decision processes, organizational consumers may apply value analysis and vendor analysis. **Value analysis** compares the benefits of different materials, components, and manufacturing processes in order to improve products, lower costs, or both.[2] Among the questions posed by value analysis are: What is an item's function? What is its present cost? What else could perform the function? Is the item's cost proportional to its usefulness? What features are necessary? Can a standard product be found?[3] **Vendor analysis** is the rating of specific suppliers in terms of quality (such as the per cent of defective merchandise), service (such as delivery speed and reliability), and price (such as credit and transportation terms).

Organizational consumers frequently lease major equipment. About 20 per cent of all capital goods, worth more than $150 billion when new, are leased in the United States.[4]

Organizational consumers frequently utilize competitive bidding and negotiation in important contracts. In **competitive bidding** sellers are independently asked to submit price quotations for specific products, projects, and/or services. In **negotiation** the buyer uses bargaining ability and order size to influence prices. Competitive bidding and negotiation are most applicable in situations where complex, custom-made products and services are involved.

In *competitive bidding* sellers submit price bids; in *negotiation* the buyer bargains to set prices.

Differences from Final Consumers Due to the Nature of the Market

Organizational consumer demand is **derived** from the demand of final consumers. For example, the demand for precision rivets used in aircraft construction is derived from the demand for new aircraft, which ultimately is derived from demand for air travel. Manufacturers utilizing channel members are aware that they sell *through* wholesalers and retailers and not *to* them. Unless demand is generated at the final consumer level, distribution pipelines become clogged quite quickly and channel members will not be able to purchase fresh goods and services. For this reason organizational consumers are less sensitive to price changes. As long as final consumers are willing to pay higher prices for goods and services, organizational consumers will not object to price increases. On the other hand, low final consumer demand will result in reduced purchases by organizational consumers, even if prices are drastically reduced. Figure 5-2 illustrates derived demand for televisions.

Organizational consumer demand is *derived* from that of final consumers.

A good example of derived demand is the situation facing General Motors' Electro-Motive Division which produces locomotives for sale to railroad companies. Although General Motors, along with General Electric, dominates the locomotive market, recent sales have been low because of a sluggish railroad industry. However, the demand for new locomotives is expected to double by the late 1980s as the industry turns around. This will be due to the railroad's fuel efficiency, deregulation, and bulk shipments (such as coal).[5]

The demand of organizational consumers tends to be more volatile than that of final consumers. A small change in the final demand for highly processed goods and services can yield a large change in organizational consumers' demand. This is attributed to the **accelerator principle,** whereby final consumer demand affects several layers of organizational consumers. For example, a decline in automobile demand by final consumers reduces dealers' demand for automobiles, car manufacturers' demand for steel and other raw materials, and steel manufacturers' demand for iron ore. In addition, major purchases by organizational consumers (such as plant and equipment) are highly influenced by the economy.

The *accelerator principle* states that final consumer demand has an impact on several layers of organizational consumers.

Figure 5-2
Derived Demand

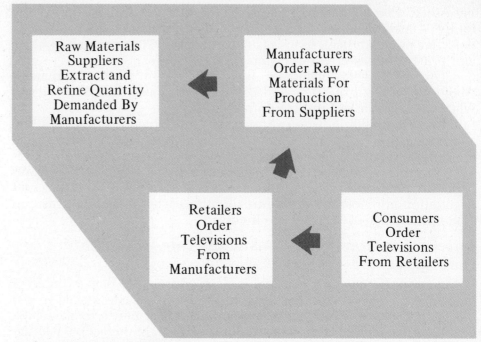

Raw Materials Suppliers Extract and Refine Quantity Demanded By Manufacturers

Manufacturers Order Raw Materials For Production From Suppliers

Retailers Order Televisions From Manufacturers

Consumers Order Televisions From Retailers

ALL INTERMEDIATE LEVELS OF DEMAND ARE DERIVED FROM FINAL CONSUMER DEMAND.

Organizational consumers tend to be large and geographically concentrated.

Organizational consumers are fewer in number than final consumers. There are about 500,000 manufacturers, 600,000 wholesalers, and 2.5 million retailers in the United States, as compared to more than 226 million final consumers. In some industries, the largest firms dominate. For example, five industries in which the four biggest firms have a great amount of sales are domestic passenger cars (99 per cent), flat glass (92 per cent), cereal breakfast foods (90 per cent), turbines and turbine engines (90 per cent), and electric lamps (90 per cent).[6] The size of these companies gives them bargaining power in dealing with sellers.

Organizational consumers also are geographically concentrated. For example, seven states (New York, California, Pennyslvania, Illinois, Ohio, New Jersey, and Michigan) contain more than half of the nation's industrial producers. Some industries (such as steel, petroleum, rubber, auto, and tobacco) are even more geographically concentrated.

Buying specialists are trained analysts who purchase and negotiate.

Because of their size and the types of products and services purchased, many organizational consumers use buying specialists. These employees often have technical backgrounds and are trained in supplier analysis and negotiating. Their full-time jobs are to purchase products and services and analyze those purchases. Expertise is quite high.

Because organizational consumers are large and geographically concentrated, purchase complex products and services, require custom-made products and services, and use buying specialists, distribution channels tend to be shorter than those for final consumers. For example, a typewriter manufacturer would deal directly with a company interested in buying 100 typewriters, and a salesperson would call on the company's purchasing agent. A company marketing typewriters to final consumers would distribute the typewriters through retail stores and expect final consumers to visit those stores.

Organizational consumers may require special services, such as extended warranties, a liberal return policy, cooperative advertising, and free credit. Two other such services are systems selling and reciprocity. In **systems selling,** a combination of goods and services is provided by a single source. This enables the buyer to have single-source accountability, one firm with which to negotiate, and assurance of the compatibility of various parts and components. IBM employs systems selling for its main computers, printing machines, supplies, computer programs, and servicing.

Through *systems selling,* organizational consumers obtain many goods and services from a single source.

Reciprocity is a procedure by which organizational consumers select suppliers who agree to purchase goods and services from them as well as sell to them. The Justice Department and the Federal Trade Commission monitor reciprocity because it may substantially lessen competition. An example of reciprocity is the way the Swiss government purchased military equipment from Northrop (a U.S. firm). The Swiss agreed to buy 72 fighter planes from Northrop. In return, Northrop promised to find $150 million worth of new business for Swiss manufacturers.[7]

***Reciprocity* is a system in which suppliers purchase as well as sell goods and/or services.**

Last, organizational consumers may be able to produce goods and services themselves, if they find purchase terms, the way they are treated, or available choices unacceptable. Sometimes, organizational consumers may suggest to suppliers that they will make their own goods in order to improve their bargaining positions.

Types of Organizational Consumers

In developing a marketing plan aimed at organizational consumers, it is necessary to research their attributes: areas of specialization, size and resources, location, and products and services purchased. Organizational consumers may be placed into five broad categories: manufacturers, wholesalers, retailers, government, and nonprofit.

For all but government, the **Standard Industrial Classification (SIC)** may be used to gather information about organizational consumers. The SIC, compiled by the U.S. Office of Management and Budget, has eight general industrial classifications: agricultural, forestry, and fishing; mining; construction; manufacturing; transportation, communication, electric, gas, and sanitary services; wholesale and retail trade; finance, insurance, and real estate; and services. Substantial data relating to SIC classifications are available from various government and commercial publications. Information on government organizations is available on a local, state, and federal level from many sources.

The *Standard Industrial Classification (SIC)* provides information on organizational consumers.

In the following subsections, the characteristics of manufacturers, wholesalers, retailers, government, and nonprofit organizations as consumers are described.

Manufacturers as Consumers

Manufacturers are firms that produce products for resale to other consumers. The *Standard Industrial Classification Manual* lists twenty major two-digit industry groups in manufacturing. Each of these major groups is divided into 150 industry groups; these industry groups are then further broken down into 450 four-digit subgroupings. For example, SIC 23 includes apparel and other textile products manufacturers; 223, women's, misses', and juniors' outer wear; and 2331, blouses.

In the United States, of the 500,000 manufacturers, more than one third have twenty or more employees. Approximately 20 million people work in manufacturing. The annual costs of materials to manufacturers exceed \$1 trillion. New capital expenditures for plant and equipment exceeded \$89 billion in 1980. Manufacturers annually use 13 trillion BTUs of energy. Annual net sales exceed \$2 trillion.[8]

Industry groups differ by geographic area. By knowing where different industries are located, a firm can concentrate its marketing efforts and not have to worry about covering dispersed geographic markets. Because the purchasing decisions of manufacturers can be made centrally at headquarters, the seller must identify the location of the proper decision maker.

As consumers, manufacturers purchase many products and services, including land and capital equipment, machinery, raw materials, component parts, trade publications, accounting services, supplies, insurance, advertising, and delivery services.

Wholesalers as Consumers

Wholesalers are organizations that buy or handle merchandise and its resale to retailers, other merchants, and/or industrial, institutional, and commercial users. They do not sell significant volume to final users. About 41 per cent of wholesale sales involve industrial, commercial, and government users; 37 per cent are made to retailers; 15 per cent are made to other wholesalers; 6 per cent are made to foreign buyers; and 1 per cent are made to final consumers and farmers.[9]

In the United States there are about 600,000 wholesalers. More than 5 million people are employed in wholesaling. Wholesalers are most prominent in New York, California, Illinois, Texas, Ohio, Pennsylvania, and New Jersey. Total annual wholesale sales (excluding agents and brokers) are well over \$1 trillion. Sales are largest for groceries and related products; machinery, equipment, and supplies; motor vehicles and automotive parts and supplies; electrical goods; lumber and other construction materials; and beer and liquor.

As consumers, wholesalers purchase or handle many products and services, including warehouses, trucks, finished products, insurance, refrigerators, trade publications, accounting services, supplies, and spare parts. A major task in dealing with wholesalers is getting them to carry the firm's product line for further resale, thereby placing the items into the distribution system. For new sellers or those with new products, gaining wholesaler cooperation may be difficult.

Retailers as Consumers

Retailers are firms that handle merchandise and services for sale to the ultimate (final) consumer. Retailers usually obtain their goods and services from a combination of manufacturers and wholesalers. Chapter 10 has a thorough discussion of both wholesaling and retailing.

In the United States there are about 2.5 million establishments that account for over $1 trillion in annual retail sales and employ 15 million people. More than 500,000 establishments are franchising arrangements (contractual agreements between central owners and local operators). Chain retailers (those operating two or more outlets) represent one sixth of all retailers but contribute about half of total sales. Major retail sales involve automotive dealers, food stores, general merchandise group stores, gasoline service stations, eating and drinking places, and drug and proprietary stores.

As consumers, retailers purchase or handle a variety of products and services, including store location, physical plant, interior design, advertising, items for resale, insurance, and trucks. On the average, retailers are more concerned about the composition and atmosphere of their stores than are wholesalers, who are more involved with the resale items themselves. This is because final consumers shop at retail stores, whereas wholesalers call on their customers. For the same reason retailers frequently buy fixtures, displays, and services to redecorate their stores.

Getting retailers to stock new items may be difficult because shelf space is limited. As an example, about 45 per cent of magazines are sold through retail outlets. For a publisher to convince a retailer to carry a new magazine, a price of 20 to 30 per cent off the cover amount must be set, wire racks must be set up (at $5 to $15 per rack), and allowances must be given for retail services.[10]

Some retailers insist that manufacturers make products under the retailers' names. For these private-label manufacturers, the continued orders of their retailers are essential. Not long ago, Star-Lite, a major producer of automotive softgoods such as mats and slip covers for seats, lost 41 per cent of its annual sales revenue (approximately $4 million) when Sears decided to phase it out as a supplier. Sears decided to make all its auto softgoods purchases from Farber Brothers.[11]

> *Retailers* handle merchandise and services for sale to the final consumer. They purchase store fixtures, advertising, insurance, and other items.

Government as Consumer

Government consumes products and services in the performance of its duties and responsibilities. Federal (1), state (50), and local (80,000) governmental units together account for the largest expenditures of any consumer group in the United States. In total, all branches spend over $1 trillion, half by the federal government. The greatest expenditures are on operations, capital outlays, military services, postal services, education, highways, public welfare, health, police, fire protection, sanitation, and natural resources. All levels of government employed 16 million people (excluding armed forces) in 1980.

Statistics on state and local expenditures by item (education, highways, public welfare, health/hospitals, police and fire protection, hous-

> *Governments* (federal, state, and local) purchase and use a variety of routine and complex products and services.

ing and urban renewal) are reported in *Government Finances* and *City Government Finances* on an annual basis.

Governmental consumers purchase a wide range of products and services, including food, military equipment, office buildings, subway cars, office supplies, clothing, and automobiles. Many of the products purchased by these organizations are standard products offered to traditional consumers; others, such as armaments, are specially made for the federal government. Firms such as Northrup and General Dynamics derive large shares of their sales from government contracts.[12]

Nonprofit Institutions as Consumers

Nonprofit institutions do not seek financial profits. They purchase items to operate their organizations.

Nonprofit institutions are those that operate in the public interest or to foster a cause and do not seek financial profits. Public hospitals, museums, most universities, political parties, civic organizations, and parks are examples of nonprofit institutions. They purchase products and services in order to run their organizations and also buy items for resale to generate additional revenues to offset costs. Nonprofit institutions are discussed in detail in Chapter 17.

There are many national nonprofit institutions, such as the American Cancer Society, Democratic and Republican Parties, Boy and Girl Scouts, Chamber of Commerce, and the Red Cross. Hospitals, museums, and universities, because of their fixed locations, tend to be among the local nonprofit institutions.

Characteristics of Organizational Consumers

The consumer behavior of manufacturers, wholesalers, retailers, government, and nonprofit institutions depends on their buying objectives, buying structure, use of the purchase, and constraints.

Buying Objectives

As stated at the beginning of this chapter, organizational buyers have several distinct objectives in purchasing goods and services. See Figure 5-3, which shows an ad for the Tycon Courthouse commercial office building in Tysons Corner, Virginia. It appeals to a combination of buying objectives for prospective business tenants.

Product availability, seller reliability, consistent quality, delivery, and price are important organizational buying objectives.

In general, for all types of organizational buyers, these **buying objectives** are important: the availability of items, reliability of sellers, consistency of quality, delivery, and price. Availability of items means that the buyer is able to secure an adequate supply of products throughout the year or whenever necessary. An organization's production or resales are not possible if purchases are unavailable at the appropriate time. Seller reliability is based on the seller's honesty in the reporting of bills or shipping orders, fairness to its customers, responsiveness to special requests, ongoing relationships, and reputation.

Consistency of quality refers to the buyer's goal of obtaining similar items on a continuous basis. For example, drill bits should have the

Figure 5-3
An Advertisement Appealing to Organizational Buying Objectives

Reprinted by permission of Tycon and Earle Palmer Brown.

same degree of hardness, transistors the same level of durability, and employee uniforms the same color each time they are purchased. Delivery objectives include minimizing or stabilizing the length of time from the placing of an order to the receipt of items, reducing the order size required by the supplier, having the seller maintain responsibility for shipments, holding down costs, and adhering to an agreed-on schedule. Price considerations involve purchase price, discounts, availability of credit, and length of payment.

Manufacturer-consumers are also quite concerned about the minimum quality standards of raw materials, component parts, and equipment. Some manufacturers like to deal with a variety of suppliers to protect against shortages from a single supplier, to foster price and service competition, and to be exposed to new merchandise lines.

Wholesalers and retailers consider the further saleability of items as the highest priority. Where possible, they also seek exclusive buying arrangements, in which only one wholesaler or retailer in each geographic area is allowed to carry merchandise. They also seek manufacturers' advertising and transportation support.

Government-consumers frequently require precise specifications for the products they purchase. For example, military tanks must be built to exact specifications. As large-volume, complex-product buyers, government-consumers are able to secure these specifications. In some cases government-consumers may also consider the economic conditions in the geographic areas of potential sellers when they make purchases. As an illustration, Grumman Aerospace of New York often bids against McDonnell Douglas of California for government contracts. Sometimes the contracts are awarded to the company that has the highest unemployment in its surrounding community.

Nonprofit consumers place the most emphasis on price, availability, reliability, and consistency. They sometimes seek special purchase terms in recognition of their nonprofit status.

Buying Structure

The **buying structure of an organization** depends on its size, resources, diversity, and level of specialization.[13] The buying structure is likely to be formalized (separate department or function) for a large, corporate, resourceful, diversified, and specialized organization. It will be less formalized for a small, independently owned, financially limited, and general organization.

Large manufacturer-consumers will normally have specialized purchasing agents who work with engineers, the production department, or the plant general manager. Large wholesaler-consumers tend to have a single purchasing department or a general manager in charge of operations. Large retailer-consumers tend to be extremely specialized and have buyers for each narrow product category. These buyers are supervised by group managers. Small manufacturers, wholesalers, and retailers have their buying functions completed by the owner-operator.

Each governmental unit (federal, state, and local) and division has a purchasing department. The General Services Administration (GSA) is the federal office responsible for centralized procurement and coordination of purchases. Each federal unit may receive merchandise from the GSA's Bureau of Federal Supply or buy directly from suppliers. In a nonprofit organization, there is usually one purchasing department or a member of the operations staff who performs the buying function.

Use of Purchases

As mentioned earlier, organizational consumers have different uses for their products. Manufacturer-consumers buy items that are used in the production process or for the operation of the company. Wholesaler-consumers purchase component parts, items for further resale, or items used in the operation of the company. Retailer-consumers buy for further resale or use in operations. Government-consumers buy items for use in the operation of the government and the enactment of various programs. Nonprofit consumers primarily buy items to be used in operations; they sometimes purchase for resale.

Constraints on Purchases

For manufacturer-consumers, wholesaler-consumers, and retailer-consumers, derived demand is the major constraint on purchase behavior. Without the demand of final consumers, production halts and sales disappear as the backward chain of demand comes into play (final consumer→retailer→wholesaler→manufacturer).

Manufacturer-consumers also are constrained by the availability of raw materials and their ability to pay for large-ticket items. Wholesaler-consumers and retailer-consumers are usually unwilling and unable to buy merchandise that does not meet minimum profit margins (profits as per cents of sales), regardless of sales potential. They are also limited by the finances available to make purchases and the level of risk they are willing to take. In this case, risk refers to the probability that wholesalers or retailers will be able to sell the merchandise they buy in a reasonable time period. Product categories such as fashion clothing have higher risks than staple merchandise such as panty hose, children's underwear, and men's leather-palm woolen gloves.

Government-consumers are constrained by the budget-setting process. Approval for categories of purchases must normally be secured well in advance, and deviations must be fully explained. Budgets must be certified by various legislative bodies. For nonprofit consumers, cash flow (timing of money coming into the organization versus money spent by it) is the major concern.

> **Final consumer demand is the major constraint on organizational purchase behavior.**

Organizational Consumer Decision Making

Organizational consumers use a decision-making procedure in much the same manner as final consumers. Figure 5-4 shows the ***organizational consumer's decision process,*** which has four major components: expectations, buying process, conflict resolution, and situational factors.[14]

> **The *organizational consumer's decision process* is like the final consumer's.**

Expectations

Organizational consumers, as represented by purchasing agents, engineers, and users, bring a set of expectations to any buying situation:

> Expectations refer to the *perceived* potential of alternative suppliers and brands to satisfy a number of explicit and implicit objectives.[15]

In order for a purchase to be made, the buyer must have favorable expectations about a supplier's product quality, availability, reliability, delivery time, and service.

Expectations are drawn from a variety of factors: background of

> **Purchase expectations are based on factors such as buyers' backgrounds, information, perception, and past experience.**

Figure 5-4
Organizational Consumer's Decision Process

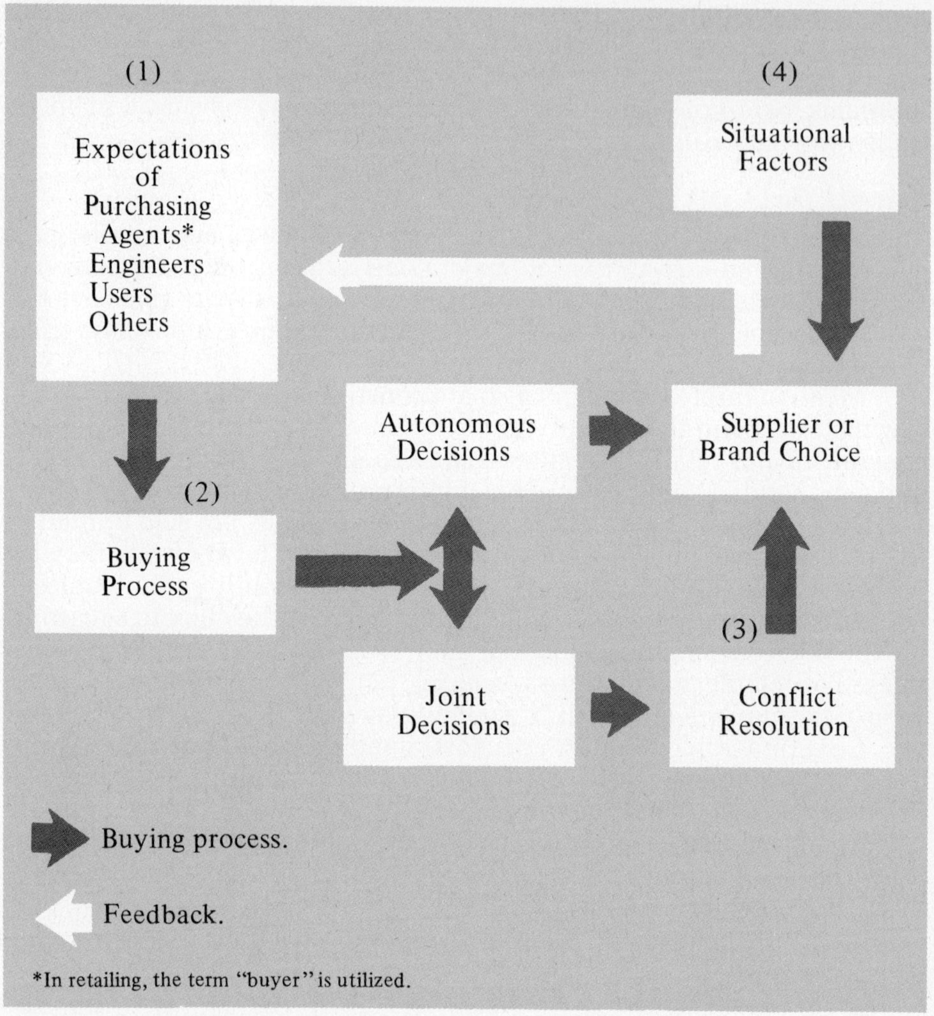

Expectations of Purchasing Agents* Engineers Users Others (1)

Situational Factors (4)

Autonomous Decisions

Supplier or Brand Choice

Buying Process (2)

Joint Decisions

Conflict Resolution (3)

➡ Buying process.

⬅ Feedback.

*In retailing, the term "buyer" is utilized.

Source: Adapted from Jagdish N. Sheth, "A Model of Industrial Buyer Behavior," *Journal of Marketing*, Vol. 37 (October 1973), p. 51. Reprinted from *Journal of Marketing*, published by the American Marketing Association.

individuals, information sources, search, perception, and satisfaction with past purchases.[16]

Buying Process

The buying process may involve autonomous (independent) or joint decision making depending on the product and the company.

The buying process may involve autonomous (independent) or joint decision making. The type of decision making depends on product-specific and company-specific factors.

Product-specific factors leading to autonomous decision making are low perceived risk, routine products, and time pressures. Joint decision making is the result of high perceived risk, unique or seldom-purchased products, and a lead time for purchases.

Company-specific factors leading to autonomous decision making are technology or production orientation, small size, and high centralization. Joint decision making is the result of low technology or production orientation, large size, and little centralization.

During the buying process, a decision to buy is initiated, information gathered, alternative suppliers evaluated, and conflicts among the different representatives of the buyer resolved. The process itself is similar to the consumer buying process shown in Figure 4-11.

Bidding is frequently used with organizational consumers: the potential seller specifies in writing all the terms and conditions of the purchase in addition to product or service attributes. With open bidding, the proposed contract can be seen by competitors. With closed bidding, contract terms are kept secret and the sellers are asked to make their best presentation in their first bids. Bidding is most often used in government purchases in order to avoid charges of unfair negotiations or bias. For these reasons, bids for government purchases are generally closed.

In open bidding the seller proposes a contract that can be seen; in closed bidding contract terms are kept secret.

Conflict Resolution

Because of the different training, role orientation, goals, and life-styles of purchasing agents, engineers, and users, joint decision making sometimes results in conflicts. **Conflict resolution** is then necessary to make a purchase decision. Four methods of resolution are possible: problem solving, persuasion, bargaining, and politicking.

Resolving conflicts due to joint decision making may be resolved through problem solving, persuasion, bargaining, or politicking.

Problem solving occurs when the members of the purchasing team decide to acquire further information before making a decision. This is the best procedure for the company. Persuasion takes place when each member of the team presents his or her reasons why a particular supplier or brand should be selected. In theory, the most logical presentation should be chosen. However, the most dynamic speaker often persuades others to follow his or her lead.

Under bargaining, team members agree to support each other's recommendations in different situations, regardless of merit. For example, one member is allowed to select the supplier of the current item. In return, another member chooses the vendor for the next item. The last, and least desirable, method of conflict resolution is politicking. With politicking, team members seek to persuade outside parties and superiors to back their positions and then seek to win at power plays.

Situational Factors

A number of **situational factors** can interrupt the decision-making process and the actual selection of a supplier or brand:

Situational factors are external variables that affect organizational consumers.

temporary economic conditions such as price controls, recession, or foreign trade; internal strikes, walkouts, machine breakdowns, and other production-related events; organizational changes such as merger or acquisition; and ad hoc changes in the market place, such as promotional efforts, new product introduction, price changes, and so on, in the supplier industries.[17]

Purchase and Feedback

After the decision process is complete and situational factors are eliminated or adapted to, a choice of supplier or brand is made and the purchase completed. The level of satisfaction with the purchase is fed back to the purchasing agent or team, and this information is stored for future use.[18] See Figure 5-5.

Figure 5-5
Purchase Feedback

Reprinted by permission of
Marketing News, published
by the American Marketing
Association.

"We're just learning to use it; what do you mean it's already outdated?"

Types of Purchases

**Organizational
consumers use *new task
purchases* for unique
items, *modified rebuys*
for infrequent items, and
straight rebuys for
regular items.**

As with final consumers, organizational buyers have three types of decision processes. A **new task** purchase process is needed for an expensive product the firm has not bought before. A large amount of decision making is undertaken. This is similar to extended behavior for a
final consumer. A **modified rebuy** purchase process is employed for
medium-priced products the firm has bought infrequently before. A
moderate amount of decision making is needed. This is similar to limited decision making for a final consumer. A **straight rebuy** purchase
process is used for inexpensive items bought on a regular basis. Reorder-
ing, not decision making, is applied. This is similar to a routine purchase for a final consumer.

Marketing Implications

Organizational and final consumers have substantial differences, as was
noted at the beginning of this chapter. They also have significant similarities. Both can be described in demographic terms, and statistical and
descriptive data can be gathered and analyzed. Both consumers have
different types of buyers, each of whom has separate needs and requirements. Both can be defined by using social and psychological factors,
such as operating style, buying structure, use of the purchase, expectations, perceived risk, and conflict resolution among buyers or purchasing agents. Both organizational and final consumers use a decision process, employ joint decision making, and face different kinds of purchase
situations.

Marketers must understand the similarities and differences between organizational and final consumers and develop their plans accordingly. Furthermore, it must be realized by manufacturers and wholesalers that they need two marketing plans—one for the intermediate buyer and another for the final consumer.

Marketers need to see that organizational purchasing agents or buyers have personal as well as company goals. These buyers seek status, approval, promotion, bonuses, and other rewards. And, these individuals bring distinct backgrounds and expectations to each buying situation, just as final consumers do.

Summary

An organizational consumer is a formal entity that purchases products or services for further production, for use in operating the entity, or for resale to other consumers. Organizational consumers seek supplier reliability and consistency and specific product attributes. They are influenced by derived demand and utilize formal purchasing departments. They are geographically concentrated, expect sellers to visit them, use joint decision making, make large purchases, require personal selling, and look for favorable purchase terms.

Organizational consumers are classified by area of specialization, size and resources, location, and products and services purchased. The major organizational consumers are manufacturers, wholesalers, retailers, government, and nonprofit. The SIC system provides much information on nongovernment consumers.

Organizational consumers can be characterized by buying objectives, buying structure, use of the purchase, and constraints. Decision making includes buyer expectations, buying process, conflict resolution, and situational factors. Of prime importance is whether the organization uses joint decision making and, if it does, how. Some form of bidding, open or closed, is frequently employed with organizational consumers (most often with the government).

When conflicts arise under joint decision making, problem solving, persuasion, bargaining, or politicking is implemented to arrive at a purchase decision. Situational factors can intervene between decision making and a purchase. These factors include strikes, economic conditions, and organizational changes.

New task, modified rebuy, and straight rebuy are the different purchase situations facing organizational consumers. Organizational consumers and final consumers have many similarities and differences. It is important for marketers to understand and adapt to them. Two marketing campaigns are necessary for manufacturers and wholesalers who sell to intermediate buyers as well as to final consumers.

Purchasing agents or buyers have personal goals, such as status, promotion, and bonuses, which have a large impact on their decision making.

KEY TERMS

After reading this chapter, you should understand these key terms:

Industrial marketing
Product specifications
Multiple-buying responsibility
Value analysis
Vendor analysis
Competitive bidding
Negotiation
Derived demand
Accelerator principle
Systems selling
Reciprocity
Standard Industrial Classification (SIC)
Manufacturers

Wholesalers
Retailers
Government
Nonprofit institutions
Organizational buying objectives
Buying structure of an organization
Organizational consumer's decision process
Conflict resolution
Situational factors
New task purchase process
Modified rebuy purchase process
Straight rebuy purchase process

QUESTIONS FOR DISCUSSION

1. Explain five differences between organizational and final consumers.
2. What is derived demand? Which organizational consumers does it affect?
3. How can derived demand be increased?
4. What is the SIC? Explain.
5. Large manufacturers dominate the tobacco, motor vehicle, and soap industries. What does this mean for suppliers to these companies?
6. Comment on this statement: "For new sellers or those with new products, gaining wholesaler cooperation may be difficult."
7. What risks do private-label manufacturers such as Star-Lite run? How can they be avoided?
8. Develop a plan for selling vacuum cleaners to your local government.
9. Dallas and New York competed for the right to host the 1984 Republican National Convention. Develop a plan for acquiring the 1988 convention for your area.
10. Describe the organizational consumer's decision process.
11. Explain the factors that make up an organizational buyer's expectations.
12. Many firms are supporters of autonomous decision making. Others favor joint decision making. Why are there opposing views?
13. Why is problem solving the preferred way of resolving conflicts?
14. What are situational factors? How do they affect purchases?

NOTES

1. Alexander Stuart, "Boeing's New Beauties Are a Tough Sell," *Fortune* (October 18, 1982), pp. 114–120.
2. Michael D. Hutt and Thomas W. Speh, *Industrial Marketing Management* (Hinsdale, Ill.: Dryden Press, 1981), pp. 32–33.
3. Anthony R. Tocco and Joseph Kaufman, "Value Engineering (Value Analysis)" in Carl Heyel (Editor), *The Encyclopedia of Management*, Third Edition (New York: Van Nostrand Reinhold, 1982). p. 1280.
4. Paul F. Anderson, "Industrial Equipment Leasing Offers Economic and Competitive Edge," *Marketing News* (April 4, 1980), p. 20.

5. Jeff Blyskal, "On the Siding," *Forbes* (May 10, 1982), pp. 105–106.

6. Paul MacAvoy, "Learning to Love Oligopolies," *New York Times* (September 18, 1980), p. F2.

7. Louis Kraar, "Everyone at Northrup Is in Marketing," *Fortune* (April 10, 1978), p. 54.

8. U.S. Bureau of Economic Analysis, *Survey of Current Business, Current Business Reports*, and annual *Survey of Manufacturers*.

9. Bert C. McCammon, Jr. and James W. Kenderine, "Mainstream Developments in Wholesaling," paper presented at the 1975 Southwestern Marketing Association Conference, p. 3.

10. N. R. Kleinfield, "Magazines Battling for Checkout Racks," *New York Times* (April 4, 1979), pp. D1, D9.

11. Chuck Wingis, "Sears Consolidates Vendors: Star-Lite Socked with Pink Slip," *Industrial Marketing* (October 1979), p. 22.

12. See "Look Who's Headed for No. 1 in Defense: Northrop," *Business Week* (April 19, 1982), pp. 70–79; and "General Dynamics: Striking It Rich on Defense," *Business Week* (May 3, 1982), pp. 102–106.

13. See Thomas C. Hayes, "New Status for Purchasing," *New York Times* (July 2, 1981), pp. D1, D6; N. R. Kleinfield, "How a Company Does Its Shopping," *New York Times* (January 17, 1982), Section 3, pp. 1, 27; and Craig Endicott, "Manager's Day Is a Changing Menu," *Advertising Age* (April 27, 1981), pp. S–20, S–22.

14. The material in this section is drawn from Jagdish N. Sheth, "A Model of Industrial Buyer Behavior," *Journal of Marketing*, Vol. 37 (October 1973), pp. 50–56.

15. Ibid., p. 52.

16. See Larry Giunipero and Gary Zenz, "Impact of Purchasing Trends on Industrial Marketers," *Industrial Marketing Management*, Vol. 11 (February 1982), pp. 17–23; and Alok K. Chakrabarti, Stephen Feinman, and William Fuentevilla, "Targeting Technical Information to Organizational Positions," *Industrial Marketing Management*, Vol. 11 (July 1982), pp. 195–203.

17. Sheth, "A Model of Industrial Buyer Behavior," p. 56.

18. See John A. Goodman and Larry M. Robinson, "Strategies for Improving the Satisfaction of Business Customers," *Business*, Vol. 32 (April–June 1982), pp. 40–44.

SENSORMATIC: MARKETING ANTISHOPLIFTING DEVICES TO RETAILERS* 1

CASES

Sensormatic Electronics Corp. manufactures and markets antishoplifting devices, which it sells to retailers. Sensormatic's plastic tags and magnetic strips are adhered to merchandise; an alarm is set off if the devices are not removed properly by store employees and a customer tries to leave the premises without paying for the merchandise. Sales of Sensormatic devices rose from $7.7 million in 1977 to $67 million in 1982. The company holds a 70 per cent market share in the industry, and is headquartered in Deerfield Beach, Florida.

Until now, Sensormatic has concentrated on general merchandise customers, such as department stores, specialty stores, and discount and variety stores. But, Ronald Assaf, Sensormatic's founder and chief executive, believes the time is ripe to market the firm's products to supermarkets. In the U.S., supermarket shoplifting is estimated at $1.2 billion annually; and supermarkets usually have extremely low profit margins (around 1 per cent.) Therefore, a reduction in supermarket shoplifting could have a dramatic effect on profitability.

Sensormatic's leading competitors, Knogo and Checkpoint, have tested their systems in supermarkets—with little success. They encountered too many

*The data in this case are drawn from "Sensormatic: Out to Quadruple Revenue by Bagging Supermarket Thieves," *Business Week* (June 14, 1982), pp. 99–100.

false alarms and too much employee resistance. However, Sensormatic has developed a new technology specifically aimed at high-turnover supermarket retailing. Sensormatic's system will be heavily promoted by a 90-person national sales force personally calling on supermarket management. Midwestern supermarkets have shown the greatest initial interest, as a result of above-average shoplifting during the recent recession. Stated one security manager, "If they can get the bugs out, the system will sell like wildfire."

Not all supermarket executives are convinced that electromagnetic antishoplifting devices will work in their industry. Regarding the possibility of false alarms, one executive commented that "Once a checkout clerk has gone through a false alarm, it is almost impossible to rebuild confidence." On the cost of the devices, another executive said "Supermarket net profit margins are simply not enough to allow us to plug an expensive tag on a can of green beans." Sensormatic feels it can counter these and any other objections that are raised.

QUESTIONS

1. Why do you think that general merchandise stores have been more interested in antishoplifting devices than supermarkets?
2. What are the buying objectives and constraints for supermarkets in the evaluation of antishoplifting devices?
3. Would the purchase of antishoplifting devices require joint decision making? Explain your answer.
4. How would you assign the 90-member sales force to supermarkets?
5. How would you answer the objections raised by supermarket executives?

2 PREMIER INDUSTRIAL: MARKETING NUTS AND BOLTS TO INDUSTRY†

Premier Industrial is a Cleveland-based manufacturer and distributor of nuts, bolts, and electrical equipment. It markets 12,000 industrial items and 90,000 electronic and electric component parts. The company prides itself on new products and innovativeness. Prices are above those of competitors. Annual sales are well in excess of $300 million.

The philosophy of Premier is summed up by Mort Mandel, its chairman:

> Our approach is classic: Find a need and fill it. We're also committed to quality. That's trite, but so is 'I love you'—and it still means something.

This philosophy is backed by sensitivity to customer requests and a sales force of 1,800. Demonstrations are emphasized in sales presentations.

An illustration of Premier's search for and development of new products involves the company's rusted screw extractor. In 1979, Premier sales personnel observed mechanics' difficulties in removing rusted screws that had been frozen in engine blocks ("Just the sort of thing that drives mechanics crazy.") Two years later, Premier was able to introduce an extractor that removed the

†The data in this case are drawn from Barbara Rudolph, "Sounds Trite, But So Does 'I Love You,'" *Forbes* (March 1, 1982), p. 66

screws easily and quickly. The extractor is now selling well at a price of $40 per set of four.

Although Premier publishes a 752-page catalog of its products, the firm concentrates on items that are not carried by larger competitors, such as Avnet and Arrow. This enables Premier to avoid price competition and become the sole distributor for a large number of its products, including many routine items like batteries and resistors.

In *Forbes* magazine, Premier was called "the kind of company that men like Peter Drucker (a well-known management professor and consultant) love because it reaffirms some basic business truths: sell quality; keep costs down; grow slowly through small but smart acquisitions."

QUESTIONS

1. How do organizational and final consumers differ in the purchase and use of nuts and bolts?
2. Would Premier use different approaches when selling products to manufacturers than when selling to retailers? Explain your answer.
3. How could organizational customers efficiently use a 752-page catalog describing over 100,000 items?
4. What is the organizational consumer decision-making process for Premier's existing products (such as nuts and bolts)? For new products (such as the rusted screw extractor)?
5. Evaluate Premier's price strategy.

Developing a Target Market

6

Chapter Preview

Chapter Objectives

1 To explain and contrast mass marketing, market segmentation, and multiple segmentation and to describe the factors to be considered in selecting a target market strategy

2 To present several applications for each method of developing a target market

3 To discuss the bases of segmentation, steps in planning a segmentation strategy, organizational consumer segments, requirements for successful segmentation, and the limitations of segmentation

4 To examine sales forecasting and its role in developing a target market

Anheuser-Busch remains the "King of Beers," despite major competitive efforts by Miller, Stroh, Heileman, and others. In 1982, Anheuser-Busch accounted for 32 per cent of total industry sales, up from 23 per cent in 1977. Miller is second with about 24 per cent of sales (compared to 15 per cent in 1977). Anheuser-Busch's sustained success is due in large part to its target market strategy.

The company offers several brands of beer in three distinct categories: Busch and Natural Light in the popular-price range; Budweiser and Budweiser Light in the premium range; and Michelob and Michelob Light in the super-premium range. See Figure 6-1. Within each of these categories are both the traditional and newer "light" beer products. The popular-price beers are aimed at value-conscious consumers. The premium-price beers are geared toward middle-class consumers, usually blue-collar workers willing to spend money on beer. The super-premium beers are sold to more affluent consumers, who are willing to pay high prices for superior beer.

The marketing of Budweiser and Budweiser Light shows the diversity of Anheuser-Busch's target market efforts. Budweiser is the company's flagship beer and the industry leader, with 20 per cent of total U.S. beer sales in 1982. Its basic appeal is to a growing middle-class market, with themes such as "For all you do, this Bud's for you." Recent commercials, oriented toward a broader market, have featured commercial artists, disc jockeys, ski instructors, and others.

Budweiser Light is a new entry in the lower-calorie beer segment. The entire segment represents about 10 to 11 per cent of industry sales. Miller Lite holds 7 per cent of the market, while Natural Light and Michelob Light hold about 2 per cent together. Since light beer appeals to white-collar twenty-five to forty-nine-year-olds and its sales are increasing much faster than traditional beer sales, Budweiser Light is intended to be more competitive with Miller Lite than either Natural Light and Michelob Light have been, stressing the slogan, "Bring out your best."[1]

Developing a Target Market Strategy

Mass marketing, market segmentation, and multiple segmentation are the three alternative methods a firm has for developing a target market. These methods are summarized in Table 6-1.

In **mass marketing,** a company seeks to appeal to a broad range of consumers by utilizing a single basic marketing program. In **market segmentation,** a company seeks to appeal to one well-defined consumer group by one marketing plan. In **multiple segmentation,** a company seeks to appeal to two or more well-defined consumer groups by different marketing plans.

Mass marketing seeks a range of consumers, market segmentation one segment, and multiple segmentation diverse segments.

Mass Marketing

A mass-marketing approach aims at a large, broad consumer market through one basic marketing plan. An early practitioner of mass marketing was Henry Ford, who created and sold one standard automobile model at a reasonable price to a large number and variety of people. The original Model T had no options and came only in black.

Mass marketing was a popular method for developing a target market when large-scale production started, but the number of companies using a pure mass-marketing approach has declined rapidly over the last several years. Among the factors contributing to its fall from use are

Figure 6-1
**The Brands of Anheuser-
Busch**

Reprinted by permission.

that competition has grown, demand is stimulated by an appeal to specific market segments, improved marketing research is able to pinpoint
the desires of different segments, and total production and marketing
costs can be reduced by segmentation.

Before an organization undertakes mass marketing, it must examine several factors. Substantial total company resources and abilities are
needed to mass produce, mass distribute, and mass advertise. There are
per unit production and marketing savings because a limited number of
products or services are offered, and different brand names are not employed. These savings may allow low competitive prices.

**A major objective of
mass marketing is to
maximize sales without
diversifying.**

A major objective of mass marketing is to maximize sales—that is,
a company attempts to sell as many units of an item as possible. National goals are usually set. Diversification is not undertaken.

For successful mass marketing, a large group of consumers must
have the desire for similar product or service attributes, so that the company can appeal to them through one marketing program. As an example, suppose all consumers buy Morton's salt because of its freshness,
quality, storability, availability, and fair price. Then, a mass marketing

Table 6-1   **Methods for Developing a Target Market**

Marketing Approach	Mass Marketing	Market Segmentation	Multiple Segmentation
Target market	Many type of consumers	One well-defined consumer group	Two or more well-defined consumer groups
Product or service	Limited number of products or services under one brand for many types of consumers	One product or service brand tailored to one consumer group	Distinct product or service brand for each consumer group
Price	One "popular" price range	One price range tailored to the consumer group	Distinct price range for each consumer group
Distribution	All possible outlets	All suitable outlets	All suitable outlets—differs by segment
Promotion	Mass media	All suitable media	All suitable media—differs by segment
Strategy emphasis	Appeal to various types of consumers through a uniform, broad-based marketing program	Appeal to one specific consumer group through a highly specialized, but uniform, marketing program	Appeal to two or more distinct market segments through different marketing plans catering to each segment

strategy is appropriate. However, if some consumers want attractive decanters, larger crystals, and smaller-sized packages, then Morton would be unable to appeal to all consumers through one marketing plan. Under mass marketing, different consumer groups are not identified and sought.

With mass marketing, the firm pursues an intensive channel strategy. Its offerings are sold at all possible outlets. Channel requirements (the needs of wholesalers and retailers) must be evaluated. Some channel members may not be pleased if the company's brand is sold at several nearby locations and may insist on carrying additional brands to fill out their product lines. It is very difficult to persuade channel members not to carry competing brands. The shelf space given to the company depends on the popularity of its brand and the promotional support given. Channel members often set final selling prices.

A mass-marketing strategy should consider total profits and long-run profits. Sometimes firms become too involved with sales and lose sight of profits. For example, for a number of years, the sales of A&P rose as the company continued its competition with Safeway for leadership in supermarket sales. Unfortunately, A&P incurred large losses during that period. Only when A&P began to close some unprofitable stores and stop pursuing sales at any cost did it start to show profits.

A company can ensure a consistent, well-known image with a mass-marketing approach. Consumers have only one image when thinking of a firm, and it is retained for a number of years.

TV Guide magazine and Sears are good examples of mass-marketing appeals. *TV Guide* is a weekly television magazine that was established over thirty years ago. It contains television program listings, descriptions, and evaluations as well as current events and articles on personalities, shows, and the industry. *TV Guide* has a circulation of more than twenty million copies per week. It is advertised on television and in newspapers and stores. *TV Guide* is relatively inexpensive and is available at several types of stores and newsstands. Many sales are through subscription. The product itself, the magazine, has undergone few changes since its inception and is recognized as the standard in the field. Consumers of varying backgrounds buy *TV Guide* for its listings and stories.

Sears is the country's largest retailer, with total company sales of $27.4 billion in 1981 and well over 300,000 employees.[2] In addition to retail stores, Sears owns and operates Allstate insurance, Dean Witter stock brokerage, and Coldwell Banker realty. Its advertising slogan is "Sears, Where America Shops." Through its product and service assortments, middle to low prices, heavy promotion ($544 million in media in 1981),[3] and geographically dispersed store locations, Sears seeks a wide range of consumers.

Other illustrations of mass-marketing approaches are Commodore digital watches priced at $7.95 to $19.95 and sold at all types of outlets (including supermarkets,[4] National Liberty Corporation selling insurance through television and direct mail advertising,[5] and the broad and varied uses of Riunite wines:

> Riunite can be used as a table wine to accompany food. It can be used as an apertif before the meal, and also as a refreshment wine that is used—apart from any food—at bars, at home, in the backyard.[6]

Market Segmentation

A market-segmentation approach aims at a narrow, specific consumer group (market segment) through one, specialized marketing plan that caters to the needs of that segment.

Market segmentation has emerged as a popular technique, particularly for small or specialized firms. With market segmentation a firm does not have to mass produce, mass distribute, or mass advertise. The firm can succeed with limited resources and abilities by specializing. A market segmentation strategy is not normally a sales-maximization approach. Instead, the firm's objective is efficiency, attracting a large portion of one market segment at controlled costs. The firm wants recognition as a specialist. It does not try to diversify.

In evaluating competition the firm must determine whether it wants to attract a market segment with no competitors or one with several strong competitors. It is essential that the company do a better job of tailoring a marketing program for its segment than competitors. Competitor strengths should be avoided and weaknesses exploited. For instance, a new fast-food restaurant that sells hamburgers would have a more difficult time in differentiating itself from competitors than a fast-food restaurant selling French onion soup and crepes.

With market segmentation, a firm can succeed with limited resources and specialization; it does not have to mass produce, mass distribute, or mass advertise.

If there are two or more available consumer groups, the firm must select the one segment that offers the greatest opportunity. While criteria for selecting a segment are detailed later in this chapter, the firm should be alert to two factors. One, the largest segment may not provide the best opportunity because of heavy competiton or high consumer satisfaction with competitor offerings (for example, the small-car segment of the auto market). A company selecting the largest segment may regret it because of the **majority fallacy,** which asserts that companies sometimes fail when they go after the largest market segment because competition is intense. See Figure 6-2. Two, a potentially profitable market segment may be one that is ignored by other firms. As an illustration, Frank Perdue is very successful in the poultry business. This has occurred because Perdue was the first chicken producer to see a market segment that desired quality, an identifiable brand name, a guarantee, and would pay premium prices. Others sold chickens as unlabeled commodities.

Market segmentation can enable a company to maximize per unit profits but not total profits, because only one segment is sought. It also enables a firm with low resources to compete effectively with larger firms for specialized markets. For example, there are many regional soda producers who can effectively compete with national manufacturers in a given region but who do not have the resources to compete on a national level. On the other hand, small shifts in population or consumer tastes can sharply affect a segmenter.

A segmenter is able to generate a specialized image for a particular brand. This encourages brand loyalty for the current offering and may be helpful if the company develops a product line under one name (such as Hellman's). As long as the firm stays within its perceived area of expertise, the image of one product (mayonnaise) will rub off on another (tartar sauce).

Bic and 7-Eleven are two examples of companies that have employed market segmentation. For many years, Bic sold one product line—inexpensive pens—aimed at an economy-conscious market segment. Because of its success with the pens and the company's image of quality at a low price, Bic was able to expand into related product lines and introduce low-priced disposable lighters and razors.

7-Eleven stores have been operated for more than fifty years by the Southland Corporation. They attract the convenience-oriented consumer who buys fill-in merchandise at erratic hours. The average 7-Eleven customer is male, under 35, and married with two children. He earns more than $10,000 per year, shops in 7-Eleven 6.1 times per month, spends $6.16 per month at 7-Eleven, and is in the store for 3.5 minutes per trip.[7]

Others using market segmentation include American Dunhill stores, which cater to affluent consumers with items such as $325 gold-plated toothbrushes and $5,000 crocodile attache cases;[8] retailers such as San Francisco's The Short Stop and Detroit's Napoleon's Closet, which concentrate on clothes for small men;[9] and *Golf Digest*, which is aimed at recreational golfers.

The *majority fallacy* states that companies may fail when they pursue the segment with the greatest competition. A better strategy may be to enter a smaller, but untapped segment.

Figure 6-2
**How the Majority Fallacy
Works**

1. A firm examines the size of two alternative market segments.

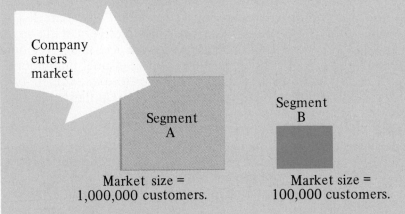

Segment A — Market size = 1,000,000 customers.

Segment B — Market size = 100,000 customers.

2. Without studying the competition in Segment A, it decides to develop a product for this segment since it is much larger.

Company enters market

Segment A — Market size = 1,000,000 customers.

Segment B — Market size = 100,000 customers.

3. The company is forced out of the market, due to heavy competition. It mistakenly ignored Segment B, which had no competitors.

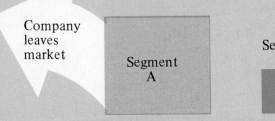

Company leaves market

Segment A — Market size = 1,000,000 customers. There are 12 competitors, including 3 national firms, (each with a 20 per cent market share).

Segment B — Market size = 100,000 customers. No firms serve this market.

Multiple Segmentation

Under a multiple-segmentation approach, a company tries to combine the best attributes of mass marketing and market segmentation. The method is similar to market segmentation, except that the firm appeals to two or more distinct market segments, with a different marketing plan for each segment. Some firms, such as General Motors, employ multiple segmentation to attract all the segments in the market and achieve the same effect as mass marketing. General Motors has five car divisions (Cadillac, Buick, Oldsmobile, Pontiac, Chevrolet) and a truck division. Other firms, such as Batus, use multiple segmentation to attract two or more, but not all, of the potential market segments. Batus operates Saks Fifth Avenue (status-conscious, high-income market) and Gimbels (middle-income market) but does not pursue discount-oriented customers. Batus uses a selective strategy in choosing market segments, General Motors an all-inclusive strategy.

In a number of cases, companies use both mass-marketing and market-segmentation approaches in their multiple-segmentation strategy. These firms have one or more major brands aimed at a wide range of consumers (the mass market) and secondary brands geared toward specific market segments. For example, Time Inc. publishes *Time, Life,* and *People* for very broad audiences and *Fortune, Money,* and *Discover* for specialized segments. Coca-Cola markets Coke to a broad spectrum of consumers, while its Tab, Fresca, Sprite, Mr. Pibb, Mello Yello, and other brands appeal to narrower groups of customers.

As with the other techniques, multiple segmentation requires a thorough analysis. Company resources and abilities must be able to produce and market two or more different sizes, brands, or products. This can be costly. Such is the case in the automobile industry. On the other hand, if the company sells its own and retailer brands, added costs are small.

Multiple segmentation should enable the firm to achieve many company objectives. It is possible to maximize sales, when a number of segments are addressed. For example, Procter & Gamble has a 50 per cent market share in the laundry and cleaning products field. This is made possible through a number of detergent brands such as Tide, Bold, Dash, Cheer, Gain, Oxydol, and Duz.[10]

Recognition as a specialist can continue as long as the firm markets a narrow product line or different brand names are used. For instance, Whirlpool maintains a distinct image under its own label; few consumers know it also makes products for Sears. Multiple segmentation also allows a firm to diversify and minimize its risks, because all the emphasis is not placed on one segment. Gerber life insurance provides an excellent hedge against a drop in the sales of baby products for that company.

Multiple segmentation does not mean that a firm has to enter markets where competitors are strongest and be subjected to the majority fallacy. Its objectives, strengths, and weaknesses must be measured against competitors. The firm's philosophy should be to choose and develop only those segments that it can handle. The company should

With multiple segmentation, a company markets two or more different sizes, brands, or products. This strategy combines the attributes of mass marketing and market segmentation.

note that the majority fallacy also works in reverse. If the firm enters a market segment before a competitor, it may prevent the competitor from successfully entering that segment in the future.

Multiple segmentation requires two or more sizable consumer groups. In each group, consumer desires must be different. For example, a firm that sells both designer jeans and store-brand jeans appeals to two distinct market segments (status conscious and affluent versus functionally oriented and price conscious). The more *clusters* (segments) facing the firm, the greater the opportunity for multiple segmentation. In many

The more separate clusters of consumers, the better the chance for successful multiple segmentation.

Figure 6-3

Using Multiple Segmentation

To appeal to different audience segments, *Runner's World* magazine has introduced its split cover marketing strategy, which began with the January 1983 issue. Subscribers, who presumably are more serious about running than other readers, saw an action shot of the New York City Marathon on the cover of their January copy (left), while newsstand purchasers found Donna Mills on their covers (right). The contents of both magazines are the same. *Runner's World* tested the concept after a review of sales figures showed the most successful issues had cover photos with broad audience appeal. "We expect to increase sales by reaching two distinct audiences while providing information relevant to both," said Bob Anderson, president and publisher.

Sources: Reprinted with permission of *Runner's World* Magazine, 1400 Stierlin Road; Mountain View, California 94043; and *Marketing News* (February 4, 1983).

cases, a firm that begins as a market segmenter is able to use multiple segmentation and pursue underdeveloped consumer segments after it becomes firmly established in one segment.

Channel members usually find multiple segmentation to be highly desirable. It enables them to reach different consumer groups, offers some degree of brand exclusivity, allows orders to be concentrated with one seller, and encourages them to carry their own private brands. From the selling firm's perspective, several channel benefits exist. Items can be sold to competing stores under different labels. Store shelf space must be provided to display each size, package, or brand. Price differentials among brands can be maintained. Competition may be kept out of the channel. Overall, multiple segmentation places the seller in a good bargaining position.

Multiple segmentation can be extremely profitable, because total profits should rise as the firm increases the number of segments it services. Per unit profits should also be high, if the firm does a good job of developing a unique market plan for each segment. Then, consumers in each segment are willing to pay a premium price for the tailor-made product or service.

Because the firm diversifies its markets under multiple segmentation, risks from a decline in any one segment are lessened. However, the firm might have to produce product variations, sell through different channels (a separate sales force for each channel may be necessary), and promote different brands. A firm must balance the additional revenues obtained from selling to multiple segments with the additional costs.

Under multiple segmentation, a company must be careful to guard its image. The firm's reputation can be hurt if it sells products and services to different segments under separate brand names and consumers find out about it. A few years ago, General Motors had such a problem when a number of Oldsmobile and Buick customers discovered that their automobiles had engines from the less-expensive Chevrolet division.

Other companies using multiple segmentation include Club Med, with separate resorts for couples only and families;[11] the Clinique division of Estee Lauder, which makes skin care products for women and for men;[12] and Safeway stores, which operates traditional supermarkets and upscale Bon Appetit stores.[13] Figure 6-3 shows how *Runner's World* magazine is using multiple segmentation.

Applying a Segmentation Approach

In this section, several aspects of segmentation are discussed: bases, steps in planning, organizational consumer segments, requirements for success, and limitations.

Bases of Segmentation

Market segments can be based on geographic demographics, personal demographics, and consumer life-styles. See Table 6-2.

Table 6-2	*Base*	*Possible Segments*
Bases for Segmentation	Geographic demographics	
	Population	
	Location	North, South, East, West
	Size	Small, medium, large
	Density	Urban, suburban, rural
	Transportation network	Mass transit, vehicular, pedestrian
	Climate	Warm, cold
	Type of commerce	Tourist, local worker, resident
	Retail establishments	Downtown shopping district, shopping mall
	Media	Local, regional, national
	Competition	Underdeveloped, saturated
	Growth pattern	Stable, negative, positive
	Legislation	Stringent, lax
	Rate of inflation	Low, moderate, high
	Personal demographics	
	Age	Child, teenager, adult, senior citizen
	Gender	Male, female
	Education	Less than high school, high school, college
	Mobility	Same residence for 2 years, changed residence in last 2 years
	Income	Low, middle, high
	Occupation	Blue-collar, white-collar, professional
	Marital status	Single, married, divorced, widowed
	Family size	1, 2, 3, 4, 5, 6 or more
	Nationality or race	European, Hispanic, American, Asian; black, white
	Consumer life-styles	
	Social class	Lower-lower to upper-upper
	Family life cycle	Bachelor to solitary survivor
	Usage rate	Light, medium, heavy
	Usage experience	None, some, extensive
	Brand loyalty	None, some, total
	Personality	Introverted-extroverted, persuasible-nonpersuasible
	Attitudes	Neutral, positive, negative
	Class consciousness	Inner-directed, outer-directed
	Motives	Benefit segmentation
	Perceived risk	Low, moderate, high
	Innovativeness	Innovator, laggard
	Opinion leadership	None, some, a lot
	Importance of purchase	Little, a great deal

Geographic Demographics

Geographic demographics describe towns, cities, states, and regions.

Geographic demographics are the basic identifiable characteristics of towns, cities, states, and regions. Figure 6-4 shows a demographic map of the United States. A company can use one or a combination of geographic demographics to segment its market. Segmentation strategies emphasize and cater to geographic differences.

Toys "R" Us and Heileman Brewing are illustrations of companies applying geographic segmentation. Toys "R" Us, the largest toy store chain in the U.S., operates more than 100 outlets in 26 markets (in 17 states). Its expansion strategy involves entering one new market, with several outlets, each year. In the evaluation of new markets, Toys "R" Us specifies that the areas must each have at least 250,000 people, in-

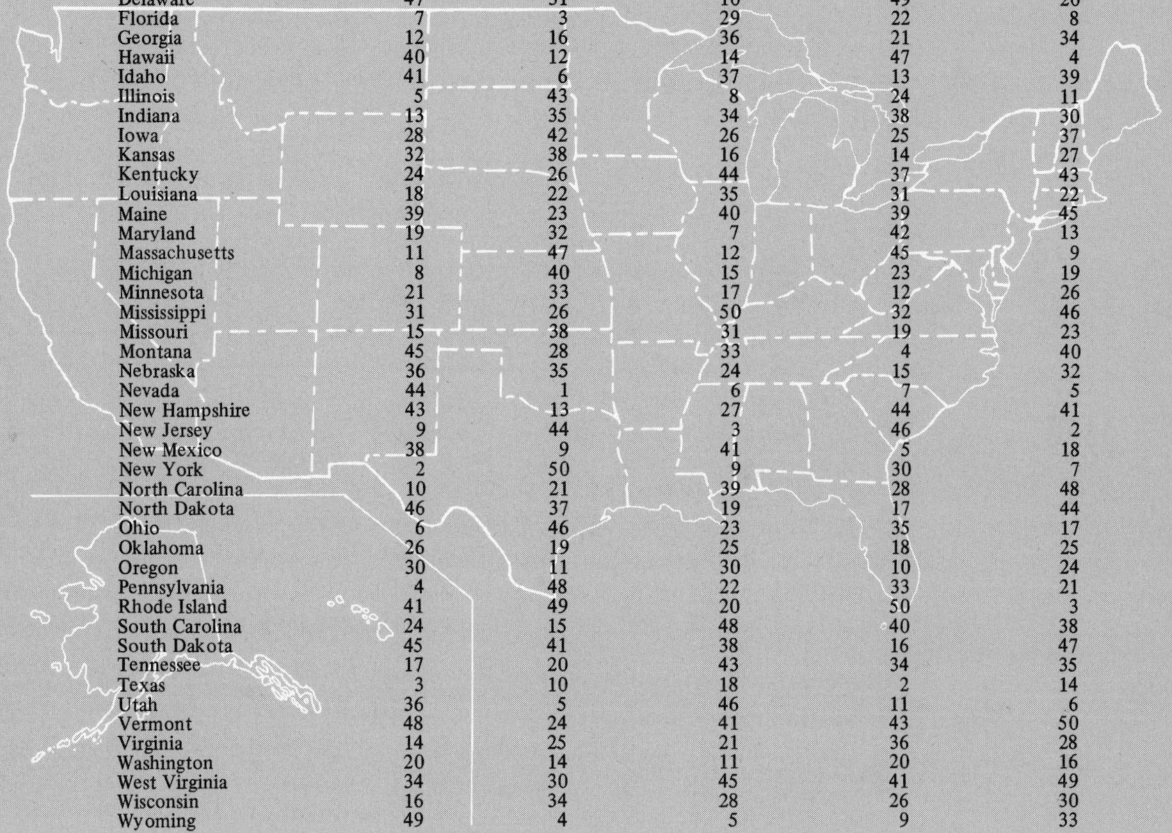

States	1980 Population Ranking	1970–1980 Population Growth Ranking	1981 Per Capita Income Ranking	1980 Geographic Size Ranking	1980 Urbanization Ranking*
Alabama	22	29	47	29	36
Alaska	50	6	1	1	29
Arizona	29	2	32	6	9
Arkansas	33	17	49	27	42
California	1	18	4	3	1
Colorado	27	8	13	8	12
Connecticut	25	45	2	48	15
Delaware	47	31	10	49	20
Florida	7	3	29	22	8
Georgia	12	16	36	21	34
Hawaii	40	12	14	47	4
Idaho	41	6	37	13	39
Illinois	5	43	8	24	11
Indiana	13	35	34	38	30
Iowa	28	42	26	25	37
Kansas	32	38	16	14	27
Kentucky	24	26	44	37	43
Louisiana	18	22	35	31	22
Maine	39	23	40	39	45
Maryland	19	32	7	42	13
Massachusetts	11	47	12	45	9
Michigan	8	40	15	23	19
Minnesota	21	33	17	12	26
Mississippi	31	26	50	32	46
Missouri	15	38	31	19	23
Montana	45	28	33	4	40
Nebraska	36	35	24	15	32
Nevada	44	1	6	7	5
New Hampshire	43	13	27	44	41
New Jersey	9	44	3	46	2
New Mexico	38	9	41	5	18
New York	2	50	9	30	7
North Carolina	10	21	39	28	48
North Dakota	46	37	19	17	44
Ohio	6	46	23	35	17
Oklahoma	26	19	25	18	25
Oregon	30	11	30	10	24
Pennsylvania	4	48	22	33	21
Rhode Island	41	49	20	50	3
South Carolina	24	15	48	40	38
South Dakota	45	41	38	16	47
Tennessee	17	20	43	34	35
Texas	3	10	18	2	14
Utah	36	5	46	11	6
Vermont	48	24	41	43	50
Virginia	14	25	21	36	28
Washington	20	14	11	20	16
West Virginia	34	30	45	41	49
Wisconsin	16	34	28	26	30
Wyoming	49	4	5	9	33

* % of population living in urban areas.

Sources: Bureau of the Census, and Bureau of Economic Analysis.

Figure 6-4
Demographic Map of the United States

cluding 25 to 28 per cent children. Toys "R" Us wants to operate stores in the largest 25 markets in the U.S.; it is now located in 15 of them.[14]

Heileman Brewing of La Crosse, Wisconsin, is the fourth largest beer manufacturer in the United States. It has acquired more than a dozen companies and markets over 30 brands of beer.[15] Most of its brands are regional and appeal to local tastes:

Flouting the conventional wisdom that nothing but nationally recognized brands could compete, Heileman over the last twenty years has aggressively acquired battered small breweries and put the power of a growing organization behind locally respected labels. . . . Heileman treats each market differently, with a lineup of brands and a pricing policy specifically fashioned for it.[16]

Personal Demographics

Personal demographics describe individual people.

Personal demographics are the basic identifiable characteristics of individual people. They are often used as the basis for segmentation, because people with different backgrounds frequently have different purchase requirements. Personal demographics may be viewed singly or in combinations.

Applications of demographic segmentation are plentiful, as these examples show. The Petersen Company publishes nine magazines, including *Hot Rod, Motor Trend, Skin Diver,* and *Photographic.* Of its audience, 74 per cent is eighteen- to thirty-four-year-old males. "No one has communicated with the eighteen to thirty-four male market as consistently and as successfully as we do."[17]

American Express concentrates on consumers with a median annual income over $25,000. Its eight million customers represent half of those families in the United States. "Because its cardholders spend more per purchase than bank-card users, Amexco is able to demand a higher percentage of the bill from merchants."[18]

Until recently, the Chevrolet Camaro was marketed as a "slab-sided boxy" car to single, young consumers with annual incomes of $20,000. Now, the redesigned Camaro offers a stylish look, a European appearance, interior comfort, good acceleration, and family roominess. As a result, the new Camaro attracts slightly-older, married consumers with annual incomes of $35,000.[19]

Modern Maturity, 50 Plus, and *Prime Time* are three magazines aimed at the forty-five and older segment. This segment is often overlooked, as firms go after the eighteen to thirty-four market. However, the segment is sizable, affluent, financially secure, and interested in products and services made especially for mature adults.

Consumer Life-Styles

As defined in Chapter 4, life-styles are the patterns in which people live and spend time and money. They include social and psychological factors. By developing life-style profiles, companies may be able to appeal to distinct market segments. Table 6-2 shows life-style segmentation for a wide range of social and psychological factors.

Life-style segmentation can be seen through these examples. Consumers who shop on Sundays can be divided into three categories: serious (necessary buying for a full-time worker), family (family members buy together), and recreational (entertainment value of buying).[20] In 1980, Bancroft introduced a new graphite tennis racquet selling for $225. Its market segment was the serious tennis player who wanted a product that would last through hard-fought tennis matches.[21] In 1982, Seven-Up started stressing in ads that its soft drink had no caffeine, "Never had it, never will." The company sought the health-conscious consumer with this orientation, an extension of its earlier "Uncola" theme.[22]

Two concepts are particularly useful in life-style segmentation: the heavy-half theory and benefit segmentation. Market segments can be based on usage rate, which refers to the amount of a product or service that a consumer buys. A consumer may use very little, some, or a great deal. In the 1960s, Dik Warren Twedt coined the term **heavy-half** to describe the market segment accounting for a large proportion of a product or service's total sales. For a wide variety of products, such as soda and shampoo, Twedt found that a heavy-user segment existed. In some cases, less than 20 per cent of the market made 80+ per cent of purchases.[23]

The *heavy-half* segment represents a much larger percentage of sales than the light-half segment.

Other applications of the heavy-half theory include the following. Singles represent 12.5 per cent of total consumers, yet account for 15.5 per cent of "eating-out" spending and car sales, and 20 per cent of alcohol sales.[24] Consumers 50 years of age and older represent 26 per cent of the population, but purchase over 42 per cent of digestive aids.[25] Four per cent of the U.S. population consumes 53 per cent of all wine bought.[26] When pursuing the heavy-half segment, a firm must be careful not to engage in the majority fallacy. Perhaps the "light" half has been underdeveloped.

Consumer motives (reasons for purchases) can be broken down into benefit segments. **Benefit segmentation** was popularized by Russell Haley in 1968:

Benefit segmentation assumes that consumers may be grouped on the basis of their reasons for using products or services.

> The belief underlying this segmentation strategy is that the benefits which people are seeking in consuming a given product are the basic reasons for the existence of true market segments.[27]

Haley studied the toothpaste market and was able to divide it into four segments. The sensory segment sought flavor and product appearance, had children, used spearmint toothpaste, favored brands like Colgate, had a degree of self-involvement, and was pleasure-oriented. The sociable segment sought bright teeth, was young, smoked, favored brands like Ultra Brite, and was highly sociable and active. The worrier segment sought decay prevention, had large families, used toothpaste heavily, favored Crest, had hypochondria, and was conservative. The independent segment sought low prices, was male, used toothpaste heavily, bought the brand on sale, and was autonomous and value-oriented.[28]

Later, Calantone and Sawyer applied benefit segmentation to bank marketing and were able to identify five distinct segments of bank customers: front runners, loan seekers, representative subgroup, value seekers, and one-stop bankers.[29] The highlights of their study are shown in Table 6-3.

An examination of Table 6-3 leads to an important overall conclusion about segmentation: A firm should normally use a combination of factors to determine and describe its market segments. A richer and more useful analysis takes place when geographic and personal demographics and consumer life-style factors are reviewed.

Table 6-3 **Benefit Segmentation of Bank Customers**

Factor	Front Runners	Loan Seekers	Representative Subgroup	Value Seekers	One-Stop Banker
			Segment		
Principal benefits sought	Large, bank for all, good advertising	Good reputation, loans easily available, low loan interest	Average on all benefits sought	High savings interest, quick services, low loan interest, plenty of parking	Wide variety of Services, convenient hours, quick service, encouragement of financial responsibility, convenient branch
Banks favored	Commercial bank A	Commercial bank B, savings bank X	Commercial banks A and B	Savings banks Y and Z	Commercial banks A and B
Demographic characteristics	Young, rent home	More transient, more blue collar		Tend to save more	Older
Life-style characteristics	High ability to manage money	Liberal about use of credit, positive about bank loans		Conservative overall life-style, conservative about use of credit, low propensity toward risk taking	Conservative about use of credit, positive toward checking account
Consumers (in %)	2.3	14.8	34.3	25.9	22.6

Source: Roger J. Calantone and Alan G. Sawyer, "The Stability of Benefit Segments," *Journal of Marketing Research*, Vol. 15 (August 1978), p. 400. Reprinted from *Journal of Marketing Research*, published by the American Marketing Association.

Planning a Segmentation Strategy

A segmentation strategy follows a series of stages.

The development of a ***segmentation strategy*** involves six steps:

1. Determining the characteristics and needs of consumers for the product or service category of the company
2. Analyzing consumer similarities and differences
3. Developing consumer group profiles
4. Selecting consumer segment(s)
5. Positioning the company's offering in relation to competition
6. Establishing an appropriate marketing plan

Characteristics and Needs of Consumers

A company should determine the characteristics and needs of consumers when it specifies the broad nature of its business. The exact product or service (such as, ladies' leather handbags or discount dental plans) should not be defined until after consumer research is undertaken. Step one is a data-collection stage.

Consumer Similarities and Differences

After determining and characterizing consumer needs, individual similarities and differences among consumers are analyzed. Where similarities exist, the firm knows it must respond to them in its marketing plan regardless of the segment(s) chosen. Where differences exist among consumers, the choice of a market segment will determine how the firm devises its marketing plan.

After assessing the individual similarities and differences among consumers, the firm is ready to assemble consumer profiles. These profiles define market segments by aggregating consumers with similar characteristics and needs and separating them from consumers with different characteristics and needs.

Consumer Group Profiles

At this point, the firm has two decisions to make: Which segment(s) offer the greatest opportunities for the company? How many segments should the firm pursue?

Selecting Consumer Segments

In deciding which segment(s) contain the greatest potential, the company must consider company objectives, company strengths, the level of competition, the size of the markets, channel relations, profits, and company image.

Once the company selects a market segment, it must identify the attributes and images of each competitor's products and select a position for its own product or service.

Positioning the Company's Offering

The last stage in the segmentation process is for the firm to develop its marketing plan, including

Establishing a Marketing Plan

1. Product
2. Distribution
3. Price
4. Promotion

Organizational Consumer Segments

In Chapter 5, the characteristics and behavior of organizational consumers (manufacturers, wholesalers, retailers, government, and non-profit institutions) were discussed and contrasted with final consumers. A firm engaging in a segmentation strategy should first examine and choose between final and organizational consumer markets. Then it should develop segments within either or both of these markets.

When segmenting, a firm should examine organizational consumers as well as final consumers. The same general segmentation criteria are used for both.

As noted in Chapter 5, organizational consumers require precise items, normally have strict price limits, frequently utilize joint decision making, buy in quantity, rate reliability and service very high, expect salespeople to visit them, and rely on trade publications. In contrast, final consumers frequently have flexibility in purchases, can vary price limits, often act alone, buy single units, may be relatively unconcerned about the future reliability of a vendor, usually go to a store, and rely on commercial media. The two markets require entirely different marketing approaches. For example, a firm selling vacuum cleaners to hospitals as well as final consumers would need vastly different marketing plans for each.

In segmenting the organizational consumer market, a company

Figure 6-5
Segmentation by a Typical Industrial Distributor

Source: H. Lee Mathews, "Stock What You Can Sell by Using Product/Customer Matrix," *Marketing News* (May 30, 1982), p. 4. Reprinted by permission.

PRODUCT LINES / CUSTOMER GROUPS	MACHINE SHOPS	FOOD INDUSTRY	FURNITURE INDUSTRY	NEW CUSTOMER SEGMENTS
CUTTING TOOLS				
ABRASIVES				
PORTABLE AIR TOOLS				
SHELVING				
NEW PRODUCT LINES				

should use the same criteria it would use for a final consumer. Geographic demographics are the features of the area in which the organizational consumer resides. Personal demographics refer to the organization and its personnel, including size, area of specialization, resources, existing contracts, past purchases, order size, and the demographics of decision maker(s). Life-style factors include the way in which the organization operates (centralized or decentralized), brand loyalty, reasons for purchases, and the social and psychological attributes of decision maker(s). These characteristics are potential bases for segmentation.

The procedure for segmenting organizational consumers is the same as that for final consumers and a company may decide on a market or multiple-segmentation strategy.

The segmentation of organizational consumer markets can be applied to many different situations, as these examples demonstrate. CT-scanners are new, three-dimensional, computerized x-ray systems marketed to hospitals. The hospitals can be divided into three segments: government, profit, and nongovernment/nonprofit.[30] The Detroit Diesel Allison Division of General Motors makes automatic transmissions for heavy-duty buses, trucks, and coaches. It segments consumers by product usage (such as trash collection) and geographic location.[31] Figure 6-5 shows how a typical industrial distributor can segment its market by customer groups and product lines.

Requirements for Successful Segmentation

In order for segmentation planning to be successful, consumer groups must meet five criteria:

Effective segmentation requires segments that are large, distinct, homogeneous, measurable, and reachable.

1. The segments must be large enough to generate sales and cover costs.
2. There must be differences among consumers, or else mass marketing would be an appropriate strategy.
3. Within each segment there must be enough consumer similarities to develop an appropriate marketing plan for the entire segment.

4. The firm must be able to measure the characteristics and needs of consumers in order to establish groups. This may be difficult for social and psychological factors.
5. The members of a segment must be reachable in an efficient manner. For example, young women can be reached through *Seventeen* magazine. It is efficient because males and older women do not read the magazine.

Limitations of Segmentation

Although segmentation is usually a consumer-oriented, efficient, and profitable marketing technique, it should not be abused. Firms can divide markets into segments that are too small, misinterpret consumer similarities and differences, become cost inefficient, spin off too many imitations of original brands, become myopic in research, be unable to use certain media, try to compete in too many disparate segments, confuse consumers, or become locked into a market segment that is declining. See Figure 6-6.

Sales Forecasting

As a company develops its target market, it should forecast the short-run (one-year) and long-run (five-year) sales of its product or service to that market. A **sales forecast** outlines expected company sales for a specific product or service to a specific consumer group over a specific period of time under a well-defined marketing program. By accurately forecasting sales, the firm is able to pinpoint areas of growth, develop a marketing budget, allocate marketing resources, measure success, analyze sales productivity, monitor the external environment, monitor competition, and modify marketing plans.

A **sales forecast** predicts company sales of a specific product to a specific consumer group over a specified period of time.

Figure 6-6
Oversegmenting the Market

Drawing by W. Miller. ©
The New Yorker Magazine,
Inc.

Figure 6-7
Developing a Sales Forecast

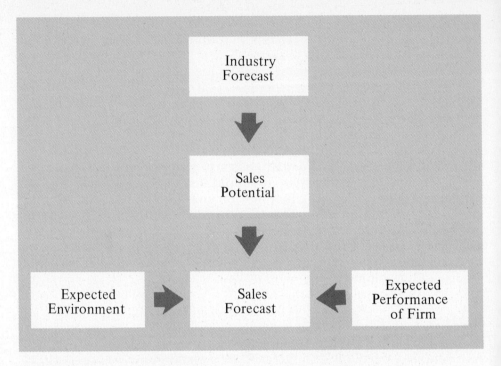

In order to estimate company sales, a firm should first look at industry forecasts, because they usually have a strong bearing on the sales of an individual company. Next, sales potential outlines the upper sales limit for the firm, based on marketing and production capacity. Then a sales forecast details a firm's realistic sales level. The forecast is based on the expected environment and performance of the firm. Figure 6-7 shows the sales forecasting process.

A sales forecast should take into account demographics (such as per capita income and number of households), economic conditions (such as the GNP and the rate of inflation), the competitive environment (such as price and advertising levels), last year's sales, and other variables. When constructing a sales forecast, precision is required. The forecast should break sales down by specific product or service (model 123), specific consumer group (adult female), time period (January through March), and type of marketing plan (market segmentation).

Data Sources

Data for forecasts may be obtained from government sources and industry and business publications.

A company has several sources available to generate the data needed for a sales forecast. The government collects and stores information on national and local population trends, past sales by industry and product type, and economic conditions. Industry trade associations put out publications and maintain libraries dealing with a variety of sales statistics. For example, the Conference Board publishes widely and maintains an extensive library for member firms. General business publications, such as *Business Week* and *Fortune*, conduct a variety of forecasts on a regular basis.

The firm can also obtain data from present and future customers, executives, sales personnel, and internal records. This information will usually center on company rather than industry predictions.

Methods of Sales Forecasting

Various methods of sales forecasting can be undertaken by a firm. The methods range from simple and unsophisticated to complex and quite sophisticated. Among the simple methods are trend analysis, market share analysis, jury of executive or expert opinion, sales force surveys, and consumer surveys. Among the more complex methods are the chain-ratio technique, market buildup method, test marketing, and statistical analyses.

Under *simple trend analysis,* the firm forecasts future sales on the basis of recent or current performance. For example, if the company's sales have increased an average of 10 per cent per year over the past five years, it forecasts next year's sales to be 10 per cent higher than this year's. The problems with simple trend analysis are that past sales fluctuations, the economy, changing consumer tastes, changing competition, and market saturation are not considered. A firm's growth rate may change as a result of these factors. In addition, all firms in an industry do not progress at the same rate.

Market share analysis is similar to simple trend analysis, except that the company bases its forecast on the assumption that its share of industry sales will remain constant. Although market share analysis has the same weaknesses as simple trend analysis, it does enable an aggressive or declining firm to adjust its forecast and marketing efforts.

The *jury of executive* or *expert opinion* is a forecasting method used when the management of a company or other well-informed persons meet, discuss the future, and set sales estimates based on the group's experience and intuition. By itself, this method excludes statistical data and relies too heavily on informal analysis. In conjunction with other methods, it is effective because it enables experts to direct, interpret, and respond to concrete data. Because management establishes objectives, sets priorities, and guides the organization's future, its input is mandatory.

The firm's employees most in touch with consumers and the external environment are sales personnel. *Sales force surveys* enable the company to obtain input in a structured way. Sales personnel are frequently able to pinpoint coming trends, strengths and weaknesses in the company's offering, competitive strategies, customer resistance, and the traits of heavy users. They can also break sales forecasts down by product category, customer grouping, and geographic area. On the other hand, sales personnel can have a limited perspective, offer biased replies, and misinterpret consumer desires.

Many market researchers believe that the best indicators of future sales are consumer attitudes. By conducting *consumer surveys,* a company can obtain a variety of information: purchase intentions, future expectations (optimistic-pessimistic), rate of consumption, brand switching, time between purchases, and reasons for purchases. Con-

Under *simple trend analysis,* a firm extends past sales into the future.

With *market share analysis,* the company assumes its share will remain.

The *jury of executive* or *expert opinion* method has well-informed people discuss and estimate sales.

Sales force surveys use market input from sales personnel, who are most directly in touch with consumers.

Through *consumer surveys,* a company can obtain attitudes and purchase intentions.

sumers are not always willing to reply to company surveys and may act differently from what they believe or state.

With the *chain-ratio method,* the firm starts with general data and develops a series of more specific market factors.

Under the **chain-ratio method,** the firm starts with general market information and then computes a series of more specific market information. These combined data yield a sales forecast. For example, the Harris Lamp Company wants to forecast sales of model A lamps to single males from January through March. General information is the total company sales forecast (1,200,000 units); specific market factors are the forecasts for the per cent of customers buying model A (33.3), the per cent of single-male customers (16.7), and the per cent of sales from January through March (25.0):

$$\begin{aligned} \text{Sales forecast} &= \text{Total sales forecast} \times \text{Per cent buying} \\ \text{(units)} &\quad \text{model A} \times \text{Per cent single male} \times \text{Per cent} \\ &\quad \text{of sales January-March} \\ \text{Sales forecast} &= (1{,}200{,}000) \times (33.3\%) \times (16.7\%) \times (25.0\%) = 16{,}667. \\ \text{(units)} \end{aligned}$$

Single males are forecast to buy 16,667 model A lamps from Harris between January and March 1985.

The chain-ratio method is only as accurate as the data plugged in for each market factor. Nonetheless, it is a useful tool because it requires management to think through the sales forecast and obtain different kinds of information.

The *market buildup method* compiles data from separate market segments to make a broad prediction.

The opposite approach to the chain-ratio method is the **market buildup method.** With the market buildup method, the firm gathers data from small, separate market segments and aggregates them. For example, the market buildup method enables a company operating in four metropolitan areas to develop a forecast by first estimating sales in each area and then adding the areas.

When using the market buildup method, a marketer must note that consumer tastes, competition, population growth, and media differ by geographic area. Areas or consumer groups of equal size may offer entirely dissimilar sales opportunities. They should not be lumped together on the basis of limited demographics.

In test marketing the firm estimates total future sales from short-run, geographically limited sales.

Test marketing provides one form of market buildup analysis in which the firm estimates total future sales from the short-run, geographically limited sales of a product or service. In test marketing, the company usually introduces a new product or service into one or a few markets for a short period of time. The full marketing campaign of the firm is carried out during the test. After the test is completed, the company forecasts future sales from test market sales.

For instance, a manufacturer of tennis shoes decides to introduce a new model in three test market locations. The sales of the shoes are $500,000 in the three areas. Last year, these areas accounted for 5 per cent of total company sales for its other shoes. A national sales forecast for the new shoes would then be ($500,000) × (100 per cent/5 per cent) = $10,000,000. As before, the firm must remember that test areas may not be representative of all locations. Furthermore, test market enthusiasm may not carry over into national distribution. Test marketing is discussed in greater depth in Chapter 8.

A number of detailed statistical analyses are available for sales forecasting. Simulation allows a company to enter several market factor statistics into a computer-based model and forecast sales under varying conditions and marketing plans. With complex trend analysis (time-series analysis), the firm includes past sales fluctuations (seasonal and long term), cyclical factors (such as economic conditions), and other factors when developing short-run and long-run sales trends. Regression and correlation techniques seek to explore the mathematical relationships between future sales and market factors, such as total family income. These methods depend on reliable data and the ability of personnel and management to use them correctly. A deeper discussion is beyond the scope of this text.

> *Detailed statistical analyses use the methods of simulation, complex trend analysis (time-series analysis), regression, and correlation.*

Additional Considerations

The method and accuracy of sales forecasting depend a great deal on the newness of a firm's offering. A forecast for a continuing product or service should utilize trend analysis, market share analysis, executive and expert opinion, and sales force surveys. Barring major changes in the economy, competition, or consumer tastes, the sales forecast should be relatively accurate.

> *A forecast for a continuing product should be the most accurate, while one for a completely new product should be the least.*

A sales forecast for a product or service that is new to the firm but continuing in the industry should utilize trade association data, executive and expert opinion, sales force surveys, consumer surveys, and test marketing. The sales forecast for the first year should be somewhat accurate, the following years more accurate. It is difficult to estimate first-year sales, because consumer acceptance and competitive reactions are difficult to gauge precisely.

A sales forecast for a product or service that is new to both the firm and the industry needs to rely on consumer surveys, test marketing, sales force surveys, executive and expert opinion, and simulation. The sales forecast for the first two to three years may be highly inaccurate, because the speed of consumer acceptance is difficult to measure precisely. Later forecasts will be more accurate. Even though the initial sales forecast may be inaccurate, it is necessary for the reasons cited earlier: pinpointing growth, budgeting, allocating resources, measuring success, monitoring the environment and competition, and setting marketing plans.

The firm must also consider sales penetration when forecasting future sales. **Sales penetration** is the degree to which a company is achieving its sales potential. It is expressed as:

> *Sales penetration describes whether a company has reached its potential. Diminishing returns may result when a firm tries to convert nonconsumers.*

Sales penetration = Actual sales ÷ Sales potential.

A firm with a high sales penetration level must realize that its market may be relatively saturated and that **diminishing returns** may occur if it attempts to convert the remaining nonconsumers of its products, because the costs of attracting these people may outweigh the revenues. Other products or segments may offer better opportunities.

Again, the company must remember that a number of factors may change and cause the sales forecast to be inaccurate unless revised. These include economic conditions, industry conditions, company performance, competition, and consumer tastes.

Summary

Mass marketing (appealing to many consumers through one basic marketing plan), market segmentation (appealing to one well-defined consumer group through one marketing program), and multiple segmentation (appealing to two or more well-defined consumer groups through different marketing plans) are the alternative methods by which a firm can develop a target market. In choosing a method, the company must examine its resources and abilities, objectives, competition, consumer characteristics and needs, channel requirements, profits, and image. In recent years, pure mass marketing has declined, whereas market and multiple segmentation have grown.

When segmenting, a company must be careful to understand the majority fallacy: selecting the largest consumer segment, which also has the greatest number of competitors and brands. Untapped, smaller segments may offer greater potential.

Segmentation can be based on one or a combination of geographic demographics, personal demographics, and life-style factors. The heavy-half theory and benefit segmentation are useful ways of defining market groups.

Six steps are necessary to create a segmentation strategy: determining consumer characteristics and needs, analyzing consumer similarities and differences, developing consumer group profiles, selecting consumer segment(s), positioning the company's offering in relation to competition, and establishing the marketing plan. Organizational consumer segments deserve separate analysis and planning by firms, even though the procedure for developing a target market is similar to that for final consumers. Successful segmentation planning requires large enough segments, differences among segments, similarities within segments, measurable consumer traits and needs, and efficiency in reaching segments.

Marketers should forecast short-run (one-year) and long-run (five-year) sales in conjunction with the development of target markets. This will enable them to pinpoint growth, compute budgets, allocate resources, measure success, analyze productivity, monitor the external environment and competition, and adjust marketing plans. A sales forecast describes the expected company sales of a specific product or service to a specific consumer group over a specific time period under a well-defined marketing program.

The company can obtain the data needed for sales forecasting from the government, industry trade associations, general publications, present and future customers, executives, experts, sales personnel, and internal records. A number of simple and complex methods are available for sales forecasting. These include simple trend analysis, market share analysis, jury of executive and expert opinion, sales force surveys, consumer surveys, chain-ratio method, market buildup method, test marketing, and detailed statistical analyses (such as simulation, complex trend analysis or time-series analysis, regression, and correlation). The best results are obtained when several methods and forecasts are combined.

The sales forecast should take into account the level of newness of the firm's offering, sales penetration, diminishing returns, and the changing nature of many variables.

KEY TERMS

After reading this chapter, you should understand these key terms:

Mass marketing	Simple trend analysis
Market segmentation	Market share analysis
Multiple segmentation	Jury of executive (expert) opinion
Majority fallacy	Sales force surveys
Geographic demographics	Consumer surveys
Personal demographics	Chain-ratio method
Heavy-half	Market buildup method
Benefit segmentation	Sales penetration
Segmentation strategy	Diminishing returns
Sales forecast	

QUESTIONS FOR DISCUSSION

1. Distinguish among mass marketing, market segmentation, and multiple segmentation.
2. Why has the use of pure mass marketing declined? Give two examples of firms that still use pure mass marketing (not described in the chapter).
3. What is the majority fallacy? Under which circumstances should a firm ignore this concept?
4. Develop a personal-demographic profile of the students in your marketing class. For what products and services would the class be a good market segment?
5. Explain the heavy-half theory. What are its implications? Relate the majority fallacy to this theory.
6. Explain benefit segmentation. What potential benefit segments exist for bicycles?
7. Briefly describe the steps in planning a segmentation strategy, and apply it to a new perfume.
8. The Johnston Company wants to sell electric clocks both to factories and final consumers. Create marketing strategies for each.
9. Explain the requirements for successful segmentation.
10. What are the limitations of segmentation?
11. Why should a company develop a sales forecast?
12. Explain the chain-ratio and market buildup methods of sales forecasting.
13. How does the level of newness of the firm's offering affect sales forecasting?
14. What is sales penetration? How does it relate to diminishing returns?

NOTES

1. Fred Gardner, "Budweiser's 'Must Win' Attitude," *Marketing & Media Decisions* (Spring 1982, Special Edition), pp. 21–30; and "Anheuser Busch: The King of Beers Still Rules," *Business Week* (July 12, 1982), pp. 50–54.

2. "The 50 Largest Retailing Companies," *Fortune* (July 12, 1982), p. 140.

3. "Sears, Roebuck & Co." *Advertising Age* (September 9, 1982), p. 162.

4. "Low-Priced Digital Wristwatches Mass Marketed Like Ball-Point Pens," *Marketing News* (August 7, 1981), p. 3.

5. Cynthia Saltzman, "Troubled Life-Insurance Companies Try Mass-Marketing Tactics to Increase Sales," *Wall Street Journal* (December 19, 1980), p. 50.

6. Jeanne Toomey, "A Citadel of Success," *Advertising Age* (July 27, 1981), p. S-43.

7. Allen Liles, *Oh Thank Heaven! The Story of the Southland Corporation* (Dallas: Southland Corporation, 1977), p. 232.

8. Isadore Barmash, "Here, You Can Spend $325 for a Toothbrush," *New York Times* (October 11, 1981), Section 3, p. 9.

9. Jeffrey H. Birnbaum, "Little Guys' Shops Separate the Men from the Boys' Dept.," *Wall Street Journal* (February 3, 1981), p. 1.

10. Carol J. Loomis, "P & G Up Against Its Wall," *Fortune* (February 23, 1981), p. 54.

11. Alan Rosenthal, "Club Med: Taking Aim at the Family," *Advertising Age* (March 15, 1982), pp. M-2–M-3.

12. "Cosmetics Makers Are Luring Men," *New York Times* (January 7, 1982), p. D3.

13. John Revett and Steve Beitler, "Safeway Goes Upscale," *Advertising Age* (January 11, 1982), p. 81.

14. "Simplified Growth: One Market Per Year," *Chain Store Age* (September 1981), p. 18; and Janet Neiman, "Retailers Should Know Their Place," *Advertising Age* (November 1, 1982), p. M-22.

15. Winston Williams, "Keeping Heileman in the Pack," *New York Times* (November 14, 1982), Section 3, p. 6; Robert Reed, "Heileman Poised, But Where's The Target?" *Advertising Age* (October 18, 1982), pp. 4, 75; and Lawrence Ingrassia, "Heileman Plans Big Expansion into South, Setting Stage for Bruising Beer-Sales Fight," *Wall Street Journal* (February 3, 1983), p. 33.

16. Gwen Kinkaid, "Heileman Toasts the Future with 34 Beers," *Fortune* (June 18, 1979), pp. 124, 126.

17. "We Deliver the Men for You" (Los Angeles: Petersen Publishing Company).

18. A. F. Ehrbar, "Hazards Down the Track for American Express," *Fortune* (November 6, 1978), p. 98.

19. Douglas R. Sease, "Camaro, Firebird Become Fast Selling Cars for GM, Helping Profit and Lifting Morale," *Wall Street Journal* (June 8, 1982), p. 37.

20. Nora Ganim Barnes, "Sunday Shoppers Divided into Three Distinct Categories: Serious, Family, and Recreational," *Marketing News* (October 1, 1982), p. 9.

21. Sam Harper, "Tennis Racquet Makers Court Serious Players," *Advertising Age* (September 24, 1979), p. 58.

22. "Seven-Up Uncaps a Cola—and an Industry Feud," *Business Week* (March 22, 1982), pp. 98, 100.

23. Dik Warren Twedt, "How Important to Marketing Is the 'Heavy User'?" *Journal of Marketing*, Vol. 28 (January 1964), pp. 71–72.

24. Gay Jervey, "Y & R Study: New Life to Singles," *Advertising Age* (October 4, 1982), p. 14.

25. Charles H. Kline & Co., "Consumption of Nonprescription Drugs by Age Group—1980," *Advertising Age* (April 6, 1981), p. 67.

26. "Creating a Mass Market for Wine," *Business Week* (March 15, 1982), p. 109.

27. Russell I. Haley, "Benefit Segmentation: A Decision-Oriented Research Tool," *Journal of Marketing*, Vol. 32 (July 1968), p. 31.

28. Ibid., p. 33.

29. Roger J. Calantone and Alan G. Sawyer, "The Stability of Benefit Segments," *Journal of Marketing Research*, Vol. 15 (August 1978), pp. 395–404.

30. Yoram Wind, Thomas S. Robertson, and Cynthia Fraser, "Industrial Product Diffusion by Market Segment," *Industrial Marketing Management*, Vol. 11 (February 1982), pp. 1–8.

31. Eric F. J. Lutz, "How One Industrial Marketer Used Market Segmentation Key to Unlock Target Markets," *Marketing News* (May 1, 1981), Section 2, p. 4.

THE LIMITED: ACTIVELY PURSUING A MULTIPLE-SEGMENTATION APPROACH*   1

CASES

For most of its twenty years, Limited Inc. operated only The Limited stores and functioned as a market segmenter. The Limited carried trendy apparel for fashion-conscious young single women who were working or attending college. The stores concentrated on a narrow assortment of traditional outfits and sportswear, but stressed large quantities and a deep selection of colors. The Limited's merchandising ability was well-respected in the industry. Through its strategy, The Limited grew to about 500 outlets with total annual sales of more than $350 million.

Then Leslie Wexner, founder and chairman of Limited Inc., decided to broaden the company's product offerings and began a multiple-segmentation approach. As a result, Limited Inc.

- Acquired Lane Bryant, a 207-store apparel chain appealing to full-size women; Bryant's Smart Size, a 32-store discount apparel division; and Bryant's $170 million per year mail-order business.
- Acquired Roaman's, a 63-store apparel chain catering to full-size women, and Roaman's 41-store discount division.
- Developed Limited Express, a 30-store apparel chain for teenage girls.
- Added clothes for upper-income career women into The Limited stores.
- Acquired Victoria's Secret, a mail-order retailer of high-priced lingerie.

Said Wexner, "Some of our competitors are thinking in terms of 1982; we're thinking in terms of 1992."

Limited Inc. considers the market for full-size women's apparel to be relatively untapped. Studies show that 14 per cent of American women aged 16 and older wear full-size clothing. To penetrate this market, Lane Bryant stores will be placed into many of the 500 shopping centers where The Limited stores are already located.

Observers wonder whether Limited Inc.'s centralized management can oversee its widening range of stores and mail-order operations, and if the optimism about the full-size market is too high.

QUESTIONS

1. If The Limited functioned so well as a marketer segmenter, why would it start a multiple-segmentation approach?
2. Name and evaluate the mix of segments at which Limited Inc. is now aiming.
3. Assess the strategy of placing Lane Bryant and The Limited stores in the same shopping centers.
4. What risks and potential problems does Limited Inc. face? How can they be avoided or solved?

*The data in this case are drawn from "Limited Inc.: Expanding Its Position to Serve the Rubenesque Woman," *Business Week* (November 22, 1982), pp. 56, 58.

2 KELLOGG: THE CEREAL COMPANY†

Kellogg, now a company with $2.2 billion in annual sales and 39 per cent of the cereal market, was founded in 1906. It was Kellogg that pioneered the modern cereal industry. Of all major food-processing companies, Kellogg remains the most dependent on cereal. Kellogg has four of the six leading brands of cereal: Corn Flakes (its original product), Sugar Frosted Flakes, Raisin Bran, and Rice Krispies. Bran Products ranks tenth.

For most of the 1970s, the industry's annual growth of cereal sales was 7 per cent. However, this dropped sharply in the late 1970s to 2 per cent. No growth is projected for the next several years as a result of population changes. The under-twenty-five age group, the largest eaters of cereal, with annual consumption of 11 pounds per capita, is shrinking. The twenty-five to fifty age group, the smallest number of eaters of cereal, with annual consumption of less than 5.5 pounds per capita, is the fastest-growing consumer segment. In addition, overall demand for sugared cereal has dropped because of government and consumer-group activities.

Rather than move more rapidly into diversification (Kellogg does one quarter of its business outside cereal and owns Salada Foods and Mrs. Smith's Pie Company, among others), Kellogg remains strongly committed to the cereal business. It has introduced several new cereal brands; the five launched in 1979 were the most it ever brought out in a single year. The company's research budget was increased 15 per cent a year in order to generate new cereal brands.

The new brands are aimed at diverse markets, as Kellogg has upgraded its use of multiple segmentation. For example, in 1979 it introduced Most, a high-fiber wheat cereal with the highest nutritional content of any cereal on the market. One serving satisfies all the federally recommended daily requirements for ten vitamins. Most is oriented toward health-conscious adults. Other new 1979 brands included Smart Start for working women, Honey & Nut Corn Flakes for teenagers, and Graham Crackos and Crunchy Loggs for children.

In 1981, Kellogg introduced Nutri-Grain, its only sugarless cereal. Nutri-Grain was produced in four varieties: corn, wheat, barley, and rye. During 1981, Kellogg spent $15 million advertising Nutri-Grain. Yet, by mid-1982, sales were just 1 per cent of total industry volume; and the rye and barley varieties were dropped (replaced by a wheat-and-raisins version). Thus far, it has not been able to raise cereal consumption among adults.

At the same time, Kellogg has been working hard to maintain the sales of sugared children's cereals. Kellogg dominates this market with brands such as presweetened Sugar Frosted Flakes, Sugar Pops, and Sugar Smacks cereals, and by using its animated Tony the Tiger.

Among competitors, General Mills has been the most active—and the most successful. Its newer cereal brands include Honey & Nut Cheerios, Crispy Wheats 'N Raisins, and Golden Grahams. Ralston-Purina has begun manufacturing a variety of private-label brands for supermarkets.

Kellogg is expanding its overseas cereal business in several countries in South America, Central America, the Middle East, and Asia, where the sales penetration of cereal has been low for cultural and other reasons.

†The data in this case are drawn from "Kellogg: Still the Cereal People," *Business Week* (November 26, 1979), pp. 80–93; John Holusha, "Outlook Brightens for Profitable Kellogg," *New York Times* (April 25, 1982), pp. D1, D6; John Koten "For Kellogg, the Hardest Part Is Getting People Out of Bed," *Wall Street Journal* (August 27, 1982), p. 31; and "Kellogg Tells New Strategy," *Advertising Age* (February 28, 1983), pp. 1, 72.

QUESTIONS

1. How can Kellogg have four different cereal brands among the six leading brands in the United States?
2. Do you think the heavy-half theory applies to cereal? Explain your answer. How can the theory be proven or disproven?
3. Will Kellogg be able to increase cereal sales in the 1980s despite unfavorable demographics? Explain your answer.
4. Illustrate how Kellogg could use the chain-ratio method to forecast the sales for a new brand of cereal for senior citizens.
5. How would you evaluate Kellogg's level of sales penetration? What does this mean?

Introduction to Part Three

In order to carry out the marketing concept (consumer satisfaction, integrated effort, and attainment of company goals), a firm must develop, implement, and monitor a systematic marketing plan. This plan centers on the four major elements of marketing: product, distribution, promotion, and price. Parts Three through Six examine each of these four elements in detail and show their interrelationship. Part Three describes product planning and its components.

Chapter 7 offers an overview of product planning, the systematic decision making pertaining to all aspects of the development and management of a firm's products. The different types of consumer and industrial products are distinguished. Width and depth of product assortment are considered and the various types of product management forms are detailed. The use of product positioning, the analysis of consumer perceptions of the firm's and competitors' products, is explained. The importance and functions of branding and packaging are covered in depth, as are the necessary decisions involving these aspects of product planning.

Chapter 8 deals with the management of products from their inception to their deletion. The role of the product life cycle is described and evaluated. The coverage of new products includes a description of new product types, why new products fail, and the new-product planning process: idea generation, product screening, concept testing, business analysis, product development, test marketing, and commercialization. The growth of products is shown in terms of the adoption and diffusion processes. Several methods for extending the lives of mature products are described. Finally, product deletion decisions and strategies are detailed.

An Overview of Product Planning

7

Chapter Preview

Chapter Objectives

1 To define product planning

2 To examine the various types of consumer and industrial products, product mixes, and product management organization forms from which a firm may select

3 To discuss product positioning and its utility for marketers

4 To study the functions and decisions involved with branding and packaging

General Mills is a diversified company with annual sales exceeding $5 billion. Among the businesses operated by General Mills are consumer foods, restaurants, toys, specialty retailing, and clothing. Company brand (store) names include Hamburger Helper, Cheerios, Betty Crocker, Yoplait yogurt, Red Lobster restaurants, Parker Brothers toys, and Izod/Lacoste clothing.

For more than twenty years, General Mills has been an advocate of the product-management system, whereby each brand is supervised by an individual manager who is responsible for its advertising, pricing, research, themes, and so on. In the consumer-foods area, General Mills has more than 30 product managers (none over thirty-five years of age)—one per brand. Annually, all brands are subjected to a three-month planning process, which results in an identification of key issues, a business review, and a budget (incorporating a marketing overview, the brand's competitive position, a sales forecast, costs, and channel strategy). Product managers develop and implement these plans.

It takes about three years of training to complete the General Mills' product-management program and become a product manager. The average manager earns a $30,000 to $40,000 salary per year plus an annual bonus averaging 15 to 25 per cent of salary. Usually a manager spends two years each on two different brands before moving up the corporate ladder. The General Mills' system is very competitive. Managers must vie with one another for financial and staff support, shelf space in stores, and promotional resources. Only 8 to 9 of the 33 current food product managers will be promoted to marketing director, the next step in product management. The remainder will be moved into other divisions or job responsibilities.

Said the president of PepsiCo, "General Mills has gone from a pretty good product-management system to one that is outstanding. It turns out an excellent end product."[1] In a recent survey of executives at 200 of the largest U.S. companies, General Mills was rated among the top ten most-admired firms by its peers.[2]

The Framework of Product Planning

Product planning involves the development and management of products. Products contain physical, image, and service aspects.

Product planning is systematic decision making relating to all aspects of the development and management of a firm's products, including branding and packaging. A **product** consists of a basic physical offering and an accompanying set of image and service features that seek to satisfy consumer needs. A well-structured product-planning process enables a company to pinpoint potential opportunities, develop appropriate marketing programs, coordinate a mix of products, maintain successful products as long as possible, reappraise faltering products, and delete undesirable products.

Chapter 7 provides an overview of product planning. It examines the basic decisions facing the firm: product types, product mix, product management organization, and product positioning. It concludes with a discussion of branding and packaging. Chapter 8 presents an in-depth description of product planning from finding new product ideas to deleting existing products. The product life cycle is examined in that chapter.

Types of Products

The most basic decision in product planning is the choice of the type(s) of products to offer. Products can be categorized on the basis of the buyer: consumer or industrial. The classification is important because it focuses on the differences in the characteristics of products and the resulting implications for marketers.

Consumer Products

Consumer products are goods and services intended for the ultimate consumer for personal, family, or household use. The use of the good or service (not the tangible nature of it) designates it as a consumer product. For example, a calculator, dinner at a restaurant, telephone service, a file cabinet, a vacuum cleaner, and an electric pencil sharpener are consumer products only if they are purchased for personal, family, or household use.

Consumer goods were first classified about sixty years ago by Melvin T. Copeland.[3] His three-category system of convenience, shopping, and specialty goods is widely employed today. The system is based on shoppers' awareness of alternative products and their characteristics prior to the shopping trip and the degree of search shoppers will undertake. It is important to recognize that placing a product into one of these categories depends on the shopper's behavior. See Table 7-1, and Figure 7-1.

   Convenience goods are those purchased with a minimum of effort, because the buyer has knowledge of product characteristics prior to shopping. Convenience goods are generally low in price and frequently purchased. The consumer does not want to search for additional information (because the item has been bought before) and will accept a substitute (Libby's instead of Green Giant canned corn) rather than have to visit more than one store.

   The tasks of marketing center on intensive distribution (all available outlets), convenient store locations, evening and weekend store hours, heavy use of mass advertising and in-store displays, well-

Consumer products include goods and services marketed to the ultimate consumer.

Consumer Goods

Convenience goods are bought in a routine manner. They may be categorized as staples, impulse goods, and emergency goods.

Table 7-1 **Characteristics of Consumer Goods**

	Type of Good		
Characteristics	*Convenience*	*Shopping*	*Specialty*
Awareness of product alternatives and their attributes prior to purchase	High	Low	High
Effort expended to acquire good	Minimal	Moderate to high	As much as necessary
Willingness of consumers to accept substitutes	High	Moderate	None
Frequency of purchase	High	Moderate or low	Varies
Information search	Low	High	Varies
Major consumer desire	Availability without effort	Comparison shopping to determine best choice	Brand loyalty regardless of price and availability

Figure 7-1
Examples of Consumer Goods

A. Convenience

1. Staples–
   Regular purchases of

2. Impulse–
   Unplanned purchases of

3. Emergency–
   Urgent purchases of

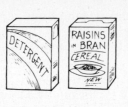 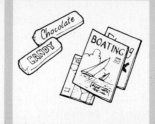 

B. Shopping

1. Attribute–Based

2. Price–based

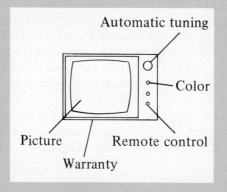

Automatic tuning

Color

Picture

Warranty

Remote control

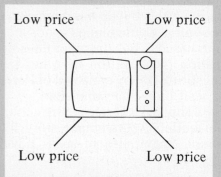

Low price   Low price

Low price   Low price

C. Specialty

Campbell's   Brand A   Brand B

designed store layouts, and self-service to minimize purchase time. Retailers often carry a number of brands of convenience goods.

Convenience goods can be further divided into staples, impulse goods, and emergency goods. Staples are low-priced items that are routinely purchased on a regular basis. Impulse goods are items that the consumer does not plan to buy on a specific trip to a store, such as candy or a record album. Emergency goods are purchased out of urgent need, such as an umbrella or a tire to replace a flat.

Shopping goods are those for which consumers must seek information about product alternatives and their attributes in order to make a purchase decision. For attribute-based shopping goods, consumers get information about and then evaluate product features, warranty, performance, options, and other factors. The good with the best combination of attributes is purchased. For price-based shopping goods, consumers judge product attributes to be similar and look around for the least expensive item. Consumers will exert effort in searching for information, because shopping goods are bought infrequently.

Shopping goods require an information search regarding product features or price.

The marketing emphasis for shopping goods is on depth of assortment (such as many colors, sizes, options), knowledgeable and persuasive sales personnel, the communication of competitive advantages through informative and persuasive advertising, well-known brands, channel enthusiasm to sell the goods, and customer warranties and follow-up service to reduce perceived risk. Shopping centers and downtown business districts ease shopping behavior by placing several stores in close proximity.

Specialty goods are those to which consumers are brand loyal. They are fully aware of these products and their attributes prior to making a purchase decision. They are willing to make a significant purchase effort to acquire the brand desired and will pay a higher price than for competitive products, if necessary. For specialty goods, consumers will not make purchases if their brand is not available.

Consumers are loyal to *specialty goods*. They will pay more and exert more effort to acquire them.

The marketing emphasis for specialty goods is on maintaining the product features that make the items unique to loyal consumers, reminder advertising, distribution appropriate for the product (Kraft mayonnaise and *Business Week* require different distribution to loyal customers: supermarkets versus home subscriptions), extension of the brand name to related products (such as Kraft salad dressing), product improvements, ongoing customer contact (such as *Friends* magazine, published for owners of Chevrolet cars), and monitoring the performance of channel members.

The consumer goods classification system is an excellent basis for segmentation. For example, Ban deodorant may be a convenience good for some consumers (who will buy Sure or Right Guard if Ban is unavailable), a shopping good for others (who read ingredient labels before selecting a brand), and a specialty good for still others (who insist on Ban regardless of price or availability). Bristol-Myers, maker of Ban, must understand how Ban fits into these different categories and plan its marketing strategy accordingly. Finally, it should be noted that this classification system can be applied to consumer services.

Consumer Services

Consumer services include *rentals, owned-goods,* and *nongoods.*

There are three broad categories of consumer services: rented goods, owned goods, and nongoods. A **rented-goods service** involves the leasing of a product for a specified period of time. Examples include car, hotel room, apartment, and boat rentals. An **owned-goods service** involves an alteration or repair of a product owned by the consumer. Examples include repair services (such as automobile, watch, and plumbing), lawn care, car wash, haircut, and dry cleaning. A **nongoods service** provides personal service on the part of the seller; it does not involve a product. Examples include accounting, legal, and tutoring services. Services are fully discussed in Chapter 17.

The marketing characteristics of services differ significantly from those of goods:

1. The intangible nature of many services makes the consumer's choice more difficult than with goods.
2. The producer and his or her services are often inseparable.
3. The perishability of services prevents storage and increases risks (for example, the revenues from an unrented hotel room are lost forever).[4]

Industrial Products

Industrial products include goods and services marketed to the organizational consumer.

Industrial products are goods or services purchased for use in the production of other goods or services, in the operation of a business, or for resale to other consumers. Industrial products include heavy machinery, raw materials, typewriters, janitorial services, and cash registers. An industrial buyer may be a manufacturer, wholesaler, retailer, or government or other nonprofit organization.

Industrial Goods

Installations and accessory equipment are expensive capital items that do not become part of the final product.

Industrial goods are categorized by the degree of decision making that is necessary in making a purchase, costs, rapidity of consumption, role in production, and change in form. Because industrial-goods sellers normally seek out potential purchasers, store shopping behavior is not a useful classification method. Installations, accessory equipment, raw materials, component materials, fabricated parts, and supplies are the types of industrial goods. See Table 7-2.

Installations and **accessory equipment** are capital items. They are used in the production process and do not become part of the final product. Installations involve a high degree of decision making (usually by several upper-level executives), are very expensive, last for many years, and do not change form. The major marketing tasks are direct selling from the manufacturer to the purchaser, lengthy negotiations about features and terms, providing complementary services such as maintenance and repair, tailoring products to the desires of the buyer, offering technical expertise, and team selling (in which various salespeople have different areas of expertise and interact with specialized executives of the buyer). Examples of installations are buildings, assembly lines, major equipment, large machine tools, and printing presses.

Accessory equipment requires a moderate amount of decision making, is less expensive than installations, lasts a number of years, and

Table 7-2 **Characteristics of Industrial Goods**

	Type of Good					
Characteristics	*Installations*	*Accessory Equipment*	*Raw Materials*	*Component Materials*	*Fabricated Parts*	*Supplies*
Degree of consumer decision making	High	Moderate	Low	Low	Low	Very low
Per unit costs	High	Moderate	Low	Low	Low	Very low
Rapidity of consumption	Very low	Low	High	High	High	High
Item becomes part of final product	No	No	Yes	Yes	Yes	No
Item undergoes changes in form	No	No	Yes	Yes	No	No
Major consumer desire	Long-term production facility	Modern equipment	Continuous, cost-efficient, graded materials	Continuous, cost-efficient, specified materials	Continuous, cost-efficient, fabricated materials	Continuous, cost-efficient supplies
Examples	Manufacturing plant, assembly line	Truck, drill press	Iron, copper	Steel, textiles	Battery, transistor	Pencils, stationery

does not become part of the final product or change its form. The major marketing tasks are tying sales to those of installations; providing a variety of choices in price, size, and capacity; employing a strong channel or sales force; stressing durability and efficiency; and providing technical and maintenance support. Examples of accessory equipment are drill presses, motor trucks, and lift trucks.

Raw materials, component materials, and ***fabricated parts*** are used in production or become part of final products. They are expense rather than capital items. They require limited decision making by the buyer, are inexpensive on a per unit basis, and are rapidly consumed. Raw materials are unprocessed primary materials from extractive and agricultural industries—minerals, crude petroleum, crops, and iron ore, for example. Component materials are semimanufactured goods that undergo further changes in form—steel, cement, wire, textiles, and basic chemicals, for example. Fabricated parts are placed into a product without further changes in form—electric motors, automobile batteries, refrigerator thermostats, and transistors, for example.

Raw materials, component materials, and fabricated parts are consumed in production and are considered expense items.

The major marketing tasks for materials and parts are to ensure continuity in shipments, quality items, and prompt delivery; actively pursue reorders; implement standardized pricing; employ active channel members or sales personnel; seek long-term contracts; and satisfy specifications set by buyers.

Industrial supplies are convenience goods that are necessary for the daily operation of the firm. These goods can be maintenance supplies, such as lightbulbs, cleaning materials, and paint; repair supplies,

Industrial supplies are used in daily operations.

such as rivets, screws, nuts, and bolts; or operating supplies, such as stationery, pens, and business cards.

Industrial supplies do not require extensive decision making by the buyer, are very inexpensive on a per unit basis, are rapidly consumed, and do not become part of the finished product. Marketing emphasis is on availability, promptness, and ease of ordering.

Industrial Services

Industrial services are maintenance and repair, and business advisory.

Industrial services are of two general types: maintenance and repair, and business advisory. Maintenance and repair services include painting, machinery repair, and janitorial services. Business advisory services include management consulting, advertising agency services, accounting services, and legal services.

Industrial services are intangible, the producer and his or her service are inseparable, and services are perishable. They are frequently purchased on a contract or retainer basis, and some firms undertake the services internally. A general principle is that services can be shifted to others, but not eliminated.

Elements of a Product Mix

A *product item* is a specific model, brand, or size of a product; a *product line* is a group of closely related items; a *product mix* is all the firm's product lines.

After determining the type(s) of products it will offer, a firm needs to outline the variety and assortment of those products. A ***product item*** is a specific model, brand, or size of a product that the company sells, such as a four-door Cutlass, Polaroid One-Step camera, or twelve-ounce can of Dr. Pepper.

Usually, a company markets many products items. A ***product line*** is a group of closely related items. For example, Beatrice Foods makes Good 'N Plenty, Good 'N Fruity, and Rothschilds candy; S. C. Johnson & Son produces Brite, Step Saver, Future, Klear, and Glo Coat floor cleaners; Macmillan publishes a number of college textbooks in marketing; and local telephone companies provide many different monthly telephone services (such as flat rate or unlimited rate) for customers.

The ***product mix*** consists of all the different product lines a firm offers. For instance, American Home Products manufactures prescription and packaged medicines, food products, home products, and housewares. Among its brands are Anacin, Dristan, Preparation H, Sleep Eze, Woolite, Easy Off, Sani-Flush, Ekco, Chef Boy-Ar-Dee, and Brach. Figure 7-2 shows Campbell Soup Company's product mix.

A product mix can be defined in terms of its *width, depth,* and *consistency.*

A product mix can be described by its ***width*** (based on the number of different product lines it has), ***depth*** (based on the number of product items within each product line), and ***consistency*** (based on the relationship among product lines in terms of their sharing a common end-use, distribution outlets, consumer group[s], and price range).

A wide mix enables a firm to diversify its products, appeal to different consumer needs, and encourage one-stop shopping. It also requires resource investments and expertise in different product categories. A deep mix can satisfy the needs of several consumer segments for the same product, maximize shelf space, prevent competitors, cover a range of prices, and sustain dealer support. It also imposes higher costs

Figure 7-2
Campbell's Product Mix

Campbell's domestic and international product lines are represented here. Included are retail operations such as H. T. McDoogal's and Pietro's restaurants. The company is divided into 5 major divisions: Campbell U. S., Vlasic Foods, Pepperidge Farm, other U. S. (such as restaurants), and International.

for inventory, product alterations, and order processing. In addition, there may be some difficulty in differentiating between two similar product items. A consistent mix is generally easier to manage than an inconsistent one. It allows the company to concentrate marketing and production expertise, create a strong image, and generate solid channel relations. However, excessive consistency may leave the firm vulnerable to environmental threats (such as resource shortages), cyclical or seasonal fluctuations, or decreased growth potential, because all the emphasis is on a limited product assortment.

The potential benefits of diversification sometimes cause firms to develop products outside their marketing and production expertise. For instance, Gillette had to abandon its pocket calculator and digital watch product lines when it found it did not possess competence in these areas. Most of Gillette's products are low-cost, repeat-purchase items.

Product Management Organizations

There are several organizational forms of product management from which a firm may choose: marketing manager, product manager, product-planning committee, new-product manager, and venture team.

All marketing reports to one manager in a *marketing-manager system*.

Under a ***marketing-manager system*** all the functional areas of marketing report to one manager. These areas include sales, advertising, sales promotion, and product planning. This type of system works well for companies with a line of similar products or one dominant product line. It may be less successful when there are many products and brands and each requires a different marketing mix. Pepsi, Purex, Eastman Kodak, and Levi Strauss are companies that use some form of marketing-manager system.

A manager handles new and existing products in one or a group of categories in the *product (brand) manager system*.

With a ***product (brand) manager system*** there is a middle manager who focuses on a single product or a small group of products. This manager handles new and existing products and is involved with everything from marketing research to package design to advertising.[5] The product-manager system allows each product or brand to receive adequate attention. It works well when there are many distinct products or brands, each requiring individual expertise and marketing decisions. There are two problems with this system: lack of authority for the product manager and inadequate attention to new products. General Mills, Nabisco, Pillsbury, Procter & Gamble, Colgate-Palmolive, Lever Brothers, and Lehn-Fink are companies using product managers.

A *product-planning committee* contains executives who handle product development part-time.

A ***product-planning committee*** is staffed by executives from functional areas, including marketing, production, engineering, finance, and research and development (R&D). The committee handles product approval, evaluation, and development on a part-time basis. Once a product is introduced in the market, the committee usually disbands and turns it over to a product manager. This system enables management to have a strong input into product decisions; however, it meets on an irregular basis and must pass projects on to line managers. The product-planning committee functions best as a supplement to other methods.

In a *new-product manager system,* there are separate managers for new and existing products.

A ***new-product manager system*** has product managers for existing products and new-product managers for new products. This ensures adequate time, resources, enthusiasm, and expertise for new products. After a new product is introduced, it is managed by a product manager. The new-product manager system can be costly, lead to conflicts, and cause discontinuity when the product is introduced. General Foods, General Electric, NCR, and Johnson & Johnson use new-product managers.

A *venture team* is an autmomous department that manages new-product development.

A ***venture team*** is a small, independent department consisting of a broad range of specialists who manage a product's entire new-product development process from idea generation to market introduction. Team members work on a full-time basis and function as a separate unit within the company. The team disbands when the product is introduced. A venture team provides adequate resources, a flexible environment, expertise, and continuity. It is also expensive to establish and operate. Xerox, Polaroid, Monsanto, Westinghouse, and Texas Instruments use venture teams.

The correct organizational form depends on the diversity of the firm's offerings, the number of new products introduced, company resources, and management expertise. A combination of forms may also be highly desirable.

Product Positioning

Product positioning enables the firm to map its offerings in terms of consumer perceptions and desires, competition, other company products, and environmental changes.[6] Consumer perceptions are the images consumers have of products, both a company's and competitors'. Consumer desires refer to the attributes consumers would like products to possess—that is, their ***ideal points***. Competitive product positioning refers to the perceptions consumers have of a firm relative to its competitors. Company product positioning shows a firm how consumers perceive the firm's different brands within the same product line and the relationship of those brands to each other.

A company must also monitor environmental changes that would alter the manner in which its products are viewed. These changes include new products by competitors, changing consumer profiles, new technology, negative publicity, and resource availability.

An illustration of product positioning is shown in Figure 7-3. Six national brands of jeans and a store brand (Levi's Gap jeans) are rated by consumers on the basis of price and status. Sasson, Calvin Klein, Jordache, and Gloria Vanderbilt are perceived as high-priced status jeans. Levi and Lee are viewed as reasonably priced "old reliables." Gap store jeans are ranked much lower in price and in status. Each of the types of jeans has carved out a distinctive product position that matches an ideal point (market segment): I_1—status seeker, I_2—dependable shopper, and I_3—economizer. There is no overlap among these categories.

An examination of competitive product positioning reveals that the status jean segment of the market is highly saturated, and that all of these jeans are viewed as relatively similar by consumers. The "old reliable" and economizing segments have much less competition. When evaluating the level of competition, the firm must consider the size of the market segments (how many consumers).

From an analysis of company product positioning, Levi sees that its traditional and Gap store jeans appeal to different market segments, and that it has no product to attract status-conscious consumers. Levi has clearly decided not to pursue the status jeans segment. It realizes that competition in this segment is intense and believes its current offerings appeal to two large and stable market segments (whereas status jeans may be more of a fad).

Product positioning is based on consumer perceptions and desires. Ideal points represent the combination of attributes desired.

Figure 7-3
Product Positioning of Jeans

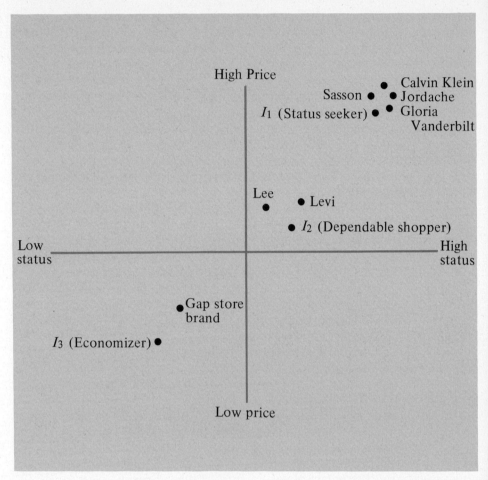

Another example of product positioning involves Glass* Plus, which Texize introduced a few years ago as a new cleaning product to compete with Windex. At that time, Windex was the undisputed leader among glass cleaners. Other new cleaners had failed to gain a major part of the market by attacking Windex directly.

Texize discovered a differential advantage of Glass* Plus through consumer usage studies. These studies showed that many customers used Windex for cleaning items other than mirrors and windows, despite its perception as a window cleaner. Consumers believed there was no other product available for cleaning shiny surfaces. By positioning Glass* Plus as the "glass, appliance, and cabinet cleaner all in one" and stressing "I don't do windows," Texize was able to attack Windex in the area where it was weakest. Today, Glass* Plus is a strong second in the market.[7] See Figure 7-4.

Branding

An important part of product planning is branding, the procedure a firm follows in researching, developing, and implementing its brand(s). A

Figure 7-4
Glass Plus

Reprinted by permission of
Morton Thiokol, Inc.

brand is a name, design, or symbol (or combination of these) that identifies the products and services of a seller or group of sellers. By using or establishing well-known brands, companies are usually able to obtain public acceptance, extensive distribution, and higher prices.

There are four types of brand designation:

1. A **brand name** is a word, a letter, a group of words, or letters that can be spoken. Examples are Lite Beer, Lipton Cup-A-Soup, and New Orleans Superdome.
2. A **brand mark** is a symbol, design, or distinctive coloring or lettering. Examples are Ralston-Purina's checkerboard and Prudential's rock.
3. A **trade character** is a brand mark that is personified. Examples are Ronald McDonald, Borden's Elsie the Cow, and Morton Salt's umbrella girl.
4. A **trademark** is a brand name, brand mark, or trade character or combination thereof that is given legal protection. When it is used, a registered trademark is followed by ®. Examples are Panasonic®, Scrabble®, and MasterCard®.

Brand names, brand marks, and trade characters are marketing designations for products and services. They do not offer legal protection against use by competitors, unless they are registered as trademarks under the regulations of the Lanham Act. Trademarks provide legal remedies against firms using "confusingly similar" names, designs, or symbols. Trademarks are discussed more fully later in this section.

In the U.S., there are over 300,000 brand names in circulation.[8] Each year, the 100 top advertisers spend about $15 billion advertising their brands.[9] Permanent media expenditures (such as a company logo,

A brand is a name, design, or symbol; the four types of brand designation are brand name, brand mark, trade character, and trademark.

stationery, brochures, business forms and cards, and vehicular and building signs) for brands are another major cost.

In countries that do not use brand names, consumers and sellers both suffer. For example, in the past, the absence of brands for television sets in the Soviet Union meant customers could not identify the factory that habitually produced "lemons." The sales of all television sets suffered as a result.[10]

There are four branding decisions a firm must undertake. These involve corporate symbols, branding philosophy, choice of brand name, and the use of trademarks.

Corporate Symbols

Corporate symbols are necessary for a company's overall image.

The selection of **corporate symbols,** such as the firm's name, logo, and trade characters, is a significant element in the creation of an overall company image. Also, when a firm sets new objectives, diversifies, expands, or feels its name is too difficult to pronounce, a new company name may be required.

Until a few years ago, Standard Oil of New Jersey was known by many names, such as Esso, Enco, Enjay, and Humble. It spent considerable time and $100 million to promote its new corporate name, Exxon. The name had to be placed on 25,000 U.S. service stations alone (at five signs per station); 300 million sales slips and other forms were replaced.

Why did Exxon undertake this massive changeover? The Esso name could not be used nationwide. The use of several brand names left the firm with no clear corporate identity. Enco and Enjay had unfortunate connotations or sounds in some languages (in Japanese, *Enco* means "stalled car").[11]

Branding Philosophy

When developing a brand strategy, a firm needs to state its branding philosophy. This philosophy outlines the use of manufacturer, dealer, and/or generic brands as well as the use of family or multiple branding.

Manufacturer, Dealer, and Generic Brands

Manufacturer brands, which are well known and heavily promoted, account for the bulk of sales in most industries.

Manufacturer (national) brands are those items that contain the name of the manufacturer. *Dealer (private) brands* are those items that contain the name of the wholesaler or retailer. *Generic brands* are those items that contain the names of the products themselves and do not emphasize manufacturer or dealer names.

Manufacturer brands represent the vast majority of sales for most product categories, such as 70 per cent in food items, all automobiles, more than two thirds of major appliances, and more than 80 per cent of gasoline. These brands appeal to a wide range of consumers who desire low risk of poor product performance, good quality, routinized purchase behavior, status, and convenient shopping. Manufacturer brands are quite well known and trusted because quality control is strictly maintained. The brand name is identifiable and presents a distinctive image to shoppers. Manufacturers normally produce a number of product alternatives under their brands.

Manufacturer brands are sold at many competing retailers. For each individual retailer, purchases (and therefore inventory investments) may be low. In addition, the presold nature of these brands makes their turnover high. Manufacturers spend large sums promoting their brands and frequently run cooperative advertisements with dealers, so that costs are shared. Prices are the highest of the three brands, with the bulk going to the manufacturer (who also receives the greatest profit). The major marketing focus for manufacturer brands is to attract and retain consumers who are loyal to the firm's offering and to control the marketing effort for the brands.

Dealer brands account for significant levels of sales in many product categories, such as 50 per cent in shoes, about a third of tires, 30 per cent of food items, and almost a third of appliance sales. Also, many retailers, such as Sears and McDonald's, generate 75 per cent or more of sales from their own brands. Dealer brands appeal to price-conscious consumers. These shoppers compare prices and ingredients with manufacturer brands. When they believe dealer brands offer good quality at a lower price, they purchase them. They are willing to accept some risk regarding quality, but store loyalty causes these consumers to believe the products are reliable. Usually, dealer brands are similar in quality to manufacturer brands, although packaging is less important. In some cases, these brands are made to dealer specifications. Assortments are limited and the brands are unknown to shoppers who do not patronize the store.[12]

Dealer brands **enable wholesalers and retailers to generate customer loyalty and to control the marketing effort.**

Dealers secure exclusive rights for their brands and are responsible for their distribution. Dealer brands require large total investments and purchases by retailers. Turnover is lower than that of manufacturer brands. Promotion is also the responsibility of the dealer and prices are controlled by the retailer. Because per unit distribution and promotion costs are less for dealer brands, retailers are able to sell these items at lower prices and still obtain higher per unit profits (their share of the final selling price is higher than for manufacturer brands). The marketing focus of dealer brands is to attract and retain customers who are loyal to the store and to exert control over the marketing plan for these brands.*

Generic brands started in the drug industry as low-cost alternatives to expensive, heavily promoted manufacturer brands. Generic food items began in a French supermarket chain in 1976, and Jewel of Chicago brought the idea to the United States. Recently, generics have expanded into flashlight batteries, tennis shoes, underwear, beer, Scotch, and motor oil. Nationally, generics represent 5 per cent of grocery sales. In those stores selling generics, sales are 8 to 10 per cent.[13] Generic brands appeal to price-conscious, careful shoppers, who are sometimes willing to accept lower quality and purchase for large families.

Generic brands **are low-priced, plain goods that are not advertised. They appeal to the most price-conscious consumers.**

Generic brands are seldom advertised and receive secondary shelf space (for example, floor level). Consumers must search out these brands. Prices are less than those of manufacturer or dealer brands by anywhere from 10 to 50 per cent. The lower prices are due to quality,

---

*Large retailers now advertise their brands extensively. Some, like Sears' Kenmore brand, have become as well known as manufacturer brands. Furthermore, some companies, like Sherwin-Williams, operate as manufacturers and retailers.

Figure 7-5
Selected Generics

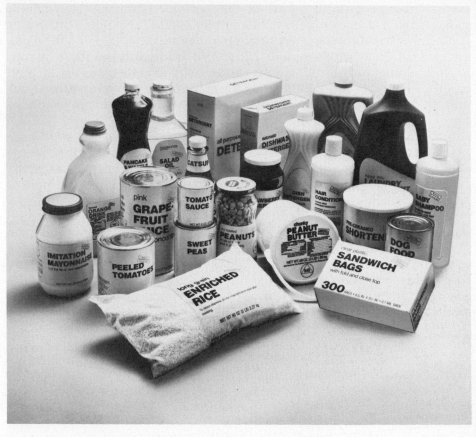

Reprinted by permission of *Chain Store Age, Supermarkets.*

packaging, assortment, distribution, and promotion economies. The major marketing goal with generics is to offer low-priced, lower-quality items to consumers interested in economy. Figure 7-5 shows an assortment of generic food products.

A *mixed-brand strategy* includes manufacturer and dealer brands, and offers advantages for each party.

Many manufacturers and retailers employ a **mixed-brand strategy,** whereby they sell a combination of manufacturer and dealer brands (and sometimes generic brands). A mixed-brand strategy provides benefits for manufacturers and retailers:

1. There is control over the brand bearing the seller's name.
2. Two or more market segments can be reached.
3. Exclusive rights to a brand can be obtained.
4. Brand and store loyalty are encouraged, shelf space and location are coordinated, and assortments are increased.
5. Production is stabilized and excess capacity utilized.
6. Channel member cooperation is enhanced.
7. Profits are equitably shared.
8. Distinct images and offerings are maintained.
9. Sales are maximized.
10. Long-run planning is coordinated.

Sometimes, manufacturer, dealer, and generic brands engage in a **battle of the brands,** in which each attempts to obtain a greater share of the consumer's dollar. Each wants to control the marketing strategy of a brand, obtain consumer loyalty, maintain exclusive rights to a brand, maximize shelf space and locations, acquire a large share of profits, create a distinctive image and offering, limit competition, optimize total costs, and maximize sales. See Figure 7-6.

In the *battle of the brands,* the brands compete for sales.

Under *family (blanket) branding* one name is used for several products. Some companies, like General Electric and Xerox, utilize family branding for their entire product mixes. Other firms employ a family brand for each category of products. For example, Sears has Kenmore appliances and Craftsman tools. Family branding can be applied to both manufacturer and dealer brands.

Family branding is most effective for specialized firms or those with specialized product lines. It enables companies to capitalize on

Family and Multiple Branding

Family branding applies one name to many products.

Figure 7-6

Battle of the Brands

"I'm better-known, more reliable, guaranteed by my manufacturer, and the best in quality."

"I'm reliable, cheaper, guaranteed by my re-tailer, of good quality, and appealing to my store's loyal shoppers."

"I'm the cheapest, with only slightly lower quality and plain packaging. Economical shoppers want me."

Brand extension **gains quick acceptance for new products, but it may blur image.**

one uniform image and promote the same name continually. Accordingly, promotion costs are kept down. Family branding is particularly effective for firms introducing new products. ***Brand extension*** is a strategy by which an established brand name is applied to new products. Quick customer acceptance is gained because customers are already familiar and happy with existing products bearing the same name. The major disadvantages of family branding are that a company's image may be adversely affected when widely different products (such as cereal and pet food, or luxury and economy cars) carry one name and multiple segmentation efforts are minimized.

Multiple branding **applies distinct names to each item or product.**

With ***multiple (individual) branding,*** separate brands are used for each item or product category sold by the firm. As an example, Ralston-Purina markets Purina Dog Chow, Bran Chex cereal, and Chicken of the Sea tuna, and owns Jack's restaurants. Not only does each have distinctive images and appeals, each must be marketed differently. Ralston-Purina must be careful not to have people confuse pet and human products.

For firms that use a mixed-brand strategy, multiple branding is necessary to secure control and secrecy. In addition, multiple branding allows a manufacturer to secure greater shelf space in a retail store. On the negative side, multiple brands require large promotional costs and there may be a loss of continuity. Economies due to mass production are lessened. New products do not benefit from an established identity.

To obtain the advantages of family and multiple branding, several companies combine the two. For example, One-A-Day is a family brand used by Miles Laboratories to designate one of its vitamin categories (the others are Flintstone and Bugs Bunny). The brand has an overall image and appeals to a specific market segment. New introductions benefit from the One-A-Day label, and there is an interrelationship among One-A-Day products. Individual names are also used, so that product differences can be identified: One-A-Day Stressguard, One-A-Day Plus Minerals, One-A-Day Essential, One-A-Day Plus Iron, and One-A-Day Plus Extra C.

Choosing a Brand Name

Sources of brand names range from existing names to *licensing agreements* with other firms.

When a firm chooses the brand name for a product, there are several potential sources:

1. Under a brand extension policy, the existing name is applied to a new product (Pepsi Free, Cracker Jacks popcorn).
2. For a dealer's brand, the dealer specifies the name.
3. When a new name is sought, these alternatives are available:
   a. Initials (IBM, ABC, J&B Whiskey).
   b. Invented name (Kleenex, Exxon).
   c. Numbers (Chanel No. 5, Phillips 66 Gasoline).
   d. Mythological character (Atlas tires).
   e. Personal name (Lipton, Heinz, Ford).
   f. Geographical name (Pittsburgh paints, Utica sheets).
   g. Dictionary name (Sunbeam appliances, Whirlpool appliances).

h. Foreign word (Nestlé, Lux).

i. Combination of words (Head and Shoulders shampoo).

4. A name can be licensed from a firm that holds the trademark on it. Under a **licensing agreement,** the company pays a fee to use a name. Examples of licensed names are Strawberry Shortcake, Annie, Care Bears, Raggedy Ann, E.T., and Donky Kong.[14]

The process of developing and testing a new brand name can involve extensive research. Procter & Gamble chose the name Pampers for its disposable diapers after eliminating many other names. Unacceptable names included Tenders, Dri Wees, Winks, Solos, and Zephyrs.[15] Pampers represented the tender, loving care felt by parents toward their babies.

In choosing a brand name, it is essential that a firm understand and plan for the consumer's **brand decision process.** For a new brand, the consumer begins with nonrecognition of the name, and the seller must make the consumer aware of the brand. Then the consumer moves to recognition, wherein the brand and its attributes are known, and the seller emphasizes persuasion. Next, the consumer develops a preference (or dislike) for the brand and purchases it; the seller's task is to achieve brand loyalty. Last, some consumers exhibit an insistence (or aversion) for the brand and become loyal to it; the seller's role is to maintain this loyalty. In many cases, consumers develop preferences toward several brands, but do not buy or insist upon one brand exclusively.

> The consumer's *brand decision process* moves from nonrecognition to recognition to preference (or dislike) to insistence (or aversion).

With a brand-extension strategy, the product begins at the preference or insistence stage, because of the carryover effect of the established name. Consumers who dislike the existing product line are unlikely to try a new product under a brand-extension strategy, but may try a product under a different brand.

Use of Trademarks

Finally a company must determine whether to apply for trademark protection under the federal Lanham Act of 1946. Trademark protection gives a firm exclusive use of a brand for as long as the brand is marketed. The protection is voluntary and requires a registration procedure.[16]

> Trademark protection legally grants a firm exclusive use of a brand for as long as it is marketed.

Any aspect of a product or its package may be registered as a trademark if the feature is nonfunctional (a functional feature may be patented for seventeen years). For example, Haig & Haig's ''pinch bottle'' for Scotch is a registered trademark. Identification marks of services (such as Weight Watchers), certification marks (such as Wool Bureau label), and trade characters (such as Elsie the Cow) can also be registered.

There are requirements for making a trademark legally protectable: it must be adhered to the product, its label, or its container; it must not be confusingly similar to other trademarks; and it cannot imply characteristics that the product does not possess. A surname cannot be registered, because anyone can do business under his or her name.

When brands become too popular, they run the risk of becoming public property. Then a firm loses its trademark position. Examples of

Figure 7-7
Selected Trademarks of R. J. Reynolds

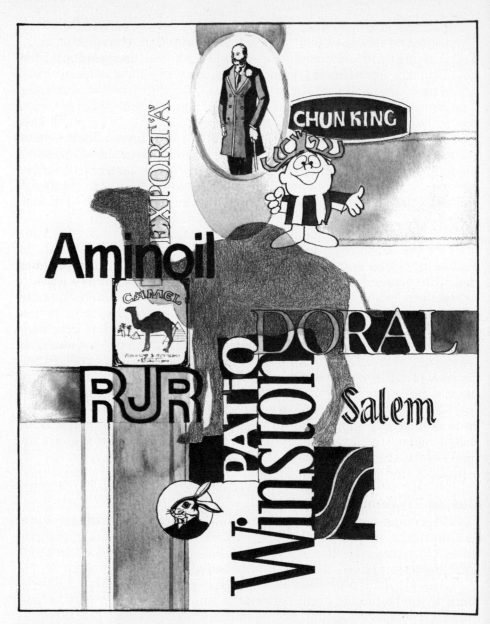

Trademark violation has become a major concern in the marketing of products. Unauthorized use of trademarks or brand names can cast a negative reflection on products and the company which makes them. Shown here are some of the trademarks of R. J. Reynolds Industries. . . Camel, Winston, Salem, and Doral cigarets; "Punchy" the Hawaiian Punch beverage character; Prince Albert pipe tobacco; Sea-Land logo; Brer Rabbit molasses; Chun King Chinese foods; Patio Mexican foods; RJR corporate logo; and Aminoil energy products. Reprinted by permission.

former trademarks that are now considered generic and therefore public property are cellophane, aspirin, shredded wheat, kerosene, cola, linoleum, and thermos. In early 1983, the U.S. Supreme Court ruled that "Monopoly" was a generic term that could be used by any game maker.[17] Brands that are fighting to remain exclusive trademarks include Xerox, Teflon, Levi's, Q-Tips, Frigidaire, Formica, and Kleenex. For example, DuPont used careful research to retain a trademark for Teflon. A company survey showing 68 per cent of the respondents identifying Teflon as a brand name was used to win a court case against a Japanese firm using the name Eflon.[18]

Trademark protection is essential to many firms because exclusive use of brands and symbols enables them to maintain long-established images and market shares. For example, Coca-Cola vigorously polices its brands. It realizes that a loss of brand recognition would be extremely harmful. As another illustration, Figure 7-7 shows a number of trademarks R. J. Reynolds strives to protect.

Packaging

Packaging is the part of product planning in which a firm researches, designs, and produces its package(s). A **package** is an item's physical container, label, and inserts. The physical container may include a cardboard box, cellophane wrapper, glass, aluminum, or plastic jar or can, paper bag, styrofoam, or a combination of these. Products frequently have more than one physical container. For example, cereal is shipped in large cardboard boxes and individually packaged in smaller cardboard boxes. Watches are shipped in plastic boxes and covered in inner cloth linings. A label contains the product's brand name, the company logo, ingredients, promotional messages, inventory control codes, and instructions for use. Inserts are (1) detailed instructions and safety information for complex or dangerous products that are carried in drug, toy, and other packages or (2) coupons, prizes, or recipe booklets.

*A **package** consists of a physical container, label, and inserts.*

There are six major **packaging functions:** containment and protection, usage, communication, market segmentation, channel cooperation, and new-product planning. Table 7-3 outlines these functions.

Packaging functions range from containment and protection to new-product planning.

Annually, well over $50 billion is spent on packaging (almost the

Function	Description	
		Table 7-3
Containment and protection	The package enables the product to be shipped, stored, and handled in a safe and reasonable manner.	**Functions of Packaging**
Usage	The package allows the product to be easily used and restored. Sometimes a package is reusable after the product is depleted.	
Communication	The package communicates a company image through its design, label, color, brand, and display. The package is a major promotion tool.	
Market segmentation	The choice of package design, color, shape, and so on allows the firm to appeal to a particular market segment or multiple segments.	
Channel cooperation	The package must satisfy wholesaler and retailer needs.	
New-product planning	A new package can be an important innovation for the firm.	

amount spent on advertising). On the average, packaging costs 10 per cent of a product's retail price. This amount is higher for such products as cosmetics (up to 40 per cent and more). The complete package redesign of a major product might cost several million dollars for machinery and production. Packaging decisions are generally complex. They must serve both channel member and ultimate consumer needs. Plans are often made in conjunction with production, logistics, and legal personnel. Errors in packaging decisions can be quite costly.

For these and other reasons, many firms exert a large effort in package design. As an example, Coca-Cola rejected 150 package designs for its new diet Coke before selecting a satisfactory package. Diet Coke's package contains red lettering on a white-striped and silver-reflective background. Among the package colors turned down by Coca-Cola executives were blue (associated with Pepsi), silver (associated with Diet Rite), and a red background (too confusing due to its similarity with Coke's design). The packaging of diet Coke was so important to the company because no other new Coca-Cola product had ever used the Coke name in the firm's 95 years of existence.[19] Figure 7-8 shows the chosen diet Coke package and some of those rejected.

Package redesign frequently occurs when a firm's current packaging receives a poor response from channel members and customers or the company seeks a new market segment, reformulates a product, or changes product positioning. For instance, Timex discovered problems with its watch packages, which had an awkward, twenty-sided shape that made gift wrapping difficult. Retailers complained that the pack-

Figure 7-8
Choosing a Package Design for Diet Coke

Reprinted by permission from the October 18, 1982 issue of *Advertising Age.* Copyright 1982 by Crain Communications, Inc.

ages were hard to open and display. In addition, costs were high. Timex employed Chajet Design Group to improve its packages. The result was a hollow, off-white box on a black pedestal. It was easy to open and display and cost half the amount of the old design.[20]

The key factors to consider in packaging are described next.

Factors Considered in Packaging

Package design has an impact on the image a company seeks for its products. Color, shape, and material all influence the consumer's perception of a company and its products. For example, when Mobil and Exxon introduced their high-priced synthetic oils they developed packages of silver and gold/white, respectively. As noted previously, plain packaging fosters a lower-priced image for generics.

What image is sought?

In family packaging a firm uses a common element on each package in its product line. Family packaging parallels family branding. Campbell Soup has virtually identical packages for every soup line. The only difference is flavor or content identification. Procter & Gamble, maker of Charmin and White Cloud toilet tissues, does not use family packaging and has significantly different packages for each tissue to attract different segments.

Should family packaging be used?

An international or multinational firm must determine whether a standardized package can be used throughout the world (with only a language change on the label). Standardization increases worldwide recognition. For this reason, Coke and Pepsi utilize standard packages in all parts of the world. With the United States converting to the metric system (already used by other countries) in the 1980s, standardization will be easier. Nonetheless, some colors, symbols, and shapes have negative connotations in certain countries. For example, white can represent purity or mourning, two vastly different images.

Should a standard package be used throughout the world?

Package costs must be considered on both a total and per unit basis. As noted earlier, total costs can run into the millions of dollars. Per unit costs can go as high as 40 per cent of a product's retail price, depending on the purpose and extent of packaging.

What should costs be?

The firm has a number of packaging materials from which to choose, such as paperboard, plastic, metal, glass, styrofoam, and cellophane. In the selection, trade-offs are probably necessary. For instance, cellophane allows products to be displayed, but it is highly susceptible to tearing; paperboard is relatively inexpensive, but it is difficult to open. Also, a company must determine how innovative it wants its package to be. For example, Ocean Spray and other companies have introduced paper bottles (aseptic packages) for beverages that allow them to be displayed and stored without refrigeration. Previously, most fruit juices and milk had to be kept cold and could be preserved for only short periods.[21]

What materials should be used? How innovative should the package be?

There is a wide range of package features from which to choose, depending on the product. These features include pour spouts, hinged lids, screw-on tops, pop-tops, see-through bags, tuck- or seal-end cartons, carry handles, product testers (for items like batteries), freshness dating, and blister cards (products are placed under a plastic dome mounted on a card with a hole in it and hung on a metal rack). Any one

What features should the package incorporate?

or combination of these features provides a firm with a differential advantage over its competition.

Next, the firm selects the size(s), color(s), and shape(s) of its packages. Included in this decision is the question of how many different packages it should offer. In selecting a package size, shelf life (how long a product retains its freshness), convenience, tradition, and competition must be considered. In the food industry, new and larger sizes have captured high sales. The choice of package color depends on the image sought for the brand. Sunkist soda, an orange-flavored soft drink made by General Cinema Corporation, has a bright blue logo on a bold orange label. Package shape also affects a product's image. Hanes created a mystique for L'eggs by creating the egg-shaped package. The number of packages for any one product depends on competition and the company's use of multiple segmentation. The sales of small, medium, large, and family packages of current detergents make it difficult and expensive for a new firm to enter, ensure maximum shelf space, and appeal to different consumers. Size, color, and shape are an integral part of a package's promotional value.

The placement, content, size, and prominence of the label must be determined. The company and brand names need to appear on the label. Package inserts range from recipes to directions for use to safety tips to coupons for future purchases. Cracker Jacks has for some time inserted toys and puzzles to boost its sales.

Multiple packaging is the coupling of two or more products in one container. This coupling may involve the same item (such as razor blades, soda, or socks) or a combination of different items (such as comb and brush, first aid kit, and tool set). The goals of multiple packaging are to increase consumption of the same item (hoarding may be a problem), get the consumer to buy an assortment of items, or have the consumer try a new item (such as a new automatic pencil packaged with an established ball-point pen).

Individually wrapping portions of a divisible product may offer a competitive advantage. It may also be quite costly. Kraft has done well with its individually wrapped cheese slices. Alka-Seltzer sells its tablets in individually wrapped tin-foil containers, as well as in a bottle without wrapping.

The versatility of the package must be determined. For example, soda cans do not have to be stored in a refrigerator until they are served. Some items need to fit into vending machine spaces (long cigarettes are troublesome here). Packages must be sturdy enough for shelf displays, yet easy enough to open. Most multiple packs, like cereal, are versatile because they can be sold as they are shipped or broken into single units.

For certain items, preprinted prices are desired by dealers. These include shirts, magazines, watches, and candy. The dealers have the option of charging those prices or adhering their own labels. Many retailers prefer only a space for the price on a package and insert their own price labels automatically. With improved computer technology for handling inventory control, more channel members are insisting on premarked inventory codes. The **Universal Product Code (UPC),** used in the food industry, and **Optical Character Recognition (OCR-A),** used

What size(s), color(s), and shape(s) should be used?

How should the label and inserts appear?

Should multiple packaging be used?

Should items be individually wrapped?

Should the package be versatile?

Should the package have a preprinted price and use the *Universal Product Code (UPC)* or *Optical Character Recognition (OCR-A)*?

in department stores, are industrywide systems for coding information onto merchandise. The UPC requires manufacturers to premark items with a series of thick and thin vertical lines; price and inventory data are contained but are not readable by employees and customers. OCR-A is readable by both machines and humans and can handle more information than the UPC. With the UPC, prices must still be marked on merchandise; OCR-A is slower to process.[22]

A variety of firms offer reusable packages, containers that can be utilized after the product is depleted. For example, Welch's often runs promotions for its jellies with a decoratively designed glass bottle that can be reused as a storage container for food products.

Should the package be reusable?

Finally, a company must be certain that package design fits in with the rest of the marketing mix. When Borden repackaged its super glue, it overcame prior problems with the package bursting and the glue drying out. The new package stood upright, was placed on attractive in-store displays, and was backed by an extensive, multi-million-dollar promotion campaign. The name was changed from Wonder Bond to Wonder Bond Plus.[23]

How does the package interrelate with other marketing variables?

Criticisms of Packaging

Packaging has been criticized and regulated in recent years because of its impact on the environment and scarce resources, rising costs, questions about the honesty of labels and confusion caused by inconsistent package sizes (e.g., large, family, super), and inadequate package safety.[24]

Packaging has been faulted for waste, misleading labels, and lack of safety.

For example, when Lever Brothers introduced Sunlight dishwashing liquid with lemon juice, it designed a package similar to Minute Maid Lemon Juice. See Figure 7-9. As a result, a number of adults and children drank Sunlight. Lever Brothers responded that the misparcep-

Figure 7-9
Confusion Over Sunlight Packaging

Reprinted by permission of *Marketing News.*

tion was very minor and continued with the Sunlight package. Said a Lever Brothers spokesperson:

> We feel we've leaned over backwards with our labeling to try to avoid this type of problem. Sunlight contains 10% real lemon juice, an attribute that sets it apart from other dishwashing liquids. We would be doing ourselves a disservice if we didn't call attention to this fact.[25]

The consumer must also bear responsibility for some of the negative results of packaging. For example, the more than $1 billion worth of shoplifting annually adds to packaging costs. Throwaway bottles (highly preferred by consumers) use 2.7 times the energy of returnable bottles.[26] In planning a packaging program, both the benefits and costs of providing environmentally safer, less confusing, and tamper-resistant packages must be weighed. Many firms are responding positively to the criticisms raised here; they will be examined in Chapter 18, "Marketing and Society."

Summary

Product planning is systematic decision making relating to all aspects of the development and management of a firm's products. It allows the firm to pinpoint opportunities, develop marketing programs, coordinate a product mix, maintain successful products, reappraise faltering products, and delete undesirable products.

Consumer products are goods or services for the final consumer. They can be classified as convenience, shopping, and specialty items. These products are differentiated on the basis of consumer awareness of alternatives and their characteristics prior to the shopping trip and the degree of search and time spent shopping. Consumer services can be categorized as rented-goods, owned-goods, or nongoods.

Industrial products are goods or services used in the production of other goods or services, in the operation of a business, or for resale. Industrial goods are divided into installations, accessory equipment, raw materials, component materials, fabricated parts, and supplies. They are differentiated on the basis of decision making, costs, rapidity of consumption, role in production, and change in form. Industrial services are maintenance/repair and business advisory.

A product item is a specific model, brand, or size of a product that the company sells. A product line is a group of closely related items sold by the firm. A product mix consists of all the different product lines a firm offers.

A firm may choose from among or combine several product management organizations: marketing-manager system, product (brand) manager, product-planning committee, new-product manager system, and venture team.

Product positioning enables the firm to map its offerings in terms of consumer perceptions, consumer desires (ideal points), competition, its own products within the same line, and the changing environment.

Branding is the procedure a firm follows in formulating its brand(s). A brand is a name, design, or symbol (or combination of these) that identifies a product or service. A brand name is a word, letter, or group of words or letters that can be spoken. A brand mark is a symbol, design, or distinctive coloring or lettering. A trade character is a personified brand mark. A trademark is a brand given legal protection under the Lanham Act.

Four decisions are necessary in branding. First, corporate symbols are determined and, if applicable, revised. Second, a branding philosophy is set. Third, a brand name is chosen from one of several sources; and the consumer's decision process moves from nonrecognition to recognition to preference (or dislike) to insistence (or aversion). Fourth, the use of trademarks is evaluated and planned.

Packaging is the procedure a firm follows in formulating its package(s). A package consists of a product's physical container, label, and inserts. Packaging has six major functions: containment and protection, usage, communication, market segmentation, channel cooperation, and new-product planning.

Packaging decisions involve image; family packaging; standardized packaging; package costs; packaging materials and innovativeness; package features; package size(s), color(s), and shape(s); package versatility; preprinted prices and inventory codes; reusable packages; and integration with marketing plan. Packaging has been criticized on the basis of environmental, safety, and other issues.

After reading this chapter, you should understand these key terms: **KEY TERMS**

Product planning	**Depth of product mix**
Product	**Consistency of product mix**
Consumer products	**Marketing-manager system**
Convenience goods	**Product (brand) manager system**
Shopping goods	**Product-planning committee**
Specialty goods	**New-product manager system**
Rented-goods services	**Venture team**
Owned-goods services	**Product positioning**
Nongoods services	**Ideal points**
Industrial products	**Brand**
Installations	**Brand name**
Accessory equipment	**Brand mark**
Raw materials	**Trade character**
Component materials	**Trademark**
Fabricated parts	**Corporate symbols**
Industrial supplies	**Manufacturer (national) brands**
Industrial services	**Dealer (private) brands**
Product item	**Generic brands**
Product line	**Mixed-brand strategy**
Product mix	**Battle of the brands**
Width of product mix	**Family (blanket) branding**

Brand extension | Packaging functions
Multiple (individual) branding | Universal Product Code (UPC)
Licensing agreement | Optical Character Recognition
Brand decision process | (OCR-A)
Package

QUESTIONS FOR DISCUSSION

1. Would you want to be a product manager for General Mills? Why or why not?
2. How are convenience and specialty goods similar? How are they dissimilar?
3. How can one product be a convenience, shopping, *and* specialty good? What does this mean to marketers?
4. Differentiate between installations and component materials.
5. Distinguish among product item, product line, and product mix.
6. Would a firm ever seek a narrow, deep product mix? Why?
7. Evaluate Campbell's product mix.
8. Distinguish among the product manager, new-product manager, and venture-team methods of product management organization.
9. Draw a product-positioning map comparing Glass* Plus and Windex.
10. What are corporate symbols? Why is the selection of these symbols the first branding decision a company makes?
11. Contrast the battle of the brands with a mixed-brand strategy.
12. What is brand extension? Why is it a useful concept?
13. Explain the six major functions of packaging.
14. Give several examples of existing products that have recently changed their packaging. Why were the changes made?

NOTES

1. Ann M. Morrison, "The General Mills Brand of Managers," *Fortune* (January 12, 1981), pp. 98–107.
2. Claire Makin, "Ranking Corporate Reputations," *Fortune* (January 10, 1983), p. 35.
3. Melvin T. Copeland, "Relation of Consumers' Buying Habits to Marketing Methods," *Harvard Business Review*, Vol. 1 (April 1923), pp. 282–289.
4. Richard M. Bessom and Donald W. Jackson, Jr., "Service Retailing: A Strategic Marketing Approach," *Journal of Retailing*, Vol. 51 (Summer 1975), pp. 75–84; and William R. George, "The Retailing of Services—A Challenging Future," *Journal of Retailing*, Vol. 53 (Fall 1977), pp. 85–98.
5. For an interesting article on product managers, see Carl McDaniel and David A. Gray, "The Product Manager," *California Management Review*, Vol. 23 (Fall 1980), pp. 87–94.
6. See David A. Aaker, "Positioning Your Product," *Business Horizons*, Vol. 25 (May–June 1982), pp. 56–62.
7. John A. Shimell, Jr., "'Thoroughness' Backs 'Creativity' Every Time," *Advertising Age* (October 15, 1979), pp. S-34–S-35.
8. Bernard F. Whalen, "Marketer Designs Permanent Media to Position Firms," *Marketing News* (November 2, 1979), p. 8.
9. Marion Elmquist, "100 Leaders Spend 14% More in 1981," *Advertising Age* (September 9, 1982), p. 1.
10. Theodore Levitt, "Branding on Trial," *Harvard Business Review*, Vol. 44 (March–April 1966), p. 28.

11. James C. Tanner, "Exxorcising Esso—Name Change Brings Exxedrin Headaches and Costs Approximately $100 Million," *Wall Street Journal* (January 9, 1973), p. 1.

12. See Theodore J. Gage, "The Labels May Be Private—But the Demand Isn't," *Advertising Age* (October 11, 1982), pp. M-44–M-45.

13. J. L. Parks, *Generics in Supermarkets: Myth or Magic?* (Chicago: A. C. Nielsen, 1981); and Fred Gardner, "The Generics Threat," *Marketing & Media Decisions* (February 1982), pp. 58–61ff.

14. Margaret Yao, "The Marketing of Licensed Characters for Kids, Or How the Lovable Care Bears Were Conceived," *Wall Street Journal* (September 24, 1982), p. 56; James P. Forkan, "Coleco Rides on Licensing," *Advertising Age* (August 23, 1982), pp. 4, 46; and Kevin Higgins, "Marketers Embrace Licensing to Move Products off Shelves," *Marketing News* (October 15, 1982), pp. 1, 4.

15. "The Pampers Story: A P&G Success," *Consumer Choice* (Cincinnati: Procter & Gamble, 1977).

16. See Frank Delano, "Keeping Your Trade Name or Trademark out of Court," *Harvard Business Review*, Vol. 60 (March–April 1982), pp. 72–74.

17. Richard L. Gordon, "Monopoly Name Doesn't Pass Go," *Advertising Age* (February 28, 1983), pp. 3, 69.

18. Sidney A. Diamond, "DuPont's Teflon Trademark Survives Attack," *Advertising Age* (July 14, 1975), p. 93.

19. Nancy Giges, "After 150 Tries Comes a Winning Design," *Advertising Age* (October 18, 1982), pp. M-4–M-5.

20. Richard Quarrell, "Designing Art Director Focuses on Marketing Oriented Packages," *Advertising Age* (November 26, 1979), p. 60.

21. Robert Ball, "Warm Milk Wakes Up the Packaging Industry," *Fortune* (August 9, 1982), pp. 78–82.

22. See Barry Berman and Joel R. Evans, *Retail Management: A Strategic Approach*, Second Edition (New York: Macmillan, 1983), pp. 175–176, 339–341.

23. "Marketing Facelift Corrects Elmer's Problem," *Marketing News* (February 8, 1980), p. 8.

24. For example, see Bill Abrams, "Packaging Often Irks Buyers, But Firms Are Slow to Change," *Wall Street Journal* (January 28, 1982), p. 29; Tom Masloski, "An Understanding of Overpackaging," *Advertising Age* (August 9, 1982), p. M-10; and "Consumers Examine Packages Very Closely Since Tylenol Tragedy," *Wall Street Journal* (November 5, 1982), pp. 1, 31.

25. Lynn G. Reiling, "Consumer Misuse Mars Sampling for Sunlight Dishwashing Liquid," *Marketing News* (September 3, 1982), pp. 1, 12.

26. R. Bruce Holmgren, "Product Packaging in an Era of Scarce Resources," *Journal of Contemporary Business*, Vol. 4 (Winter 1975), p. 20.

WD-40 COMPANY: RELYING ON ONE PRODUCT* 1 CASES

A chemist for the Rocket Chemical Company invented WD-40 as a lubricant and rust and corrosion preventative for the U.S. government's Atlas missiles in the 1950s. WD-40 was applied to the stainless steel skins of the missiles to protect them.

Soon thereafter, company employees began informally experimenting with WD-40 on their personal property. They used the product on items such as squeaky chairs, engines, and rifles. Rocket Chemical "realized it had a diamond in the rough."

Then in the 1960s, cans of WD-40 were sold to an organization that sent gift packs to American soldiers in Vietnam. The soldiers rubbed WD-40 on their rifles, cooking utensils, etc.; and, they became the biggest fans of the product.

*The data in this case are drawn from Ellen Paris, "The One-Mystique Company," *Forbes* (April 26, 1982), p. 103.

Upon their return home, these users of WD-40 quickly found new applications for it, lubricating and protecting tools, equipment, and even home appliances.

While WD-40 was gaining popularity in the late 1960s, John Barry (who formerly worked in new products for 3M) became Rocket's chief executive and changed the company's name to WD-40. Since Barry has been in charge, the firm has not developed or marketed any products other than WD-40. Worldwide, more than 50 million people use WD-40; and sales have increased for 20 straight years—to about $50 million in 1982. Each dollar of WD-40's sales is divided as follows:

- 44 cents for ingredients and packaging
- 23 cents for overhead and advertising
- 17 cents for earnings
- 16 cents for taxes

WD-40 has 36 employees. It operates one manufacturing facility in San Diego, "where the secret ingredients are mixed in a single vat." WD-40 works with independent contractors who package the product in blue-and-yellow cans and send it to wholesalers and distributors. A large amount of sales are through mail orders.

When questioned about his one-product strategy, Barry replied:

> We're already breaking all the Harvard Business School rules. You're not even supposed to have a one-product company. How can we follow this act? There's fabulous female potential out there. I dream of being under the kitchen sink, I dream of being in the back closet. . . .

QUESTIONS

1. In the past few years, 3M, DuPont, and Borden each introduced products to compete with WD-40; yet, none succeeded. How is small WD-40 (for example, DuPont's annual sales are about $33 billion) able to continue to dominate its market?
2. Will WD-40 triumph with the female market? Explain your answer.
3. Evaluate John Barry's one-product philosophy.
4. What long-term advice would you give John Barry?

2 NISSAN MOTOR CO.: SHOULD A COMPANY CHANGE A STRONG BRAND NAME?†

During 1981, Nissan Motor Co. had U.S. sales of its Datsun cars and trucks that totaled almost $16 billion. Worldwide, Nissan was the fourth largest motor company, behind General Motors, Ford, and Toyota.

Nonetheless, in mid-1981, Nissan announced that it would phase out the Datsun name for its products and replace it with the corporate name. This decision raised a number of doubts among observers and analysts.

Nissan believed that its new brand strategy was vital to long-term growth:

†The data in this case are drawn from "A Worldwide Brand for Nissan," *Business Week* (August 24, 1981), p. 104.

"It's essential to unify the name of the company and the brand name in order to pursue our global strategy and to fulfill the kind of social responsibility requested [of us] by society and governments." Worldwide, Nissan had ventures with Italy's Alfa Romeo, Germany's Volkswagen, Spain's Motor Iberica, and plans for a $500 million plant in Great Britain. It was also concerned that consumers did not link the brand Datsun with the company.

Nissan used a gradual approach. Ads for 1982 Datsun models mentioned Nissan as the manufacturer. The 1982 Nissan Stanza and Sentra contained a Datsun logo. It was estimated that a total $150 million would eventually be spent in advertising the name change in the U.S.

Many U.S. Datsun dealers and others did not understand Nissan's strategy. They felt the Datsun name represented quality at a good price. 1981 marketing research studies showed an 85 per cent recognition of the Datsun name versus 10 to 15 per cent for Nissan.

One Japanese competitor, critical of Nissan's approach, commented that: "If I were Ishihara (Nissan's president), I'd change the name of the company to Datsun." This competitor pointed out that Sony and Olympus changed their corporate names rather than their popular brands. Another competitor added: "Anytime you have a brand name and pull the rug out from under it, you kiss off years of marketing."

A vice president of Datsun U.S.A. summarized the positions: "Some dealers feel that the name of Datsun has been part of their success and are concerned about losing their image. Others feel that one name identification will be better for everybody. Only time will tell. . . ."

QUESTIONS

1. Evaluate Nissan's strategy.
2. Under what conditions should a company change its name? Retain its name?
3. What level of input should the 1,100 U.S. Datsun dealers have in decisions such as these?
4. Compare Nissan's strategy to the five-divisional (Chevrolet, Pontiac, Buick, Oldsmobile, Cadillac) arrangement of General Motors.

Product Planning: From New Products to Product Deletion

8

Chapter Objectives

1. To study how products are created and managed, with an emphasis on the product life cycle

2. To describe the stages in the new-product planning process

3. To analyze the growth and maturity of products, including the adoption process, the diffusion process, and extension strategies

4. To examine product deletion

The Sony Walkman, a portable stereo with headphones for personal use, was introduced in mid-1979. During 1982, more than 3.5 million Walkmans were sold worldwide.

The development of the Walkman began in late 1978, when Sony staff members connected a compact recorder to a pair of heavy and large headphones, and discovered that sound quality was excellent. Then, lightweight headphones were substituted. Other features, such as a volume suppressor, were added. Preliminary research showed that 50 per cent of potential customers would use the product for enhancing activities and the other half would use it for escapism.

After determining that a great potential existed for the Walkman, Sony's chairman assembled a 10-person "Walkman Team" from various Sony divisions: product planning, design, advertising, sales, production, and export. The team was responsible for final product design and reducing costs to ensure a large teenage market. Several names were evaluated, including "Hot-Line," "Stereo Walkie," and "Sound-About," before Walkman was selected. The product reached the market six months after the initial concept was proposed, a year and one half faster than usual.

Beginning in early 1981, Sony replaced the original Walkman with more advanced products: Walkman I, a low-priced tape player with headphones; Walkman II, a smaller and fancier version of Walkman I; and FM Walkman, a radio with headphones. To support these models, more than $2 million was spent on advertising in 1981 and in 1982.

Since the Walkman was introduced in 1979, over 50 manufacturers have produced their own versions of the product. Thus far, these competitors have made little dent in Sony's market. Said Sony's advertising manager: "We're clearly number one. I don't know how close our biggest competitor is, but the Walkman is recognized as the leader throughout the industry. Our marketing efforts for the Walkman have been fueled by the visual and word-of-mouth boost we've been getting. They all work together. And, as far as we're concerned, it's Sony, the one and only Walkman!"[1] Figure 8-1 shows a Sony Walkman.

Figure 8-1
The Sony Walkman

Reprinted by permission.

Developing and Managing Products

Product planning involves both new and continuing products.

In this chapter the development of new products and their management throughout the product life cycle are discussed. Emphasis is placed on new-product development, growing and mature products, and the termination of undesirable products.

As previously defined, a product is an entity with an accompanying set of image and service features that seeks to satisfy consumer needs. A ***new product*** involves a modification of an existing product or an innovation that the consumer perceives as meaningful. For a new product to succeed, it must have desirable attributes, be unique, and be able to have its features communicated to consumers. Full marketing support is necessary.

A *new product* is perceived as new and may be a modification of minor or major innovation.

Modifications are alterations in a company's existing products and include new models, styles, colors, product improvements, and new brands. Minor innovations are items that have not been previously sold by the firm but have been sold by others (such as Kodak's introducing a self-developing camera). Major innovations are items that have not been previously sold by the company or any other firm (such as the first home computer). As a company moves from modifications to major innovations, costs, risks, and time required for profitability all increase.

New products may be developed by the company itself or purchased from another firm. In the latter case the company may buy a firm outright, purchase the product, or enter into a licensing agreement (whereby it pays the founder a royalty fee based on sales). Acquisitions reduce risks and time requirements but rely on outside parties for innovations and require large investments.

After introduction, products are managed during their growth, maturity, and decline.

During the course of a product's life, there is usually a solid period of strong sales growth, as more and more consumers purchase and repurchase it. This is an exciting and profitable period. Next, the market becomes saturated, and competition intensifies. At this point, the company can maintain a high level of sales by adding features that provide convenience and durability, using new materials in product construction, emphasizing new packaging and product safety, offering a range of models, and adding customer services. It can also reposition the product, enter untapped geographic markets, demonstrate new product uses, offer new brands, set lower prices, use new media, and appeal to new market segments. Then, at some point, the company must determine whether the product has outlived its usefulness and is a candidate for deletion.

Product Life Cycle

The *product life cycle* describes each stage in its life.

The ***product life cycle*** is a concept that attempts to describe a product's sales, profits, customers, competitors, and marketing emphasis from its beginning until it is removed from the market.

Marketers are interested in the product life cycle for several reasons. One, some analysts state that product lives are shorter now than previously. Two, new products are requiring increased investments. Three, the product life cycle enables a marketer to anticipate changes in consumer tastes, competition, and channel support and adjust the marketing plan accordingly. Four, the product life cycle concept enables the marketer to consider the mix of products the firm will offer; many firms seek to attain a **balanced product portfolio,** whereby a combination of new, growing, and mature products is maintained.

Companies often desire a balanced product portfolio.

The product life-cycle concept may be applied to a product class (watches), a product form (quartz watches), and a brand (Seiko quartz watches). However, product forms generally follow the traditional product life cycle more closely than product classes or brands, which are more erratic.

Product life-cycle patterns may vary a lot, both in length of time and shape.[2] Figure 8-2 shows several product life-cycle patterns. The traditional curve contains distinctive periods of introduction, growth, maturity, and decline. The boom, or classic, curve describes an ex-

Product life cycle types are traditional, boom or classic, fad, extended fad, seasonal or fashion, revival or nostalgia, and bust.

Figure 8-2
Selected Product Life-Cycle Patterns

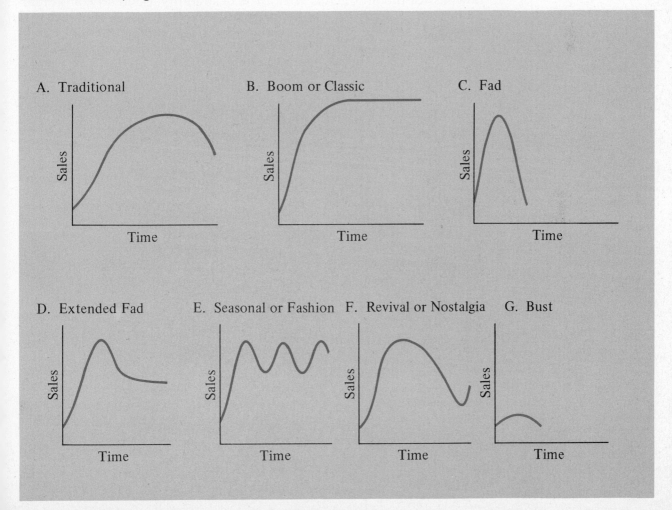

tremely popular product that attains steady sales over a long period of time. A fad curve represents a product that has quick popularity and a sudden decline. An extended fad is like a fad, except that sales continue at a fraction of earlier sales after the initial success. A seasonal or fashion curve results when a product sells well during nonconsecutive time periods. With a revival, or nostalgia, curve, a seemingly obsolete product achieves new popularity. A bust curve occurs for a product that is not successful at all.

Stages in the Product Life Cycle

The stages and characteristics of the traditional product life cycle are shown in Figure 8-3 and Table 8-1, which refer to total industry performance during the cycle. The performance of an individual firm will vary from that of the industry, depending on its specific goals, resources, marketing plans, location, competitive environment, level of success, and stage of entry.

In *introduction,* the goal is to establish a consumer market.

During the ***introduction stage,*** the objective is to develop a customer market for a new product. The rate of sales growth depends on the newness of the product as well as its desirability. Generally, a product modification generates faster sales than a major innovation. At this stage, only one firm has entered the market and competition is limited.

Figure 8-3

Stages of the Traditional Product Life Cycle

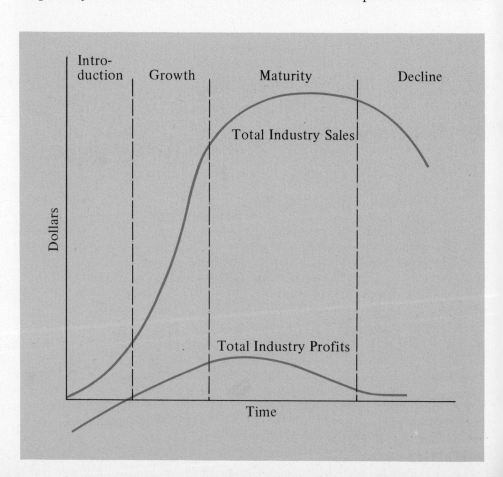

Table 8-1 **Characteristics of the Traditional Product Life Cycle**

	Stage in Life Cycle			
Characteristics	*Introduction*	*Growth*	*Maturity*	*Decline*
Marketing objective	Attract innovators and opinion leaders to new product	Expand distribution and product line	Maintain differential advantage	(a) Cut back, (b) revive, (c) terminate
Industry sales	Increasing	Rapidly increasing	Stable	Decreasing
Competition	None or small	Some	Many	Few
Industry profits	Negative	Increasing	Decreasing	Decreasing
Profit margins	Low	High	Decreasing	Decreasing
Customers	Innovators	Affluent mass market	Mass market	Laggards
Product mix	One basic model	Expanding line	Full product line	Best sellers
Distribution	Depends on product	Expanding number of outlets	Expanding number of outlets	Decreasing number of outlets
Pricing	Depends on product	Expanding to match product mix	Full line	Selected prices
Promotion	Informative	Persuasive	Competitive	Informative

Losses are taken because of high production and marketing costs; similarly, profit margins (unit profits) are low. Initial customers are innovators who are willing to take risks, can afford to take them, and like the status of buying first. Because only one firm dominates the market and costs are high, one basic model of the product is sold. For a convenience item, like a new cereal, distribution is extensive. For a luxury item, like a new boat, distribution is exclusive. Depending on the product and choice of consumer market, the firm may start with a high status price or a low mass-market price. Promotion must be informative and free samples may be desirable.

In the **growth stage,** the marketing objective is to expand distribution and the range of available product alternatives. Industry sales increase rapidly as a few more firms enter a highly profitable market that has substantial potential. Unit profits are high because an affluent mass market buys distinctive products from a limited group of firms and is willing to pay for them. To accommodate the growing market, modified versions of the basic model are offered, distribution is expanded, a range of prices is available, and persuasive mass advertising is utilized.

During growth, firms expand distribution, enlarge the market, and offer alternatives.

During the **maturity stage,** companies try to maintain a differential advantage (such as a lower price, product features, or extended warranty). Industry sales stabilize as the market becomes saturated and many firms enter to capitalize on the still sizable demand. Competition is at its highest level. Therefore, total industry and unit profits decline because discounting becomes popular. At this stage, the average-income mass market makes its purchases. A full line of products is made available at many outlets and many price levels. Promotion becomes very competitive.

In maturity, firms work hard to sustain a differential advantage and stabilize sales.

During *decline,* companies cut back on marketing, revive the product, or terminate the product completely.

In the **decline stage,** firms have three alternate courses of action. They can cut back on their marketing programs, thereby reducing the range of products they make, the outlets they sell through, and the promotions they use; they can revive the product by repositioning, repackaging, or otherwise remarketing it; or they can terminate the product. At this stage, industry sales decline and many firms leave the market because customers are fewer and they have less income to spend. The product mix concentrates on best sellers, selected outlets and prices, and promotion that stresses, in an informative way, availability and price.

The pocket calculator is a good example of a product that has recently moved through the life cycle. It went from an exclusive, expensive item to a widespread, moderately priced item to a mass-marketed, inexpensive item in just a few years. Its characteristics during the life cycle closely paralleled those in Table 8-1.

Evaluating the Product Life Cycle Concept

As mentioned earlier, the product life cycle is an interesting and useful concept for marketers; but, although it provides a framework for product planning, it has not proven useful in forecasting. First, the stages of the life cycle, the time span of the entire life cycle, and the shape of the cycle (such as flat, erratic, or sharply inclined) vary by product.

Second, external factors such as the economy, rate of inflation, and consumer life-styles may have a major impact on the performance of a product and shorten or lengthen its life cycle.

Third, a company may not only be able to manage the product life cycle, it may also be able to extend it. Effective marketing may attract a new market segment, find a new use for the product, or generate increased dealer support.

A *self-fulfilling prophecy* may occur when a firm reduces marketing.

Fourth, some companies may engage in **self-fulfilling prophecies,** whereby they predict sales will decline and then make sure this will occur by removing marketing support. With adequate support, these products might have healthy sales for many years.

Importance of New Products

New products account for a large percentage of total company sales.

A firm's product policy must always look to the future and recognize that all products, no matter how successful, are mortal—that is, they will eventually have to be withdrawn from the market. Therefore, replacements need to be constantly planned.

According to a recent Booz, Allen & Hamilton survey, consumer and industrial goods companies expected new products to account for about 35 per cent of their total sales by 1986. These companies planned to double the number of new products they introduced each year.[3] Another study, by SAMI (Selling Areas-Marketing Inc.), reported that one fifth of all food brands with annual sales of $1+ million have been brought out since January 1, 1970.[4]

Companies have several objectives in introducing new products:

sales, profits, less dependence on one product or product line, use of an existing distribution system, use of waste materials from current production, and image.[5]

For companies with cyclical or seasonal sales, new products can stabilize sales and costs throughout the year. Union Carbide diversified into agriculture, fish, and medical-testing equipment in an attempt to reduce its dependence on the cyclical chemicals business. Black & Decker, the world's largest maker of power tools, limited its output of lawn mowers and hedge trimmers and looked for new opportunities in its more traditional, stable product lines:

> Business could collapse if it rained during the key months and you can't use that as an excuse to your stockholders if you call yourself a growth company. So Black & Decker cut back sharply on outdoor products.[6]

New products can stabilize company sales or contribute to sales growth.

Planning for sales growth must take into account the time required for a new product to move from the idea stage to full commercialization. For instance, in 1965, a scientist for Searle first discovered that aspartame could be used as a nonsugar, low-calorie sweetener. After years of product development and thorough testing, Searle filed for Food and Drug Administration (FDA) approval of aspartame in 1973. Yet, while aspartame was approved by countries around the world, it was not permitted to be marketed in the U.S. until the end of 1981 (and then only in tablets and powder form and as a food additive). Not until July 1983 was aspartame allowed in diet soda. Then, Coca-Cola and others quickly signed agreements with Searle. At the same time, controversial saccharin continued to be allowed in dietary products.[7] Figure 8-4 shows Searle's Equal brand of aspartame artificial sweetener.

New products can lead to large profits and enable the firm to gain control over price. For example, General Motors spent about $150 million in developing its Seville model Cadillac. In return, initial per unit profit on each Seville was $4,000 (as compared with $1,250 profit for each Chevrolet Malibu).[8] Since their introduction in 1975, more than 350,000 Sevilles have been sold. Today, their retail selling price is over $25,000.

New products can increase profits and control over price.

To limit risk, many firms seek new products to reduce dependence on one product or product line. As an illustration, at one time Ocean Spray concentrated its sales on cranberry products. Just before Thanksgiving in 1959, the U.S. government announced that a herbicide used by cranberry growers had caused cancer in laboratory rats. Although the government eventually acknowledged that only a small portion of cranberries were affected and paid growers a $10 million indemnity, industry sales were depressed for years. The incident led to Ocean Spray Grapefruit Juice and the bottling of prune juice in Ocean Spray factories.[9]

Risk may be lessened through product diversity.

Some companies look to maximize their established distribution systems by introducing new products into them. This enables the firms to spread sales, advertising, and distribution costs among several products, obtain dealer support, and preclude potential competitors from entering the distribution network. Companies such as Nabisco, Dart &

Often, companies add new products into established channels.

Figure 8-4
Equal Artificial Sweetener by Searle

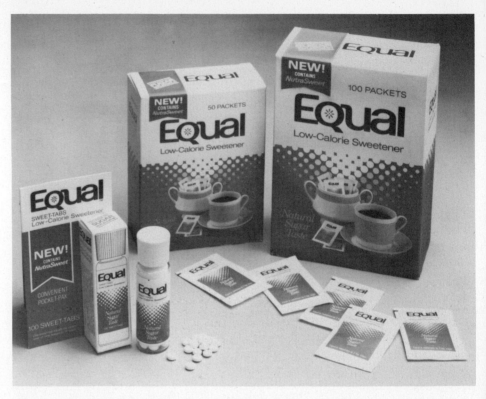

About 17 years after a new type of artificial sweetener was discovered by a Searle scientist, the company was allowed to market a variety of Equal products in the U.S. Reprinted by permission of G. D. Searle.

Kraft, and Revlon are able to place new products in many outlets quickly and obtain dealer support for them.

Waste materials may be used for new products.

A number of firms seek to find uses for waste materials from existing products. For example, fish packers found that by-products could be used for cat food. Cosmetics firms and dairy-products companies discovered that by-products could result in new cosmetic and dairy products. Vasoline is a by-product of petroleum.

New products can build up and broaden a firm's image.

Frequently, new products enhance a firm's image, as this example shows. Long known only for its Crayola crayons, Binney & Smith is now viewed as a "company in the business of providing assorted products that are fun to use and inspire self-expression." Binney & Smith currently markets coloring books, markers, and more than 30 other children's activity items. Just 45 per cent of sales are from crayons.[10]

Good, long-run new-product planning requires systematic research and development, matching the requirements of new-product opportunities against company abilities, emphasis on consumers' perceived product attributes, sizable expenditures of time and money, and defensive as well as offensive planning. In addition, a firm must be willing to accept that some new products will fail because of competition and changing customers; a progressive firm will take risks.

Why New Products Fail

Despite improved marketing technology, the failure rate of new products remains as high as it was thirty years ago. Studies have shown new-product failure rates ranging from 20 per cent for some industrial products to 80 per cent for some consumer products.[11] A comprehensive Booz, Allen & Hamilton survey completed in 1981 found an overall failure rate of 35 per cent for a combination of industrial and consumer products.[12]

Product failure can be defined in absolute and relative terms. **Absolute product failure** occurs when a company is unable to regain its production and marketing costs. It incurs a financial loss. **Relative product failure** occurs when a company is able to make a profit on an item but the product does not reach profit objectives and/or adversely affects the firm's image. In computing profits and losses, the impact of the new product on the sales of other company items must be measured. Even firms with good new-product performance records have had failures along with their successes. Table 8-2 lists some examples of modern product failures.

Under *absolute product failure*, costs are not regained. Under *relative product failure*, goals are not reached.

There are a number of factors that lead to new-product failure or unsatisfactory performance. Among the most important are lack of a differential advantage, poor planning, poor timing, and excessive enthusiasm by the product sponsor. Illustrations of failures or weak performance caused by these factors follow.

Factors leading to product failure include lack of a differential advantage, poor planning and timing, and excessive enthusiasm.

Johnson & Johnson disposable diapers were unable to compete with Procter & Gamble's Pampers and Luvs, and Kimberly-Clark's Huggies. Consumers observed no differential advantage, since Johnson

Table 8-2 **Examples of Modern Product Failures**

Food Items	Health and Beauty Aids	Other Products
Campbell's Red Kettle Soups	Colgate's Cue Toothpaste	Real cigarettes
Best Foods' Knoor Soups	Aerosol Ipana Toothpaste	Sylvania's Colorside TV Viewer
Post Cereals with Freeze-Dried Fruit	Bristol-Myers' Resolve Analgesic	Stanley Works' Garden Tool Line
Gablinger's Beer	Scott Paper's Babyscott Diapers	Edsel
Hunt-Wesson's Suprema Spaghetti	Nine Flags Men's Cologne	Dupont's Corfam (leather substitute)
Sauce	Warner-Lambert's Reef Mouthwash	Golden Esso Extra
Heinz's Great American Soup	Colgate's 007 Men's Cologne	Gillette's calculators and watches
Rheingold's California Gold Label	Revlon's Super Natural Hairspray	Westinghouse's white goods*
Beer	Procter & Gamble's Hidden Magic	Prestone Long-Life Coolant
Seagram's Four Roses Premium	Hairspray	Corvair
Light Whiskey	Crazy Legs (shaving cream for	DuPont's 270 Material Dye Products
Gourmet Foods	women	
	Us (unisex deodorant)	
	Rely tampons	
	Johnson & Johnson's Huggies disposal	
	diapers	

* White goods are major home appliances, such as refrigerators, washing machines, dishwashers, ranges, and dryers.

& Johnson diapers represented a "Cadillac," while Pampers was seen as a "Chevy" and Luvs and Huggies were perceived as "Mercedes." Johnson & Johnson was outpositioned.[13]

While 3M is a large and diversified company, most of its successes have been in industrial marketing (with the notable exception of Scotch-brand tape). Less than ten per cent of its sales are in consumer products. As a result, its product planning for consumer goods can sometimes misfire. In early 1980, 3M began marketing "Mmm! What a Tan!"—a long-lasting suntan lotion that could be removed only with soap and water. The product worked, although consumers complained that it smelled like insect repellent. The lotion received little advertising support, and made no impact on the market. Commented an observer, "It's as though they're afraid to get into the fray and have a product bomb. It would be too embarrassing to have a public failure."[14]

As noted in Chapter 5, Boeing introduced its new 767 jet in 1981 during a very poor year for the airline industry. The timing of Boeing's introduction resulted in the sales of only two 767s over the first two years. Boeing has been willing to wait until the airline industry turns around, which could be quite a while longer.[15]

Excessive enthusiasm caused Procter & Gamble to lose over $200 million on Pringle's potato chips—and still keep them on the market. After reducing advertising costs to $340,000 in 1980, the company spent $8 million on advertising in 1981. Although introduced in 1968, Pringle's had just a 5 per cent market share in 1980 (compared to 30 per cent for Frito-Lay). Among the problems encountered by Pringle's were a bland, processed taste; consumer perceptions of a high price and fewer potato chips than in competitors' bags; and an advertising campaign by competitors that stressed their natural ingredients. 1981's "new" Pringle's featured a better flavor; regular, light, and rippled potato chips; and no artificial ingredients (which had been removed in 1977).[16]

New-Product Planning

The *new-product planning process* includes all the stages from idea generation to commercialization.

The **new-product planning process** involves seven steps: idea generation, product screening, concept testing, business analysis, product development, test marketing, and commercialization. See Figure 8-5. During the process, the company generates several potential opportunities, evaluates them, weeds out the least attractive ones, obtains consumer perceptions, develops the product, tests it, and introduces it into the marketplace. The termination of an idea can occur at any point; costs increase the further into the process the company goes.

In 1968, U.S. manufacturing companies reported that it took 58 product ideas to yield one successful new product. In 1981, these firms stated that it took only 7 product ideas to produce one successful new product. This improvement was due to more systematic and careful product planning.[17]

Figure 8-5
New-Product Planning Process

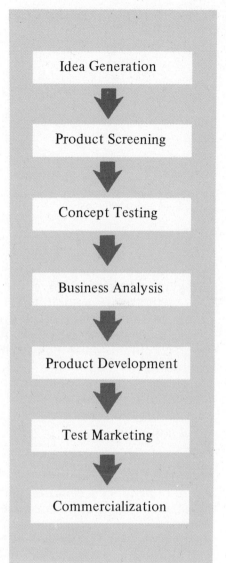

Idea Generation

Idea generation is the continuous, systematic search for new product opportunities. It involves determining the sources of new ideas and methods for generating them.

Sources of new product ideas may be employees, channel members, competitors, government, and others. It is important to distinguish between market-oriented and laboratory-oriented sources. Market-oriented sources identify opportunities on the basis of consumer needs and wants; then laboratory research is directed to satisfying defined consumer requirements. Filter cigarettes, roll-on deodorants, and easy-opening beer and soda cans evolved from market-oriented sources. Laboratory-oriented sources identify opportunities on the basis of pure re-

Idea generation is the search for new product opportunities, through market-oriented and laboratory sources.

Figure 8-6
Searching for New-Product Ideas

ROTHCO
ORIGINAL

Reprinted by permission of Rothco.

"What we need is a brand new idea that has been thoroughly tested."

search (which seeks to gain knowledge and indirectly leads to specific, new product ideas) or applied research (which uses existing scientific techniques to develop new product ideas). Penicillin, antifreeze, teflon, and synthetic fibers evolved from laboratory-oriented sources.

Methods for generating new ideas include brainstorming (small-group sessions where open discussions encourage a wide range of ideas), analysis of existing products, and surveys. When new ideas are being compiled, these points should be followed: ideas should not be criticized, no matter how foolish they may seem; creative concepts should be sought; a large number of ideas should be generated; and the ideas of different people should be combined. Many marketing analysts suggest that an open perspective is essential for generating new ideas. See Figure 8-6.

Product Screening

Product screening eliminates undesirable ideas, often using a screening checklist.

After the firm has identified a set of potential products, it must screen them. In **product screening,** poor, unsuitable, or otherwise unattractive ideas are weeded out from further consideration. Today, many companies use a new-product screening checklist for preliminary evaluation. In the checklist, the firms list the attributes of new products they consider most important and rate each product idea for those attributes. The checklist is a standardized form that allows several product ideas to be compared with one another. See Figure 8-7.

A patent permits exclusive rights for a new product for 17 years.

During the screening stage the potential for product patentability must be determined. A **patent** grants the inventor of a useful product or process exclusive selling rights for a period of 17 years. In the United States any product or process can be patented through the Patent Office if it is novel and useful and plans for a working model are provided. A patent holder has the right to sell his or her invention or receive licensing fees from it. When patents are filed, the information pertaining to them becomes public.

Concept Testing

Concept testing determines attitudes before expensive development.

A firm needs to acquire consumer feedback about its product ideas. **Concept testing** presents the consumer with a proposed product and measures purchase intention at this early stage of development.

Figure 8-7
New-Product Screening Checklist

General Characteristics of New Product   Rating*

Profit potential   _____
Existing competition   _____
Potential competition   _____
Size of market   _____
Level of investment   _____
Patentability   _____
Level of risk   _____

Marketing Characteristics of New Product

Fit with marketing capabilities   _____
Effect on existing products (brands)   _____
Appeal to current consumer markets   _____
Potential length of product life cycle   _____
Existence of differential advantage   _____
Impact on image   _____
Resistance to seasonal factors   _____

Production Characteristics of New Product

Fit with production capabilities   _____
Length of time to commercialization   _____
Ease of product manufacture   _____
Availability of labor and material resources   _____
Ability to produce at competitive prices   _____

*Each characteristic is rated on a 1-10 scale.
 1 = outstanding; 10 = very poor.

Note: Companies will usually weight these characteristics,
      since they are not all of equal value (e.g.,
      differential advantage is more important than
      resistance to seasonal factors).

Concept testing is a quick and inexpensive tool for measuring consumer enthusiasm. It involves asking potential consumers to react to a picture, written statement, or oral description of a product, thus enabling the firm to determine overall attitudes prior to expensive, time-consuming product development.

Business Analysis

Business analysis for the remaining product ideas centers on demand projections, costs, competition, investment requirements, and profits.

Business analysis investigates demand, costs, competition, and other factors.

Business analysis is much more time consuming and detailed than product screening.

Because the next step is the expensive and time-consuming product-development stage, critical use of business analysis is essential to eliminate marginal items.

Product Development

The ***product development*** stage converts a product idea into a physical form and identifies a basic marketing strategy. Product development involves product construction, packaging, branding, product and brand positioning, and attitude and usage testing.

Product development can be quite costly. Innovative consumer products often cost a million dollars or more for development. General Motors spent $2.7 billion in developing its "x-body" series of cars, which were subsequently named Oldsmobile Omega, Pontiac Phoenix, Chevrolet Citation, and Buick Skylark.[18]

Sometimes product development is a difficult process. For example, Gillette developed Dry Idea, a new roll-on antiperspirant that "goes on dry," after concept testing attracted consumer interest. Consumers liked the idea of a strong antiperspirant that was dry on application.

Gillette's problem was to develop the product as desired by consumers. It had to find a replacement for water in the antiperspirant formulation. One ingredient dissolved the ball in the applicator. Another was too oily. A third had a short shelf-life—it became rock-hard after four months. Finally, a proper ingredient was found and tested with women who sat in a 100-degree "hot room" for several hours. It was also smeared on rabbits' skins and fed to rats to test its safety.

Next, packaging was needed. The first package developed was egg-shaped; it made the product feel too dry when applied and allowed the contents to leak. Engineers gave the applicator a texture and built a clicking noise into it to enable consumers to know it was working. After all this, Gillette then decided to continue with a modified conventional roll-on bottle, shown in Figure 8-8.

Last, a brand name had to be determined. More than a dozen names were tested on consumers. Among those rejected were Dry a Mite (sounded too much like a drain cleaner), Feel Free (sounded like a tampon), and Omni and Horizon (automobile names). Dry Idea was selected, and positioned for women aged twenty to forty-five.[19]

Test Marketing

Test marketing involves placing a product for sale in one or more selected areas and observing its sales performance under the proposed marketing plan. The purpose of the test is to evaluate the product and pretest the firm's marketing plan prior to a full-scale introduction of the product.

Test marketing enables the product to be analyzed in a real setting. Rather than inquire about intentions, test marketing allows actual consumer behavior to be observed. The firm can also learn about competi-

Figure 8-8
Regular Scent and Unscented Dry Idea

Reprinted by permission of Gillette.

tive reactions and the response of channel members. On the basis of test marketing, the firm can go ahead with its plans on a larger scale, modify the product and then expand its effort, modify the marketing plan and then expand its effort, or drop the product. Figure 8-9 shows the most popular test markets in the U.S. and some recent brands that Procter & Gamble test marketed.

Although test marketing has been successful in many cases, some companies now question its effectiveness and downplay or skip this stage in the new-product planning process. Dissatisfaction with test marketing arises from its costs, the time delays before full introduction, information being provided to competitors, an inability to predict national results based on one or two test market cities, and the impact of external factors, such as the economy and competition, on test results.

Test marketing has been criticized by some.

Frequently test marketing allows nontesting competitors to catch up with the innovative firm by the time the product is ready for national distribution. In these five cases, test marketing actually enabled competitors to reach the national market before the original firm:[20]

Test Market Brand	First in National Introduction
Arm in Arm Deodorant (Helene Curtis)	Arm & Hammer Deodorant (Church & Dwight)
Maxim (General Foods)	Taster's Choice (Nestlé)
High Yield Coffee (Hills Brothers)	Folgers' Flakes (Procter & Gamble)
Prima Salsa Tomato Sauce (Hunt-Wesson)	Ragu Extra Thick & Zesty (Chesebrough-Pond)
Cooking Ease (Clorox)	Mazola No-Stick (CPC International)

Figure 8-9
***Test Marketing and Procter &
Gamble***

© 1982 by The New York Times Company. Reprinted by permission.

Commercialization

*Commercialization
occurs when the product
is made available to the
entire market.*

After all testing is completed, the firm is ready to introduce the product
to its full target market. This is known as ***commercialization*** and corresponds to the introductory stage of the product life cycle. Commercialization involves implementation of a total marketing plan and mass production.

The commercialization stage often requires considerable expenditures and rapid decision making. For example, Campbell began regional
marketing of Prego bottled spaghetti sauce in 1981, with an advertising
budget of $15 million. Advertising was increased to $25 million for
1982, when Campbell started national marketing in October; this
amounted to about 25 per cent of sales. In response to Campbell,
Chesebrough-Pond (maker of the leading spaghetti sauce, Ragu) added a
new Ragu Homestyle spaghetti sauce and spent $20 million to promote

it. 75-cent discount coupons were also distributed for regular Ragu. Said an observer, "These two brands are beating each other's brains out."[21]

Among the factors to be considered in the commercialization stage are the speed of acceptance by consumers, the speed of acceptance by channel members, the intensity of distribution (how many outlets), production capabilities, the promotional mix, prices, competition, the time period until profitability occurs, and the costs of commercialization.

Growing Products

The growth rate and total sales level of new products rely heavily on two related consumer behavior concepts: the adoption process and the diffusion process.

The **adoption process** is the procedure an individual consumer goes through when learning about and purchasing a new product. It includes the mental and behavioral sequence through which consumers progress, potentially leading to the acceptance and continued use of a product or brand.[22] The adoption process is in six stages:

*The **adoption process** explains the new-product purchase behavior of individual consumers.*

1. Awareness: the person learns of the existence of a product but does not have information about it.
2. Interest: the person is motivated to seek information.
3. Evaluation: the person decides whether to try the product.
4. Trial: the person buys the product and tests its usefulness.
5. Adoption: the person uses the product on a regular basis.
6. Confirmation: the person seeks reinforcement and may reverse the decision if exposed to conflicting messages.[23]

The rate (speed) of adoption depends on the traits of consumers, the product, and the firm's marketing effort. The rate of adoption will be faster if consumers have high discretionary income and are willing to try new offerings; the product presents little physical, social, or financial risk; the product has an advantage over other items already on the market; the product is a modification of an existing idea and not a major innovation; the product is compatible with current consumer life-styles; the attributes of the product can be easily communicated; the importance of the product is low; the product can be tried in small quantities; mass advertising and distribution are used; the product is consumed quickly; the product is easy to use; and the marketer responds to the changing needs of the consumer as he or she moves through the adoption process and seeks to satisfy those needs.

The **diffusion process** describes the manner in which different segments of the market often accept and purchase a product. The process spans the time from product introduction until market saturation. It is in five stages:

*The **diffusion process** describes when different market segments are likely to purchase a product.*

1. Innovators are the first consumers to accept a new product. They are venturesome, willing to accept risk, socially aggressive, communicative, and cosmopolitan. As detailed in Chapter 4, it is necessary to determine which innovators are opinion leaders—those

who influence others to purchase. This group represents 2.5 per cent of the market.

2. Early adopters are the next group of consumers to accept a new product. They enjoy the leadership, prestige, and respect that early purchases bring. These consumers tend to be opinion leaders. They adopt new ideas early but use discretion. This group represents 13.5 per cent of the market.

3. The early majority is the first part of the mass market to buy a product. They have status in their social class and are outgoing, communicative, and attentive to information cues. This group represents 34 per cent of the market.

4. The late majority is the second part of the mass market to buy a product. They are less cosmopolitan and responsive to change. The late majority includes people with ethnic backgrounds and lower economic and social status, those past middle age, and skeptics. This group represents 34 per cent of the market.

5. Laggards are the last people to purchase a product. They are price conscious, extremely suspicious of novelty and change, low in income and status, tradition bound, and conservative. Laggards do not adopt a product until it reaches maturity. From a profit perspective, it may be wise for some firms to ignore laggards because it could be extremely expensive to reach and market a product to this small group. On the other hand, a market segmenter might do well to concentrate on a line of products for laggards. This group represents 16 per cent of the market.[24]

The rate and level of growth for a major innovation may be slow at first because there is an extended adoption process and the early majority may be hesitant to purchase. It may then rise quite quickly. Figure 8-10 shows the growth of color televisions in the United States for the thirty-year period from 1950 to 1980. These sets were first marketed in the early 1950s. Yet only 340,000 households (less than 1 per cent of all U.S. households) owned one by 1960. At this point, sales began to expand rapidly, because of reduced prices, better-quality sets, improved programming, increased competition, and the transition from innovators to early majority. As of 1980, more than 80 per cent of U.S. households had at least one color set.

The home video recorder, another major innovation, succeeded much more quickly than color television, although sales penetration was not immediate. Sony mastered the technology for the home video recorder in 1976. The recorders were priced at well over $1,000 each; and only 30,000 units were sold in 1976. 200,000 recorders were sold in 1977. In 1980, 800,000 recorders were sold. Since then, more than 1 million units have been sold annually in the U.S. There are over a dozen major competitors, a wide variety of models, and prices starting as low as $350.

For minor innovations or product modifications, growth is even quicker. As an example, Polaroid has sold self-developing cameras for more than thirty years and is the recognized leader in the field. In 1981, it introduced a new automatic-focus Sun camera. Because of its past

Source: "Trends in Television, 1950 to Date, "Television Bureau of Advertising, Inc. (January 1981), pp. 2-3. Reprinted by permission.

reputation, intensive distribution, and multimillion dollar advertising campaign, Polaroid was able to generate high initial sales for the new camera and expected saturation in fewer than two years.

Among the many products now in the growth stage, personal home computers, videodisc players, and large-screen rear-projection television sets will be interesting to observe over the next several years.

Mature Products

When products reach the late majority and laggard markets, they are in the maturity stage of the product life cycle. Company goals turn from growth to maintenance. Because new products are so costly and risky, more and more firms are placing their marketing emphasis on mature products that offer steady sales and profits with minimal risk.

In the analysis of mature products, a company should consider these factors: the size of the existing market, the characteristics and needs of present customers, untapped market segments, competition, product modifications, the availability of a new product to replace the

Although mature products have reached their sales peak, with proper marketing they can frequently be maintained for many years.

mature one, profit margins, the marketing effort necessary for each sale, channel satisfaction, the promotional mix, the importance of the products in the overall product line, the products' effect on company image, the number of remaining years for the products, and the management effort needed.

The makers of Listerine, Ivory Snow, *Reader's Digest*, Bayer aspirin, M&Ms, Tide, Mustang, Scrabble, Barbie dolls, Juicy Fruit gum, Rice Krispies, and other brands have worked hard to sustain the sales of these items (in some cases for decades). Each of the brands provides its company with a large, loyal group of customers and a stable, profitable position in the market. The most successful companies offer products that remain in maturity for long periods of time.

For instance, Arm & Hammer baking soda was developed in 1846. Until 1969, the product was marketed simply as a baking soda to be used in cooking. It was called a "sleepy, one-dimensional brand." Because of changing consumer life-styles, sales were stagnating. Then, an aggressive marketing effort was enacted:

- Intensive advertising resulted in 97 per cent of U.S. female heads of households knowing the Arm & Hammer name.
- Arm & Hammer baking soda was repositioned, and different product uses were promoted: refrigerator freshener, freezer freshener, kitchen drain deodorizer, bath water additive, laundry additive, placque remover for dental plates, cat litter deodorizer, etc.
- New products, such as detergent, were introduced under the Arm & Hammer name.

By 1981, Arm & Hammer baking soda was used for baking by only 6 per cent of its customers. The total sales of Church & Dwight, maker of Arm & Hammer, rose from $15.6 million in 1969 to $150 million in 1982.[25] Figure 8-11 shows the basic Arm & Hammer package (with the captions "Guaranteed pure" and "Absorbs refrigerator odors.").

There are several strategies available for extending the mature stage of the product life cycle. Table 8-3 presents seven such strategies and provides examples of each.

Figure 8-11

Arm & Hammer Baking Soda: Extended Uses Lead to Extended Sales

ARM & HAMMER is a registered trademark of Church & Dwight Co., Inc. This picture was reproduced with permission of Church & Dwight Co., Inc.

Strategy	Examples	*Table 8-3*
1. Develop new uses for the product	Jell-O used in garden salads Arm & Hammer baking soda used as a refrigerator deodorant	**Strategies for Extending the Mature Stage of the Product Life Cycle**
2. Develop new product features and refinements	Automatic 35 mm cameras Battery-powered televisions	
3. Increase market segmentation	Family and individual sizes for food products Regional editions of major magazines	
4. Find new classes of consumers for the present product	Nylon carpeting for institutional markets Johnson & Johnson's baby shampoo used by adults Coca-Cola and Pepsi-Cola in less-developed nations	
5. Find new classes of consumers for the modified product	Breakfast menu at McDonald's Industrial power tools altered for the do-it-yourself market	
6. Increase product usage among current users	Multiple packages for soda and beer Jeans promoted for wear at social gatherings Season tickets for sports and entertainment events	
7. Change marketing strategy	Hosiery sold in supermarkets Electronic games priced at $30 (down from $100) *Reader's Digest* advertising on television	

Not all mature products can be revitalized or extended. The consumer's need may disappear, as occurred when frozen orange juice replaced orange juice squeezers. Better, cheaper, and more convenient products may be developed, such as electronic calculators to replace mechanical ones and plastic furniture moldings to replace wooden ones. Competitors may secure a strategic advantage, such as Xerox getting a large government order for traditional electric typewriters. Finally, the market may be saturated and additional marketing efforts may be unable to generate sufficient sales to justify time and cost expenditures.

Product Deletion

When products offer limited sales and profit potential, involve large amounts of management time, tie up resources that could be used for other opportunities, create channel dissatisfaction due to low turnover, reflect poorly on the company, and divert attention from long-term goals, these products should be deleted from the firm's offerings.

Some products do not merit resources and should be deleted.

However, there are a number of factors to consider before deleting a product:

1. As a product matures, it blends in with existing items and becomes part of the total product line.

2.   Customers and channel members may be hurt if the item is withdrawn.
3.   The firm may not want competitors to have the only product for customers.
4.   Poor current sales and profits may be only temporary.
5.   The marketing strategy, not the product, may be the cause of bad results.

Ralph S. Alexander, the first marketer to write in depth about product deletion, proposed a systematic, four-step procedure for eliminating products: (1) selecting products that are candidates for deletion, (2) gathering and analyzing information about these products, (3) making deletion decisions, and (4) removing products from the line.[26]

Low-margin or rapidly declining products are often dropped or de-emphasized, as these recent examples show. Between 1979 and 1982, Firestone reduced the number of tires it marketed from 7,300 to 2,600.[27] In 1980, after 10-year sales of almost 3 million units, Ford removed the Pinto from its product line.[28] In August 1981, the *Washington Star* newspaper ceased publication, after 128 years.[29]

When discontinuing a product, the firm must remember to consider replacement parts, notification time for customers and channel members, and honoring of guarantees.

Summary

Product planning deals with the creation of new products, which begin as modifications of existing products or innovations, and their management as they are offered in the marketplace. The product life cycle is a concept that seeks to describe an individual product's sales, profits, customers, competitors, and marketing emphasis from its inception until its removal from the market. Many firms desire a balanced product portfolio, with products in various stages of the life cycle. There are several derivations of the product life cycle: traditional, boom or classic, fad, extended fad, seasonal or fashion, revival or nostalgia, and bust. The traditional life cycle goes through four stages: introduction, growth, maturity, and decline. During each stage, the marketing objectives, industry sales, competition, industry profits, profit margins, customers, and marketing plan change. Although the life cycle is useful as a planning tool, it should not be employed as a forecasting tool.

Company objectives for introducing new products relate to sales, profits, less dependence on one product or product line, use of an established distribution system, use of waste materials, and/or image. When the company suffers a financial loss, a product is an absolute failure. When the company makes a profit but does not attain its objectives, a product is a relative failure. Failures occur because of a lack of a significant competitive advantage, poor planning, poor timing, and excessive enthusiasm by the product sponsor.

Proper new-product planning involves a comprehensive, seven-step process: idea generation, product screening, concept testing, business analysis, product development, test marketing, and commercialization. It should be noted that a new product can be stopped or modified at any point in the process.

The growth rate and level of a new product are highly dependent on the adoption process, which describes how a single consumer learns about and purchases a product, and the diffusion process, which describes how different segments of the market learn about and purchase a product. The adoption and diffusion processes are quicker for certain consumers, products, and marketing strategies.

Mature products provide companies with stable sales and profits and loyal consumers. They do not require the risks and costs of new products. There are several factors to consider and alternative strategies from which to choose when planning to sustain mature products. It may not be possible to retain these products if consumer needs disappear, new products make them obsolete, competitors exhibit too much strength, or the market becomes too saturated.

Product deletion is necessary for weak products. It may be difficult because of the interrelation of products, the impact on customers and channel members, and other factors. Product deletion should be conducted in a systematic manner.

KEY TERMS

After reading this chapter, you should understand these key terms:

New product   **Idea generation**
Product life cycle   **Product screening**
Balanced product portfolio   **Patent**
Introduction stage   **Concept testing**
Growth stage   **Business analysis**
Maturity stage   **Product development**
Decline stage   **Test marketing**
Self-fulfilling prophecies   **Commercialization**
Absolute product failure   **Adoption process**
Relative product failure   **Diffusion process**
New-product planning process

QUESTIONS FOR DISCUSSION

1. Why is it important to understand the product life cycle? What are its shortcomings?
2. Give an illustration for each of these product life cycles:
   a. Boom
   b. Fad
   c. Extended fad
   d. Fashion
   e. Bust
3. At what stage of the product life cycle is the Sony Walkman? Explain your answer.
4. Why is a major innovation more risky than a modification? Why does it have greater potential?

5. Comment on the following statement: "We never worry about relative product failures because we make a profit on them. We only worry about absolute product failures."

6. What factors cause new products to fail? Can they be overcome? If so, how?

7. How do market-oriented new-product idea sources differ from laboratory-oriented ones?

8. Develop a ten-question screening checklist for a new alarm clock.

9. How does business analysis differ from product screening?

10. Why is test marketing not used by some companies? Under what circumstances would you recommend test marketing?

11. How would a consumer use the adoption process differently when purchasing a home computer from buying a television set?

12. Is the maturity stage a good or bad position for a product to occupy? Explain.

13. Select a product that has been in existence for ten or more years and explain why it cannot be rejuvenated.

14. Why is product deletion so difficult?

NOTES

1. Madeleine Dreyfack, "Sony Walkman Off to a Running Start," *Marketing & Media Decisions* (October 1981), pp. 70ff.; and Shu Ueyama, "The Selling of the 'Walkman' (or It Almost Got Called 'Sound-About')," *Advertising Age* (March 22, 1982), pp. M-2, M-3, M-37.

2. For example, see John E. Swan and David R. Rink, "Fitting Marketing Strategy to Varying Product Life Cycles," *Business Horizons*, Vol. 25 (January–February 1982), pp. 72–76.

3. Thomas D. Kuczmarksi and Steven J. Silver, "Strategy: The Key to Successful New Product Development," *Management Review*, Vol. 71 (July 1982), pp. 26–40.

4. "SAMI Says: 19% of $1 Million Food Store Brands Were Introduced in Last 12 Years," *Marketing News* (April 2, 1982), p. 16.

5. Adapted from George A. Steiner, *Top Management Planning* (New York: Macmillan, 1969).

6. Paul W. Sturm, "Keep 'Em Coming," *Forbes* (February 5, 1979), p. 56.

7. Leslie Wayne, "Searle's Push into Sweeteners," *New York Times* (October 24, 1982), Section 3, p. 4; and Jennifer Alter, "Something Old, Something New Sweeten Searle's Sales Picture," *Advertising Age* (February 14, 1983), pp. 4, 64.

8. "The Mark of Dominance," *Forbes* (April 1, 1977), pp. 62–64.

9. Michael Knight, "Ocean Spray's Aggressive Marketing Plan Pays Off," *New York Times* (May 28, 1978), pp. C1, C7.

10. Gay Jervey, "New Products Painting Rosy Future for Crayola," *Advertising Age* (January 11, 1982), p. 4.

11. C. Merle Crawford, "Marketing Research and the New Product Failure Rate," *Journal of Marketing*, Vol. 41 (April 1977), p. 51.

12. Kuczmarksi and Silver, "Strategy: The Key to Successful New Product Development," p. 40.

13. "Diaper Rash at Johnson & Johnson," *Business Week* (June 16, 1980), pp. 63–64.

14. Lee Smith, "The Lures and Limits of Innovation," *Fortune* (October 20, 1980), pp. 84–94.

15. Alexander Stuart, "Boeing's New Beauties Are a Tough Sell," *Fortune* (October 18, 1982), pp. 114–120.

16. Dean Rotbart, "In Spite of Huge Losses, Procter & Gamble Tries Once More to Revive Pringle's Chips," *Wall Street Journal* (October 7, 1981), pp. 29, 42.

17. *Product Management in the 1980s* (New York: Booz, Allen & Hamilton, 1982).

18. Pamela G. Hollie, "G.M. Previews Fuel-Saving Car," *New York Times* (April 4, 1979), p. D5.

19. Neil Ulman, "Sweating It Out: Time, Risk, Ingenuity All Go into Launching New Personal Product," *Wall Street Journal* (November 17, 1978), pp. 1, 41.

20. B. G. Yovovich, "Competition Jumps the Gun," *Advertising Age* (February 9, 1981), p. S-21.

21. Betsy Morris, "New Campbell Entry Sets Off a Big Spaghetti Sauce Battle," *Wall Street Journal* (December 2, 1982), p. 31.

22. Leon Schiffman and Leslie Lazar Kanuk, *Consumer Behavior* (Englewood Cliffs, N.J.: Prentice-Hall, 1978), p. 262.

23. Everett M. Rogers, *Diffusion of Innovation* (New York: Free Press, 1962), pp. 81–86; and Everett M. Rogers and F. Floyd Shoemaker, *Communication of Innovations*, Second Edition (New York: Free Press, 1971), p. 103.

24. Rogers, *Diffusion of Innovation*.

25. Jack J. Honomichl, "The Ongoing Saga of 'Mother Baking Soda'," *Advertising Age* (September 20, 1982), pp. M-2, M-3, M-22.

26. Ralph S. Alexander, "The Death and Burial of 'Sick' Products," *Journal of Marketing*, Vol. 28 (April 1964), pp. 1–7.

27. "A Shrunken Firestone Picks Its Turf in Tires," *Business Week* (April 26, 1982), pp. 74–76.

28. Ralph Gray, "Putting the Pinto Out to Pasture After a Decade," *Advertising Age* (April 7, 1980), p. 64.

29. Joseph M. Winski, "Why Washington's Star Fell," *Advertising Age* (September 21, 1981), pp. 55–56, 60.

KODAK: A STEADY STREAM OF NEW CAMERA PRODUCTS* 1   CASES

In order to maintain its leadership position in the photography field, Kodak regularly modifies its cameras and film and periodically introduces major new products. Kodak realizes that amateur photographers tend to use less film as their cameras get older. So the firm brings out new cameras that are increasingly more convenient to use and more reliable, thus stimulating higher film sales.

Over the past twenty years, Kodak has marketed these major new camera products:

- 1963—Instamatic, with the first film cartridge.
- 1972—110 Instamatic, a pocket camera.
- 1976—Colorburst, a self-developing camera.
- 1982—Disc, the easiest to use and best pocket camera yet produced by Kodak.

The new disc camera took more than five years to commercialize and cost over $600 million. The camera offered consumers an automatic built-in flash (guaranteed for five years), automatic film advance and exposure control, closer-range pictures, and a very high rate of good pictures (about 95 per cent). In addition, the pocket-size camera relied on a revolutionary film disc cartridge. The camera's models had list prices ranging from $70 to $140.

Consumers were quickly attracted to the disc camera. About 8 million cameras were sold in 1982 (75 per cent during the holiday season); and Kodak predicted 1983 sales of 12 million units. The company also estimated that an average of 130 film discs would be purchased by each disc camera owner

---

*The data in this case are drawn from Linda Snyder Hayes, "What's Kodak Developing Now?" *Fortune* (March 23, 1981), pp. 78–91; "Kodak Fights Back," *Business Week* (February 1, 1982), pp. 48–54; Lydia Chavez, "Why Kodak Went for the Disc," *New York Times* (December 26, 1982), Section 3, pp. 1, 22; and "Credit Success of Kodak Disc Camera to Research," *Marketing News* (January 21, 1983), Section 1, pp. 8–9.

within five years after the camera was bought; and Kodak makes a 50 per cent gross profit on the sales of color film.

Competitors have taken strong actions to make sure Kodak does not dominate amateur photography in the 1980s. Fuji Film acquired sponsorship of the 1984 Summer Olympics (outbidding Kodak) and started marketing a disc film in 1983. Polaroid spent large sums promoting its new line of Sun cameras. And, a number of new, inexpensive automatic 35-millimeter cameras were introduced by a variety of firms (including Canon and Minolta). The latter did not disturb Kodak, since it sold 90 per cent of all 35-millimeter film.

QUESTIONS

1. Evaluate Kodak's strategy of bringing out major new cameras every several years.
2. Did the disc camera represent a financial risk for Kodak? Explain your answer.
3. Polaroid still has a 70 per cent share of the self-developing camera market, and industry sales of instant cameras have dropped steadily for several years. Therefore, why would Kodak enter this market (at a cost of $200 million)?
4. What should Kodak do with its 110 Instamatic?
5. Would you describe the disc camera as a major innovation? Why or why not?

2 ROBBINS & MYERS: THE MARKET FOR CEILING FANS TURNS SOUR†

Robbins & Myers began manufacturing ceiling fans in 1910. It acquired the Hunter Fan & Motor Corp., producer of the Hunter fan (the "Cadillac" of ceiling fans), in 1949. Over the years, Robbins & Myers added floor fans, baseboard heaters, pumps, electric motors, and materials-handling machinery to its product mix.

During the early 1900s, ceiling fans sold well. However, in the late 1940s, air conditioners began to cut into the market; and eventually, the sales of ceiling fans fell drastically. It was at this point that Robbins & Myers started placing greater emphasis on the other items in its product mix.

Suddenly, beginning in the mid-1970s, a revival of consumer interest in ceiling fans pushed industry sales to their highest levels ever. Nearly 7.5 million ceiling fans were sold in 1981, up from 250,000 in 1976. This surge was due to nostalgia, caused by such movies as *Casablanca,* and the energy efficiency of ceiling fans (which could reduce electricity costs by 15 per cent or more).

At the forefront of this boom was Robbins & Myers, which totaled $250 million in revenues during fiscal 1981. The company dropped its baseboard heaters and floor fans, and expanded production capacity of ceiling fans from 50,000 to 900,000 units per year. It abandoned plans for other new products, such as kerosene heaters and automatic thermostats.

Robbins & Myers' fans were of top quality, having a quiet motor, a self-lubricating central shaft, and a cast-iron housing (compared with aluminum for

†The data in this case are drawn from Damon Darlin, "Sales Plateau in Ceiling Fans Hurts Concern," *Wall Street Journal* (November 8, 1982), pp. 31, 35.

most competitors). The fans were priced at $175 to $300, about twice the prices of competitors. Between 1976 and 1981, 130 firms entered the industry.

Then, as suddenly as the demand for ceiling fans rose, high prices and the recession caused industry sales to flatten out in 1982. And, Robbins & Myers, with its top-of-the-line fans, was hurt the most as many consumers turned to do-it-yourself models. Robbins & Myers responded by selling directly to large retailers to reduce prices (which alienated wholesalers) and promoting customer rebates (which only cleared out stores' inventories and did not result in reorders). During 1982, the firm lost $2.6 million (after $13.4 million in profits for 1981) and discharged one third of its workers.

Regarding the future of ceiling fans, Robbins & Myers' chief executive said:

> We think they're here to stay, and all the marketing research we've done indicates that. It just won't be the leading growth market that it was.

QUESTIONS

1. What are the most significant flaws in Robbins & Myers' product strategy? Why did they occur?
2. Apply the product life-cycle concept to ceiling fans. What stage do you believe these fans are in now? Explain your answer.
3. Describe the adoption and diffusion processes for ceiling fans.
4. Develop a five-year product plan for Robbins & Myers. Include both a general plan and a specific ceiling fan plan.

Part
Four

Distribution
Planning

Introduction to Part Four

Part Four deals with the second major element of marketing, distribution. Chapter 9 presents an overview of distribution planning, the systematic decision making relating to the physical movement and transfer of ownership of a product or service from producer to consumer. The chapter explores the functions of distribution, the role of middlemen, manufacturer/channel member contracts, channel cooperation and conflict, and the industrial channel of distribution. The elements of physical distribution, especially transportation and inventory management, are also discussed in detail.

Chapter 10 examines the wholesaling and retailing aspects of distribution. Wholesaling encompasses the buying and handling of merchandise and its resale to retailers, organizational consumers, and other wholesalers—but not sales to final consumers. Retailing includes all the business activities involved in the sale of goods and services to the final consumer. The functions and types of wholesalers and retailers are each studied in depth.

An Overview of Distribution Planning and Physical Distribution

9

Chapter Preview

Chapter Objectives

1 To define distribution planning and explain its functions

2 To describe the different types of distribution channels, their characteristics, and the factors used in selecting a channel of distribution

3 To study cooperation and conflict in a channel of distribution

4 To show the special considerations relating to a distribution channel for industrial products

5 To examine physical distribution and demonstrate its significance for marketing

Film studios and their retailers are in conflict over the marketing of movies on videocassettes. Each party wants to increase its control and share of the profits in this emerging area.

Until recently, film studios sold videocassettes of their movies to retailers, with the expectation that the cassettes would be resold to final consumers. Originally, the cassettes were purchased by retailers for $50 to $60 each and resold to consumers for $75 to $100. However, retailers quickly determined that consumers were more interested in renting movies for about $5 apiece, than in purchasing them.

This meant that retailers could purchase a limited quantity of several different titles (some video stores carry 1,500 or more titles) and make a profit after the tenth time each cassette was rented. It also meant that cassette sales by film studios would be low. The Copyright Act of 1976 encouraged this practice under a clause stating that "once a purchaser has bought a copyrighted work, he is allowed to do with it whatever he pleases."

To combat these retail activities, some large film studios have begun leasing cassettes to video stores. The stores are required to pay a deposit of up to $100 per tape, a rental fee, and a purchase fee. In total, they are being charged about $250 to buy a tape that used to cost them $50. Retailers believe they will have to double their rental charges to customers in order to remain profitable.

Film studios have also started releasing their movies to cable television at the same time they lease cassettes to retailers. This can affect the retailers' business, since first-run movies are available for television viewing more quickly.

Most of these conflicts are caused by the new and uncertain relationships among film studios and retail stores, misunderstanding the consumer market, and the number of small video stores that opened up virtually overnight. Recognizing each other's problems and making compromises on both sides are needed to ensure long-run profitability in the industry.[1]

Distribution Planning

Distribution planning involves physical movement and ownership transfer in a *channel of distribution,* consisting of the *channel members* in the process.

Distribution planning is systematic decision making regarding the physical movement and transfer of ownership of a product or service from producer to consumer. It includes transportation, storage, and customer transactions.

Distribution functions are carried out through a ***channel of distribution,*** which is comprised of all the organizations or people involved with the movement and exchange of products or services. The organizations or people in the distribution process are known as ***channel members*** or ***middlemen.***

A channel of distribution can be simple or complex. It can be based on a handshake agreement between a small manufacturer and a local retailer or require detailed written contracts among a number of manufacturers, wholesalers, and retailers.

Many firms, such as Mattel and General Mills, are interested in widespread distribution. They need independent retailers to carry their merchandise and perform distribution tasks. Other firms, like Avon and Electrolux, desire direct contact with consumers and do not use independent channel members. Industrial channels of distribution usually have more direct contact between manufacturers and customers than do final consumer channels.

This chapter presents an overview of distribution and the role of physical distribution. Chapter 10 covers the areas of wholesaling and retailing.

Importance of Distribution Planning

Distribution decisions have a broad impact on the operations and marketing program of a firm. For example, a decision to use independent channel members and the kind of distribution channel employed both affect a firm's marketing efforts. Because middlemen can provide a wide variety of marketing functions, the firm's marketing plan will differ if it sells direct rather than through channel members. Similarly, a decision to sell through retail stores rather than through the mail requires a different marketing orientation and tasks.

In many cases the choice of a channel of distribution is the most important one a firm will make for several reasons. First, good relationships with channel members take a long time to develop and are difficult to change. Second, where established channels exist, it is hard for a new firm to enter. Third, once a firm has good channel relationships, suitable new products are easier to place into distribution. Fourth, channel members need to plan and implement strategies in a coordinated manner. Fifth, strong distributors greatly aid manufacturers' marketing capabilities. Sixth, consumers like to purchase products or services in the same manner over time.

Operating costs as well as profits are influenced by the selection and use of a distribution channel. A firm undertaking all channel functions must pay for these functions; in return, the firm reaps whatever profits are earned. A firm that uses independent (outside) channel members is able to reduce its per unit distribution costs; however, it also reduces its per unit profits because channel members must receive their share. With the latter type of channel, total profits can rise if channel members help bring in higher sales than the firm could accomplish itself.

Channels of distribution tend to be traditional in a number of product categories. For example, in the beverage and food industry, manufacturers normally sell through wholesalers who deal with retailers. Automobile makers sell through franchised dealers. Mail-order firms line up products, print catalogs, and sell directly to consumers. Firms must conform to these channel patterns.

The size and nature of a firm's market are influenced by the location of channel members, the number of channel members, geographic penetration, channel members' image and product selection, channel services provided, and the overall marketing program of channel members. In addition, the more middlemen a firm employs, the less customer contact it achieves and the lower its control over the marketing plan.

These examples show the scope and importance of distribution planning. After 30 years of renting its trucks and trailers through commissioned dealerships (usually at service stations), U-Haul decided to establish its own national chain of retail outlets. U-Haul soon discov-

> The choice of a distribution channel may be the most important one a company makes.

ered that company-owned outlets were expensive to build and that its former service stations had turned to renting competitors' vehicles. As a result, it has now returned to commissioned dealerships.[2]

Neutrogena markets a $2.00 medicinal soap bar, positioned between Ivory soap and Clinique. It has 16 salespeople call on dermatologists and leave samples, in the expectation that the doctors will recommend Neutrogena to their patients. In addition, Neutrogena sells mini-bars to 300 resort and luxury hotels, thus sampling the product to more consumers. Through this distinctive distribution approach, Neutrogena has established its brand ($30 million in annual sales.)[3]

From 1971 to fall 1982, Chrysler had exclusive U.S. distribution rights for Mitsubishi vehicles. But Mitsubishi became increasingly unhappy with the sales performance of Chrysler's dealer network. This caused Mitsubishi to alter its long-standing agreement with Chrysler and set up its own dealer network in 16 states, at a cost of several million dollars. The new Mitsubishi dealers would provide complete service and maintain a good supply of replacement parts. As can be seen in Figure 9-1, customer service became a key part of Mitsubishi's revised distribution strategy. During 1983, Chrysler dealers were still expected to make the great majority of Mitsubishi's U.S. sales.[4]

Basic *channel functions* must be performed by some member of the distribution channel.

Channel Functions and the Role of Middlemen

For the great majority of products and services, these *channel functions* must be provided:

Figure 9-1
The Mitsubishi Dealer Network: Emphasizing Customer Service

The Service Marketing Program is evident in the Mitsubishi Motors dealers' store interior. The total design communicates to the consumer that this is the place to bring a Mitsubishi product for quality service. Reprinted by permission.

1. Marketing research—analyzing customer characteristics and needs
2. Buying—purchasing arrangements and terms for items acquired by channel members
3. Promotion—advertising, personal selling, and special sales and events
4. Consumer services—delivery, credit, in-home purchases, etc.
5. Product planning—product testing, product positioning, and product deletion
6. Pricing—setting intermediate and final prices
7. Distribution—transporting, warehousing, and customer contact

These functions must be completed by some member of the distribution channel (the manufacturer, if no middlemen are used) and responsibility for them assigned.

When they are used, independent middlemen have a major role in distribution. Due to their closeness to the market, they have good insights into the characteristics and needs of customers. This customer contact eases the marketing research process.

In some cases, wholesalers and retailers purchase merchandise upon its receipt; in others, the middlemen are consigned the items and do not pay for them until after a sale has been made. Furthermore, purchase terms may range from net cash (payment due immediately) to net sixty days (payment not due for sixty days) or longer. Ownership and credit arrangements are key areas in channel arrangements. When the middleman does not pay for merchandise from the manufacturer until after its resale, the manufacturer risks a poor cash flow, high merchandise returns, product obsolescence, spoilage, multiple transactions with wholesalers and retailers, and potentially low sales to customers.

In assigning promotion responsibility, manufacturers usually take care of national advertising. Wholesalers sometimes motivate and train a retailer's sales staff and help coordinate local promotion among retailers. Retailers undertake local advertising, personal selling, and special events.

Consumer services include delivery, credit, in-home purchases, warranties and guarantees, and return policies. Again, these services can be provided by a channel member or a combination of channel members.

Channel members contribute to product planning in several ways. Channel personnel act as expert opinion leaders and provide their views of products. Test marketing requires the cooperation of channel members. Finally, middlemen can be quite helpful in properly positioning products against competitors and suggesting which products to delete.

Channel members usually have strong input into pricing decisions. They stipulate their required markups and generally prefer to price mark their own merchandise. Court decisions have severely restricted manufacturers' ability to control final prices. Therefore, channel members have great flexibility in setting final prices and their method of payment.

Distribution incorporates three factors: transporting, warehousing,

Middlemen can reduce costs, provide early payments, offer expertise, open new markets, and lower risks.

and customer contact. Merchandise must be shipped from the manufacturer to channel members and then to final consumers. Because production frequently exceeds immediate demand, items need to be warehoused. Last, products and services are sold to consumers. This requires a store or seller location, hours of operation, fixtures, and inventory management.

Through the sorting process, middlemen can help manufacturers complete the distribution function. The **sorting process** consists of accumulation, allocation, sorting, and assorting.[5] It resolves the differences in the goals of manufacturers and final consumers.

Accumulation is the wholesaler function of collecting small shipments from several manufacturers so that they can be transported more economically. Allocation is the wholesaler/retailer function of distributing items to various consumer markets; it is an apportionment activity. Sorting is the wholesaler/retailer function of separating merchandise into grades, colors, and sizes. Assorting is the retailer function of acquiring a broad range of merchandise so that the consumer is able to choose from among different brands, price ranges, and models.

Often, manufacturers would like to produce a limited variety of an item in large quantity and make as few transactions as possible to sell their entire production output. However, a final consumer would like a variety of brands, colors, sizes, and qualities from which to choose and wants to buy a small amount of an item at a time. In addition, manufacturers would prefer to sell merchandise from the factory, maintain nine-to-five hours and spartan fixtures, and have a limited sales force. The consumer wants to shop at a nearby location, wants to be able to visit a store on weekends and evenings, appreciates store atmosphere, and frequently desires sales help. With the sorting process, middlemen eliminate these differences between manufacturers and consumers.

Types of Channels

There are two basic types of channel of distribution: direct and indirect. A **direct channel of distribution** involves the movement of goods and services from manufacturer to consumer without the use of independent middlemen. An **indirect channel of distribution** involves the movement of goods and services from manufacturer to independent channel member to consumer. Figure 9-2A shows a direct channel for final and organizational goods. Figure 9-2B shows the most common indirect channels for consumer and organizational goods.

A direct channel is most frequently used by companies that want to control their entire marketing program, desire close customer contact, and have limited target markets. An indirect channel is usually used by companies that want to enlarge their markets, increase sales volume, give up many distribution functions and costs, and are willing to relinquish some channel control and customer contact.

Two points are important. First, when a manufacturer sells to consumers through company stores (for example, Melville's Thom McAn shoe stores or Singer-owned home products stores), this is a direct channel of distribution. Second, with an indirect channel, a manufacturer may employ several layers of wholesalers (for example, regional, state,

The sorting process coordinates the goals of manufacturers and consumers; it includes accumulation, allocation, sorting, and assorting.

In a direct channel of distribution, the manufacturer performs all functions. In an indirect channel of distribution, independent wholesalers or retailers are used.

Figure 9-2
Channels of Distribution

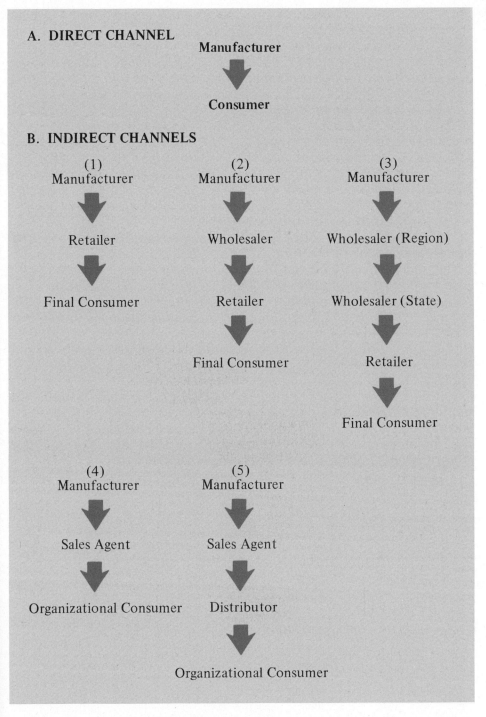

and local) and sell through different kinds of retailers (such as discount, department, and specialty stores).

Because an indirect channel has independent members, a method for developing an overall marketing plan and assigning responsibilities is needed. This may be accomplished by a contractual arrangement or

A *contractual arrangement* outlines all terms for each channel member.

an administered channel. With a ***contractual arrangement,*** all the terms regarding distribution functions, prices, and other factors are clearly specified in writing for each channel member. For example, a manufacturer and a retailer would sign an agreement stating delivery dates, quantity discounts, commissions, payment terms, promotional support, and merchandise handling, marking, and displays.

The most powerful firm sets policy in an *administered channel.*

In an ***administered channel,*** the dominant firm in the distribution process plans the marketing program and itemizes responsibilities. Depending on their relative strength, a manufacturer, wholesaler, or retailer could be the channel leader. For example, a manufacturer of a strong national brand would set its image, price range, and method of selling. It could refuse to sell through uncooperative channel members. Similarly, a powerful retailer could decline to stock an item because suppliers did not conform to its requests.

Channel length describes the number of levels of independent channel members. *Channel width* refers to the number of independents at any level.

In describing a channel of distribution, ***length*** refers to the number of independent members along the channel. In Figure 9-2, A represents a short channel, while B2, B3, and B5 show long channels. Sometimes, a firm shortens its channel by acquiring a company at another stage in the channel, such as a manufacturer purchasing a wholesaler. This enables the firm to be more self-sufficient, ensure supply, lower middleman costs, control channel members, and coordinate timing of products through the channel. Critics of this practice believe that it limits competition, fosters inefficiency, and does not result in lower prices to consumers.

Width refers to the number of independent channel members at any stage of the distribution process. A narrow channel is one in which the manufacturer sells through few channel members; in a wide channel, the manufacturer sells through many channel members. Distribution can be exclusive, selective, or intensive. See Table 9-1.

Under ***exclusive distribution,*** the firm severely limits the whole-

Table 9-1 **Amount of Channel Coverage**

Characteristics	Exclusive Distribution	Selective Distribution	Intensive Distribution
Objectives	Strong image, channel control and loyalty, price stability	Moderate market coverage, solid image, some channel control and loyalty	Widespread market coverage, channel acceptance, volume sales
Channel members	Few in number, well-established, reputable stores	Moderate in number, well-established better stores	Many in number, all types of outlets
Customers	Few in number, trend setters, willing to travel to store, brand loyal	Moderate in number, brand conscious, somewhat willing to travel to store	Many in number, convenience-oriented
Marketing emphasis	Personal selling, pleasant shopping conditions, good service	Promotional mix, pleasant shopping conditions, good service	Mass advertising, nearby location, items in stock
Examples	Automobiles, designer clothes, caviar	Furniture, clothing, watches	Groceries, household products, magazines

Table 9-2

			Considerations in Choosing a Channel of Distribution

A. Consumer
  1. Characteristics
  2. Needs
  3. Segments
 	
B. Company
  1. Goals
  2. Resources
  3. Expertise
  4. Experience
	C. Product or service
	  1. Value
	  2. Complexity
	  3. Perishability
	  4. Bulk
	
	D. Competition
	  1. Characteristics
	  2. Tactics
		E. Distribution channels
		  1. Alternatives
		  2. Characteristics
		  3. Availability
		
		F. Legalities	

salers and retailers it utilizes in a geographic area, perhaps employing only one or two retailers within a specific shopping district. Unit sales are low and unit profits are high. With **selective distribution,** the firm employs a moderate number of wholesalers and retailers. It tries to combine channel control and a prestige image with good sales volume. In **intensive distribution,** the firm uses a large number of wholesalers and retailers. Its objectives are to obtain widespread market coverage, channel acceptance, and high-volume sales. Unit sales and total profits are high and per unit profits are small. Intensive distribution is a channel strategy aimed at the mass market, particularly at consumers interested in convenience.

The use of exclusive, selective, or intensive distribution depends on company objectives, channel members, customers, and marketing emphasis.

Some additional factors are important in studying channel coverage. First, a firm may use a **dual channel of distribution.** Under this system, the firm appeals to different market segments or diversifies its business by selling through two or more different channels. For example, a manufacturer may use selective distribution for a prestige brand of watches and intensive distribution for a discount brand. Second, a firm may move from exclusive to selective to intensive distribution as a product passes through its life cycle. However, it would be extremely difficult to go from intensive to selective to exclusive distribution. As an example, designer jeans moved rapidly from prestige stores to better stores to all types of outlets. This process would not have worked in reverse. Third, a company may distribute its products in a new way and achieve considerable success. L'eggs, a division of Hanes, revolutionized the sale of women's hosiery by placing the product in supermarkets.

A dual channel of distribution allows the company to reach different segments of the market or to diversify its offerings.

The major considerations in the selection of a channel of distribution are shown in Table 9-2.

Manufacturer/Channel Member Contracts

Manufacturer/channel member contracts focus on five components: price policy, conditions of sale, territorial rights, services/responsibility mix, and contract length and conditions of termination. The highlights of a basic contract follow.

Manufacturer/channel member contracts cover key issues.

Price policy largely deals with the discounts provided to channel members for performing trade functions, quantity purchases, and cash payments and with commission rates. Trade (functional) discounts are deductions from list prices given to channel members for performing storage, handling, transportation, selling, and other activities. Some-

Price policy outlines discounts as well as commission rates.

times, commissions are paid to channel members (such as agents and brokers) for performing functions. Quantity discounts are deductions for large-volume purchases. Cash discounts are deductions for immediate or early payment of goods.

Conditions of sale describe guarantees, terms, unsaleable items, and other factors.

Conditions of sale cover price and quality guarantees, payment and shipping terms, reimbursement for unsaleable merchandise, and return allowances. Of particular importance is the guarantee against a price decline. With this guarantee, a channel member is protected against paying a high price for an item that is then offered to other firms at a lower price. If prices are reduced, the original buyer receives a rebate so that the cost of its merchandise is similar to that of competitors. Otherwise, it could not meet the prices competitors charge customers.

Territorial rights set selling areas or outline the market.

Territorial rights outline the geographic areas (such as greater San Diego) in which channel members may operate and/or the target markets (such as small business accounts) that may be contacted by these firms. In some cases, wholesalers and retailers receive exclusive territories, such as McDonald's franchisees; in others, many competitive firms are granted territorial rights for the same areas, such as retailers selling Sharp calculators.

The services/ responsibility mix details the obligations of each channel member.

The services/responsibility mix describes the services and responsibilities each channel member provides to the others. Included in the mix are sales force training, accounting systems assistance, inventory level requirements, delivery standards, and communication. Frequently, manufacturers/suppliers employ full-line forcing, whereby wholesalers and retailers are required to carry an entire line of products. This is legal as long as wholesalers and retailers are not prevented from purchasing competitive products from other suppliers. A hold-harmless agreement protects wholesalers and retailers in product liability cases. Under it, manufacturers assume responsibility for legal suits arising from poor product design or negligence in production.

Length of the contract and conditions of termination protect all parties.

The length of the contract and conditions of termination protect a wholesaler or retailer against a manufacturer/supplier prematurely bypassing it after a territory has been built up. The manufacturer is protected by limiting the duration of the contract and specifying the factors leading to termination.

It should be remembered that not all relationships among channel members are formal. Sometimes firms operate with handshake agreements. However, without a contract, the danger exists that there will be misunderstandings regarding objectives, compensation, services to be provided, and the length of the agreement. The one constraint of a written contract may be its inflexibility under changing market conditions.

Channel Cooperation and Conflict

Channel member goals need to be balanced and differences settled in an equitable manner.

All channel members have the same general objectives: profitability, access to products and services, efficient distribution, and customer loyalty. However, the way these and other objectives are accomplished frequently leads to differing views. See Figure 9-3. For example: How

Dennis Kendrick

Figure 9-3
Manufacturers and Channel Members: Different Perspectives

Procter & Gamble closely monitors in-store displays—but it is becoming more flexible.

Reprinted from *Business Week* by special permission. © McGraw-Hill, Inc.

are profits allocated along the channel? How can manufacturers sell products through many competing retailers and expect the retailers not to carry other brands? Who coordinates channel decisions? To whom are consumers loyal, manufacturers or retailers?

It should be recognized that there are natural differences among channel members by virtue of their positions in the channel, the functions performed, and the desire of every firm to maximize its own profits and control its strategy. The successful channel will be able to maximize cooperation and minimize conflict. Table 9-3 shows ways channel members can cooperate with one another.

In the past, manufacturers tended to dominate channels because they had national market coverage and recognition, and retailers were small and localized. Today, with the growth of large national retail chains, the balance of power has shifted somewhat toward retailers. Now, the control in any given channel depends on the attributes of its members.

Retailers are becoming more powerful and demanding.

When conflicts arise, they may be resolved in a cooperative manner in which channel members discuss their problems and accept mutual responsibility for solving them, or conflicts may lead to confrontations. These may result in a manufacturer shipping late, refusing to deal with certain middlemen, limiting financing, withdrawing promotional support, and other tactics. Similarly, a retailer may make late payments, provide poor shelf space, refuse to carry items, return many products, and apply other tactics. A channel cannot function well within a confrontational framework.

Table 9-3 **Methods of Channel Cooperation**

Factor	Manufacturer Action	Wholesaler/Retailer Action
New-product introduction	Thorough testing, adequate promotional support	Good shelf location and space, enthusiasm for product, assistance in test marketing
Delivery	Prompt filling of orders, adherence to scheduled dates	Proper time allowed for delivery, shipments immediately checked for accuracy
Marketing research	Data provided to wholesalers and retailers	Data provided to manufacturers
Pricing	Prices to wholesalers and retailers enable them to achieve reasonable profits, dealer flexibility allowed	Infrequent sales from regular prices, maintenance of proper image
Promotion	Sales force training, sales force incentives, development of national advertising campaigns, cooperative advertising programs	Attractive in-store displays, knowledgeable salespeople, participation in cooperative programs
Financing	Liberal financial terms	Adherence to financial terms
Product quality	Product guarantees	Proper installation and servicing of products
Channel control	Shared and specified decision marking	Shared and specified decision making

Following are some recent examples of channel conflict:

- Apple Computer tried to stop mail-order sales of its products. The affected retailers responded that Apple was engaging in restraint of trade.[6] Eventually, Apple cut off mail-order retailers and was sued by them.
- Anheuser-Busch prohibited its beer distributors from selling company products outside their territories. Discount retailers were thus unable to shop around for the lowest distributor's prices. As a result, beer prices to final consumers rose.[7]
- Jordache filed a lawsuit against K mart, claiming that the retailer was selling counterfeit Jordache jeans. In response, K mart ordered the removal of Jordache jeans from its shelves.[8]

In a *pushing strategy*, a manufacturer and channel members cooperate. In a *pulling strategy*, a manufacturer generates demand before channel support.

An existing manufacturer is usually able to secure dealer support and enthusiasm when introducing a new product. This occurs because the dealer know the manufacturer's past track record, the type of promotional support that will be provided, and the manufacturer's reliability in future deliveries. Accordingly, the channel members cooperate in what is a ***pushing strategy***.

On the other hand, it will be difficult for a new manufacturer to break into an existing channel. The dealer will be unfamiliar with the manufacturer, be unable to gauge its sales potential, and wonder about its support and future deliveries. Because of these factors, the new firm

Figure 9-4
Pushing Versus Pulling Strategies

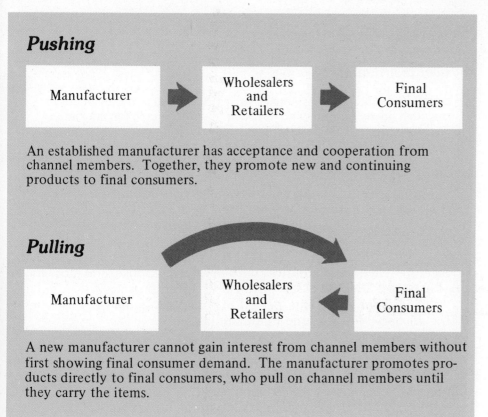

Pushing

Manufacturer → **Wholesalers and Retailers** → **Final Consumers**

An established manufacturer has acceptance and cooperation from channel members. Together, they promote new and continuing products to final consumers.

Pulling

Manufacturer   **Wholesalers and Retailers** ← **Final Consumers**

A new manufacturer cannot gain interest from channel members without first showing final consumer demand. The manufacturer promotes products directly to final consumers, who pull on channel members until they carry the items.

must embark on a **pulling strategy.** With that approach, the company first develops consumer demand and then secures dealer support. This requires heavy promotional expenses, paid entirely by the manufacturer; frequently, it must offer retailers guarantees of minimum sales or profits (and make up any shortages from these guarantees). Figure 9-4 contrasts pushing and pulling strategies.

Industrial Channel of Distribution

The distribution channel for industrial products differs from that for consumer products in the following ways:

An industrial channel has several unique characteristics.

1. Retailers are usually not employed.
2. Direct channels are more readily used.
3. Transactions are fewer and orders are larger.
4. Specification selling is more prevalent.
5. Independent channel members are more knowledgeable.
6. Team selling (two or more salespeople) may be necessary.
7. Different channel members specialize in industrial products than in consumer products.
8. Leasing, rather than selling, may be required.

Physical Distribution

Physical distribution involves deliveries to the right place, at the right time, and in good condition.

Physical distribution describes the

> broad range of activities concerned with the efficient movement of finished goods from the end of the production line to the consumer, and in some cases includes the movement of raw materials from the source of supply to the beginning of the production line.[9]

Physical distribution is involved with delivering goods (raw materials, parts, semifinished items, and finished goods and services) to the designated place, at the designated time, and in proper condition. It is undertaken by manufacturers, wholesalers, and retailers.

An order cycle covers many distribution activities.

Physical distribution includes customer service, warehousing, shipping, inventory controls, private trucking fleet operations, packaging, receiving, materials handling, and plant, warehouse, and store location. Figure 9-5 illustrates the physical distribution activities involved in a typical **order cycle** (the period of time that spans the customer's placing an order to receiving merchandise).

Importance of Physical Distribution

Physical distribution is important for a number of reasons: its costs, the value of distribution service in obtaining and keeping customers, and the relationship of physical distribution to the other functional areas of a company.

Costs

Distribution costs vary widely by industry. For example, in the food industry these costs account for nearly one third of the retail price, whereas for wood products and textiles the costs are closer to one sixth of the retail price.[10]

As energy costs have risen, the expenditures on transportation have increased sharply. According to one report, from 1972 to 1981, physical distribution costs doubled[11], before stablizing during 1982 and 1983.

It is essential for marketers to be able to identify the symptoms of a poor physical distribution system, since it could result in high costs and/or poor customer service. These symptoms are shown in Table 9-4.

Customer Service

A major part of any firm's distribution program is its level of customer service. Physical distribution services include frequent deliveries, the speed and consistency of deliveries, emergency shipment policies, accepting small orders, warehousing, coordinating assortments, and providing order progress reports. Poor performance in these areas can result in lost customers.

Efficient customer service is vital. Therefore, distribution standards are needed.

Accordingly, **distribution standards** must be developed that are clear and measurable. Examples are filling 90 per cent of orders from existing inventory, responding to customer requests for order informa-

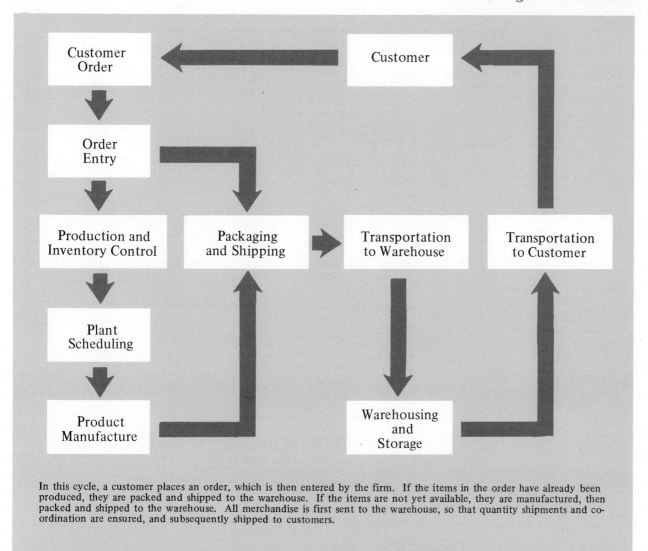

In this cycle, a customer places an order, which is then entered by the firm. If the items in the order have already been produced, they are packed and shipped to the warehouse. If the items are not yet available, they are manufactured, then packed and shipped to the warehouse. All merchandise is first sent to the warehouse, so that quantity shipments and coordination are ensured, and subsequently shipped to customers.

Sources: Adapted from Stephen B. Oresman and Charles D. Scudder. "A Remedy for Maldistribution," *Business Horizons*, Vol. 17 (June 1974), p.62, © 1974, *Business Horizons*.

Figure 9-5
Physical Distribution Activities Involved in a Typical Order Cycle

tion within three hours, filling orders with 99 per cent accuracy, and limiting merchandise damaged in transit to 3 per cent.

One way to determine the optimal customer service level is through the **total-cost approach.** Under this approach, the distribution service level with the lowest total costs—including freight, warehousing, and the cost of lost business—is the optimal service level. The ideal system seeks a balance between low distribution costs and high opportunities for sales. Seldom will this balance be achieved at the lowest level of distribution costs; lost sales will be too great.

The *total-cost approach* considers both costs and opportunities.

Table 9-4

	Symptom	Explanation
Symptoms of a Poor Physical Distribution System	1. Slow-turning inventories	Inventory turnover should be comparable to that of similar firms.
	2. Inefficient customer service	Costs are high compared to the value of shipments; warehouses are poorly situated; inventory levels are not tied to customer demand.
	3. A large number of interwarehouse shipments	Merchandise transfers increase physical distribution costs because they must be handled (packed, unpacked, stored, and verified) at each warehouse.
	4. Frequent use of emergency shipments	Extra charges add significantly to physical distribution costs.
	5. Erratic customer service	Large variations in the order cycle exist; customers cannot depend on the supplier for consistent delivery times.
	6. Too-high inventory levels	Too much capital is tied up in inventory. The firm must bear high insurance costs, interest expense, and high risks of pilferage and product obsolescence. Merchandise may not be fresh.
	7. No backhaul opportunities	The firm uses its own trucking facilities; however, trucks are only full one way.
	8. Peripheral hauls	The firm uses its own trucking facility; however, many hauls are peripheral or too spread out.
	9. Large group of small orders	Small orders often are unprofitable. Many distribution costs are fixed.

Research has shown the importance of physical distribution services in obtaining and retaining customers. One analysis of industrial purchasing agents found more than half stating that they stopped using a supplier because of slow or unreliable service.[12] Another investigation of purchasing managers showed that physical distribution ranked second only to product quality as a major reason for buying from a particular firm.[13] A study of purchasing managers in small firms revealed these problem areas with vendors: failure to deliver on time, the quantity and quality of items delivered not the same as those ordered, and the unwillingness of some sellers to call on and sell to smaller firms.[14]

Physical Distribution and Other Functional Areas

Physical distribution must be coordinated with other marketing and nonmarketing areas.

Physical distribution interacts with every aspect of marketing as well as other functional areas within the company.

Product differentiation—which focuses on many variations in product color, size, features, quality, and style—imposes a heavy burden on a company's distribution facilities. Greater variety means lower volume per item, which increases unit shipping and warehousing costs. The stocking of a broader range of replacement parts also becomes necessary.

The high costs of transportation have motivated some manufacturers to seek methods for reducing the water concentration in products like soft drinks, beer, canned juice, and fresh meat. For example, Procter

& Gamble has developed a dry mix which, when reconstituted with water, will produce a carbonated beverage.[15]

Distribution policy must be closely aligned with promotion. Because promotion campaigns are often planned weeks in advance, it is essential that distribution to wholesalers and retailers be carried out at the proper times to ensure ample stocks of goods. Retailers may receive consumer complaints for not carrying or having sufficient quantities of the items they advertise, even though the manufacturer is at fault. Some new products fail because of poor initial distribution.

Physical distribution is related to overall channel strategy. A firm seeking extensive distribution needs many dispersed warehouses. One involved with perishables needs to be sure that a large proportion of a product's salable life is not spent in transit.

Physical distribution also plays an important part in pricing decisions. A firm with quick, reliable delivery and an ample supply of replacement parts that will ship small orders and provide emergency shipments may be able to charge higher prices than a company that provides less service.

A distribution strategy has an important overlap with production and financial functions. For example, many meat processors are able to reduce transportation costs by centralizing their cutting operations because less waste is shipped to each store. High freight costs and the uncertainty of continuous fuel supplies encourage firms to locate plants closer to markets. Low average inventories in stock enable companies to reduce finance charges. Public warehouse receipts can be used as collateral for loans, and the utilization of bonded warehouses defers the payment of excise taxes and import duties until goods are sold.

There are many decisions to be made in the development of a **physical distribution strategy:** the transportation form or forms to be used, inventory levels and warehouse form(s), and the number and locations of plants, warehouses, and retail locations.

A physical distribution strategy involves transportation, inventory, and facilities.

A physical distribution strategy can be fairly simple. A firm can have one plant, focus attention on one geographic market, and ship directly to customers without the use of decentralized warehouses. At the other extreme, a physical distribution strategy can include multiple plants, assembly locations in each geographic market, thousands of customer locations, and the integration of many transportation forms.

The remainder of this chapter deals with the two central components of physical distribution strategy: transportation and inventory management (which includes warehousing).

Transportation

Since 1950, the relative importance of railroads has declined substantially, despite their continuing leadership in ton miles. Motor trucks have increased their share of ton miles by 50 per cent during this period. Waterway shipments have had a stable share for the last thirty years. The share of ton miles shipped via pipelines has more than doubled since 1950. Despite the growth of airlines, freight deliveries through the airways remain at less than 1 per cent of all shipments.

Figure 9-6 ranks these transportation forms on the basis of six oper-

Operating Characteristics[1]	Railroads	Motor trucks	Waterways	Pipelines	Airways
Speed[2]	3	2	4	5	1
Availability[3]	2	1	4	5	3
Dependability[4]	3	2	4	1	5
Capability[5]	2	3	1	5	4
Frequency[6]	4	2	5	1	3
Cost per ton mile[7]	3	4	2	1	5

[1] 1 = high rank; 5 = lowest rank
[2] Speed = Door-to-door delivery time
[3] Availability = Number of geographic points served
[4] Dependability = Ability to meet schedules on time
[5] Capability = Ability to handle various products
[6] Frequency = Scheduled shipments per day
[7] Cost per ton mile = Illustrative costs per ton mile are pipeline, $ .27; waterways, $ .30; railroad, $1.43; motor truck, $7.70; and airways, $21.88.

Source: Adapted from Donald J. Bowersox, *Logistical Management,* Second Edition (New York: Macmillian, 1978), p. 120. (Copyright © 1978, Donald J Bowersox); reprinted by permission.

Figure 9-6
Relative Operating Characteristics of Five Basic Transportation Forms

Transportation forms may be rated on speed, availability, dependability, capability, frequency, and cost.

ating statistics. Airways have the best rating for speed. Pipelines are superior in dependability (time schedules met), frequency (shipments per day), and cost per ton mile. Waterways are able to handle the most different products. Motor trucks have the highest availability in terms of number of geographic points served.

Each transportation form and such transportation services as parcel post are studied next.

Railroads

Railroads **transport 35 per cent of U.S. freight, mostly heavy items over long distances.**

Railroads usually carry heavy, bulky items that are low in value (relative to their weight) over long distances. Railroads ship items whose weight is too heavy for trucks.

Despite their dominant position in ton miles shipped, railroads have been beset by a variety of problems in recent years. Fixed costs are high because of investments in facilities. Shippers face railroad car shortages during high demand months for agricultural goods. Some tracks and railroad cars are in serious need of repair. Trucks are faster, more flexible, and are packed more easily. In response to these difficulties, the railroads are relying on three solutions to improve their outlook: new shipping techniques, deregulation, and mergers. See Figure 9-7.

Motor trucks predominantly transport small shipments over short distances. They handle about 80 per cent of the country's shipments of less than 500 or 1,000 pounds. Seventy per cent of all trucks are used for local deliveries and 50 per cent of total truck miles are local.

Trucks are more flexible than rail because they can pick up packages at the factory or warehouse and deliver them to the customer's door. For example, General Motors moves half its total shipments by trucks, which carry parts from one plant right to the assembly area of another.[16] In addition, trucks are faster than rail for short distances.

Motor Trucks

Motor trucks handle 25 per cent of U.S. freight, emphasizing small shipments over short distances.

Figure 9-7
Railroads Respond to Deregulation

Reprinted by permission of the Association of American Railroads (AAR), Washington, D.C., 1982.

The trucking industry has been deregulated since 1980. This has expanded competition in the industry.[17]

Waterways

Waterways involve the movement of goods on barges via inland rivers and on tankers and general merchandise freighters through the Great Lakes, intercoastal shipping, and the St. Lawrence Seaway. Waterways are used primarily for transporting low-value, high-bulk freight (such as coal, iron ore, gravel, grain, and cement). Although this type of transportation is slow and may be closed by ice during the winter, the rates are extremely low.

Various improvements in vessel design have recently occurred. For example, many "supervessels" are now operating on the Great Lakes. These supervessels can each carry 61,000 gross tons of iron-bearing rock in one trip. The conveyor system is twice as efficient as the one on older boats. One supervessel can annually deliver three and one-half million gross tons of rock along a route from Lake Superior to Gary, Indiana. This is enough to keep Gary's blast furnaces operating for 160 days.[18]

Pipelines

Within *pipelines,* there is continuous movement and there are no interruptions, inventories (except those held by a carrier), and intermediate storage locations. Thus, handling and labor costs are minimized. Even though pipelines are very reliable, only certain commodities can be moved through them. In the past, emphasis was on gas and petroleum-based products. Recently, pipelines have been modified to accept coal and wood chips, which are transported in a semiliquid state. Nonetheless, lack of flexibility limits the potential of pipelines.

Some pipelines are enormous in size. For example, the Alaska Natural Gas Transportation System (ANGTS) will eventually cover 4,800 miles and deliver 2.4 billion cubic feet of natural gas per day to the lower 48 states.[19] It is estimated that this pipeline has cost $10 billion to construct.

Airways

Airways are the fastest, most expensive form of transportation. As a result, high-value products, perishable goods, and emergency goods dominate air shipments. Even though air transit is costly, it may lower other costs, such as the need for outlying or regional warehouses. The costs of packing, unpacking, and preparing goods for transportation are lower than for other forms.

Airfreight has been deregulated since late 1977. As a result, some airlines have stepped up cargo operations, while others have curtailed them. Many carriers now employ wide-bodied jets that can handle large containers. In addition, modern communications and sorting equipment have been added to airfreight operations. Firms specializing in air shipments have done well by emphasizing fast, guaranteed service at reasonable prices.

Transportation Services

Transportation service companies handle the shipments of moderate-sized packages. Some pick up packages from the shipping firm's office and deliver direct to the addressee. Others require packages to be brought to a service company outlet. The three major kinds of service companies are government parcel post, private parcel, and express.

Government parcel post operates from post offices and utilizes rates based on postal zones, of which there are eight. Parcel post can be insured or sent COD (collect on delivery). Special handling is available to expedite shipments. Express mail is available for next-day service from a post office to an addressee.

Private parcel services specialize in small-package delivery, usually less than 50-pound shipments. Most services ship from manufacturers, wholesalers, distributors, and retailers to their customers within a several-state area. The largest private firm is United Parcel Service (UPS), a multibillion dollar, national company.

Express companies, such as Federal Express, Emery Air Freight, Burlington North Air Freight, and Purolator Courier Corporation, generally provide guaranteed nationwide delivery of small packages for the morning after pickup. The average express delivery is 10 pounds.

> These *transportation service companies* ship medium-sized packages: government parcel post, private parcel, and express.

Coordination of Transportation

Because a single shipment may involve a combination of transportation forms, coordination is necessary. Two major innovations that improve a firm's ability to coordinate shipments are containerization and freight forwarding.

Under **containerization,** goods are packed into sturdy containers that can be placed on trains, trucks, ships, or planes. These marked containers are sealed until delivered, thereby reducing damage and pilferage. Their progress and destination are frequently monitored. The containers are mobile warehouses that can be moved from manufacturing plants to receiving docks, where they remain until the contents are needed.

> With *containerization,* nonbreakable containers are sealed until the final destination.

Freight forwarders consolidate small shipments (usually less than 500 pounds each) from several companies. They pick up merchandise at the shipper's place of business and arrange for delivery at the buyer's door. Freight forwarders prosper because less than carload (lcl) rates are sharply higher than carload (cl) rates. Freight forwarders also provide traffic management services, such as selecting the best transportation form at the most reasonable rate.

> *Freight forwarders* accumulate shipments from several companies.

Legal Status of Transportation Firms

Transportation firms are categorized as common, contract, exempt, or private carriers. **Common carriers** must provide service between designated points on a fixed schedule. They are not permitted to change operating schedules or rates without permission, and they cannot refuse to transport the goods of anyone unless a carrier's rules are violated. Common carriers must obtain franchises from the appropriate regulatory agency. The main agencies are

> *Common carriers* are licensed by the government and must provide service to all who request it.

Interstate Commerce Commission (ICC) for railroads, motor trucks, and inland waterway carriers.
Civil Aeronautics Board (CAB) and Federal Aviation Agency (FAA) for air carriers.

Federal Maritime Commission (FMC) for ocean-going water carriers.

Federal Power Commission (FPC) for pipelines.

All railroads and petroleum pipelines and some air, motor-truck, and water transporters are common carriers. Recent deregulation has generally increased price competition.

Contract carriers provide one or a few shippers with transportation services based on individual agreements. Although contract carriers must obtain certificates in order to operate, they are not required to maintain fixed routes or schedules, and rates may be negotiated. Many motor-truck, inland-waterway, and airfreight transporters are contract carriers.

Exempt carriers are excused from economic regulations and must only comply with safety requirements. Exempt carriers are specified by law. Some commodities moved by water, such as coal, and most agricultural goods are exempt from economic restrictions.

Private carriers are shippers who possess their own transportation facilities. They are subject to safety rules. Private carriers are common in the automobile industry.

Inventory Management

The intent of **inventory management** is to provide a continuous flow of goods and to match the quantity of goods kept in inventory with sales demand. When production or consumption is seasonal or erratic, this can be difficult.

Therefore, inventory management (including warehousing) has broad implications for the firm. It is vital that sufficient quantities be on hand when they are advertised by a retailer. A producer cannot afford to run out of a crucial item that could put a halt to production. On the other hand, inventory should not be too large, since the costs of storing products for a year (floor space, insurance, supervision, and credit) are estimated by one source to be 36 per cent of the goods' costs.[20] In situations where models change yearly, as with automobiles, large inventories of year-old cars can adversely affect new-car sales. Finally, large inventories may result in stale goods, cause the firm to mark down prices due to product obsolescence, and tie up working capital.

Four aspects of inventory management are explained in the following subsections: stock turnover, when to reorder, how much to reorder, and warehousing.

Stock Turnover

The balance between sales and inventory on hand is expressed by **stock turnover,** which represents the number of times during a specified period (usually one year) that the average inventory on hand is sold. Stock turnover is calculated in units or dollars:

$$\text{Annual rate of stock turnover (in units)} = \frac{\text{Number of units sold during year}}{\text{Average inventory on hand (in units)}}$$

$$\text{Annual rate of stock turnover (in dollars)} = \frac{\text{Net yearly sales (in retail dollars)}}{\text{Average inventory on hand (in retail dollars).}}$$

Annual stock turnover rates range from 3.0 in jewelry stores to 16.0 in grocery stores.[21]

There are many advantages to fast inventory turnover: inventory investments are productive, merchandise is fresh, losses from changes in styles and fashion are reduced, and the costs of maintaining inventory (such as insurance, breakage, warehousing, and credit) are lessened.

Turnover can be improved by reducing product assortments, eliminating slow-selling items, maintaining minimal inventories for some items, and purchasing from suppliers who deliver on time. According to the purchasing manager for U.S. Borax and Chemical Corp. in Los Angeles:

> While people think of inventories as "something in a warehouse" . . . 65% of our inventory is in conveyance somewhere—the biggest warehouse in the world is on wheels.[22]

Too high a turnover can also negatively affect a firm for several reasons. Small-quantity purchases can cause the loss of volume discounts. Low product assortment can reduce sales if consumers are unable to compare brands or related items are not carried. Low prices may be necessary to stimulate sufficient purchases. The chances of running out of stock rise when average inventory size is lowered. As the purchasing chief at Pfizer commented: "If you have too much inventory, you get yelled at; if you shut the plant because you don't have it, you get fired."[23]

Knowing when to reorder merchandise helps protect against stockouts while minimizing inventory investments.

When to Reorder Inventory

The reorder point sets a level at which orders must be placed—based on lead time, usage, and safety stock.

The **reorder point** establishes an inventory level at which new orders must be placed. The reorder point depends on order lead time, usage rate, and safety stock.

Order lead time is the period from the date an order is placed until the date merchandise is ready for sale (received, checked against the order, and altered, if necessary). Usage rate refers to the average sales in units per day (for a wholesaler or retailer) or the rate at which a product is used in a production process (for a manufacturer). Safety stock is the extra merchandise kept on hand to protect against out-of-stock conditions resulting from unexpectedly high demand, greater-than-anticipated production volume, and delivery delays. Safety stock must be planned in accordance with the marketer's policy toward running out of merchandise.

The reorder point formula is

Reorder point = (Order lead time × Usage rate) + (Safety stock).

A firm that needs four days for an order to be completed, sells 10 items per day, and wants to have 10 extra items on hand in case of a delivery delay of one day has a reorder point of 50[(4 × 10) + 10)]. Without the safety stock, the firm will lose 10 sales if it orders when inventory is 40 items and the order takes five days to complete.

How Much to Reorder

Order size depends on discounts, company resources, stock turnover, and costs.

Order size depends on several factors: the availability of quantity discounts, the resources of the firm, inventory turnover, the costs of processing each order, and the costs of maintaining goods in inventory. When orders are large, quantity discounts are usually available, a large portion of a firm's finances are tied up in inventory, stock turnover is relatively low, per-order processing costs are reduced, and inventory costs are generally high. The firm is also less likely to run out of goods. The opposite is true for small orders.

Economic order quantity (EOQ) balances ordering and inventory costs.

Many companies seek to balance their order-processing costs (filling out forms, computer utilization, and merchandise handling) and their inventory-holding costs (warehouse expenses, interest charges, insurance, deterioration, and pilferage). Processing costs per unit decline as orders get bigger while inventory costs rise. The **economic order quantity** (EOQ) is the order volume corresponding to the lowest sum of order-processing and inventory-holding costs.

Warehousing

Warehouses store and dispatch goods.

Warehouses receive, identify, and sort merchandise. They store goods, implement product-recall programs, select goods for shipment, coordinate shipments, and dispatch orders.

Firms operate private warehouses to handle their own items.

Private warehouses are owned and operated by firms which store and distribute their own products. Private warehouses are mostly used by companies with stable inventory levels and long-run expectations to serve the same geographic markets. Figure 9-8 shows the automatic storage retrieval systems used in a warehouse owned and operated by W. W. Grainger, an industrial distributor of motors and other items.

Public warehouses rent storage space and offer distribution services to any interested party.

Public warehouses provide storage and related physical distribution services to any interested individual or firm on a rental basis. Public warehouses are used by firms that desire additional storage space (because their private warehouses are filled) or firms entering new geographic markets (where test marketing or preopening space is needed). If a product is recalled, a public warehouse can be utilized as a collection point, where products are segregated, disposed of, or salvaged.

Public warehouses can provide transportation economies for users by allowing carload shipments to local markets before warehouse distribution to customers. Firms are able to reduce capital expenditures and maximize flexibility by using public warehouses, which are adapted easily to new or expanding markets. Public warehouses are available in major urban areas and in many smaller cities; there are about 15,000 public warehouses in the United States.

A *bonded warehouse* can store imported or taxable goods. *Field warehousing* provides receipts for private or in-transit items.

Bonded warehousing and field warehousing are also available through public warehouses. In a **bonded warehouse,** imported or taxable merchandise is stored and can be released for sale only after appropriate taxes are paid. A bonded warehouse allows firms to postpone tax payments until they are ready to make deliveries to customers. Ciga-

Reprinted by permission.

rettes, liquor, and various imported products are often stored in a bonded warehouse.

With **field warehousing** a receipt is issued by the public warehouse for goods stored in a private warehouse or in transit to consumers. These goods are usually placed in a special area, and the field warehouser takes responsibility for the merchandise. A firm uses field warehousing because the warehouse receipt serves as collateral for a loan.

For many firms a combination of private and public warehouses may be optimal. This enables the private warehouse to be full at almost all times and the public warehouse to stock items for peak seasons, bonded goods, and merchandise for geographic areas with low concentrations of customers.

The coordination of a firm's transportation and inventory management strategies is known as a **physical distribution system**.

A physical distribution system is useful.

Summary

Distribution planning is systematic decision making relating to the physical movement and transfer of ownership of a product or service from producer to consumer. A channel of distribution contains the organizations or people involved with the movement and exchange of products or services.

Regardless of who performs them, channel functions include marketing research, buying, promotion, customer services, product planning, price planning, and distribution. Independent channel members can play an important role by performing various functions and resolving the differences between manufacturers' and consumers' goals.

A direct channel requires the manufacturer to perform all distribution functions, while in an indirect channel these activities are carried out by both the manufacturer and independent middlemen. In comparing the two methods, the firm must balance its costs and abilities against control and total sales. An indirect channel may use a contractual arrangement or an administered agreement.

A long channel has a number of levels of independent middlemen; it can be shortened if the firm increases the functions it performs. A wide channel has a large number of firms at any stage in the channel, such as retailers. The distribution channel may be exclusive, selective, or intensive, depending on the firm's goals, channel members, customers, and marketing emphasis. A dual channel allows a company to operate through two or more distribution methods.

In contracts between manufacturers and other channel members, price policy, conditions of sale, territorial rights, services/responsibility mix, and contract length and conditions of termination are specified. Cooperation and conflict both occur in a channel of distribution. Conflicts need to be settled fairly, since confrontation leads to hostility and negative actions by all parties. A pushing strategy, based on channel cooperation, is available to established, successful firms. A pulling strategy, based on proving the existence of consumer demand prior to channel support or acceptance, must be used by many new companies.

The channel of distribution for industrial products normally does not use retailers but tends to be direct, involve few transactions and large orders, require specification selling and knowledgeable channel members, utilize team selling and different channel members, and include leasing arrangements.

Physical distribution is involved with getting goods delivered to the designated place, at the designated time, and in proper condition. There are a number of reasons for studying physical distribution: costs, importance of customer service, and its relationship with other functional areas of the organization.

In a physical distribution strategy, decisions are made regarding transportation, inventory levels, warehousing, and location of facilities. Railroads typically carry goods for long distances and ship bulky items that are low in value in relation to their weight. Motor trucks dominate in transporting small shipments over short distances. Waterways are used primarily for the shipment of low-value freight. Pipelines provide reliable and continuous movement of liquid, gaseous, and semiliquid products. Airways offer fast, expensive movement of perishables and high-value items.

Inventory management is needed to regulate product supplies and distribution. Stock turnover is the number of times during a year that the average inventory on hand is sold. The reorder point is based on a pre-established minimum inventory level at which merchandise must be reordered. The economic order quantity formula determines the optimal quantity of goods to order based on total order-processing and holding costs. Warehousing decisions include selecting a private or public warehouse and examining the availability of public warehouse services.

After reading this chapter, you should understand these key terms: **KEY TERMS**

Distribution planning   **Physical distribution strategy**
Channel of distribution   **Railroads**
Channel members (middlemen)   **Motor trucks**
Channel functions   **Waterways**
Sorting process   **Pipelines**
Direct channel of distribution   **Airways**
Indirect channel of distribution   **Transportation service companies**
Contractual arrangement   **Containerization**
Administered channel   **Freight forwarders**
Channel length   **Common carriers**
Channel width   **Contract carriers**
Exclusive distribution   **Exempt carriers**
Selective distribution   **Private carriers**
Intensive distribution   **Inventory management**
Dual channel of distribution   **Stock turnover**
Manufacturer/channel member   **Reorder point**
  contracts   **Order size**
Pushing strategy   **Economic order quantity (EOQ)**
Pulling strategy   **Warehouses**
Physical distribution   **Bonded warehouse**
Order cycle   **Field warehousing**
Distribution standards   **Physical distribution system**
Total-cost approach

QUESTIONS FOR DISCUSSION

1. Define a channel of distribution.
2. Are independent channel members always necessary? Explain your answer.
3. Why do some firms consider the selection of a channel of distribution to be their most important decision?
4. How can a refrigerator cost $150 to make and yet retail for $500?
5. Explain the sorting process. What are the differences between manufacturers' and consumers' goals?
6. Why would a manufacturer utilize both direct and indirect distribution channels?
7. Give an illustration of a product moving from exclusive to selective to intensive distribution.
8. How may the manufacturer, wholesaler, and retailer of a line of candy cooperate with each other? How may they be in conflict with each other?

9. Devise a distribution channel for the sale of
    a. An industrial photocopier.
    b. A $10 camera.
    c. Office stationery.
    d. A residential house.
10. List five symptoms of a poor physical distribution strategy. Explain why each symptom is included on your list.
11. Develop five clear levels of service standards for a department store. Develop five for a washing machine manufacturer.
12. How can air freight be an economical means of transporting cargo using a total-cost approach?
13. Differentiate among a common carrier, a contract carrier, and a private carrier.
14. What are the problems for a firm having too high an inventory turnover? Give an example where this situation has occurred.

NOTES

1. "A No-Win War in Videocassettes," *Business Week* (May 24, 1982), p. 152; and Laura Landro, "Film Studios' Plans to Lease Videocassettes Bring Big Outcry from Squeezed Retailers," *Wall Street Journal* (January 18, 1982), p. 25.
2. "U-Haul Strategy Reversal Moves It Back to Gas Stations," *Business Week* (May 4, 1981), pp. 162, 164.
3. William Harris, "If I Have the Doctor," *Forbes* (March 30, 1981), pp. 63–64, 67.
4. "Mitsubishi Revs Up to Go Solo," *Business Week* (May 3, 1982), pp. 131–132.
5. Wroe Alderson, *Marketing Behavior and Executive Action* (Homewood, Ill.: Richard D. Irwin, 1957), Chapter 7.
6. Marilyn Chase, "Apple Computer Tries to Ban Mail Business, Drawing Angry Charges of Trade Restraint," *Wall Street Journal* (December 7, 1981), p. 37.
7. Richard Sandomir, "King Bud's New Rules," *Newsday* (October 18, 1982), Part III, pp. 1, 13.
8. "Jordache Sues K mart in Its Battle to Halt Jeans Counterfeiting," *Wall Street Journal* (December 13, 1982), p. 38.
9. National Council of Physical Distribution Management, Chicago, Ill.
10. Ronald H. Ballou, *Basic Business Logistics* (Englewood Cliffs, N.Y.: Prentice-Hall, 1978), pp. 17–18.
11. "New Distribution Strategies Needed to Combat Skyrocketing Energy Costs," *Marketing News* (February 8, 1980), p. 14.
12. "Physical Distribution: The Right Time, the Right Place," *Sales & Marketing Management* (June 14, 1976), p. 48.
13. William D. Perreault, Jr., and Frederick A. Russ, "Physical Distribution Service in Industrial Purchase Decisions," *Journal of Marketing*, Vol. 40 (April 1976), p. 5.
14. Monroe Murphy Bird, "Small Industrial Buyers Call Late Delivery Worst Problem," *Marketing News* (April 4, 1980), p. 24.
15. Rudolf Struse, "High Cost of Shipping Water to Spur Dry Mix Food Forms," *Marketing News* (December 28, 1979), p. 1.
16. "Getting Ready: Businessmen Brace for a Trucking Strike, But There's a Limit to What They Can Do," *Wall Street Journal* (March 29, 1979), p. 46.
17. For example, see Robert Raissman, "Deregulated Truckers Taking Ad Route," *Advertising Age* (February 22, 1982), pp. 45, 52.
18. Seth Cropsey, "King of the Ore Boats," *Fortune* (March 10, 1980), pp. 104–106; and "Shippers Are in the Driver's Seat," *Business Week* (October 18, 1982), pp. 182–186.
19. "McMillian: A Tough Pipeliner Vs. the Producers," *Business Week* (March 31, 1980), pp. 62, 65.

20. Richard F. Janssen and John Koten, "Leaner Inventories Than in Prior Slumps Could Lessen Severity of This Recession," *Wall Street Journal* (May 23, 1980), p. 48.

21. For a good discussion of stock turnover, see "Inventories and Stock Turns: How Do They Balance?" *Nielsen Researcher* (November 3, 1982), pp. 2–12.

22. Janssen and Koten, "Leaner Inventories Than in Prior Slumps Could Lessen Severity of This Recession."

23. Ibid.

RADIO SHACK: CONTROLLING ITS OWN DESTINY* 1

CASES

Radio Shack (a division of Tandy Corporation), unlike almost all of its competitors, performs every channel function—from manufacturing to retailing—for the electronics and computer products it markets. Others in the industry operate as either manufacturers or as retailers. As a Radio Shack vice-president noted:

> If we manufacture a product . . . we are already assured that we will be able to distribute it to an established, nationwide chain of retail outlets. If RCA or G.E. or any of our other competitors comes up with a product, they have to put together a distribution system store by store.

The company manufactures most of the products it offers under its own private labels and sells them only through Radio Shack stores. Some items sold in the stores are special purchases from a variety of sources. Radio Shack owns and operates 4,300 U.S. stores. In addition, there are 2,000 independently owned Radio Shack outlets in the U.S.; however, these stores must follow the same policies as company-owned stores.

Over the past several years, Radio Shack has developed a good reputation for its home-computer line. It was the first nationwide retailer to market an inexpensive home computer. Today, it markets a full line of small business and home computers. In order to better concentrate on computer sales, Radio Shack has opened 500 retail stores specializing only in these products. During 1982, computers and related equipment accounted for over 30 per cent of total sales.

To maintain control over marketing efforts, Radio Shack develops its own catalogues and has a large in-company advertising department. The firm also plans each store's layout, hours, product mix, and selling practices. Radio Shack believes this strategy results in one uniform image and generates customer trust. After all, how many other manufacturers have several thousand of their own stores to handle customer service?

QUESTIONS

1. Evaluate Radio Shack's overall distribution strategy. Consider both pros and cons.

*The data in this case are drawn from Craig Reiss, "Advantages of Being Self-Contained," *Marketing & Media Decisions* (Spring 1982, Special Edition), pp. 69–74; Howard Rudnitsky and Toni Mack, "Sometimes We Are Innovators, Sometimes Not," *Forbes* (March 29, 1982), pp. 66–70; and David Stipp, "Computer Boom Lifts Tandy Sales Even as Its Market Share Declines," *Wall Street Journal* (February 14, 1983), p. 19.

2. Why do you think that RCA and G.E. have not followed Radio Shack's approach in operating their own stores nationwide?
3. Comment on Radio Shack's opening specialized computer stores.
4. Does Radio Shack's distribution approach eliminate channel conflict? Explain your answer.

2 CHUCK SANDERS: INVENTORY PROBLEMS FOR AN INTERNATIONAL HARVESTER DEALER†

Chuck Sanders operates a farm-equipment dealership, specializing in International Harvester products, in Urbana, Ohio. For ten years, Sanders' business earned good profits; then, in 1981, he took a loss as sales declined sharply. 1982 sales were even worse. The poor sales were a result of the weak 1981–82 economy and uncertainty that International Harvester would remain in business. Customers did not want to buy expensive machinery that they believed could not be easily serviced or repaired. J. I. Case and Deere & Co., two competitors of International Harvester, were in much better financial condition.

At the end of 1982, Chuck Sanders had an inventory-on-hand worth almost $2 million, about double the amount at which his firm could operate efficiently. The inventory included 27 new plows, 5 combines (machines that harvest grains and soybeans), 6 corn planters, more than a dozen large tractors, and a lot of smaller equipment (such as 11 cultivators).

The excessive inventory caused these problems for Sanders:

- Equipment had to be priced at just above cost. For example, he sold a tractor for $41,500, 5 per cent above dealer cost.
- Interest charges reached $12,000 per month.
- Interest charges of $110,000 were accumulated.
- Receipt of new equipment was not scheduled until customer orders were placed.
- Personnel were cut back considerably.

With the support of International Harvester, Chuck Sanders has been working hard to turn the situation around. International Harvester agreed to defer interest charges and sponsored discount price programs. Sanders and his banker drafted plans for Small Business Administration assistance, while he introduced special offers, participated in the local county fair, and actively promoted his equipment. For Sanders, the continued existence of his company is at stake.

QUESTIONS

1. Could Chuck Sanders have avoided the problems he faced in 1981–82? If so, how?
2. What else could Sanders do to reduce inventory?
3. Develop a plan for Chuck Sanders to plan next year's inventory levels.
4. How easy will it be for Sanders to sell new farm equipment that sits in inventory for two or three years? Compare this with the sale of new 1982-model automobiles in 1984.

†The data in this are drawn from Claudia Waterloo, "Harvester Dealer Struggles to Overcome His Supplier's Troubles and the Recession," *Wall Street Journal* (November 30, 1982), p. 56.

Wholesaling and Retailing

10

Chapter Preview

Chapter Objectives

1 To describe wholesaling, explore its scope and functions, and examine wholesaler relationships with suppliers and customers

2 To explain the three broad categories of wholesaling and the specific types of firms within each category

3 To describe retailing and consider the special characteristics that distinguish it from other areas of marketing

4 To study retail ownership forms, strategy mixes, and nonstore retailing

5 To examine several major considerations in retail planning

loan's is the fastest growing and most profitable supermarket chain in Manhattan. Under the leadership of Julie Rose, its chief executive, the chain has thrived despite a reputation as the area's most expensive supermarket. Annually, Sloan's 42 stores account for 15 per cent of Manhattan's $1.5 billion in grocery sales.

While Sloan's has prospered, a number of large supermarket chains were forced to pull out of the New York market. Among them were Safeway, Finast, Big Apple, Bohack, and International. These retailers just could not earn an adequate profit in New York.

Succeeding in the supermarket business is difficult, particularly in Manhattan. Profit margins (net profits as per cents of sales) are about seven tenths of 1 per cent as compared to 4 per cent for department stores. In crowded city stores, there is no room for the higher-margin nonfood items suburban chains use to increase profits. High rents and small stores mean that Manhattan food shoppers are not offered cooking demonstrations, free samples, specialty departments, and fancy displays. One of every three U.S. food dollars is now spent on fast food. The Manhattan market has different market segments that vary in family size, income, ethnic background, and life-styles.

The dominance of Sloan's is attributable to several factors:

1. Doubling the number of supermarkets in a five-year period (leading to a tripling of sales).
2. Maintaining a quality image and product line.
3. Appealing to New Yorkers through a campaign strategy "We're New York's Own" on plastic shopping bags.
4. Advertising through ethnic festivals, cheese promotions, and gourmet-bread deals.
5. Rose shopping in his own stores and staying in touch with managers via a small squawk box on his desk.
6. Sending a trouble-shooting team to stores where sales volume does not keep rising. The team (comprised of a meat person, produce person, store operations expert, and advertising expert) visits the area, checks competitors, examines the Sloan's outlet, and surveys customers.
7. Adapting marketing strategy to each neighborhood location, based on family structure, ethnic makeup, and income.[1]

Characteristics and Importance of Wholesaling

Wholesaling covers buying and selling items for resale to channel members or other organizational consumers, but not sales to final consumers.

Wholesaling involves the buying and handling of merchandise and its resale to retailers, organizational users, and/or other wholesalers but not the sale of significant volume to final consumers.[2] According to one study, wholesale sales are divided as follows: 40.7 per cent to industrial, commercial, and government users; 37.2 per cent to retailers; 15.0 per cent to other wholesalers; and 7.1 per cent to others.[3]

There are about 600,000 wholesalers with total annual sales above $1 trillion in the U.S. Although wholesale revenues are higher than those in retailing, there are more than three times as many retailers as wholesalers. High wholesale sales occur because some products move through several layers of wholesalers; and there is only one level of retailing. Therefore, an item can be sold twice or more at the wholesale level (e.g., regionally, then locally), yet just once at the retail level. There are more retailers because they service small and geographically dispersed final consumer groups; wholesalers deal with fewer, larger, more geographically concentrated consumers.

From a cost perspective, wholesalers have a significant impact on the price of merchandise. For example, 25.6 per cent of the price a jewelry wholesaler charges its retailers covers the wholesaler's operations and other expenses (21.2 per cent) and pretax profit (4.4 per cent). Operating costs include inventory charges, sales force salaries, advertising, and rent.[4]

The use of wholesalers varies widely. While most consumer products, industrial machinery, equipment maintenance, and replacement parts are funneled through independent channel members, some manufacturers bypass independent wholesalers. The following wholesaling activities are usually required whether they are performed by the manufacturer or an independent wholesaler: developing contacts, selling and servicing accounts, managing and paying for a sales force, maintaining inventories, shipping goods, and handling payments and returns. Independent wholesalers are sometimes in a difficult position because they are located between manufacturers and retailers, and must determine their responsibilities to each.

Without wholesalers, retailers and other organizational consumers may have to deal with a number of manufacturers and coordinate shipments, develop supplier contacts, perform more distribution functions, stock greater quantities, and place more emphasis on an internal purchasing agent or department. In addition, many small retailers and organizational customers might be avoided because they would not be profitably reached by a manufacturer/supplier; and these small retailers and organizational customers might not be able to purchase necessary items elsewhere.

As an illustration of the value of wholesaling, in the auto parts industry there is now an orderly system of independent distributors (wholesalers) to perform functions for manufacturers and their retailer customers. Before this system was introduced, there were thousands of manufacturers producing a wide range of products and marketing them through a multitude of selling organizations. Customers, mostly garages and service stations, were constantly interrupted by salespeople. Sales costs were high for the manufacturers. A smoother, less costly arrangement exists today with the organized use of a moderate number of independent distributors.

Independent wholesalers can perform a number of functions, but are sometimes caught between their manufacturers and their retailers.

Types of Wholesaling

The three broad categories of wholesaling are outlined in Figure 10-1: manufacturer wholesaling, merchant wholesaling, and agents and brokers.

Manufacturer Wholesaling

With ***manufacturer wholesaling,*** the producer undertakes all wholesaling functions itself. This occurs when the firm believes it is most able to reach its retailers and other organizational customers effectively by

Figure 10-1
Broad Categories of Whole-saling

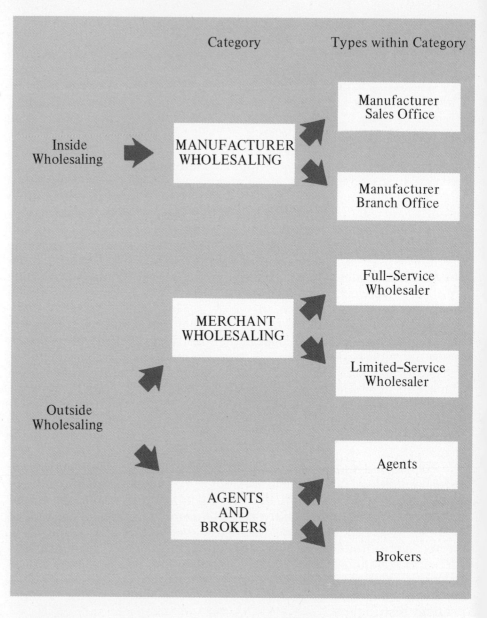

Category   Types within Category

Inside Wholesaling → **MANUFACTURER WHOLESALING** → Manufacturer Sales Office / Manufacturer Branch Office

Outside Wholesaling → **MERCHANT WHOLESALING** → Full–Service Wholesaler / Limited–Service Wholesaler

AGENTS AND BROKERS → Agents / Brokers

assuming responsibility and completing wholesaling tasks. Table 10-1 lists several conditions that favor the performance of wholesale activities by manufacturers.

Manufacturers' wholesale sales volume is between 35 and 40 per cent of total wholesale revenues; they operate approximately 45,000 to 50,000 outlets. Wholesale activities by manufacturers may be conducted in either a sales office or branch office. A manufacturer's sales office is located at the company's production facilities or a site close to the market. No inventory is carried at the sales office. In contrast, a manufacturer's branch office includes facilities for warehousing goods as well as for selling them.

In *manufacturer wholesaling*, a firm completes all wholesaling activities through its own sales or branch offices.

Table 10-1

1. Existence of large-scale retailers
2. Large-volume purchases by small retailers
3. Small number of customers
4. Geographically concentrated customers
5. High product perishability
6. High product unit value
7. Highly technical products, requiring specialized installation and repair services
8. Manufacturer having a long line of products
9. High financial strength of manufacturer
10. Independent wholesalers either inefficient, incompetent, or unavailable

Conditions That Favor the Performance of Wholesale Functions by Manufacturers

Source: Adapted from James C. McKeon, "Conflicting Patterns of Structural Change in Wholesaling," *Economic and Business Bulletin* (Winter 1972), pp. 37–48. © *Economic and Business Bulletin*, 1972; reprinted by permission.

Manufacturer wholesaling is often necessary when no satisfactory independent wholesaler is available. This took place for both R. J. Reynolds and Philip Morris, who found no existing wholesale channel for marketing their tobacco products in Brazil. And their wholesaling activities proved costly. According to the president of Philip Morris' Brazilian subsidiary, "Selling direct is cheap if you have a large share of market, but with 8 per cent its expensive."[5]

Merchant Wholesaling

Merchant wholesalers buy, take title, and take possession of products for further resale. They represent the largest category of wholesalers in terms of sales—roughly 50 per cent of the total—and establishments—more than three quarters of the total.

Merchant wholesalers may be full service or limited service. ***Full-service merchant wholesalers*** assemble an assortment of products in a given place. They provide trade credit, store and deliver merchandise, offer merchandising and promotion assistance, provide a personal sales force, and offer research and planning support. Information is available for suppliers and customers. Installation and repair services are given. Full-service merchant wholesalers act like the sales arms of their manufacturers. They are prevalent for grocery products, tobacco, alcoholic beverages, hardware, plumbing equipment, and drugs.

Limited-service merchant wholesalers buy and take title to merchandise. However, they do not perform all the functions of full-service merchant wholesalers. For example, they may not provide credit, merchandising assistance, or marketing research data. Limited-service wholesalers are popular for construction materials, coal, lumber, perishables, and specialty foods.

On the average, full-service merchant wholesalers require higher compensation than limited-service merchant wholesalers, because they perform greater functions. Figure 10-2 shows the different types of merchant wholesalers, which are described next. Table 10-2 contrasts the marketing strategies of the two kinds of merchant wholesalers for medical supplies.

Merchant wholesalers purchase products for resale. They may be full service or limited service.

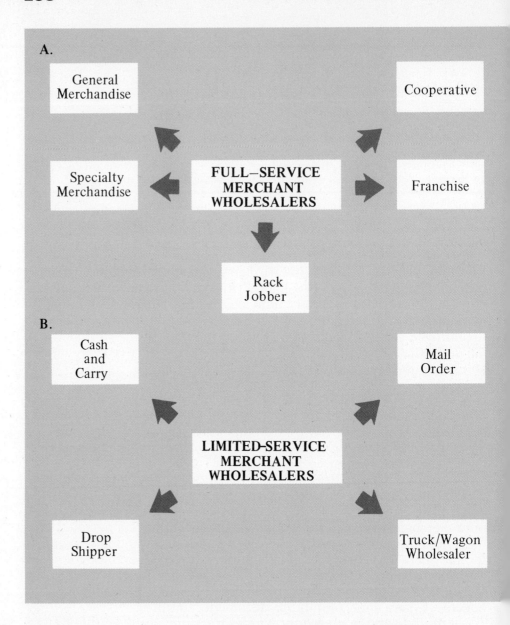

Full-Service Merchant Wholesalers

General-merchandise wholesalers sell a wide range of items, and try to secure exclusivity.

Specialty-merchandise wholesalers concentrate efforts on a narrow but deep product line.

Full-service merchant wholesalers can be divided into general merchandise, specialty merchandise, rack jobber, franchise, and cooperative types.

General-merchandise (full-line) wholesalers carry a wide assortment of products, nearly all the items needed by the retailers to which they cater. For example, general-merchandise hardware, drug, and clothing wholesalers stock many items for their customers, but not much depth within any specific product line. These wholesalers seek to sell their retailers or other organizational customers all or most of their products and develop strong loyalty and exclusivity with them.

Specialty-merchandise (limited-line) wholesalers concentrate efforts on a relatively narrow range of products and have an extensive

Full-Service Medical-Supply Wholesaler

Table 10-2

- Provides special services for physicians, such as frequent sales calls, emergency and small-order delivery, and liberal credit terms
- Guarantees zero out-of-stock policy for key health care items through an inventory control system
- Prepares an ideal inventory model for accounts and agrees to manage inventory to maintain appropriate stock levels
- Uses a sales contract or prime vendor contract whereby the hospital agrees to do the majority of its purchasing through the contracting wholesaler
- Maintains an inventory of 8,000–10,000 items
- Is paid, on average, every 50 days

Contrasting Strategies of Full-Service and Limited-Service Medical-Supply Merchant Wholesalers

Limited-Service Medical-Supply Wholesaler

- Offers the lowest market price as the primary means of generating sales; gross profit margin is 10% of sales, compared to the industry average of 20%
- Uses multiyear supply contracts with hospitals, reducing need for field sales support; average selling costs as a per cent of new sales are 2.0%, compared with the industry average of 5.5%
- Seeks sales contracts only from largest-volume hospitals
- Deals only in high-volume medical commodities
- Uses high levels of computer cost controls and accounting controls
- Maintains an inventory of 1,500–3,000 items
- Is paid, on average, in fewer than 30 days

Source: Adapted from P. Ronald Stephenson, "Wholesale Distribution: An Analysis of Structure, Strategy, and Profit Performance," in Arch G. Woodside *et al.* (Editors), *Foundations of Marketing Channels* (Austin, Texas: Lone Star Publishers, 1978), pp. 103–107. © Lone Star Publishers, 1978; reprinted with permission.

assortment within that range. These wholesalers offer expertise and many sizes, colors, and models in their product categories. The specialty wholesaler provides functions similar to general-merchandise and other full-service merchant wholesalers. Specialty wholesaling is popular for health foods, seafood, retailers' store displays, and frozen foods.

Rack jobbers furnish the racks or shelves on which merchandise is displayed. The rack jobber owns the merchandise on its racks, selling the items on a consignment basis, so that the retailer pays after the goods are sold. Unsold merchandise is taken back. The jobber sets up displays, refills shelves, price marks merchandise, maintains inventory records, and computes the amount due from the retailer. Heavily advertised, branded merchandise that is sold on a self-service basis is most frequently handled. Included are health and beauty aids, drugs, cosmetics, magazines, hand tools, toys, housewares, and stationery. See Figure 10-3.

Rack jobbers set up displays, price-mark merchandise, receive payments after sales, and take returns.

In *franchise wholesaling,* independent retailers affiliate with an existing wholesaler in order to use a standardized storefront design, business format, name, and purchase system. In many instances, suppliers produce goods according to specifications set by the franchise wholesaler. This form of wholesaling is utilized for hardware, auto parts, and groceries. Major franchise wholesalers include Independent Grocers Affiliate (IGA), Ben Franklin Stores, Western Auto, Rexall, Walgreen, and Super Valu Stores.[6]

With *franchise wholesaling,* retailers join with a wholesaler.

Figure 10-3
Rack Jobbing by Harlequin Books

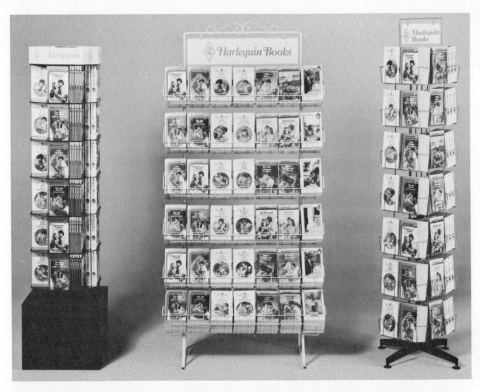

Proper maintenance of the Harlequin "booktique" rack and other displays is an important element in the romance publisher's success. Unlike trade publishers, Harlequin controls all aspects of distribution and display for the retailer as part of its packaged goods approach to bookselling. It uses a number of independent rack jobbers to service its retailers. Sources: Harlequin Books and *Marketing News* (December 24, 1982), p. 5. Reprinted by permission.

A number of manufacturers or retailers can establish a *wholesale cooperative*.

A ***wholesale cooperative*** is owned by its member firms to economize functions and offer broad support. Producer-owned wholesale cooperatives are popular in farming. For example, Sunkist Growers is made up of 7,300 small producers. It ships one half of all fresh oranges and 80 per cent of all fresh lemons consumed in the United States.[7] Producer cooperatives not only market, transport, and process farm products, they also manufacture and distribute farm supplies. In many instances, cooperatives sell to supermarkets under their own names, such as Welch's and Ocean Spray.

Retailer-owned wholesale cooperatives appear when independent retailers form associations that purchase, lease, or build wholesale facilities. The cooperative takes title to merchandise, handles cooperative advertising, and negotiates with suppliers. Retailer-owned cooperatives are used by hardware and grocery stores.

Limited-Service Merchant Wholesalers

Limited-service merchant wholesalers can be divided into cash and carry, drop shipper, truck/wagon, and mail-order types.

With ***cash-and-carry wholesaling,*** a small businessperson is able to drive his or her truck to a wholesaler, order products, and take them back to the store or business. Cash-and-carry wholesaling emerged in the 1920s and 1930s as a result of the growing threat of chain stores against independent retailers. Cash-and-carry wholesalers offer no credit or delivery, provide no merchandising and promotion assistance, have no outside sales force, and do not aid in marketing research or planning. They are important for fill-in items, have low prices, and allow immediate product availability. Cash-and-carry wholesalers are common for construction materials, electrical supplies, office supplies, auto supplies, hardware products, and groceries.

In *cash-and-carry
wholesaling,* the
customer drives to a
wholesaler, orders
products, and takes
them back.

Drop shippers (desk jobbers) purchase goods from manufacturers or suppliers and arrange for their shipment to retailers or industrial users. While the drop shipper has legal ownership of the products, it does not take physical possession of them and has no facilities for storing them. A drop shipper buys items, leaves them at manufacturers' plants, contacts customers by telephone, coordinates carload shipments from manufacturers directly to its customers, and assumes responsibility for items that cannot be sold. Trade credit, a personal sales force, and some research and planning assistance are provided; merchandising and promotional support are not. Drop shippers are frequently used for coal, coke, and building materials. These goods have high freight costs in relation to their unit value, because of their weight. Therefore, direct shipments from suppliers to customers are needed.

Drop shippers buy goods
and arrange for their
shipment to customers.
They do not take
possession of goods.

Truck/wagon wholesalers generally have a regular sales route, offer items from the truck or wagon, and deliver goods at the same time they are sold. They also provide merchandising and promotion support. This wholesaler is considered to offer limited service because it usually does not extend credit and offers little research and planning help. High operating costs are required because of the personalized services performed and low average sales. A truck or wagon wholesaler often deals with goods requiring special handling or those that are highly perishable. These include bakery products, tobacco, meat, candy, potato chips, and dairy products.

Truck/wagon wholesalers
offer items from their
vehicles and deliver
goods on a sales route.

Mail-order wholesalers utilize catalogs, instead of a personal sales force, to promote products and communicate with their customers. Generally, they do not provide credit or merchandising and promotion support. They do store and deliver goods and offer some research and planning assistance. Mail-order wholesaling is found with jewelry, cosmetics, auto parts, specialty food product lines, business supplies, and small office equipment.

Mail-order wholesalers
sell through catalogs.

Agents and Brokers

Agents and *brokers* provide many wholesaling functions, but they do not purchase or take title to goods. Unlike merchant wholesalers, who receive profits from the sales of goods they own, agents and brokers work for commissions or fees as payment for their services. Roughly 10 to 12 per cent of wholesale sales are handled by agents and brokers. The principal difference between agents and brokers is that agents are more likely to be used on a permanent basis, whereas brokers are employed on a temporary basis.

Agents and brokers offer three major advantages: they allow a man-

Agents and *brokers* do
not take title to goods;
relationships with
agents are usually more
permanent.

ufacturer or supplier to expand sales despite limited resources; their selling costs are a predetermined per cent of sales; and they provide a trained sales force.

Agents are comprised of manufacturers' agents, selling agents, and commission (factor) merchants. ***Manufacturers' agents*** are organizations that work for several manufacturers and carry noncompetitive, complementary products in exclusive territories. By selling noncompetitive items, agents are able to eliminate conflict-of-interest situations. By selling complementary goods, agents are able to stock a fairly complete line of products for their market areas. These agents do not offer credit but sometimes store and deliver products and provide limited research and planning aid. Merchandising and promotion support are given.

Manufacturers' agents work for several manufacturers and carry noncompetitive, complementary products in exclusive territories.

Manufacturers' agents may supplement the sales efforts of manufacturers, help introduce new products, enter geographically dispersed markets, and sell products with low average sales. They usually carry only a portion of a manufacturer's products. A manufacturer may employ many agents, each with a unique product-territorial mix. Larger firms might use a different agent for every major product line. Manufacturers' agents have little input into a manufacturer's marketing program and price structure. Manufacturers' agents are important wholesalers of automotive products, iron, steel, footwear, and textile products. They generally earn commissions of 5 to 10 per cent of sales.

Selling agents assume responsibility for marketing the entire output of a manufacturer under a contractual agreement. In effect, selling agents become the marketing departments for their manufacturers/suppliers and are empowered to negotiate price and other conditions of sale, such as credit and delivery. They perform all wholesale functions except taking title to merchandise. While a manufacturer may use several manufacturers' agents, it may employ only one sales agent. Commissions vary widely, depending on the services performed.

Selling agents market all the products of a manufacturer under contractual agreement. They offer many services.

Selling agents are more likely to work for small manufacturers than large ones. These agents are common for textile manufacturing, canned foods, metals, home furnishings, apparel, lumber, and metal products.

Commission (factor) merchants receive goods on consignment from producers, accumulate them from local markets, and arrange for their sale in a central market location. These markets sometimes offer credit, store and deliver goods, provide a sales force, and offer research and planning help. They normally do not assist in merchandising and promotion.

Commission merchants assemble goods from local markets and sell them in a large market.

Commission merchants can negotiate selling prices with buyers, providing the prices are not below the seller's stated minimums. They may operate in an auction setting. The merchants deduct their commission, freight charges, and other expenses after the products are sold. The balance is sent to the producer or supplier. Commission merchants are used for agricultural and seafood products, furniture, and art.

Food brokers unite buyers and sellers in the food industry to conclude sales.

Brokers are very common in the food industry. ***Food brokers*** introduce buyers and sellers to one another and bring them together to complete a sale. They are well informed about market conditions, terms of sale, sources of credit, price setting, potential buyers, and the art of negotiating. They do not actually provide credit but sometimes store and deliver goods. Brokers also do not take title to goods and usually are not allowed to conclude a transaction without formal approval. Brokers generally represent the seller, who pays their commission.[8]

Food brokers, like manufacturers' agents, operate in specific geographic locations and work for a limited number of food producers within these areas. Their sales force calls on chain-store buyers, store managers, and institutional purchasing agents. Brokers work closely with advertising agencies. The average commission for food brokers is 5 per cent of sales.

Characteristics and Importance of Retailing

Retailing encompasses those business activities involved in the sale of goods and services to the ultimate (final) consumer for personal, family, or household use. It is the last stage in a channel of distribution.

Retailing, the last stage in a channel, includes the activities in selling to final consumers.

Retailing includes products, such as automobiles and televisions, as well as services, such as life insurance and appliance repair. It involves store and nonstore (vending machine, direct-to-home, mail order) sales. Manufacturers, importers, and others act as retailers when they sell products directly to the final consumer.

In general, retailers perform four functions: they collect an assortment of products and services from a wide variety of suppliers and offer them for sale; they provide information to consumers, as well as to other channel members; they frequently store merchandise, mark prices on it, and pay for items prior to selling them to final consumers; and they conclude transactions with final consumers.

The functions of retailing include collecting an assortment, circulating information, preparing items for sale, and completing a sale.

Retail sales and employment are sizable. While less than wholesale sales, annual retail sales volume exceeds $1 trillion. About 17 per cent of the nonagricultural U.S. work force is employed in the country's 2.5 million retail establishments. People are involved in store management, merchandising, ownership of businesses, and other retail occupations.

From another perspective—costs—retailing is a significant field of study. For example, on the average, about 41 cents of every dollar a customer spends in a department or specialty store goes to the store as compensation for the activities it performs.[9] This compensation, known as gross margin, is for rent, taxes, fuel, advertising, inventory management, personnel, and other retail costs, as well as profits.

The average size of a retail sale is small, $19.50 for department stores and $31.67 for specialty stores in 1980. Convenience stores, like 7-Eleven, have average sales under $2.00. Medium-sized supermarkets average $9.45.[10] Accordingly, retailers need to increase sales through one-stop shopping appeals, broadened merchandise assortments, increased frequency of shopping, and attracting more family members to go on shopping trips. Inventory controls, automated material handling, and electronic cash registers are needed to reduce transaction costs.

Despite low average sales, more than 50 per cent of department and specialty store sales are on credit. For example, Sears has more than 25 million active credit card customers who buy over $6 billion of merchandise on credit each year.[11] The use of credit necessitates bank or store credit plans and reasonable credit terms but leads to increased sales.

Whereas salespeople regularly visit organizational consumers to initiate and conclude transactions, most final consumers patronize stores. This makes the location of the store, product assortment, store hours, store fixtures, sales personnel, delivery, and other factors critical tools in drawing customers to the store.

Final consumers make many unplanned purchases. In contrast, those who buy for resale or use in manufacturing are more systematic in their purchasing. Therefore, retailers need to place impulse items in high-traffic locations, organize store layout, train sales personnel in suggestion selling, place related items next to each other, and sponsor special events.

Types of Retailers

Retailers can be categorized by ownership, strategy mix, nonstore operations, and service retailing.* The categories are overlapping; that is, a retailer can be correctly placed in more than one grouping. For example, 7-Eleven can be classified as a chain, a franchise, and a convenience store.

An examination of retailers by category provides information about their attributes, relative sizes and importance, different strategies, and the impact of environmental factors.

By Ownership

Retail ownership can be independent, chain, franchise, leased department, and/or cooperative, as shown in Figure 10-4.

An ***independent retailer*** operates only one retail outlet. It offers personal service, a convenient location, and close customer contact. Dry cleaners, butcher shops, furniture stores, independent service stations, barber shops, and many neighborhood stores are independents. About 85 per cent of all retailers are independents. This large number is the result of the ease of entry in retailing. For many kinds of retailing, investment requirements, state licensing standards, and technical knowledge requirements are low, and, therefore, competition is plentiful. Many retailers may fail because of ease of entry, poor management skills, and inadequate capital. Annually, several thousand firms fail, including about one third of those in business three years or less. The economy of the early 1980s has been particularly hard on independents.[12]

A ***chain*** involves common ownership of multiple retail units. It usually employs centralized purchasing and decision making. Independents have simple organizations, but chains have specialization, standardization, and elaborate control systems. Because of these factors,

An *independent retailer* operates one retail outlet and offers personal service and a good location.

In a *chain,* one firm operates multiple retail outlets. Chains account for 45 per cent of retail store sales, yet represent only 15 per cent of retailers.

*Service retailing is discussed fully in Chapter 17. Types of services were classified in Chapter 7. This chapter does not deal with service retailing.

Figure 10-4
Retail Ownership Forms

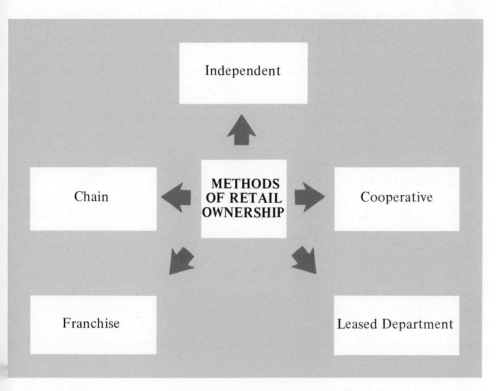

chains are able to serve a large, geographically dispersed target market and maintain a well-known company name. Although chains represent only about 15 per cent of all retailers, they account for over 45 per cent of total retail store sales. Only a few hundred chains operate one hundred or more units, yet they are responsible for over one quarter of total store sales. Chains are widespread for supermarkets, department stores, variety stores, and fast-food restaurants, among others. Examples of large chains are Sears, K mart, and Safeway.

Retail franchising is a contractual arrangement between a franchisor (who may be a manufacturer, wholesaler, or service sponsor) and a retail franchisee, which allows the franchisee to conduct a certain form of business under an established name and according to a specific set of rules. It is a form of chain ownership. Franchising allows a small businessperson to benefit from the experience, buying capabilities, and image of a large multiunit chain retailer. The franchisee also receives management training, participates in cooperative buying and advertising, and acquires a well-established company name. The franchisor benefits by obtaining franchise fees and royalties, fast payments for goods and services, strict controls over operations, consistency among outlets, and motivated owner-operators. Annually, franchises account for more than $300 billion in sales through nearly 500,000 establishments.[13] Franchising is particularly popular for auto and truck dealers, fast-food outlets, health spas, and convenience-foods stores. Examples of franchises are McDonald's, Jack LaLanne health spas, and Chevrolet dealers.

Retail franchising involves an arrangement between a franchisor and a franchisee to employ an established name and operate under certain rules.

A *leased department* in a store is rented to an outside party that provides expertise and management skills.

A *leased department* is a department in a retail store (usually a department, discount, or specialty store) that is rented to an outside party. The manager of a leased department is responsible for all aspects of its operation and pays a percentage of sales as rent. As in franchising, the leasing retailer places strict rules on the leased department operator. Leasors benefit because of the expertise of department operators, reduced risk and inventory investment, lucrative lease terms, increased store traffic, and an appeal to one-stop shopping convenience. Leasees benefit from the existence of an established location, the prestige of the leasor's name, the store traffic generated by the leasor, the one-stop customers attracted by the store as a whole, and whatever services (advertising, accounting, etc.) the leasor provides by mutual agreement. Leased departments are popular for beauty salons, jewelry, photographic studios, shoe repairs, and cosmetics. On average, leased departments contribute 7.0 per cent of department store sales and 11.0 per cent of specialty store sales.[14]

With a *retail cooperative*, independent stores organize to share costs, functions, and planning.

A cooperative is a retail organization that is operated by several independent retailers or by a group of consumers. In a *retail cooperative*, independent retailers share purchases, storage and shipping facilities, advertising, planning, and other functions. The individual stores retain their independence but agree on broad, common policies. Retail cooperatives are growing in response to the domination of independents by chains. Retail cooperatives are common for liquor stores, hardware stores, and some grocery stores. Ace Hardware, Associated Food Stores, and Western Auto are retail cooperatives. As pointed out earlier, wholesalers frequently aid retailers in setting up cooperatives.

With a *consumer cooperative*, consumer members invest in and operate a retail firm.

In a *consumer cooperative*, a retailer is owned and operated by consumer members. A group of consumers invests, receives stock certificates, elects officers, manages operations, and shares profits or savings. The goal is to offer reduced prices to members. Consumer cooperatives have been most prevalent with food products, particularly produce items. However, the cooperatives represent less than 1 per cent of total supermarket sales or supermarket produce sales. They have not grown further because they involve a lot of consumer initiative, profits have been low, and consumer expertise as owner-operators has been lacking.

By Strategy Mix

The *retail strategy mix* is the combination of prices, products, etc. that a retailer offers.

Retailers can be classified by *retail strategy mix*, the combination of prices, products, sales personnel, displays, and other factors they employ. Retail strategy mixes differ for convenience stores, supermarkets, superstores, specialty stores, variety stores, department stores, full-line discount stores, and retail catalog showrooms. See Figure 10-5.

A *convenience store* has long hours and carries a limited number of items.

A *convenience store* is a store featuring food items that is open long hours and carries a limited number of items. In the U.S., convenience stores have annual sales of $25 billion, including gasoline. The average convenience store has sales that are less than one fifth of those of the average supermarket.[15] Consumers use a convenience store for fill-in merchandise, often at off-hours. Bread, milk, ice cream, newspapers, and now gasoline are popular items at convenience stores (with

Figure 10-5
Retail Strategy Mixes

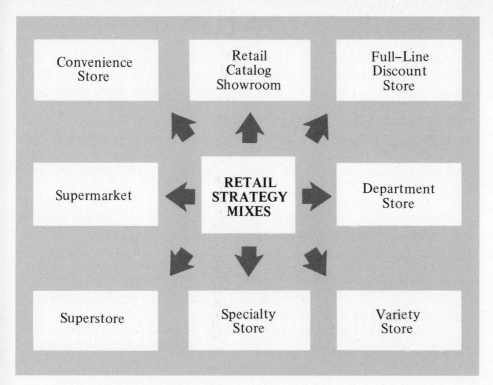

gasoline contributing one third of all sales). 7-Eleven, Arco, and Dairy Barn operate convenience stores.

A **supermarket** is a departmentalized food store with minimum annual sales of $2 million. The supermarket originated in the 1930s, when food retailers realized that a large-scale operation would enable them to combine volume sales, self-service, low prices, impulse buying, and one-stop food shopping. The automobile and refrigerator contributed to the supermarket's success by lowering travel costs and adding to the life span of perishable items. During the past twenty years, supermarket sales have stabilized at about 72 to 75 per cent of total grocery sales. Annually, supermarkets have sales of over $175 billion, 60 per cent of which is provided by chains.[16] In response to convenience stores, some supermarkets have lengthened their hours of operation. The largest supermarkets are Safeway, Kroger, and A&P.

A **superstore** is a large food-based retailer that is much more diversified than a supermarket. Superstores typically carry garden supplies, televisions, clothing, wine, boutique items, bakery products, and household appliances—in addition to a full line of supermarket items. While the average supermarket occupies 18,000 square feet of space, the typical superstore utilizes 30,000 square feet. Several factors are causing a number of supermarkets to switch to superstores: an interest in total one-stop shopping, the leveling off of food sales as a result of population stability and competition from restaurants and fast-food stores, improved transportation networks, and the higher margins on general merchandise (more than double those of food items). Grand Bazaar in Chicago and Hyper-Marche Laval in Montreal, Canada, are two superstores.

A **supermarket** is a large food store, with annual sales of at least $2 million. It is self-service and offers low prices.

A **superstore** stocks supermarket items and a variety of other products to attract one-stop shoppers.

A *specialty store* concentrates on the sale of one merchandise line, such as apparel and its accessories, sewing machines, or high-fidelity equipment. Consumers like specialty stores because they are not confronted with racks of merchandise, do not have to walk or search through several departments, can select from tailored assortments, and usually avoid crowds. Specialty stores are most successful in the apparel, gourmet food, appliance, toy, electronics, and sports product lines. In some cases department stores have reacted by creating boutiques and specialty shops within their stores. Specialty store sales exceed $50 billion per year. Successful specialty stores include Radio Shack, The Limited, and Toys ''R'' Us.

A *variety store* sells a wide assortment of low and popularly priced merchandise. It features stationery, gift items, women's accessories, toilet articles, light hardware, toys, housewares, and confectionaries. Variety-store sales are about $9 billion per year. With the growth of other retail strategy mixes, variety stores have fallen on hard times. In the mid-1970s W. T. Grant went bankrupt, the largest bankruptcy in retailing history. F. W. Woolworth, the country's twelfth largest retailer, dominates the variety-store category.

A *department store* is a large retailer that employs at least 25 people and usually sells a general line of apparel for the family, household linens and dry goods, and furniture, home furnishings, appliances, radios, and television sets. It is organized into separate departments for purposes of buying, promotion, service, and control. A department store has the greatest assortment of any retailer, provides many customer services, is a fashion leader, and dominates the stores around it. Because most department stores are parts of chains, they have high name recognition and can utilize all forms of media. In recent years department stores have set up many boutiques, theme displays, and designer departments to compete with other retailers. Annual total department store sales including mail order, are about $100 billion. Examples of department store chains are Federated, Dayton Hudson, May, Carter Hawley Hale, and R. H. Macy.

A *full-line discount store* has low prices, a relatively broad merchandise assortment, low-rent location, self-service, brand-name merchandise, wide aisles, shopping carts, and most merchandise displayed on the selling floor. Annually, discount stores sell over $50 billion in merchandise. Discount stores are the largest retailers of general merchandise, housewares, sporting goods, luggage, linens and domestics, toys, and children's wear.[17]

Another discount retailer is a *retail catalog showroom,* in which consumers select merchandise from a catalog and shop at a warehouse location. Customers frequently write up their own orders, products are usually stocked in a back room, and there are limited displays. Catalog showrooms specialize in national brands. Annual sales are about $9 billion.[18] Best Products, Service Merchandise, and Consumers Distributing are among the largest catalog showrooms.

During recent years, a number of other forms of low-price retailing have grown. These include limited-line and warehouse food stores, factory outlet stores, off-price chains, discount drugstores, and flea mar-

Table 10-3   **Retail Strategy Mixes—A Discount Store Versus a Department Store**

Discount-Store Strategy	Department-Store Strategy
1. Inexpensive rental location—low level of pedestrian traffic (Note: full-line discount stores are increasingly using more expensive locations)	1. Expensive rental location in shopping center or district—high level of pedestrian traffic
2. Simple fixtures, linoleum floor, centralized dressing room, few interior or window displays	2. Elaborate fixtures, carpeted floor, individual dressing rooms, many interior and exterior displays
3. Promotional emphasis on price. Some discounters do not advertise brand names, but state "famous brand"	3. Promotional emphasis on full service, quality brands, and fashion leadership
4. No alterations, telephone orders, delivery, or gift wrapping; limited credit	4. Alterations included in clothing prices, telephone ordering, and home delivery at little or no fee; credit widely available
5. Reliance on self-service, dump-bin displays (plain cases with piles of merchandise), and rack displays; all merchandise visible	5. Extensive sales force assistance, attractive merchandise displays, most storage in back room
6. Emphasis on branded merchandise. Selection probably not complete (not all models and colors); featuring "seconds," removal of labels from merchandise if required by manufacturer, and stocking of low-price nonbranded items	6. Emphasis on a full selection of branded and privately branded first-quality merchandise; will not stock closeouts, discontinued lines, or seconds
7. Year-round use of low prices	7. Sales limited to end-of-season clearance and special events

kets. These retailers reduce prices by limiting inventory, using plain store fixtures, locating at inexpensive sites, and offering few customer services.[19] Table 10-3 shows the basic differences between most discount and department store strategies.

By Nonstore Operations

Nonstore retailing refers to retailers who do not utilize conventional store facilities. It includes vending machines, direct-to-home sales, and mail order.

A *vending machine* uses coin-operated machinery, eliminates the need for sales personnel, allows around-the-clock sales, and can be placed outside rather than inside a store. Vending-machine sales are concentrated in a narrow product line. Beverages and cigarettes yield two thirds of sales. Less than 10 per cent of sales come from nonfood items. Machines require intensive servicing because of breakdowns, stock-outs, and vandalism. Although annual sales exceed $14 billion, vending machines have limited growth potential.[20]

Direct-to-home retailers sell directly to consumers in their homes. Cosmetics, vacuum cleaners, encyclopedias, dairy products, and newspapers are successfully sold direct-to-home. This form of retailing can be either on a cold canvass (Electrolux), referral (Avon), or party (Tupperware) basis. In a cold canvass the salesperson goes through an area and knocks on each door in search of customers. With a referral system, past buyers recommend friends for the salesperson to call on. In the

Nonstore retailing does not use traditional facilities.

Vending machines eliminate a sales force, allow 24-hour sales, and can be placed outside a store.

Direct-to-home retailers use cold canvassing, referrals, or party plans to sell to consumers in their homes.

party method one consumer acts as host and invites friends and acquaintances to a sales demonstration in his or her home. It is estimated that direct-to-home sales are about $10 billion per year.

Mail order retailing occurs when the seller seeks orders through television, radio, printed media, or the mail, receives orders through the mail or telephone, and ships merchandise to the customer's home. There are general-merchandise mail-order firms, stores offering mail order as a supplement to regular business, and novelty or specialty mail-order firms. The most popular mail-order items are ready-to-wear clothing, insurance, magazines, and books. Annual mail-order sales are approximately $35 billion. This form of retailing offers convenience for consumers, low operating costs, coverage of a wide geographic area, and new market segments. Large mail-order firms are Spiegel, L. L. Bean, Montgomery Ward, and Sears.

> With *mail order retailing*, a seller seeks orders through the media and ships merchandise to the consumer at home.

Considerations in Retail Planning

There are many factors for retailers to consider when developing and implementing their marketing plans. Five of the most important factors are store location, atmosphere, scrambled merchandising, the wheel of retailing, and technological advances.

Store Location

Store location is important to retailers because it helps determine the customer mix and competition. It is also highly inflexible.[21] These are the basic forms of store location: the isolated store, the unplanned business district, and the planned shopping center.

An *isolated store* is a free-standing retail outlet located on either a highway or side street. This type of store location is used by discount stores because of low rent and manufacturers' desires for them to be far enough away from traditional specialty and department stores that sell goods at full prices. Although there are no adjacent stores with which the firm must compete, there are also no stores to help draw consumer traffic. The difficulty of attracting and holding consumers is the reason why large retailers are usually best suited for an isolated location. Customers are unwilling to travel to an isolated store that does not have a wide assortment of products and an established reputation. See Figure 10-6.

> An *isolated store* is a free-standing outlet on a highway or side street. There are no other stores next to it.

An *unplanned business district* exists where a group of stores are located close to one another and the combination of stores is not based on prior planning. There are four kinds of unplanned business district: central business district, secondary business district, neighborhood business district, and string.

> In an *unplanned business district*, stores locate together with no planning.

A central business district (CBD) is the hub of retailing in a city and is synonymous with the term downtown. It contains the largest commercial and shopping facilities in a city. Cultural, employment, and entertainment facilities surround it. There is at least one major department store and a broad grouping of specialty and convenience stores. CBDs have had some problems with crowding, lack of parking, old

> A central business district (CBD) is the largest "downtown" area of a city with commercial and shopping facilities.

Figure 10-6
A Very Isolated Store Location

"LET'S FACE IT, IRV. WE'RE IN A <u>TOO LOW</u> RENT DISTRICT."

Reprinted by permission of Rothco.

buildings, crime, and other factors. However, CBD sales remain strong. Among the innovations used to strengthen CBDs are closing streets to vehicular traffic, modernizing storefronts and equipment, developing strong merchant associations, planting trees to make the area more attractive, improving transportation, and integrating a commercial and residential environment.

A secondary business district (SBD) is a shopping area that is usually bounded by the intersection of two major streets. Cities generally have several SBDs, each having at least one junior department store, a variety store, and several small service shops. In comparison with the CBD, the SBD has less merchandise assortment, a smaller trading area (the geographic area from which a store draws its customers), and sells more convenience items.

A secondary business district (SBD) is bounded by two major streets. It has a junior department store.

A neighborhood business district (NBD) satisfies the convenience shopping needs of a neighborhood. The NBD contains a number of small stores, with the major retailer being a supermarket or variety store. An NBD is located on the major street in a residential area.

A neighborhood business district (NBD) satisfies local needs.

A string is usually composed of a group of stores with similar or compatible product lines. However, because this location is unplanned, various store combinations are possible. It is located along a street or highway. Car dealers, antique stores, and clothing stores are retailers that frequently locate in a string.

A string contains closely grouped stores on a highway or street.

A *planned shopping center* is centrally owned or managed, planned and operated as an entity, surrounded by parking, and based on balanced tenancy. *Balanced tenancy* means that the type and number of stores within any planned center are related to the overall needs of the surrounding population. The various stores complement each other in the quality and variety of merchandise. To ensure balance, a center

A *planned shopping center* is centrally planned, suits the area, and has *balanced tenancy,* which relates stores to the population.

may limit the merchandise lines any store carries. Planned centers account for approximately 43 per cent of total retail store sales; isolated stores and unplanned business districts account for the remaining 57 per cent. The three types of planned center are regional, community, and neighborhood.

A regional shopping center sells mostly shopping goods to a geographically dispersed market. A regional center has at least one or two department stores and up to one hundred or more small retailers. Customers are willing to drive up to a half hour to reach a regional center.

A community shopping center has a variety store and/or small department store as its major retailer, with several smaller stores. This center sells both convenience and shopping items. A neighborhood shopping center sells mostly convenience products. The largest store is a supermarket and/or drugstore, with a few smaller stores.

A regional shopping center sells shopping goods to a large market.

A community center has some variety of stores; a neighborhood center sells convenience goods.

Atmosphere

Atmosphere is the sum total of the physical characteristics of a retail store that are used to develop an image and draw customers. The overall atmosphere of a store helps determine the customers it will attract, sets the mood for shopping, encourages impulse purchases, and sets a long-term image for the store. Atmosphere is closely related to the strategy mix a retailer selects, as described earlier in the chapter. For example, a discounter will have linoleum floors, crowded displays, centrally located cash registers, and shopping carts. A prestige department store will have carpeted floors, wide aisles and attractive displays, recessed cash registers, and sales personnel to help carry purchases.

There are four components of a store's atmosphere: exterior, general interior, store layout, and interior displays. The exterior of a store encompasses its storefront, marquee, entrances, display windows, visibility from the street or highway, uniqueness, surrounding area, surrounding stores, and traffic congestion. The general interior includes a store's flooring, colors, scents, lighting, fixtures, wall textures, temperature, width of aisles, dressing facilities, vertical transportation, personnel, and placement of cash registers.

Store layout refers to the floor space allocated for customers, selling, and storage, the groupings of products, department locations, and arrangements within departments. Interior (or point-of-purchase) displays involve the types of cases and racks used to show merchandise, mobiles, in-store advertising, mannequins, and wall decorations.

Recently, Safeway opened an innovative 61,000-square-foot food and general merchandise store in Arlington, Texas. A major objective set by Safeway was to change the atmosphere consumers faced when entering traditional food stores. According to the store's designer:

Atmosphere refers to the physical characteristics of a store. It consists of a store's exterior, general interior, layout, and displays.

> We set out to create something with pizazz, something that isn't mundane and something which puts some fun and interest into shopping. There's a little less merchandise per square foot than Safeway normally would get into a store, but we've made it more inviting for people to come into the store.[22]

Reprinted by permission.

To establish the atmosphere it sought, Safeway created a number of small shops in the center of the store, used photos as aisle signs, and set up a simulated sidewalk cafe (with seating for 36 customers) inside the store. The store cost $3 million to build. Figure 10-7 shows the store's indoor cafe.

Scrambled Merchandising

Scrambled merchandising occurs when a retailer adds products or product lines that are unrelated to each other and the retailer's original business. Examples of scrambled merchandising are supermarkets carrying nonfood items like toys, panty hose, nonprescription drugs, and magazines; gasoline service stations selling food items; and drugstores selling film and gift items.

There are three reasons for the popularity of scrambled merchandising: retailers seek to convert their stores to one-stop shopping centers; scrambled merchandise is often fast selling, generates store traffic, and yields high profit margins; and impulse purchasing is increased.

Scrambled merchandising spreads quickly and frequently leads to competition among unrelated stores. For example, when supermarkets branched into nonfood personal care items, they created a decline in drugstore sales. Drugstores were then forced to scramble into small appliances and toys. This had an impact on specialty store sales, and so on.

There are limits to scrambled merchandising, especially if the addition of unrelated items lowers buying, selling, and servicing expertise. Furthermore, a low turnover of certain products can occur, should the

*In scrambled
merchandising, a retailer
adds unrelated products
in order to obtain one-
stop shopping, higher
margins, and more
impulse purchases.*

Courtesy of Sears, Roebuck and Co.

retailer expand into too many diverse product categories. Finally, store image may become fuzzy as consumers fail to see a retailer stressing any one product category or group.

Sears provides a good example of scrambled merchandising. In addition to the regular goods and services that department stores offer, Sears now provides insurance (Allstate), real estate brokerage (Coldwell Banker), and stock brokerage (Dean Witter) in many stores. While some observers refer to Sears as "Socks 'n' Stocks," the firm has been quite successful with its strategy.[23] Figure 10-8 shows the Sears Financial Network.

Wheel of Retailing

**The *wheel of retailing*
shows how retail
strategies change over
time, thus leaving
opportunities for new
firms.**

The ***wheel of retailing*** describes how low-end (discount) strategies can turn into high-end (full service, high price) strategies and thus provide opportunities for new firms to enter as discounters. According to the wheel, retail innovators often first appear as low-price operators with low profit-margin requirements. As time passes, these innovators look to increase sales and their customer base. They upgrade product offerings, facilities, and services and develop into more traditional retailers. They may expand sales force support, utilize a more costly location, and introduce delivery, credit, and alterations. These improvements lead to higher costs, which in turn lead to higher prices. This creates opportunities for new retailers to emerge by appealing to price-conscious consumers.

Figure 10-9 shows the wheel of retailing in action.

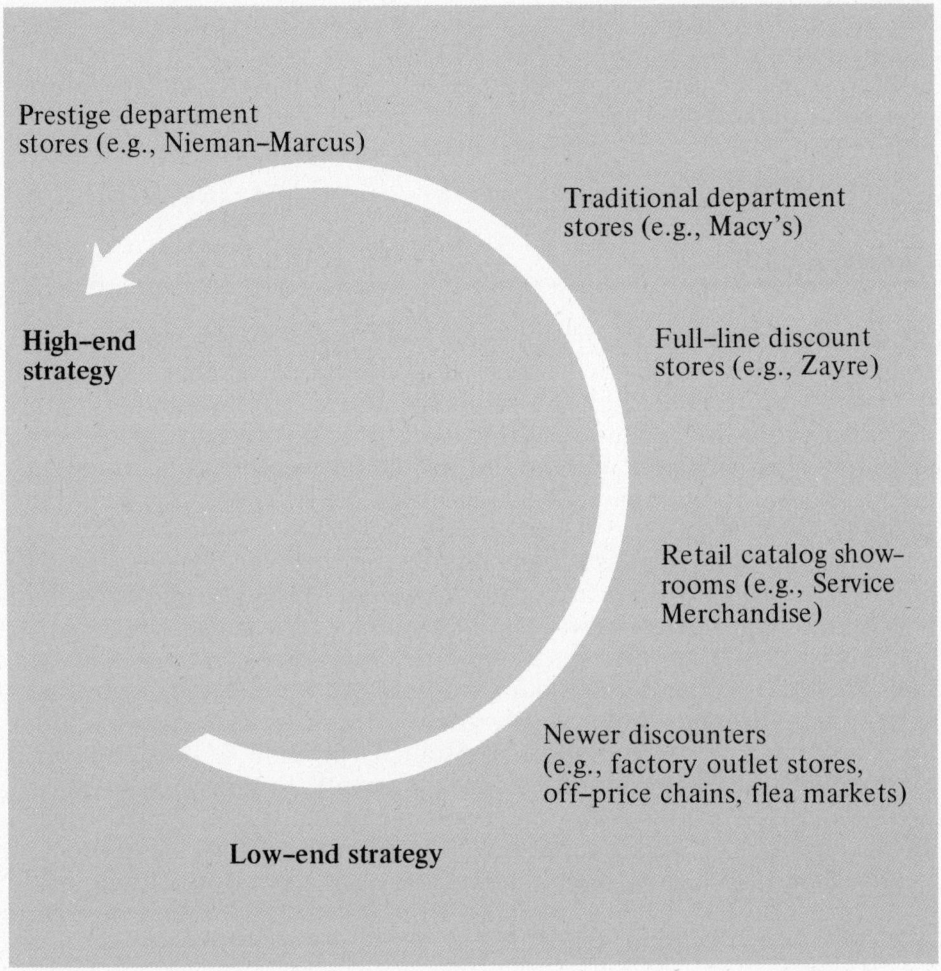

Figure 10-9
The Wheel of Retailing in Action

Prestige department stores (e.g., Nieman–Marcus)

Traditional department stores (e.g., Macy's)

High–end strategy

Full–line discount stores (e.g., Zayre)

Retail catalog show-rooms (e.g., Service Merchandise)

Newer discounters (e.g., factory outlet stores, off–price chains, flea markets)

Low-end strategy

Technological Advances

During the past several years, a number of technological advances have emerged in retailing, many as the result of growing computerization. Among the major advances are

- Computerized-checkout systems (utilizing the UPC or OCR-A), that speed up transactions, record data, and reduce cashier errors.
- Antishoplifting tags, that are attached to merchandise and set off an alarm if not properly removed by employees.
- Automatic energy-control systems, that carefully monitor store temperature and reduce fuel costs.
- Computerized site-selection programs, which are able to evaluate the characteristics of many potential store locations.
- Improved credit systems, that allow faster processing of credit authorizations and efficient transfers of funds.
- Computerized inventory systems, that reduce the need for physical inventory counts.

Technological advances in retailing are improving efficiency and performance.

In general, these advances enable retailers to improve efficiency, obtain more accurate and quicker information, hold down labor costs, minimize losses due to employee errors and customer and employee theft, and make better decisions. Nonetheless, new technology can be quite expensive, require break-in periods, and encounter employee and customer resistence.

Summary

Wholesaling involves the buying and handling of merchandise and its resale to retailers, organizational users, and/or other wholesalers but not the sale of significant volume to final consumers. Wholesaling functions include developing contacts, selling and servicing accounts, operating a sales force, distribution, and handling payments and returns. Independent wholesalers must balance the requests of their manufacturers and retailers.

Manufacturer wholesaling is conducted through sales and branch offices. The sales office carries no inventory. Through either or both offices, manufacturers carry out all wholesale functions.

Merchant wholesalers buy, take title, and possess products for further resale. Full-service merchant wholesalers assemble an assortment of products, provide trade credit, store and deliver merchandise, offer merchandising and promotion assistance, provide a personal sales force, and offer research and planning support. Full-service merchant wholesalers fall into general merchandise, specialty merchandise, rack jobber, franchise, and cooperative types. Limited-service merchant wholesalers take title to merchandise but do not provide all wholesale functions. Limited-service merchant wholesalers are divided into cash and carry, drop shipper, truck/wagon, and mail-order types.

Agents and brokers provide many wholesaling functions, but do not purchase goods. Agents are used on a more permanent basis than brokers. Types of agents are manufacturers' agents, selling agents, and commission (factor) merchants. Food brokers dominate brokerage.

Retailing encompasses those business activities involved with the sale of goods and services to the ultimate (final) consumer for personal, family, or household use. It includes products and services, and store and nonstore sales. The primary functions of retailing are collecting assortments, providing information, handling and paying for merchandise, and concluding customer transactions.

Retailers may be categorized in several ways. Ownership types are independent, chain, franchise, leased department, and cooperative. The ease of entry into retailing fosters competition and results in many new firms failing. Different strategy mixes are used by convenience stores, supermarkets, superstores, specialty stores, variety stores, department stores, full-line discount stores, and retail catalog showrooms. Nonstore retailing involves vending machines, direct-to-home, and mail order. Service retailing includes rental goods, owned goods, and nongoods categories (discussed in Chapters 7 and 17).

In retail planning, store location, atmosphere, scrambled merchandising, the wheel of retailing, and technological advances need to be considered. Locational alternatives are isolated stores, unplanned business districts, and planned shopping centers. Only the planned centers utilize balanced tenancy. Atmosphere is the sum total of a store's physical characteristics that help develop an image and attract customers. Scrambled merchandising is the addition of products unrelated to the retailer's original business. The wheel of retailing explains low-end and high-end retail strategies and how they emerge. Technological advances include computerized checkouts, antishoplifting tags, energy-control systems, site-selection programs, credit systems, and inventory systems.

KEY TERMS

After reading this chapter, you should understand these key terms:

Wholesaling
Manufacturer wholesaling
Merchant wholesalers
Full-service merchant wholesalers
Limited-service merchant wholesalers
General-merchandise wholesalers
Specialty-merchandise wholesalers
Rack jobbers
Franchise wholesaling
Wholesale cooperative
Cash-and-carry wholesaling
Drop shippers (desk jobbers)
Truck/wagon wholesalers
Mail-order wholesalers
Agents
Brokers
Manufacturers' agents
Selling agents
Commission merchants
Food brokers
Retailing
Independent retailer
Chain

Retail franchising
Leased department
Retail cooperative
Consumer cooperative
Retail strategy mix
Convenience store
Supermarket
Superstore
Specialty store
Variety store
Department store
Full-line discount store
Retail catalog showroom
Nonstore retailing
Vending machine
Direct-to-home retailers
Mail order retailing
Isolated store
Unplanned business district
Planned shopping center
Balanced tenancy
Atmosphere
Scrambled merchandising
Wheel of retailing

QUESTIONS FOR DISCUSSION

1. Explain why wholesale sales volume exceeds retail sales volume.
2. "Wholesalers are very much in the middle, often not fully knowing whether their loyalty should be to the manufacturer/supplier or the customer." Comment on this statement.
3. Why are rack jobbers common for supermarket products such as magazines?
4. Why would a manufacturer use an agent rather than a merchant wholesaler?
5. How do manufacturers' agents and selling agents differ?

6. Develop a short checklist a manufacturer could use to evaluate independent wholesalers.
7. Why do final consumers usually visit retail stores, when organizational consumers generally have salespeople call on them?
8. How can independents successfully compete with chains?
9. At one time most of McDonald's outlets operated under franchise agreements. Today many of McDonald's outlets are owned by the firm itself.
   a. Why was franchising a correct strategy for McDonald's in its early years?
   b. Why would McDonald's want to buy back its franchises now?
10. Compare the strategies of convenience stores, supermarkets, and superstores.
11. Develop a discount strategy for a high-fidelity equipment retailer. How would it compete with a high-priced specialty store?
12. Compare the attributes of a central business district with those of a regional shopping center.
13. Explain the appropriate atmosphere for a retailer of fine jewelry.
14. Give two examples of the wheel of retailing working in your area.

NOTES

1. Geri Hirshey, "The Supermarket That's Eating Manhattan," *New York* (March 17, 1980), pp. 48–52; and Charles Paikert, "Jules Rose: Manhattan's Food Market Maven," *Chain Store Age Executive* (January 1982), pp. 48ff.
2. Adapted from Ralph S. Alexander (Chairman), *Marketing Definitions: Report of Definitions Committee* (Chicago: American Marketing Association, 1960), p. 47.
3. Bert C. McCammon, Jr., and James W. Kenderine, "Mainstream Developments in Wholesaling," paper presented at the 1975 Conference of the Southwestern Marketing Association, p. 3.
4. *'80 Annual Statement Studies* (Philadelphia: Robert Morris Associates, 1980).
5. "Marketing Observer," *Business Week* (October 4, 1976), p. 104.
6. See "A Food Supplier's Bigger Bite," *Business Week* (February 22, 1982), p. 136 to learn how IGA and its major wholesaler operate.
7. Hal Lancaster, "Giant Sunkist Co-Op Beset by Government, Business, and Growers," *Wall Street Journal* (July 24, 1978), p. 1.
8. See Nancy Giges, "Grocers' 'Middlemen' Step to the Forefront," *Advertising Age* (October 11, 1982), pp. M-18–M-21.
9. "Retailing: Department, Discount, Specialty, and Drug Stores," *Standard & Poor's Industry Analysis* (November 26, 1981), p. R119.
10. Ibid.; Pamela G. Hollie, "Food Is Pumping Up Net at Arco," *New York Times* (March 3, 1980), p. D5; and "48th Annual Report of the Grocery Industry," *Progressive Grocer* (April 1981), p. 128.
11. "The New Sears," *Business Week* (November 16, 1981), p. 143.
12. See Claudia Ricci and John Curley, "Troubled Retailers," *Wall Street Journal* (December 17, 1982), pp. 1, 12.
13. Andrew Kostecka, "Restaurant Franchising in the Economy," *Restaurant Business* (March 15, 1981), p. 104.
14. "At Your Service—Outlook for Leased Departments: Brightest and Best in Service Areas," *Stores* (December 1977), p. 44.
15. "1982 Convenience Store Industry Report," *Convenience Store News*.
16. "Grocery Industry for 1981," *Progressive Grocer* (April 1982), pp. 51–52.
17. "Retailing: Department, Discount, Specialty, and Drug Stores," p. R122.
18. For a 10-year analysis of showrooms, see Jody Long, "Catalog Firms Faring Well in Recession," *Wall Street Journal* (March 23, 1982), pp. 37, 43.
19. See "Outlets' Balancing Act: Low Price Vs. Quality," *Chain Store Age Executive* (May 1982),

pp. 110, 113; "K mart Sets Off-Price Brand Units," *Advertising Age* (November 1, 1982), p. 6; Marianne Maloney, "No-Frills Outlet Stores Trying Mall Concept," *Advertising Age* (March 29, 1982); and "Ward's Latest Formula: Hybrid Discounting," *Business Week* (November 2, 1981), pp. 77, 80, 82.

20. "Hard Times in Vending Field," *New York Times* (January 29, 1982), pp. D1, D4.

21. For a look at how several retailers select store locations, see Janet Neiman, "Retailers Should Know Their Place," *Advertising Age* (November 1, 1982), p. M-22.

22. Kevin Higgins, "Safeway Enters Quest for Supermarket of Future," *Marketing News* (January 7, 1983), pp. 1, 6.

23. Tim Carrington, "Socks 'n' Stocks," *Wall Street Journal* (November 19, 1982), pp. 1, 21.

MALONE & HYDE: A FOOD WHOLESALER DIVERSIFIES* 1 — CASES

Malone & Hyde is the nation's third-largest food wholesaler, with annual sales exceeding $2 billion. It serves 2,200 independent grocery stores in 16 states, from Florida to Texas and north to Indiana. Malone & Hyde provides its grocers with a full line of food and related products, trading stamps, and services (such as accounting assistance and property, life, and health insurance).

Overall, food wholesalers in the U.S. supply about $75 billion worth of products to about 115,000 independent supermarkets. Despite this high sales volume, the food-wholesaling industry is facing several problems:

1. There is little potential for increasing the number of independents using wholesalers, since many are already linked to brokers.
2. There has been a decline in independent supermarkets, as many have gone out of business and others have formed cooperative affiliations for buying purposes.
3. U.S. grocery sales are leveling off, because the population has stabilized and more people eat out.
4. Refrigeration, rent, shipping, and labor costs have risen significantly in recent years.
5. More grocers expect their wholesalers to help them with financing.
6. Modernization of distribution facilities will be expensive.

There are 300 fewer food wholesalers now than in 1976.

In order to sustain its own growth, Malone & Hyde has engaged in a major diversification effort. Among the firms it has acquired are

- Piggly Wiggly supermarkets in Texas, Oklahoma, Arkansas, and Louisiana.
- Super D drugstores in the Southeast.
- Sunset and Wolfe's sporting-goods chains, with stores from Arizona to Washington.
- Auto Shack, an auto-parts retailer in the Southeast.

Malone & Hyde has also upgraded its distribution facilities. For example, it built a 500,000 square-foot facility in Miami for $20 million. Through this facility, Malone & Hyde hopes to expand its business with supermarket chains.

*The data in this case are drawn from Steven Flax, "Wholesalers," *Forbes* (January 4, 1982), pp. 222–223; Thomas Jaffe, "A Self-Inflicted Wound," *Forbes* (February 1, 1982), pp. 81, 84; and "Malone & Hyde Buys 80% of Piggly Wiggly Red River Inc. Stock," *Wall Street Journal* (December 20, 1982), p. 27.

Joseph R. Hyde, III, the company's chief executive, believes these new ventures will succeed because, like food distribution, they "all deal with the management of inventories—how to move goods through a warehouse."

QUESTIONS

1. Evaluate Malone & Hyde's new ventures in relation to the company's original role as a food wholesaler.
2. What factors should Malone & Hyde consider in making further expansion plans?
3. Is there a conflict of interest in Malone & Hyde acting as a food wholesaler as well as a supermarket owner?
4. Are wholesaling and retailing skills the same? Explain your answer and relate it to Mr. Hyde's statement.

2   DAYTON HUDSON: TAKING RISKS TO EXPAND†

Dayton Hudson is the sixteenth largest retailer in the U.S., with annual sales exceeding $5 billion and about 1,000 stores nationwide. While the company began when two department-store chains merged (Dayton's of Minneapolis and J. L. Hudson of Detroit), it has since branched out into discount, apparel, bookstore, and jewelry retailing. See Table 1. Today, only one quarter of its total sales come from department stores.

Dayton Hudson is very thorough and systematic in its planning. It focuses on an annual long-term return on investment goal of 15–16 per cent. One day a month, executives meet to discuss long-range plans. The company has a decentralized management structure, which places great control in the hands of the managers for each of the nine store chains it owns. Marketing research studies are conducted regularly.

Over the years, Dayton Hudson has had some disappointments, in addition to its large success. It dropped mail-order, cosmetics, and catalog showroom

†The data in this case are drawn from Stanley H. Slom, "Dayton Hudson Unveils Five-Year Plan," *Chain Store Age Executive* (January 1982), pp. 66–67; and John Curley and Larry Ingrassia, "Big Retailer Seeks Profits in Discounting," *Wall Street Journal* (October 6, 1982), p. 35.

Table 1	Divisions	Stores
The Divisions and Stores of Dayton Hudson	Apparel store	Mervyn's
	Bookstore	B. Dalton Bookseller
	Department store	Dayton's Diamonds Hudson's John A. Brown
	Discount store	Plums Target
	Home and leisure products store	Lechmere
	Jewelry store	Dayton Hudson Jewelers

businesses less than one year after they were acquired. In 1979, Lipman's department stores were sold (despite being profitable) because sales were too small. A current disappointment is Diamonds, a Phoenix-based department store chain, which has had a decline in return on investment.

To continue its sales and profit growth, Dayton Hudson has very ambitious plans. After reviewing a 100-page research report on a study it commissioned, the firm decided to open five off-price fashion stores named Plums in Los Angeles during 1983. These stores would feature name brands at low prices. Three of Dayton Hudson's chains will be expanded significantly by 1986: Target, from 151 to 265 stores; Mervyn's, from 78 to 178 stores; and B. Dalton Bookseller, from 563 to 1,100 stores. Hudson's will go from 18 to 20 stores. Total expansion will cost $2.5 billion.

QUESTIONS

1. How can Dayton Hudson effectively manage so many different divisions?
2. What are the potential benefits and risks in Dayton Hudson's expansion plans?
3. Dayton Hudson expects only to maintain department store sales. It forecasts little growth in that area. Comment on this.
4. Develop a list of environmental factors Dayton Hudson should monitor during the next five years. Do these factors and their effects differ by division? Explain your answer.

Part
Five

Promotion
Planning

Introduction to Part Five

Part Five deals with the third major element of marketing, promotion. Chapter 11 provides an overview of promotion planning, the systematic decision making relating to the communication used by a firm to inform, persuade, or remind people about its products, services, image, ideas, community involvement, or impact on society. The basic types of promotion are described: advertising, publicity, personal selling, and sales promotion. The channel of communication through which a company sends a message to its audience is fully explained. Next, the steps in the development of an overall promotion plan are described. These include establishing objectives, setting a budget, and developing a promotion mix. The chapter concludes with discussions regarding the legal environment of promotion and criticisms and defenses of promotion.

Chapter 12 examines the two mass communication forms of promotion, advertising and publicity. Advertising is defined as the paid, nonpersonal presentation and promotion of ideas, goods, and services by an identified sponsor. Publicity is defined as the nonpaid, nonpersonal presentation and promotion of ideas, goods, and services by an independent source. The scope of advertising and publicity and their positive and negative attributes are detailed. There are comprehensive descriptions of the development of advertising and publicity plans, from objectives to evaluation of success or failure.

Chapter 13 concentrates on personal selling and sales promotion. Personal selling is defined as that part of promotion involving an oral presentation in a conversation with one or more prospective buyers for the purpose of a sale. Sales promotion consists of the marketing activities, other than advertising, publicity, or personal selling, that stimulate consumer purchases and dealer effectiveness. In this chapter the scope, characteristics, and stages in planning are described for both personal selling and sales promotion.

An Overview of Promotion Planning

11

Chapter Preview

Chapter Objectives

1 To define promotion and show its importance

2 To describe the general characteristics of advertising, publicity, personal selling, and sales promotion

3 To explain the channel of communication and how it functions

4 To examine the components of a promotion plan: objectives, budget, and mix of elements

5 To study the legal environment and the criticisms and defenses of promotion

Vermont Castings Inc. is a manufacturer of wood- and coal-burning stoves. Founded in 1975, the company now sells more than 50,000 stoves (priced at $400 to $800) each year. It accomplishes this despite almost no distribution in retail stores and a sales force operating only in Randolph, Vermont, where the firm is located. Vermont Castings Inc.'s success is due to a well-organized promotion effort and extensive referrals by satisfied customers.

The company opened just after the 1973–74 oil embargo, at a time when consumers began purchasing stoves for heating their homes. Initial advertising was placed in New England magazines, and drew tremendous responses. Expanded direct mail advertising eliminated the need for retailers and a field sales force. Instead, telephone sales personnel were used to handle all inquiries and resolve outstanding questions. Past customers helped out by providing leads.

To maintain customer loyalty and generate further referrals, Vermont Castings Inc. publishes a quarterly newsletter; each customer is given a lifetime subscription. The newsletter reports on such topics as the manufacturing of stoves, employee profiles, recreational activities, letters from stove owners, and advice on stove maintenance. The firm also makes customers feel welcome at its Randolph showroom by giving away apples or zucchini, and selling maple syrup made by employees in their free time.

Not long ago, the company sponsored a picnic attended by 10,000 people, from as far away as Michigan and Texas. The picnic included plant tours, lectures on wood and coal burning, square dancing, barbequed chicken, ballooning, woodchopping demonstrations, and lots of conversation among stove owners. Said Duncan Syme, the firm's founder, "When was the last time your refrigerator maker invited you to a picnic?"[1]

Characteristics and Importance of Promotion

Promotion planning focuses on the total promotion effort— including information, persuasion, and reminding.

Promotion planning is systematic decision making relating to all aspects of the development and management of a firm's promotional effort. **Promotion** is any form of communication used by a firm to inform, persuade, or remind people about its products, services, image, ideas, community involvement, or impact on society. The components of this definition are explained in the following paragraphs.

Promotion includes brand names, packaging, store marquees, personal sales force, trading stamps, coupons, and mass media (newspapers, television, radio, direct mail, billboards, magazines, and transit). It can be company sponsored or controlled by independent media. Messages may emphasize information, persuasion, fear, sociability, product performance, humor, and/or comparisons with competitors.

With new products, customers must be informed about the items and their attributes before they can develop favorable attitudes toward them. For products that have a solid level of consumer awareness, the promotional thrust is on persuasion—converting product knowledge to product liking. For well-entrenched products, the emphasis is on reminder promotion—reinforcing existing consumer beliefs.

The people to whom a firm's promotional effort can be addressed fall into several categories: consumers, stockholders, consumer organizations and lobbies, government, channel members, employees, and the general public. It is important to realize that communication goes on

between a firm and each of these groups, not just with its consumers. In
addition, the communication with each will be different because the
groups have distinct goals, knowledge, and needs. Within groups, a firm
must identify and appeal to opinion leaders. It needs to understand the
mechanisms of **word-of-mouth communication,** the process by which
people express their opinions and product-related experiences to one
another. Without sustained positive word-of-mouth, it is difficult for a
company to succeed in the long run.

A firm's promotional plan usually stresses individual products and
services, with the objective of moving consumers from awareness to
purchase. However, a company may also seek to communicate its overall image (such as industry innovator), views on ideas (such as nuclear
energy), community involvement (such as the funding of a new hospital), or impact on society (for example, the number of workers employed).

A good promotion plan complements the product, distribution,
and price components of marketing. Table 11-1 shows the role of promotion in the marketing mix. For example, a prestige retailer would use
elegant store fixtures, nonprice advertising, plentiful salespeople, high
prices, and status brands. A discount retailer would use plain fixtures,
price advertising, self-service, low prices, and popular brands.

These are well-conceived promotion plans that have proven very
successful for their companies:[2]

- Pepsi conducted blind (disguised) taste tests comparing Pepsi with
  Coke. The results showed a strong preference for Pepsi. The company then developed an ad campaign around these tests, and issued its now famous "Pepsi challenge"—encouraging consumers
  to take the test themselves. See Figure 11-1.
- Spic 'n Span, as a cleaning product in the mature stage of the product life cycle, was facing declining sales. Consumers used Spic 'n

*Word-of-mouth
communication* occurs
when people relate
opinions to one another.

**Promotion enables a
firm to sell products, set
an image, express views,
and complement other
functions.**

Table 11-1

Promotion

**The Role of
Promotion**

— Establishes a company or product/service image, such as prestige, discount, or
  innovative.
— Communicates product or service features.
— Creates awareness for new products or services.
— Keeps existing products or services popular.
— Can reposition the images or uses of faltering products or services.
— Generates enthusiasm from channel members.
— Explains where products or services can be purchased.
— Convinces consumers to trade up from one product or service to a more ex-
  pensive one.
— Alerts consumers to sales.
— Justifies product or service prices.
— Answers consumer questions.
— Closes transactions.
— Provides afterservice for consumers.
— Places the company and its products or services in a favorable light, relative to
  competitors.

Figure 11-1

The Pepsi Challenge

Reprinted by permission.

Span, mixed with water, to wash walls and floors. They rarely used it in dry form to clean bathroom tubs and sinks. So, a promotion campaign was launched to increase awareness of dry-form uses. Easy-pour canisters, given away free, and extensive advertising revived Spic 'n Span.

- J. M. Smucker, a manufacturer of jellies and jams, created a two-pronged strategy—one aimed at children and one at adults. For children, Smucker had a tie-in with Walt Disney movies (offering items such as free drinking mugs containing characters from the films) and ran other sales promotions. For adults, Smucker gave away cookbooks and other premiums. All the promotions were related to product purchases by consumers.

The importance of promotion is also evident from the expenditures and employment of people in this area, as these figures indicate. The top 100 advertisers spent $15 billion on national advertising in 1981, up 14 per cent over the 1980 total. More than six million people are employed in some aspect of sales. Over 100 billion coupons are annually distributed. The yearly sales volume for trading stamps exceeds $500 million.[3]

In this chapter an overview of promotion planning is provided. Included are discussions on the types of promotion, channel of communication, promotion planning, the legal environment, and criticisms and defenses of promotion. Chapter 12 covers advertising and publicity—the paid and nonpaid forms of mass communication. Chapter 13 deals with personal selling and sales promotion—the individual and supplemental forms of promotion.

Types of Promotion

In its communications program, a firm can utilize one or a combination of four basic types of promotion: advertising, publicity, personal selling, and sales promotion.

   Advertising is any paid form of nonpersonal presentation and promotion of ideas, goods, and services by an identified sponsor. **Publicity** is the nonpersonal stimulation of demand for a product, service, or business by placing commercially significant news about it in a published medium or obtaining favorable presentation on radio, television, or stage that is not paid for by an identified sponsor. **Personal selling** is an oral presentation in a conversation with one or more prospective buyers for the purpose of making sales. **Sales promotion** involves marketing activities, other than advertising, publicity, or personal selling, that stimulate consumer purchases and dealer effectiveness. Included are shows, demonstrations, and various nonrecurrent selling efforts not in the ordinary promotion routine.[4]

   The general characteristics of each type of promotion are shown in Table 11-2. As discussed later in the chapter, many firms combine these four types in an integrated promotional blend. This enables them to reach the entire target market, present both persuasive and believable messages, have personal contact with customers, sponsor special events, and balance the promotional budget.

Advertising and *publicity* are nonpersonal types of promotion. *Personal selling* involves one-to-one contact. *Sales promotion* includes supplemental techniques.

Channel of Communication

In order to develop a promotion mix properly and communicate effectively with consumers, a firm must understand the channel of communication shown in Figure 11-2. Through the **channel of communication (communication process),** a source sends a message to its audience. A communication channel consists of the source, encoding, the message, the medium, decoding, the audience, feedback, and noise. These are discussed next.

A message is sent to an audience through a *channel of communication.*

Source

The **source** of communication is the company, independent institution, or opinion leader that seeks to present a message to an audience. The company communicates through a company spokesperson, celebrity, actor playing a role, representative consumer, and/or salesperson.

   A company spokesperson is usually a high-ranking employee of the firm who represents it in advertisements. The spokesperson provides an aura of sincerity, commitment, and expertise. Eastern Airlines' Frank Borman and Chrysler's Lee Iacocca have been particularly effective.[5]

   A celebrity is used to gain the attention of the audience and improve product awareness. Problems can arise if consumers perceive the celebrity as insincere or unknowledgeable. Among the most popular

The *source* presents a message.

Company sources are spokespersons, celebrities, actors playing roles, representative consumers, and salespersons.

Table 11-2   **Characteristics of Promotional Types**

Factor	Advertising	Publicity	Personal Selling	Sales Promotion
Audience	Mass	Mass	Small (one-to-one)	Varies
Message	Uniform	Uniform	Specific	Varies
Cost	Low per viewer or reader	None for media space and time; can be moderate costs for press releases and publicity materials	High per customer	Moderate per customer
Sponsor	Company	No formal sponsor in that media are not paid	Company	Company
Flexibility	Moderate	Low	High	Moderate
Control over content and placement	High	None	High	High
Credibility	Moderate	High	Moderate	Moderate
Major goal	To appeal to a mass audience at a reasonable cost, and create awareness and favorable attitudes	To reach a mass audience with an independently reported message	To deal with individual consumers, to resolve questions, to close sales	To stimulate short-run sales, to increase impulse purchases
Example	Newspaper ad emphasizing Bloomingdale's use of a China theme and displaying Chinese products	Newspaper article reporting on the background and characteristics of Bloomingdale's China theme	Sales personnel explaining the craftsmanship of Chinese rugs	Demonstration of Chinese cooking sponsored by Bloomingdale's

celebrity sources are James Garner and Mariette Hartley for Polaroid, Bill Cosby for Texas Instruments, Lauren Hutton for Revlon, and athletes such as Chris Evert and Jimmy Connors for Converse (see Figure 11-3).

Figure 11-2
Channel of Communication

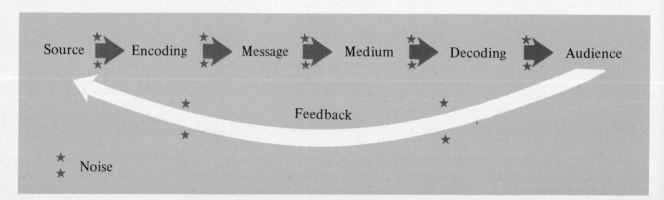

Figure 11-3
Celebrity Endorsements

Many advertisements use actors playing roles rather than celebrity spokespeople. In these commercials emphasis is placed on presenting a message about a product or service, rather than on the consumer recognizing a celebrity. The hope is that the consumer will learn more about product or service attributes.

A representative consumer is one who likes the product and recommends it in an advertisement. This person is shown with his or her name and general address. The intent is to show a real consumer in an actual situation. A hidden camera or blind taste test is often used with the representative consumer. Today a number of viewers are skeptical about how "representative" the endorser is.[6]

Finally, the company may be represented by a salesperson who communicates with consumers. Most salespeople are knowledgeable, aggressive, and persuasive. However, consumers question their objectivity and fairness. Car salespeople rate particularly low in consumer surveys.

An independent institution is not controlled by the companies on

An independent institution is not paid by the firm on which it reports.

which it reports. It evaluates and presents information on the operations and products of companies in a professional, nonpaid (by the companies) manner. Consumers Union, Consumers' Research, and the local newspaper food critic are examples of independent sources. They usually have great credibility for their readers because they point out both good and bad points, but large segments of the population may not be exposed to these sources. The information presented may differ from that contained in a firm's commercials.

Opinion leaders influence others through the *two-step flow of communication*. These leaders are also influenced in a *multistep flow*.

Opinion leaders are people who have face-to-face contact with and influence potential consumers. Because they deal on a personal level, opinion leaders usually have strong persuasive impact and believability. They are able to offer social acceptance and status for followers. The firm should address its initial messages to opinion leaders, who then provide word-of-mouth communication about the product to other consumers. This is the **two-step flow of communication** (company to opinion leader to target market). Marketers further believe that opinion leaders not only influence but also are influenced by the general public (opinion receivers); they need approval for their decisions. This is the **multistep flow of communication.**

In assessing the qualities of a source, these questions are most critical: Is the source believable? Is the source convincing? Does the source present an image consistent with the firm? Do consumers value the message of the source? Is the source perceived as knowledgeable? Does the source complement the product or service it communicates about or does the source overwhelm it? Do significant parts of the market dislike the source?

Encoding

During *encoding,* the source translates a thought or idea into a message.

Encoding is the process whereby a thought or idea is translated into a message by the source. At this stage, preliminary decisions are made regarding message content, such as the use of symbolism and wording. It is vital that the thought or idea be translated exactly as the source desires. For example, a firm wanting to stress the prestige of its product would include the concepts of status, exclusive ownership, and special features in a message. It would not emphasize a price lower than competitors, availability in discount stores, or the millions of people who have already purchased it.

Message

A *message* combines words and symbols, and contains various information features.

The **message** is the combination of words and symbols transmitted to an audience. The focus of message content depends on whether the firm's goal is to inform, persuade, or remind its audience. This is examined later in the chapter.

In almost all messages, this information would be presented:

1. Company name
2. Product or service name
3. Image
4. Differential advantage
5. Product or service attributes and benefits

Additionally, a firm would provide information about availability and price somewhere in the communication process.

Most communication involves one-sided messages, in which the firm mentions only the benefits of its product or service. Few companies use two-sided messages, in which both benefits and limitations are discussed. Companies are not anxious to point out their own shortcomings, even though consumer perceptions of honesty are improved through two-sided messages. For example, a few years ago a new deodorant named Stay Dry was marketed. In the commercials for the product, the spokesperson said it should have been called Stay Drier. He explained that although Stay Dry could keep people drier than any other deodorant, no deodorant could keep them dry. The product did not sell well.

> **With one-sided messages, only benefits are mentioned; two-sided messages describe both benefits and limitations.**

Many messages use symbolism and try to relate safety, social acceptance, or sexual appeal to the purchase of a product. For example, in commercials, life insurance provides safety for family members; clothing styles offer acceptance by peers; and toothpaste brightens teeth and makes a person more sexually attractive. With symbolic messages the firm stresses psychological benefits rather than tangible product performance, such as miles per gallon.

> **Symbolism relates the message to a product's safety, social value, or sexual appeal.**

One type of symbolism, the use of fear appeals, has had mixed results. Although consumers respond to moderate fear appeals, strong messages yield few favorable responses. For example, the Highway Traffic and Safety Commission found that a commercial for safety belts showing mangled cars and broken bones was too overpowering for people, causing them to avoid viewing it. A subsequent campaign based on "If you love me, you'll show me" sent out the same message, but in a milder way. Similarly, several years ago Allstate ran a life insurance commercial picturing a young man playing basketball with his son. Suddenly, the man's face was blacked out and the life insurance pitch made. This message was also succeeded by a softer one. Detergents, toothpaste, and deodorants have done well with moderate fear appeals.

Humor is sometimes used to gain audience attention and retain it. Some examples of humor are Don Rickles and Lynda Carter teasing each other about "good taste" in a diet 7-Up commercial, Mr. Whipple advising shoppers not to squeeze the Charmin, and George Steinbrenner (N.Y. Yankees owner) telling Billy Martin (the three-time Yankee manager) he is fired again in a Miller Lite commercial. The firm needs to be careful to get across the intended message when using humor. The humor should not make fun of the company, its products, or services; and, it should not dominate the message so that the brand name or attributes of the item go unnoticed. A good use of humor is shown in Figure 11-4.

> **Humor in messages can attract attention, but it should not detract from image.**

In recent years comparative messages have substantially increased in number. Comparative messages contrast the firm's offerings against those of competitors. Some use a brand X or leading brand campaign (such as "Our fabric softener is more effective than other leading brands"). Others utilize direct comparisons (such as Minute Maid lemonade calling Country Time the "no-lemon lemonade."). Salespeople frequently compare the characteristics of their products with those of competitors. An interesting comparative message is shown in Figure 11-5.

> **Comparative messages position the firm's offerings versus competitors'.**

Figure 11-4
A Clever Use of Humor in Advertising

There's only one wagon with better mileage than the Civic Wagon.

The other wagon gets about a year out of two pairs of sneakers. Just a guess, of course.

With our wagon, however, we can be more precise. A gallon of gas takes you an EPA estimated 35 miles with the 5-speed transmission. Estimated 46 miles highway.*

And our mileage figures are better than any other gasoline or diesel powered station wagon.

The Honda Civic 4-Door Wagon is also generous with interior space. Its rear seatback folds down for a longer, completely carpeted cargo area. And a wide opening liftgate makes loading and unloading easier.

There's no driveshaft running through the Civic Wagon because it has front-wheel drive. You get even more legroom and load room.

Our roomy station wagon handles like a passenger car. It's easy to park.

It's also easy on your budget. Because the Civic Wagon is one of the lowest priced wagons in America. And we've loaded it with practical standard equipment.

Like our energetic 1488cc engine with 5-speed transmission. Steel-belted radial tires. Remote control outside rearview mirror. Front door and rear window defrosters and tinted glass. The front bucket seats fully recline. And the rear seatback adjusts for comfort.

You have the option of ordering Honda's 3-speed automatic transmission. Even with automatic, no other wagon gets better mileage around town than the Civic Wagon.†

Well, with one exception.

*Use estimated mpg for comparison only. Actual highway mileage probably less. Your mileage may differ depending on speed, weather and trip length. California figures will be lower.
† 31 est. mpg. 49-state only. Comparison excludes est. hwy.

HONDA
We make it simple.

Reprinted by permission.

A message must be desirable, exclusive, and believable.

The content of a message must be presented in a desirable, exclusive, and believable manner.[7] The product, service, or idea needs to be perceived by the audience as something worth purchasing or accepting. It also needs to be considered unique to the company—that is, it cannot be obtained elsewhere. Finally, the message must contain believable statements and claims.

The use of *massed* or *distributed promotion* and the *wearout rate* must be carefully planned.

The timing of messages must be carefully planned. First, during what periods in the year should the firm advertise, add salespeople, or run promotions? With **massed promotion,** communication is concentrated in peak periods, like holidays. With **distributed promotion,** communication is spread throughout the year.

Second, the **wearout rate** (the period of time it takes for a message to lose its effectiveness) must be determined. Some messages wear out quickly, while others may last for months or years. The wearout rate depends on the frequency of communications, the quality of the message, the number of messages used by the company, and other factors. When measuring wearout, it must be noted that effective messages can be used over a long period of time. For example Wisk's "ring around the collar" message has been around since 1967; and as the slogan's author noted:

Figure 11-5
**A Comparative Message
from Fiat**

Are you watching where your dollars are going, going, gone?

If money's no object, you can buy any car in the world.
But, if you're careful about investing, spending
and saving, here's an interesting
investment alternative.

Mercedes Benz 380 SL
☐ Electronic fuel injection ☐ Overhead cam engine
☐ Power steering ☐ Independent front and rear suspension
☐ Sliding electric roof ☐ Tinted glass
☐ Air conditioning, climate control ☐ Tachometer
☐ Power brakes ☐ Steel belted radials
☐ Adjustable front bucket seats (Electric seat adjuster)

Fiat Spider 2000
☐ Electronic fuel injection ☐ Double overhead cam engine
☐ Worm and roller steering ☐ Independent front suspension
☐ One-hand fully convertible top ☐ Tinted glass
☐ Multi-level heating/ventilating ☐ Tachometer
☐ Power assisted 4-wheel disc brakes ☐ Radial ply tires
☐ Adjustable bucket seats

The Mercedes Benz 380SL List price

$41,773

Down payments (20%). **$8,347**
Balance to be financed . . . **$33,386**
Monthly payments **$1,194****
Total interest paid **$9,598**
You pay a total of **$51,331.00**

The Fiat Spider 2000 List price

$12,290

Down payment (20%). **$2,458**
Balance to be financed . . **$9,832**
Monthly payments **$350****
Total interest paid **$2,768**
You pay a total of **$15,058.00**

☐Savings on down payment with Spider **$5,889** ☐Monthly savings with Spider **$844** ☐Total savings **$36,273.00**

Of course, the Mercedes Benz 380SL has every luxury
feature imaginable. It costs $41,773 and is worth it.
The Fiat Spider 2000 is a true convertible
sportscar. It costs $12,290 and it's worth more.
It's enough to make you stop and think, isn't it?

It all comes down to the price you put on fun.
You can test drive and test price a classic Fiat
Spider convertible, designed and built by Pininfarina,
at your local Fiat dealer today.

FIAT

Nothing moves you like a Fiat Sportscar.

*1982 Comparisons POE East Coast. Comparisons based upon manufacturers information available as of October, 1982. Prices are suggested list exclusive of freight, dealer prep, taxes, title, license fees and optional equipment. **Financing has been calculated at an APR of 17.25%,
36 months. The method of calculation by financial institutions varies slightly. All figures are approximate.*

This eye-catching advertisement demonstrates that comparative messages are not limited to inexpensive or convenience products and services. Reprinted by permission. Produced by Hank Forssberg Advertising, Two University Plaza, Hackensack, New Jersey 07601. Telephone: (201) 488-4800.

It would be fair to call that commercial a screeching commercial, an abrasive commercial, an intrusive commercial. But the one thing you can't call it is a bad commercial because the purpose of a commercial is to do a commercial job.[8]

A storyboard from a recent Wisk television commercial is shown in Figure 11-6.

Medium

The *medium* is the personal or nonpersonal channel used to send a message. Personal media are company salespeople and other representatives as well as opinion leaders. Nonpersonal media include newspapers, television, radio, direct mail, billboards, magazines, and transit.

Personal media offer one-to-one contact with the audience. They are flexible, able to adapt messages to individual needs, and can answer questions. They also appeal to a small audience and work best with a concentrated target market.

Nonpersonal (mass) media provide a large audience and low per customer costs. They are inflexible and not as dynamic as one-to-one presentations. They work best with a dispersed target market.

When deciding between personal and nonpersonal media, the firm

*The medium is the
personal or nonpersonal
channel for a message.*

Figure 11-6
"Ring Around the Collar"

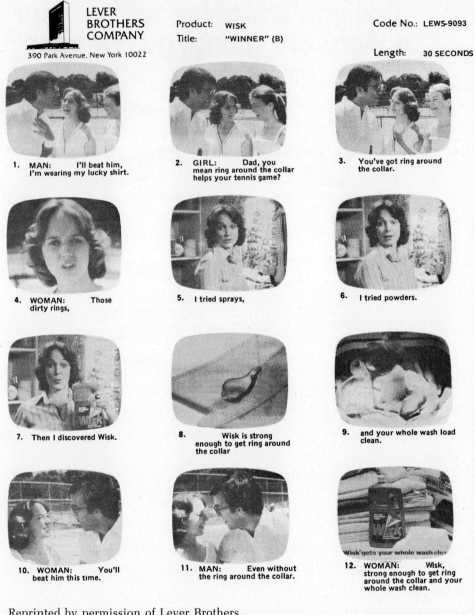

LEVER BROTHERS COMPANY

390 Park Avenue, New York 10022

Product: WISK
Title: "WINNER" (B)

Code No.: LEWS-9093

Length: 30 SECONDS

1. MAN: I'll beat him, I'm wearing my lucky shirt.

2. GIRL: Dad, you mean ring around the collar helps your tennis game?

3. You've got ring around the collar.

4. WOMAN: Those dirty rings,

5. I tried sprays,

6. I tried powders.

7. Then I discovered Wisk.

8. Wisk is strong enough to get ring around the collar

9. and your whole wash load clean.

10. WOMAN: You'll beat him this time.

11. MAN: Even without the ring around the collar.

12. WOMAN: Wisk, strong enough to get ring around the collar and your whole wash clean.

Reprinted by permission of Lever Brothers.

should consider total and per unit costs, product or service complexity, audience attributes, and communication goals. The two types of media also work well together, because nonpersonal media generate consumer interest and personal media help close sales.

Decoding

In *decoding*, the audience translates the message sent by the source.

Decoding is the process by which the message sent by the source is interpreted by the audience. Members of the audience interpret the message according to their background and the clarity of message content.

As noted earlier in the chapter, it is essential that a message be decoded in the manner desired by the source (encoding = decoding).

The background of the audience—demographics and life-styles—affects the way it decodes messages. For example, a housewife and a working woman might have different interpretations of a message on the value of day-care centers. An upper-class consumer would view Cadillac commercials differently from a middle-class consumer.

Clarity of message content also influences decoding. Usually, as symbolism increases, clarity decreases. Some ambiguous messages are "We circle the world (MasterCard)," "Out front. Pulling away (Goodyear)," "Think what we can do for you (Bank of America)," and "A powerful part of your life (Westinghouse)." Clearer messages are "Now is the closest thing to a tar-free cigarette" and "C&C is half the price of Coke and Pepsi."

Finally, **subliminal advertising** is a highly controversial type of promotion because it does not enable a consumer to consciously decode a message. In subliminal advertising, visual or verbal messages are presented so quickly that consumers do not see or hear them or remember them. Yet, consumers are expected to buy goods and services because of subconscious impulses. Ads of this type stress symbolism, and sometimes sexual themes, to increase sales. The overwhelming evidence shows that subliminal advertising cannot get consumers to buy products they do not want. In addition, subliminal ads are often misinterpreted; and clear, well-labeled ads are much more effective.[9] In the U.S., self-regulation by advertising associations (such as the National Association of Broadcasters) has all but eliminated subliminal ads.

Subliminal advertising, which is seldom used in the U.S., aims at the consumer's subconscious.

Audience

The **audience** is the object of the source's message. In most marketing situations, the audience is the target market. However, the source may also want to communicate an idea, build an image, or provide information to stockholders, consumer groups, independent media, the public, or government officials.

The audience is usually the target market; but it can also be investors, government officials, or others.

The types of communication channels used by a firm depend on the size and dispersion of the audience, demographic and life-style audience traits, and the availability of media appropriate for the audience. The total communication process must be keyed to the audience.

The findings of a 1980 survey of the American public show that

1. Seventy per cent are disturbed about distortion and exaggeration in advertising and do not believe business has been responsive to consumer concerns.
2. Seventy per cent believe advertising should be more heavily regulated and balanced (two-sided) messages used more frequently[10]

One California car dealer has found the right way to interact with his customers and is representative of the new orientation of business:

My sales techniques and service philosophies are founded upon the ways I'd like to be treated if I was buying a car. I've adopted a more consumer-oriented approach to selling cars. There was a time when high-pressure selling and leader ads worked. But today you must have respect for the intelligence of the consumer.[11]

Feedback

Feedback is the response the audience makes to the firm's message. It may take one of three forms: purchase, attitude change, or nonpurchase. A company must understand that any of these three alternative responses is possible and develop a procedure for monitoring them.

The most desirable kind of feedback occurs when a consumer purchases a product or service after communications with or from the firm. This means the message is effective enough to stimulate a transaction.

A second type of feedback takes place when the firm determines that its promotional efforts have caused a favorable attitude change toward the company or its offerings by the audience. With new products or services, favorable attitudes must be created prior to consumer purchases (awareness→favorable attitude→purchase). With existing products, immediate purchases may not be possible because consumers may have bought a competing brand before the message was received or they may be temporarily out of funds. Developing favorable attitudes by these consumers may lead to future purchases.

The least desirable feedback is when the audience neither purchases an item nor develops a favorable attitude. This may happen for one of several reasons: no recall of message, contentment with present product, message not believed, or no differential advantage shown.

Noise

Noise is interference at any stage along the channel of communication. Because of noise, messages are sometimes encoded or decoded incorrectly or weak responses are made. Examples of noise are

1. A telephone call interrupting the company's marketing manager while he or she is developing a promotional theme.
2. A salesperson misidentifying a product and giving the wrong sales presentation.
3. An impatient customer interrupting a sales presentation.
4. Conversation between two consumers during a television commercial.
5. A direct-mail ad being opened by the wrong person.
6. A consumer seeing a sale on a competitor's item while waiting at a supermarket checkout counter.

See Figure 11-7.

Promotion Planning

After a firm has gained an understanding of the communication process, it is ready to develop an overall promotion plan. The plan consists of three parts: objectives, budget, and mix of elements.

Figure 11-7
Noise in a Channel of Communication

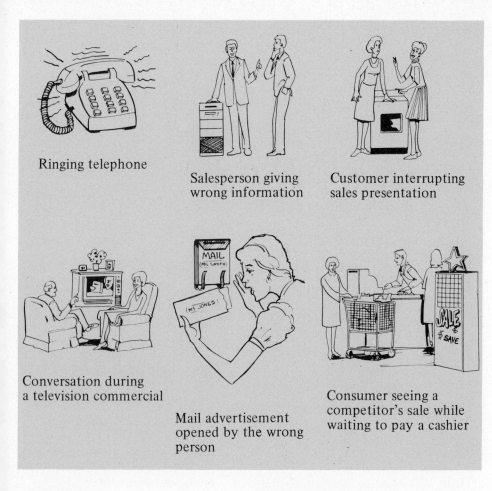

Ringing telephone

Salesperson giving wrong information

Customer interrupting sales presentation

Conversation during a television commercial

Mail advertisement opened by the wrong person

Consumer seeing a competitor's sale while waiting to pay a cashier

Objectives

The objectives of promotion can be divided into two general categories: stimulating demand and enhancing company image.

In setting specific demand objectives (such as increasing sales by 12 per cent through a $1 million promotion campaign), a firm should understand the **hierarchy-of-effects model.**[12] This model outlines the intermediate and long-term promotional objectives the firm should pursue: awareness, knowledge, liking, preference, conviction, and purchase. Attaining a consumer purchase is based on achieving each of the steps before it. Figure 11-8 shows the hierarchy-of-effects model and relates it to promotional objectives and tools.

Using the hierarchy-of-effects model, a firm can move from informing to persuading and then to reminding consumers about its offerings. At the early stages, when the product or service is little known, primary demand should be sought. **Primary demand** is consumer demand for a product category, such as canned peaches or dietetic candy. At later stages, when preference is the goal, selective demand should be sought. **Selective demand** is consumer demand for a particular brand of a product. As an example, the Florida Orange Growers sponsor a series of primary demand ads aimed at increasing the consumption of Florida

The objectives of promotion are to stimulate demand and enhance company image. The hierarchy-of-effects model outlines demand objectives.

Primary demand is for a product category; selective demand is for a brand.

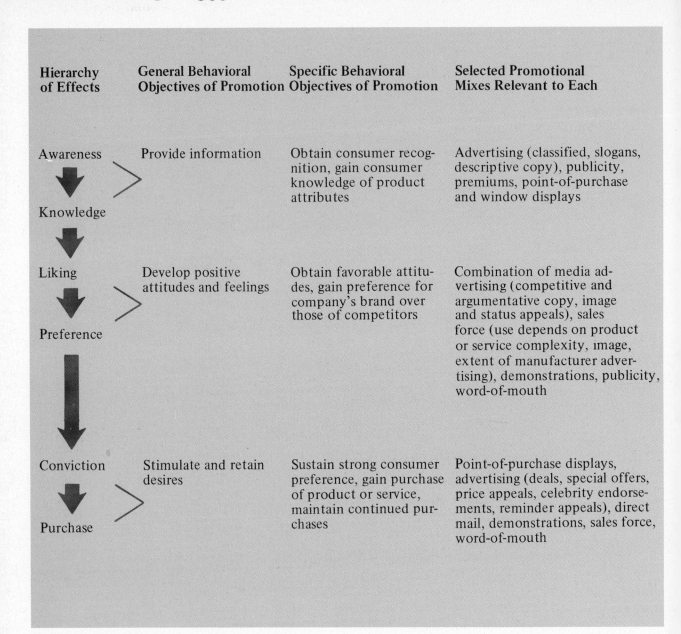

Hierarchy of Effects	General Behavioral Objectives of Promotion	Specific Behavioral Objectives of Promotion	Selected Promotional Mixes Relevant to Each
Awareness ⬇ Knowledge	Provide information	Obtain consumer recognition, gain consumer knowledge of product attributes	Advertising (classified, slogans, descriptive copy), publicity, premiums, point-of-purchase and window displays
Liking ⬇ Preference	Develop positive attitudes and feelings	Obtain favorable attitudes, gain preference for company's brand over those of competitors	Combination of media advertising (competitive and argumentative copy, image and status appeals), sales force (use depends on product or service complexity, image, extent of manufacturer advertising), demonstrations, publicity, word-of-mouth
Conviction ⬇ Purchase	Stimulate and retain desires	Sustain strong consumer preference, gain purchase of product or service, maintain continued purchases	Point-of-purchase displays, advertising (deals, special offers, price appeals, celebrity endorsements, reminder appeals), direct mail, demonstrations, sales force, word-of-mouth

Figure 11-8
Promotion and the Hierarchy-of-Effects Model

orange products. Tropicana sponsors additional ads aimed at increasing selective demand for its brand of orange products.

Institutional advertising seeks to improve image.

Enhancing company image is the second major promotional objective. In this case firms utilize ***institutional advertising,*** for which the goal is improved corporate image and not the sales of products or services.

For example, as the price of gasoline rose, public criticism of oil

Why does gasoline cost so much?

Figure 11-9
An Institutional Advertisement

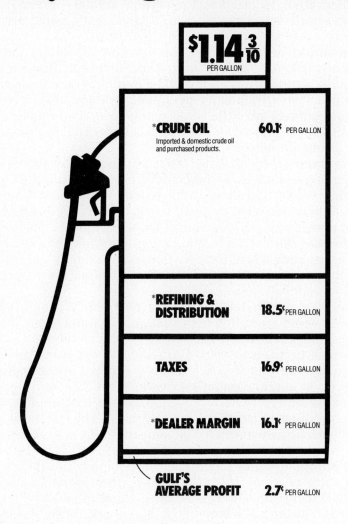

$1.14 3/10 PER GALLON

*CRUDE OIL   60.1¢ PER GALLON
Imported & domestic crude oil
and purchased products.

*REFINING &
DISTRIBUTION   18.5¢ PER GALLON

TAXES   16.9¢ PER GALLON

*DEALER MARGIN   16.1¢ PER GALLON

GULF'S
AVERAGE PROFIT   2.7¢ PER GALLON

GULF OIL CORPORATION

companies increased. To enhance their images, many oil companies placed advertisements explaining how small their profits were as per cents of sales. Figure 11-9 shows an ad used by Gulf Oil.

Annually, General Telephone & Electronics (GTE) spends several million dollars on institutional advertising. According to GTE's vice-president for advertising, these ads

> reflect our belief that customers buy more than products. They "buy" the company that makes the product. They "buy" its size, its integrity, and the confidence they have in a familiar corporate name.[13]

Promotion Budget

There are five alternative techniques for setting a total promotion budget: all you can afford, incremental, competitive parity, percentage of sales, and objective and task.

In the ***all-you-can-afford technique,*** the firm first allocates funds for every element of marketing except promotion. Whatever funds are left over are placed in a promotion budget. This method is the weakest of the five and is used most frequently by small, production-oriented companies. Its shortcomings are little importance given to promotion, expenditures not linked to objectives, and the risk of having no promotion budget if no funds are left over.

With the ***incremental technique,*** the company bases its new budget on previous expenditures. A percentage is either added to or subtracted from this year's budget in order to determine next year's budget. This technique is also used by small firms. It offers these advantages: provision of a reference point, a budget based on a firm's feelings about past successes and future trends, and easy calculations. Important disadvantages do exist: budget size is rarely tied to objectives, "gut feelings" are overemphasized, and there is difficulty in evaluating success or failure.

In the ***competitive parity technique,*** the company's promotion budget is raised or lowered according to the actions of competitors. It is useful for both large and small firms. The benefits of the method are that it provides a reference point, it is market-oriented, and it is conservative. The shortcomings are that it is a following and not a leadership strategy, it is difficult to obtain competitors' promotion data, and there is the assumption of a similarity between the firm and its competitors (years in business, products or services, image, prices). The last point is particularly important; firms usually have major differences from competitors.

With the ***percentage-of-sales technique,*** the company ties the promotion budget to sales revenue. In the first year a promotion-to-sales ratio is established. During suceeding years, the per cent of promotion to sales dollars remains constant. The benefits of this procedure are the use of sales as a base, adaptability, and the interrelationship of sales and promotion. The weaknesses are that there is no relationship to objectives, promotion is used as a sales follower and not a sales leader, and automatic promotion decreases are applied in poor sales periods (when increases could be beneficial). This technique provides too large a budget during high sales periods and too small a budget during low sales periods.

Under the ***objective-and-task technique,*** the firm clearly outlines its promotional objectives, determines the tasks needed to satisfy those objectives, and then establishes the appropriate budget. It is the best of the five methods. The advantages are that it clearly states objectives, expenditures are related to the completion of goal-oriented tasks, it offers adaptability, and it is relatively easy to evaluate success or failure. The major weakness is the complexity of setting goals and specific tasks, especially for small companies.

The selection of a budgeting technique depends on the individual requirements and constraints of the individual firm. Promotional budgets generally range from 1 to 5 per cent for some industrial goods companies, and up to 20 to 30 per cent for some consumer goods companies.

Promotion Mix

After establishing a total promotion budget, the company must determine its promotion mix. The ***promotion mix*** is the overall and specific communication program of the firm, consisting of a combination of advertising, publicity, personal selling, and/or sales promotion.

It is rare for a company to use only one type of promotion—for example, a mail-order firm relying on advertising, a hospital on publicity, or a flea market vendor on personal selling. In most cases a mix of promotion types is used. For example, General Foods has a sales force that visits every supermarket in which its products are stocked, advertises in newspapers and magazines and on television, and distributes cents-off coupons. IBM has a large technical sales force, advertises heavily in business and trade publications, and sends representatives to trade shows.

It is important to remember that each type of promotion serves a different function, and therefore complements the other types. Advertisements appeal to large audiences and create awareness; without them, the personal sales effort is much more difficult, time consuming, and expensive. Publicity provides credible information to a wide audience, but its content and timing cannot be controlled by the firm. Personal selling offers one-to-one contact, flexibility, and the ability to close sales; without it, the initial interest caused by ads would be wasted. Sales promotion stimulates short-run sales and supplements advertising and selling.

The promotion mix varies by type of company. A small firm is restricted in the kinds of ads it can afford or use efficiently. It would emphasize personal selling. A large firm covering a sizable geographic area would stress advertising as well as personal selling. A nonprofit firm would seek as much publicity as possible. A consumer company would rely heavily on advertising its brands. An industrial company would count on a major personal selling effort.

It is the responsibility of the company's marketing director (or vice-president) to establish a promotion budget and promotion mix and then allocate resources and effort to each aspect of promotion. In large firms, there are separate managers for advertising, personal selling, and sales promotion. They report to and have their efforts coordinated by the marketing director.

The *promotion mix* is a combination of advertising, publicity, personal selling, and/or sales promotion.

Legal Environment of Promotion

Federal and local governments have enacted many laws and rules that affect a firm's promotional mix. They range from banning some products from media (cigarettes cannot be advertised on television or radio) to prohibiting media performance (billboards are not allowed in many

Table 11-3	Factor	Legal Environment
Legal Environment of Promotion	Access	• Cigarettes, liquor, and billboards have restricted access. • Legal, medical, and other professions have been given the right to advertise.
	Deception	It is illegal to use false or misleading promotional messages.
	Bait-and-switch	It is illegal to lure a customer to a store with an advertisement for a low-priced item and then, after the customer is in the store, to use a strong sales pitch intentionally to switch the shopper to a more expensive item.
	Direct-to-home sales	• Many locales restrict direct-to-home sales practices. • A cooling-off period allows a consumer to cancel a direct-to-home sale up to three days after an agreement is reached.
	Promotional allowances	Promotional allowances must be available to channel members in a fair and equitable manner.
	Comparative advertisements	• Claims must be substantiated. • The Federal Trade Commission favors naming competitors in ads (not citing a competitor as brand X).
	Testimonials or endorsements	The celebrity or expert endorser must actually use the product if advertisements make such a claim.

locations) to ordering corrective ads (messages clearing up past falsities or misrepresentations) to issuing fines for deceptive and dishonest practices (such as overstating the effectiveness of a pain remedy). The major federal agency involved with promotion is the Federal Trade Commission. Table 11-3 outlines the impact of the legal environment on promotion.

There are five major ways in which the legal environment protects consumers and competing firms against unsatisfactory promotion practices: full disclosure, substantiation, cease-and-desist orders, corrective advertising, and fines.

Full disclosure requires that all data necessary for a consumer to make a safe and informed decision be provided. For example, Alka Seltzer must mention that its regular product contains aspirin, and diet products must note that they include saccharin. In this way consumers are able to assess the overall benefits and risks of a purchase.

Substantiation requires a firm to be able to prove all the claims it makes. This means thorough testing and evidence of performance are needed prior to making claims. For example, a tire company that says its brand will last for 70,000 miles must be able to prove this assertion with test results.

Under a *cease-and-desist order,* a firm must discontinue deceptive practices and modify its promotion messages. It is not forced to admit guilt or pay fines. For example, Sears agreed not to use bait-and-switch practices (explained in Table 11-3) to sell major home appliances.

Corrective advertising requires a firm to run new advertisements to correct the false impressions left by previous ones. For example,

Full disclosure, substantiation, cease-and-desist orders, corrective advertising, and fines are major governmental limits on promotion activities.

Listerine was told to spend $10.2 million on advertising to correct previ-
ous messages claiming the product was a cold remedy. Listerine decided to run the ads after learning that it would not be able to continue
any advertising without them.

The last major remedy is *fines,* which are dollar penalties levied on
a firm for deceptive promotion. A company may be required to pay a
large sum to the government, as in the case of STP, or forced to provide
consumer refunds, as in the case of mail-order firms who do not meet
delivery dates. STP was fined $700,000 for misrepresenting the effec-
tiveness of its product in raising auto gas mileage.

In addition to government restrictions, the media place voluntary
controls on promotion. For example, the National Association of Broadcasters monitors the ads placed on television and radio. General groups,
such as the Better Business Bureau, also contribute to self-regulation.

Criticisms and Defenses of Promotion

Promotion is probably the most heavily criticized area of marketing.
Detractors feel that promotion

**Promotion controversies
center on materialism,
honesty, prices,
symbolism, and
expectations.**

- Creates an obsession with material possessions.
- Is basically dishonest.
- Raises the prices of products and services.
- Overemphasizes symbolism and status.
- Causes excessively high expectations.

In defense of promotion, marketers offer these rebuttals. Promotion

- Responds to consumer desires for material possessions. In an affluent society, these items are plentiful and paid for with discretionary earnings.
- Is basically honest. The great majority of companies abide by all
  laws and set strict self-regulations. A few dishonest firms give a
  bad name to all.
- Holds down the prices of products and services. By increasing consumer demand, promotion enables manufacturers to fully utilize
  mass production and reduce per unit costs. In addition, employment is higher when demand is stimulated.
- Differentiates products and services through symbolic and status
  appeals. Consumers desire distinctiveness and product benefits.
- Keeps expectations high; it thereby sustains consumer motivation
  and worker productivity in order to satisfy expectations.

Summary

Promotion informs, persuades, or reminds people about a firm's products, services, ideas, community involvement, or impact on society. Its
major elements are advertising, publicity, personal selling, and sales
promotion.

Through the channel of communication, a source sends a message to its audience. The channel consists of source, encoding, message, medium, decoding, audience, feedback, and noise. The source is the company, independent institution, or opinion leader that seeks to present a message to an audience. In choosing a source, credibility, expertise, and other factors must be considered.

Encoding is the process by which a thought or an idea is translated into a message by the source. The message is the combination of words and symbols transmitted to the audience; it must be presented in a desirable, exclusive, and believable manner. Timing must be carefully planned. The medium is the personal or nonpersonal channel used to convey a message. Decoding is the process through which the message sent by the source is translated by the audience.

The audience is the target of the source's message. Although it is usually the target market, it may also be stockholders, consumer groups, independent media, the public, or government officials. Feedback is the response the audience makes to the firm's message: purchase, attitude change, or nonpurchase. Noise is the interference at any stage along the channel of communication.

Promotion objectives may be demand or image oriented. Demand objectives should parallel the hierarchy-of-effects model, moving from awareness to purchase. Primary demand is total product demand; selective demand is for the company's brand. Institutional advertising is used to enhance company image.

There are five methods for setting a promotion budget: all you can afford, incremental, competitive parity, percentage of sales, and objective and task. The weakest is the all-you-can-afford technique. The best is the objective-and-task technique.

The promotion mix is the overall and specific communication program of the firm, combining advertising, publicity, personal selling, and/or sales promotion. A number of factors should be considered in the development of a promotion mix.

There are many laws and rules affecting promotion. The major ways unsatisfactory promotion is guarded against are full disclosure, substantiation, cease-and-desist orders, corrective advertising, and fines. Critics are strong in their complaints about promotion. Marketers are equally firm in their defenses.

KEY TERMS

After reading this chapter, you should understand these key terms:

Promotion planning	**Two-step flow of communication**
Promotion	**Multistep flow of communication**
Word-of-mouth communication	**Encoding**
Advertising	**Message**
Publicity	**Massed promotion**
Personal selling	**Distributed promotion**
Sales promotion	**Wearout rate**
Channel of communication	**Medium**
Source	**Decoding**

Subliminal advertising

Audience

Feedback

Noise

Hierarchy-of-effects model

Primary demand

Selective demand

Institutional advertising

All-you-can-afford technique

Incremental technique

Competitive parity technique

Percentage-of-sales technique

Objective-and-task technique

Promotion mix

Full disclosure

Substantiation

Cease-and-desist orders

Corrective advertising

Fines

QUESTIONS FOR DISCUSSION

1. Explain the full range of a firm's promotional activities.
2. What is word-of-mouth? Why is it so important?
3. Distinguish among advertising, publicity, personal selling, and sales promotion.
4. Evaluate the use of O. J. Simpson as a spokesperson for Hertz car rental company.
5. Describe a recent advertisement that you saw that could be misunderstood by the audience.
6. Comment on the use of fear appeals and humor in messages. Offer examples of each.
7. Give a recent example of a comparative message and evaluate it.
8. A consumer views an advertisement but does not make a purchase. Has the ad failed? Explain your answer.
9. Explain the hierarchy-of-effects model. How is it related to demand objectives?
10. What is the role of institutional advertising?
11. Evaluate the five methods of promotional budgeting.
12. Develop a promotion mix for
    a. A local florist.
    b. Burger King.
    c. TWA.
    d. Xerox (office machines division).
13. Comment on this statement: "Full disclosure only confuses consumers by giving them too much information. It also raises costs."
14. Evaluate the criticisms and defenses of promotion.

NOTES

1. William L. Bulkeley, "Wood-Stove Maker Has Hot Love Affair with Its Customers," *Wall Street Journal* (September 9, 1981), pp. 1, 25.
2. "How Four Companies Used Strategic Promotion Planning," *Marketing News* (October 30, 1981), p. 13.
3. Marion Elmquist, "100 Leaders Spend 14% More in 1981," *Advertising Age* (September 9, 1982), p. 1; *Employment and Earnings* (Washington, D.C.: U.S. Bureau of Labor Statistics, 1980); "Analyzing Promotions," *Nielsen Researcher* (November 4, 1982), p. 17; and Jeffrey H. Birnbaum, "Industry Blues Fail to Deter S & H Stamps," *Wall Street Journal* (August 5, 1980), p. 29.
4. Ralph S. Alexander (Chairman), *Marketing Definitions: A Glossary of Marketing Terms* (Chicago: American Marketing Association, 1960), pp. 9, 18, 19, 20.

5. "Putting the Boss in TV Commercials," *New York Times* (August 8, 1982), Section 3, p. 21; and Ann Morrison, "The Boss as Pitchman," *Fortune* (August 25, 1980), pp. 66–73.

6. See "'Real People' Work Best in Ads with Real Product Stories," *Marketing News* (August 21, 1981), pp. 1, 4.

7. Dik Warren Twedt, "How to Plan New Products, Improve Old Ones, and Create Better Advertising," *Journal of Marketing*, Vol. 33 (January 1969), pp. 53–57.

8. Bill Abrams, "'Ring Around the Collar' Ads Irritate Many Yet Get Results," *Wall Street Journal* (November 4, 1982), p. 33.

9. See Timothy E. Moore, "Subliminal Advertising: What You See Is What You Get," *Journal of Marketing*, Vol. 46 (Spring 1982), pp. 37–47.

10. Jennifer Alter, "Public Is Still Wary of Ads: Study," *Advertising Age* (June 23, 1980), pp. 3, 94.

11. "Car Dealer Increases Sales with Honest Ads, Respect for Shoppers," *Marketing News* (August 24, 1979), p. 12.

12. Robert Lavidge and Gary A. Steiner, "A Model for Predictive Measurements of Advertising Effectiveness," *Journal of Marketing*, Vol. 25 (October 1967), pp. 59–62.

13. "GTE to Spend $7,000,000 for Corporate Ads," *Industrial Marketing* (January 1979), p. 8.

CASES

1 PROMOTION PLANNING AT GENERAL MOTORS*

General Motors is the world's largest automobile manufacturer. In addition, it produces buses, trucks, diesel engines, gas turbines, locomotive parts, tractors, and other items. 1981 sales totaled $63 billion. Promotion planning at General Motors is extensive and complex. This is a result of the variety of its product lines and the size of its promotion expenditures. For example, it spends more than $400 million each year just for advertising.

One former General Motors' president summed up the company's view of promotion:

> First you have to advertise in such a way that the dealer and the salesman recognize that you're out front with your products. . . . I think it's maybe more important that our dealers and our salesmen are the target of our advertising as much or more so than are the customers . . . it is tremendously important for a salesman to come in in the morning and say to his fellow salesmen in the dealership, "Did you see that ad on our car on TV?"

> The other part of advertising, of course, is to let our customers know the kinds of products we make and what we do, and we're also trying to get the kind of image of ourselves and our business that we can, too, so the whole thing is a package.

Each auto division (Cadillac, Buick, Oldsmobile, Pontiac, and Chevrolet) has a separate advertising budget, advertising staff, and sales force. Ads are screened by divisional sales managers, general managers, the overall general director of advertising, and the vice-president of corporate marketing. Divisional promotion plans are reviewed by the GM Marketing Policy Group.

There are also separate sales promotion budgets for dealer-incentive contests,

*The data in this case are drawn from "Marketing and Advertising at GM," *Industrial Marketing* (March 1979), pp. 68–70, 74; and "General Motors Corp.," *Advertising Age* (September 9, 1982), pp. 92, 94, 98.

dealer-announcement shows, posters, window displays, and auto shows. Publicity is sought each time a new model or innovation is introduced. GM institutional advertising is handled by a public relations department. These ads stress the company's commitment to building better products and holding down insurance costs.

QUESTIONS

1. Evaluate General Motors' view of promotion.
2. Assess General Motors' promotion mix.
3. Should General Motors use the same promotional approach for each of its product lines?
4. Could a small firm apply the promotional concepts used by General Motors? Explain your answer.

MARZETTI: A PROMOTION STRATEGY FOR A SMALL SALAD-DRESSING COMPANY†   2

Marzetti is a successful regional manufacturer of salad dressing. The company markets a full line of dressings and sells them through grocery stores. Competitors are large firms with sizable advertising budgets, such as Dart and Kraft (Kraft dressings) and Anderson Clayton Foods (Seven Seas dressings). Industry sales exceed $1 billion per year.

Not long ago, Marzetti introduced a new line of low-calorie salad dressing called Marzetti Lights. These products are positioned between diet and regular salad dressings. The promotion theme is "Half the calories and all of the flavor of regular dressings." Marzetti has been aggressive in placing Marzetti Lights in shelf spaces already occupied by competitors.

Marzetti supplies its food brokers and district managers with complete sales kits. The kits include market research results, salad dressing sales by category, consumer life-styles and changes, data on the shifts in the salad dressing market, and sheets describing promotional allowances. The kits also contain information to help merchandise Marzetti products: advertising summary sheets, media schedules by market, color descriptions of television commercials, preprints of newspaper coupons, and advertising sheets.

In addition, Marzetti uses a projector to show television commercials in buyer offices. Taste testing accompanies the commercials. Finally, packages (containing three varieties of Marzetti Lights, a ceramic salad bowl, and a nice note) are given to key buyers.

Ron Gowman, consultant to Marzetti concludes:

(1) Without distribution, the media advertising would be useless, and (2) You can make a limited ad budget go a lot further by devoting at least as much attention to sales support programs as you normally devote to the consumer advertising program. Marzetti's growth and continuous success are testimony to this approach.

†The data in this case are drawn from Ron Gowman, "How Managers Maximize Limited Advertising Budgets," *Marketing News* (May 30, 1980), pp. 10–11; and Carol Galginaitis, "Dressings Blend into Bountiful Market," *Advertising Age* (March 15, 1982), pp. M-14, M-16.

QUESTIONS

1. Why does Marzetti give so much importance to promoting its products to brokers and district managers?
2. How can Marzetti generate high sales of its low-calorie dressing with a very low advertising budget?
3. How may Marzetti and its large competitors have vastly different promotion strategies yet both succeed?
4. What risks does Marzetti take if it does not utilize advertising to final consumers?

Advertising and Publicity

12

Chapter Preview

Chapter Objectives

1 To examine the scope, importance, and characteristics of advertising

2 To study the elements in an advertising plan: objectives, responsibility, budget, themes, media, advertisements, timing, cooperative efforts, and evaluation of success or failure

3 To examine the scope, importance, and characteristics of publicity

4 To study the elements in a publicity plan: objectives, responsibility, types, media, messages, timing, and evaluation of success or failure

Milton Hershey, who founded the company named after him about 85 years ago, had this view about advertising: "Whenever he spotted a Hershey-bar wrapper on the ground, he always checked to see if the Hershey name was up. If it wasn't, he would pick up the wrapper, carefully smooth it out if necessary and place it back on the ground with the name clearly visible. That was Mr. Hershey's idea of good advertising." Hershey believed he did not have to advertise since he made a product of consistent quality and kept stores well stocked. This generated word-of-mouth communication among customers.

In 1969, twenty-four years after Hershey died at age 88, his company began to advertise in the U.S. This action was spurred by the success of M&M/Mars (which had replaced Hershey as the leader in candy bars),

Beatrice Foods, Standard Brands (now Nabisco Brands), and Nestlé. By 1981, Hershey was spending about $57 million annually on advertising, increasing expenditures by about 34 per cent over a five-year period. 1981 sales and earnings set records for the company.

During 1982, Hershey agreed to allow Reese's Pieces to be used in a tie-in with the movie "E.T." after Mars (the maker of M&M's) turned down a request from Universal Pictures. The publicity generated from the appearance of Reese's Pieces in the movie caused sales to rise 70 per cent in one month, secured distribution in over 800 theaters (where the product was not previously sold), and resulted in stories in *People* magazine, the "Today" show, and several newspapers.[1] See Figure 12-1.

Overview

This chapter examines the two mass communication forms of promotion available to a firm, advertising and publicity. As defined in Chapter 11, advertising is the paid, nonpersonal presentation and promotion of ideas, goods, and services by an identified sponsor. The distinguishing features of advertising are that the firm pays for its message, a set format is delivered to the entire audience through mass media, the name of the sponsor is clearly presented, and the company controls the message.

Publicity is the nonpaid, nonpersonal presentation and promotion of ideas, goods, and services by an independent source. Its unique features are that the firm does not pay for a message, a set format is delivered to the entire audience through mass media, the message is presented by a source not affiliated with the company, and the independent source controls the message.

The differences between advertising and publicity are in part shown by the statement "Advertising is paid for, publicity is prayed for."

Scope and Importance of Advertising

The leading advertising media are newspapers, television, and direct mail.

In 1982, more than $67 billion was spent on advertising media. Table 12-1 shows the expenditures by medium and the changing emphasis since 1950. The leading medium throughout this period has been newspapers; however newspapers' share of advertising has dropped substantially since 1950. The second leading medium is now television, whose

Figure 12-1
Reese's Pieces and E.T.

Reprinted by permission of Universal City Studios.

relative size has grown significantly since 1950. Direct mail is also gaining in popularity, while magazines and radio continue to decline.

Advertising as a per cent of sales varies by industry and company. Overall, advertising as a per cent of sales is quite low. During 1981, the 100 leading national advertisers in the U.S. (excluding the federal government) had advertising expenditures that averaged 1.6 per cent of their sales.[2] Table 12-2 shows the ten leading advertisers in 1981 and the per cent of sales they allotted to advertising.

On average, firms spend less than 2 per cent of sales on advertising.

Table 12-1

Advertising Expenditures, 1950–1982, by Medium (in Billions)

Medium	1950		1982	
	$	%	$	%
Newspapers	2.07	36.3	18.70	27.8
Magazines	.48	8.4	3.74	5.6
Farm publications	.06	1.1	0.16	0.2
Television	.17	3.0	14.20	21.1
Radio	.61	10.7	4.55	6.8
Direct mail	.80	14.0	10.20	15.1
Business papers	.25	4.4	2.00	3.0
Outdoor	.14	2.5	0.70	1.0
Miscellaneous	1.12	19.6	13.10	19.5
Total	5.70	100.0	67.35	100.0*

*Rounding error.

Source: Adapted from *Advertising Age* (September 1979) and *New York Times* (December 13, 1982).

Ads are most important for new and existing consumer products that have a low selling price.

A comprehensive study involving more than one thousand consumer and industrial products investigated the conditions under which a strong emphasis is placed on advertising. It found that standardized products with large markets and small average purchase amounts receive substantial advertising. Companies are likely to advertise if they have high gross margins, relatively small market shares, and/or surplus production capacity. In addition, new products and those sold through independent channel members obtain high advertising support.[3]

Another advertising research study, by Joseph E. Seagram & Sons and Time Inc., was conducted over a three-year period and involved 20,000 consumers. It found that

- Behavior is easier to change than attitudes.
- Recall is a weak measure of advertising effectiveness.
- One ad can have a strong effect on brand awareness.
- It is easier to improve the favorable rating for a little-known product by extended advertising than a well-known product.
- Advertising effectiveness grows during extended campaigns.[4]

Table 12-2

Ten Leading U.S. Advertisers, 1981

Company	Advertising Expenditures	Advertising as a Per Cent of Sales
Procter & Gamble	$671,800,000	5.6%
Sears	544,100,000	2.0
General Foods	456,800,000	5.5
Philip Morris	433,000,000	4.0
General Motors	401,000,000	0.6
K mart	349,600,000	2.1
Nabisco Brands	341,000,000	5.9
R. J. Reynolds	321,300,000	2.7
American Telephone & Telegraph	297,000,000	0.5
Mobil	293,100,000	4.3

Source: "100 Leaders' Advertising As a Per Cent of Sales," *Advertising Age* (September 9, 1982), p. 8

Characteristics of Advertising

Advertising offers a number of positive and negative characteristics. On the positive side, advertising attracts a large and geographically dispersed market. For print media, circulation is supplemented by the passing of a copy from one reader to another.

The costs per viewer or listener are low. For example, a single 30-second television ad that attracts 30 million viewers and costs $150,000 to air has per-viewer costs of $0.005 (this figure includes media time only and not commercial production costs).

A broad range of media is available: from national television to local newspapers. Therefore, the objectives of a firm and its resources may be matched with the most appropriate medium. For example, see Figure 12-2.

The firm has control over all aspects of advertising, including mes-

Advertising attracts a large audience, has low per customer costs, offers many media, is controllable, may be surrounded by noncommercial information, and aids selling.

Figure 12-2
How Outdoor Advertising Satisfies Company Promotion Objectives

Reprinted with permission of the Institute of Outdoor Advertising.

sage content, graphics, timing, size or length of message, and the demographics of the audience. In addition, a uniform message is delivered to all members of the audience. And, with print media, consumers can study and restudy messages.

With advertising, editorial content (a news story or segment of a television show) often surrounds an advertisement. This will increase readership or viewing, enhance the company's or product's image, and create the proper mood for the advertisement. It is for these reasons that firms seek specialized media or sections of media (such as the sports section of a newspaper for a men's clothing ad).

Advertising eases the way for personal selling by obtaining audience awareness and liking for a firm's brands. In addition, advertising both allows reduced-service and self-service retailers to operate and sustains an entire industry—mail order. With a pulling strategy, advertising enables a firm to show its channel members that consumer demand exists.

Advertising is inflexible and has high total costs, wasted audience segments, limited information, and weak feedback.

On the negative side, because advertising messages are standardized, they are inflexible. This makes it difficult to adapt to consumer needs and differences. Furthermore, questions consumers have about a product or service cannot be answered. Because the audiences for most mass media are quite diverse, inflexibility is a significant problem.

Some types of advertising require high total expenditures, even though costs per viewer or reader are low. This may exclude smaller firms from utilizing certain media. In the preceding example, a television ad cost $.005 per viewer. Nonetheless, total costs (excluding production expenses) are $150,000 and this is for one ad placed once.

Many media appeal to large geographical areas. This may result in wasted viewing or circulation for a small or moderate-sized firm. For example, a single-unit discount store or a beer manufacturer distributing locally might find that only 60 per cent of a newspaper's readers live within its shopping areas. Also, because audiences for advertisements are diversified, a large amount of readership or viewership may be wasted. A dress manufacturer of clothes designed for fifteen- to eighteen-year-old females might find only magazines with broader readership profiles, for example, thirteen- to twenty-five-year-old females.

Mass media attract many people who do not view or listen to commercials, read advertisements, or keep circulars or mail ads. These people watch television, read magazines and newspapers, and keep up with first-class mail; but they do not pay attention to advertising.

The majority of advertisements do not provide the audience with much information, because high costs lead to brief messages. In particular, television commercials are short, averaging thirty or less seconds; few are longer than one minute.

Last, because advertising is nonpersonal, feedback is difficult to obtain and usually it is not immediately available.

Developing an Advertising Plan

The development of an advertising plan consists of the nine steps shown in Figure 12-3. The steps are highlighted in the following subsections.

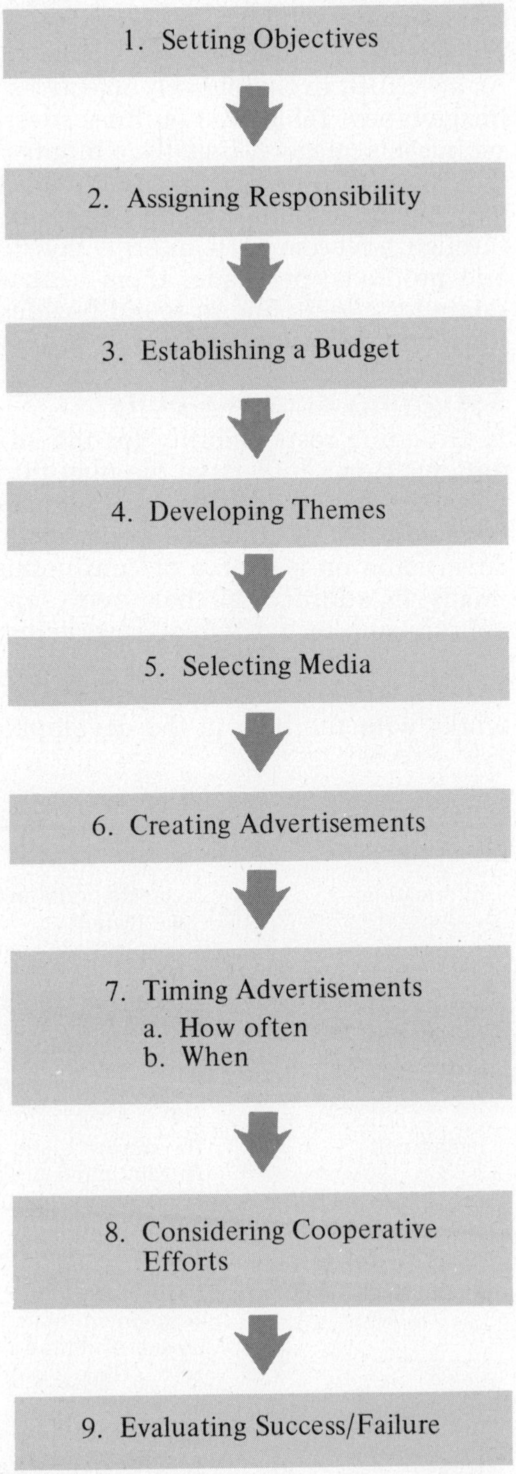

Figure 12-3
**Developing an Advertising
Plan**

1. Setting Objectives

2. Assigning Responsibility

3. Establishing a Budget

4. Developing Themes

5. Selecting Media

6. Creating Advertisements

7. Timing Advertisements
   a. How often
   b. When

8. Considering Cooperative
   Efforts

9. Evaluating Success/Failure

Setting Objectives

The advertising objectives set by a firm guide its entire advertising plan. As described in Chapter 11, objectives can be divided into demand and image types. Table 12-3 outlines several specific objectives a firm may set in each category. Usually, a number of these objectives are combined and pursued through the advertising plan.

As an example, AT&T seeks to achieve a variety of objectives through advertising. It informs consumers of new telephone services and products, persuades them to increase long-distance calling, uses reminder advertising to retain business customers, and places institutional ads detailing the overall value of the company.

Assigning Responsibility

In assigning responsibility for the advertising plan, the firm has two options. It can undertake the plan through an in-house advertising department or hire an outside advertising agency. Although a number of companies have in-house departments, most of those involved with advertising on a sizable or continuous basis employ outside agencies (many in addition to their own departments). Diversified firms frequently employ a different advertising agency for each of their product lines.

An ***advertising agency*** offers a variety of functions. It usually works with the firm in the development of its advertising plan. This

An *advertising agency* may work with a firm to develop its advertising plan, conduct research, or complete other tasks.

Table 12-3	*Type of Objective*	*Illustrations*
Illustrations of Specific Advertising Objectives	**Demand oriented**	
	Information	To create brand awareness of a new product by the target market
		To explain the characteristics of a new product or service
		To acquaint consumers with new store hours
		To reduce the time it takes for salespeople to answer basic questions
		To expand the existing base of customers by appealing to new geographic areas or market segments
	Persuasion	To improve brand ratings
		To gain brand preference
		To increase store traffic
		To increase sales
		To achieve brand loyalty
	Reminding (retention)	To stabilize sales
		To maintain brand loyalty
		To sustain brand recognition and image
		To reinforce customers' brand preferences
	Image oriented	
	Industry	To develop and maintain a favorable industry image
		To generate primary demand for products or services
	Company	To develop and maintain a favorable company image
		To generate selective demand for products or services

Agency	Selected Clients	Table 12-4
Young & Rubicam	CBS Publishing, U.S. Postal Service, C.I.T. Financial, Merrill Lynch, Southland	**Leading U.S. Advertising Agencies***
J. Walter Thompson	Ford, Eastman Kodak, Quaker Oats, Reader's Digest, McDonnell-Douglas	
Ogilvy & Mather	Baskin-Robbins, Pepperidge Farms, General Foods, Sears, Shell Oil	
McCann-Erickson	Coca-Cola, Exxon, General Electric, General Motors, Gillette	
Ted Bates	Colgate-Palmolive, ITT Continental Baking, Mars, Warner-Lambert, Warner Amex	
BBDO	Dow Jones, DuPont, PepsiCo, 3M, Armstrong Cork	
Leo Burnett	Allstate, Green Giant, Kellogg, Maytag, Procter & Gamble	
SSC&B	Lipton, Noxell, Olympus Camera, Lever Bros., Sheraton	
Foote, Cone & Belding	Clairol, Hughes Aircraft, Levi Strauss, Sunkist Growers, Zenith	
Doyle Dane Bernbach	Polaroid, Joseph E. Seagram, Volkswagen of America, IBM, American Tourister	

*Based on worldwide billings.
  Source: John J. O'Connor, "1981 Income Tops $5 Billion," *Advertising Age* (March 24, 1982), p. 1, and "Some Major Agencies and Their Longtime Clients," *Advertising Age* (July 12, 1982), p. 41.

includes themes, media selection, copywriting, and other tasks. The large agencies offer a full complement of market research, product planning, consumer research, public relations, and other services. For many years, agencies received 15 per cent of advertising expenditures as their commissions for basic functions and added charges for additional services. Although the 15 per cent rate is no longer mandatory, it is still the most common compensation arrangement. The firm's decision to use an outside agency depends on its own expertise and resources, and the role for advertising.[5] Table 12-4 shows the largest 10 U.S. advertising agencies and some of their major clients.

Establishing a Budget

After determining the overall expenditures to be allocated to advertising by the all-you-can-afford, incremental, competitive parity, percentage-of-sales, or objective-and-task method, the firm establishes a detailed advertising budget. It must outline the funds for each type of advertising (such as product and institutional messages) and each medium (such as newspapers and radio). Table 12-5 shows the 1981 advertising budget for American Home Products, maker of Anacin, Dristan, Woolite, Chef Boy-ar-dee, and a variety of other products.

A firm must proceed very carefully before reducing advertising expenditures for a product. As an example, the tobacco industry has been able to sustain the sales of cigarettes despite long-running bans against television advertising. Instead of reducing expenditures when excluded from certain media, total advertising increased as more magazine, newspaper, and other print ads were used.

Developing Themes

Next, the firm develops **advertising themes,** the overall appeals for its campaign. A product or service appeal centers on the item and its attri-

Table 12-5	*Medium*	*Advertising Budget*	*Per Cent of Budget*
Advertising Budget for American Home Products, 1981	Newspapers	$ 1,681,200	0.8
	Magazines	10,262,200	4.9
	Farm publications	519,500	0.2
	Spot television	40,376,700	19.3
	Network television	131,449,800	62.9
	Spot radio	1,840,200	0.8
	Network radio	4,135,100	2.0
	Other (including production costs, direct mail, etc.)	18,776,000	9.0
	Total	$209,040,700	100.0*

1981 sales = $4,131,237,000.
Advertising as a % of sales = 5.1.

*Rounding error.
Source: "American Home Products," *Advertising Age* (September 9, 1982), p. 22.

The basic *advertising themes* are the product or service, consumer, and/or nonconsumer appeal.

butes. A consumer appeal describes the product or service in terms of consumer benefits rather than product or service characteristics. A non-consumer or nonproduct or nonservice appeal deals with institutional advertising and corporate image.[6] Coca-Cola combines all three themes in the advertisement shown in Figure 12-4. Table 12-6 presents the full range of advertising themes from which the firm may select.

Selecting Media

The firm has a wide variety of media from which to choose. The characteristics of the leading media are shown in Table 12-7.

Figure 12-4
Advertising Themes for Coca-Cola

Reprinted by permission of Coca-Cola.

Table 12-6 **Advertising Themes**

Theme	Explanation	Example
Product- or service-related		
1. Product or service features	Dominant features described	Maytag washers emphasize dependability and durability.
2. Product or service competitive advantages	Competitive advantages cited	Ford stresses the quiet ride of its cars versus competitors cars.
3. Product or service prices	Price used as dominant feature	Suave beauty products advertise low prices.
4. Product or service news	News or information domination	New-model cars point out improvements in gas mileage.
5. Product or service popularity	Size of market detailed	Hertz emphasizes its leading position in car rentals.
6. Generic	Primary demand sought	Grapes are advertised.
Consumer-related		
1. Consumer uses	Product or service uses explained	Pillsbury ads show cake recipes.
2. Savings through uses	Cost benefits of product or service shown	Owens-Corning shows how consumers reduce heating bills with fiberglas insulation.
3. Consumer self-enhancement	Emphasis on how product or service helps consumer improve	Listerine advertises that it eliminates bad breath.
4. Fear	Threatening situation displayed	American Express points out the risks of carrying cash.
5. Subsidized product or service trials	Incentives given to encourage product or service purchases	An ad mentions $1 off the purchase price as an introductory offer for a new brand of coffee.
Nonconsumer or nonproduct/ service-related		
1. Corporate citizenship	Favorable image sought	Exxon shows how it is searching for new energy sources.
2. Investor solicitations	Growth, profits, and potential described to attract investors	Full-page ads are taken in business sections of major newspapers.

When selecting media, these factors should be considered: cost, reach, frequency, message permanence, persuasive impact, and lead time.

Advertising costs should be assessed in three ways. First, the total costs of a medium are calculated—for example, $30,000 for a full-page color ad in a national magazine. Second, per reader or viewer costs are computed. Costs are expressed on a per thousand basis, except by newspapers which use a cost per million base. If the $30,000 ad is placed in a magazine with a circulation of 500,000, the cost per thousand is $60. Third, *waste,* the portion of the audience that is not in the firm's target market, is analyzed. Because media appeal to mass audiences, waste is a significant factor in advertising.

Reach refers to the number of viewers or readers in the audience. For television and radio, reach is the total number of people who are exposed to an advertisement. For print media, reach has two components, circulation and passalong rate. Circulation is the number of cop-

Advertising costs must be examined on the basis of total costs, costs per reader or viewer, and *waste*.

Reach is the size of the audience. It includes circulation and passalong rate.

Table 12-7 **Advertising Media**

Medium	Market Coverage	Best Uses	Advantages	Disadvantages
Daily newspaper	Entire metropolitan area, local editions sometimes used	Large retailers	Short lead time, concentrated market, flexible, passalongs, surrounded by content	General audience, heavy ad competition, limited color, limited creativity
Weekly newspaper	One community	Local retailers	Same as daily	Heavy ad competition, limited color, limited creativity, small market
Television	Regional or national	Regional manufacturers and large retailers, national manufacturers and largest retailers	Reach, low cost per viewer, persuasive impact, creative options, flexible, surrounded by programs	High minimum total costs, general audience, lead time, short message, limited availability
Direct mail	Advertiser selects market	New products, book clubs, financial services, catalog sales	Precise audience, flexible, personal approach, no clutter from other messages	High throwaway rate, receipt by wrong person, low credibility
Magazines	National (most with regional editions) or local	National manufacturers, mail order firms, local service retailers	Color, creative options, affluent audience, permanence of message, passalongs, flexible, surrounded by content	Long lead time, poor frequency, ad clutter, geographically dispersed audience
Radio	Entire metropolitan area	Local or regional retailers	Low costs, selective market, high frequency, immediacy of messages, surrounded by content	No visual impact, commercial clutter, channel switching, consumer distractions
Business paper	National or regional	Corporate advertising, industrial manufacturers	Selective market, high readability, surrounded by content, permanence of message, passalongs	Restricted product or service applicatons, not final-consumer-oriented

***Table 12-7* Advertising Media (contd.)**

Medium	Market Coverage	Best Uses	Advantages	Disadvantages
Outdoor	Entire metropolitan area or one location	Brand-name products, nearby retailers, reminder ads	Large size, color, creative options, frequency, no clutter of competing messages, permanence of message	Legal restrictions, consumer distractions, general audience, inflexible
Transit	Urban community with a transit system	Firms located along transit routes	Concentrated market, permanence of messages, frequency, action orientation, color, creative options	Clutter of ads, consumer distractions, limited audience
Telephone directories	Entire metropolitan area (with local supplements)	All types of retailers, professionals, service companies	Low costs, permanence of message, coverage of market, specialized listings, action-oriented	Clutter of ads, limited creativity, long lead time, low appeal to passive consumers
Flyers	Single neighborhood	Local retailers	Low cost, market coverage, little waste, flexible	High throwaway rate, poor image

ies sold or distributed to consumers. Passalong rate is the number of times each copy is placed with another reader. For example, each copy of *Newsweek* is read by about six people. The passalong rate for magazines is much higher than for daily newspapers.

Frequency is how often a medium can be used. It is greatest for newspapers, radio, and television, where ads may appear daily and advertising strategy may be easily changed. Telephone directories, outdoor ads, and magazines have the poorest frequency. A Yellow Pages ad may be placed or changed only once per year.

Message permanence refers to the number of exposures one advertisement generates and how long it remains with the audience. Outdoor ads, transit ads, and telephone directories yield many exposures per message. In addition, magazines are retained by consumers for long periods of time. On the other hand, radio and television ads last only 5 to 60 seconds and are over.

Persuasive impact is the ability of a medium to stimulate consumers. Television often has the highest persuasive impact because it is able to combine audio, video, color, animation, and other appeals. Magazines also have high persuasive impact.

Frequency is highest for newspapers, radio, and television.

Exposures per ad involve message permanence.

Persuasive impact is highest for television.

**Lead time is needed by a
medium for placing an
advertisement.**

Lead time is the time required by the medium for placing an advertisement. It is shortest for newspapers and longest for magazines and telephone directories. A long lead time means a firm must plan its advertising program six months or more in advance, and risk incorrect messages in a changing environment. Television may also require a long lead time, because the number of ads it can carry is limited.

In recent years there have been many media innovations. These include regional editions and zip-code marketing (ads placed in specific geographic areas) to revive magazines; newspapers improving their computer skills in placing ads; advertising on cable television; televised commercials in supermarkets, movie theaters, and airplanes; and specialized Yellow Pages.[7]

Creating Advertisements

**Creating advertisements
involves message
content, production
schedule, message
variations, and
placement in the
medium.**

Creating advertisements involves four fundamental decisions:

1. Message content must be determined. Each advertisement needs a headline or opening that creates consumer interest, such as "Finally, a copier for the most important person in my life. Me." and copy that presents the message:

   > To you, I'm Jack Klugman the Actor. To my agent, business manager, and accountant, I'm Jack Klugman the Corporation. They have copiers. Why shouldn't I?

   See Figure 12-5. Content decisions also involve the use of color and illustrations, ad size or length, the source, and the use of symbolism. These factors depend on the firm's goals and resources.
2. A production schedule must be outlined. This schedule should allow for all copy and artwork and be based on the lead time needed for the chosen medium.
3. The firm needs to determine how many variations of its basic message to utilize. This depends on the frequency of presentation and the quality of the ad.
4. The location of an ad in a broadcast program or print medium must be determined. For men, newspaper placement in the sports section increases readership. Women read the entertainment and food and cooking sections more frequently. As costs have risen, more and more companies have become concerned about improved ad placement.[8]

Timing Advertisements

**Timing advertisements
involves how often an
advertisement is shown
and when to advertise
during the year.**

Timing advertisements requires two major decisions: how often a particular ad is shown and when to advertise during the year. In the first decision the firm must balance audience awareness and knowledge versus irritation if it places an ad a number of times in a short period. For example, McDonald's runs its ads repeatedly, but changes them very often.

Second, the firm determines whether to advertise throughout the year or in concentrated periods. Distributed advertising maintains company and brand recognition, balances sales, and increases sales in

Figure 12-5
*Interesting and Informative
Message Content*

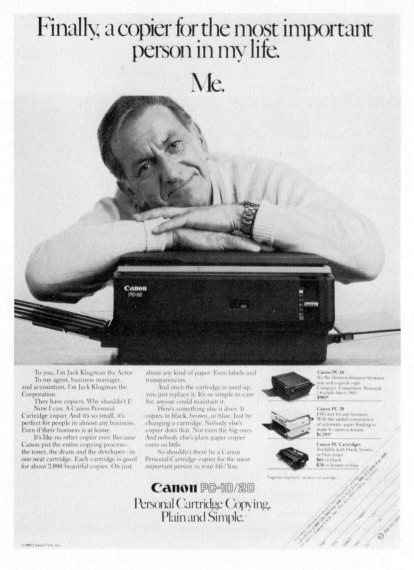

Reprinted by permission.

nonpeak periods. It is used by most manufacturers and general-merchandise retailers. Massed advertising concentrates advertising during peak periods, maximizes seasonal sales, generates short-run consumer enthusiasm, and ignores sales in nonpeak periods. Specialty manufacturers and retailers use this method.

Other timing considerations are when to advertise new products, when to stop advertising existing products, how to coordinate advertising and other promotional tools, when to change basic themes, and how to relate messages to the hierarchy-of-effects process.

Considering Cooperative Efforts

In order to stimulate channel members and expand advertising efforts, the firm should consider cooperative efforts. Under a ***cooperative advertising plan,*** channel members share the costs of some aspects of

Figure 12-6
***Cooperative Advertising
Benefits All Parties***

MANUFACTURER ⟷ MEDIA ⟷ RETAILER

Three's no crowd

Source: Reprinted by permission from the August 17, 1981
issue of *Advertising Age*. Copyright 1981 by Crain Communications, Inc.

With a *cooperative advertising* plan, costs are shared by channel members. Cooperative arrangements may be vertical or horizontal.

advertising. In a vertical cooperative-advertising agreement, channel members at different stages share costs (for example, manufacturer and retailer). With a horizontal cooperative-advertising agreement, two or more channel members at the same stage share costs (for example, two retailers).

Good cooperative agreements state the share of costs paid by each party, functions and responsibilities of each party, advertisements to be covered, and basis for termination. They also benefit each participant.[9] See Figure 12-6.

An example of cooperative advertising involves the National Bowling Council, a federation of bowling lane proprietors and bowling companies. The council developed a program whereby local proprietors, the council, and the Bowling Proprietors Association shared advertising costs. If the local proprietors raised $10,000, the council contributed $2,500 and the Association another $1,250. The council also placed ads for the proprietors.[10] The council encouraged both vertical and horizontal cooperation.

Evaluation of success or failure must relate performance to objectives.

Evaluating Success or Failure

The success or failure of advertising depends on how well it helps the company achieve promotion objectives. Creating customer awareness and increasing sales are two distinct goals; success or failure in attaining them must be measured differently. Furthermore, advertising is extremely difficult to isolate as the single factor leading to a certain image or sales level.

Following are a variety of examples dealing with the evaluation of advertising success or failure:

- Igloo, a division of Anderson, Clayton, & Co., tested an advertising campaign for its Playmate personal-size ice chest. It found that the campaign increased brand awareness by 300 to 400 per cent, and sales rose by 25 per cent.[11]
- In the first *Advertising Age* poll on advertising awareness, the top ten were Coca-Cola, Pepsi-Cola, McDonald's, Miller beer, Ford, Chrysler, Peter Pan peanut butter, 7 Up, Budweiser, and Chevrolet. This ranking was based on consumer recall of ads for the previous month.[12]
- A study on two AT&T commercials revealed that "cost of visit" ads (which stressed the economy of long-distance calls) generated greater revenues than "reach out and touch someone" ads.[13]
- An analysis of more than 800 commercials found that celebrities were not overly effective in gaining brand preference, but they did contribute to higher levels of recall about the ads in which they appeared.[14]

Scope and Importance of Publicity

Every company would like to receive favorable publicity about its offerings or the company itself, such as "This news station rates the Honda Accord as a superior effort" or "State Farm Insurance is considered one of the five best homeowners' insurance companies by this magazine."

Accordingly, the competition for publicity is intense. After all, there are only four national television networks (ABC, CBS, NBC, and PBS) and a few national periodicals. It is difficult to make the network news. However, there are numerous opportunities for publicity because there are 4,600 AM radio stations, 4,300 FM radio stations, 1,100 independent television stations, and 10,000 newspapers and periodicals located throughout the United States. In addition, the number of cable television stations is rising rapidly.

Unfortunately, many firms have poor or ineffective policies for dealing with the independent media or developing a sustained publicity campaign. Table 12-8 shows a variety of publicity-related situations and the alternate ways a firm could deal with them. From this table it should be clear that unfavorable as well as favorable publicity can occur and the firm must be prepared to handle it in the best way possible. Negative publicity can occur for any company; but the successful one will have a contingency plan to handle it.

It is important for the relationship of advertising, public relations, and publicity to be understood. Advertising is paid mass communication that is demand or image directed. ***Public relations*** is mass and

Public relations is any communication on behalf of a firm that is image directed—paid or nonpaid. Publicity is nonpaid and may be demand or image oriented.

Table 12-8 **Publicity-Related Situations and How a Firm Could Respond to Them**

Situation	Poor Response	Good Response
Fire breaks out in a company plant	Requests for information by media are ignored.	Company spokesperson explains the cause of the fire and company precautions to avoid it and answers questions.
New product introduced	Advertising is used without publicity.	Preintroduction news releases, product samples, and testimonials are used.
News story about product defects	Requests for information by media are ignored, blanket denials are issued, hostility is exhibited toward reporter of story.	Company spokesperson states that tests are being conducted on products, describes procedure for handling defects, and answers questions.
Competitor introduces new product	The advertising campaign is stepped up.	Extensive news releases, statistics, and spokespersons are made available to media to present company's competitive features.
High profits reported	Profits are rationalized and defended.	Profitability is explained, data (historical and current) are provided, uses of profits are detailed: research, community development.
Overall view of publicity	There is an infrequent need for publicity; crisis fighting is used when bad reports are circulated.	There is an ongoing need for publicity, strong planning, and contingency plans for bad reports.

personal communication that is demand or image directed. Public relations efforts include institutional advertising, publicity, and personal appearances to enhance a firm's image. Publicity is nonpaid mass communication that is demand or image directed. Figure 12-7 contains examples of the three concepts.

Characteristics of Publicity

Publicity has no space or message costs, high credibility, an attentive audience, and a mass audience.

Publicity offers several benefits. There are no costs for message time or space. An advertisement in prime-time television may cost $200,000 to $300,000 or more per minute, whereas a five-minute report on a network newscast would not cost anything. However, publicity should not be viewed as entirely cost free. There are costs for news releases, a publicity department, and other items.

Credibility about messages is high, because they are reported in independent media. A newspaper review of a movie has a higher level of believability than an ad in the same paper, because the reader knows the review is not sponsored by the movie producer. The audience associates independence with objectivity.

Similarly, people are more likely to pay attention to news reports than to clearly identified ads. For example, *Women's Wear Daily* has many fashion reports and advertisements. Readers spend time reading the stories, but they flip through the ads. In the same vein, there may be ten commercials during a half-hour television program or hundreds of ads in a magazine. Feature stories are much fewer in number and stand out clearly.

Concept	Examples
Advertising	An ad for Time magazine (paid, demand directed)
	An ad showing the growth of Time Inc. (paid, image directed)
Public relations	An ad showing the growth of Time Inc. (paid, image directed)
	A report on the local news about the success of Time Inc. (nonpaid, image directed)
	A speech at a local college by a representative of Time Inc.'s *Life* magazine (personal contact, image directed)
Publicity	A newspaper article citing Time Inc.'s Book-of-The-Month Club as the outstanding mail-order book club (nonpaid, demand directed)
	A report on the local news about the success of Time Inc. (nonpaid, image directed)

As with advertisements, publicity reaches a mass audience. Within a short period of time, new products or company policies can be known by most of the target market.

Publicity also has some significant limitations. A firm has little control over messages, their timing, their placement, or their coverage by a given medium. A company may issue detailed news releases and find only portions cited by the media. In particular, media have the ability to be much more critical than a company would like. Furthermore, media usually find disasters (fires, auto crashes, product side effects) more newsworthy than routine statements distributed by the firm.

Publicity cannot be controlled, planned, or timed accurately by the firm.

For example, in 1982, Procter & Gamble faced a substantial publicity problem over the meaning of the firm's 123-year-old company logo. A small number of ministers and other private citizens believed that the symbol was based on Satanism and therefore sacrilegious. These beliefs were covered extensively by the media and resulted in the firm receiving 15,000 phone calls about the rumor in June alone. To combat this negative publicity, Procter & Gamble issued news releases featuring prominent clergy (such as Jerry Falwell) that refuted the rumors, threatened to sue those people spreading the stories, and had a spokesperson appear on "Good Morning America." The media cooperated with the company and ultimately the false rumors were put to rest, with no adverse affect on sales.[15] Figure 12-8 shows the rumored symbolism and Procter & Gamble's explanation.

A firm may also want publicity during certain periods, such as

Figure 12-8
**Procter & Gamble:
Countering Negative
Publicity**

**Rumored
symbolism**

Connected to one another,
the stars form the number 666,
a symbol of the Antichrist.
Curls in the "sorcerer's" beard
also form 666 when the logo
is held up to a mirror.

P&G's explanation

The man-in-the-moon was
"a popular decorative fancy"
adopted in an early version
of the logo in 1859.
The 13 stars represent the
original United States colonies.

Source: Reprinted from the
August 9, 1982 issue of *Advertising Age*. Copyright
1981 by Crain Communications, Inc.

when a new product is introduced or a new store opened, but the media
may not cover the introduction or opening until after the time it would
aid the firm. Similarly, media determine the placement of a story; it may
follow a report on crime or sports. Finally, the media ascertain whether
to cover a story at all and the amount of coverage to be devoted to it. A
company-sponsored jobs program might go unreported or received
three-sentence coverage in a local newspaper.

Finally, it is difficult to plan publicity in advance, because newsworthy happenings take place quickly. Therefore, short-run plans are
most applicable. Publicity must be viewed as complementary to advertising and not a substitute for it. The characteristics of both (credibility
and low costs for publicity, control and coverage for advertising) are
needed for an effective communications program.

Developing a Publicity Plan

Developing a publicity plan is much like developing an advertising
plan. It consists of the steps shown in Figure 12-9 and described in the
following subsections.

Setting Objectives

The objectives of publicity are the same as those for advertising—they
can be demand oriented (information, persuasion, reminding) and/or
image oriented (industry, company). The objectives guide the entire
publicity plan.

As an example, the publicity objectives for the *American Heritage*

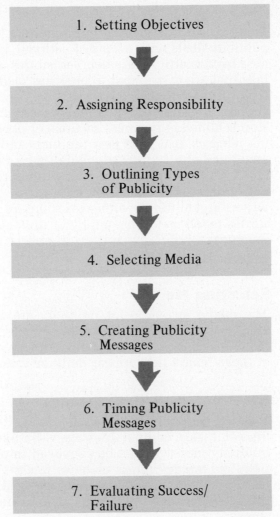

Figure 12-9
Developing a Publicity Plan

1. Setting Objectives

2. Assigning Responsibility

3. Outlining Types of Publicity

4. Selecting Media

5. Creating Publicity Messages

6. Timing Publicity Messages

7. Evaluating Success/ Failure

Dictionary when it was first introduced were inclusion on national best-seller lists for as long as possible, placement of company personnel on leading broadcast interview programs, publication of print interviews in major daily newspapers in twelve key cities, placement of stories and book reviews on a national basis, and acceptance by editors as a worthwhile, innovative working tool.[16]

Assigning Responsibility

A firm has three options for assigning promotion responsibility: it may employ an in-house public relations or publicity department to enact the entire publicity plan; it may have its outside advertising agency handle publicity; or it may hire a specialized public relations or publicity firm. The in-house department ensures greater secrecy until releases are distributed. The outside firm has better contacts and expertise. Each approach is popular.

A firm can use an in-house department, hire an outside ad agency, or hire a specialized firm.

Outlining Types of Publicity

There are several general ***publicity types*** available to the firm.[17] News publicity deals with events of national, regional, or local interest. Business feature articles are detailed stories about the company or its offerings that are distributed to business media. Service feature articles are lighter stories that focus on personal care, household items, and recipes and are distributed to newspapers and magazines. Finance releases are stories aimed at business sections of newspapers and magazines. Product releases deal with new products and product improvements. They are aimed at all forms of media.

Pictorial releases are illustrations or pictures supplied to media. Background editorial material is extra information provided to media writers and editors; it enhances standard releases and provides filler for stories (such as the biography of the chief executive of the company). Emergency publicity consists of special releases keyed to disasters or serious problems.

Selecting Media

The media available for publicity are newspapers, television, magazines, radio, and business papers. Because of the infrequent nature of many magazines and some business papers, publicity is usually aimed at those media that appear daily or weekly.

Creating Publicity Messages

Creating publicity messages involves the same factors as in advertising— message content, message variations, and a production schedule. Publicity messages can be conveyed in one or a combination of forms: news conference, press or news release, phone calls or personal contacts, press kit (a combination of materials about a story), special events (Macy's Thanksgiving Parade, an appearance on the "Today" show), or films.

Timing Publicity Messages

Publicity should precede the introduction of new products and generate excitement for them. For emergencies, press releases and spokespeople should be immediately available. For ongoing publicity, messages should be properly spaced throughout the year. As noted previously, a company may have difficulty anticipating the timing of both unanticipated and planned publicity since the media control timing.

Evaluating Success or Failure

There are several straightforward methods for evaluating the success or failure of a publicity campaign. The firm can count the media covering each story, analyze the length and placement of coverage, correlate desired with actual timing, evaluate audience reactions to publicity, and/or compute the cost of comparable advertising.

Summary

Advertising and publicity are the two forms of mass communication available to a firm. Advertising expenditures exceed $67 billion annually through such media as newspapers, magazines, farm publications, television, radio, direct mail, and outdoor.

The advantages of advertising are appeal to a large and geographically dispersed audience, low per customer costs, availability of a broad variety of media, control over all aspects of a message, surrounding editorial content, and how it complements personal selling. Disadvantages are inflexibility of messages, high total expenditures for some media, wasted viewers or readers, low audience involvement and high throwaway rates, limited information provided, and difficulty in obtaining audience feedback.

An advertising plan has nine steps: (1) setting objectives, (2) assigning responsibility, (3) establishing a budget, (4) developing themes, (5) selecting media, (6) creating advertisements, (7) timing advertisements, (8) considering cooperative efforts, and (9) evaluating success or failure.

Firms seek to obtain favorable publicity and avoid or minimize negative publicity. Competition is intense for placing publicity releases. The advantages of publicity are no costs for message time and content, high level of credibility, audience attentiveness, and mass audience. The disadvantages are lack of control by the firm and the difficulty of planning in advance. Public relations is mass and personal communication aimed at company image. It uses advertising, publicity, and personal contact.

A publicity plan has seven steps: (1) setting objectives, (2) assigning responsibility, (3) outlining types of publicity, (4) selecting media, (5) creating publicity messages, (6) timing publicity messages, and (7) evaluating success or failure.

KEY TERMS

After reading this chapter, you should understand these key terms:

Advertising agency
Advertising themes
Waste
Reach
Frequency
Message permanence

Persuasive impact
Lead time
Cooperative advertising plan
Public relations
Publicity types

QUESTIONS FOR DISCUSSION

1. Compare and contrast advertising and publicity.
2. Comment on the advertising media trends since 1950. Why did you think they have occurred? Refer to Table 12-1.
3. Why would the U.S. government rank 26th among the largest advertisers?

4. Under what circumstances is advertising most likely to be used?

5. List five objectives of advertising and give an example of how each may be accomplished.

6. Why should a company hire an outside advertising agency? Which companies should not hire an agency? Explain your answer.

7. A firm has an overall budget of $100,000 for advertising. What specific decisions must it make in allocating the budget?

8. Some companies rely on national television advertising, others on magazine advertising, and still others on newspaper advertising. Why? What factors would you use to decide on the proper medium for advertising?

9. Distinguish among these media concepts: reach, frequency, and waste.

10. Develop a persuasive magazine ad for a Sony portable television.

11. What problems can arise with horizontal-cooperative advertising? With vertical-cooperative advertising?

12. Differentiate between publicity and public relations.

13. Some critics believe Procter & Gamble overreacted to the rumors about its company symbol, and thereby made more people aware of the controversy. Evaluate Procter & Gamble's reaction.

14. Give an example for each of these:
    a. News publicity
    b. Emergency publicity
    c. Finance release
    d. Background editorial material
    e. Service feature article

NOTES

1. Joseph M. Winski, "Once-Holdout Hershey Becomes Big Advertiser," *Advertising Age* (September 7, 1981), pp. 3, 67–68; and Joseph M. Winski, "Hershey Befriends Extra-Terrestial," *Advertising Age* (July 19, 1982), pp. 1, 66.

2. "100 Leaders' Advertising as a Per Cent of Sales," *Advertising Age* (September 9, 1982), p. 8.

3. Paul W. Farris and Robert D. Buzzell, "Why Advertising and Promotional Costs Vary: Some Cross-Sectional Analyses," *Journal of Marketing*, Vol. 43 (Fall 1979), p. 120.

4. Stuart Emmrich, "Major Study Details Ads' Effect on Sales," *Advertising Age* (June 21, 1982), pp. 1, 80.

5. See Jo-Ann Zbytniewski, "Ad Agencies—Who Needs 'Em?" *Progressive Grocer* (May 1981), pp. 103–110; and Bill Abrams, "Promising More," *Wall Street Journal* (March 2, 1982), pp. 1, 15.

6. This classification was developed by William H. Weilbacher, *Advertising* (New York: Macmillan, 1979), pp. 216–231.

7. See *Zip*, the monthly magazine for zip-code marketing; Cindy Ris, "Electronic Newspapers Could Alter Shape of the $4.6 Billion Classified Ad Market," *Wall Street Journal* (August 11, 1980), p. 15; "Only Use Cable to Reach Narrow Audience, Experiment, or Improve Coverage," *Marketing News* (May 28, 1982), p. 1; Bernard F. Whalen, "On-Line Markets New Mass Advertising Medium," *Marketing News* (December 28, 1979), pp. 1, 4; Richard Kreisman, "Airlines Deciding on In-Flight Ad Formats," *Advertising Age* (June 28, 1982), p. 10; and Richard Davis, "Specialty Yellow Pages Making Debut," *Advertising Age* (August 17, 1981), p. 26.

8. Stuart Emmrich, "Magazines Pressed on Positioning of Ads," *Advertising Age* (September 28, 1981), pp. 3, 92.

9. See Renee Blakkan, "Partnership Perks Up Profits," *Advertising Age* (August 17, 1981), pp. S-1, S-16; and Martin Everett, "Just the Weapon for a Tough Fight," *Sales & Marketing Management* (May 17, 1982), pp. 62–82.

10. Christy Marshall, "Co-Op Ads, New Gear Lead Bowlers Down Alley," *Advertising Age* (September 8, 1978), pp. 48, 78.

11. Tom Bayer, "Igloo Is Taking Its Case to Consumer in Ad Drive," *Advertising Age* (June 21, 1982), p. 4.

12. Joseph M. Winski, "Coke Is It in First Ad Age Poll," *Advertising Age* (May 17, 1982), p. 1.

13. Robert Raissman, "Study Says 'Reach Out' Not AT&T's Best," *Advertising Age* (November 1, 1982), p. 20.

14. David Ogilvy and Joel Raphaelson, "Research on Advertising Techniques That Work—And Don't Work," *Harvard Business Review*, Vol. 60 (July–August 1982), p. 15.

15. Sandra Salmans, "P&G's Battles With Rumors," *New York Times* (July 22, 1982), pp. D1, D4; and "P&G Rumor Blitz Looks Like a Bomb," *Advertising Age* (August 9, 1982), pp. 1, 68–69.

16. Arthur M. Merims, "Marketing's Stepchild: Product Publicity," *Harvard Business Review*, Vol. 50 (November–December 1972), p. 110.

17. N. Frazier Moore and Bertrand R. Canfield, *Public Relations: Principles, Cases, and Problems*, Seventh Edition (Homewood, Ill.: Richard D. Irwin, 1977), pp. 140–147.

LONGINES-WITTNAUER: INNOVATIVE ADVERTISING FOR EXPENSIVE WATCHES* 1

CASES

Longines-Wittnauer is a manufacturer of top-quality watches that retail from $275 to $25,000. Until 1976, the firm avoided television advertising, since it believed magazines aimed at upper-income consumers were more effective. Then, Ogilvy & Mather, Longines' advertising agency, persuaded the company that television could be a useful medium. As an Ogilvy & Mather executive commented later, "We were the first to prove you could sell an expensive watch on television."

In 1979, Longines began running its most popular television commercial. It showed a husband giving his wife a new watch as a gift; but the wife was obviously disappointed. Finally, she said "I was hoping for a Longines."

During 1981, Longines introduced a new $550 watch, named Mirage, and backed it with the company's most extensive and innovative advertising strategy. Within a short time, sales were 2½ times better than Longines' previous bestseller. The Mirage campaign included

- Larger-than-life pictures of just one watch. Traditional industry ads usually had actual-size pictures and emphasized a full line of watches.
- Comparing the new watch with a $4,800 18-carat Longines watch.
- A full range of television and radio advertising.
- Ads in *Playboy, Ebony, Esquire, Fortune, Gentleman's Quarterly, Vogue,* and airline magazines.
- Cooperative ads with retailers (including some billboards).
- Two-page ads in trade publications, such as *Jewelers Circular Keystone* and *National Jeweler.*

On a companywide level, Longines actively participates in promotional tie-ins, especially in the areas of fashion and sports. For example, it has presented watches during the Miss Universe pageant and served as the official timekeeper of the Olympics. These tactics are consistent with the company's goal of appealing to younger customers, those twenty-five to fifty-four years old earning $35,000+ annually.

*The data in this case are drawn from "Wristwatch Marketer Watches Sales Skyrocket; Ad Innovations Created," *Marketing News* (November 13, 1981), p. 8.

QUESTIONS

1. What were the potential benefits and risks with Longines' initial television advertising efforts?
2. Evaluate Longines' advertising approach for its Mirage watch. Be specific.
3. Why would a firm use comparative advertising involving a comparison with its own $4,800 brand?
4. How do you think advertising strategies for Timex (moderately priced) and Longines' watches should differ? Consider all the elements of an advertising plan.

2 ARTESIA WATERS: USING PUBLICITY TO COMPETE WITH PERRIER†

In early 1980, Rick Scoville entered the sparkling water business, with a loan of $25,000 and an aging, small bottling plant in San Antonio, Texas. Scoville's goal was to have his Artesia Waters compete head on with Perrier for the Texas market. His major problem—Scoville had no money to advertise.

To make up for his inability to advertise, Scoville mounted an aggressive publicity campaign to secure media attention, following the plan outlined in Table 1. Initially, Scoville wrote letters to media describing his product; this resulted in newspaper stories in Dallas, Houston, and San Antonio. He reproduced a story from a Houston paper and mailed it to other publications. A follow-up telephone call to the *Wall Street Journal* led to a one-paragraph article on page one.

The, *Texas Monthly* printed a feature story on Artesia. This earned Scoville an invitation to a bottled water taste test; and Artesia won the test. Coverage on Texas television stations increased rapidly, and sales tripled the day after the first telecast.

Artesia's image was carefully developed, "We tell Perrier drinkers, 'We're chic. We're American. We're Texan. We're good. And we cost less.'" Scoville played up the theme of the small American firm versus the large foreign firm. And fancy bottling and labeling added to Artesia's image.

Sales during 1980 were $102,000; they jumped to $1.5 million in 1981. Artesia gained a strong market share in Texas, taking up to 30 per cent of

†The data in this case are drawn from John Sharkey, "Kicking Perrier in the Derriere," *Inc.* (September 1981), pp. 165–166.

Table 1

Artesia Water's Guidelines for Generating Publicity	1. Place stories directly with newspapers, trade magazines, and radio and television stations. 2. Send letters to the editors and program directors for local media. They are frequently on the lookout for interesting stories. 3. Write short pieces, emphasizing newsworthy factors. 4. Reproduce and forward copies of early stories that have been placed in the media to news organizations. This establishes credibility and leads to further placements. 5. Create an angle (e.g., small company makes good). 6. Design product packaging for maximum attention. 7. Be patient, flexible, and persistent.

Perrier's sales. Based upon his early success, Scoville started advertising in 1981, setting a budget of $270,000. Advertising centered on direct mail, outdoor, and print media.

QUESTIONS

1. Evaluate Table 1.
2. Why would the *Wall Street Journal* carry a story on a small, unknown bottled water company?
3. What would have happened to Artesia Waters if it lost the televised taste test?
4. In 1981, Scoville decided to reduce the role of publicity and began advertising. Why? Was this action correct?

Personal Selling and Sales Promotion

13

Chapter Preview

Chapter Objectives

1 To examine the scope, importance, and characteristics of personal selling

2 To study the elements in a personal selling plan: objectives, responsibility, budget, type(s) of sales positions, sales techniques, sales tasks, and implementation

3 To examine the scope, importance, and characteristics of sales promotion

4 To study the elements in a sales promotion plan: objectives, responsibility, overall plan, types of sales promotion, coordination, and evaluation of success or failure

Ray Henderson is a traveling salesperson who regularly visits doctors' offices and medical centers in northeast Tennessee for his employer, Merck & Co. He is a "detail man," one of 25,000 such medical representatives in the U.S., who promotes new and existing medicines to doctors and tries to convince them to prescribe Merck products to their patients.

Ray began with Merck in 1960, after working for a medical-supply house. He travels about 25,000 miles each year and distributes large amounts of drug samples to the doctors in his territory. Twice, Ray has been the highest-producing salesperson at Merck. He is at the top of the company's $25,000 to $50,000 annual compensation range.

The communication between Ray Henderson and his doctors is two-sided. In a quiet manner, Ray explains the uses and benefits of Merck's medicines. The doctors raise questions about adverse side effects and the circumstances under which certain drugs should or should not be used. To aid the process, Ray also helps to set up medical symposiums, bringing together local doctors with invited guest lecturers from outside the geographic area.

Henderson works hard to ensure that doctors respect him and his company. He spends many hours learning about Merck's new products and refreshing his memory about existing products (at Merck, a detail person spends 12 weeks during his or her first year in formal courses and in rounds with interns and residents at a teaching hospital). Every year, all sales personnel are tested four times and must attend four regional tutorials conducted by medical experts.

Despite Ray Henderson's high standards and low-key approach, some doctors and others criticize the general role of the detail person in promoting drugs. They fear that overzealous salesmanship can sometimes overstate actual product effectiveness. Nonetheless, "even the critics of detail men agree that most drug salespeople are ethical and straightforward"; and many companies have clear policies that tone down the sales presentations of detail persons.[1]

Scope and Importance of Personal Selling

As defined in Chapter 11, personal selling is that part of promotion involving an oral presentation in a conversation with one or more prospective buyers for the purpose of making a sale. Unlike advertising and publicity, selling relies on personal contact. The goals of personal selling are similar to other promotion types: information, persuasion, and/or reminding.

Personal selling utilizes oral presentations to prospective buyers.

In the United States, more than six million people are employed in the sales positions defined by the Bureau of Labor Statistics. Included are professional sales personnel and clerical sales personnel. Salesworkers may be involved with complex selling arrangements or perform routine tasks.

Professional sales personnel generate customer accounts, find out customer needs, interact with consumers, emphasize knowledge as well as persuasion, and provide substantial service. Top salespeople can earn more than $100,000 per year. Examples of professional sales personnel are stockbrokers, manufacturing sales representatives, insurance agents, and real estate brokers.

Professional sales personnel build accounts. Clerical sales personnel complete transactions.

Clerical sales personnel answer telephone and in-person inquiries, obtain stock from inventory, recommend the best brand in a product category, and complete transactions by receiving payments and packing products. Examples are retail, wholesale, and manufacturer sales clerks.

Personal selling goes far beyond the six million workers identified as salespersons by the Bureau of Labor Statistics, because every contact between a company representative and a current or potential customer involves some degree of personal interaction. For example, lawyers, plumbers, hairdressers, and cashiers are not defined as sales workers. Yet, each occupation involves a great degree of customer contact.

In a variety of situations, a strong emphasis on personal selling is usually needed. Large-volume customers require special attention and handling. With direct company to consumer sales, channel members are not hired to complete transactions; the company is responsible for personal selling. Geographically concentrated consumers may be more efficiently served by a sales force than through advertisements in mass media. Custom-made, expensive, and/or complex products or services require detailed consumer information, demonstrations, and follow-up calls. Sales services, such as gift wrapping, delivery, and installation, may be requested. If ads do not provide enough information, questions can be resolved only through personal selling. New products may require personal selling to gain channel acceptance. Finally, industrial customers expect a high level of personal contact and service. In general, the decision to stress personal selling rather than other promotion tools should be based on audience size, audience needs, the firm's desire for flexibility, and company resources.

> **Personal selling is stressed when orders are large, special handling is needed, a direct channel is used, consumers are concentrated, items are expensive or new, or service is required.**

The costs of personal selling are much higher than advertising for most companies. On the average, selling costs are 3 per cent of sales for consumer-goods companies and 3.4 per cent for industrial-goods companies. These costs cover compensation, travel, and expenses. In 1981 the average cost of a single sales call was $106.91 (about $170 for each industrial sales call); and it took four visits to complete a sale. The average experienced salesperson earned more than $30,000 per year, while semiexperienced personnel earned about $24,000 per year in 1981.[2]

> **The average cost of a single sales call is well over $100. This has led to a greater concern for efficiency.**

In order to keep selling costs down and improve sales force efficiency, a number of firms have developed revised strategies, as these examples show:[3]

- GTE-Sylvania sales personnel use computer terminals to determine the lighting needs of commercial customers, instead of making manual computations.
- Skil's Power Tool Group replaced some salespeople who worked on a salary-plus-commission basis with others who were paid only commissions.
- Xerox opened a chain of business computer stores, eliminating the need for sales personnel to call on small accounts.
- Toyota began using telephone calls to gain initial appointments for its commercial truck salespersons. This cut down on wasted sales trips.

Characteristics of Personal Selling

Personal selling has a number of positive and negative attributes. On the positive side, personal selling provides individual attention for each

Figure 13-1
The Buyer-Seller Dyad

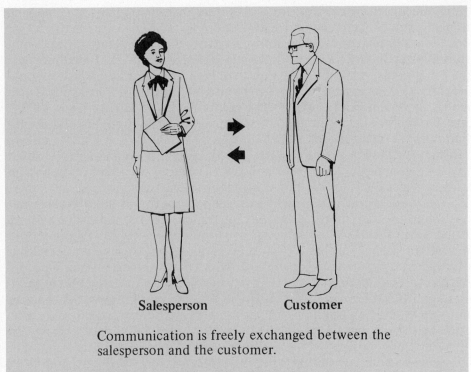

Salesperson   Customer

Communication is freely exchanged between the salesperson and the customer.

consumer and is able to pass along a lot of information. There is a dynamic, rather than passive, interaction between buyer and seller. This enables the firm to apply the concept of a ***buyer-seller dyad,*** which is a two-way flow of communication between both parties. See Figure 13-1. This interaction is not possible with advertising.

The *buyer-seller dyad* is the two-way flow of communication between the buyer and the seller.

Personal selling approaches can be flexible and adapted to the needs of specific consumers. For example, a real estate broker would make a different sales presentation to a couple looking for a year-round home than to a couple looking for a weekend retreat. The salesperson can use as much persuasion as necessary and balance it against the need for information.

Personal selling is flexible, has little waste, closes sales, and provides fast feedback.

There is less waste with most forms of selling than with advertising. Personal selling centers on a more defined and concentrated target market. In addition, customers who walk into a store or who are contacted by a salesperson are more likely to purchase a product or service than those watching an advertisement on television. Finally, because advertising stimulates consumers, those who make it to the personal selling stage are key members of the target market. Direct-to-home selling, where unsolicited, has the highest amount of wasted audience in personal selling.

Personal selling closes sales and is often the last stage in the consumer's decision process, taking place after an information search and exposure to advertisements. It holds on to repeat customers and customers already convinced by advertising and resolves any doubts or concerns of undecided consumers. Personal selling answers any remaining questions about price, warranty, and other factors. It also settles service issues, such as delivery and installation.

Feedback is immediate and clear-cut with personal selling. Consumers may be asked about company policies or product attributes, or they may register complaints about the firm or its products. Salespeople are able to determine the strengths and weaknesses of a marketing program, such as a firm's advertising campaign.

Personal selling reaches a limited audience, has high per customer costs, does little in creating awareness, and has a poor image to some.

On the negative side, personal selling can accommodate only a limited number of consumers at a given time. For example, a retail furniture salesperson may be able to handle less than twenty consumers per day if the average length of a presentation is 15 minutes to a half hour. Industrial salespeople may handle even fewer customers.

As mentioned in the previous section, personal selling costs per customer are high. This is because of the one-to-one nature of selling. An in-store furniture salesperson who interacts with 20 customers per day might cost a company $3 per presentation ($60/day compensation divided by 20), an amount much higher than the cost of contacting a person through advertising. For outside sales personnel, expenses associated with travel such as hotel, meals, and car rental can easily amount to more than $100 per day per salesperson, and compensation must be added to these costs.

Personal selling is an ineffective tool for obtaining consumer awareness about a product or service. This role is better assumed by advertising. Similarly, many consumers attracted by advertising desire self-service. This is discouraged by some aggressive salespeople.

Finally, personal selling, particularly on the retail level, has a poor image in the eyes of a number of consumers. It is criticized for a lack of honesty, strong-pressure sales pitches, and pushing consumers to make premature decisions. These criticisms may be overcome by improved sales force training and the use of modern marketing (consumer oriented) rather than selling (seller oriented) practices.

Developing a Personal Selling Plan

The development of a personal selling plan can be broken down into the seven steps shown in Figure 13-2. These are highlighted in the following subsections.

Setting Objectives

Personal selling objectives can be demand or image oriented. Illustrations of each type of objective appear in Table 13-1.

Although most firms have information, reminding, and image goals for personal selling, the major goal is persuasion: converting consumer interest into a sale.

Assigning Responsibility

Depending on the size of the company, there may be one or more sales managers who are responsible for all aspects of personal selling, includ-

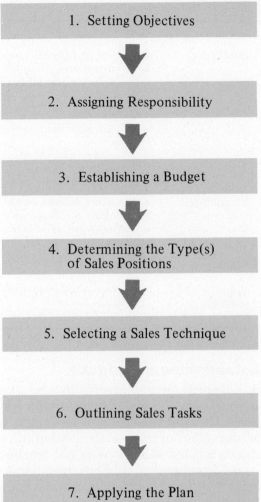

Figure 13-2
Developing a Personal Selling Plan

1. Setting Objectives

2. Assigning Responsibility

3. Establishing a Budget

4. Determining the Type(s) of Sales Positions

5. Selecting a Sales Technique

6. Outlining Sales Tasks

7. Applying the Plan

ing budgeting, types of selling, types of salespeople, selling tasks, and sales force management.

For a small or specialized firm, there is usually one sales manager. For a large or diversified firm, there are generally several sales managers, classified by geographic area (east, west), customer type (industrial, consumer), and/or product line (furniture, appliances).

An inadequate number of sales managers can have a strong impact on sales force performance. For example, Avon recently revised its approach to sales management, as the result of an annual employee turnover rate of 125 per cent. Avon had hired inexperienced workers and given them little training and supervision. Each district manager was responsible for 150 salespeople. Under its new program, Avon added a layer of district sales coordinators, who were each responsible for 10 to 15 salespeople. These coordinators were given extra commission for improving the performance of their employees.[4]

Table 13-1   *Type of Objective*   *Illustrations*

Specific Personal Selling Objectives	**Demand oriented**	
	Information	• To explain fully all product and service attributes • To answer any questions • To probe for any further questions
	Persuasion	• To distinguish clearly product or service attributes from those of competitors • To maximize the number of sales as a per cent of presentations • To convert undecided consumers into buyers • To sell complementary items, e.g., film with a camera • To placate dissatisfied customers
	Reminding	• To ensure delivery, installation, etc. • To follow up after a product or service has been used • To follow up when a repurchase is near • To reassure previous customers when making a new purchase
	Image oriented	
	Industry and company	• To maintain a good appearance by all personnel in contact with consumers • To follow acceptable sales practices

Establishing a Budget

A sales-expense budget apportions expenditures for a specific period.

A **sales-expense budget** allocates expenditures among salespeople, products, customers, and geographic areas for a given period of time. A budget is usually based on a sales forecast and relates selling tasks to the achievement of sales goals. It should have some flexibility in the event the forecasted sales level is not reached or is exceeded.

These items should be covered in a sales-expense budget: projected sales, overhead (manager's compensation, office costs), sales force compensation, sales expenses (travel, lodging, entertainment), sales meetings, selling aids, and sales management (employee selection and training) costs.

The size of the sales-expense budget depends on many factors. It will tend to be larger if customers are geographically dispersed and extensive travel is necessary. Complex products and services require time-consuming sales calls and result in fewer calls per salesperson. An expanding sales force needs expenditures for the recruitment and training of new salespeople. Table 13-2 shows a sales budget for a small, specialized firm.

Determining Type(s) of Sales Positions

Salespeople can be broadly classified as order takers, order getters, or support personnel. Some companies utilize one type of salesperson, others a combination of all three types.

An order taker handles routine orders and sells items that are presold.

An **order taker** processes routine orders and reorders. The job is more clerical than creative selling. The order taker usually handles products or services that are presold. He or she arranges displays, restocks merchandise, answers simple questions, writes up orders, and

Table 13-2

		A Sales-Expense Budget
Overhead (1 sales manager, office rental, 1 secretary)	$ 70,000	**for Emery Office**
Sales force compensation (3 salespeople)	54,000	**Supplies, 1984 (Based**
Sales expenses	40,000	**on Expected Sales of**
Sales meetings	1,000	**$3 Million)**
Selling aids	1,500	
Sales management costs (e.g., training)	3,300	
Total sales budget	$169,800	

completes transactions. An order taker may work inside a store (retail clerk or cashier) or call on customers (a field salesperson dealing with liquor stores).

An ***order getter*** is involved with generating customer leads, providing information, persuading customers, and closing sales. High-priced, complex, or new products generally require an order getter. Like the order taker, an order getter may be inside (automobile salesperson) or outside (IBM salesperson). In 1981, the average order getter was thirty-seven years of age, had attended college, had been with the company for 7.5 years, cost $12,633 to train, spent 16 hours per week in nonselling activities, and was paid over $30,000 per year in salary and commission.[5] Figure 13-3 describes a typical order-getter salesperson. Figure 13-4 contrasts order getters and order takers.

Support personnel supplement the basic sales force by providing a variety of functions. A ***missionary salesperson*** is used to distribute information about new products or services. This person does not sell but describes the attributes of the new item, answers questions, and leaves written data. The missionary salesperson paves the way for later sales. This is most commonly used with pharmaceuticals and other medical products. A ***sales engineer*** may accompany an order getter

An order getter gets customer leads, provides information, persuades customers, and closes sales.

Missionary salespersons, sales engineers, and service salespersons are support personnel.

Figure 13-3
Profile of a Typical Order-Getter Salesperson

After obtaining his MBA in 1977, Robert Taaffe joined the Xerox Corporation as a sales representative. He began by selling small copiers valued at under $20,000 to doctors, lawyers, and shop owners. In 1980 Taaffe became a sales specialist for $100,000+ Xerox machines that could produce 25,000 to 500,000 copies each month.

A typical sale would involve several months of effort, joint sales presentations with other Xerox personnel, and a number of meetings with a customer's executives. An important part of Taaffe's sales analysis was uncovering the customer's decision process:

It's a mistake to leave any stone unturned. One thing I'm always trying to figure out is the decision-making process within a given company: who the key people are. It often has nothing to do with a person's nominal title.

During 1980, three years after entering the Xerox sales force, Taaffe earned between $40,000 and $50,000. One third was in salary and the remainder in commission.

Source: Steve Lohr, "How Companies Sell to Companies," *New York Times* (December 7, 1980), Section 3, p. 15.

Figure 13-4
Order Getters and Order Takers

when a highly technical or complex item is being sold. This salesperson explains product specifications, alternatives, and long-range uses. The order getter initially contacts customers and closes sales for these products. A ***service salesperson*** usually interacts with customers after sales are completed. Delivery, installation, or other follow-up tasks are undertaken.

Selecting a Sales Technique

There are two basic techniques for selling: the canned sales presentation and the need-satisfaction approach. The ***canned sales presentation*** is a memorized, repetitive presentation given to all customers interested in a particular item. This approach does not adapt to customer needs or traits but presumes that a general presentation will appeal to all customers. Although the method has been criticized for its inflexibility and nonmarketing orientation, it still retains some value:

> Logically, inexperienced salespeople who are lacking in selling instinct and confidence will benefit from the professionalism, anticipation of questions and objections, and other fail-safe mechanisms that are often inherent in a company-prepared memorized, audiovisual, or flip chart presentation. Consequently, this method should be considered when qualified new salespeople are scarce and when brevity of training is essential.[6]

The ***need-satisfaction approach*** is a higher-level method based on the principle that each customer has different characteristics and wants, and therefore the sales presentation should be adapted to each individual consumer. With need satisfaction, the salesperson first asks questions of the consumer, such as: What type of product are you looking for? Have you ever purchased this product before? What price range are you considering? Then the sales presentation can be more responsive to the particular customer. Under this method a new shopper would be treated quite differently from an experienced shopper. The need-satisfaction approach is the most popular and customer-oriented technique; however, it requires more training and better-skilled sales personnel.[7] Figure 13-5 shows the two techniques.

The canned sales presentation works best with inexpensive, routine items that are heavily advertised and usually presold. The need-satisfaction approach works best with more expensive, more complex items that have moderate advertising and require substantial additional information for consumers.

Outlining Sales Tasks

The tasks to be performed by the personal sales force need to be outlined. The ***selling process*** involves prospecting for customer leads, approaching customers, determining customer wants, giving a sales presentation, answering questions, closing the sale, and following up. Figure 13-6 shows examples for each of these stages.

Outside selling requires a procedure for generating a list of customer leads. This procedure is known as ***prospecting.*** Blind prospecting relies on telephone directories and other general listings of potential customers. Lead prospecting depends on past customers and others for referrals. Inside selling usually does not involve prospecting, because

The *canned sales presentation* is a memorized, nonadaptive technique used for all customers.

The *need-satisfaction approach* adapts the sales presentation to suit the needs and wants of individual consumers.

The *selling process* moves from prospecting for leads to following up.

Prospecting involves creating customer leads.

Figure 13-5
Selling Techniques

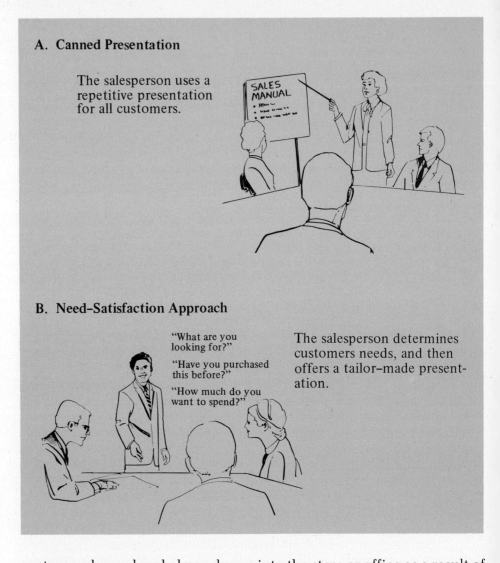

A. **Canned Presentation**

The salesperson uses a repetitive presentation for all customers.

B. **Need–Satisfaction Approach**

"What are you looking for?"

"Have you purchased this before?"

"How much do you want to spend?"

The salesperson determines customers needs, and then offers a tailor–made presentation.

customers have already been drawn into the store or office as a result of advertisements or past purchase experience.

The preapproach and greeting are each part of approaching customers.

Approaching customers is a two-stage procedure: preapproach and greeting. During the preapproach, the salesperson tries to obtain information about the customer's characteristics from census and other secondary data, as well as from referrals. Inside retail salespeople are frequently unable to use a preapproach; and therefore they know nothing about a consumer until he or she enters the store. In the greeting the salesperson begins a conversation with the customer. The intention is to put the customer at ease and build a rapport.

The next step is to determine customer wants by asking a variety of questions regarding past experience, price, product or service features, intended uses, and the kinds of information still needed.

The *sales presentation* converts an uncertain consumer.

The *sales presentation* includes a description of the product or service, its benefits, available options and models, price, associated services such as delivery and warranty, and a demonstration (if neces-

Stages	Examples

Stages

Examples

1. Prospecting
   a. Blind
   b. Lead

a. Send a direct mail piece to all people residing in an area. Wait for replies.
b. Ask each customer within the last six months for the names of two friends who would be interested in the product or service.

2. Approach
   a. Preapproach
   b. Greeting

a. Determine customer demographics from available census data.
b. "Good morning. I'm Bill Case from the American Camera House, the area's largest seller of camera equipment. Your next-door neighbor, Jack Dean, just bought a camera from us. Jack said you were over at his house last night and remarked that you were interested in a similar camera. May we talk?"

3. Customer Wants

"Do you have a specific camera in mind?" "For what purpose is it to be used?" "What price range are you considering?" "Have you ever bought a camera of this type before?" "What would you like to know about the different brands?"

4. Sales Presentation

"This camera comes in three models, for beginners, intermediates, and experts. The beginner model is the least complex and costs $150. The others are more complex and take better pictures. Their prices are $200 and $400. Each camera has a one-year limited warranty."

5. Answering Questions
   a. Questions
   b. Objections

a. "The beginner model has fewer parts and a simple focusing mechanism. These are the basic differences."
b. "I understand that you feel $400 is expensive for this type of camera, but it is comparable to competitors' prices and takes excellent pictures."

6. Close

"I agree with your choice. The expert camera is best suited to your ability and interests. Would you like to pay cash or charge it?"

7. Follow Up
   a. Satisfaction
   b. Referrals
   c. Repurchase

a. "Hi. This is Bill from the American Camera House. How are you enjoying the camera you bought two weeks ago?"
b. "We are running a workshop for camera buffs. Would you like to come and bring two or three of your friends?"
c. "Hi. This is Bill from American Camera. We just got in an upgraded model of the camera you bought last year. If you are interested, we will give you a $140 trade-in on your present camera."

Figure 13-6
The Selling Process

sary). As explained earlier, the presentation may involve a canned sales or need-satisfaction method. The purpose of the sales presentation is to convert an undecided consumer into a purchaser.

After the presentation the salesperson usually must answer questions from the consumer. These questions are of two kinds: the first require further information, and the second raise objections that must be settled before a sale is made.

The *closing* clinches the sale.

Once the questions have been answered, the salesperson is ready for the major goal: ***closing the sale.*** This involves getting the customer to agree to a purchase. The salesperson must be sure that no major questions remain before attempting to close a sale. In addition, the salesperson should not argue with the consumer.

Finally, for major purchases, salespeople should follow up after the sale to ensure that the customer is satisfied. This accomplishes three objectives: the customer gains short-run satisfaction, referrals are stimulated, and, in the long run, repurchases are more likely.

Sales personnel may be required to perform a variety of nonselling tasks.

Besides the tasks accomplished through the selling process, the firm must clearly outline the nonselling tasks it wants the sales force to perform. Among the nonselling tasks that may be required are setting up displays, writing up information sheets, pricing merchandise, checking competitors' strategies, conducting such marketing research as consumer surveys, and training new employees.

Applying the Plan

The application of the plan is accomplished through the firm's sales management structure. ***Sales management*** is the planning, analysis, and control of the personal sales function. It covers employee selection, training, territory allocation, compensation, and supervision.[8]

In the selection of sales personnel, a number of factors need to be considered. First, contrary to earlier beliefs, it is now generally accepted that good salespeople are not necessarily born, they are carefully selected and trained. Personality is only one attribute to be considered when choosing salespeople.

Second, the traits of salespeople must be matched with those of customers. As noted earlier in the chapter, the buyer-seller dyad is the interaction between the customer and the salesperson. The two relate better when their characteristics are similar. A recent study showed that buyer-seller similarities were most important for high financial purchases and for racial backgrounds.[9]

Third, the traits of salespeople must be matched to the requirements of the product or service being sold. For example, an automobile salesperson would have different traits from a computer salesperson. The latter would need much more formal education, technical training, and utilize a longer, more informational sales process.[10]

Sales personnel selection includes determining attributes for new salespeople, contacting sources of employees, and interviewing candidates.

After these factors are studied, the firm would develop a formal selection procedure. It would outline the personal attributes sought, sources of employees (such as colleges and employment agencies), and methods for selection (such as interviews, application forms, and testing). This procedure would be based on the firm's overall sales program and needs.

The training of sales personnel may take one or a combination of forms. A formal program utilizes a trainer, classroom setting, lectures, and printed materials. This program may also include role playing, in which trainees act out parts to improve skills, and case analysis. Field trips take trainees out on actual calls so they can observe skilled salespeople in action. On-the-job training places trainees in their own selling situations under the close supervision of the trainer or senior salesperson.

Training usually covers a wide range of material. It should teach necessary selling skills and also include information about the company and its offerings, the industry, and employee responsibilities. In addition to initial training, many companies use continuous training or retraining of sales personnel in order to teach new techniques, explain new products, or improve performance. This is particularly important for highly technical products and services.

Next, territory size and salesperson allocation are determined. A territory consists of the geographic area, customers, and/or product lines assigned to a salesperson. When territories are assigned on the basis of customer type (such as large or small) or product type (such as computers or photocopiers), two or more salespeople may cover the same geographic area. Territory size depends on the geographic concentration of customers, order size, travel time and expenses, the time needed for each sales call, the number of yearly visits for each account, and the amount of hours per year each salesperson has available for selling tasks. The allocation of a salesperson to a specific territory depends on his or her ability, the buyer-seller dyad, the mix of selling and nonselling functions (for example, one salesperson may do a lot of training of new employees), and seniority.

Proper territory size and allocation provide adequate coverage of customers, minimize territory overlap and salesperson conflict, recognize natural geographic boundaries, minimize travel expenses, encourage solicitation of new accounts, provide a large enough sales potential for a good salesperson to be well rewarded, and offer equity among salespeople in terms of territorial sales potential and workload.

Sales compensation can take one of three general formats: straight salary, straight commission, or a combination of salary and commission. Under the **straight-salary plan,** the salesperson is paid a flat fee per week, month, or year. Earnings are not tied to sales. The advantages of the plan are that both selling and nonselling tasks are specified and controlled, there is security for salespeople, and expenses are known in advance. The disadvantages of the plan are low sales force incentive to increase sales, expenses not tied to productivity, and continued costs even if there are low sales. Order takers are usually paid straight salaries.

With a **straight-commission plan,** a salesperson's earnings are directly related to sales or profits. The commission rate is often keyed to a quota, which is a performance standard for the salesperson. A quota can be based on total sales, total profit, customers serviced, products sold, or some other criterion. The advantages of this plan are motivated salespeople, no fixed costs, and expenses tied to productivity. The disadvan-

Sales training must cover selling skills and company characteristics and requirements.

A territory contains the area, customers, and/or products assigned to a salesperson; salesperson allocation depends on ability, the buyer-seller dyad, functions, and seniority.

Sales compensation may be *straight salary,* *straight commission,* or a *combination* of the two.

tages of the plan are lack of control over nonselling tasks performed, instability of a company's dollar expenses and employee earnings, and the risk to employees. Real estate, insurance, and direct-to-home order getters are often paid on a straight commission basis. For example, a real-estate salesperson might receive a 3 per cent commission of $3,000 for selling a $100,000 house.

To combine the advantages of salary and commissions plans, many companies use *combination compensation plans.* These plans balance control, flexibility, and employee incentives. Sometimes bonuses are stipulated for outstanding individual or company performance. All types of order getters work on a combination basis. For example, Robert Taaffe, the Xerox salesperson noted in Figure 13-3, is compensated by one-third salary and two-thirds commission.

The combination plan is used by 54 per cent of the firms analyzed in *Dartnell's 21st Biennial Survey of Sales Personnel.* Straight salary is utilized by 26 per cent of the firms. Straight-commission plans are used by 20 per cent. On average, sales personnel paid via a combination plan earn the most and those on a straight-salary plan the least.

Sales force supervision involves motivation, performance measurement, nonselling tasks, and modifying poor behavior.

Supervision incorporates four aspects of sales management: sales force motivation, measurement of performance, completion of nonselling tasks, and initiating behavior changes. First, sales personnel must be motivated to fulfill their jobs. A recent study showed that motivation is related to task clarity (what must be done), the salesperson's need for achievement, the incentive provided for each task (such as compensation), and good management (such as all sales personnel treated equitably and outstanding performance recognized).[11]

Second, performance must be measured.[12] To do this, achievements must be gauged against objectives such as total sales and calls per day. This analysis should take into account territory size, travel time, experience, and other factors. Third, the sales manager must make sure that all nonselling tasks are completed, even if sales personnel are not rewarded for them. Fourth, poor behavior should be modified. For example, salespeople go through career cycles similar to those of products[13]—that is, at the maturity and decline stages, enthusiasm and productivity fall. The manager should rekindle enthusiasm through increased compensation, retraining, new territories, added responsibilities, or promotion.

Scope and Importance of Sales Promotion

Sales promotion consists of activities that stimulate customer purchases and dealer effectiveness.

As defined in Chapter 11, sales promotion involves the marketing activities, other than advertising, publicity, or personal selling, that stimulate consumer purchases and dealer effectiveness. Types of sales promotion include samples, coupons, special sales, contests, trading stamps, trade shows, and many additional activities. In 1981 sales promotion expenditures were about $50 billion.

The level of sales promotion activities can be shown through the following:

- More than 100 million coupons are distributed annually. Although 80 per cent of American households use coupons, redemption rates are relatively low (ranging from 2.1 per cent for Sunday supplements to 10.5 per cent for direct mail).[14]
- Each year, more than $500 million worth of trading stamps are given out. About 20 per cent of U.S. supermarkets now handle trading stamps, down from a peak of 65 per cent.[15] Consumers have become more price conscious and less interested in stamps.
- Trade show attendance exceeds 30 million people per year; there are more than 8,000 shows containing ten exhibits or more. The average attendee spends 7.5 hours at a show and visits 19 exhibits.[16]
- In 1981, there were about 1,000 nationally advertised sweepstakes. They awarded well over $150 million in prizes.[17]
- Annually, Macy's sponsors a Thanksgiving Day parade, which attracts heavy media coverage throughout the U.S. and signals the start of the Christmas selling season. It generates a great deal of consumer and channel member enthusiasm. Figure 13-7 shows a scene from a recent Macy's parade.

Several factors have contributed to the growth of sales promotion. The various forms of promotions are now more acceptable to firms, channel members, and consumers. Executives are better qualified to di-

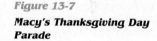

Sales promotion is growing rapidly, as it becomes more acceptable.

Figure 13-7

Macy's Thanksgiving Day Parade

Reprinted by permission.

rect sales promotion. Quick returns are possible. As competition increases, promotions increase. During economic recessions consumers look for promotions, and channel members put more pressure on manufacturers for promotions.[18] Sales promotions are also adaptive, and can be used to increase purchases without changing prices.

Despite the factors mentioned here, many companies treat sales promotion haphazardly and do not appreciate its usefulness. As a leading analyst of sales promotion stated:

> It has been virtually ignored. . . . Objectives for sales promotion programs are rarely established and, when they are established, are not likely to be in quantitative terms. This shortcoming applies to the plan as a whole and to individual programs. Promotions may be scheduled simply because "there was one last year," or because competitors have them, or because of demands from the sales force for something to be done in their region.[19]

Characteristics of Sales Promotion

Sales promotion lures customers, maintains loyalty, provides value, increases impulse purchases, creates excitement, is often keyed to patronage, and appeals to channel members.

Sales promotion has a number of advantages for the firm. It helps attract customer traffic and maintain brand or store loyalty. For example, new-product samples or trial offers draw customers. A manufacturer can retain brand loyalty through gifts to regular customers or coupons for its brands. A retailer can retain store loyalty by giving store trading stamps or store coupons. Quick results can be achieved.

Some forms of sales promotion provide value to the consumer and are retained by them. They provide a reminder function. These include calendars, matchbooks, T-shirts, pens, and posters with the firm's name.

Impulse purchases can be increased through in-store displays. For example, an attractive display for batteries in a supermarket can significantly increase sales. In addition, a good display can lead to a larger-volume purchase than originally intended by the consumer.

Excitement is created through certain short-run promotions involving gifts, contests, or sweepstakes. In particular, high-value items or high payoffs encourage consumers to participate. Contests offer the further benefit of customer involvement (through the completion of a puzzle or some other skill-oriented activity).

Many types of sales promotion are keyed to customer patronage. Some promotions, such as coupons, trading stamps, and referral gifts, are directly related to sales. In these cases the promotions are a fixed percentage of sales and their costs are not incurred until sales are completed.

Sales promotion may hurt image, cause consumers to wait for special offers, and shift the focus from the product.

Finally, channel members cooperate better with manufacturers when sales-promotion support is provided in the form of displays, manufacturers' coupons, manufacturers' rebates, joint training of the retail sales force, and trade allowances.

There are also several limitations to sales promotion. The image of the firm may be lessened if it continuously runs special deals. Consumers may view the discounts as representing a decline in product or

Figure 13-8
Aggressive Sales Promotion

"The earliest known sales promotion tool . . . "

Reprinted by permission of *Marketing News,* published by the American Marketing Association.

service quality and believe the firm could not sell its offerings without them.

When coupons, rebates, or other special deals are used frequently, consumers may not make purchases if the items are sold at regular prices. Instead, they will stock up each time there is a special offer. In addition, consumers may interpret the regular price as a price hike for items that are heavily promoted.

Sometimes sales promotions shift the focus away from the product or service onto secondary factors. Consumers may be attracted by calendars, coupons, or sweepstakes instead of by the product or service's quality, functions, and durability. In the short run this generates consumer enthusiasm. In the long run this may have adverse effects on a brand's image and on sales, because a product-related differential advantage has not been developed. See Figure 13-8.

It must be remembered that sales promotion is a supplement to the other forms of promotion. It enhances, but does not replace, advertising, personal selling, and publicity.

Developing a Sales Promotion Plan

The development of a sales promotion plan consists of the steps shown in Figure 13-9 and explained in the following subsections.

Setting Objectives

Sales promotion objectives are almost always demand-oriented. These objectives may be related to channel members or consumers.

Objectives pertaining to channel members include obtaining distri-

Figure 13-9
***Developing a Sales
Promotion Plan***

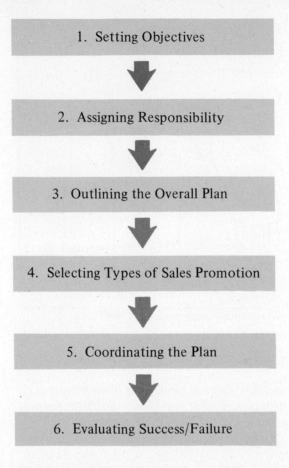

bution, receiving adequate store shelf space, increasing dealer enthusiasm, increasing sales, and cooperating in sales-promotion expenditures.

Objectives pertaining to customers include increasing brand awareness, increasing trial of a product or service, increasing average purchases, stimulating repurchases, obtaining impulse sales, emphasizing
novelty, and supplementing other promotional tools.

Assigning Responsibility

The responsibility for sales promotion is usually shared by advertising
and sales managers. Each directs the promotions regarding his or her
area. For example, the advertising manager would be involved with
coupons, contests, trading stamps, matchbooks, calendars, and other
mass-promotion tools. The sales manager would be involved with trade
shows, special sales, trade allowances, cooperative promotions, special
events, demonstrations, and other efforts requiring individualized attention directed at channel members or final consumers.

Outlining the Overall Plan

The overall sales promotion plan should be outlined and include a
budget, an orientation or theme, conditions, media, duration or timing,
and cooperative efforts.

When establishing the sales-promotion budget, it is important to include all costs. For example, the average face value of a coupon was 20 cents in 1981. In addition, manufacturers had to pay retailers a 7 to 10 cent handling charge for each coupon they redeemed, and they had to cover printing, mailing, advertising, and handling costs.

Sales promotion orientation refers to its focus: channel members or final consumers. Promotions directed at channel members should increase product knowledge, provide sales support, offer rewards for sales, and aim to increase cooperation and productivity. Promotions directed at final consumers should stimulate impulse and larger-volume sales, sustain brand-name recognition, and gain audience participation. The theme of sales promotion refers to its underlying message, such as a special sale, store opening, new-product introduction, holiday celebration, or new-customer recruitment.

Sales promotion conditions are the requirements channel members or final customers must meet to be eligible for a sales promotion. These may include minimum purchases, performance provisions, and minimum age. For example, a channel member may have to stock merchandise and set up advertising displays in order to receive a display case from a manufacturer. A final consumer may have to send in proof of purchase in order to receive a refund or gift. In most situations, strict time limits are set that define the closing dates for participation in a sales promotion.

The media are the vehicles through which sales promotions reach channel members or final consumers. Media include direct mail, newspapers, store displays, television, personal selling, and group meetings.

The duration of a sales promotion may be short or long. Supermarket and fast-food coupons usually have quick closing dates. Trading stamps normally have no closing dates. The duration must be keyed to objectives. Coupons are used to increase store traffic, and trading stamps are used to maintain loyalty. As noted earlier, when sales promotions are lengthy or are offered frequently, consumers may come to expect them as a basic part of a purchase. Some promotions are seasonal, and for these timing is crucial. The promotions must be tied to the introduction of seasonal activities such as school openings or model or style changes.

Finally, the firm should determine the value of shared sales promotions. With cooperative efforts, each channel member pays part of the promotion cost and receives benefits. In retailing, cooperative sales promotions are frequently sponsored by merchants via shopping-center associations. For example, a group of merchants may share the costs of running a children's petting zoo located in a regional shopping center.

Selecting Types of Sales Promotion

There is a wide range of sales promotion tools available to a firm. The characteristics of channel-member sales promotion tools are shown in Table 13-3. The characteristics of final-consumer sales promotion tools are displayed in Table 13-4. Examples for each tool are provided in these figures.

The selection of sales promotions should be based on company

Table 13-3   **Types of Sales Promotions Directed at Channel Members**

Type	Characteristics	Illustration
Trade shows or meetings	One or a group of manufacturers invites channel members to attend sessions where products are displayed and explained.	The annual National Home Center Show attracts more than 1,200 exhibitors and thousands of attendees.
Training	The manufacturer provides training for channel members' personnel.	Bell & Howell/Mamiya trained several thousand retail salespeople about its cameras.
Trade allowances or special offers	Channel members are given discounts or rebates for performing specified functions or purchasing during certain time periods.	A local retailer receives a discount for setting up a special display for GE lightbulbs.
Point-of-purchase displays	The manufacturer or wholesaler gives the retailer a fully equipped display for its products and sets it up.	Coca-Cola provides refrigerators with its name on them to retailers carrying minimum quantities of Coca-Cola products.
Push money	Channel members or their salespeople are given bonuses for pushing the brand of a particular manufacturer. Retailers may not like this practice if salespeople shift their loyalty to the manufacturer.	A salesperson in a television store is paid an extra $50 for every console of a particular brand that is sold.
Sales contests	Prizes or bonuses are distributed if certain performance levels are met.	A retailer receives an extra $1,000 for selling 1,000 radios in a month.
Free merchandise	Discounts or allowances are provided in the form of merchandise.	A retailer gets one case of soda free for every ten cases purchased.
Demonstration models	A free item is given to the wholesaler or retailer for demonstration purposes.	A vacuum-cleaner manufacturer offers retailers a floor demonstrator.
Gifts	Channel members are given gifts for carrying items or performing functions.	During one two-month period, Sherwood Medical Industries offered wholesalers purchasing a $6,000 syringe package a choice of a color television, microwave oven, or freezer filled with steaks.
Cooperative promotions	Two or more channel members share the costs of a promotion.	A manufacturer and retailer each pay part of the costs for pens with the retailer's name embossed.

image, objectives, costs, participation requirements, and channel or customer enthusiasm.[20]

Coordinating the Plan

In coordinating the plan, advertising and sales promotion should be integrated.

It is essential that sales promotion activities be well coordinated with other elements of the promotion mix. In particular, advertising and sales promotion plans should be integrated. The sales force should be notified of all promotions well in advance and trained to implement them. For special events, such as the appearance of a major celebrity, publicity should be obtained. Sales promotions should also be consistent with channel-member activities.

Table 13-4   **Types of Sales Promotions Directed at Final Consumers**

Type	Characteristics	Illustration
Coupons	Manufacturers or retailers advertise special discounts for customers who redeem coupons.	P&G mails consumers a 25-cents-off coupon for Sure deodorant, which could be redeemed at any supermarket.
Refund or rebate	A consumer submits proof-of-purchase (usually to the manufacturer) and receives an extra discount.	First Alert home fire alarms provides $5 rebates to consumers submitting proof of purchase.
Samples	Free merchandise or services are given to consumers, generally for new items.	When Sunlight dishwashing liquid was introduced, free samples were mailed to consumers.
Trading stamps	Consumers are given free stamps based on dollar purchases. Stamps are accumulated and exchanged for gifts or money.	Some A&P supermarkets distribute S&H Trading Stamps.
Contests or sweepstakes	Consumers compete for prizes by answering questions (contests) or fill out forms for random drawings of prizes (sweepstakes).	Publishers Clearinghouse sponsors annual sweepstakes and awards automobiles, houses, and other prizes.
Bonus or multipacks	Consumers receive discounts for purchasing in quantity.	Some stores run one-cent sales, whereby the consumer buys one item and gets a second one for a penny.
Shows or exhibits	Many manufacturers cosponsor exhibitions for consumers.	The Auto Show is annually scheduled for the public in New York.
Point-of-purchase displays	In-store displays remind customers and generate impulse purchases.	Chewing gum sales in supermarkets are high because displays are placed at checkout counters.
Special events	Manufacturers or retailers sponsor celebrity appearances, fashion shows, and other activities.	Virtually every major league baseball team has an annual "Old Timers' Day," which attracts large crowds.
Gifts	Consumers are given gifts for making a purchase or opening a new account.	Hertz awards gifts to consumers, based on the number of car rentals.
Referral gifts	Existing customers are given gifts for referring their friends to the company.	Tupperware awards gifts to the woman hosting a Tupperware party in her home.
Demonstrations	Products or services are shown in action.	The Evelyn Woods' reading course technique is demonstrated in a complimentary lesson.

Evaluating Success or Failure

The success or failure of many types of sales promotions is relatively straightforward to measure because promotions are so closely linked to performance or sales. By analyzing before-and-after data, the usefulness of promotions should be apparent.

The success or failure of sales promotions is often simple to measure.

For example, companies are able to verify changes in sales due to their dealer-training programs. Firms using coupons examine sales and compare redemption rates with industry averages. Attitudinal surveys of channel members and final consumers indicate satisfaction with various kinds of promotions, suggestions for improvements, and the effect of promotions on image.

Some promotions, such as calendars, pens, and special events, are more difficult to evaluate because objectives are less definitive.

Summary

More than six million people are employed in personal selling occupations. This number understates the value of personal selling, because every contact between a company representative and a customer involves some amount of personal selling. Selling costs as a percentage of sales fall between 3 and 3.4 per cent. The average cost of one sales call is over $100.

Personal selling sets up a buyer-seller dyad (the two-way flow of communication between both parties), offers flexibility and adaptability, results in little waste in terms of audience, closes sales, and provides immediate feedback. However, personal selling can handle only a limited number of customers at a time, has high costs per customer, is ineffective for creating consumer awareness, and has a poor image for some consumers.

A personal selling plan involves (1) setting objectives, (2) assigning responsibility, (3) establishing a budget, (4) determining the type(s) of sales positions, (5) selecting a sales technique, (6) outlining sales tasks, and (7) applying the plan.

Sales promotion encompasses all forms of promotion not defined as advertising, publicity, and personal selling. Sales promotion has annual expenditures of about $50 billion. The growth of sales promotion is the result of greater firm and consumer acceptance, better management, quick responses, competition, economic conditions, and demands by channel members.

Sales promotion helps attract customer traffic and loyalty, provides value to consumers and is sometimes retained by them, increases impulse purchases, creates excitement, is keyed to customer patronage, and improves channel-member cooperation. On the other hand, sales promotion may hurt the firm's image, encourage consumers to wait for promotions before making purchases, and shift the focus away from product or service attributes. Sales promotion cannot replace other forms of promotion.

A sales promotion plan includes (1) setting objectives, (2) assigning responsibility, (3) outlining the overall plan, (4) selecting types of sales promotion, (5) coordinating the plan, and (6) evaluating success or failure. Types of sales promotion include trade shows, training, allowances, free merchandise, and cooperative promotions for channel members and coupons, refunds, samples, stamps, and gifts for final consumers.

KEY TERMS

After reading this chapter, you should understand these key terms:

Buyer-seller dyad	**Order getter**
Sales-expense budget	**Missionary salesperson**
Order taker	**Sales engineer**

Service salesperson
Canned sales presentation
Need-satisfaction approach
Selling process
Prospecting
Approaching customers
Sales presentation

Closing the sale
Sales management
Straight-salary plan
Straight-commission plan
Combination compensation plan
Sales promotion orientation
Sales promotion conditions

QUESTIONS FOR DISCUSSION

1. The Bureau of Labor Statistics lists six million people in sales positions. Why does this figure understate the importance of personal selling?
2. Under what circumstances should a firm emphasize personal selling?
3. How do personal selling objectives compare with those for advertising?
4. Distinguish among and give an example of an order taker, support salesperson, and order getter.
5. In what situations is a canned sales presentation acceptable? When is it not acceptable?
6. Develop a lead-prospecting plan for a real estate broker.
7. How would you evaluate the sales presentations of a company's personnel? What criteria would you use?
8. What characteristics are desirable in a salesperson? Are they the same for all categories of sales personnel?
9. Develop a one-month advertising and sales promotion plan for Sears' television department.
10. How do sales promotion objectives differ from personal selling objectives?
11. What are meant by the conditions of sales promotion? Why do so many sweepstakes not require proof of purchase?
12. A local restaurant places two-for-one dinner coupons in the Sunday newspaper each week. What are the potential benefits and risks associated with this strategy?
13. Wrigley is introducing a new chewing gum. Recommend several channel-member and final-consumer promotions.
14. How would you measure the effectiveness of participating in a trade show aimed at electronics retailers?

NOTES

1. Michael Waldholz, "How a 'Detail Man' Promotes New Drugs to Tennessee Doctors," *Wall Street Journal* (November 8, 1982), pp. 1, 25.
2. "Survey of Selling Costs," *Sales & Marketing Management;* and *Compensation of Salesmen: Dartnell's 21st Biennial Survey* (Chicago: Dartnell Institute of Financial Research, Dartnell Corporation, 1982).
3. Lad Kuzela, "Slicing Costs with Smarter Selling," *Industry Week* (February 22, 1982). See also Lauren R. Januz, "Use Telemarketing System to Generate, Qualify Sales Leads," *Marketing News* (April 30, 1982), p. 4.
4. Gail Bronson, "Avon Lady Will Be Getting New Look in Drive for More Fashionable Image," *Wall Street Journal* (January 1, 1981), p. 12.
5. *Compensation of Salesmen: Dartnell's 21st Biennial Survey.*
6. Marvin A. Jolson, "The Underestimated Potential of the Canned Sales Presentation," *Journal of Marketing*, Vol. 39 (January 1975), p. 78.

7. See Kenneth A. Meyers, "The Selling Professional of the 1980s," *Business*, Vol. 32 (October–December 1982), pp. 44–46.

8. See Alan J. Dubinsky and Thomas E. Barry, "A Survey of Sales Management Practices," *Industrial Marketing Management*, Vol. 11 (April 1982), pp. 133–141.

9. Ishmael P. Akaah, "Dyadic Similarity and Its Influence on Customer Preferences: An Experimental Study," in Richard P. Bagozzi et al. (Editors), *Marketing in the '80s* (Chicago: American Marketing Association, 1980), pp. 114–117.

10. For a look at a modern salesperson, see Hugh D. Menzies, "The New Life of a Salesman," *Fortune* (August 11, 1980), pp. 172–180.

11. Stephen X. Doyle and Benson P. Shapiro, "What Counts Most in Motivating Your Sales Force," *Harvard Business Review*, Vol. 58 (May–June 1980), pp. 133–140.

12. See Douglas N. Behrman and William D. Perreault, Jr., "Measuring the Performance of Industrial Salespersons," *Journal of Business Research*, Vol. 10 (September 1982), pp. 355–370.

13. Marvin A. Jolson, "The Salesman's Career Cycle," *Journal of Marketing*, Vol. 38 (July 1974), pp. 39–46.

14. "Analyzing Promotions," *Nielsen Researcher* (Number 4, 1982), p. 17.

15. Daniel Kahn, "Trading Stamps Make LI Comeback," *Newsday* (May 12, 1981), p. 35; and Jeffrey H. Birnbaum, "Industry Blues Fail to Deter S&H Stamps," *Wall Street Journal* (August 5, 1980), p. 29.

16. "Trade Show Industry Still Growing, But at Slower Rate," *Marketing News* (April 30, 1982), p. 1; and Richard K. Swandby and Jonathan (Skip) Cox, "How Trade Shows Served the '70s," *Industrial Marketing* (April 1980), pp. 72–78.

17. Franklynn Peterson and Judi Kesselman-Turkel, "Catching Customers with Sweepstakes," *Fortune* (February 8, 1982), p. 84.

18. Roger A. Strang, "Sales Promotion—Fast Growth, Faulty Management," *Harvard Business Review*, Vol. 54 (July–August 1976), pp. 117–119.

19. Ibid., p. 119.

20. For an excellent discussion of sales promotion tools, see William A. Robinson, "What Are Promos' Weak, Strong Points?" *Advertising Age* (April 7, 1980), pp. 53–54.

CASES   1   INSURANCE SALES: TURNING TO COMPUTERS TO IMPROVE EFFICIENCY*

In the U.S., there are 65,000 independent insurance agencies who sell policies for large insurance companies, such as Fireman's Fund Insurance and Aetna Life & Casualty. The agencies average less than $1 million per year in sales and they may represent a dozen or more insurance companies.

Paper flow and other costs have risen drastically for these agencies during the past several years. As a result, insurance companies that sell directly to consumers without independent agencies, such as State Farm Insurance and Allstate Insurance, have been able to underprice the agencies. Since 1969, the market share of independent insurance agencies has fallen from 80 per cent to just over 40 per cent. Over the next decade, 20,000 agencies are expected to merge, sell out, or go out of business.

Until recently, the agencies and their insurance companies did little to reduce the paper flow between the two. It was estimated that 25 per cent of insurance premiums, about $40 billion annually, was needed to cover paper-flow costs alone. Most agencies relied on typewriters and the postal service.

*The data in this case are drawn from "Insurance Agents Go Electronic," *Business Week* (November 19, 1979), pp. 142–150; and Daniel Hertzberg, "Insurance Relying More on Automation," *Wall Street Journal* (November 9, 1982), pp. 37, 42.

This led to delays of up to four months in the delivery of policies, in addition to costs. Policies frequently went back and forth between agents and their companies six times. With each transfer, coding and rating errors occurred. Up to one sixth of transactions were rejected because of errors; these cost an average of $5 to $7 to correct.

Now, with the assistance of their insurance companies, the agencies are automating their sales procedures. Computers reduce transactions, costs, and errors. Information is fed into a computer once, where it is permanently stored. Policies can be delivered in a few minutes or by the next day. Among them, Aetna, Fireman's Fund, and Travelers are committed to spending $220 million to automate their independent agencies.

Agents are pleased with the new systems. As one commented: "There's no postage, no necessity for follow-up, there's more accuracy, and you have the policy by the next day." Also, a system that ties into all insurance companies will enable agents to increase their business. For the agents, this is necessary because commissions have fallen 25 per cent since the mid-1970s. On the other hand, the insurance companies desire systems that are unique (where an agent may only hook up to one firm).

QUESTIONS

1. Develop a program for training veteran salespeople who are reluctant to learn a new method of selling.
2. Describe the procedure you would use for selling a $100,000 life-insurance policy. In which phases would you use a computer? In which phases would you not use a computer?
3. List several types of information, useful to an insurance salesperson, that would be immediately available through a computer.
4. What criteria would you use in hiring new insurance sales personnel?

AMERICAN AIRLINES: USING SALES PROMOTION TO INCREASE PASSENGER LOYALTY† 2

Many travelers have limited loyalty toward any individual airline company. Instead, they readily switch companies on the basis of flight availability and price. This situation is of great concern to the airline industry, particularly since it often leads to price wars that hurt all the firms.

In order to increase customer loyalty, American Airlines (as well as its major competitors) has frequently turned to sales promotions that are linked to continued patronage of the firm. An example of this is the frequent traveler program (American's version is called AAdvantage) which gives passengers rewards for repeated travel on a single airline.

The frequent traveler market is extremely important to the airline industry. While there are only one million frequent fliers, those who fly 12,000 or more miles per year account for 65 per cent of domestic revenue.

AAdvantage, started in May 1981, has attracted 800,000 participants. 75,000 of these fly 30,000 miles or more per year. The plan works as follows:

†The data in this case are drawn from Stratford P. Sherman, "The Airlines? Flying Jackpots," *Fortune* (November 29, 1982), pp. 103–108.

1. A passenger flies 12,000 to 75,000 miles on American Airlines during any 12-month period.
2. Discounts are given for Hertz rental cars, British Airways Flights, Holland American Cruises, and Hyatt hotel rooms.
3. Free or reduced-price tickets for American Airlines flights are provided. The top prize is awarded to any passenger flying 75,000 miles in twelve months: two first-class round-trip tickets to almost anywhere.

Although the frequent flyer program seems to be working so far, American Airlines has three concerns. First, price wars in the airline industry have continued. For example, in early 1983, flights between most large U.S. cities were priced at $99 or less each way. Second, American remembers well that its last significant sales promotion ultimately cost the firm $50 million in lost revenue. In 1979, it matched United's sales promotion featuring a half-price coupon for a future flight for every ticket purchased (even inexpensive, short-flight tickets). Third, frequent flyers sometimes use their free or reduced-price tickets on popular flights, causing American to give up full-fare sales.

QUESTIONS

1. Evaluate the frequent-traveler sales promotion.
2. Comment on American's concerns.
3. How would you determine the success or failure of AAdvantage?
4. What other techniques could American use to attract more business? Consider both channel- and consumer-oriented sales promotions.

Part Six

Price Planning

Introduction to Part Six

Part Six covers the fourth and final major element of marketing, pricing. Chapter 14 presents an overview of price planning, the systematic decision making pertaining to all aspects of pricing by the organization. The role of pricing in allocating goods and services among purchasers, its importance in transactions, and its interrelation with other marketing variables are described. The differences between price and nonprice competition are explained. Each of the factors affecting price decisions are studied: consumers, government, channel members, competitors, and costs. Included are discussions of consumer sensitivity to price, legal restrictions, channel requirements, types of competitive environments, and the impact of costs on prices.

Chapter 15 details how a pricing strategy is developed. It distinguishes among sales, profit, and status quo objectives. The use of a broad price policy is studied. The three basic types of pricing strategy are outlined: cost, demand, and competition. Pricing techniques are explained and illustrated. The importance of an integrated price strategy is stressed. A number of pricing tactics, such as customary and odd pricing, are examined. The various methods for adjusting prices are noted.

An Overview of Price Planning

14

Chapter Preview

Chapter Objectives

1 To define price and price-planning terms

2 To show the importance of price and its relationship to other marketing variables

3 To differentiate between price and nonprice competition

4 To examine the factors affecting pricing decisions: consumers, government, channel members, competition, and costs

For decades, Timex stressed a utilitarian image and low prices for its watches. It featured John Cameron Swayse in commercials showing the watches' durability, with the slogan "takes a licking and keeps on ticking." The company's traditional price range was $15 to $25.

But, beginning in 1972, Timex's sales stagnated. First, despite competitors' popularity with digital watches and then quartz analog watches, Timex stayed with mechanical watches. During the early 1970s, 90 per cent of Timex watches were mechanical; the number was still 60 per cent by the end of 1981. Second, Texas Instruments introduced a variety of low-priced watches in 1976. The watches were originally priced at $20, which soon dropped to $10 to $11. Third, Timex paid inadequate attention to watch fashion and was unable to gain distribution of its products through trendier jewelry stores.

To improve its position, Timex then hired an aggressive group of executives and increased expenditures for research, design, and advertising. A new approach has emerged, which is centered on several strategy revisions. By 1986, mechanical watches are planned to account for only 30 per cent of sales, with digital and quartz watches contributing 70 per cent. Styling and design have greater importance, and are being used to expand distribution at jewelry stores. Fancier models of watches are priced at $50 and up, far above customary Timex prices. Advertising outlays doubled between 1980 and 1982, from $11.9 million to more than $20 million, and are expected to rise further. Figure 14-1 shows one of Timex's newer quartz watches.

The Timex goal is to "stand for more than affordable, plain-Jane watches." Said its U.S. marketing director, "Timex is never going to mean fine jewelry, but it can mean fashionability." However, as one rival commented, "Timex is still associated with a less-expensive brand. I don't know if it's possible for them to overcome that."[1]

Price Planning Defined

A *price* places a value on a product or service. *Price planning* deals with all the elements of pricing.

A **price** represents the value of a product or service for both the seller and the buyer. **Price planning** is systematic decision making by an organization regarding all aspects of pricing.

The value of a product or service to an organizational or final customer can involve both tangible and intangible factors. An example of a tangible factor is the cost savings obtained by the purchase of a new bottling machine by a soda manufacturer. An example of an intangible factor is a consumer's pride in the ownership of a Nikon rather than another brand camera.

Many words are substitutes for the term price: admission fee, membership fee, rate, tuition, service charge, donation, rent, salary, interest, retainer, and assessment.

A price can be expressed in monetary or nonmonetary terms.

A price can also refer to a nonmonetary exchange of goods and services: the price of a new iron may be ten books of trading stamps. Monetary and nonmonetary exchange may be combined, as is common with automobiles, where the consumer gives the seller money plus a trade-in. This combination allows a reduction in the monetary price.

A price contains all the terms of purchase: monetary and nonmonetary charges, discounts, handling and shipping fees, credit charges and other forms of interest, and late-payment penalties.

Exchange takes place only when the buyer and the seller are satisfied with the price.

For an exchange to take place, both the buyer and seller must feel that the price of a product or service provides an equitable value. To the

Figure 14-1
A Newly-Designed Timex Quartz Watch

Reprinted by permission.

buyer, the payment of a price reduces purchasing power available for other items. To the seller, receipt of a price is a source of revenue and an important determinant of sales and profit levels.

From a broader perspective, price is the mechanism for allocating goods and services among potential purchasers and for ensuring competition among sellers in an open market economy. If there is an excess of demand over supply, prices are usually bid up by consumers. If there is an excess of supply over demand, prices are usually reduced by sellers.

In this chapter, the importance of price and its relationship to other marketing variables, price and nonprice competition, and the factors affecting price decisions are examined. Chapter 15 deals with the development and implementation of a price strategy.

Importance of Price and Its Relationship to Other Marketing Variables

The importance of price to marketing executives has risen substantially over the past 20 years. In a 1964 study, they ranked pricing as the sixth most important of twelve marketing factors, behind product planning, marketing research, sales management, advertising and sales promotion, and customer services. Half of the executives did not consider pricing to be one of the five most vital areas.[2] However in 1975 and 1980 studies, marketing executives rated pricing as the first or second most crucial marketing activity.[3]

The rise in the relative significance of price is attributable to rapid cost increases, more competition for many products and services,

The importance of price has risen because of cost increases, competition, consumer price awareness, and product shortages.

greater price awareness on the part of consumers, and shortages leading to high prices in some product categories. Because price in a monetary or nonmonetary form is a key component of exchange, it appears in every marketing transaction.

Since a price places a value on the overall combination of marketing variables offered to consumers (such as product features, image, store location, customer service, etc.), pricing decisions must be made in conjunction with product, distribution, and promotion plans. An incorrect price can misstate the value of a product or service and result in diminished sales and profits. A correct price can present an equitable value to consumers and maximize sales and profits. Following are some examples of how pricing is related to other marketing and firm variables:

Price decisions must be interrelated with product, distribution, and promotion to ensure a consistent offering.

- Prices frequently vary over the life cycle of a product, from high introductory prices to gain status-conscious innovators to low prices to attract the mass market.
- Customer service levels are affected by prices. Low prices are usually associated with little customer service.
- From a distribution perspective, the prices charged to channel members must adequately compensate them for their functions, yet be low enough to be competitive with other brands at the retail level.
- There may be channel conflict if the manufacturer tries to control or suggest final prices.
- Product lines with different prices attract different market segments.
- The personal sales force needs some flexibility in negotiating prices and terms.
- The efforts of marketing and finance personnel need to be coordinated. Marketers usually begin with final consumer prices and work backward to determine channel member prices and acceptable production costs. Finance people typically start with costs and add desired profits to come up with selling prices.

Price and Nonprice Competition

Price competition occurs when sellers influence demand through price changes; nonprice competition emphasizes marketing factors other than price.

With **price competition,** sellers influence demand primarily through changes in price levels. **Nonprice competition** minimizes price as a consideration in consumer demand. This is accomplished by creating a distinctive product or service through promotion, packaging, delivery, customer service, availability, and other marketing factors. The more unique a product or service offering is perceived to be by consumers, the greater is the freedom of a marketer to set prices above competitors.

In price competition, sellers move along a demand curve by raising or lowering their prices. Price competition is a flexible marketing tool because prices can be adjusted quickly and easily to reflect demand, cost, or competitive factors. However, of all the controllable marketing variables, a pricing strategy is the easiest for a competitor to duplicate.

This may result in a "me-too" strategy or even in a price war. Furthermore, the government monitors price strategies.

In nonprice competition, sellers shift the demand curves of consumers to the right by stressing the distinctive attributes of their products or services. This enables firms to increase unit sales at a given price or to sell their original supply at a higher price. The risk with a nonprice strategy is that consumers may not perceive the seller's product or service attributes as better than the competition's. In this case the consumer will buy the lower-priced item he or she believes is similar to the higher-priced item. See Figures 14-2, 14-3, and 14-4 for illustrations of price and nonprice competition.

Arco (Atlantic Richfield Company) operates a large chain of gasoline stations that follows a price competition strategy. Arco stations do not accept credit cards and stress low gasoline prices:

> An Arco ad showed a man ripping open a huge brown shopping bag to reveal a life-size Arco gasoline pump, making the point that a consumer can shop for fuel just as he does for food. The company also distributed bumper stickers with the message: "I love Arco prices."[4]

Hewlett-Packard, a producer of programmable calculators and advanced office machines, employs a nonprice strategy. It has carved out a distinctive niche in the highly competitive portable calculator market. Hewlett-Packard sells expensive products that are equipped with special features and sets premium prices for them. As a consequence of this strategy, Hewlett-Packard continually varies its product line and introduces new models in order to stay ahead of competition.[5]

Factors Affecting Pricing Decisions

Before a firm develops a pricing strategy (which will be described in Chapter 15), it should analyze the outside factors affecting price decisions. Like channel-of-distribution decisions, price decisions depend heavily on elements external to the firm. This contrasts with product and promotion decisions, which are more directly controlled by the firm.

The outside factors affecting price should be studied before enacting a price strategy.

The major factors affecting price decisions are consumers, government, channel members, competitors, and costs. Sometimes the factors severely limit the company's ability to set prices; in other instances, the factors have little impact. Figure 14-5 outlines the factors.

Consumers

A marketer should understand the relationship between price and consumer purchases and perceptions. This relationship is explained by two economic principles—the law of demand and price elasticity of demand—and market segmentation.

The **law of demand** states that consumers usually purchase more units at a low price than at a high price. The **price elasticity of demand** defines the sensitivity of buyers to price changes in terms of the quantities they will purchase.

According to the law of demand, more units are bought at low prices than at high ones; price elasticity of demand explains the reactions of buyers to price changes.

Figure 14-2
Price and Nonprice Competition

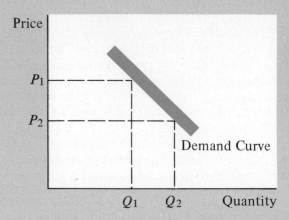

PRICE COMPETITION

At price P_1, quantity Q_1 is demanded.
At price P_2, quantity Q_2 is demanded.
A company operating at P_1Q_1 may increase sales by lowering its price to P_2. This increases demand to Q_2. A firm relying on price competition must lower prices to increase sales.

NONPRICE COMPETITION

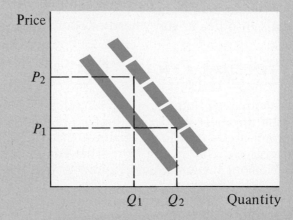

Demand curve after successful product differentiation
Demand curve for relatively undifferentiated product

At P_1, the firm is able to shift demand from Q_1 to Q_2.
At Q_1, the firm is able to shift price from P_1 to P_2.
Through nonprice competition, the firm shifts the consumer demand curve to the right by successfully differentiating its products/services from competitors. This enables the firm to:
(a) increase demand from Q_1 to Q_2 at price P_1, or
(b) raise the price from P_1 to P_2 while maintaining a demand of Q_1.

Figure 14-3
**Price Competition Approach
of Sunshine**

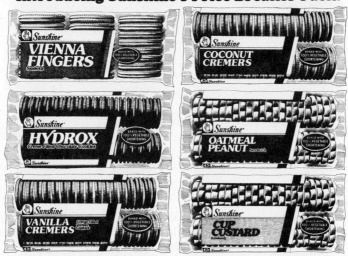

Reprinted by permission.

Price elasticity is computed by dividing the percentage change in quantity demanded by the percentage change in price charged:

$$\text{Price elasticity} = \frac{\dfrac{\text{Quantity 1} - \text{Quantity 2}}{\text{Quantity 1} + \text{Quantity 2}}}{\dfrac{\text{Price 1} - \text{Price 2}}{\text{Price 1} + \text{Price 2}}}$$

Figure 14-4
Nonprice Competition at American Dunhill Stores

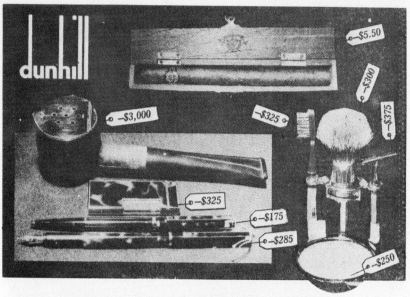

At American Dunhill Stores, high prices are used to attract affluent consumers. © The New York Times Company. Reprinted by permission.

Consumers may be sensitive to price changes *(elastic demand)* or relatively insensitive to price changes *(inelastic demand)*. This depends on substitutes and urgency of needs.

This formula shows the percentage change in quantity demanded for each 1 per cent change in price. Because quantity demanded usually decreases as price increases, elasticity is a negative number. However, for purposes of simplicity, elasticity calculations are usually expressed as positive numbers.*

Elastic demand occurs if relatively small changes in price result in large changes in quantity demanded. Numerically, price elasticity is greater than one. With elastic demand, total revenue goes up when prices are decreased and goes down when prices rise. **Inelastic demand**

---

*An example of how to compute price elasticity is contained in Appendix B at the end of the text.

Figure 14-5
Factors Affecting Price Decisions

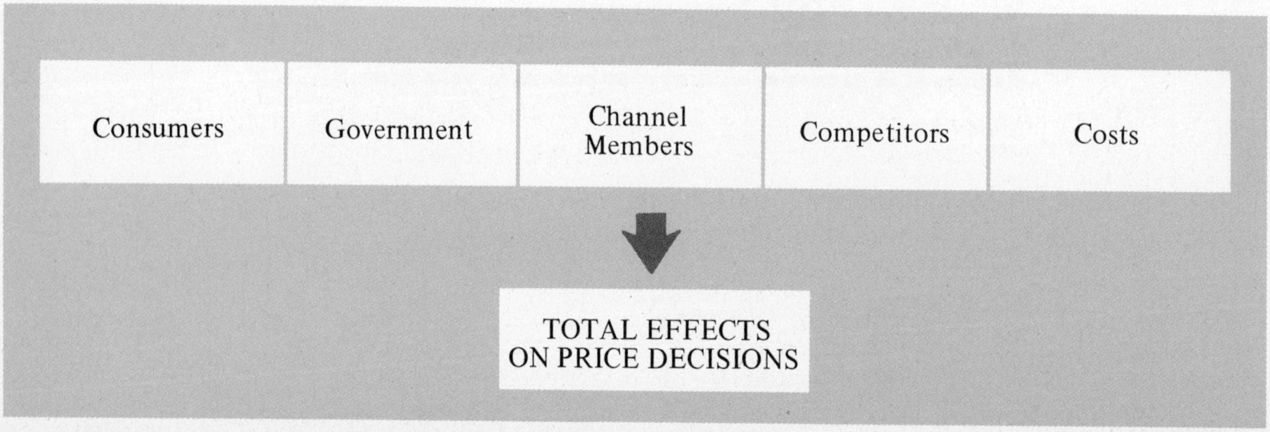

Consumers	Government	Channel Members	Competitors	Costs

TOTAL EFFECTS
ON PRICE DECISIONS

takes place if price changes have little impact on quantity demanded. Price elasticity is less than one. With inelastic demand, total revenue goes up when prices are raised and goes down when prices decline.

The type of demand that exists is based on two criteria: availability of substitutes and urgency of need. When the consumer believes there are many similar products or services from which to choose or there is no urgency to make a purchase, demand is elastic and highly influenced by price changes. A price increase will lead to the purchase of a substitute or a delayed purchase. A price decrease will expand sales as customers are drawn from competitors or move up the date of their purchases. For many customers the airfare for a vacation is highly elastic. If prices go up the consumer may travel by car or postpone the trip.

When the consumer believes the firm's product or service offering is unique or there is an urgency to make a purchase, demand is inelastic and little influenced by price changes. Neither a price increase nor a price decline will have much impact on demand. For example, if mass transit fares are increased or decreased, demand remains relatively constant because there is often no acceptable substitute and the same number of people must get to work each day. Brand loyalty also leads to inelastic demand because consumers perceive their brand as distinctive and will not buy substitutes. Finally, emergency conditions often cause inelastic demand. A consumer with a flat tire would pay more for a replacement than a consumer with time to shop around. Figure 14-6 shows elastic and inelastic demand.

It is also necessary to understand the importance of price by market segment. Not all consumers are equally price conscious. On the basis of a classic study, consumers can be divided into four categories or segments, depending on their shopping orientation:

1. Economical shopper: Primarily interested in shopping for values and extremely sensitive to price, quality, and merchandise assortment

2. Personalizing shopper: emphasizes product or service image, personal service, and treatment by firms; less concerned with price

3. Ethical shopper: willing to sacrifice low prices and wide assortments in order to patronize a small firm

4. Apathetic shopper: major concern for convenience, whatever the price[6]

Consumers can be divided into four categories: economical, personalizing, ethical, and apathetic.

Research confirms that not all consumers use price as the dominant purchase determinant. One study showed that price is not an overriding factor for products for which consumers have a strong brand preference.[7] Another study demonstrated that a convenient store location and a close relationship with local merchants are significant determinants in a purchase.[8] A third study found that a consumer's perception of price **(subjective price)** may be more important than actual price. A consumer may believe that a company has higher prices than its competitors, and, even though an item may actually have a low price, purchase from a competitor.[9]

The consumer's perception of a price level is the subjective price.

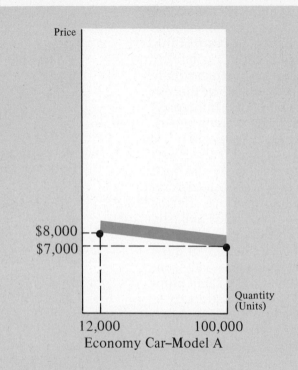

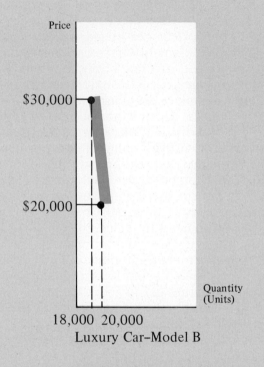

The purchasers of an economy car are highly sensitive to price. They perceive many models as interchangeable and demand will suffer significantly if the car is priced too high. At $7,000, 100,000 models may be sold (revenues are $700 million). A small increase to $8,000 will cause demand to fall to 12,000 units (revenues are $96 million).

The purchasers of a luxury car have little sensitivity to price. They perceive their model as quite distinctive and will pay a premium price for it. At $20,000, 20,000 models may be sold (revenues are $400 million). A large increase in price, to $30,000, will have a small effect on demand, 18,000 units (revenues are $540 million).

Figure 14-6

Demand Elasticity for Two Models of Automobiles

Government

Government actions relating to price can be divided into five major areas: price fixing, price discrimination, minimum prices, unit pricing, and price advertising. Each of these is discussed in the following subsections.

Price Fixing

Horizontal price fixing is illegal and results from agreements among companies at the same stage in a channel.

The government places limitations on horizontal and vertical price fixing. *Horizontal price fixing* results from agreements among manufacturers, among wholesalers, or among retailers to set prices at their stage in a channel of distribution. Such agreements are illegal according to the Sherman Antitrust Act and the Federal Trade Commission Act, regardless of how "reasonable" the price is.

377 An Overview of Price Planning

An example of a horizontal price agreement and its legal ramifications occurred in the folding-carton industry. The Justice Department charged that a widespread conspiracy, mainly among plant managers, existed east of the Rocky Mountains. The managers were said to have fixed the prices of corrugated cardboard boxes and folding cartons. The criminal case was the largest such antitrust action ever brought by the Justice Department. Companies representing 70 per cent of the $1.5 billion in annual industry sales were convicted. A federal judge imposed fines, probation, or jail terms on 47 of 48 executives in 22 companies. One company reported that legal fees alone exceeded earnings over the previous five-year period.[10]

In order to avoid price-fixing charges, a company must be careful not to

1. Coordinate discounts, credit terms, or conditions of sale with competitors;
2. Discuss prices, markups, and costs at trade association meetings;
3. Arrange with competitors to issue new price lists at the same date;
4. Arrange with competitors to rotate low bids on contracts; or
5. Agree with competitors to uniformly restrict production to maintain high prices.[11]

Vertical price fixing occurs when manufacturers or wholesalers are able to control the retail prices of their products or services. Until 1975 the Miller-Tydings Act (in conjunction with the McGuire Act) enabled these firms to strictly set and enforce retail prices if they desired. This practice was known as fair trade. It protected small retailers against price discounting by larger competitors and maintained manufacturers' brand images by forcing all retailers within fair-trade states to charge the same price for affected products.

Under *vertical price fixing,* manufacturers or wholesalers try to control retail prices. Today this practice is limited.

Fair trade was heavily criticized by consumer groups, many retailers, and a number of manufacturers for being noncompetitive, keeping prices artificially high, and rewarding retailer inefficiency. On December 12, 1975, President Gerald Ford signed the Consumer Goods Pricing Act of 1975. This law terminated all interstate utilization of fair trade or resale price maintenance as of March 11, 1976.[12]

Today, retailers cannot be required to adhere to list prices developed by manufacturers or wholesalers. In most cases, retailers are free to establish final selling prices. Manufacturers or wholesalers may control retail prices only through one of these methods:

1. Manufacturer or wholesaler ownership of retail facilities
2. Consignment selling, whereby the manufacturer or wholesaler owns items until they are sold and assumes all costs normally associated with the retailer, such as advertising and selling
3. Careful screening of the retailers through which products or services are sold
4. Suggesting realistic retail list prices
5. Preprinting prices on products
6. Establishing a customary price (such as 25 cents for a newspaper) that is accepted by consumers

Price Discrimination

The *Robinson-Patman Act* prohibits manufacturers and wholesalers from discriminating in price when selling to channel members.

The ***Robinson-Patman Act*** prohibits manufacturers and wholesalers from price discrimination in dealing with different channel-member purchasers of products of "like quality" if the effect of such discrimination is to injure competition. Covered by the Robinson-Patman Act are prices, discounts, rebates, premiums, guarantees, delivery, warehousing, and credit terms. Terms and conditions of sale must be made available to all competing channel members on a proportionately equal basis.

The Robinson-Patman Act was enacted in 1936 in order to protect small retailers from unfair price competition from large chains. It was feared that small retailers would be driven out of business due to the superior bargaining power of large chains with product suppliers. The Robinson-Patman Act required price differences to be limited to a manufacturer's cost savings in dealing with different retailers. The Robinson-Patman Act remains a major legal restriction on pricing.

There are some exceptions to the Robinson-Patman Act. Price discrimination within a channel is permissible if each buyer purchases products with substantial physical differences, if noncompeting buyers are involved, if prices do not injure competition, if price differences are justified by costs, if market conditions change (such as production costs rising), or if the seller reduces price to meet another supplier's bid.

Discounts are acceptable if the seller demonstrates that they are available to all competitive channel buyers on a proportionate basis, that they are sufficiently graduated so that small as well as large buyers can qualify, or that they are cost-justified. For example, the seller must prove that discounts for cumulative purchases (total volume during the year) or multistore purchases by retail chains are based on cost savings.

Although the Robinson-Patman Act is oriented toward sellers, it provides specific liabilities for purchasing firms under Section 2(F):

> it shall be unlawful for any person engaged in commerce, in the course of such commerce, knowingly to induce or receive a discrimination in price which is prohibited in this section.

Minimum Prices

Unfair-sales acts prevent large retailers from setting low prices in order to drive small firms out of business (*predatory pricing*).

Several states have enacted **unfair-sales acts (minimum price laws)** that prevent retailers from selling merchandise for less than the cost of the product plus a fixed percentage that covers overhead and profit. Unfair-sales acts are intended to protect small retailers from predatory pricing by larger competitors. Under **predatory pricing,** large firms attempt to drive small firms out of business by setting extremely low prices.

At the federal level, predatory pricing is banned by the Sherman and Clayton Acts. No channel member is allowed to set low prices for the purpose of forcing competitors out of the market. Manufacturers, wholesalers, and retailers are all subject to these acts.

Loss leaders are items priced below cost to attract customers.

Loss leaders, items priced below cost to draw customer traffic into a store, are restricted by unfair-sales acts in about twenty-five states. Retailers use loss leaders, typically well-known and heavily advertised brands, to increase overall store sales. They assume that customers who are drawn by loss leaders will also purchase nonsale items. Because consumers normally benefit from loss leaders, the laws are rarely enforced.

In addition to general unfair-sales acts, several states have laws that set minimum prices for specific items. For example, Pennsylvania regulates milk and liquor prices.

The lack of uniformity and consistency in package sizes has led to the enactment of unit-pricing legislation in a number of states. ***Unit pricing*** enables consumers to compare price per quantity for competing brands and for various sizes of the same brand.

Food stores are most affected by unit pricing. In many cases the stores must express price per unit of measure as well as total price. For example, unit pricing would show that a 12-ounce can of soda selling for 30 cents is priced at 2.5 cents per ounce, whereas a 67.6-ounce (2 liter) bottle of the same brand of soda selling for $1.39 is priced at 2.1 cents per ounce. The larger size is cheaper than the smaller.

The costs of unit pricing to retailers include per unit price computations, printing of shelf labels, and computer records. Costs are influenced by the number of stores in a chain, sales per store, the number of items under unit pricing, and the frequency of price changes. For smaller stores, unit pricing costs as much as 26 per cent of sales.[13] On the other hand, Giant Foods, a large Washington-based supermarket chain, found that it attained considerable savings through reductions in marking errors, better inventory control, and improved space management.[14]

Guidelines for price advertising have been developed by the Federal Trade Commission (FTC) and various trade associations, such as the Better Business Bureau. The FTC's guidelines specify standards of permissible conduct in five broad categories.[15]

A company may not claim or imply that a price has been reduced from a former level unless the original price was offered to the public on a regular basis during a reasonable, recent period of time.

A firm may not claim that its price is lower than that of competitors or the manufacturer's list price without verifying, through price comparisons involving large quantities of merchandise, that the price of an item at other outlets in the same trading area is in fact higher.

A suggested list price or a premarked price cannot be advertised as a reference point for a sale or a comparison with other products unless the advertised product has actually been sold at the list or premarked price.

Bargain offers such as "free," "buy one, get one free," "two-for-one sale," "half-price sale," and "one-cent sale" are frequently used by companies. These practices are considered deceptive by the FTC if the terms of an offer are not disclosed at the beginning of a sales presentation or advertisement, the stated regular price of an item is inflated to create an impression of savings, or the quality or quantity of merchandise is reduced without informing the consumer of the change. In addition, it is considered deceptive to continuously advertise the same product as being on sale.

Unit Pricing

With *unit pricing,* consumers can easily compare price per quantity for different-size packages.

Price Advertising

FTC guidelines deal with comparing new prices with former prices, comparing competitors' prices, suggested retail prices, advertised bargains, and bait-and-switch.

Under *bait-and-switch advertising,* retailers illegally draw customers into a store with no intention of selling the advertised product.

Bait-and-switch advertising is an illegal procedure in which a retailer lures customers into a store by advertising items at exceptionally low prices and then tells the customers that the items are out of stock or are of inferior quality. The salesperson attempts to switch the customers to more expensive substitutes, and there is no intention of selling the advertised item. Signs of bait-and-switch are refusal to demonstrate requested products, belittling of products, insufficient quantity to meet reasonable demand, refusal to take orders, demonstration of defective products, and a compensation plan encouraging salespeople to engage in the practice. In the late 1970s Sears was criticized for its methods of selling appliances. In particular, sales personnel failed to show advertised items, pointed out faults in low-price merchandise, and failed to make a sincere sales effort for certain models. Sears changed these practices under government prodding.

Each of the FTC's guidelines requires careful record keeping and documentation for all advertising claims that are made.

Channel Members

Every channel member wants a role in setting prices in order to meet its own goals.

Each channel member seeks to play a significant role in setting prices in order to build sales volume, obtain adequate profit margins, establish a suitable image, obtain repeat purchases, and meet specific goals.

There often are conflicts among manufacturers, wholesalers, and retailers regarding price policies. The manufacturer wants to cover production costs and make a profit, establish a brand image, and have input into final selling prices. It is particularly fearful of continued discounts or price cutting that may hurt brand image. The wholesaler wants to cover selling costs and make a profit, be competitive with other wholesalers, and have input into final selling prices. Wholesale prices are based on the costs, goals, and strengths of individual wholesalers. The retailer wants to cover selling costs and make a profit, be competitive with other retailers, and control final selling prices. It sets prices based on individual image, objectives, method of operations, and cost considerations.

Different channel members at the same stage in the channel have the right to charge different prices for an identical brand. For example, a stereo may be sold at four stores in a downtown shopping area and have a distinct price at each. The prices at each store are based on the target market attracted, locational costs, the level of sales help, profit requirements, company resources, store image, inventory turnover, and other factors.

A manufacturer can gain stronger control over price by using an exclusive distribution system or minimizing sales through price-cutting retailers, preticketing prices on merchandise, opening its own retail outlets, offering goods on consignment, providing adequate margins to channel members, and most importantly by developing strong national brands that consumers have brand loyalty toward whatever final price is charged.

A wholesaler or retailer can gain stronger control over price by stressing its importance as a customer to the manufacturer, linking its resale support (displays, personal selling) to the profit margins allowed by the manufacturer, refusing to carry unprofitable products, stocking competitive items, and developing strong wholesaler or retailer brands so that consumers are loyal to the seller and not the manufacturer.

To ensure channel cooperation with price decisions, the manufacturer should first determine the final selling price consumers will pay and the profit margins required by wholesalers or retailers. Then, the manufacturer's price should be set. An attempt by the manufacturer to cut the traditional markups for wholesalers or retailers may lose their cooperation and perhaps find them unwilling to carry the product.

To obtain support for prices, the manufacturer should consider channel member profits.

Sometimes retailers engage in **selling against the brand,** whereby they stock merchandise, place high prices on it, and then sell other brands for lower prices. This is often done to increase the sales of private (store) brands. The practice is disliked by manufacturers because the sales of their brands decline.

To increase private brand sales, some retailers *sell against the brand.*

In other cases, wholesalers and retailers seek price guarantees to maintain inventory values and profit. As explained in Chapter 9, **price guarantees** assure wholesalers or retailers that the prices they pay are the lowest available. Any discount given to competitors will also be given to the original purchasers. Guarantees are most frequently provided by new firms or new products that want to gain entry into an established channel of distribution.

Price guarantees reassure channel members.

Finally, the impact of price increases on channel-member behavior should be evaluated. Usually, when manufacturers raise prices to channel members, the increases are passed along to final consumers. This practice is more difficult for items with customary prices, such as candy or newspapers, where small cost rises may be absorbed by the channel members. In any event, cooperation depends on an equitable distribution of costs and profit within the channel. See Figure 14-7.

Competition

Another element contributing to the degree of control a firm has over prices is the competitive environment within which it operates: market-controlled, company-controlled, and government-controlled.

A **market-controlled price environment** is characterized by a high level of competition, similar products and services, and little control over price by individual companies. Firms attempting to charge more than the going competitive price would attract few customers, because demand for any single firm is weak enough that customers would switch to a competitor if prices were raised. Similarly, a firm would gain little by selling for less than its competition. Its profits would be reduced because it could sell its items at the market price.

In a *market-controlled price environment,* there is strong competition and little price control by individual firms.

A **company-controlled price environment** is characterized by a moderate level of competition, well-differentiated products and services, and strong control over price by individual firms. In this environment firms may succeed with high prices because consumers view their offerings as unique. Differentiation may be based on brand image, features, associated services, assortment, or other factors. Discounters also can carve out a niche in this environment by attracting consumers interested in low prices. The choice of a price depends on the firm's strategy and target market.

In a *company-controlled price environment,* there is moderate competition and strong price control by individual firms.

Figure 14-7
Pricing Through the Channel

"HMM, LET'S SEE... FACTORY PRICE, WHOLESALE PRICE, DISTRIBUTOR'S
PRICE, JOBBER'S PRICE, RETAIL PRICE. WELL, TOUGH LUCK... YOU HAVE
TO PAY THE RETAIL PRICE!"

Reprinted by permission of Rothco.

In a government-controlled price environment, prices are regulated by the government.

A ***government-controlled price environment*** is characterized by prices set or directed by the government. Examples are public utilities, municipal buses, taxis, and state universities. In each of these cases, government bodies or agencies determine or approve prices after obtaining input from the affected companies, institutions, or industries as well as other interested parties (such as consumer groups).

Firms may have to adapt to changes in the competitive environment in their industry. For example, the environment facing railroads, air travel, and the trucking industry shifted from government-controlled to market-controlled.

Because price strategies are relatively easy and quick to copy, the reaction of competition is predictable if the firm initiating price changes is successful. Accordingly, a marketer should view price from both short-run and long-run perspectives.

Price wars occur when competing firms frequently lower prices.

Excessive price competition may lead to long and costly ***price wars,*** in which various firms continually try to undercut each other's prices to draw customers. These wars usually result in low profits or even losses for the participants and in some companies being forced out of business.

A good example of this is the long-running price war among supermarkets in San Antonio, Texas. When Kroger entered the market in 1979, it developed a price campaign that offered to pay customers triple the difference between their prices and competitors' prices if the customers could find lower prices for a similar product assortment at any competitor's store. H. E. Butt, a 156-unit regional chain, countered by setting its prices below Kroger's. This set off a price war that reduced gross operating margins from 16–18 per cent to 5 to 6 per cent of sales; and profits vanished. By 1981, several competitors had withdrawn from the area (Fedmart, Eagle Stores) or gone out of business (Deluxe Supermarkets). Another, Handy Andy, closed some stores and filed for bankruptcy; its president commented, "Who wants to sell goods at a loss forever?"[16]

Costs

The costs of raw materials, supplies, labor, advertising, transportation, and other items are frequently beyond the control of the firm. Yet, these costs have a great influence on final prices.[17]

Over the past decade, costs have increased dramatically in many areas, making it difficult for firms to manage their prices effectively.

From the early 1970s through 1981, many costs rose rapidly and pushed prices to high levels. For example,

- Fuel costs went up almost 500 per cent. This placed pressure on airlines, the trucking industry, and the automobile industry.
- Silver and gold prices were extremely volatile. Silver went from $6 per ounce to more than $50 per ounce, before settling at $10 to $15 per ounce. This created difficulties for the photography industry which used silver as a prime ingredient in film. Gold went from $45 per ounce to about $1,000 per ounce, before settling at $400 to $600 per ounce. This had an effect on dentists and jewelers.
- The minimum wage rose from $1.60 per hour in 1970 to $3.35 per hour on January 1, 1981. This affected fast-food retailers and other firms who rely on unskilled labor.
- Mortgage interest rates more than doubled between 1977 and 1981. This severely dampened the housing market.
- The cost of prime-time television commercials went up dramatically. As an illustration, a 30-second commercial on the 1973 Super Bowl cost $103,500. In 1983, the cost was $400,000.

In 1982, cost increases tapered off. For the year, wholesale prices increased by only 3.5 per cent, the lowest amount in over a decade. This meant better cost control for marketers and more stable prices.

In the face of rising costs, companies pass along increases to customers, alter products or services, or delete some items.

During periods of rapidly rising costs, companies can react in one or more ways. They can leave their products and services unchanged and pass along all of their cost increases to consumers, leave their products and services unchanged and pass along part of their increases and absorb part of them, modify products and services to hold down costs and maintain prices (by reducing size, offering fewer options, or using lesser-quality materials), modify products and services to gain consumer support for higher prices (by increasing size, offering more options, or using better-quality materials), and/or abandon unprofitable products and services.

Sometimes, despite a company's or industry's best intentions, it may take several years to get runaway costs (and prices) under control. A good illustration of this is the automobile industry, where costs and prices have gone up drastically since 1970. At that time, an average U.S. automobile had a retail price of under $4,000; today, the average

Figure 14-8
*How a Small Car's Price
Grows from the Assembly
Line to the Showroom*

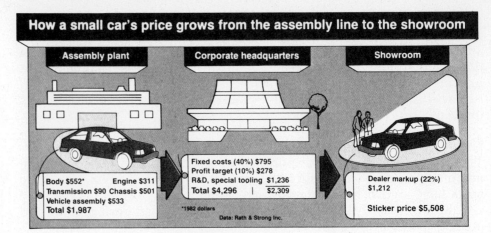

Reprinted from *Business Week* by special permission. © McGraw-Hill, Inc.

price is about $10,000. Among the costs auto executives have had to deal with are

1. $80 billion in retooling from large to small cars.
2. High fixed costs—plant, equipment, unionized labor.
3. Hundreds of millions of dollars for anti-pollution devices and safety features.
4. $1,500 per car higher costs for U.S. cars than for Japanese cars.
5. Up to $1 billion or more to develop a single major new car model.

As a result, pricing decisions have to be made well in advance; little flexibility is possible.[18] Figure 14-8 shows the costs and sticker price of a 1982 U.S. compact car.

Cost decreases can have positive benefits for marketing strategies.

It should be noted that cost declines also can occur and enable firms to lower selling prices or raise profit margins, as these illustrations show:

- The use of microprocessors in personal computers has reduced their costs significantly by requiring less wiring and assembly time during production, improving durability, and enlarging information-processing capability.[19] Prices have been steadily lowered, thus expanding the market considerably.
- The drop in sugar prices during 1981 and 1982 allowed candy manufacturers to increase package size (and profits) without raising prices.

Summary

A price represents the value of a product or service for both the seller and the buyer. Price planning is systematic decision making relating to all aspects of pricing by a company; it involves tangible and intangible factors and can refer to the nonmonetary exchange of goods and services. A price contains all the terms of a purchase. Exchange does not take place unless both the buyer and seller agree that a price represents an equitable value. Price also balances supply and demand. The increased importance of price is the result of cost rises, foreign competition, consumer awareness, and shortages.

Under price competition, sellers influence demand primarily through changes in price levels. With nonprice competition, sellers minimize price and emphasize other marketing characteristics such as image, packaging, and features.

Several factors affect a firm's pricing decisions: consumers, government, channel members, competition, and costs. The law of demand states that consumers usually purchase more units at a low price than at a high price. Price elasticity of demand explains the sensitivity of buyers to price changes in terms of the quantities they purchase. Elastic demand occurs if relatively small changes in price result in large changes in quantity demanded, and inelastic demand results if price changes have little impact on quantity demanded. Demand is influenced by the availability of substitutes and urgency of need. Consumers can be divided into economical, personalizing, ethical, and apathetic market segments.

Government is active in a broad variety of pricing areas. Price fixing, both horizontal and vertical, is subject to severe restrictions. The Robinson-Patman Act bans most forms of price discrimination to channel members that are not justified by costs. A number of states have unfair-sales acts (minimum price laws) to protect small firms against predatory pricing. Unit pricing requires specified retailers to post prices in terms of quantity. The Federal Trade Commission has a series of guidelines for price advertising.

Each channel member seeks a major role in setting prices in order to generate sales, obtain adequate profit margins, sustain a suitable image, ensure repeat purchases, and meet its own goals. Manufacturers exert control through exclusive distribution, preticketing, opening their own outlets, offering goods on consignment, providing adequate margins, and having strong brands. Wholesalers and retailers exert control by making large purchases, linking sales support to margins, refusing to carry items, stocking competitive brands, and developing their own brands. Cooperation can be gained by first determining final selling price, then working back to the manufacturer's price, and making sure that channel members receive sufficient markups.

A market-controlled price environment has a high level of competition, similar products and services, and little control over price by individual firms. A company-controlled price environment has a moderate level of competition, well-differentiated products and services, and strong control over price by individual firms. In a government-controlled price environment, the government sets prices. Some competitive actions may result in price wars, in which firms try to undercut each other's prices.

The costs of raw materials, supplies, labor, advertising, transportation, and other items affect prices. During the past decade, costs have risen significantly in many areas. This has caused companies to pass along increases to consumers, modify products and services, and abandon some offerings. Cost declines can benefit marketing strategies by improving the firm's ability to plan prices.

KEY TERMS

After reading this chapter, you should understand these key terms:

Price	Predatory pricing
Price planning	Loss leaders
Price competition	Unit pricing
Nonprice competition	Bait-and-switch advertising
Law of demand	Selling against the brand
Price elasticity of demand	Price guarantees
Elastic demand	Market-controlled price
Inelastic demand	environment
Subjective price	Company-controlled price
Horizontal price fixing	environment
Vertical price fixing	Government-controlled price
Robinson-Patman Act	environment
Unfair-sales acts	Price wars
(minimum price laws)	

QUESTIONS FOR DISCUSSION

1. Evaluate Timex's new price strategy.
2. "The value of a product or service to a customer can be determined by both tangible and intangible factors." Explain this statement.
3. Why is price such an important marketing variable?
4. Differentiate between price and nonprice competition. Give an example of each.
5. Give five examples of products or services with elastic demand. Explain why their demand is elastic.
6. What two criteria determine the elasticity of demand? Explain your answer.
7. Develop a price strategy for a personalizing shopper interested in a new air conditioner.
8. Distinguish between subjective and actual prices. Which is more important?
9. Why have most types of price fixing been declared illegal?
10. What are the exceptions to the Robinson-Patman Act?
11. How may different channel members control price? Give examples.
12. Why would a price war develop? How could it be avoided?
13. When would you pass along a full cost increase to consumers? When would you absorb the increase?
14. Which is determined first, product quality or price? Explain your answer.

NOTES

1. Jeffrey H. Birnbaum, "Falling Profit Prompts Timex to Shed Its Utilitarian Image," *Wall Street Journal* (September 17, 1981), p. 29.
2. Jon G. Udell, "How Important Is Pricing in Competitive Strategy?" *Journal of Marketing*, Vol. 28 (January 1964), pp. 44–48.
3. Robert A. Robicheaux, "How Important Is Pricing in Competitive Strategy?" in Henry W. Nash and Donald P. Robin (Editors), *Proceedings: Southern Marketing Association* (January 1976),

pp. 55–57; and Saeed Samiee, "Elements of Marketing Strategy: How Important Are They from the Executive Viewpoint?" *Journal of the Academy of Marketing Science,* Vol. 8 (Winter 1980), pp. 40–50.

4. Maria Shao, "Oil Companies Hustling Again as Price of Gasoline Declines," *Wall Street Journal* (January 6, 1983), p. 19.

5. "Flexible Pricing," *Business Week* (December 12, 1977), p. 84; and "When 'Calculator' Is a Dirty Word," *Business Week* (June 14, 1982), p. 62.

6. Gregory P. Stone, "City Shoppers and Urban Identification: Observation on the Social Psychology of City Life," *American Journal of Sociology,* Vol. 60 (July 1954), pp. 36–45.

7. Evan E. Anderson, "The Effectiveness of Retail Price Reductions: A Comparison for Alternative Expressions of Price," *Journal of Marketing Research,* Vol. 11 (August 1974), pp. 327–330.

8. Robert F. Hartley, "The Importance of Price in Small Town Shopping Behavior," *Southern Journal of Business,* Vol. 5 (April 1970), pp. 24–32.

9. Kent B. Monroe, "Buyers' Subjective Perceptions of Price," *Journal of Marketing Research,* Vol. 10 (February 1973), pp. 73–80.

10. Winston Williams, "Cardboard Makers to Pay $300 Million to End Pricing Suit," *New York Times* (May 2, 1979), pp. 1, D4; and Jeffrey Sonnenfeld and Paul R. Lawrence, "Why Do Companies Succumb to Price Fixing?" *Harvard Business Review,* Vol. 56 (July–August 1978), p. 147.

11. "Price Fixing; Crackdown Under Way," *Business Week* (June 2, 1975), pp. 42–48.

12. See L. Louise Luchsinger and Patrick M. Dunne, "Fair Trade Laws—How Fair?" *Journal of Marketing,* Vol. 42 (January 1978), pp. 50–53; and Richard Sandomir, "Retailers Fear Price-Fixing Return," *Newsday* (October 3, 1982), p. 92.

13. Kent B. Monroe and Peter G. LaPlaca, "What Are the Benefits of Unit Pricing?" *Journal of Marketing,* Vol. 36 (July 1972), p. 17.

14. Esther Peterson, "Consumerism as a Retailer's Asset," *Harvard Business Review,* Vol. 52 (May–June 1974), p. 97.

15. Earl W. Kintner, *A Primer on the Law of Deceptive Practices* (New York: Macmillan, 1978), pp. 213–226. See also, Joe L. Welch, *Marketing Law* (Tulsa, Ok.: PPC Books, 1981), pp. 82–112.

16. Richard Erickson, "Grocers Aiming Low in City Price War," *Advertising Age* (November 23, 1981), p. 45.

17. See, for example, Mary Louise Hatten, "Don't Get Caught with Your Prices Down: Pricing in Inflationary Times," *Business Horizons,* Vol. 22 (March–April 1982), pp. 23–28; Carol J. Loomis, "How GE Manages Inflation," *Fortune* (May 4, 1981), pp. 121–124; and Michael L. King, "Inflation Forces Mortgage Lenders to Find New Pricing Methods That Prevent Losses," *Wall Street Journal* (January 5, 1982), p. 33.

18. "Why Detroit Can't Cut Prices," *Business Week* (March 1, 1982) pp. 110–111; and John Holusha, "Detroit Bows to Sticker Shock," *New York Times* (August 5, 1982), pp. D1, D5.

19. William M. Bulkeley, "New, Powerful Personal Computers Force Price Cuts and Alter Market," *Wall Street Journal* (May 11, 1982), p. 33.

GASOLINE MARKETING: PRICE AND NONPRICE STRATEGIES*   1   **CASES**

From the 1950s through the early 1970s, gasoline was in full supply. Service stations frequently engaged in price wars and regularly ran sales promotions to attract customers. Then, the oil embargo in 1973 and later cutbacks in oil production by OPEC (Organization of Petroleum Exporting Countries) reduced the supply of gasoline and caused prices to rise sharply. A gallon of gasoline that

*The data in this case are drawn from Maria Shao, "Gasoline Concerns Scramble to Sign Up Competitors' Credit-Card Customers," *Wall Street Journal* (November 12, 1982), p. 19; and Maria Shao, "Oil Companies Hustling Again as Price of Gasoline Declines," *Wall Street Journal* (January 6, 1983), p. 19.

Table 1	Company	Has Own Cards	Honors Other Oil-Company Cards	Honors Bank Cards	Gives Discounts For Cash	Accepts Only Cash
Credit-Card Policies of Selected Oil Companies (as of early 1983)	Amoco	X			X	
	Arco					X
	Chevron	X	X	X	X	
	Exxon	X		X	X	
	Getty			X		
	Gulf	X				
	Mobil	X	X	X	X	
	Shell	X	X	X		
	Sun	X	X			
	Texaco	X		X		

sold for $.30 at retail before the embargo reached $1.33 in December 1981. Accordingly, service stations turned away from price competition and did not sponsor sales promotions; they were able to sell all the gasoline they were allotted at high prices.

But during 1982, the situation changed once again as gasoline supplies grew steadily and consumers continued to hold down their fuel consumption. By December 1982, prices had fallen an average of eight cents per gallon. And, for the first time since the embargo, the major oil companies began aggressively competing for sales through both price and nonprice strategies.

To appeal to price-sensitive consumers, some companies used self-service, cash-only sales, free credit-card sales, and discounts for cash in order to offer the lowest prices possible. To appeal to consumers who were less price-sensitive, other companies provided full-service, promotional giveaways (such as Gillette razors and iced-tea glasses), one-stop shopping (by stocking convenience items), and extended station hours; their gasoline prices were higher.

Still other companies, combined these approaches (for example, having one self-service pump and one full-service pump). Table 1 shows the different ways that oil companies handled credit cards.

QUESTIONS

1. What are the strengths and weaknesses of price-oriented gasoline strategies? Nonprice-oriented strategies?
2. Why have the same pricing strategies not been applied to home heating oil as to gasoline?
3. Many oil companies that have their own credit cards absorb the costs involved in extending credit (about 6 to 9 cents per gallon). Comment on this approach. Why is it considered a price-oriented strategy?
4. Comment on Table 1. If you were an oil company executive, which strategy would you select? Explain your answer.

2 **IBM: A CHANGE IN PRICING PHILOSOPHY†**

IBM, despite some inroads by competitors, is by far the world's largest computer company. Its annual sales are expected to reach $50 billion by 1987.

†The data in this case are drawn from Andrew Pollack, "I.B.M.'s Aggressive Pricing," *New York Times* (August 9, 1982), pp. D1, D7.

Until recently, IBM had a very structured pricing philosophy. As the industry leader, it stressed product quality and assortment and the expertise of its huge service force. Prices were relatively high and not open to negotiation. While other firms allowed their sales personnel to bargain with customers over price, IBM's sales force could not. As one observer noted, "It was like the Sears or Montgomery Ward catalogue."

During the late 1970s, IBM made the first modification in its pricing strategy. Price discounts were allowed for quantity purchases of selected items. Eventually, more and more products were eligible for the discounts. However, the sales force was still not allowed to negotiate price with buyers; discount schedules were published and available to anyone.

Finally in 1982, IBM adopted a more flexible approach to pricing. For the first time, salespeople were permitted to negotiate prices. Industry analysts believe this shift was caused by the federal government's antitrust suit against IBM being dismissed in January 1982. This enabled IBM to be more active in competing with other firms, without fear of government intervention. Throughout the 13 years of the government's suit, IBM had been "extra conservative."

Under its new flexible pricing strategy, IBM recently completed two large orders—1,000 personal computers for Connecticut Mutual Life Insurance Company and an undisclosed number of series 4300 computers for Exxon. In both cases, contract provisions prohibited the buyers from disclosing purchase terms.

While sales have increased, profit margins are now lower. As one marketing researcher commented:

> It's one thing to gain market share and another thing to do it profitably. A lot of these strategies are opposite to the ones I.B.M. used in the past, which have proven to be successful.

QUESTIONS

1. Evaluate IBM's former and current pricing philosophies.
2. Does IBM's revised pricing approach mean that it has abandoned its traditional marketing emphasis on product quality and assortment along with a comprehensive service staff? Explain your answer.
3. Should IBM use flexible pricing in marketing personal computers to final consumers? Why or why not?
4. How can IBM make sure that it does not end up in a price war with its competitors?

Developing a Pricing Strategy

15

Chapter Preview

Chapter Objectives

1. To study the overall process for developing a pricing strategy

2. To examine sales-based, profit-based, and status quo-based pricing objectives

3. To describe the elements in a broad price policy and cost, demand, and competitive pricing techniques

4. To show how a pricing strategy can be implemented

5. To present the major ways that prices can be adjusted

Competitive pricing in the silverware industry is causing large-scale discounting, channel member disputes, and court litigation. These activities have escalated since 1980, as consumer demand for sterling silver flatware has begun to fall drastically. Explained one manufacturer, "When the pie isn't dramatically getting any larger, and when there are only eight companies selling sterling flatware, it becomes a very competitive thing."

The basic pricing tactic used by silverware manufacturers is called "deep discounting," whereby merchandise is sold to final consumers for 40 to 85 per cent below manufacturers' suggested retail prices. For example, Towle encourages deep discounts of 60 per cent or more. A Towle fork with a suggested retail price of $215 normally sells for $86 (this still enables retailers to take a 40 per cent markup).

Many retailers object to deep discounting as causing customer confusion and being deceptive. Yet as one retailer remarked, "We stayed away from playing those games for a long time, but as much as I disagree with the darn thing, [after reinstating deep discounts] we did a year's worth of business in a week." Manufacturers not deep discounting have encountered much resistance from their retailers.

The leading opponent of deep discounting is Reed & Barton, one of the eight largest silverware manufacturers. Reed & Barton is anxious about the industry's image, the deceptive aspects of deep discounting, and deteriorating channel relations. Accordingly, it has taken a two-pronged approach. The company is suing five of its competitors, charging them with "false advertising concerning the price of their products." It is also trying to convince retailers that deep discounting is illegal and to drop the practice. One major retail chain, Allied Stores, has toned down deep discounting in its 222 department stores.

As a result of Reed & Barton's persistence, the Federal Trade Commission and a number of state consumer protection agencies have been investigating. Michigan's attorney general has shown particular interest.[1]

Developing a Pricing Strategy

There are five stages in developing a pricing strategy: objectives, broad policy, strategy, implementation, and adjustments. See Figure 15-1. It is important to recognize that all aspects of the process are affected by the external factors discussed in Chapter 14.

Like any planning activity, price strategy begins with a clear statement of objectives and ends with an adaptive or corrective mechanism. It is essential that pricing decisions be integrated with the firm's overall marketing program. This is done in the broad price-policy phase shown in Figure 15-1.

The construction of a pricing strategy is not a one-time occurrence. The strategy needs to be re-examined when a new product is developed, a product is revised, the competitive environment changes, a product moves through its life cycle, a competitor initiates a price change, costs rise, or the firm's prices come under government scrutiny.

This chapter describes each of the components of a pricing strategy in detail.

Developing a pricing strategy involves objectives, broad policy, strategy, implementation, and adjustments.

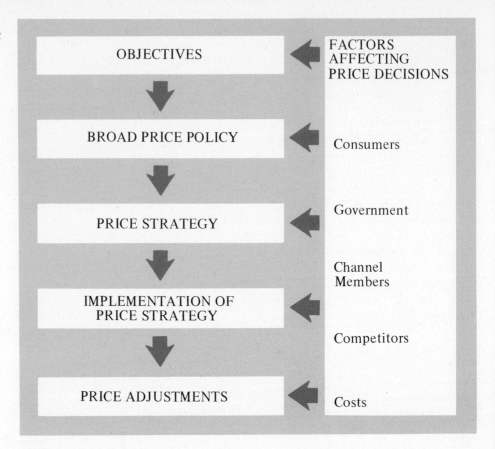

Pricing Objectives

A pricing strategy should be consistent with and reflect overall company objectives. It is possible for different firms in the same industry to have dissimilar objectives and, therefore, different pricing strategies. For example, in the ice cream industry, Baskin-Robbins appeals to middle-class families and seeks to maximize sales. It has 2,500 franchised outlets, offering more than 500 rotating ice cream flavors (31 are sold each month) and accounting for over $400 million in annual sales. For the most part, Baskin-Robbins' stores have no sit-down facilities and price a single-dip cone at $.55. In contrast, Häagen-Daz caters to a "largely adult, more sophisticated, and better-heeled market" through its 200 retail outlets, which have annual sales of $60 million. Häagen-Daz stores have attractive sit-down facilities and feature 20 flavors of top-of-the-line ice cream. A single-dip cone sells for $1.00 and up.[2]

Pricing objectives can be sales-, profit-, and/or status quo-based.

There are three general pricing objectives from which a firm may select: sales-based, profit-based, and status quo-based. With sales-based objectives, the firm is interested in sales growth or maximizing market share. With profit-based objectives, the firm is interested in maximizing profit, earning a satisfactory profit, optimizing the return on investment, or securing an early recovery of cash. With status quo-based objectives, the firm seeks to avoid unfavorable government actions, minimize the effects of competitor actions, maintain good channel relations, discourage the entry of competitors, reduce demands from suppliers, or stabilize prices.

A company may pursue more than one pricing objective at the same time, such as maximizing market share and earning at least a specified net profit before taxes. A firm may also set different short-run and long-run objectives. For example, in the short run, it may want to secure an early recovery of cash; in the long run, it may seek to discourage the entry of competitors.

Sales-Based Objectives

A company with **sales-based objectives** is oriented toward high sales volume or expanding its share of sales relative to competitors. A firm would focus on sales-based objectives for either of three reasons. One, it is interested in market saturation or sales growth as a major step leading to market control and sustained profits. Two, it seeks to maximize unit sales and is willing to trade low per unit profits for larger total profits. Three, it assumes that higher sales will enable the firm to have lower per unit costs.

Sales-based objectives seek high sales volume or increased market share.

In order to achieve high sales, a penetration pricing strategy is frequently used. A **penetration price** is a low price intended to capture the mass market for a product or service. It is a proper strategy when customers are highly sensitive to price, low prices discourage actual and potential competitors, there are economies of scale (per unit production and distribution costs decrease as sales increase), and a large consumer market exists. Penetration pricing also recognizes that a high price may leave a product vulnerable to competition.

A penetration price is a low price aimed at the mass market.

A penetration strategy was followed when the Timex-Sinclair 1000 personal home computer was introduced in mid-1982. See Figure 15-2. The Timex-Sinclair had a limited information-processing capability and few features compared to its major competitors (such as Texas Instruments and Commodore). However, it had a list price of $100 and sold for $40 or less by mid-1983. The lowest-priced Texas Instruments and Commodore personal computers sold for two to three times as much. As a result of its pricing strategy, 600,000 Timex-Sinclair computers were sold in their first five months.[3]

In many cases, penetration pricing may tap markets that were not originally anticipated. For example, few people forecast that electronic hand-held calculators would reach the sales volume attained during their peak. The market expanded rapidly after prices fell below $100. It grew again as new models were introduced for $20 and less.

Profit-Based Objectives

A company with **profit-based objectives** orients its strategy toward some type of profit goal. Profit-maximization objectives are used when a firm designates high dollar profit as a goal, such as $1 million before taxes. Satisfactory-profit objectives are used by a firm seeking stable profits over a period of time. Rather than maximize profits in any given year, which could result in declines in nonpeak years, the firm sets a steady

Profit-based objectives seek maximization, satisfactory profit, return on investment, and/or recovery of cash.

Figure 15-2
**Timex-Sinclair: A Penetration
Price Strategy**

When introduced, the Timex-Sinclair 1000 computer was sold
for less than $100. It quickly dropped to under $40 in many
stores. Reprinted by permission of Timex.

profit goal for a number of years, such as $700,000 per year for five
years. With return-on-investment objectives, the firm states that profits
must relate to investment costs. This objective is frequently used by
regulated utilities as a means of justifying rate-increase requests. Early-
recovery-of-cash objectives are used by firms that desire high initial
profits because they are short of funds or uncertain about the future.

**Profit goals can be
related to per unit profit
or total profit.**

Profit may be expressed in per unit or total terms. Per unit profit
equals the revenue a seller receives for one unit sold minus costs. An
item like perfume would have a high unit profit. Total profit equals the
revenue a seller receives for all items sold minus costs. It is computed
by multiplying per unit profit times the number of units sold. An item
like milk would have a low unit profit. Its profitability is based on the
number of units that are sold (turnover). High per unit profits usually
rely on skimming prices. High total profits usually involve penetration
pricing.

**A *skimming price* is
aimed at consumers
interested in quality. It
can be followed by a
penetration price.**

A ***skimming price*** is a high price intended to attract the market
segment that is more concerned with product quality, uniqueness, or
status than price. It is a proper strategy if competition can be kept out or
minimized (through patent protection, brand loyalty, raw material control, or high capital requirements), funds are needed for early recovery
of cash or further expansion, the market is insensitive to price or willing
to pay a high initial price, and unit production and distribution costs
remain equal or increase as sales increase (economies of scale are ab-
sent).

Figure 15-3
Rolex: A Skimming Price
Strategy

Time's Golden Rule:
The Classic Rolex Day-Date

Forged by six decades of watchmaking integrity, and carved from a solid block of 18kt. gold, today's handcrafted Rolex Day-Date blends tradition with uncompromising technology. Elegant, impregnable, this self-winding superlative chronometer is pressure-proof down to 165 feet in its seamless Oyster case. Its matching President bracelet with classic, satin finish clasp may be engraved with your own initials to subtly stress a personal commitment to quality.

This watch retails for over $2,000. Reprinted by permission.

Rolex uses skimming prices for its watches, which are sold at prices ranging from several hundred to several thousand dollars. They appeal to status-conscious and upper-income consumers. Figure 15-3 shows a typical watch from the Rolex line.

A common strategy is first to employ a skimming price and then to apply penetration pricing. There are several advantages to this strategy. One, a high price is charged when competition is limited. Two, a high price helps defray research and development and introductory advertising costs. Three, the first group of customers to purchase a new product is usually less sensitive to price than later groups. Four, a high initial price portrays a high-quality image for a product. Five, raising an initial price often encounters market resistance; lowering a price is viewed favorably. Six, after the initial market segment is saturated, penetration pricing can be used to appeal to the mass market and expand total sales volume.

Following are several examples of companies beginning with a skimming price and then switching to a penetration price in order to increase sales volume and respond to competition:

- RCA originally priced SelectaVision, its Videodisc player, at $499. It soon reduced the price to $299 to expand the size of its market.[4]
- Xerox usually introduces new photocopiers at relatively high prices and later lowers them to meet competition. Its model 3109 was first priced at $7,495. Eventually the price dropped to $4,175.[5]
- Nimslo Corp. introduced a 3-D camera in 1982 and priced it at $200. In order to improve sluggish sales and appeal to more price-conscious consumers, Nimslo cut the price in half during early 1983.[6]
- U.S. auto dealers generally set high prices at the beginning of the new selling year and reduce these prices at the end of the selling season to attract price-sensitive consumers.

Status Quo-Based Objectives

Status quo-based objectives **seek stability and favorable business conditions.**

Status quo-based objectives are sought by a firm interested in stability or in continuing a favorable climate for its operations. Pricing strategy is oriented toward avoiding declines in sales and minimizing the impact of such outside parties as government, competitors, and channel members.

It should not be inferred that status quo objectives require no effort on the part of the firm. For example, a manufacturer would instruct salespeople not to offer different terms to competing retailers, or else the government may accuse the company of a Robinson-Patman Act violation. In order to retain customers, a wholesaler may have to match the price cuts of its competitors. To maintain channel cooperation, a manufacturer may have to lower its markup in the face of rising costs. A retailer may have to charge low prices to discourage competitors from stocking certain product lines.

Broad Price Policy

A ***broad price policy*** **links prices with the target market, company image, and other marketing elements.**

A ***broad price policy*** coordinates pricing decisions with the firm's target market, image, and marketing mix. It generates a coordinated series of actions, a consistent image, and a strategy that incorporates short- and long-term goals.

The company outlines its broad price policy by placing individual price decisions into an integrated framework. For example, the firm would decide on the interrelationship of prices for goods within a product line, how often special discounts are used, how prices compare to

Table 15-1 **Broad Price Policies for Price- and Nonprice-Oriented Manufacturers**

Price Oriented	*Nonprice Oriented*

1. Target market
  a. Discount seekers
  b. Economy seekers
  c. Price very important
	1. Target market
	  a. Status seekers
	  b. Quality seekers
	  c. Price not important

2. Image
  a. No frills
  b. Low (discount)
  c. Price cutter
	2. Image
	  a. Elaborate
	  b. Prestige
	  c. High prices

3. Marketing mix
  a. Prices 10–15% below competitors
  b. All competitive prices met
  c. Volume sales encouraged by low prices on key items
  d. Frequent sales
  e. Distribution through discount and other high-volume stores
  f. Promotional emphasis on low prices and self-service
  g. Products concentrated on best-sellers
	3. Marketing mix
	  a. Prices 10–15% above competitors
	  b. Competitive prices met if firms involved have similar markets and images
	  c. Substantial gross profit margins on all items
	  d. Sales limited to end-of-season clearances and close-outs
	  e. Distribution through prestige retailers
	  f. Promotional emphasis on style, quality, service, and personal interest in consumers
	  g. Full-product line

competition, the frequency of price changes, and the method for setting the prices of new products.

Table 15-1 contains illustrations of two broad price policies, one for a price-oriented manufacturer and the other for a nonprice-oriented firm.

Price Strategy

A price strategy may be cost-based, demand-based, or competition-based. Overall, competitive pricing is used by more than half of firms, cost-based policies by more than 25 per cent, and demand-based methods by about 15 per cent. Pricing according to government rules and regulations accounts for the balance of the firms.[7]

Competitive pricing is used by the majority of firms.

Cost-Based Pricing

With **cost-based pricing,** the marketer determines prices by computing merchandise, service, and overhead costs and then adding an amount to cover the firm's profit goal. Table 15-2 defines the key concepts in costs and how they may be applied to bicycles.

Cost-based prices are relatively easy to implement, because there is no need to estimate elasticity of demand or competitive reactions to price changes. There is also more certainty about costs than demand or competitor responses to prices. Finally, cost pricing seeks to attain reasonable profits, because it is geared to covering all types of costs.

Cost-based pricing does have some significant limitations. It does

Cost-based pricing is simple to use, based on relative certainty, and tied to a reasonable profit. However, it does not consider market conditions, plant capacity, competitors, and other factors.

Table 15-2 **Key Cost Concepts and How They May Be Applied to Bicycles**

Cost Concept	Definition	Examples	Sources of Information	Method of Computation
Total fixed costs	Ongoing costs that are unrelated to volume. These costs are generally constant over a given range of output within a specified period of time.	Rent, administrative salaries, electricity, real-estate taxes, plant, and equipment.	Accounting data, bills, cost estimates.	Addition of all fixed cost components.
Total variable costs	Costs that change with increases or decreases in output (volume).	Bicycle parts (such as gears, frames, wheels, brakes, tires), hourly employees who assemble bicycles, and sales commissions.	Cost data from suppliers, estimates of labor productivity, sales estimates.	Addition of all variable cost components.
Total costs	Sum of total fixed and total variable costs.	See above.	See above.	Addition of all fixed and variable cost components.
Average fixed costs	Average fixed costs per unit.	See above under total fixed costs.	Total fixed costs and sales estimates.	Total fixed costs/ quantity produced in units.
Average variable costs	Average variable costs per unit.	See above under total variable costs.	Total variable costs and sales estimates.	Total variable costs/ quantity produced in units.
Average total costs	Sum of average fixed costs and average variable costs.	See above under total fixed and total variable costs.	Total costs and sales estimates.	Average fixed costs + average variable costs *or* Total costs/quantity produced in units.
Marginal costs	Costs of producing an additional unit.	See above under total fixed and total variable costs.	Accounting data, bills, cost estimates of labor and materials.	Total costs of producing increased quantity − total costs of producing current quantity.

not consider market conditions, the existence of excess plant capacity, competitive prices, the product's phase in its life cycle, market share goals, consumers' ability to pay, and other factors.[8] For example, U.S. Steel passes cost increases on to consumers no matter how large the increases are. According to an outside marketing expert, U.S. Steel "kept prices high enough to allow 10 to 12 smaller companies to take a substantial share of the market."[9] From 1910 to the mid-1950s, U.S. Steel's market share dropped from 48 to 34 per cent. By the late 1970s, it had fallen to 23 per cent.

In some situations it is difficult to calculate the overhead costs that should be attributed to individual products. When a company makes or sells a variety of products, it must determine how rent, lighting, personnel, and other general costs are allocated to each product. Overhead costs are often assigned on the basis of product sales or personnel time associated with each item. For instance, if product A accounts for 10 per cent of company sales, it might be allocated 10 per cent of overhead costs. If product A receives 20 per cent of personnel time, it might be allocated 20 per cent of overhead costs.

In the following subsections, four cost-based pricing techniques are discussed in detail: cost-plus, markup, target, and traditional break-even. At the end of these subsections, Table 15-3 shows an illustration of each technique.

With **cost-plus pricing,** prices are determined by adding a predetermined profit to costs. It is the simplest form of cost-based pricing.

In general the steps for computing cost-plus pricing are to estimate the number of units to be produced, calculate fixed and variable costs, and add a predetermined profit to costs. The formula for cost-plus pricing is

Cost-Plus Pricing

Cost-plus pricing is the easiest form of pricing, based on units produced, total costs, and profit.

$$\text{Price} = \frac{\text{Total fixed costs} + \text{Total variable costs} + \text{Projected profit}}{\text{Units produced}}.$$

Although the cost-plus method is easy to compute, it has several shortcomings. Profit is not expressed as a per cent of sales but as a per cent of cost, and price is not tied to consumer demand. Adjustments for rising costs are poorly conceived, and there are no plans for using excess capacity. There is little incentive for the firm to improve efficiency to hold down costs, and marginal costs are rarely analyzed.

Cost-plus pricing is most effective when price fluctuations have little influence on sales and when the manufacturer is able to control price. For example, the prices of custom-made furniture, airplanes, ships, heavy machinery, and extracted minerals depend on the costs that are necessary to produce these items. Manufacturers set prices by determining costs and adding a reasonable profit. In many instances, cost-plus pricing allows manufacturers to receive orders, produce items, and then derive prices after total costs are known. This protects sellers against cost increases during time-consuming production periods and where the prices of raw materials fluctuate widely.

In **markup pricing** the firm sets prices by calculating per unit merchandise costs and then determining the markup percentages that are needed to cover selling costs and profit. Markup pricing is most commonly used by wholesalers and retailers. The formula for markup pricing is

Markup Pricing

Markup pricing considers per unit merchandise costs and the markups required to cover selling costs and profits.

$$\text{Price} = \frac{\text{Merchandise costs}}{(100 - \text{Markup per cent})/100}.^{*}$$

*Markup can be calculated by transposing the above formula into

$$\text{Markup percentage (on selling price)} = \frac{\text{Selling price} - \text{Merchandise cost}}{\text{Selling price}} \times 100.$$

Markups are expressed in terms of selling price rather than cost.

There are several reasons why markups are usually expressed in terms of selling price instead of cost. First, expenses, markdowns, and profits are always computed as percentages of sales. When markups are per cents of sales they aid in profit planning. Second, manufacturers quote their selling prices and trade discounts to channel members as percentage reductions from retail list prices. Third, retail sales price information is more readily available than cost information. Fourth, profitability appears to be smaller if based on price rather than cost. This can be useful in avoiding criticism over high profits.

The size of a markup depends on traditional profit margins, retail expenses, manufacturers' suggested list prices, inventory turnover, competition, the extent to which products must be altered or otherwise serviced, and the effort needed to complete sales.

A *variable markup policy* responds to differences in selling costs among products by using distinct markups.

In order to respond to differences in selling costs among products, firms sometimes use a ***variable markup policy,*** whereby separate categories of goods and services receive different percentage markups. Variable markups recognize that some items require greater personal selling efforts, customer service, alterations, and end-of-season markdowns than others. For example, computer stores often have two price levels. A full-service price level offers consumers an analysis of their individual needs, computer installation, and training assistance. A "no-frills" price level provides no need analysis, installation, or training.

Markup pricing, while having many of the limitations of cost-plus pricing, remains very popular for wholesalers and retailers. It is fairly simple, especially for firms that use the same markup for a number of items. It offers channel members equitable profits. Price competition is reduced when retailers adhere to simlar markups. Channel members are able to compare their prices with manufacturers' suggested list prices. Price adjustments can be made when costs rise. Variable markups are responsive to selling cost differences among products or channel members.

Target Pricing

Target pricing sets prices that enable a rate of return on investment to be earned for a standard volume of production.

In ***target pricing,*** prices are set to provide a specified rate of return on investment for a standard volume of production, which is the level of production the firm plans for the year. For target pricing to operate properly, the company must sell its entire standard volume at specified prices.

Target pricing was introduced by General Motors in the 1920s and worked well for the company through the 1960s. Then during the 1970s, problems with target pricing began because costs rose rapidly, competition expanded and forced lower prices, and demand leveled off. General Motors saw inventories rise and was unable to sell its entire standard volume at the prices it set.

Target pricing is used by capital-intensive firms (such as auto makers) and public utilities (such as power and light companies). The prices charged by public utilities are based on fair rates of return on invested assets and must be approved by regulatory commissions.

Mathematically, target pricing is computed as

$$\text{Price} = \left(\frac{\text{Investment costs} \times \text{Target return on investment (\%)}}{\text{Standard volume}} + \left(\text{Average total costs (at standard volume)} \right) \right).$$

Target pricing has four major limitations. One, it is not useful for firms with low capital investments because it will undervalue selling price. Two, because prices are not keyed to demand, the entire standard volume may not be sold at the target price. Three, production problems may hamper output and the standard volume may not be attained. Four, price reductions to handle overstocked inventory are not planned under this approach. Therefore, inventory may be priced too high at peak production levels and too low at limited production levels.

Like target pricing, traditional break-even analysis examines the relationship among costs, revenues, and profits. While target pricing yields the price that results in a specified return on investment, ***traditional break-even analysis*** determines the sales quantity in units or dollars that is necessary for total revenues (price × units sold) to equal total costs (fixed and variable) at a given price. When sales exceed the break-even quantity, the firm earns a profit. When sales are less than the break-even quantity, the firm loses money. Traditional break-even analysis does not consider return on investment or the dollar value of investment. It can be extended to take profit planning into account, and it is used by all types of channel members.

The break-even point can be computed in terms of units or sales dollars:

Traditional Break-Even Analysis

Traditional break-even analysis describes the unit or dollar sales needed to break even at a specific price.

$$\text{Break-even point (units)} = \frac{\text{Total fixed costs}}{\text{Price} - \text{Variable costs (per unit)}}.$$

$$\text{Break-even point (sales dollars)} = \frac{\text{Total fixed costs}}{1 - \dfrac{\text{Variable costs (per unit)}}{\text{Price}}}.$$

These formulas are derived from the equation: Price × Quantity = Total fixed costs + (Variable costs per unit × Quantity).

There are some limitations to traditional break-even analysis. One, as with all forms of cost-based pricing, it does not consider demand. The assumption is that wide variations in quantity can be sold at the same price, and this is highly unlikely. Two, traditional break-even analysis assumes all costs can be divided into fixed and variable categories. Some costs, like advertising, are difficult to define as fixed or variable because they can be placed in either category, depending on the situation. Advertising can be fixed or a per cent of sales. Three, traditional break-even formulas presume that variable costs per unit are constant

Table 15-3

Examples of Cost-Based Pricing Techniques

Cost-Plus Pricing

A custom-sofa manufacturer has total fixed costs of $50,000, variable costs of $500 per sofa, desires $10,000 in profits, and plans to produce 100 couches. What is the selling price for each couch?

$$\text{Price} = \frac{\text{Total fixed costs} + \text{Total variable costs} + \text{Projected profit}}{\text{Units produced}}$$

$$= \frac{\$50,000 + \$500(100) + \$10,000}{100} = \underline{\underline{\$1,100}}$$

Markup Pricing

A retailer pays $30 for touch-tone telephones. The retailer wants a markup on selling price of 40 per cent (30 per cent for selling costs and 10 per cent for profit). What is the final selling price for each telephone?

$$\text{Price} = \frac{\text{Merchandise costs}}{(100 - \text{Markup per cent})/100} = \frac{\$30}{(100 - 40)/100} = \underline{\underline{\$50}}$$

Target Pricing

An auto company has just spent $80,000,000 for a new plant. It has a 20 per cent target return on investment. Standard production volume for the year is 5,000 units. Average total costs, excluding the new plant, are $4,000 for each car (at a production level of 5,000 cars). What is the selling price to the company's retail dealers?

$$\text{Price} = \left(\frac{\text{Investment costs} \times \text{Target return on investment (\%)}}{\text{Standard volume}} \right) +$$

$$\left(\text{Average total costs (at standard volume)} \right)$$

$$= \left(\frac{\$80,000,000 \times .20}{5,000} \right) + \$4,000 = \underline{\underline{\$7,200}}$$

Traditional Break-Even Analysis

A candy manufacturer has total fixed costs of $100,000 and variable costs per unit of $.10. The firm sells its candy for $.15 per bar. What is the break-even point in units? In sales dollars?

$$\frac{\text{Break-even point}}{\text{(units)}} = \frac{\text{Total fixed costs}}{\text{Price} - \text{Variable costs (per unit)}}$$

$$= \frac{\$100,000}{\$.15 - \$.10} = \underline{\underline{2,000,000}}$$

$$\frac{\text{Break-even point}}{\text{(sales dollars)}} = \frac{\text{Total fixed costs}}{1 - \dfrac{\text{Variable costs (per unit)}}{\text{Price}}}$$

$$= \frac{\$100,000}{1 - \dfrac{\$.10}{\$.15}} = \underline{\underline{\$300,000}}$$

over a range of quantities. However, quantity and shipping discounts or overtime wages may alter these costs. Fourth, it is assumed that fixed costs remain constant. Yet, increases in production may lead to higher costs for lighting, salaried employees, and other items.

By including demand considerations, each of the cost-based techniques can be improved. Demand-based pricing techniques are discussed next.

Demand-Based Pricing

With **demand-based pricing,** the firm first finds out the prices final consumers and channel members will pay for products and services, then calculates the markups it will need to cover selling expenses and profits, and finally, determines the maximum it can spend producing its offering. In this way, both prices and costs are linked to consumer preferences and channel needs, and a specific product image is sought.

Demand-based techniques require consumer research regarding the quantities that will be purchased at various prices, the elasticity of demand (sensitivity to price changes), the existence of market segments, and consumers' ability to pay for products or services. It must be realized that demand estimations are usually less precise and more subject to change than cost estimations. In addition, firms that do inadequate research on costs and rely on demand-oriented data may end up losing money, because they make unrealistically low assumptions about costs.

With demand-based pricing, highly competitive situations result in small markups and low prices because consumers are willing to purchase substitutes. In these cases it is necessary for costs to be held down or else prices will be too high. For example, if a firm desires a 50 per cent markup on selling price and it knows from research that consumers will pay $10 for an item, the costs of producing the item must be $5 or less. At a lower cost, the firm will be satisfied; markup will be greater than 50 per cent. Costs above $5 are not satisfactory because customers will not accept a price above $10 and markup will be less than 50 per cent. In the latter situation the firm would either switch to a more profitable item, substitute cheaper materials to reduce costs, or decide to tolerate lower per cent profits.

Noncompetitive situations allow firms to achieve large markups and high prices because demand is relatively inelastic. Companies would place little emphasis on costs when setting prices in these situations. For example, a firm that knows consumers will pay $20 for an item costing $7 will achieve a 65 per cent markup on selling price and receive a large profit per unit. With cost-based pricing, the firm would be likely to set prices that are too low in noncompetitive markets.

In the following subsections, four demand-based pricing techniques are examined: demand-minus, chain-markup, modified breakeven, and price discrimination. At the end of these subsections, Table 15-4 contains an illustration of each technique.

In **demand-minus (demand-backward) pricing,** the firm ascertains the appropriate final selling price and works backward to compute costs. This approach stipulates that price decisions revolve around consumer

Under *demand-based pricing,* prices are linked to consumer desires, channel needs, and product image.

Demand-Minus Pricing

In *demand-minus pricing,* final selling price, then markup, and finally maximum merchandise costs are computed.

demand rather than internal company operations. It is used by companies that sell directly to consumers.

Demand-minus pricing is comprised of three steps. One, final selling price is determined through consumer surveys or other research techniques. Two, the markup percentage is derived from selling expenses and desired profits. Three, maximum acceptable merchandise costs are computed.

The formula used in demand-minus pricing is

Maximum merchandise costs = Price × [(100 − Markup per cent)/100].

As noted, this formula shows that costs are calculated after selling price and markup are set.

The difficulty in demand-minus pricing is that market research may be time consuming or complex, particularly if many items are involved. Also, new-product pricing research may be particularly inaccurate.

Chain-Markup Pricing

Chain-markup pricing traces demand-minus calculations from the retailer to the manufacturer.

Chain-markup pricing extends demand-minus calculations from the retailer all the way back to the manufacturer. With chain-markup pricing, final selling price is determined, markups for each channel member are examined, and the maximum acceptable costs to each member are computed. It is used when there are independent channel members.

In a traditional channel, the chain is composed of

1. Maximum selling price to retailer = Final selling price × [(100 − Retailer's markup)/100].

2. Maximum selling price to wholesaler = Selling price to retailer × [(100 − Wholesaler's markup)/100].

3. Maximum merchandise costs to manufacturer = Selling price to wholesaler × [(100 − Manufacturer's markup)/100].

Through chain-markup pricing, price decisions are related to consumer demand and each channel member is able to see the effects of price changes on the total system. The interdependence of members becomes clear; channel members cannot set prices independently of one another.

Modified Break-Even Analysis

Combining traditional break-even analysis with demand evaluation at various prices is *modified break-even analysis.*

Modified break-even analysis combines traditional break-even analysis with an evaluation of demand at various levels of price. Traditional analysis focuses on the sales needed to break even at a given price. It does not indicate the likely level of demand at that price, examine how demand responds to different levels of price, consider that the break-even point can vary greatly depending on the price the firm happens to select, or calculate the price that maximizes profits.

Whereas traditional analysis defines the sales needed to break even at a specific price, modified analysis reveals the price-quantity mix that maximizes profits. It demonstrates that profits do not necessarily rise as quantity sold increases, because lower prices are needed to increase demand. It also verifies that a firm should examine various levels of price and select the one that maximizes profits. Finally, it relates demand to price, rather than assuming that the same volume could be sold at any price.

Price discrimination enables a firm to set two or more distinct prices for a product or service in order to appeal to different final consumer or organizational consumer market segments. With price discrimination, higher prices are established for inelastic consumer segments and lower prices for elastic segments. Price discrimination can be customer-based, product-based, time-based, or place-based.

In customer-based price discrimination, prices differ by customer category for the same product or service. Price differentials may relate to a consumer's ability to pay (physicians, lawyers, and accountants partially set prices in this manner), negotiating ability (the final price of a new or used car is usually established by bargaining), or buying power (discounts are given for large purchases).

Under product-based price discrimination, the firm offers a number of features, styles, qualities, brands, or sizes of a product or service and sets a different price for each one. Price differentials are greater than cost differentials for the various product or service versions. For example, one type of haircut may be priced at $7 and take 20 minutes to complete (35 cents per minute); another may be priced at $12 and take 30 minutes to complete (40 cents per minute). A dishwasher may be priced at $300 in white and $320 in brown, although the brown color costs the manufacturer only $3 more. In both situations there is inelastic demand by customers desiring special features or services, and the product or service versions are priced accordingly.

With time-based price discrimination, the company varies prices by day versus evening (movie theater tickets), time of day (telephone and utility rates), or season (hotel rates). Consumers that insist on prime time use of a product or service pay higher prices than those who are willing to make their purchases during nonpeak times.

In place-based price discrimination, prices differ by seat location (sports and entertainment events), floor location (office buildings, hotels), or geographic location (resort cities). The demand for locations near the stage, elevators, or warm climates drives the prices of these locations up. General admission tickets, basement offices, and moderate-temperature resorts are priced lower in order to attract consumers to make otherwise less desirable purchases.

Price discrimination methods can be combined. For example, automobile prices are frequently different on the West Coast from those on the East Coast. Profit margins on accessory equipment are generally greater than on basic car prices. Different body styles (two-door, hatchback, station wagon) have different profit margins. Also, final prices are agreed on after bargaining between buyers and sellers.

Before employing price discrimination, the marketer should consider these points. Are there distinct market segments? Do consumers

---

Price Discrimination

Setting distinct prices for a product or service to reach different market segments is *price discrimination.*

Table 15-4   *Demand-Minus Pricing*

Examples of Demand-Based Pricing Techniques

An encyclopedia publisher has conducted consumer research and found that people are willing to spend $800.00 for a complete set of its brand. The firm's selling expenses and profits are expected to be 30 per cent of the selling price. What is the maximum amount the company can spend to produce each set of encyclopedias?

$$\text{Maximum merchandise costs} = \text{Price} \times [(100 - \text{Markup per cent})/100]$$
$$= \$800.00 \times [(100 - 30)/100] = \underline{\underline{\$560.00}}$$

Chain-Markup Pricing

A ladies' shoe manufacturer has determined that consumers will pay $50.00 for a pair of its shoes. The company sells through a channel of wholesalers and retailers. Each requires a markup of 30 per cent; the manufacturer requires a 25 per cent markup. (a) What is the maximum price that retailers and wholesalers will spend for a pair of shoes? (b) What is the maximum amount the manufacturer can spend to make each pair of shoes?

(a)
$$\text{Maximum selling price to retailer} = \text{Final selling price} \times [(100 - \text{Retailer's markup})/100]$$
$$= \$50.00 \times [(100 - 30)/100]$$
$$= \underline{\underline{\$35.00}}$$

$$\text{Maximum selling price to wholesaler} = \text{Selling price to retailer} \times [(100 - \text{Wholesaler's markup})/100]$$
$$= \$35.00 \times [(100 - 30)/100]$$
$$= \underline{\underline{\$21.45}}$$

(b)
$$\text{Maximum merchandise costs to manufacturer} = \text{Selling price to wholesaler} \times [(100 - \text{Manufacturer's markup})/100]$$
$$= \$21.45 \times [(100 - 25)/100]$$
$$= \underline{\underline{\$16.09}}$$

Modified Break-Even Analysis

An aspirin manufacturer has total fixed costs of $2,000,000 and variable costs of $.50 per bottle. Its research shows the following demand schedule: $2.50 price—1,200,000 units would be purchased; $2.00—2,000,000 units would be purchased; $1.50—3,200,000 units would be purchased; $1.00—5,000,000 units would be purchased; $ .50—10,000,000 units would be purchased. At what price should the company sell its aspirin?

Selling Price	Quantity Demanded	Total Revenue	Total Cost	Total Profit (Loss)	
$2.50	1,200,000	$3,000,000	$2,600,000	$ 400,000	
2.00	2,000,000	4,000,000	3,000,000	1,000,000	
1.50	3,200,000	4,800,000	3,600,000	1,200,000	← Maximum
1.00	5,000,000	5,000,000	4,500,000	500,000	profit
.50	10,000,000	5,000,000	7,000,000	(2,000,000)	at price of $1.50

A book publisher estimates that it can sell 100,000 copies of a hardcover novel at $12.95, if it does not release the book in paperback at a later date. The firm also estimates that it can sell 50,000 copies of the hardcover novel at $12.95, if it later releases the book in paperback. The paperback version would sell 200,000 copies at $3.95. It costs $8.25 to manufacture and market the hardcover book, and $2.50 for the paperback. Will the firm benefit from a price-discrimination strategy?

Examples of Demand-Based Pricing Techniques (contd.)

Hardcover only:

Total revenues	$1,295,000
Total costs	− 825,000
Total profit	$ 470,000

Hardcover and paperback:

Hardcover revenues	$ 647,500
Hardcover costs	− 412,500
Hardcover profit	$ 235,000

+

Paperback revenues	$790,000
Paperback costs	− 500,000
Paperback profit	$290,000
Total profit	$525,000

Additional profit from sale of both hard cover and paperback: $55,000

---

communicate with each other about product features and prices? Can product versions be differentiated? Will some consumers choose low-priced models when they might otherwise buy high-priced models if they are the only ones available? How do marginal costs of creating additional product alternatives compare with marginal revenues? Will channel members stock all models? How difficult is it to explain product differences to consumers? Under what conditions is price discrimination legal (the firm would not want to violate the Robinson-Patman Act)?

Competition-Based Pricing

In ***competition-based pricing,*** the firm uses competitors' prices rather than demand or cost considerations as its primary guideposts. With this approach, the company may not respond to changes in demand or costs unless they have an effect on competitors' prices. A company may set prices below the market, at the market, or above the market, depending on its customers, image, overall marketing mix, consumer loyalty, and other factors.

Setting prices on the basis of competition is competition-based pricing.

Competition-based pricing is popular for several reasons. It is simple, with no calculations of demand curves, price elasticity, or costs per unit. The ongoing market price level is assumed to be fair for both consumers and companies. Pricing at the market level does not disrupt competition and, therefore, does not lead to retaliations. However, it may lead to complacency.

Two aspects of competition-based pricing are discussed in the following subsections: price leadership and competitive bidding.

Price Leadership

In price leadership, some firms initiate price changes in an industry; they are effective when other firms follow.

Before assuming *price leadership,* a firm must determine whether it has the interests and the ability to be an initiator of price changes (leader) or a reactor to other firms' changes (follower). Price leaders are firms that have significant market shares, well-established positions, respect from competitors, and the desire to implement price changes. Price followers are those who are conservative or indecisive, as well as those who are small or have limited market shares.

Price leaders are usually the dominant firms in their respective industries, such as IBM and General Motors. Competitors often follow the pricing strategies of these firms. This eliminates severe price competition and the possibility of price wars. In addition, the threat of predatory pricing (the setting of low prices, often below cost, to drive out competitors) is reduced.

During the past several years, the role of the price leader has been substantially reduced in many industries, including steel, chemical, and glass container. For example, when Owens-Illinois (larger than its next five competitors combined) raised list prices by 4.5 per cent, its competitors offered huge discounts on glass bottles. The smaller firms feared the higher prices would hurt sales to breweries that had just begun to switch to glass bottles. Said one glass company president, "In effect, the smaller companies become the price leaders in order to entice the brewers."[10] This action also showed that the smaller firms were after Owen-Illinois' market share.

Announcements of price changes must be communicated through independent media or company publicity releases. It is illegal for firms to confer with one another regarding price setting.

Competitive Bidding

Competitive bidding balances potential profits against the probability of winning a bid.

With *competitive bidding,* two or more companies independently submit prices for specific products, projects, and/or services. Generally, sealed bids are offered in response to precise government or other organizational consumer requests, and each seller has one chance to make its best offer.

Various mathematical models have been applied to competitive bidding. All of them utilize the expected profit concept, which states that as the bid price increases the profit to a firm increases but the probability of its winning the contract decreases. It is often difficult to measure the probability of getting a contract (or underbidding all other qualified competitors).

Combining Techniques

It is beneficial for companies to combine cost, demand, and competitive pricing techniques.

Although cost-, demand-, and competition-based pricing techniques have been discussed separately throughout this chapter, in practice the three approaches are often combined. The cost method sets a price floor and outlines the various costs incurred in doing business. It establishes profit margins, target prices, and/or break-even quantities. The demand approach determines the appropriate final price and the ceiling prices for each channel member. It develops the price-quantity mix that maximizes profits and allows a firm to reach different market segments. The competition approach examines the appropriate price level for the firm in relation to competitors.

Unless the techniques are combined, critical decisions are likely to be overlooked. The following group of questions demonstrates the interrelation of cost-, demand-, and competition-based methods of deriving prices:

1. Will a given price level allow us to attain the desired profit? (Cost-based)
2. If we sell in quantity, will there be cost savings that can be passed on to customers? (Cost-based)
3. If we increase prices by 10 per cent, how much will unit sales decrease? (Demand-based)
4. Should we conduct off-season sales to attract customers? (Demand-based)
5. If we give quantity discounts, will competitors do nothing, match prices, or beat the prices? (Competition-based)
6. Should we change prices before or after competitors? (Competition-based)

This group of questions is not complete, but it should give some idea of how a marketer integrates demand, cost, and competitive orientations to pricing.

Implementating Price Strategy

Implementating a price strategy involves a wide variety of separate but interlocking specific concepts in addition to the broad issues discussed previously. In the following subsections, these concepts are described in detail. See Figure 15-4.

Customary and Variable Pricing

Customary pricing occurs when a channel member sets product or service prices and seeks to maintain them over an extended period of time. Prices are not changed during this time period.

With customary pricing, the same price is kept for a long time.

Customary pricing is used for items like candy, gum, magazines, restaurant food, and mass transit. Instead of modifying prices to reflect cost increases, organizations reduce package size, change ingredients, or "impose a stricter transfer policy among bus lines." The assumption is that consumers prefer one of these modifications over a price hike.

Between 1971 and 1982, Wrigley raised the price of its chewing gum only three times, from 10 to 15 cents, from 15 to 20 cents, and from 20 to 25 cents, despite steadily higher costs for sugar, gum base, and wrapping material. In order to minimize consumer resistance to the first

Customary Pricing

PRICE MAINTAINED
OVER TIME

Variable Pricing

PRICES RESPOND TO
COSTS AND DEMAND

One-Price Policy

ALL BLOUSES
$12.95

ONE PRICE FOR ALL
CUSTOMERS

Flexible Pricing

SPECIAL SALE
MAKE US AN
OFFER

PRICES DEPEND
ON CUSTOMER
BARGAINING

Odd Pricing

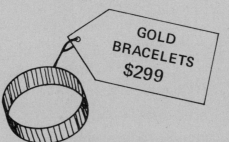

GOLD
BRACELETS
$299

PRICING BELOW
EVEN DOLLAR
VALUES

Prestige Pricing

SHOP THE BEST!
OUR PRODUCTS ARE
BETTER, SO OUR
PRICES ARE HIGHER

APPEALING TO QUALITY

Leader Pricing

Kodak film, no
one beats our
prices!

LOW PRICES
TO ATTRACT
CUSTOMER TRAFFIC

Multiple-Unit Pricing

CAMPELL'S SOUP—
3 FOR $1.89

PRICE DISCOUNTS
GIVEN FOR
QUANTITY PURCHASES

Price Lining

RUNNING
SHOES—
$12.95,
$22.95,
$35.95

DISTINCT PRICE
POINTS SET
WITHIN A SPECIFIC
RANGE

Figure 15-4
Selected Pricing Strategies

increase from 10 to 15 cents, Wrigley changed the package size from five- to seven-stick packs. Wrigley could have raised prices without changing package size and incurring the expense of modifying its wrapping machine, but it was concerned with consumer perceptions about value.

With *variable pricing,* the firm intentionally alters prices to respond to cost fluctuations or differences in consumer demand. When costs fluctuate, prices are lowered or raised to reflect the changes; cost fluctuations are not absorbed and product quality is not modified in order to maintain customary prices. Through price discrimination, a company offers distinct prices to appeal to different market segments, as noted previously. In this case, the prices charged to various consumers are not based on costs. Most firms use some form of variable pricing.

> Under *variable pricing,* prices reflect cost changes or differences in demand.

It is possible to combine customary and variable pricing. For example, a magazine may be priced at $2 per single copy and be available for $20 per year's subscription ($1.67 an issue). Under this strategy two customary prices are charged, and the consumer selects the offer that he or she finds most attractive.

One-Price Policy and Flexible Pricing

With a *one-price policy* a firm charges the same price to all customers who seek to purchase a product or service under similar conditions. Price may vary according to quantity purchased, time of purchase, and services obtained (such as delivery, installation, and an extended guarantee); but all consumers are given the opportunity to pay the same price for an identical combination of product and service. A one-price policy builds consumer confidence, is easy to administer, eliminates bargaining, and permits self-service and catalog sales.

> A firm charges the same price to all customers buying the same product or service under a *one-price policy.*

The one-price policy was begun by John Wanamaker, who was the first retailer to mark prices clearly on each item in stock. Throughout the United States, one-price policies are the rule for most retailers. In industrial marketing, a firm with a one-price policy does not permit its sales personnel to deviate from a published price list.

Flexible pricing allows the company to adjust prices based on the consumer's ability to negotiate or on the buying power of a large customer. Consumers who are knowledgeable or who are good bargainers pay lower prices than those who are not knowledgeable or are poorer bargainers. Jewelry stores, automobile dealers, flea markets, real estate brokers, and antique shops frequently use flexible pricing. In some cases, commissions are paid to sales personnel on the basis of the profitability of each order. This encourages sales personnel to solicit higher prices. Flexible prices to channel members based on their buying power are subject to the Robinson-Patman restrictions explained in Chapter 14.

> With *flexible pricing,* different customers may pay different prices for the same product or service.

Odd Pricing

An *odd-pricing strategy* is used when final selling prices are set at levels below even dollar values, such as 49 cents, $4.95, and $199. Odd pricing has proven popular for several reasons. Consumers like receiving change. And because the cashier must make change, employers ensure that transactions are properly recorded and receipts are

> In an *odd-pricing strategy,* prices are set below even dollar values.

placed in the cash register. Consumers gain the impression that the firm thinks carefully about its prices and sets them as low as possible. Consumers may also believe that odd prices represent price reductions; a price of $8.95 may be viewed as a discount from $10.[11]

Odd prices that are one or two cents below the next even price (29 cents, $2.98) are common up to $4. Beyond that point and up to $50, five-cent reductions from the highest even price ($19.95, $49.95) are more usual. For expensive items, odd endings are typically in dollars ($499, $5995).

Odd prices encourage consumers to stay within their price limits and still buy the best items available. A shopper willing to spend "less than $10" for a tie will be attracted to a $9.95 tie and be as likely to purchase it as a tie selling for $9, because it is within the defined price range. The imposition of sales tax in most states has the effect of raising odd prices into higher dollar levels and may reduce the effectiveness of odd pricing as a selling tool.

Price-Quality Association

The *price-quality association* indicates that consumers often believe there is a relationship between price and quality.

The ***price-quality association*** is a concept stating that consumers may believe high prices mean high quality and low prices mean low quality. In setting prices, the price-quality association is particularly important for situations where quality is difficult for consumers to judge on bases other than price, buyers perceive large differences in quality among brands, buyers have little experience or confidence in judging quality (as in the case of a new product), high prices exclude the mass market, brand names are unknown, or brand names require certain price levels to sustain their images. It is essential that prices properly reflect the quality and image the company seeks for its offerings.

***Prestige pricing* indicates that consumers may not buy a product when its price is too low.**

With ***prestige pricing,*** a theory drawn from the price-quality association, it is assumed that consumers do not buy products or services at prices considered too low. Consumers set price floors and will not make purchases at prices below those floors. They feel quality and status are inferior at extremely low prices. Consumers also set upper limits for prices they consider acceptable for particular products or services. Above the price ceilings, the items are perceived as too expensive. For each product or service, the firm must set its price within the acceptable range between the floor and ceiling.

In *psychological pricing,* certain prices are most effective.

When consumers are perceptually sensitive to certain prices and departures from these prices in either direction result in decreases in demand, they are responding to ***psychological pricing.*** Customary, odd, and prestige pricing are all forms of psychological pricing.

Leader Pricing

Selling key items at lower than usual prices to attract customers is *leader pricing.*

Under ***leader pricing,*** a firm advertises and sells key items in its product assortment at less than their usual profit margins. For a retailer the objective of leader pricing is to increase customer traffic into a store. For a manufacturer the objective is to gain greater consumer interest in its overall product line. In both cases it is hoped that consumers will purchase regularly priced merchandise in addition to the specially priced items that draw them to the store or manufacturer's display.

Leader pricing is most often used with nationally branded, high-turnover, frequently purchased products. For example, in drugstores, the best-selling items in terms of dollar sales are Kodak and Polaroid film. In order to stimulate customer traffic into their stores, druggists price film at very low markups; in some cases, it is sold at close to cost. According to a vice-president at Peoples, a $440 million drugstore chain with 500 stores in 13 states:

> We sell it at less than a 20 per cent markup and near 5 per cent or cost when it is on sale. Our position is that we offer some kind of photo-related item—film, flash bulbs, and so forth—every week in our ads.[12]

Film is a good item for leader pricing because consumers are able to detect low prices and they are attracted into a store by a discount on the item, which regularly sells for several dollars.

There are two kinds of leader pricing: loss leaders and prices higher than cost but lower than regular prices. As described in Chapter 14, the use of loss leaders is illegal in a number of states.

Multiple-Unit Pricing

Multiple-unit pricing is a practice whereby a company offers consumers discounts for buying in quantity in order to increase its sales volume. For example, by offering items at two for 99 cents or six for $1.39, the firm attempts to sell more units than at 50 cents or 25 cents each.

There are four major reasons for using multiple-unit pricing. First, customers may increase their immediate purchases if they believe a bargain is achieved through a multiple-unit purchase. Second, customers may increase their overall consumption if they make quantity purchases. For instance, the multiple-unit pricing of soda may encourage greater consumption. Third, competitors' customers may be attracted by the firm's discounts. Fourth, the firm may be able to clear out slow-moving and end-of-season merchandise.

Multiple-unit pricing will not achieve its goals if consumers merely shift their purchases and do not increase consumption of a company's brand. For example, multiple-unit pricing for Heinz catsup will probably not result in consumers using more catsup with their meals. It will not raise total dollar sales and will cause consumers to buy catsup less frequently because it will be stored. Short-run sales will be good, but long-run sales will not increase.

With multiple-unit pricing, quantity discounts are intended to result in higher overall sales volume.

Price Lining

Price lining involves selling merchandise at a range of prices, with each price representing a distinct level of quality. Instead of setting one price for a single model of a product, the firm sells two or more models (at different quality levels) at different prices. Price lining involves two decisions: defining the price range of the firm's offerings (floor and ceiling) and establishing specific price points within the price range.

Price lining establishes a range of selling prices and price points within that range.

The price range may be defined as low, intermediate, or high. For example, inexpensive radios may be priced from $8 to $20, moderately priced radios from $22 to $50, and expensive radios from $55 to $120.

After the range is determined, a limited number of price points is set within it. These prices must be distinct and not too close together. Inexpensive radios could be priced at $8, $12, and $20. They would not be priced at $8, $9, $10, $11, $12, $13, $14, $15, $16, $17, $18, $19, and $20. This would confuse consumers and be inefficient for the firm.

When developing a price line, the marketer must consider the following factors. One, price points must be spaced far enough apart so that customers perceive quality differences among models, otherwise consumers will view the price floor as the price they should pay and believe that there is no difference among models. Two, price points should be spaced farther apart at higher prices, because consumer demand becomes more inelastic. Three, the relationships of price points must be maintained when costs rise, so that clear differences are retained. For example, if radio costs rise 25 per cent, prices should be $10, $15, and $25.

Price lining benefits both channel members and consumers. Channel members are able to offer an assortment of products, attract market segments, trade up consumers within a price range, control inventory by price point, exclude competitors from the channel by offering models throughout the price range, and increase overall sales volume. Consumers are given an assortment from which to choose, confusion is minimized, comparisons may be made, and quality alternatives are available within the desired price range.

Geographic Pricing

Geographic pricing assigns transportation costs.

Geographic pricing outlines the responsibility for transportation charges. Generally, geographic pricing is not negotiated but depends on the traditional practices in the industry in which the firm operates. All firms in an industry normally conform to the same geographic pricing format. Table 15-5 describes the basic methods of geographic pricing.

Terms

Terms outline all pricing provisions.

Discounts are reductions from final price for performing functions, paying in cash, quantity buying, and off-season purchases.

Terms are the provisions of price agreements, including discounts, timing of payments, and credit arrangements.

Discounts are reductions from final selling price that are available to channel members and final consumers for performing certain functions, paying in cash, buying large quantities, purchasing in off-seasons, or enhancing promotions. For example, a wholesaler could purchase goods at 40 per cent off the manufacturer's suggested list price. This would cover the wholesaler's selling expenses, profit, and discount to the retailer. The retailer could purchase goods for 25 per cent off list (the wholesaler would retain 15 per cent for costs and profit).

The total discounts a firm offers its customers are typically quoted in the form of a chain. Cash, quantity, seasonal, and promotional discounts are deducted after the functional or trade discount has been de-

Method	Characteristics	Table 15-5
FOB mill or factory pricing	The buyer selects the transportation form and pays all freight charges. The seller pays the costs of loading the goods (hence, "free on board") and nets the same amount regardless of the buyer's location. The delivered price to the buyer depends on freight charges.	**Methods of Geographic Pricing**
Uniform delivered pricing	All buyers pay the same delivered price for the same quantity of goods, regardless of their location. The seller pays for shipping and receives varying net prices on each sale, based on its distribution costs. This method is used when transit costs are a small part of total manufacturing costs. It aids in maintaining customary prices and allows uniform prices to be advertised.	
Zone pricing	All buyers within a geographic zone pay a uniform delivered price. In a single-zone system, any buyer within the seller's entire market area is charged the same price. In a multiple-zone system, delivered prices vary by zone. Freight charges are the average costs within a zone area. The manufacturer determines the mode of transportation and pays costs.	
Base-point pricing	The firms in an industry establish basing points from which the costs of shipping are computed. The basing points are usually the areas of greatest production. The delivered price to a buyer reflects the cost of transporting goods from the basing point nearest to the buyer, regardless of the actual site of supply. Only multiple base-point pricing is now legal, because it minimizes freight charges for shipping not actually provided by placing basing points nearer to buyers.	

termined. Transportation costs are not discounted; they are added to the final price to the channel member or consumer.

Table 15-6 shows the calculation of a series of channel discounts using the chain method of discounting. The individual discounts in this table are 40, 10, 2, 5, and 5 per cent. However, the discounts do not total 62 per cent. They total 52.2 per cent, because the discounts are computed upon successive balances. For example, the 10 per cent quantity discount is computed on $165, which is the selling price after the functional discount is deducted.

Channel members are quite interested in the timing of payments and negotiate for the best terms. For example, terms of net 30 mean that goods do not have to be paid for until thirty days after receipt. At that point, they must be paid for in full. Terms of 2/10, net 30 mean that a buyer receives a 2 per cent discount if the full bill is paid within ten days after the end of the month in which an order is placed or pays the face value within thirty days after the end of the month. A wide variety of time terms is available.

Timing of payments is important.

A firm that allows credit purchases may use an open account or revolving credit. With an open account, the buyer receives a monthly bill for goods bought during the preceding month. The account must be paid in full each month. With a revolving account, the buyer agrees to make minimum payments during an extended period of time and pays interest on outstanding balances.

A firm can offer open and/or revolving credit accounts.

Table 15-6

Calculation of Discounts Using the Chain Method

Discounts Offered by Manufacturer (in %)	
Functional	40
Quantity	10
Cash	2
Seasonal	5
Promotional	5

Suggested Final Selling Price	$275.00

Shipping Charges	$ 15.30

Computation of Price Paid by Channel Member

List price	$275.00
Less functional discount ($275.00 × .40)	110.00
Balance	$165.00
Less quantity discount ($165.00 × .10)	16.50
Balance	$148.50
Less cash discount ($148.50 × .02)	2.97
Balance	$145.53
Less seasonal discount ($145.53 × .05)	7.28
Balance	$138.25
Less promotional discount ($138.25 × .05)	6.91
Balance after all discounts	$131.34
Plus shipping charges	15.30
Price to channel member	$146.64

Total of Discounts (275.00 − $131.34)	$143.66

Total Discount % ($143.66/$275)	52.2

Price Adjustments

When costs, competition, or demand changes, price strategy must be modified.

After a price strategy is implemented, it usually requires continuous fine tuning to reflect changes in costs, competitive conditions, and demand considerations. Prices can be adjusted through changes in list prices, escalator clauses and surcharges, added markups, markdowns, and rebates. It is important that price be used as an adaptive mechanism.

List prices, escalator clauses, surcharges, additional markups, markdowns, and rebates must be used properly.

List prices are the regularly quoted prices provided to customers. They are preprinted on price tags, in catalogs, and in dealer purchase orders. Modifications in list prices are necessary if there are sustained changes in labor costs, raw material costs, and market segments and as a product moves through its life cycle. Because these events are long term in nature, they enable customary prices to be revised, new catalogs to be printed, and adjustments to be completed in an orderly fashion.

In some cases, costs or economic conditions are so volatile that revised list prices cannot be printed or distributed efficiently. Then, escalator clauses or surcharges can be used. Each of these allows prices to be adjusted quickly. With an **escalator clause,** the firm is contract-

Figure 15-5
Markdowns to Clear Out Merchandise

Drawing by Ed Arno. © The New Yorker Magazine, Inc.

ually allowed to raise the price of an item to reflect higher costs in the item's essential ingredients without changing printed list prices. **Surcharges** are across-the-board published price increases that supplement list prices. These are frequently used with catalogs because of their simplicity; an insert is distributed with the catalog.

When list prices are not involved, **additional markups** can be used to raise regular retail prices because demand is unexpectedly high or costs are rising. There is a risk to additional markups. For example, supermarkets have received adverse publicity for relabeling low-cost existing inventories at higher prices so that they match those of newer merchandise purchased at higher costs.

Markdowns are reductions from the original selling prices of items. Both manufacturers and retailers use markdowns to meet the lower prices of competitors, counteract overstocking of merchandise, clear out shopworn merchandise, deplete assortments of odds and ends, and increase customer traffic. See Figure 15-5.

While manufacturers give discounts to wholesalers and retailers on a regular basis, they may periodically offer cash rebates to customers to stimulate consumption of an item or a group of items. **Rebates** are flexible, do not alter basic list prices, and increase direct communication between consumers and manufacturers (because rebates are sent to consumers by manufacturers). Price cuts by individual retailers do not generate the same kind of consumer enthusiasm. The recent popularity of rebates can be traced to their usage by the auto industry to help cut down on inventory surpluses. Rebates have also been used by Fedders, Gillette, Polaroid, Minolta, and a number of other companies, in addition to all the U.S. auto makers.

Whenever price adjustments are necessary, channel members should cooperatively determine their individual roles. Price hikes or cuts should not be unilaterally imposed.

Summary

Developing a pricing strategy consists of objectives, broad policy, strategy, implementation, and adjustments. Pricing objectives may be sales-, profit-, or status quo-based. Sales objectives center on growth or market share. A penetration price is a low price intended to capture the mass market. Profit objectives center on profit maximization, satisfactory profits, optimizing return on investment, or early cash recovery. Profit can be expressed in per unit or total dollar terms. A skimming price is a high price intended to capture the market segment less concerned with price than quality or status. A firm may use a skimming and then a penetration pricing strategy. Status quo objectives are geared toward avoiding declines in business and minimizing the impact of outside parties. Objectives may be combined.

A broad price policy integrates pricing decisions with the firm's target market, image, and marketing mix. Within its broad price policy, the company determines whether it is price or nonprice oriented.

A price strategy may be cost-, demand-, or competition-based. With cost-based pricing, prices are computed by adding desired profits to the costs of production and selling. Cost-based techniques are cost-plus, markup, target, and traditional break-even. In demand-based pricing, final prices are based on consumer research. The firm works backward to determine the costs it can afford to incur and still sell an item at the price sought by consumers. Demand-based techniques are demand-minus, chain-markup, modified break-even, and price discrimination. Under competition-based pricing, prices are set below, at, or higher than those of competitors. All three approaches should be integrated when establishing a price strategy.

Implementing a price strategy involves a variety of separate but interlocking specific concepts. These include customary and variable pricing, a one-price policy and flexible pricing, odd pricing, the price-quality association, leader pricing, multiple-unit pricing, price lining, geographic pricing, and terms.

After a price strategy is implemented, it usually requires regular fine tuning to reflect cost, competition, or demand changes. Prices can be adjusted by changing list prices, including escalator clauses and surcharges in contracts, marking prices up or down, and offering direct manufacturer rebates.

KEY TERMS

After reading this chapter, you should understand these key terms:

Sales-based objectives	**Cost-based pricing**
Penetration price	**Cost-plus pricing**
Profit-based objectives	**Markup pricing**
Skimming price	**Variable markup policy**
Status quo-based objectives	**Target pricing**
Broad price policy	**Traditional break-even analysis**

Demand-based pricing	**Prestige pricing**
Demand-minus pricing	**Psychological pricing**
Chain-markup pricing	**Leader pricing**
Modified break-even analysis	**Multiple-unit pricing**
Price discrimination	**Price lining**
Competition-based pricing	**Geographic pricing**
Price leadership	**Terms**
Competitive bidding	**Discounts**
Customary pricing	**List prices**
Variable pricing	**Escalator clause**
One-price policy	**Surcharges**
Flexible pricing	**Additional markups**
Odd pricing	**Markdowns**
Price-quality association	**Rebates**

QUESTIONS FOR DISCUSSION

1. Evaluate the use of "deep discounting" in the silverware industry.
2. Give an example of how a firm can pursue two pricing objectives at the same time.
3. How could a dress manufacturer pursue either a penetration or skimming strategy? How could the manufacturer combine the approaches?
4. What are the advantages and limitations of cost-based pricing techniques?
5. What are the benefits and limitations of demand-based pricing?
6. From a chain markup perspective, explain how a microwave oven could have a retail price of $600 and yet cost the manufacturer only $200 to produce.
7. Under what circumstances should a firm not use price discrimination? Give an example.
8. How can customary and variable pricing be combined?
9. Few firms in the United States use flexible pricing. Most utilize one-price policies. Why?
10. Evaluate odd pricing.
11. Explain how prestige pricing could be applied to luggage.
12. Under what circumstances would multiple-unit pricing be a poor strategy?
13. How does price lining benefit manufacturers? How does it benefit retailers? How does it benefit consumers?
14. What do you think are the disadvantages of rebates?

NOTES

1. "The Silverware Price Wars," *Business Week* (March 29, 1982), pp. 160, 165.
2. "The Scoop on Ice Cream Sales," *Business Week* (September 20, 1982), p. 73.
3. Bob Davis, "Sinclair Heads into Tough Fight With Its New Low-Cost Computer," *Wall Street Journal* (January 7, 1983), pp. 19, 24.
4. Laura Landro, "Home Videodisc Players Sell Slowly, So Firms Look to Industrial Market," *Wall Street Journal* (May 18, 1982), p. 33.
5. Dylan Landis, "Xerox Slashes Copier Prices," *New York Times* (July 1, 1982), p. D5.
6. Gay Jervey, "Slow Sales Prompt Nimslo Price Cut," *Advertising Age* (January 24, 1983), p. 14.
7. Jon G. Udell, "The Pricing Strategies of United States Industry," in Thomas V. Greer (Editor), *Combined Proceedings of the American Marketing Association, 1973* (Chicago: American Marketing Association, 1974), p. 152.

8. See Seymour E. Heymann, "Consider Other Factors Than Cost When Pricing Industrial Products," *Marketing News* (April 4, 1980), p. 11.

9. "Flexible Pricing," *Business Week* (December 12, 1977), p. 84.

10. Ibid., p. 81.

11. See Bernard F. Whalen, "Strategic Mix of Odd, Even Prices Can Lead to Increased Retail Profits," *Marketing News* (March 7, 1980), p. 24.

12. Barbara Ettore, "A New Picture at Drugstores," *New York Times* (August 2, 1980), p. 27.

CASES

1 HELENE CURTIS: ADDING PREMIUM-PRICE HAIR PRODUCTS*

For ten years, Helene Curtis' consumer products division marketed one major product line, Suave shampoos and hair conditioners. The Suave products were low-cost imitations of leading brands. Advertising used the theme "Suave does what yours does for a lot less." This penetration pricing strategy enabled Suave to become the leading seller of shampoo in ounces (Head & Shoulders by Procter & Gamble is the revenue leader).

Consumers viewed Suave as a national brand that could be trusted. Yet, it was priced just above private-label brands and just below other manufacturer brands. A good degree of brand loyalty has been developed by Suave.

In 1982, Helene Curtis decided to also seek a position in the more expensive end of the market and introduced a high-priced hair conditioner named Finesse. It spent $35 million to develop and launch this product. In addition to a large advertising campaign, Helene Curtis mailed 30 million free samples to consumers and offered discounts through coupons. Within a year, Finesse attained a 6 per cent market share, placing it fourth in the industry behind Revlon's Flex, Vidal Sassoon, and Gillette's Silkience. Said one observer, "Finesse has taken Curtis from a second-rate imitator to a first-class marketer."

In response to Finesse's early success, competitors raised their advertising budgets considerably for 1983. They believed Finesse's growth would be short-lived. As a Gillette executive commented, "It's noteworthy that Finesse—a spinoff of Silkience—has captured only half the share we got over the same period of time."

Helene Curtis was confident the Finesse brand would be as profitable in the premium-price segment of the conditioner market as Suave was in the low-price segment. It was so optimistic that a Finesse shampoo was planned for an early 1983 market entry. Finesse shampoo and conditioner products were to receive more than $50 million in 1983 promotional support.

QUESTIONS

1. Based on Suave's 10-year record of achievement, why change from a pure penetration price strategy?
2. Why would consumers buy Finesse from Helene Curtis when they could buy Suave for a lower price?
3. Should Helene Curtis be a price leader or follower?
4. As a competitor of Finesse, what pricing tactics would you use to limit the sales of the new shampoo? As Helene Curtis, how would you react to these? (Remember, no predatory pricing. It is illegal!)

*The data in this case are drawn from "The Big Gamble at Helene Curtis," *Business Week* (January 24, 1983), pp. 60, 62; and Jennifer Alter, "Curtis Finesses Way into High-End Haircare," *Advertising Age* (January 31, 1983), p. 12.

GENERAL ELECTRIC: HAVE CASH REBATES BEEN OVERUSED?[†] 2

General Electric (GE) has frequently used cash rebates to stimulate consumer interest and gain retailer enthusiasm. GE began offering cash rebates on radios and tape recorders in 1974. By 1982, it was providing rebates on 23 refrigerators and ovens, 4 lighting fixtures, 62 small appliances, and selected televisions and stereos.

GE's increased emphasis on cash rebates followed a general industry pattern. For example, during the last quarter of 1977, 10 per cent of durable-goods manufacturers offered cash rebates; this rose to 70 per cent of those companies in 1982. These are representative of the 1982 offers:

- $4 rebate on a $25 GE iron
- $5 rebate on a $110 Sunbeam food processor
- $50 rebate on a $200 Intellivision master video game component
- $100 rebate on a $300 Texas Instruments home computer

The popularity of cash rebates by manufacturers was due to several factors. One, consumers were attracted by limited-time-only refunds. Two, permanent price reductions did not have to be implemented. Three, retailers had a greater incentive to promote a firm's brand. Four, customers were encouraged to communicate directly with the manufacturer. Five, they were effective during weak economic periods.

But, because of the proliferation and long-term nature of many recent rebate programs, GE and other firms have become concerned that this strategy is being overused. They believe that consumers now delay purchases until rebates are announced, rebates have led to a form of price wars, and retailers are getting tired of the required paperwork. As one GE executive said:

> We have reached the point where rebates are a hassle for us. The novelty and freshness have worn off.

For 1983, GE planned to cut rebate offers from 62 small appliances to 30. It intended to provide cash incentives to its top retailers and invest in more cooperative advertising with its retailers. No other price reduction plans were expected.

QUESTIONS

1. How would you determine the success of GE's rebate program?
2. Comment on the following statement about rebates: "We'd like to find a way out of this. The person who thinks up an alternative will be a real hero."
3. Do you think GE will be able to act as a price leader and move other durable-goods manufacturers away from cash rebates? Explain your answer.
4. Besides rebates, what other strategies can durable-goods companies use to attract price-sensitive consumers?

[†]The data in this case are drawn from Robert Johnson, "Rebating Rises, But Unhappy Firms Can't Think of a Good Alternative," *Wall Street Journal* (December 9, 1982), p. 31.

Part
Seven

**Expanding the
Scope of
Marketing**

Introduction to Part Seven

In Part Seven, the scope of marketing is broadened. Chapter 16 examines international marketing and how marketing principles can be applied in foreign markets. International and multinational marketing are defined, and the factors behind the growth of international marketing are explored. The cultural, economic, political and legal, and technological factors facing international marketers are assessed. The stages in the development of an international marketing strategy are detailed. These are the degree of standardization, company organization, and product, distribution, promotion, and price planning.

Chapter 17 extends marketing to service and nonprofit organizations. The first half of the chapter deals with the marketing of services. The differences in service and product marketing are explained. The characteristics of services, their role in the economy, and special considerations for service marketing are noted. Service marketing strategies are discussed for hotels, car repair and maintenance services, and legal services. The second half of the chapter concentrates on nonprofit marketing. The differences between nonprofit and profit marketing are described, and the characteristics of nonprofit marketing and its role in the economy are enumerated. Nonprofit marketing strategies are discussed for the United States Postal Service, colleges and universities, and public libraries.

In Chapter 18 the interaction of marketing and society is examined. The chapter is divided into two sections. The first section evaluates the concept of social responsibility and its meaning for marketers. The depletion of natural resources, marring of the landscape, ethics, and the benefits and costs of social responsibility are discussed. The second section describes consumerism and its meaning for marketers. Consumer information and education, consumer safety, consumer choice, consumers' right to be heard, and the responses of business to consumer issues are each detailed. The trend toward greater deregulation is noted.

International Marketing 16

Chapter Preview

Chapter Objectives

1 To define international and multinational marketing

2 To explain why international marketing has developed and study its scope

3 To explore the cultural, economic, political and legal, and technological environments facing international marketers

4 To study the components of an international marketing strategy: the degree of standardization, company organization, and product, distribution, promotion, and price planning

With about 1.2 billion people, China is the most-populated country in the world. In fact, approximately 25 per cent of the world's population resides in China. Yet, until recently, foreign marketers have had limited access to the Chinese market. Now, the situation is changing, as Avon Products has discovered. In late 1982, Avon reached an agreement with the Chinese government allowing the company to sell facial cream in China. Avon thus became the first Western cosmetics firm to enter the Chinese market. See Figure 16-1.

Negotiations between Avon and Chinese officials took more than three years to complete, with Avon agreeing to several strategy modifications. One, the facial cream is being sold in department stores. This marks the first time Avon is not distributing products on a direct-to-home basis (and Avon operates in the U.S. and 32 other foreign markets). Two, only one of Avon's 700 products is permitted in Chinese stores. Three, Chinese packaging and branding are used. The cream's name in China is Ai Fang, which means "Love Fragrance." Four, since just one product is being sold, Avon is relying on word-of-mouth communication rather than paid advertising. Five, Avon provides expertise in manufacturing, some raw materials, and plant machinery. In return, it receives 7.5 per cent of profits.

While Avon estimates a potential market of 2 million Chinese women for Ai Fang (which sells for an expensive $1.50 in terms of Chinese income), it is clearly looking toward the future. Avon's long-term goals are to expand its product lines, utilize direct-to-home selling, and advertise extensively in China. As an Avon spokesperson said, "We're quite proud to be welcomed into China."[1]

Overview

Marketing outside the firm's home country is *international marketing; multinational marketing* includes many foreign countries.

International marketing involves the marketing of goods and services outside an organization's home country. *Multinational marketing* is a complex form of international marketing that involves an organization engaged in marketing operations in many foreign countries. Multinational firms include Nestlé, Lever Brothers, Shell, ITT, Exxon, and Coca-Cola. These companies have brand names that are known throughout the world and extensive worldwide operations. Large multinational organizations often allocate company resources without regard to national boundaries, even though they have a home country in terms of ownership and top management.

The watch industry typifies the multinational approach to marketing:

> A watch might be designed in Switzerland, have its electronic parts manufactured in Japan, have its timekeeping module assembled in Hong Kong, its watch case produced in the U.S., its face produced in Japan, and its final assembly completed in the Virgin Islands before being sold in the U.S.
>
> Thus, a brand name which formerly represented the perceived excellence of Swiss or American craftsmanship now stands for managerial excellence in coordinating labor and logistics in many nations to assure high standards of quality and service.[2]

The Ford Escort provides another illustration of a multinational orientation to marketing. The Escort has parts from the U.S. and nine

Figure 16-1
Avon in China

This Avon Moisturizing Cream is manufactured in Beijing, China and marketed throughout China. Reprinted by permission.

other countries and is assembled in three countries. Figure 16-2 shows the countries supplying parts for the Escort.

International efforts vary widely. At one end a firm may limit itself to one or a few foreign markets, manufacture goods domestically, and market them to foreign countries with little or no adaptation of the domestic marketing plan. At the opposite end, a multinational firm may have a global orientation, operate in many different countries, and use foreign manufacturing and marketing subsidiaries to cater to individual markets.

Figure 16-2
Ford's Escort: A World Car

Source: Ford Motor Company. Photo courtesy of Ford.

Ten countries supply parts for the economical Escort:

BRAZIL	Rear brake assembly
BRITAIN	Steering gears
FRANCE	Hub and bearing clutch assembly
ITALY	Engine cylinder heads
JAPAN	Manual transaxles
MEXICO	Door lift assembly
SPAIN	Shock absorber struts
TAIWAN	Wiring
WEST GERMANY	Valve-guide bushing
UNITED STATES	All other parts

For international companies to succeed in the 1980s, it is vital that they research and understand the similarities and differences among countries and adapt their strategies accordingly. No longer can small or large American firms prosper by merely exporting to foreign markets products that have sold well in the United States. Competition is too intense and cultures too distinct.

This chapter focuses on how to adapt marketing principles to foreign markets. The chapter examines the development and scope of international marketing, its environment, and the components of an international marketing strategy.

Why International Marketing Has Developed

There are several reasons why countries and individual firms engage in international marketing, including: comparative advantage, economic trends, demographic conditions, competition at home, the stage in the product life cycle, and tax structures.[3]

Countries trade items in which they have a *comparative advantage* for those in shortage.

The concept of **comparative advantage** states that countries have different rates of productivity for different products because of resources, specialization, mechanization, or climate. Therefore, countries can benefit by exchanging goods in which they have relative production advantages for those in which they have relative disadvantages. For example, the United States exports computer technology, wheat, and aircraft. It imports petroleum, coffee, and clothing.

International marketing may help a firm minimize unfavorable domestic economic conditions or appeal to areas with growing populations.

Economic trends vary by country. A firm may minimize adverse domestic conditions such as high inflation or unemployment by marketing goods and services in countries with good economic conditions. In this way annual sales can be stablized. During the late 1970s and early 1980s, the economic climate in some parts of Europe and Asia was better than that in the United States, thus increasing the importance of those markets.

Demographic conditions also differ by country. A firm in a country with a small or stagnant population base may find new business by entering foreign markets with undersatisfied market segments. In the 1970s Gerber baby foods began operations in growing foreign markets because the birth rate in the United States was declining. Between 1980 and 2000 most of the world's population growth is forecast to be in less-developed countries.

International expansion may result from heavy competition in the domestic market.

Competition in the home market may become intense, thereby leading to international expansion. Gillette found that its U.S. business was overly dependent on the highly competitive razor blade market. In addition, the Justice Department and the Federal Trade Commission limited U.S. mergers and acquisitions by Gillette. Foreign markets were quite different. Competition was relatively weak, undercapitalized, and used antiquated family-style management practices.[4]

International marketing may extend the product life cycle or dispose of discontinued items.

In many instances products are in different stages in the life cycle in different countries. Exporting may provide opportunities for prolonging product growth. For example, foreign manufacturers of small refrigerators found that those units could be sold in the United States for dens, bars, dormitories, and studio apartments. In their home countries, they were used only as the major refrigerators for families.

International marketing can provide for the disposal of discontinued merchandise, seconds, and manufacturer remakes (products that have been repaired). These items can be sold abroad without spoiling the domestic market for full-price, first-quality merchandise. However, companies must be careful not to dump unsafe products on foreign markets. This creates ill will and diminishes a firm's image.

There may be some tax advantages through international marketing. A number of countries entice new business from foreign companies by offering tax incentives in the form of reduced property, import, and income taxes for an initial time period. In addition, multinational firms may adjust prices so that the largest profits are recorded in the countries with the lowest tax rates.

Some firms are attracted to international marketing because of tax benefits.

Scope of International Marketing

The United States is one of the largest exporters in the world. In 1981 U.S. exports totaled $236 billion, about 12 percent of total world exports. During the same period West German exports were more than $176 billion, and Japanese exports were $152 billion. U.S. exports represent roughly 8 per cent of the American gross national product. Leading U.S. exports are chemicals, industrial equipment, motor vehicles, tobacco, and earth-moving machinery. Services make up one third of exports. These include air travel, tourist expenditures in the United States, ocean shipping, insurance, management fees, and military expenses.[5]

The United States accounts for 12 per cent of world exports.

The involvement of United States firms in international marketing varies greatly. One Department of Commerce study found that 92 per cent of United States companies confined themselves to domestic markets.[6] Nonetheless, more than 21,000 companies with fewer than 100 employees were expected to export goods and services in 1980.[7] During 1981, the fifty largest United States exporters accounted for almost $63 billion in foreign sales.[8] The latter figure is deceptively low because it does not include returns on foreign investments and sales by foreign subsidiaries. Among the leading firms, exports range from 1 (Exxon) to 62 (Boeing) per cent of sales.

The United States is also the world's largest importer. In 1981 imports totaled $264 billion. Examples of other major importers are West Germany, France, and Japan. Leading U.S. imports are petroleum, machinery, transport equipment, and iron and steel mill products.[9]

During 1981 the United States had a **trade deficit** of $28 billion. This means that the value of imports exceeded the value of exports by $28 billion. Trade deficits are relatively recent in the United States. Between 1954 and 1970 the balance of trade was positive in every year.[10]

In 1981, the value of U.S. imports was about $28 billion greater than the value of exports, resulting in a *trade deficit*.

The trade deficit is attributable to a variety of factors, including: huge increases in foreign oil prices, the dollar's convertability into gold, increased competition in foreign markets, less than optimal quality control for U.S. products, and the U.S. dollar's rise in value which caused the prices of exports to rise. Furthermore, the U.S. market has been and remains a very lucrative one for foreign companies; its per capita consumption is the highest of any country in the world for most products and services.

Because U.S. trade deficits have been so high over the past few years, many American companies have called for tighter controls on imports and more open access to restricted foreign markets. The U.S. government has been negotiating with foreign governments to improve the situation. For example, Japan has agreed to a number of trade provisions to improve its balance of trade with the U.S.[11] In 1981, the U.S. had a trade deficit of $16 billion with Japan.

Many non-U.S. firms are becoming much more active in international marketing. For example, in 1964 only twelve of the world's fifty largest industrial companies were European. By 1981 this figure had risen to twenty.[12] Among the largest non-U.S. firms are Royal Dutch/ Shell Group, British Petroleum, ENI, and Unilever. As one observer noted:

> The main event in international business during the past decade has been the dramatic gain in international competitive position achieved by non-American and particularly by Continental (European) and Japanese companies.[13]

Of the ten leading firms in the world, seven are American.

Despite these trends the U.S. remains a very dominant force in international marketing. In 1981, of the world's fifty largest industrial firms, American companies comprised twenty-one. Seven of the ten leaders were American, and these seven had worldwide sales of over $400 billion.[14]

Environment of International Marketing

Although the basic marketing principles described in this text apply to international marketing, there are significant environmental differences between domestic and foreign markets, and marketing practices should be adapted accordingly. Each market should be evaluated separately:

> There is no such thing as a multinational market. We have domestic markets worldwide but no multinational markets. Each market is unique, unlike any other market, and therefore each is a domestic market.[15]

The major cultural, economic, political and legal, and technological environments facing international marketers are discussed in the succeeding subsections.

Cultural Environment

International marketers need to be aware of each market's cultural environment. As defined in Chapter 4, culture refers to a group of people sharing a distinctive heritage. This heritage teaches behavior standards, language, life-styles, and goals. A culture is passed down from generation to generation and is not easily changed. Almost every country in the world has a different culture, and continental differences exist as well. A domestic firm unfamiliar with or insensitive to a foreign culture may try to market products or services that are unacceptable to or misunderstood by that culture. For example, beef or pork products are rejected by some cultures.

Table 16-1 illustrates the errors a firm engaged in international marketing may commit as a result of a lack of awareness about foreign cultures that is rooted in inadequate data. In some cases the firm is at fault because it functions out of a domestic home office and receives little local foreign input. In other cases, such as marketing in less-developed countries, information is limited because a low level of population data or marketing research skill exists, and people are reluctant to participate in surveys. Sometimes, mail and telephone service are poor. Thus, marketing research, which could determine the hidden meanings and the ease of pronunciation of brand names and slogans, the rate of product consumption, and reasons for purchases, is not fully utilized.

Cultural awareness can be improved by employing foreign personnel in key positions, hiring foreign marketing research specialists, locating company offices in each country of operations, actively studying cultural differences, and being responsive to cultural changes. Table 16-2 shows several cultural opportunities.

> **Firms must be familiar with the cultures of the countries in which they operate.**

> **Inadequate information about foreign cultures is a common cause of errors.**

Table 16-1

Pepsodent was unsuccessful in Southeast Asia because it promised white teeth to a culture where black or yellow teeth are symbols of prestige.

In Quebec, a canned fish manufacturer tried to promote a product by showing a woman dressed in shorts, golfing with her husband, and planning to serve canned fish for dinner. These activities violated cultural norms.

Maxwell House advertised itself as the "great American coffee" in Germany. It found out that Germans have little respect for American coffee.

In Puerto Rico, the Chevrolet Nova (meaning "star") was translated as "no va"—"it doesn't go."

General Motors' "Body by Fisher" slogan became "Corpse by Fisher" when translated into Japanese.

In Brazil, Gerber could not convince mothers that baby food was a good alternative to food the mothers made themselves.

African men were upset by a commercial for men's deodorant that showed a happy male being chased by women. They thought the deodorant would make them weak and overrun by women.

Illustrations of Errors In International Marketing Because of Lack of Cultural Awareness

Sources: David A. Ricks, *Big Business Blunders* (Homewood, Ill.: Richard D. Irwin, 1983); and Ann Helming, "Culture Shocks," *Advertising Age* (May 17, 1982), pp. M-8–M-9.

Table 16-2

Examples of Cultural Opportunities for International Marketers	Hong Kong is said to have the world's highest per capita consumption of Cognac. "The belief has been established that it's good for you. You'll have old ladies who get up in the morning and have a glass of it."
	In Germany, beer communicates, "Let's meet over a beer." The average annual per capita consumption of beer is 153.4 quarts, about 68 six packs of twelve-ounce cans, in West Germany. It is 97.2 quarts in the United States.
	In Japan, Western soups are popular for breakfast, while cereals are not. Corn potage is most in demand.
	In France, chocolate is used in cooking. Italians serve chocolate as a snack for children, placing it between two slices of bread.
	Tropical area residents apply Vicks Vaporub as a mosquito repellent.

Sources: Nicole Seligman, "Be Sure Not to Wear a Green Hat If You Visit Hong Kong," *Wall Street Journal* (May 10, 1979), p. 41; John M. Gross, "The Germans Drink a Great Deal of Beer, But Not Enough to Suit the Beer Makers," *Wall Street Journal* (August 28, 1980), p. 38; George Fields, "How to Scale the Cultural Fence," *Advertising Age* (December 13, 1982), pp. M-11–M-12; and Saul Sands, "Can You Standardize International Marketing Strategy?," *Journal of the Academy of Marketing Science*, Vol. 7 (Winter, Spring 1979), p. 120.

Economic Environment

A country's economic environment indicates its present and potential capacities for consuming goods and services. Measures of economic performance include the standard of living, Gross National Product (GNP), and stage of economic development.

The quality of life in a country is measured by the *standard of living.*

The ***standard of living*** refers to the average quantity and quality of goods and services consumed in a country. Recently, the United Nations studied the per capita consumption of goods and services in countries throughout the world. It gave the United States an index number of 100 and rated the other countries in relation to this figure. The ratings were 68 for France, 66 for West Germany, 57 for Great Britain, 56 for Japan, and 46 for Italy. The report concluded that the United States has the highest standard of living for any main industrial country.[16]

The total value of goods and services produced in a country each year is the *Gross National Product (GNP).*

The ***Gross National Product (GNP)*** indicates the total value of goods and services produced in a country each year. Total and per capita GNP are the most frequently used measures of a country's wealth, because they are regularly published and easy to calculate and compare with other countries. However, per capita GNP figures may be misleading for two reasons. First, these figures represent means and not income distributions. A few wealthy citizens may boost the per capita GNP even though the bulk of the population has low income. Second, incomes purchase different standards of living in each country; an income of $10,000 in the United States may represent the same standard of living as an income of $5,000 in another country.

Countries can be classified as *industrialized, developing,* and *less-developed.*

Marketing opportunities often can be highlighted by evaluating a country's stage of economic growth. One method for categorizing the economic growth of countries is to divide them into industrialized, developing, and less-developed classes. ***Industrialized countries*** include the United States, Canada, Japan, the USSR, and nations in

Oceania and Western Europe. These countries have high literacy, modern technology, and per capita income of several thousand dollars. ***Developing countries*** include many Latin American nations. Education and technology are rising, and per capita income is about $1,500. Developing countries have 20 per cent of the world's population and almost one third of its income. ***Less-developed countries*** include a number of countries in Africa and South Asia. Literacy is low, technology limited, and per capita GNP is generally below $500. These countries have two thirds of the world's population but less than 15 per cent of world income.

The development of Hong Kong illustrates the process of economic growth. Over a twenty-year period, Hong Kong changed from a port dependent only on trade to an export-oriented country producing goods of increasing quality for world markets. The per capita GNP increased 2.5 times during this period.[17]

The greatest marketing opportunities generally occur in industrialized countries because of their higher discretionary income and standard of living. However, industrialized countries usually have stable population bases, and sales of some product categories may already be saturated. Developing and less-developed countries have expanding population bases and currently purchase limited amounts of imports. There is long-run potential for international marketers in these nations.

By examining product ownership per thousand population, a marketer can obtain a good estimate of the current size of consumer demand in a country. Table 16-3 shows ownership per 1,000 people of cars, televisions, meat, gasoline, electricity, and telephones for nine major industrialized countries. As already noted, there is usually long-run potential in countries where consumers presently have few products and services. For example, Argentina has 100 automobiles per 1,000 population, Nigeria has 3 per 1,000, and India has fewer than 3 per 1,000. The one-billion-plus people of China own only 37,000 cars. Of all the automobiles in the world, 40 per cent are in the United States; 83 per cent of the global population has only 12 per cent of the cars.[18]

> The size of consumer demand can be estimated by studying product ownership. Untapped markets should also be noted.

	Cars (Per 1,000 People)	Tele- visions (Per 1,000 People)	Meat (Lbs. Per Year Eaten)	Gasoline (Lbs.* Per Year Used)	Electricity (Kilowatt Hours Used Per Year (Per Person)	Tele- phones (Per 100 People)	
							Table 16-3
United States	507	571	211	2,968	9,456	69	**Product and Service**
Britain	260	315	163	622	4,934	38	**Consumption in Nine**
Denmark	260	308	146	904	4,710	45	**Major Industrialized**
France	300	235	172	659	3,900	26	**Countries, 1981**
Italy	283	213	68	454	2,865	26	
Japan	164	233	15	423	4,470	40	
Sweden	350	348	113	1,131	9,970	66	
Switzerland	271	264	133	886	5,670	61	
West Germany	307	297	133	734	5,710	32	

*Standard unit of international measure
Source: United Nations

Stability of currency is important because re-evaluation could affect a firm's foreign sales and profit.

Currency stability is another economic factor a firm would consider in international marketing, because sales and profits could be affected if a foreign country revalues its currency in relation to the company's home currency. For example, in 1982, an extremely weak Mexican economy caused that country's peso to be devalued by 160 per cent. This meant that Mexican goods became much cheaper for consumers in other countries, while making it very expensive for Mexican consumers to purchase any foreign products. As a result, U.S. firms had great difficulties exporting products to Mexico during this period, because their prices were relatively high.[19]

Political and Legal Environment

In each country, a unique political and legal environment exists. Among the key political and legal factors to examine are nationalism, government stability, trade restrictions, and trade agreements.

Nationalism involves a host country's attempts to promote its own interests.

Nationalism refers to a country's efforts to become self-reliant and raise its status in the eyes of the world community. Frequently, nationalism leads to tight restrictions on foreign companies and fosters the development of domestic industry at their expense. In recent years some countries have seized the assets of multinational firms, revoked their licenses to operate, prevented the transfer of funds from one currency to another, increased taxes, or unilaterally changed contract terms.

For continued success in a foreign market, *government stability* is needed.

Government stability should be examined on the basis of two factors: consistency of policies and orderliness in installing leaders. First, do government policies regarding taxes, company expansion, profits, and so on remain relatively unchanged over time? Second, is there an orderly process for selecting and empowering new government leaders? Companies will be unable to function properly unless both of these factors are positive.

For example, in 1976 Aris Gloves, a division of Consolidated Foods, selected a new manufacturing location that "everyone, including the U.S. embassy, described as a happy, sleepy country."[20] The country was El Salvador. Within two years, dissidents held the division's president and about 120 employees as hostages until the firm agreed to wage-increase demands. Aris Gloves left El Salvador in 1979.

An international firm can protect itself against the adverse effects of nationalism and political instability. It can measure domestic instability (riots, government purges, excessive strikes), foreign conflict (diplomatic expulsions, military activity), the political climate (stability of political parties, manner of selecting government officials), and the economic climate (currency stability, economic strength, extent of government intervention) prior to entering a foreign market.[21]

Investments may also be protected through insurance. The U.S. government's Overseas Private Investment Corporation (OPIC) insures investments in friendly underdeveloped countries against such perils as war damage and inconvertibility of earnings. In addition, private underwriters insure foreign investments.

Last, the risks of nationalism and political unrest can be reduced by taking foreign partners, borrowing money from foreign governments or banks, and/or utilizing one of various organizational modes such as licensing, contract manufacturing, and management contracting. These modes are discussed later in this chapter.

Another aspect of the political and legal environment encompasses trade restrictions. The most common form of restriction is a **tariff,** which is a tax placed on imported goods by a foreign government. The second major restriction is a **trade quota,** which sets limits on the amounts of goods that can be imported into a country. The strictest form of quota is an **embargo,** which refuses entry of specified products into the country.

Tariffs, trade quotas, and embargos are forms of trade restrictions.

Other regulations also restrict trade. For example, France, Germany, and the Netherlands have laws setting low maximum speed limits on tractors. These laws protect domestic manufacturers, because foreign products must implement costly modifications in their tractors.

Although the United States accepts the results of pollution tests that Japanese car manufacturers run on their autos, Japanese regulations mandate that each American car sold in Japan must be brought down to the local registration office for another series of tests.[22] For Ford, this occurs even though it brings a team of Japanese engineers to the United States every year to "witness test" vehicles for export.

In many cases trade barriers among nations have been reduced or eliminated through multilateral agreements and economic communities. In 1948 twenty-three nations, including the United States, accepted the idea of multilateral agreements by signing the **General Agreement on Tariffs and Trade (GATT).** The main contribution of GATT is the **most-favored nation principle,** which allows every nation covered by the agreement to obtain the best contract terms received by any single nation. GATT members agree to meet every two years and to negotiate for tariff reductions. By 1982, 88 nations representing more than 90 per cent of the total volume of international trade participated in GATT.

Trade agreements can reduce or eliminate trade barriers. GATT introduced the most-favored nation principle.

In November 1982, GATT member countries met in Geneva, Switzerland to try to overcome their differences due to nationalism, the worldwide recession, and trade barriers. A consensus was reached that free trade was desirable and needed to be promoted through more cooperation among countries. Despite this understanding, some trade tensions are expected to continue, as countries seek to protect their self-interests.[23] See Figure 16-3.

Since its founding, GATT has allowed a few exceptions to the most-favored nation principle. For example, regional trade associations or economic communities can be established by GATT members provided that such communities do not result in increased discrimination against other GATT members.

The most important economic community is the **European Community (EC),** the Common Market. EC members are Belgium, Denmark, France, Great Britain, Greece, Ireland, Italy, Luxembourg, the Netherlands, and West Germany. Spain and Portugal are scheduled to join in 1984. The Common Market agreement calls for no tariffs among members and a uniform tariff with nonmember nations. In addition, there are common standards for food additives, labeling requirements, and package sizes and a free flow of labor and capital. The combined GNP of

The European Community (EC) joins several countries in trade and other agreements.

Figure 16-3
The Goal of GATT

"CAN'T YOU LOWER IT JUST A LITTLE MORE?"

Reprinted by permission of Rothco.

Common Market members is about three quarters that of the United States. The combined population is roughly 120 per cent of the U.S. population.

Other significant economic communities are the Latin American Integration Association, Central American Common Market, Council for Mutual Economic Assistance (made up of Eastern European countries), Andean Common Market, East Africa Community, Asian Common Market, and Caribbean Common Market.

Technological Environment

International marketing may require adjustments in production or measures.

Technological factors such as production and measurement systems influence international marketing. Foreign workers must frequently be trained to operate and maintain unfamiliar equipment. Problems occur if maintenance standards or practices vary by country or adverse production conditions exist, such as high humidity, extreme hot or cold weather, or air pollution. Furthermore, electrical power needs may vary by country and require modifications in products. For example, U.S. appliances work on 110 volts; in Europe, appliances work on 220 volts.

Although the metric system has been adopted by most of the world, the United States, Borneo, Burma, Liberia, and South Yemen still use ounces, pounds, inches, and feet. At the present time the United States is in the process of converting to the metric system in order to be consistent with its major trading partners. General Motors, major tire manufacturers, all large soda and liquor bottlers, and other U.S. firms have recently converted or begun conversion to metric standards. As the United States converts to the metric system, the American market will have to be re-educated about measurement and learn the value of meters, liters, and other metric standards.

Developing an International Marketing Strategy

In the following subsections, the vital parts of an international marketing strategy are explored: the degree of standardization, company organization, and product, distribution, promotion, and price planning.

Standardizing Plans

A firm engaged in international marketing activities must determine the degree to which its plans should be standardized. Both standardized and nonstandardized plans have benefits and limitations.

With a **pure standardized approach,** the company utilizes a common marketing plan for all countries in which it operates. There are usually marketing and production economies because product design, assembly, advertising, packaging, and other costs are spread over a large product base. A uniform image is presented, training of foreign personnel is reduced, and centralized control is applied. It works best when few foreign markets are involved and they are similar to the home country. However, this approach is not sensitive to individual market needs, and the input from foreign personnel is limited. For example, Campbell tried to market its soups in Brazil in the same way that they were marketed in the U.S. This strategy failed, since Brazilians were used to dehydrated soup mixes or homemade soup. One critic commented on "The Campbell Syndrome":

> Campbell thought "All Brazilians have to eat my soups because they're the finest soups in the world and I'm the biggest soup manufacturer."

After selling "the wrong product too expensively" for three years, Campbell withdrew from the Brazilian market.[24]

A **pure nonstandardized approach** assumes that each market is different and requires a distinct marketing plan. This strategy is sensitive to local needs and provides opportunities for the development of foreign managers. Decentralized control is undertaken. It works best when distinctive major foreign markets are involved and/or the company has many product lines. For example, Massey-Ferguson is a Canadian-based manufacturer of farm and industrial equipment. It operates nine relatively autonomous subsidiaries in major foreign markets.[25] The pure nonstandardized approach can result in increased design and promotion costs, different company images throughout the world, and limited centralized direction.

In recent years, more and more international firms have turned to a **mixed approach** for marketing planning. Under a mixed approach, a

Under a pure standardized approach, a common marketing plan is used in each country in which a firm operates. Under a pure nonstandardized approach, each country is given a separate marketing plan. A mixed approach is a combination strategy.

combination of standardized and nonstandardized efforts enable companies to maximize production efficiencies, maintain a consistent image, exercise home-office control, and yet be sensitive and responsive to local needs. As an illustration, 7-Eleven stores in Japan emphasize the same convenience store features as their U.S. counterparts: fill-in merchandise and long hours. However, the Japanese stores carry a somewhat different assortment of products and promote the slogan "7-Eleven —for people whose time is precious." The long-running U.S. slogan has been "Oh, thank Heaven for 7-Eleven."[26]

When determining a marketing approach, a firm would evaluate whether differences among countries are sufficiently great to warrant changes in marketing plans, which elements of marketing can be standardized, whether the size of each foreign market will result in profitable adaptation, and if modifications can be made on a regional rather than a country basis.

Organizing

There are three international organizational formats from which a company may choose: exporting, joint venture, and direct ownership. These formats can be combined. For example, a firm could use an exporting organization in a country that has a history of taking over the assets of foreign firms and a direct ownership organization in a country that provides tax advantages for plant construction.

Exporting **enables a domestic manufacturer to reach international markets without foreign production.**

With *exporting,* a company reaches international markets by selling directly through its own sales force or indirectly through foreign merchants or agents. In direct selling, the firm situates its sales force in a home office or foreign branch offices. This technique is prominent when customers are easy to locate or come to the seller. In indirect selling, the firm hires outside specialists to search out and contact customers. These specialists are based in the home or foreign country. Indirect selling is applied in situations where customers are hard to locate, the exporting company has limited resources, or local customs are unique.

An exporting structure requires minimal investment in foreign facilities. There is no foreign production by the firm. The exporter may modify its packages, labels, or catalogs at its domestic facilities in response to foreign market needs. Exporting represents the lowest level of commitment to international marketing. As an illustration, Paul Masson wines are made in California and exported to many European countries. Foreign wholesalers market the wines through grocery stores and wine shops.[27]

In a *joint venture,* **a firm shares efforts with a foreign company. It can be based on licensing, contract manufacturing, management contracting, or joint ownership.**

In a *joint venture,* the firm agrees to combine some aspect of its manufacturing or marketing efforts with those of a foreign company in order to share expertise, costs, and connections with important persons. A joint venture may also result in reduced costs and favorable trade terms from a foreign government if products are produced locally and foreign ownership is established. For example, Gillette changed its policy of 100 per cent ownership after developing countries began to erect trade barriers that restricted imported razor blades. Now Gillette manufactures locally and sometimes operates as the minority owner (in countries where the government demands local participation).[28]

A joint venture can take the form of licensing, contract manufacturing, management contracting, or joint ownership. Licensing gives a foreign firm the rights to a manufacturing process, trademark, patent, and/or trade secret in exchange for a commission, fee, or royalty. Coca-Cola and PepsiCo license their products. Under contract manufacturing, the firm agrees to have a foreign company make its products locally. The firm markets the products itself and provides management expertise. This is common in book publishing.

In management contracting, the firm acts as a consultant to foreign companies. Many hotel chains, such as Hilton, engage in management contracting. With joint ownership, a firm agrees to manufacture and market products in partnership with a foreign company in order to reduce costs and spread risk. A foreign government may require joint ownership with local businesses as a condition for entry. For example, in Canada, outsiders must use joint ownership arrangements with Canadian firms for new ventures. In February 1983, General Motors and Toyota announced plans to jointly operate a small-car plant in California.[29]

Direct ownership involves the full undertaking and control of all international operations. The company owns production, marketing, and other facilities in foreign countries without any partners. In some cases international operations are organized into wholly owned subsidiaries. For example, Atari operates wholly owned subsidiaries for its video games in the United Kingdom, France, Germany, and the Netherlands.[30] The firm has all the benefits and risks associated with ownership. There are savings in labor, and marketing plans are more sensitive to local needs. Profit potential is high, although costs are also high. The possibility of nationalistic acts is raised, and government restrictions are likely to be more stringent. This is the riskiest form of organization.

Direct ownership involves total control of foreign operations and facilities by a firm.

Frequently, companies combine organizational formats. For instance, McDonald's engages in joint ventures and direct ownership. See Figure 16-4.

Product Planning

International product planning can be based on straight extension, product adaptation, backward invention, and/or forward-invention strategies.[31] In a ***straight-extension*** strategy, the company manufactures the same products for domestic and foreign sales. The firm is confident that successful products can be sold abroad without any modifications in brand name, formulations, or labeling. It is a simple, straightforward approach. However, it does not take into account differences in laws, customs, technology, and other factors. Beer companies apply straight extension strategies. In fact, imported beer often has a higher status than domestic beer.

With a ***product-adaptation*** strategy, domestic products are modified to meet foreign conditions, taste preferences, electrical require-

Straight extension, product adaptation, backward invention, and forward invention are the basic methods of international product planning.

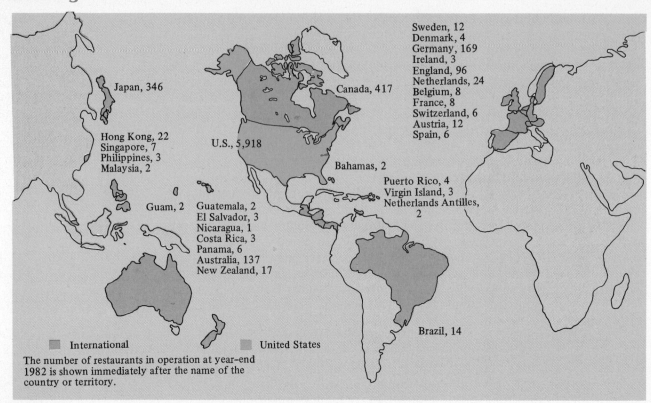

Sweden, 12
Denmark, 4
Germany, 169
Ireland, 3
England, 96
Netherlands, 24
Belgium, 8
France, 8
Switzerland, 6
Austria, 12
Spain, 6

Japan, 346

Hong Kong, 22
Singapore, 7
Philippines, 3
Malaysia, 2

Canada, 417

U.S., 5,918

Bahamas, 2

Puerto Rico, 4
Virgin Island, 3
Netherlands Antilles, 2

Guam, 2

Guatemala, 2
El Salvador, 3
Nicaragua, 1
Costa Rica, 3
Panama, 6
Australia, 137
New Zealand, 17

Brazil, 14

■ International ■ United States

The number of restaurants in operation at year-end 1982 is shown immediately after the name of the country or territory.

Figure 16-4
International Map of McDonald's
International expansion is carried out by developing restaurants operated by 1) McDonald's, 2) individual franchisees, and 3) affiliates (where 50% or more of ownership is controlled by resident nationals). Reprinted by permission.

ments, water conditions, or legal regulations. This is a relatively simple way to plan products for international markets, because it is assumed that new products are not necessary and minor changes are sufficient. Product adaptation is the most frequently used strategy in international marketing.

A product-adaptation strategy is appropriate for gasoline formulations, which must vary according to a country's weather conditions; detergent formulations, which must be changed to satisfy a country's water hardness; and electrical appliances, which are changed to accommodate voltage requirements. Sometimes adaptation is needed because a product's function differs by country. For example, a consumer lawn mower would be modified if it were to be used as a commercial mower in a foreign country.

In order to sell electric drills in West Germany, U.S. firms must modify their products. The heavier masonry in West German buildings creates a demand for more powerful, more expensive electric drills than those sold in the United States. West Germans also desire greater technical sophistication than American consumers. Although the average German homeowner uses a power drill only thirty minutes per year, he or she buys a drill with a life of about one hundred hours.[32]

With **backward invention,** the firm appeals to developing countries by making products that are less complex than the ones it sells in its domestic market. An example of backward invention is the sale of manual cash registers and nonelectric sewing machines in countries without widespread electricity. See Figure 16-5.

In **forward invention** the company develops new products for its international markets. This plan is more risky and time-consuming and requires higher capital investments than the other strategies. It also provides the firm with profit potential and, in some situations, worldwide recognition for its beneficial practices. A few years ago General Motors developed a new car exclusively for developing nations. The car was simple in design, contained many standardized parts made in the United States, had an exterior of sheet metal, and was assembled locally. General Motors worked with firms in foreign countries and minimized these firms' investment costs.

Distribution Planning

International distribution planning encompasses the selection of channel members and the physical movement of products. As noted earlier in this chapter, a firm may sell products directly through its own sales force or hire outside middlemen to complete transactions. In the selection of a distribution channel, the company would examine traditional relationships, the availability of appropriate middlemen, differences in wholesaling and retailing patterns from those in the home country, government restrictions, and costs.

For example, in Japan, American firms may distribute directly to retailers or sell through importing agents. Retail establishments range

International distribution planning involves channel members, transportation, storage, and special arrangements.

Figure 16-5
Backward Invention by Singer

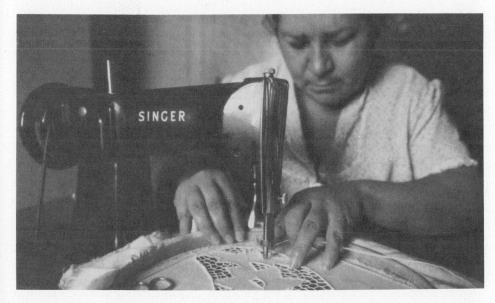

Manual Singer sewing machines, such as the one shown here in Iturbide, Mexico, enable residents of rural foreign communities to create products that generate income and improve the local economy. Courtesy of the Singer Company.

from supermarkets, department stores, and specialty stores to mail order. As one observer noted:

> Powerful Japanese trading companies *(sogo shosha)* stand ready to help U.S. exports enter the Japanese market . . . . They have enormous capabilities in international trade, in that they collect and process information, and organize business projects. However, *soga shosha* generally have dealt in bulk commodities; they only recently have started to emphasize consumer goods imports and now are organizing operations aimed at handling such goods, which normally involve small lot shipments of a great variety of merchandise.[33]

The physical distribution of products into international markets often requires special planning. The processing of marine insurance, government documents, and other papers may be time-consuming, and transportation modes may be unavailable or inefficient. For example, a foreign country may have inadequate docking facilities, poor highways, or too few motor vehicles. Finally, distribution by ship is lengthy and subject to schedule delays.

Inventory management should take into account the value and availability of warehousing and the costs of shipping in small quantities. For example, Champion spark plugs had difficulties because it had to airfreight its products to Japan to service the Honda Motors account properly. At that time Champion had no facilities in Japan. The costs of shipping were several times the value of the spark plugs.[34] Champion now has warehouse facilities in Japan.

Promotion Planning

International promotion planning depends on the overlap of audiences and languages and the availability of media.

Promotional campaigns can be standardized, mixed, or nonstandardized. Figure 16-6 shows examples of all three approaches to advertising in foreign countries. Most companies combine standardized and nonstandardized themes into mixed promotion plans. For example, Exxon's "Put a Tiger in Your Tank" campaign has been widely used. The tiger represents an internationally recognized symbol of power. Avis Rent-A-Car has used its "We Try Harder" theme throughout Europe as well as the United States. Both companies also create commercials and messages for individual foreign markets.

For companies marketing in different European countries, some degree of standardization in promotion is important because of the overlap of readership and viewers in these nations. For instance, West German television broadcasts are received by about 40 per cent of Dutch homes with televisions. The magazine *Paris Match* has substantial readership in Belgium, Switzerland, Luxembourg, Germany, Italy, and Holland.

There are also reasons for utilizing some nonstandardized promotion techniques. Many countries have cultural differences that are not satisfied through a single promotion campaign. These differences include customs, language, the meaning of colors and symbols, and the level of literacy. Media may be unavailable or inappropriate. In a number of countries there are few televisions in operation, no advertising is permitted, or mailing lists are not current. Finally, national pride some-

(a)

(b)

Figure 16-6

Approaches to Advertising in Foreign Countries

(a) Standardized—
Xerox in Canada. This English language ad is used in North America.

(b) Mixed—
Burroughs in West Germany. This ad combines German and Burroughs' English slogan.

(c) Nonstandardized—
Black and Decker in Brazil.

All advertisements reprinted by permission.

In this Black & Decker poster by Standard, Ogilvy & Mather, the proposal is to make a gift of something to make gifts with. Not a bad idea in Brazil where do-it-yourself is a new idea and a Barbie doll sells for $45.

(c)

times requires that individual promotions be used. Companies such as Unilever and Procter & Gamble "preserve a degree of local autonomy." This autonomy is greatest in highly developed markets.[35]

In 1980, total annual advertising expenditures in the noncommunist world exceeded $110 billion (about one half of it spent in the United States). Ten countries accounted for 80 per cent of international expenditures. While overall per capita expenditures averaged $42, U.S. expenditures were over $200 per resident and many European countries

Table 16-4 **Comparison of Eight Countries' Advertising Expenditures by Medium, 1980 (in Per Cent)**

COMPARISON OF ADVERTISING EXPENDITURES (PERCENTAGE)

	United States	Brazil	Britain	France	Greece	Japan	Norway	West Germany
Cinema	NA	1	1	1	2	NA	2	1
Radio	7	20	2	6	5	5	*	3
Television	20	40	24	9	47	35	*	11
Print	38	31	61	39	45	37	78	65
All other (outdoor, direct, etc.)	35	8	12	45	1	23	20	20
Total	100	100	100	100	100	100	100	100

NA: Statistics not available
* Advertising prohibited
Source: International Advertising Association

averaged over $100 per resident. The lowest per capita expenditures were in Africa and Asia. They were four cents per person in Ethiopia.[36]

Media habits vary by country. For example, 36 per cent of the French population watches less than one hour of television per week. Only 9 per cent of the U.S. population watches this little television. French residents subscribe to 2.4 magazines, while U.S. residents subscribe to 3.7.[37] Table 16-4 shows advertising expenditures by medium for eight foreign countries.

Finally, as a result of cultural distinctions, consumers abroad may be attracted by different advertising themes than American consumers. As an illustration, a comparison of French and American consumers revealed that each desires separate attributes for toothpaste. French consumers value "Kills germs in mouth" and "Removes particles from between teeth." American consumers stress "Well-known brand," "Freshens mouth," and "Brightens teeth" appeals.[38]

Price Planning

Major decisions in international price planning involve standardization, levels, currency, and sales terms. *Dumping* is disliked by host countries.

The basic considerations in international price planning are whether prices should be standardized, the level at which prices are set, the currency in which prices are quoted, and terms of sale.

Standardization of prices is difficult unless a firm operates within an economic community, such as the Common Market. Taxes, tariffs, and currency exchange charges are among the added costs a company incurs when engaged in international marketing. For example, West German consumers spend the equivalent of $1.65 for a 13-ounce package of corn flakes that sells for about $1.05 in the United States. The higher German price is due to extra labor costs and the steep import duties placed on the cereal.[39]

When setting a price level, a firm would consider local economic conditions such as per capita GNP. For this reason, many firms try to hold down prices in developing and less-developed countries by marketing simplified product versions or employing less-expensive local labor. On the other hand, higher prices in industrialized countries such as West Germany reflect product quality and the added costs of international marketing.

Some firms set lower prices in foreign countries in order to dispose of outmoded products or remove excess supply from the home market and preserve the home market's price structure. In the latter case, dumping is involved. ***Dumping*** is defined as selling a product in a foreign country at a price lower than that prevailing in the exporter's home market, below the cost of production, or both. In the United States and other countries, duties may be levied on products that are dumped by foreign companies. In the steel industry, the Commerce Department monitors a trigger-price program in which imported steel prices are investigated automatically once they fall below minimum levels.

A third fundamental pricing decision relates to the currency in which prices are quoted. If a firm sets prices on the basis of its own nation's currency, the risk of a foreign currency devaluation is passed on to the buyer and better control is maintained. However, this strategy also has limitations. For example, consumers may be confused or unable to convert the price into their currency, or a foreign government may insist that transactions be quoted and completed in its currency.

Finally, terms of sale need to be determined. This involves such judgments as what middlemen discounts are needed, when ownership is transferred, what form of payment will be required, how much time customers will have to pay bills, and what constitutes an appropriate refund policy.

Summary

International marketing involves the marketing of goods and services outside the organization's home country. Multinational marketing is a complex form of international marketing that engages an organization in marketing operations in many countries. For international companies to succeed in the 1980s, it is vital that they research and understand the similarities and differences among countries and adapt their strategies accordingly.

International marketing has developed for several reasons. Countries are interested in exchanging products with which they have comparative advantages for those with which they do not. Firms seek to minimize adverse economic conditions, attract growing markets, avoid intense domestic competition, extend the product life cycle, dispose of discontinued items, and utilize tax breaks.

The United States accounts for 12 per cent of the world's exports. Yet, more than 90 per cent of United States firms do not engage in international marketing. The United States also imports well over $260 billion in goods annually, causing a substantial trade deficit. Non-U.S. firms are rapidly increasing their role in international marketing.

International marketers work within several environments. The cultural environment includes the behavior standards, language, lifestyles, and goals of a country's citizens. The economic environment incorporates a country's standard of living, GNP, stage of economic development, demand for products, and stability of currency. The political and legal environment encompasses nationalism, government stability, restrictions, and trade agreements such as the Common Market. The technological environment refers to a country's production and measurement systems. These environments create opportunities as well as problems and vary by country.

In the development of an international marketing strategy, the firm may adopt a standardized, nonstandardized, or mixed approach to marketing. The company may emphasize exporting, engage in joint ventures, or directly own foreign subsidiaries.

Product planning would extend existing products into foreign markets, modify existing products to local needs, produce less sophisticated items for developing nations, or invent new products specifically for foreign markets. Distribution planning would investigate channel relationships and establish a formal network for direct sales or middlemen. In addition, physical distribution features would be analyzed and the proper modifications made. Promotion planning would stress standardized, mixed, or nonstandardized campaigns. Media use varies greatly by country. Price planning would outline whether prices should be standardized, the level at which prices are set, the currency in which prices are quoted, and the terms of sale.

KEY TERMS

After reading this chapter, you should understand these key terms:

International marketing	**General Agreement on Tariffs and**
Multinational marketing	**Trade (GATT)**
Comparative advantage	**Most-favored nation principle**
Trade deficit	**European Community (EC)**
Standard of living	**Pure standardized approach**
Gross National Product (GNP)	**Pure nonstandardized approach**
Industrialized countries	**Mixed approach**
Developing countries	**Exporting**
Less-developed countries	**Joint venture**
Currency stability	**Direct ownership**
Nationalism	**Straight extension**
Government stability	**Product adaptation**
Tariff	**Backward invention**
Trade quota	**Forward invention**
Embargo	**Dumping**

QUESTIONS FOR DISCUSSION

1. What potential benefits and risks does Avon face by entering the Chinese market?
2. Describe the principle of comparative advantage. Present three examples.
3. Why would a U.S.-based television manufacturer engage in marketing its products to a less-developed country?
4. What environmental factors might affect a U.S. company marketing women's blouses in Latin America?

5. Why do companies make culture-based marketing errors? How can they be avoided?

6. Illustrate how a country's stage of economic development influences consumer demand for goods and services.

7. What effect does currency devaluation have on an international marketer? How can these effects be minimized?

8. Develop a plan for limiting the negative consequences of nationalism.

9. Explain the most-favored nation principle in GATT.

10. Develop a standardized marketing strategy for a producer of clock radios.

11. Distinguish among straight extension, product adaptation, backward invention, and forward-invention product planning.

12. Given the risks, why would a firm utilize direct ownership in foreign countries?

13. How can one international advertising plan be both standardized and non-standardized?

14. As an American manufacturer of large computers, explain the criteria you would use to determine the foreign markets that present the greatest opportunities.

NOTES

1. "Avon Adds China to Its List of Foreign Markets," *Marketing News* (October 15, 1982), p. 1.

2. Russell M. Moore, "International Marketing's Competitive Arena Now Features Battle of World Firms, World Brands," *Marketing News* (October 17, 1980), Section 1, p. 10.

3. See Douglas G. Norvell and Sim Raveed, "Eleven Reasons for Firms to 'Go International,'" *Marketing News* (October 17, 1980), Section 1, pp. 1–2.

4. Bro Uttal, "Gillette Swings a Mighty Blade Abroad," *Fortune* (November 1974), p. 173.

5. Bureau of Economic Analysis, U.S. Commerce Department, 1982; and Office of Planning and Research, U.S. Commerce Department, 1982.

6. Deborah A. Randolph, "Small Firms Go Multinational, Find Niches in Foreign Markets," *Wall Street Journal* (September 8, 1980), p. 33.

7. *Seven Surprising Facts About Exporting* (Washington, D.C.: U.S. Department of Commerce, Bureau of International Commerce, 1977), p. 1.

8. Jaclyn Fierman, "The 50 Leading Exporters," *Fortune* (August 9, 1982), pp. 68–69.

9. Bureau of Economic Analysis, U.S. Commerce Department, 1982; and Office of Planning and Research, U.S. Commerce Department, 1982.

10. Ibid.

11. Masayoshi Kanabayashi and Urban C. Lehner, "Japanese Adopt Another Package to Open Market," *Wall Street Journal* (January 14, 1983), p. 26; and Douglas R. Sease and Amal Nag, "Third Year of U.S. Curbs on Japan's Cars Likely to Raise Prices, Delay New Entries," *Wall Street Journal* (February 14, 1983), p. 3.

12. "The Largest Industrial Companies in the World," *Fortune* (August 23, 1982), p. 181.

13. Lawrence G. Franko, "Multinationals: The End of Dominance," *Harvard Business Review*, Vol. 56 (November–December 1978), p. 95.

14. "The Largest Industrial Companies in the World," p. 181.

15. Warren J. Keegan, "A Conceptual Framework for Multinational Marketing," *Columbia Journal of World Business*, Vol. 7 (November 1972), p. 67.

16. Alfred L. Malabre, Jr., "Despite the Dollar's Decline, U.S. Retains Top Living Standard Among Major Nations," *Wall Street Journal* (May 1, 1979), p. 48.

17. Charles F. Steilen and Clint Laurent, "Special Skills Needed to Tap Growing Hong Kong Market," *Marketing News* (November 2, 1979), p. 7.

18. Thomas A. Staudt, "Rise of World Companies, Expanding Overseas Markets, New Vehicles to Mark 1980s," *Marketing News* (July 11, 1980), p. 8.

19. See Stephen Downer and Christy Marshall, "Currency Chaos Stills Marketers in Mexico," *Advertising Age* (August 23, 1982), pp. 1, 51; and Letitia Baldwin, "Marketers in Mexico Face Money Bind," *Advertising Age* (December 13, 1982), p. 12.

20. Louis Kraar, "The Multinationals Get Smarter About Political Risks," *Fortune* (March 24, 1980), p. 87.

21. R. J. Rummel and David A. Heenan, "How Multinationals Analyze Political Risk," *Harvard Business Review*, Vol. 56 (January–February 1978), p. 71.

22. "Japan: Barriers That Slow Ford Escort Sales," *Business Week* (December 1, 1980), p. 64.

23. See David B. Tinnin, "Trying to Restart the Engine," *Fortune* (November 29, 1982), pp. 52–56.

24. Laura Wentz, "How Big Advertisers Flopped in Brazil," *Advertising Age* (July 5, 1982), p. M-25.

25. Philip R. Cateora, *International Marketing*, Fifth Edition (Homewood, Ill.: Richard D. Irwin, 1983), p. 385.

26. Nancy Ukai and Jack Burton, "7-Eleven Japan Sets Bullish Image," *Advertising Age* (November 8, 1982), p. 34.

27. "Masson Leads Cal. Wines in Europe," *Advertising Age* (September 13, 1982), p. 26.

28. Uttal, "Gillette Swings a Mighty Blade Abroad."

29. John Koten, "GM, Toyota Unveil U.S. Small-Car Plan; Signing of Tentative Pact Due Thursday," *Wall Street Journal* (February 15, 1983), p. 3; and John Holusha, "Why G.M. Needs Toyota," *New York Times* (February 16, 1983), pp. D1, D8.

30. Howard Sharman, "Atari's Pac-Man Gobbling Up Interest in U.K., "*Advertising Age* (June 7, 1982), p. 62.

31. See Warren J. Keegan, "Multinational Product Planning: Strategic Alternatives," *Journal of Marketing*, Vol. 33 (January 1969), pp. 58–62.

32. John Tagliabue, "Tool Maker Thrives in Europe," *New York Times* (July 7, 1980), p. D1.

33. Frank Meissner, "Americans Must Practice the Marketing They Preach to Succeed in Japan's Mass Markets," *Marketing News* (October 17, 1980), Section 1, p. 5.

34. Kenneth H. Bacon, "U.S. Auto-Parts Firms Face Tough Times in Japan Despite Tariff-Bar Removal," *Wall Street Journal* (December 9, 1980), p. 30.

35. S. Watson Dunn, "Effect of National Identity on Multinational Promotion Strategy in Europe," *Journal of Marketing*, Vol. 40 (October 1976), p. 50.

36. *World Advertising Expenditures*, 16th Edition (New York: Starch INRA Hooper, 1981).

37. Robert T. Green and Eric Langeard, "A Cross-National Comparison of Consumer Habits and Innovator Characteristics," *Journal of Marketing*, Vol. 39 (July 1975), p. 39.

38. Robert T. Green, William Cunningham, and Isabella C. M. Cunningham, "The Effectiveness of Standardized Global Advertising," *Journal of Advertising*, Vol. 4 (Summer 1975), pp. 25–30.

39. John Tagliabue, "Kellogg Expanding in Europe," *New York Times* (October 22, 1980), p. D4.

CASES

1 LEVI STRAUSS: MARKETING JEANS IN EUROPE*

Levi Strauss has marketed jeans in Europe since the 1960s, when it began operating a warehouse and distribution center in Belgium. Its first European manufacturing plant was opened in Belgium during 1968. By 1981, Levi jeans were the most popular in Europe with sales of about $88,000,000 (compared with annual U.S. Levi jeans sales of almost $1 billion).

Despite its European success, Levi Strauss and its competitors have been unable to duplicate the U.S. consumption of jeans. Annual per capita jeans purchases in Europe are only 40 per cent of those in the U.S. See Table 1.

*The data in this case are drawn from Anika Michalowska, "Jeans Stretch Across Europe," *Advertising Age* (April 12, 1982), pp. M-2–M-3.

	All Groups	Adults Men	Adults Women	Age −15	Age 15–24	Age 25+	
							Table 1
Austria	0.5	0.6	0.3	1.1	1.2	0.3	**Per Capita Jeans**
Britain	1.1	1.1	0.8	1.3	2.6	0.6	**Consumption in Europe**
Denmark	1.3	0.9	0.9	2.9	2.1	0.3	**(Annual)**
France	0.9	0.8	0.5	1.4	1.5	0.4	
Holland	1.3	1.1	0.9	2.5	2.5	0.6	
Italy	1.0	0.9	0.6	1.4	2.5	0.4	
Norway	1.2	0.6	0.9	2.4	1.9	0.5	
Spain	0.6	0.5	0.4	1.0	1.5	0.2	
Sweden	1.6	0.9	0.9	3.8	2.2	0.6	
Switzerland	0.8	0.7	0.6	1.5	1.5	0.3	
West Germany	1.2	1.0	0.8	2.5	2.0	0.6	
Total Europe	1.0	0.9	0.7	1.7	2.0	0.5	
U.S.	2.5	2.4	1.3	4.7	3.7	1.2	

NOTE: Adults are defined as those of age 15 and over; children are below age 15. The 15–24 age group is regarded as the prime advertising target for purchasers, although the age group for main sales extends from 15 to 35.

Source: Euromonitor

Until recently, almost all jeans manufacturers believed in a "pan-European" (mass-marketing) approach. They felt jeans were ageless, genderless, and classless. But as Table 1 shows, this was not totally correct.

Now, the leading jeans makers are following one of two basic strategies: pan-European or regional (country). Levi is using the pan-European method, with one marketing program for all of Europe:

> We have the same strategy as Coca-Cola with a bit more flexibility in local approaches since we deal with fashion.

Wrangler is applying a regional orientation, with three independent divisions:

> Our strategy is not to have a pan-European advertising campaign. By doing so, there is a danger of losing specific appeal . . . . A lot depends on whether you have a uniform image and a uniform line of products.

In order to broaden its appeal, Levi expanded the types of jeans it offered in Europe from two in 1977 to twenty in 1982. Nonetheless, 80 to 85 per cent of total European jeans sales involve traditional denim styles.

QUESTIONS

1. Comment on Table 1. Be complete.
2. What criteria would you use to determine the European countries with the greatest potential for increased jeans sales?
3. Compare the Levi and Wrangler approaches to marketing jeans in Europe.
4. Evaluate the expansion of Levi's jeans line, from two styles to twenty.

2 PROCTER & GAMBLE: NOT MEETING EXPECTATIONS IN JAPAN†

With a great deal of optimism, Procter & Gamble (P&G) entered the Japanese market in 1973 with Cheer detergent. Shortly thereafter, it introduced Pampers disposable diapers. But despite an aggressive marketing effort, P&G lost $100 million in Japan between 1973 and 1979. Then, just when the company believed its products were ready to show sharp growth, the total Japanese detergent market dropped by 17 per cent and cultural factors caused Pampers sales to stagnate. From 1980 through 1982, P&G made no real progress.

Procter & Gamble's failure to become profitable in Japan after a full decade of trying can be traced to several poor marketing practices and other factors. Specific problems with Cheer were that

1. P&G could not effectively gain entry into the complex Japanese distribution system. It mistakenly purchased a declining Japanese soap company to promote Cheer.
2. P&G priced it far below the level set by Japanese firms, who had been practicing nonprice competition. These firms started a costly price war.
3. Commercials were too "hard sell" for Japanese consumers, who prefer more subtle "mood" ads. These commercials were on the most-hated list of Japanese viewers.
4. P&G was told very late by the Japanese government that nonphosphate detergent rules would be enacted. Japanese competitors knew in advance and gained sales until Cheer could be modified.

Similar predicaments occurred with Pampers. First, the success of Pampers in the U.S. was based upon household laundry being done once or twice a week. In Japan, laundry is washed almost every day, limiting the uses of Pampers. Second, a Japanese firm developed a disposable diaper that took away some of Pampers' sales. P&G's market share fell from 80 to 60–65 per cent.

As a result of these setbacks, P&G has delayed the introduction of a line of skincare products and other items. Said one Japanese competitor:

> Here is an American powerhouse with plenty of money and muscle entering an Asian country, thinking they can dominate the market by using the sales techniques that proved successful in the U.S. and Europe. But they face an unmitigated disaster by breaking every rule in the book when it comes to Japanese market practices.

QUESTIONS

1. Could P&G have avoided its problems in Japan? Explain your answer.
2. How were the situations P&G encountered for Cheer and Pampers different?
3. Evaluate the statement made by a P&G competitor.
4. Will P&G eventually succeed in Japan? Why or why not?

†The data in this case are drawn from Jack Burton and Dennis Chase, "Sun Still Not Shining on P&G in Japan," *Advertising Age* (December 20, 1982), pp. 4, 36.

Service and Nonprofit Marketing

17

Chapter Preview

Chapter Objectives

1   To differentiate between the marketing of services and products

2   To describe the characteristics of services, their role in the U.S. economy, special considerations for service marketers, and applications of service marketing

3   To distinguish between nonprofit and profit-oriented marketing

4   To discuss the characteristics of nonprofit marketing, its role in the U.S. economy, and applications of nonprofit marketing

In one television advertisement, Merrill Lynch's famous bull is seen walking slowly through a group of haystacks. Suddenly, the bull stops at a particular haystack. He digs in his hoofs, searching for something. Then, he uncovers a golden needle in this haystack. The symbolism is clear. Merrill Lynch can help investors find the legendary "needle in a haystack." (See Figure 17-1).

When it comes to marketing its financial services, Merrill Lynch is certainly a "breed apart." For more than forty years, the company has used aggressive marketing practices to expand its business (from 50,000 customers in 1940 to 3.3 million customers now). Today, Merrill Lynch is a financial services supermarket, offering a money market fund, a cash management account, insurance, real estate brokerage and mortgages, executive relocation planning, and a broad range of its traditional stock brokerage services. In 1982 alone, the firm spent $20 mil-lion on television, magazine, newspaper, radio, and direct mail advertising.

Merrill Lynch uses a multiple segmentation approach, appealing to both institutional investors (such as corporations) and individual investors. Services are packaged differently for the two segments; print advertisements are split between publications that reach business and those that reach retail customers. In targeting its advertising efforts, Merrill Lynch recognizes that 10 per cent of its customers do 90 per cent of the investing. The company wants to be sure it is adequately addressing the needs of the heavy investor, while offering programs to attract smaller investors.

Said a Merrill Lynch executive, "In an environment of increased competition, it's going to become critical for firms in this business to understand their customers, to understand what delivery systems best accomplish that, and finally to know how to price those products so that customers are going to be interested in purchasing them."[1]

Figure 17-1

The Merrill Lynch Bull Searching for the Golden Needle

This picture shows the filming of the television commercial in which the Merrill Lynch bull discovers the haystack which contains the golden needle of success. Reprinted by permission.

Overview

This chapter examines the marketing of services as well as the marketing of nonprofit organizations. Service and nonprofit marketing are distinct and different from product- and profit-oriented marketing. These differences require separate chapter coverage of these areas.

There is a substantial interaction between service and nonprofit marketing, because many nonprofit organizations are involved with services. Examples are colleges and universities, health clinics, and libraries.

Service Marketing: Definition and Scope

As defined in Chapter 7, *service marketing* encompasses the rental of products, the alteration or repair of products owned by consumers, and personal services. Generally, services have four characteristics that distinguish them from products: intangibility, perishability, inseparability from the service provider, and variability in quality. Table 17-1 contrasts these characteristics for services and products.

The *intangibility* of services means they often cannot be displayed, transported, stored, packaged, or inspected before buying. This occurs for repair services and personal services. The service operator can only describe the benefits that can be derived from the service experience.[2] The *perishability* of many services means they cannot be stored for future sale. Unused capacity cannot be shifted from one time period to

Service marketing consists of personal services and the rental and repair of products.

Intangibility, perishability, inseparability, and *variability* differentiate service from product marketing.

Services	Products	Table 17-1
1. *Services are often intangible.* Services are acts, deeds, performances, efforts. Most services cannot be physically possessed. The value of a service is based on an experience; there is no transfer of title.	1. *Products are tangible.* Products are objects, things, materials. The value of a product is based on ownership; transfer of title takes place.	**Basic Differences Between Services and Products**
2. *Services are usually perishable.* Unused capacity cannot be stored or shifted from one time to another.	2. *Products can be stored.* Product surpluses in one period can be applied against product shortages in another period.	
3. *Services are frequently inseparable.* One cannot separate the quality of many services from the service provider.	3. *Products can be graded or built to specifications.* The quality of a product can be differentiated from a channel member's quality.	
4. *Services may vary in quality over time.* It is difficult to standardize some services because of their labor intensiveness and the involvement of the service user in diagnosing his or her service needs.	4. *Products can be standardized.* Mass production and quality control can be used.	

another. For example, if a house painter who needs eight hours to paint a single house is idle on Monday, he or she will not be able to paint two houses on Tuesday. Monday's idle time is just lost. The service supplier must try to regulate consumer usage so there is consistent demand throughout various time periods.

Services are usually *inseparable* from the service provider. For example, the quality of a car repair depends on the skill of the mechanic, and the quality of legal services depends on the skill of an attorney. *Variability* in quality often occurs even if services are completed by the same operator. Variations may be due to the difficulty in diagnosing a problem (for repairs), the inability of the customer to verbalize his or her service needs, and the lack of standardization and mass production for most services.

The impact of these characteristics is greatest for personal services. They are more intangible, more perishable, more inseparable from the service provider, and have more quality variations than product-rental services or owned-goods services.

Although services have different characteristics from products, their sales are often connected. In service marketing, the service dominates the offering and the product augments it. For example, the major cost of a lawn-care service is the time of the operator, not the machinery used. Repair-service firms exist to install, modify, or fix all types of products from televisions to plumbing. Some independent service firms aid consumers in their purchases. These include credit card companies such as American Express and Visa and delivery firms such as United Parcel and Emery. In some instances, such as car rental and leasing, an alternative to product purchase is provided.

Service marketing can be examined in terms of a classification system, the extent of services in the economy, and the use of marketing by service firms.

Classification of Services

Services are classified on the basis of market, tangibility, skill, goals, regulation, labor intensiveness, and customer contact.

Figure 17-2 shows a detailed, seven-way classification system for services. Services are categorized by market, degree of tangibility, skill of the service provider, goal of the service provider, degree of regulation, labor intensiveness, and amount of customer contact. The classification system is a useful way of showing the diversity of service marketing.

In selecting a market, a firm should recognize that consumer and industrial segments have similarities as well as differences, as detailed in Chapter 5. The same basic service (for example, carpet cleaning, typewriter repair, lawn care, and air travel) may be offered to each market. Both markets use consumer decision making to select a service, although buying influences may be different. Each segment can counter high prices or poor service levels by performing some tasks themselves. The major differences between the segments are the reasons for the service, the quantity of service required, and the complexity of the service performed.

Services differ significantly in terms of their tangibility. In general, the less tangible the service, the less service marketing resembles product marketing. For nongoods services, performance can be judged only

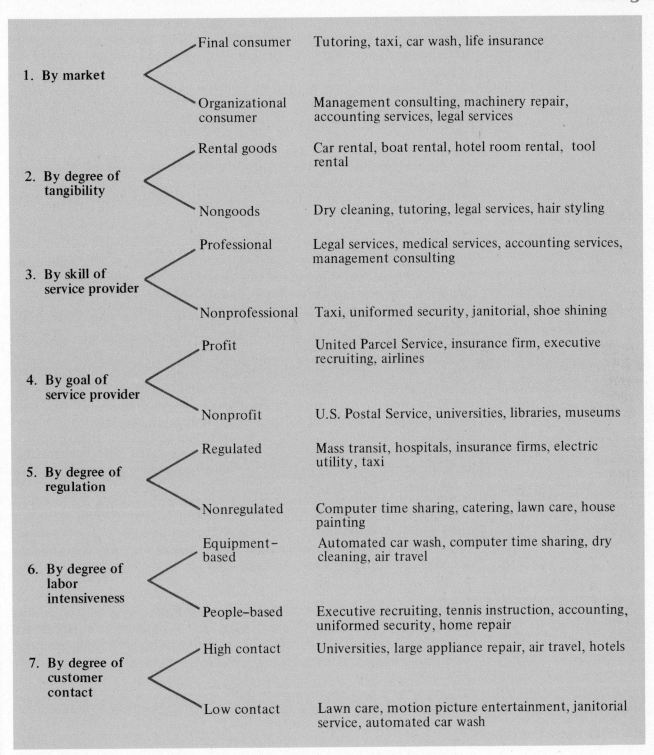

1. **By market**
   - Final consumer — Tutoring, taxi, car wash, life insurance
   - Organizational consumer — Management consulting, machinery repair, accounting services, legal services

2. **By degree of tangibility**
   - Rental goods — Car rental, boat rental, hotel room rental, tool rental
   - Nongoods — Dry cleaning, tutoring, legal services, hair styling

3. **By skill of service provider**
   - Professional — Legal services, medical services, accounting services, management consulting
   - Nonprofessional — Taxi, uniformed security, janitorial, shoe shining

4. **By goal of service provider**
   - Profit — United Parcel Service, insurance firm, executive recruiting, airlines
   - Nonprofit — U.S. Postal Service, universities, libraries, museums

5. **By degree of regulation**
   - Regulated — Mass transit, hospitals, insurance firms, electric utility, taxi
   - Nonregulated — Computer time sharing, catering, lawn care, house painting

6. **By degree of labor intensiveness**
   - Equipment-based — Automated car wash, computer time sharing, dry cleaning, air travel
   - People-based — Executive recruiting, tennis instruction, accounting, uniformed security, home repair

7. **By degree of customer contact**
   - High contact — Universities, large appliance repair, air travel, hotels
   - Low contact — Lawn care, motion picture entertainment, janitorial service, automated car wash

Figure 17-2
Classification System for Services

after the service is completed; and a consistent service level is difficult to maintain. Rentals involve physical products and are more tangible than nongoods services; thus they may be marketed in a manner similar to products.

Services may be provided by persons of greatly varying skills. For services requiring high levels of skills, customers are quite selective in their choice of provider. That is why professionals often achieve customer loyalty. For services requiring low levels of skill, the range of acceptable substitutes is usually much greater.

Service marketing may be profit or nonprofit oriented. Nonprofit-service marketing may be undertaken by government or private organizations. Nonprofit marketing is discussed in depth in the second part of this chapter.

Service marketing also varies by the extent of regulation. Some organizations, such as utilities and hospitals, are highly regulated. Others, such as caterers and house painters, are subject to limited regulation.

The traditional view of services has been that they are something performed by one individual for another. However, this view is too narrow. Services do differ in their labor intensity—for example, an automated versus a manual car wash or teller-oriented versus automated bank services. Labor intensity increases when highly skilled personnel are involved and/or services must be provided at the customer's home or place of business. Some labor-intensive services may be performed by do-it-yourself consumers (for example, home repair).

Last, service marketing can be classified by the degree of customer contact. When customer contact is high, training personnel in interpersonal skills is essential. This is in addition to the technical training needed to properly perform a service. Many service providers mistakenly ignore interpersonal training. They must realize that appliance repairpeople, car mechanics, and other service personnel also function as salespeople and complaint handlers. They may be the only contact a consumer has with the firm. When customer contact is low, technical skills are most essential.

It is important to note that an organization is normally classified on the basis of a combination of these factors. For example, a firm that tutors students for college-board exams appeals to final consumers, offers an intangible service, requires skill by the service provider, is profit oriented, is not regulated, employs many trainers, and has high customer contact. A company can also operate in more than one part of a category. For example, an accountant may deal with both final and organizational consumer markets.

Extent of Services in the Economy

The average American family spends almost half of its budget on services.

The United States has been described as the leading service economy in the world. In the private sector two thirds of the labor force is now employed in a service capacity. During 1960, the typical family spent 40 per cent of its budget on services. By 1981, the figure exceeded 47 per cent. Over this period, service expenditures rose from $131 billion to almost $900 billion. Housing, medical care, and household operations account for almost 70 per cent of consumer service spending.[3]

Various reasons have been cited for the growth of final consumer-related services, including the increased prosperity of the population, the need for specialized repairs and the installation of complex products, the growing quality of services, and the leisure orientation of U.S. consumers.

In the industrial sector, the original value of equipment being leased is about $150 billion, and leasing accounts for 20 per cent of all capital goods in the United States.[4] As purchase prices have risen, leasing has become more attractive. Among the types of equipment that can be leased are communication satellites, supertankers, oil rigs, and computers.

Despite these sizable figures, the data on services are underestimated. They do not include the **hidden service sector** that encompasses the systems planning, preinstallation support, software, repair, maintenance, delivery, collection, and bookkeeping services of firms that emphasize product sales. For example, although IBM is classified as a manufacturing company, many of its employees install or repair machines, train customers, or write computer programs.

The following illustrations show the scope of service marketing:

- Citibank offers a broad assortment of banking services for final and business consumers. Citibank makes extensive use of advertising, has implemented a huge automatic teller system, and is an innovator in services (such as money market funds for small investors). Recently, Citibank introduced a segmentation strategy aimed at wealthy consumers, emphasizing convenience and personal service.[5]
- The Department of Health and Human Services predicts a surplus of 70,000 doctors by 1990. As a result, physicians are beginning to learn marketing skills. Many of them attend seminars, employ marketing consultants, analyze census data when opening offices, and mail medical columns to patients and prospective patients. Few are yet active in advertising.[6]
- MCI Communications, founded in 1968, operates in the long-distance telephone service industry. It faces 200 competitors, including AT&T which has 96 per cent of industry sales (MCI is second with 2.5 per cent). MCI emphasizes its discount rates through a large advertising effort. See Figure 17-3. By the end of 1982, MCI had a base of 1 million customers (including 200,000 business accounts) in 200 metropolitan areas. The firm is looking into diversification, because of the level of competition.[7]
- In order to train consumers in how to use their new computers, hundreds of service firms are entering the market. They provide seminars, classroom instruction, and on-site company courses. The role of training in computer literacy is significant. As one potential customer said, "I would love to buy a personal computer for my business if I weren't so intimidated by it and someone could show me how to use it." Between 1983 and 1986, it is expected that $3 billion will be spent on computer training.[8]

The *hidden service sector* includes services by manufacturers in the course of their businesses.

You have a choice. You can contribute to Bell's profits. Or yours.

LONG DISTANCE CALLS	MINS	BELL	MCI	SAVINGS
New York City to Trenton	15	$4.40	$2.90	34.1%
Washington D.C. to Atlanta	2	1.05	.75	28.6
Erie to Cleveland	3	1.31	.98	25.2
Philadelphia to Wilmington	20	5.80	3.87	33.3
Chicago to Milwaukee	5	2.05	1.64	20.0
Boston to Providence	2	.76	.39	48.7
Hartford to Springfield, MA	17	4.96	3.29	33.6
New Haven to New York City	1	.57	.25	56.1
Scranton to Newark	7	2.79	2.30	17.6
Richmond to Baltimore	1	.58	.34	41.4
Cincinnati to Louisville	4	1.68	1.31	22.0
Cheyenne to Fort Collins	30	8.60	5.81	32.4

Rates show comparative pricing between Bell's business day rate and MCI's business day rate. Final rate authorities on all tariffed services are MCI Tariff FCC 1 and AT&T Tariff FCC 263

Usually, there are a lot of pros and cons to any decision.

With this decision, there are all pros and no cons.

You can keep paying the full rate to Bell. Or you can join MCI and cut your long distance costs 15 to 50%.

Without giving up anything.

You'll be in good company. Today, half the Fortune 500 and 170,000 other companies are enjoying the savings you see on the chart.

How can MCI charge less than Bell?

Very simply, MCI operates a long distance system more efficiently than Bell. We're a newer company and we're not saddled with outdated equipment. We work to keep our costs low, so we can pass the savings along to you.

We're also able to offer you flexibility. Every business has different needs. So we have a number of different plans for you to choose from.

They all have one thing in common. You save on every phone call you make. From 15 to 50%.

The total savings over a year can be enormous. A computer company saved a million dollars. An airline, $800,000. A bank, $750,000.

No capital investment. No installation. No nothing.

You get these savings with absolutely no capital investment. No new equipment of any kind. So, from the first moment you start using MCI, the savings are pure profit.

All you need are the same push-button phones you're using now. You punch a few extra buttons. That's it. Everything else is exactly the same. Except you start paying a lot less.

MCI now provides service to over 80% of the nation's area codes. To and from over 4000 cities across the country. And every day, another little piece of America's geography is being added.

Naturally, you may have some questions about MCI. We'd be happy to send you a free brochure. Simply fill out the coupon and mail it to us.

Or call your local MCI sales office.

And start putting your money into your profits.

Instead of Bell's.

MCI
The nation's long distance phone company.

MCI Telecommunications Corp.
1133 19th Street, N.W.
Washington, D.C. 20036 Attn: P. Colpitts

Please send me more information on how to cut long distance costs 15 to 50%.

Name
Title
Company
Address   City
State   Zip

Figure 17-3
MCI's Marketing Approach

Reprinted by permission.

Use of Marketing by Service Firms

Service firms are not as involved with marketing as manufacturing firms.

Service firms have typically lagged behind manufacturing firms in developing and using marketing. One study of 400 service and manufacturing companies concluded that service companies were less likely to have marketing activities performed by a marketing department, have an overall sales plan, use sales training programs, use marketing research firms and marketing consultants, spend as much on marketing as a per cent of sales, and handle their advertising through an outside agency.[9]

In another study, it was determined that banks and airlines utilized some marketing. Less marketing was used by insurance, brokerage, and public transportation firms. Still less usage was found for law, management consulting, medicine, architecture, and engineering. However, an overall trend toward increased applications of marketing by service firms was discovered.[10]

Several factors explain the lower use of marketing by service organizations and professionals. One, many services firms stress technical expertise. Often, these firms were started because of specialized skills, such as repairing plumbing systems, preparing food, or having knowledge of the law. Two, most service firms are so small that marketing specialists cannot be used. Three, strict licensing provisions sometimes limit competition and the need for marketing. Four, consumers have held a variety of service professionals, particularly doctors and lawyers, in such high esteem that marketing has not been needed. Five, in the past a number of associations prohibited advertising by their members. This was changed by Supreme Court rulings in the late 1970s that permitted advertising by professionals. Finally, there are still a number of service professionals who have a dislike for marketing, lack a full understanding of it, or question the use of marketing practices, such as advertising, in their fields.

> The lower use of marketing is due to an emphasis on technical expertise, small size, limited competition, and negative attitudes toward marketing.

    Over the next several years, it is expected that the use of marketing by service firms will increase dramatically, as a result of deregulation in many industries (such as banking, transportation, and communication), growing competition among service providers (such as dental services in retail stores versus traditional dentists), the recent growth in the do-it-yourself market segment due to the rising costs of services, and the expanding number of service professionals with formal business training. See Figure 17-4.

Applying Marketing to Services

The first part of this section assesses some of the special considerations in applying marketing to services. The second part contains illustrations of service marketing in three different areas: hotels, car repair and servicing, and legal services.

Figure 17-4
The Increasing Use of Marketing by Service Firms

Drawing by Robert Mankoff. © The New York Magazine, Inc.

Special Considerations for Service Marketers

The marketing of services involves a variety of special considerations, several of which are discussed in this subsection.[11]

Many services cannot be stockpiled. For example, if a movie theater has 500 seats, it cannot admit more than 500 customers to a Saturday night showing even though a Wednesday matinee had 400 empty seats. It is clear that the empty seats during a Wednesday movie cannot be used to increase theater capacity during the Saturday peak demand period. In order to match demand with supply, a service firm must alter the timing of demand and/or exert better control over the supply of the service offering. It should avoid excess demand that goes unsatisfied as well as excess capacity that results in an unproductive use of resources. Following are a number of methods for matching demand with supply:[12]

Balance the timing of demand by
1. Adding attractive services in off-peak periods, such as a hotel providing convention-meeting rooms at reduced prices.
2. Utilizing a reservation system to spread out demand.
3. Employing price discrimination, with lower prices for off-peak periods.
4. Providing customers with peripheral services while they are waiting, such as a cocktail lounge in a restaurant.

Balance supply by
1. Using part-time employees at peak periods.
2. Training employees in different skills so they can be shifted to whatever task has the greatest demand at any point in time, thus avoiding a bottleneck.
3. Increasing consumer participation in the completion of services, such as self-service buffets and direct dialing for long-distance calls.
4. Sharing capacity with other service providers, such as hospitals sharing expensive, but seldom-used, diagnostic equipment.

For some services, only a small portion of the service mix is visible to the consumer. As an example, in-store repairs are normally not seen by consumers. Although the repairperson may spend three hours on a television and insert two parts priced at $6, the consumer sees a bill for $37 and does not realize the amount of service involved. Therefore, service time and functions must be explained to customers.

The intangibility of services makes pricing difficult. For example, should an automobile mechanic set a price for the repair of a transmission on the basis of a standardized price list or place a value on his or her time and set a specific price after the transmission is repaired? How should the price be broken down into problem analysis and service components? Should prices vary for repairs performed by the head mechanic versus regular mechanics? In setting routine prices, what is covered in the basic service? Services that are equipment-based and routine in nature may be suited to cost-oriented pricing. Other services should rely on competitive pricing.[13]

The intangibility of services also makes promotion difficult. Unlike product promotion, which may stress tangible attributes and encourage customer analysis prior to a purchase, much service promotion must rely on performance attributes, which can be measured only after a purchase is made. There are three fundamental ways to promote a service:[14]

1. Develop a tangible representation of the service. For example, a credit card, although not a financial service itself, still serves as a physical product with its own image and benefits.
2. Associate the intangible service with a tangible object more easily perceived by the customer.
   For example: "You're in good *hands* with Allstate."
   "I've got a piece of the *rock*."
   "Under the Traveler's *umbrella*."
   "The Nationwide *blanket* of protection."
3. Focus on the relationship between the seller of the service and the user of the service and away from the intangible itself. Sell the competence, skill, and concern of the agent or service employee to develop a client relationship.

As noted earlier, the existence of a close service provider–consumer relationship makes employee interpersonal skills important. The workforce must be trained to interact well with consumers and be consistent in responses. Employee appearance and mannerisms have a much greater impact on service firms than on product firms. All employee-customer contacts should be performed properly, including sales, credit, delivery, and repair.

Interpersonal skills are important due to the relationship between consumer and service provider.

Many services have high costs and low reliability. One solution to this problem is the **industrialization of services** using hard, soft, and hybrid technologies.[15] **Hard technologies** substitute machinery for people, such as the implementation of an electronic credit authorization system instead of manual credit checks. Hard technologies cannot be applied to services requiring extensive personal skill and contact such as medical, legal, and hairstyling services.

The industrialization of services can involve hard technologies, soft technologies, or hybrid technologies.

Soft technologies substitute preplanned systems for individual services. For example, many travel agents sell prepackaged vacation tours. This standardizes transportation, accommodations, food, and sightseeing. **Hybrid technologies** combine hard and soft technologies. Examples include computer-based truck routing and specialized low-priced repair facilities, such as muffler repair shops.

Service reliability can also be improved by setting higher-level standards and by tying employee pay, promotions, and retention to performance levels. As an example, American Airlines developed a series of standards that enabled the company to become the preferred domestic airline, according to a recent Airline Passengers Association survey:[16]

1. Reservation phones must be answered within 20 seconds.
2. 85 per cent of passengers should not have to stand in line more than 5 minutes.

3. Flights must take off within 5 minutes of departure time.
4. Cabins must have their proper supply of magazines.
5. 85 per cent of flights should land within 15 minutes of arrival time.
6. Doors are to be opened 70 seconds after the plane stops rolling.
7. The last baggage should reach the terminal not more than 17 minutes after passengers begin to disembark from the plane.

Peripheral services add to the basic offering and can create a competitive advantage.

Peripheral services are complementary services that are needed to supplement the basic service offering. For example, while a tourist hotel markets rooms for travelers, it will also need an adequate reservation system, cleaning personnel, parking facilities, recreation facilities, restaurants, and connections to transportation terminals. Peripheral services increase a service firm's investment, require additional employee and management skills, and may be time consuming. However, they may also enable the company to create and sustain a competitive advantage.

Illustrations of Service Marketing

This subsection examines service marketing for hotels, car repairs and servicing, and legal services. These three examples represent a rented-goods service, an owned-goods service, and a nongoods service. They differ by degree of tangibility, skill of service provider, degree of labor intensiveness, and level of customer contact.

Hotels may appeal to one or more consumer segments from among business travelers, through tourists (who stay one night), regular tourists (who stay two or more nights), and conventioneers. Each segment would require different services. The business traveler seeks efficient service, a desk in the room, and convenient meeting rooms. The through tourist seeks a convenient location, low prices, and fast-food service. The regular tourist seeks a nice room, recreational facilities, and connections for sightseeing. Conventioneers seek large meeting rooms, pre-planned sight-seeing, and hospitality suites.

To attract and retain customers, hotels have been adding new services and improving their marketing efforts. First-run movies that can be viewed in the room, an indoor health spa, and casino gambling (where legal) are some of the services being added. Marketing efforts involve more television advertising and the use of well-conceived slogans, such as Holiday Inn's "no excuses guarantee."[17]

Hotels are also trying to resolve consumer complaints more effectively. For example, frequent business travelers are most concerned about overbooking—even those with guaranteed reservations could get turned away; long waiting lines; late check-in times; and unresponsive or discourteous staffs. In addition, female business travelers are concerned about personal safety and are reluctant to eat alone in restaurants. Some of these complaints have been caused by elements over which hotels have control, such as inadequate or poorly trained staff. Others are uncontrollable, such as guests overstaying their reservations.[18]

Hotels are responding in several ways. Many offer express checkouts, whereby bills are mailed to guests' businesses or homes. Some hotels place women traveling alone on certain floors and patrol those floors more frequently. A number of hotels are increasing the lighting in lobbies so that women will be more comfortable. Also, questionnaires are used to measure consumer satisfaction with hotel performance.

Automobile repairs and servicing are carried out through two basic formats: manufacturer-owned or sponsored dealerships or independent service centers. For example, General Motors' cars can be repaired and serviced through the company's "Mr. Goodwrench" program, which is available at approved dealerships. To qualify for the Mr. Goodwrench program, dealers must satisfy a number of specific quality standards. General Motors supports this program by providing mass advertising, supervising the dealers, and improving service techniques.[19] General Motors' cars can also be repaired and serviced through independent service stations. These stations handle a wide variety of makes and models. They emphasize a convenient location, personalized service, more flexible prices, faster service time, and longer hours.

The growth in foreign car sales has resulted in more service stations, garages, and mass merchandisers (such as Sears) servicing these automobiles. Some firms specialize in foreign car work because of higher profit margins. Others accept imports only grudgingly, because of difficulties with getting parts, the metric system, and the relatively small working space under the hood.

Long waiting lists at foreign car dealers and relatively high prices have shifted many foreign car owners from dealer service centers to independent firms. In an attempt to gain this business back, one foreign car manufacturer has urged its dealers to accept credit cards, advertise specials, stress quality control, extend service hours, and provide more accurate repair estimates.[20]

In 1977 the Supreme Court ruled that attorneys could not be prohibited from advertising their services and fee structures.[21] Since then, the advertising of legal services has increased significantly and a number of marketing innovations have been implemented. Lawyers now advertise on television and radio and in newspapers and magazines. Figure 17-5 shows a television ad for legal services.

Law clinics and franchised law firms have developed. These operations feature a large staff of attorneys, convenient locations (such as in shopping centers), standardized fees and services (such as $100 for a simple will), plain fixtures and furniture, and word-processing systems. The companies concentrate on routine legal services.

One leading law chain is Jacoby & Meyers, with more than 75 offices in California and New York. Jacoby & Meyers

- Offers the services of over 160 attorneys.
- Has a base of 120,000 clients.
- Has very low prices (e.g., $300 for a divorce compared with $750 to $1,500 for traditional competitors).
- Provides written estimates of charges in advance.
- Uses specialists for more complex cases.
- Spends 12 per cent of revenues on advertising.

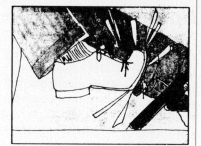

Storyboard shows opening sequences of 30-second TV commercial for Law Offices of James Sokolove, an ad co-op of 16 Massachusetts legal firms.

Spot starts with "driver's eye" shot through windshield as car moves along two-lane street. Down the road, two cars appear, one behind the other, coming

from the opposite direction. As the oncoming cars move closer, one pulls out to pass the other. Then foot is shown hitting brake pedal. The car attempting to pass

fails to move out of lane. Accident is imminent. Hands are shown clenching steering wheel. Brakes squeal. Just before head-on-collison occurs, camera cuts

to Sokolove, who reminds viewers that they have a legal right to collect for their injuries and losses resulting from such accidents. At end of spot, toll-

free number of law offices appears at bottom of screen along with offer of free consultation.

Source: Bernard Whalen, "Legal Services Marketing Enters New Era with Ad Co-Op's 'Slick,' Professional TV Commercial," *Marketing News* (March 5, 1982), p.1.

Figure 17-5
Television Advertising of Legal Services

Reprinted by permission.

- Expects to expand to 750 offices.
- Earns a pretax profit of 25 to 35 per cent of revenues.[22]

The marketing of legal services has been met with resistance and objections from many attorneys. They criticize price advertising for stressing price at the expense of quality and mass-marketing techniques as eliminating personalized counseling. They also believe the public's confidence in the profession will decline, information in ads may not be accurate, and overly high consumer expectations will be created. Attorneys applying marketing techniques state that they are making legal services available to new groups of consumers and those who could not otherwise afford them.[23] The majority of attorneys still do not advertise; they rely on referrals.

Nonprofit Marketing: Definition and Scope

As defined in Chapter 5, **nonprofit marketing** is conducted in the public interest or to foster a cause and does not seek financial profits. It may involve organizations, people, places, and ideas, as well as products and services. Although nonprofit organizations conduct exchanges, they are not necessarily in the form of dollars for goods and services. Politicians request votes in exchange for promises of better and more effective government services. The Postal Service wants increased use of zip codes in exchange for improved service and lower rate hikes. The American Cancer Society seeks funds for cancer research and treatment programs.

    In many cases the prices charged by nonprofit organizations have no relationship to the cost or value of services. For example, the Girl Scouts of America sells cookies to raise funds, but only part of the purchase price goes for the cookies. On the other hand, the price of a chest X ray at a local health clinic may be below its cost or even free.

    Nonprofit marketing can be examined in terms of a comparison with profit-oriented marketing, a classification system, and its extent in the economy. Three examples of nonprofit marketing are examined in depth: the Postal Service, colleges and universities, and public libraries.

Nonprofit marketing serves the public interest and does not seek profits.

Nonprofit Versus Profit-Oriented Marketing

Table 17-2 outlines the basic differences between nonprofit and profit-oriented marketing. Nonprofit marketing is much more prone to promote social programs and ideas than is profit-oriented marketing. Exam-

Nonprofit marketing is broad in scope and is frequently involved with social marketing.

Nonprofit Marketing	*Profit-Oriented Marketing*	*Table 17-2*
1. Nonprofit marketing is concerned with organizations, people, places, and ideas, as well as products and services.	1. Profit-oriented marketing is largely concerned with goods and services.	**Basic Differences Between Nonprofit and Profit-Oriented Marketing**
2. Exchanges can be in the form of votes in return for better government or the use of a zip code in return for improved service and lower rate increases.	2. Exchanges are generally in the form of dollars for goods and services.	
3. Objectives are more complex because success or failure cannot be measured strictly in financial terms.	3. Objectives are generally stated in terms of sales, profits, and recovery of cash.	
4. The benefits of nonprofit services are often not related to consumer payments.	4. The benefits of profit-oriented marketing are usually related to consumer payments.	
5. Nonprofit organizations may be expected or required to serve economically unfeasible market segments.	5. Profit-oriented marketing seeks to serve only those market segments that are profitable.	
6. Nonprofit organizations typically have two constituencies: clients and donors.	6. Profit-oriented marketing has one constituency: clients.	

Table 17-3   *Exchange Process*

Illustrations of Exchange Process for Organizations, People, Places, and Ideas

Organizations		
College fraternities	Benefits to members: social experience, convenient place to live, assistance from upper classmen and graduates	Benefits to fraternities: membership dues, greater on-campus exposure, improved facilities
People		
Political candidates	Benefits to voters: efficient government, better services, election of candidates with similar views	Benefits to candidates: election, prestige, power
Places		
Major cities as sites for conventions	Benefits to attendees: central locations, cultural facilities, superior accommodations and transportation	Benefits to cities: revenues, prestige, lessening of tax burdens for residents
Ideas		
Nonsmoking campaigns	Benefits to smokers: improved health, better self-image, increased social acceptance	Benefits to nonsmokers: cleaner environment, longer life span for loved ones, lower costs for medical system

ples include recycling, highway safety, family planning, gun control, and energy conservation. The use of marketing to increase the acceptability of social ideas is referred to as ***social marketing***.[24] Table 17-3 contains illustrations of the exchange process for organizations, people, places, and ideas.

Nonprofit marketing often relies on fund-raising efforts.

Nonprofit marketing may not generate revenues in day-to-day exchanges. Instead it may rely on infrequent fund-raising efforts. In addition, a successful marketing campaign may actually lose money if services or products are provided at less than cost. It is necessary for operating budgets to be large enough to serve the number of anticipated clients, so that none are poorly treated or turned away.

Objectives for nonprofit organizations go beyond financial goals.

Objectives for nonprofit organizations are sometimes complex, because success or failure cannot be measured strictly in financial terms. There is also less accountability, because there are no owners. A nonprofit organization might have this combination of objectives: raise $300,000 from government grants, increase client usage, find a cure for a disease, change public attitudes, and raise $500,000 from private donors. Objectives must include the number of clients to be served, the amount of service to be rendered, and the quality of service to be provided.

While the general public supports nonprofit organizations, benefits may be distributed unequally.

The benefits of nonprofit organizations are often not distributed on the basis of consumer payments. Only a small portion of the population contracts a disease, requires humanitarian services, visits a museum, uses a public library, or goes to a health clinic in a given year; yet, the general public pays to find cures, support fellow citizens, or otherwise assist nonprofit organizations. With profit organizations, benefits are usually distributed equitably, based on consumers' direct payments in exchange for products or services.

Nonprofit organizations are frequently expected, or even required, to serve market segments that a profit-oriented organization would find uneconomical. For example, the U.S. Postal Service must maintain rural post offices and Amtrack must provide passenger rail service on routes across sparsely populated areas. This may give profit-oriented firms an advantage, because they can concentrate their efforts on the most lucrative market segments.[25]

Nonprofit organizations often serve markets that are uneconomical for profit-oriented firms.

While profit-oriented firms have one primary constituency to which they offer goods and services and from which they receive payment, the typical nonprofit organization has two constituencies: *clients*—for whom it provides membership, elected officials, locations, ideas, products, and services—and ***donors***—from whom it receives resources (which may be time from volunteers or money from foundations and individuals). Often, there is little overlap between clients and donors.

Nonprofit organizations have two primary constituencies: *clients* and *donors*.

Private nonprofit organizations have also been granted a number of legal advantages over their profit-oriented counterparts. These include tax-deductible contributions from donors, exemptions from most sales and real-estate taxes, and special reduced postal rates.

Classification of Nonprofit Marketing

Nonprofit marketing may be classified on the basis of tangibility, organization structure, objectives, and constituency. This four-way classification is shown in Figure 17-6. As in the service-marketing classification, a nonprofit organization would be categorized by a combination of these factors. For example, postage stamps for collectors are tangible products, distributed by the federal government, intended to reduce the yearly deficit of the Postal Service, and aimed at a market segment of the general public.

The classification of nonprofit marketing is based on tangibility, organization structure, objectives, and constituency.

As noted earlier, nonprofit marketing may involve organizations, people, places, ideas, products, and services. For example, organizations include foundations, universities, religious institutions, and government; people include politicians and volunteers; places include resorts and industrial centers; ideas include family planning and patriotism; products include postage stamps and professional journals; and services include medical care, child care, and education.

Nonprofit organizations may have one of three alternate structures: government (federal, state, local), private, or cooperative. For example, the federal government markets military service to potential recruits, postal services, and other products and services. State governments market universities and employment services. Local governments market colleges, libraries, and sports arenas. In addition, government marketing is often used to increase voter registration, secure approval of bonds, and obtain passage of school and library budgets. Private organi-

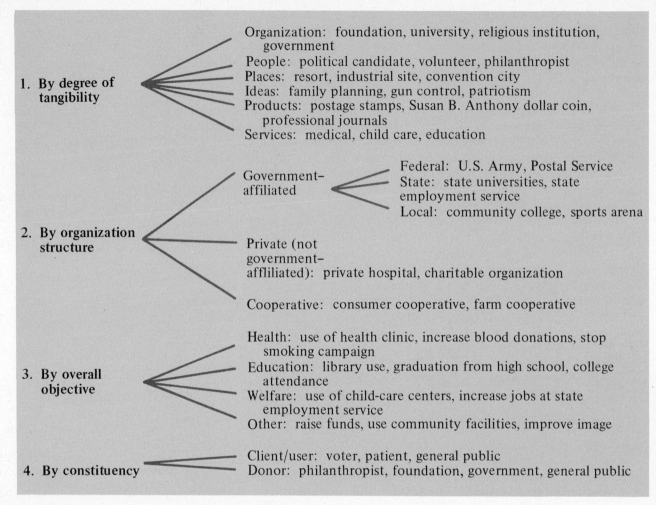

1. **By degree of tangibility**
   - Organization: foundation, university, religious institution, government
   - People: political candidate, volunteer, philanthropist
   - Places: resort, industrial site, convention city
   - Ideas: family planning, gun control, patriotism
   - Products: postage stamps, Susan B. Anthony dollar coin, professional journals
   - Services: medical, child care, education

2. **By organization structure**
   - Government-affiliated
     - Federal: U.S. Army, Postal Service
     - State: state universities, state employment service
     - Local: community college, sports arena
   - Private (not government-affliliated): private hospital, charitable organization
   - Cooperative: consumer cooperative, farm cooperative

3. **By overall objective**
   - Health: use of health clinic, increase blood donations, stop smoking campaign
   - Education: library use, graduation from high school, college attendance
   - Welfare: use of child-care centers, increase jobs at state employment service
   - Other: raise funds, use community facilities, improve image

4. **By constituency**
   - Client/user: voter, patient, general public
   - Donor: philanthropist, foundation, government, general public

Figure 17-6
A Classification System for Nonprofit Marketing

zations market hospitals, charities, social services, and other products and services. They also use marketing to increase membership and donations. Cooperative organizations aid people such as consumers and farmers. The success of cooperatives depends on their ability to attract and maintain a large membership base and on their efficiency in performing distribution functions.

Overall nonprofit marketing objectives can be divided into health (increase the number of nonsmokers), education (increase the usage of the local library), welfare (list more job openings at a state employment office), and other (increase membership in the Boy Scouts) components.

Last, nonprofit organizations must remember that they usually require the support of two distinct constituencies: clients/users and donors. Clients/users are interested in the direct benefits they obtain from participation with an organization, such as their improved health, education, or welfare. Donors are concerned about efficiency of operations, success rates, availability of products and services, and recognition of their contributions. For each constituency, the organization must correctly pinpoint its target market. As an example, the League of Women Voters might concentrate on unregistered voters during an enrollment drive, and seek funds from corporate foundations.

Extent of Nonprofit Marketing in the Economy

Thousands of nonprofit organizations operate in the United States, and their use of marketing varies widely, as these examples show:

Nonprofit organizations are diverse in their focus and use of marketing.

- In 1881, the American Association of the Red Cross was founded. Throughout its existence, the Red Cross has actively promoted its humanitarian goals. In World War I, it produced 2,000 parades and advertised in many media to raise funds. In World War II, movie and Broadway stars made announcements and appearances. In 1982–83, the Red Cross used a sophisticated television, radio, newspaper, and magazine ad campaign. It received free advertising space valued at more than $35 million during 1982–83.[26]
- The Educational Testing Service (ETS) administers the Scholastic Aptitude Test (SAT) and a number of other standardized exams. Now that the college-age population has stopped growing and government grants have dried up, ETS is turning to increased marketing. ETS has hired the Booz Allen & Hamilton consulting firm, begun searching for new markets (such as state licensing of professionals), and developed a sales force to determine the needs of potential corporate clients.[27]
- In 1976, visitors to New York State spent $5.2 billion on tourism. As a result of the popular "I Love New York" campaign, this figure rose to $10.5 billion in 1981. Resort occupancy rose by nearly 70 per cent, while Broadway ticket sales doubled during this time. The campaign ran on television and radio and in print media, and featured celebrities and New York landmarks.[28] New York was the first state to promote itself so aggressively. Others have now followed.
- In 1981 the U.S. government spent about $189 million for national advertising, making it the twenty-sixth largest advertiser in the country.[29] The federal government spent more on advertising than firms such as Gillette, General Electric, Revlon, and American Express. The largest federal expenditures were for military recruitment, the Postal Service, and Amtrack.
- In 1982, the average cost of an election for the U.S. Senate was more than $1 million. An average House of Representatives election cost over $300,000. In total, $314 million was spent on congressional races in 1982 (up 37 per cent from 1980).[30] A large amount of these funds went to television and direct-mail advertising.

A conservative estimate would place the total annual advertising expenditures of nonprofit organizations at $10 billion. This estimate does not include the costs of marketing research such as political polling, point-of-sale displays, and sales personnel, nor the value of volunteers and free advertising.

Illustrations of Nonprofit Marketing

This subsection examines nonprofit marketing for the Postal Service, colleges and universities, and public libraries. The activities of these organizations differ because of their degree of tangibility, structure, objectives, and constituency.

The Postal Reorganization Act of 1970 created the U.S. Postal Service as an independent agency and called on it to become a self-supporting enterprise. Previously, it was a government agency with no mandate to improve its marketing efforts. While the Postal Service continues to have annual losses and postage increases have occurred with some regularity since 1970, the agency has made significant progress.

New services have been developed and established services have been expanded. For example, Express Mail delivers packages and letters to distant cities overnight; these items can be dropped at specially designated collection boxes (thus eliminating waiting on lines). Self-service stamp vending machines are available in shopping centers. A commemorative stamp program was started in 1975; annual sales now exceed $100 million. Figure 17-7 shows a 1983 print advertisement for

Figure 17-7

Marketing and the U.S. Postal Service

Reprinted by permission.

commemorative stamps. Many post offices sell inexpensive hand-held scales, padded envelopes for small packages, airmail markers, and a device for adhering stamps to envelopes. An electronic mail system, which would transmit letters via wire, radio, or satellite, is in an early stage of use.

The Postal Service had an advertising budget of $19 million in 1982, with a large portion of this going to Express Mail, direct mail ads for business accounts, and commemorative stamps. Young & Rubicam was used as an advertising agency. Despite these efforts, the Postal Service faces strong competition from a number of express delivery firms and others (such as Western Union).[31]

Colleges and universities are aware that the years of rapid growth in overall enrollments are over. Between 1980 and 1985 the number of high school graduates will decline by almost 20 per cent. Accordingly, new markets are being sought and marketing is being used more aggressively.[32]

Many schools are actively seeking the adult market. The National Center for Educational Statistics estimates that about 20 million adults are now involved in some type of higher education program at colleges, universities, and private companies. The adult market requires class times that do not infringe on work commitments and convenient locations (at work, at a neighborhood library, in a business district).

Traditional students are also being actively pursued. In 1973 public institutions spent $113 per new student on admissions. This figure more than doubled by 1982. Annually, over 1,000 schools purchase direct-mailing lists of prospective students from the Educational Testing Service (the organization that administers college-board examinations); the number of schools purchasing lists in 1971 was only 125.

The expansion of marketing in higher education is not confined to poor- or average-quality institutions. For example, Barnard College in New York has spent more than $100,000 for mailings, posters, and an 18-minute slide presentation. The campaign has helped draw more applications.

Most studies of the public library market support the view that a relatively small proportion of adults are regular library users. Research by Gallup found that 23 per cent of those questioned had not visited a public library during the preceding year; an additional 54 per cent used a public library only once.[33] Demographic trends are not favorable for long-run increases in the library's market, because libraries have been most successful with children (a declining proportion of the population).

To satisfy donors (the local communities that fund them) and respond to the changing composition of the market, public libraries will have to appeal to groups they have served poorly or not at all in the past. These groups include people in low-income households, those with less than high-school educations, disabled persons, young adults, and retired persons.[34]

There is evidence that an effective marketing program can substantially expand library patronage. For example, a two-year program at the Public Library of Columbus and Franklin County, Ohio, raised library

Table 17-4	*I. General Population*
Examples of Innovative Marketing Programs to Attract People to Public Libraries	Piano and organ practice room Calisthenics Swap discount coupon room Lend-out reproduction of sculptures Tax return help by accounting students Drive-in book pick-up station Home delivery of books Extension of library hours Operation of a year-round store for used books
	II. Children
	Lend a guinea pig (for a week) Use of children's advisory council to help run juvenile section Lend-out toys Dial library for a 3-minute recorded story Karate instruction Bicycle-safety programs Guitar sessions in library rooms
	III. Other Populations
	Special programs for bicultural constituents Tool lending for artisans Instruction in "survival English" Improvement of staff expertise in dealing with inner-city residents Handling requests for transportation by physically handicapped persons Bookmobile service to hospitals, nursing homes, and institutions Exercise programs for senior citizens

Source: Adapted from Barry Berman and Joel R. Evans, "The Marketing Audit: A New Tool for Public Libraries," *LJ Special Report 18*. Reprinted from *Library Journal Special Report*, March 15, 1981. Published by R. R. Bowker Co. (a Xerox company), copyright © 1981 by Xerox Corporation.

membership 98 per cent, reference use by 43 per cent and book circulation by 19 per cent. The program included creating more attractive facilities, expanding media availability, extending library hours, and adding book delivery by mail.[35] Table 17-4 contains examples of innovative marketing programs for attracting people to public libraries.

Summary

Service marketing involves product rental, product alteration and repair, and personal services. In general, services are less tangible, more perishable, less separable from their provider, and more variable in quality than products that are sold. Service and product marketing may be interconnected.

Services can be categorized by market, degree of tangibility, skill of the service provider, goal of the service provider, degree of regulation, labor intensiveness, and amount of customer contact. An organization would be classified on the basis of a combination of these factors.

The United States is the leading service economy in the world, with two thirds of the American private labor force employed in services. United States families spend more than 47 per cent of their income on services. Twenty per cent of all industrial capital goods are leased.

Service firms have lagged behind manufacturing firms in the use of marketing because of technical emphasis, small size, less competition, the lack of a need for marketing, past prohibitions on advertising, and a dislike of marketing by some service professionals. Special considerations in service marketing are an inability to stockpile, lack of visibility of effort, difficulties in pricing and promotion, importance of customer relations, the cost/reliability mix, and peripheral services.

Nonprofit marketing is conducted by organizations that operate in the public interest or to foster a cause and do not seek financial profits. It may involve organizations, people, places, ideas, products, and services. Exchanges do not have to involve money, and objectives can be difficult to formulate. Benefits are often distributed unequally, and economically unfeasible market segments may be served. Two constituencies must be satisfied: clients and donors.

Nonprofit marketing can be classified on the basis of tangibility, organization structure, objectives, and constituency. In 1981 the U.S. government spent $189 million for national advertising. Total advertising for nonprofit institutions is probably about $10 billion per year.

After reading this chapter, you should understand these key terms:

KEY TERMS

Service marketing
Intangibility
Perishability
Inseparability
Variability
Hidden service sector
Industrialization of services
Hard technologies

Soft technologies
Hybrid technologies
Peripheral services
Nonprofit marketing
Social marketing
Clients
Donors

QUESTIONS FOR DISCUSSION

1. Why does Merrill Lynch feature a bull in its advertising?
2. Describe the characteristics of service marketing that distinguish it from product marketing.
3. Classify an automated car wash and a health spa using Figure 17-2.
4. Why have service firms lagged behind manufacturers in the development and use of marketing?
5. What peripheral services are needed for an indoor tennis center?
6. Present three ways a film-processing company can match demand and supply on days following holidays.
7. Differentiate among hard, soft, and hybrid technologies for industrializing services.
8. Explain this statement: "While nonprofit marketing involves exchanges, they are not necessarily in the form of dollars for goods and services."

9. What is social marketing? Offer an example.

10. Why is it difficult to formulate objectives in nonprofit organizations?

11. Under what circumstances should nonprofit organizations serve uneconomical market segments?

12. Describe a potential conflict that could arise between the users and donors of a playground.

13. Present several innovative marketing programs for your state's tourist office to utilize.

14. What advantages and disadvantages does the U.S. Postal Service have in relation to its profit-oriented competitors?

NOTES

1. Rebecca Fannin, "The Bull Who Walks by Himself," *Marketing & Media Decisions* (Spring 1982, Special Edition), pp. 99–108.

2. See Theodore Levitt, "Marketing Intangible Products and Product Intangibles," *Harvard Business Review*, Vol. 59 (May–June 1981), pp. 96–102.

3. Bureau of Economic Analysis, U.S. Commerce Department, 1982.

4. Paul F. Anderson, "Industrial Leasing Offers Economic and Competitive Edge," *Marketing News* (April 4, 1980), p. 20.

5. Jeremy Main, "How Banks Lure the Rich," *Fortune* (November 1, 1982), pp. 60–64.

6. Susan Tompor, "Doctors Turn to Marketing to Get Patients," *Wall Street Journal* (September 1, 1981), p. 33.

7. Brian O'Reilly, "More Than Cheap Talk Propels MCI," *Fortune* (January 24, 1983), pp. 68–72; and Robert Raissman, "MCI: Can Its Fabled Past Help Foretell Its Future?" *Advertising Age* (November 29, 1982), pp. 84–85.

8. "Training: A Built-in Market Worth Billions," *Business Week* (November 1, 1982), pp. 84–85.

9. Richard M. Bessom and Donald W. Jackson, Jr., "Service Retailing: A Strategic Marketing Approach," *Journal of Retailing*, Vol. 51 (Summer 1975), pp. 75–84.

10. Philip Kotler and Richard A. Connor, Jr., "Marketing Professional Services," *Journal of Marketing*, Vol. 41 (January 1977), p. 71.

11. For a good overview of service planning, see J. Patrick Kelley and William R. George, "Strategic Management Issues for the Retailing of Services," *Journal of Retailing*, Vol. 58 (Summer 1982), pp. 26–43.

12. W. Earl Sasser, "Match Supply and Demand in Service Industries," *Harvard Business Review*, Vol. 54 (November–December 1976), pp. 133–140.

13. Dan R. E. Thomas, "Strategy's Different in Service Businesses," *Harvard Business Review*, Vol. 56 (July–August 1978), p. 163.

14. James H. Donnelly, Jr., "Use Three Methods to Help Market Intangible Service," *Marketing News* (October 19, 1979), p. 5.

15. Theodore Levitt, "The Industrialization of Services," *Harvard Business Review*, Vol. 54 (July–August 1976), pp. 63–74.

16. Jeremy Main, "Toward Service Without a Snarl," *Fortune* (March 23, 1981), p. 61.

17. Susan Spillman, "Movie Outlets Checking into Hotel Market," *Advertising Age* (August 16, 1982), p. 50; "Hilton Hotels: Ready to Grow Again After Years of Caution," *Business Week* (July 5, 1982), pp. 91–92; Daniel F. Cuff, "Wake-Up Call at Quality Inns," *New York Times* (September 13, 1981), Section 3, p. 8; and Holiday Inn advertisements.

18. "As Hotel Rates Climb, Service Keeps Falling, Many Travelers Gripe," *Wall Street Journal* (June 9, 1980), pp. 1, 26; and "Women Travelers Find Safety and Harrassment Can Be Major Problems," *Wall Street Journal* (March 5, 1980), pp. 1, 32.

19. Gregory D. Upah, "Mass Marketing in Service Retailing: A Review and Synthesis of Major Methods," *Journal of Retailing*, Vol. 56 (Fall 1980) pp. 73–75.

20. Ronald Alsop, "As Imported-Car Service Market Grows, Mechanics Tool Up for the Business," *Wall Street Journal* (September 4, 1979) p. 44.

21. Today all professionals are able to advertise their services.

22. Jeff Blyskal, "Can Law Firms Go Public?" *Forbes* (February 15, 1982) pp. 42–43.

23. For perspectives on both sides of the issue of legal advertising, see Robert F. Dyer and Terence A. Shimp, "Reactions to Legal Advertising," *Journal of Advertising Research*, Vol. 20 (April 1980), pp. 43–51; and Larry T. Patterson and Robert A. Swerdlow, "Should Lawyers Advertise? A Study of Consumer Attitudes," *Journal of the Academy of Marketing Science*, Vol. 10 (Summer 1982), pp. 314–326.

24. See Paul N. Bloom and William D. Novelli, "Problems and Challenges in Social Marketing," *Journal of Marketing*, Vol. 45 (Spring 1981), pp. 79–88.

25. See Christopher H. Lovelock and Charles B. Weinberg, "Public and Nonprofit Marketing Comes of Age," *Review of Marketing 1978* (Chicago: American Marketing Association, 1978), pp. 413–452; and Alan R. Andreasen, "Nonprofits: Check Your Attention to Customers," *Harvard Business Review*, Vol. 60 (May-June 1982), pp. 105–110.

26. Jamie Talan, "Getting a Message of Help Across," *Advertising Age* (August 2, 1982), p. M-29.

27. Virginia Inman, "Educational Testing Service Adopts Tactics from Business World as Old Markets Shrink," *Wall Street Journal* (November 20, 1982), p. 33.

28. Rob Howe, "Luring 'Em with Brass and Class," *Marketing & Media Decisions* (Spring 1982, Special Edition), pp. 189–200.

29. "U.S. Government," *Advertising Age* (September 9, 1982), pp. 176–177.

30. Federal Election Commission, January 1983; and Laura Jereski, "Politics and Paid Media," *Marketing & Media Decisions* (November 1982), pp. 72–73ff.

31. Fred Gardener, "Squeeze of Federal Ad Budgets," *Marketing & Media Decisions* (January 1982), pp. 62–63ff; and "U.S. Government," p. 176.

32. Bruce Allen and William H. Peters, "College Presidents Are Receptive to Strategic Planning Techniques," *Marketing News* (October 15, 1982), p. 9; William M. Bulkeley, " 'Baby Bust' Enrollment Drop Seen Having an Uneven Effect," *Wall Street Journal* (December 14, 1982), p. 33; "Earning an Undergraduate Degree at the Plant," *Business Week* (August 4, 1980), pp. 76–77; Erik Larson, "Colleges Are Learning Fine Art of Hard Sell as Fast Growth Ebbs," *Wall Street Journal* (April 15, 1980), pp. 1, 41; and "Richard Moll, Student-Getter," *Chronicle of Higher Education* (June 16, 1980), p. 3.

33. "Americans Read and Use Libraries: Says Gallup," *Library Journal*, Vol. 103 (December 15, 1978), p. 2466.

34. See Joseph Eisner (Editor), *Beyond PR: Marketing for Public Libraries*, L.J. Special Report 18 (New York : Library Journal, 1981).

35. "Ways to Up City Branch Use Charted by Ohio Study," *Library Journal*, Vol. 102 (November 1, 1977), p. 2208.

H&R BLOCK: POPULARIZING TAX PREPARATION SERVICES* 1   CASES

Before Henry and Robert Bloch started the company that bears their name in 1955, consumers either completed their own tax returns or employed relatively expensive accountants (often CPAs) to process the returns. There were no large, standardized tax-preparation services that catered to lower and middle-class consumers.

H&R Block revolutionized the field of tax preparation by mass marketing these services. Block's enormous success has been due to several factors:

1. It offered uniform tax-preparation services and placed offices throughout the country.

*"H&R Block: Expanding Beyond Taxes for Faster Growth," *Business Week* (December 8, 1980), pp. 76, 78; and William M. Reddig Jr., "As H&R Block Sees It, the New Tax Law Isn't Much of a Break," *New York Times* (September 27, 1981), Section 3, pp. 4–5.

2. An extensive advertising campaign utilizing Henry Bloch developed name recognition, described specific services provided by the firm, and presented a theme of quality service at a reasonable price.
3. Frequent changes in tax laws and the growing complexities of tax-return forms encouraged more consumers to use outside tax preparers.
4. Its tax centers were located in convenient shopping centers as well as more recently in Sears stores.
5. It used franchising for half its 8,000 + outlets. This increased professionalism, reduced company risk, and ensured a 10 per cent royalty fee.
6. Its own 75-hour tax course trained personnel and attracted 70,000 to 85,000 students each year (who paid $100 to $125 each).

Annually, H&R Block prepares more than 9 million tax returns. Of the company's $300 million in yearly revenues, 65 per cent comes from tax preparation fees. The balance is from a franchised employment agency (Personnel Pool of America) and franchised legal services (Hyatt Legal Services). Beneficial Corp. is second in the tax-preparation industry, but processes only 250,000 returns annually.

The typical new H&R Block customer waits until April 1st to visit a storefront office and is a thirty-eight-year-old male who previously prepared his own tax forms. He has been employed by the same company as a skilled worker for ten years, and together with a working wife earns about $25,000 per year. He usually requires the more complex long tax form (1040) for the first time. Seventy-two per cent of these customers are satisfied with Block and return the following year.

Due to the unique nature of the tax preparation business, Block employs 43,000 people during the peak season and about 2,250 year-round. However, store leases must be maintained throughout the year. The company is planning greater computerization of its operations throughout the 1980s.

QUESTIONS

1. Although H&R Block handles over 9 million tax returns each year, 55 million taxpayers file their own returns.
   a. Why do so many people complete their own returns?
   b. How can Block win over some of the "do-it-yourselfers"?
2. Compare H&R Block's strategy to that of a CPA firm.
3. What other market segments could H&R Block attract besides the one described in the case?
4. Tax preparation is a highly seasonal business. How can H&R Block plan for and respond to this?

2 MARKETING: NO LONGER A DIRTY WORD FOR MUSEUMS†

According to Sandra Horrocks, manager of public relations for the Philadelphia Museum of Art, "Marketing is no longer a dirty word. We use it freely." Until recently, this was a far different view from that held by most people associated with museums. Instead, they believed that museums were "treasure houses of culture that should not be sullied with crass sales techniques."

†Alan Rosenthal, "Museums Jump into the Marketing Game," *Advertising Age* (September 27, 1982) pp. M-2–M-3.

What has caused the change in attitude toward marketing? There are several reasons. New museum professionals have had more formal training in marketing and are more interested in it. The value of marketing in communicating with the public and with donors is now recognized. Museum directors realize that their target markets must be broadened. Operating and other costs have increased rapidly, while traditional funding from government, foundations, corporations, and individuals has leveled off (for example, cuts in federal programs are expected to amount to $27 million between 1982 and 1986). There is rising competition from other leisure-time activities, such as amusement parks, sporting events, and home gardening.

A number of museums have become quite aggressive in their marketing approaches, as these illustrations show:

- The Philadelphia Museum of Art has a five-year marketing plan intended to raise attendance and persuade the public that the museum is a fun place to visit.
- The Boston Museum of Fine Arts (known as "the old gray lady on Huntington Avenue") uses marketing surveys, advertises widely, has a publicity program, and sponsors special events.
- The Henry Ford Museum and Greenfield Village in Dearborn, Michigan has a department of marketing and public relations. In addition to its regular advertising program, the museum has exhibitions at shopping malls and hotel lobbies, promotes food sales on museum grounds, and offers products in museum shops and through a mail-order catalog. In 1981, $60,000 was spent on television advertising.
- The Children's Museum of Denver generates 95 per cent of its revenues from publications, traveling exhibits, special promotions, admissions, and memberships. It has used shopping bag tie-ins with Safeway supermarkets, promoted a booklet titled "The Baby Sitter's Guide," published a monthly family newspaper (with a nationwide circulation of 2 million), and participated in cooperative efforts with the media and business.

While museums have adopted a number of marketing practices, they recognize that "Dignity and decorum have to be maintained. We have to remember to maintain good taste when we sell, but still get across the idea that this is a place for fun. For example, we wouldn't create a musical jingle for a museum, as we might for a theme park." (Tom Murray, a consultant for Henry Ford Museum and Greenfield Village)

QUESTIONS

1. Four donor categories were mentioned in the case (government, foundations, corporations, and individuals).
   a. Why would these donors contribute to museums?
   b. What do they expect in return for their contribution?
   c. How do their expectations differ from clients/users of museums?
2. Identify five market segments of clients/users that a museum could seek and present a brief marketing plan aimed at each.
3. Would you create a musical jingle for a museum? Explain your answer.

Marketing and Society

18

Chapter Preview

Chapter Objectives

1 To provide an overview of marketing and society

2 To study social responsibility and consider its benefits and costs

3 To define consumerism and examine the consumer bill of rights

4 To discuss the responses of manufacturers, retailers, and trade associations to consumerism

5 To explore the future of consumerism

In September and October 1982, tragedy struck as seven Chicago people died from cyanide-laced Extra-Strength Tylenol capsules. Although the cyanide was placed in the capsules by a person or persons in no way connected with the manufacture of the product, Johnson & Johnson (maker of Tylenol) was confronted with a difficult situation that was unprecedented in U.S. business history.

Never before had a firm been in a position where the market's leading brand faced almost immediate extinction through no fault of its own. At the time of the tragedy, Tylenol held an overwhelming 40 per cent share of the nonprescription analgesic market. Said Jerry Della Femina, a prominent advertising executive:

> I don't think they can ever sell another product under that name. There may be an advertising person who thinks he can solve this, and if they find him I want to hire him, because then I want him to turn our water cooler into a wine cooler.

Johnson & Johnson acted quickly and responsibly. All Tylenol capsules were withdrawn from retail shelves and the production of capsules was halted. The company announced a $100,000 reward for information leading to the arrest and conviction of the person(s) guilty of the poisonings. An extensive newspaper campaign offered to exchange Tylenol tablets for any Tylenol capsules consumers may have purchased. After a short moratorium on television advertising, Johnson & Johnson ran low-key institutional ads asking consumers "to continue to trust Tylenol." Two million pieces of literature were mailed to medical professionals. The company's chief executive appeared on the *Phil Donahue Show* and *Sixty Minutes*.

Next, Johnson & Johnson engaged in activities to restore Tylenol's sales, which had fallen to 6.5 per cent of industry sales the week after poisonings (these sales were of tablets only). In November and December 1982, newspaper ads offered consumers $2.50 coupons toward the purchase of any Tylenol product, good through December 21, 1983. Totally new packaging for Tylenol capsules was developed and then introduced in December 1982, as production of the capsules resumed. The packaging featured a sealed cardboard box, a sealed plastic bottle top, and an inner seal covering the bottle. In addition, the label stated "Do not use if safety seals are broken." See Figure 18-1. Repackaging was estimated to cost Johnson & Johnson about $100 million, which it said would be absorbed and not passed along to consumers. Product advertising resumed in January 1983.

Johnson & Johnson's rapid and conscientious actions had a positive impact on consumers. Within a month after the poisonings, Tylenol tablets had recaptured a 17.9 per cent market share of industry sales (the tablets had a 22.2 per cent share before the poisonings) and 77 per cent of regular Tylenol users stated that they would purchase the product in a tamper-resistant package. By nine weeks after the tragedy, Tylenol tablets had a market share of almost 30 per cent, nearly double the next brand. Many observers believed the company had achieved a minor miracle.[1]

Overview

Marketing has a strong impact on the society which it serves. It has the potential for both positive and negative consequences regarding areas such as

Marketing can have both a positive and a negative impact on society.

- The quality of life (standard of living).
- Consumer expectations and satisfaction with goods and services.
- Consumer choice.

Figure 18-1
New Safety Packaging for Tylenol Capsules

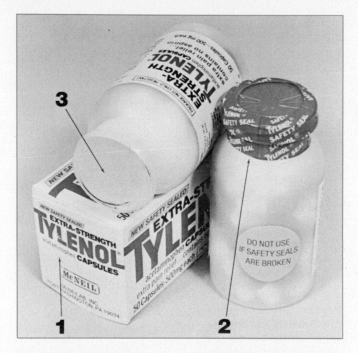

New Tylenol packaging includes (1) glued flaps on box, (2) plastic neck seal, and (3) inner foil seal. There is also a warning label cautioning about broken seals. Reprinted by permission of Johnson & Johnson.

- Product design and safety.
- Product durability.
- Product and distribution costs.
- Final prices.
- Competition.
- Natural resources, the landscape, and environmental pollution.
- Communications with consumers.
- Employment.
- Innovation.
- Deceptive practices.

For example, in the U.S., marketing practices have made a wide variety of goods and services available at relatively low prices and through convenient locations. These include food products, transportation products and services, clothing, entertainment, books, insurance, banking, television sets, furniture, and personal computers. On the other hand, marketing activities can sometimes create unrealistic consumer expectations, result in costly minor product design changes, or adversely affect the environment.

A large number of persons feel that marketing practices are not always satisfactory.

People's perceptions of marketing are mixed, at best. Studies by R. H. Bruskin and A. C. Nielsen show that at least one third of Americans feel cheated by purchases. The figure may actually approach two thirds of Americans. Others have reported that consumers may believe they are being "ripped off" when prices rise. Finally, marketers need to recognize that consumer dissatisfaction is not always transmitted to the firm. Consumers can boycott a product and privately complain to friends. Only 3 per cent of disgruntled consumers actually take the time to write to offending companies.[2] The true level of dissatisfaction may be "hidden." Many consumers believe companies operate as shown in Figure 18-2.

In this chapter the discussion of marketing and society is broken into two broad categories: social responsibility as it involves the general public, competition, employees, stockholders, and others; and consumerism as it involves consumers of a firm's offering.

Social Responsibility

Social responsibility is the "possession of a 'corporate conscience' or a response to social problems based on a sense of moral obligation."[3] Social responsibility requires that a marketing decision not only serve the interests of business but also protect and enhance society's interests. This calls for business to be accountable to society for its actions and for consumers to act responsibly.

Social responsibility involves marketing practices that serve society's best interests.

The **socioecological view of marketing** includes all the stages of a product's life span from raw materials to junkpile and incorporates the interests of all consumers who are influenced by the use of a product or service, including involuntary consumers who must share the consequences of someone else's consumption.[4] See Figure 18-3.

The socioecological view of marketing considers the environment and involuntary consumers.

There are times when social responsibility poses dilemmas for the marketer, because various products and services may have potential adverse effects on the consumer's or society's well-being. Examples of items that offer such dilemmas are cigarettes, no-return bottles, food

THE WALL STREET JOURNAL

Figure 18-2
A Cynical View of Marketing

"Well, as a last ditch measure, we could improve the corporate image by improving the product."

Source: *Wall Street Journal* (January 17, 1983). Reprinted by permission of Cartoon Features Syndicate.

Figure 18-3
The Socioecological View of Marketing

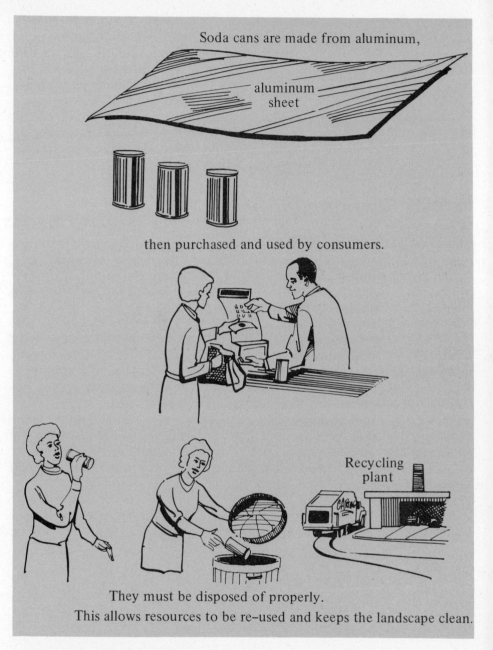

Soda cans are made from aluminum,

aluminum sheet

then purchased and used by consumers.

Recycling plant

They must be disposed of properly.
This allows resources to be re–used and keeps the landscape clean.

with high taste appeal but low nutritional content, shoes with high heels, and crash diet plans.

Until the 1960s it was accepted that the marketer's role was limited to satisfying consumers and generating profits. Environmental resources, such as air, water, energy, and paper, were viewed as limitless. Responsibility to the general public was rarely considered. Now the marketer realizes that he or she must respond to the general public, environment, employees, channel members, stockholders, and competitors, as well as consumers. Table 18-1 contains examples of marketing's social responsibility in these areas.

Table 18-1

Examples of Socially Responsible Marketing Practices

Regarding the General Public and the Environment

Recycling of products
Elimination of offensive signs and billboards
Proper disposal of waste
Use of products and services requiring low levels of environmental resources
Hiring of hard-core unemployed
Involvement in community
Donations to nonprofit organizations

Regarding Employees

Ample internal communications
Input into decisions encouraged
Training about social issues and the appropriate responses to them
No reprisals for uncovering questionable company policies
Recognition of socially responsible employees

Regarding Channel Members

Honoring verbal as well as written commitments
Fair distribution of scarce goods
Adherence to fair requests of channel members
Not forcing channel members to act irresponsibly
No coercion
Cooperative programs addressed at the general public and the environment

Regarding Stockholders

Honest reporting and financial disclosure
Publicity of company activities
Participation in setting socially responsible policy
Explanation of social issues affecting the company
Earning a responsible profit

Regarding Competitors

Adherence to high standards of performance
No illegal or unethical acts to hinder competitors
Cooperative programs for the general public and the environment
No actions that would lead competitors to waste resources

Both business and consumer activities have a significant impact on natural resources, the landscape, pollution, and standards of ethics. Each of these areas is discussed in the following subsections.

Natural Resources

In the last several years, there have been growing resource shortages, as some natural resources have become depleted. Both consumers and marketers have contributed to these shortages.

Packaging materials absorb large amounts of natural resources. Since World War II the consumption of these materials has increased five times faster than the population. Packaging now accounts for 30 to 40 per cent of all refuse. Annual packaging costs exceed $25 billion; yet, 90 per cent of packaging is thrown away. In addition, about $2.0 billion is spent to collect and dispose of packaging materials each year.

Some resources are being used up. Depletion can be slowed by reducing consumption, improving efficiency, limiting disposable packages, and lengthening products' lives.

Americans throw out more than 160 million tons of materials yearly, about 1,400 pounds for every man, woman, and child. The United States has 5 per cent of the world's population but generates more than half of the world's trash. Included in the United States' annual refuse are 85 billion cans, 40 billion glass bottles, 45 million tons of paper, 5 million tons of plastic, 200 million tires, 10 million tons of appliances, 200,000 tons of copper, 1 million tons of aluminum, and 20 million tons of grass and leaves.[5]

In general the depletion of natural resources can be reduced if the consumption of scarce materials is lessened and more efficient alternatives are purchased; fewer throwaway or disposable items, such as soda bottles and cans, pens, cigarette lighters, and carbon typewriter ribbons are bought; products are given longer life spans; and styles are changed less frequently. Convenient recycling and repair facilities, better trade-in arrangements, common facilities such as apartments, and less packaging also contribute to more efficient use of resources. An example of the positive effect one firm can have on resources is the cardboard recycling facility built by Giant Food. The facility recycles all of Giant's packaging and saves about 250,000 trees per year.[6]

Progressive actions require cooperation among business, stockholders, government, employees, the general public, consumers, and others. They also involve changes in life-styles and values. For instance, since 1978 Americans have reduced their automobile driving by more than 5 per cent in response to rising gasoline prices and shortages. In addition, the use of mass transit has risen.

The Landscape

Littering has become a major factor in marring the landscape. Various states and municipalities have introduced regulations to lessen it.

No-deposit beverage containers and abandoned automobiles are examples of items that mar the landscape. Thirty years ago virtually all beverage containers were recycled. Then manufacturers developed no-return bottles and cans. As a result, littering at roadsides and other areas became a major problem. In an attempt to reduce litter, many states, including Oregon, Vermont, Maine, Iowa, Connecticut, and Michigan, have enacted laws requiring beverage containers to have deposit fees that are refunded to consumers when they return empty containers. Many manufacturers and retailers believe these laws unfairly hold them responsible for the disposal of their products; littering is conducted by consumers. Also, labor and recycling costs associated with container returns have caused beverage prices to rise slightly. Nonetheless, a consumer study in Michigan found that, on balance, beverage container returns work very well.[7]

Cars are frequently abandoned on highways and streets, where they are subsequently stripped of usable parts. One suggestion is to include an amount to cover the disposal of the car in its original price or in a transfer tax. For example, Maryland imposes a small fee on title transfers to aid in the removal of abandoned cars.

Other means of reducing the marring of the landscape include bans on billboards and roadside signs, fines for littering, and better trade-ins for automobiles and appliances. Neighborhood block associations, merchant self-regulation, area planning and zoning, and consumer education may increase appreciation for the landscape. Maintaining an attractive landscape is a cooperative effort. A merchant clean-up patrol cannot overcome pedestrians who throw litter on the street rather than in waste baskets.

Environmental Pollution

Dangerous pollutants need to be eliminated and safe substitutes found. For example, until the late 1970s fluorocarbon propellants were used in most spray cans, such as insecticide, deodorant, hairspray, and paint. Scientists found that these propellants drifted into the upper atmosphere where they could decompose and destroy the ozone layer that shields the earth from most of the sun's ultraviolet radiation. A 5 per cent reduction in the ozone layer could lead to several thousand additional cases of skin cancer in the United States each year. Socially conscious companies, such as S. C. Johnson (maker of Raid), voluntarily discontinued fluorocarbon use. Ban deodorant, by Bristol-Myers, introduced pump-spray deodorants without fluorocarbons. Eventually, the federal government prohibited the use of fluorocarbon propellants.

> **Both government and business actions are needed to reduce dangerous environmental pollution.**

Pesticides often threaten the environment. As an illustration, in February 1979, the Environmental Protection Agency (EPA) issued a ban on 2,4,5T and 2,4,5TP herbicides, which were widely used in the United States. These herbicides were used along roadways and under rights-of-way of power lines, in forests to kill hardwood trees, in rangelands to give cattle more grass, and in rice fields to kill a weed called curly indigo. The EPA believed the herbicides were contaminated with cancer-causing dioxin. The Agency acted because of widespread reports of stillbirths in Alsea, Oregon, the scene of much spraying.

Another major source of pollution is industrial waste. The EPA estimates that heavy industry and the chemical, electroplating, textile, rubber, refining, and plastics industries generate the greatest amounts of hazardous waste. According to the EPA, less than 10 per cent of the forty million tons of annual dangerous waste in the United States is disposed of adequately.[8] In many cases the problem of industrial waste is compounded by porous soil and dependence on underground water supplies. The potential dangers of nuclear power were shown at Three Mile Island.

Even though reducing pollution is difficult, many firms have made notable attempts to do so. Waste fluoride compounds produced by Allied Chemical are transported to Occidental Chemical, where they are used in making toothpaste. Dow Chemical has developed a product stewardship concept in which it anticipates and attempts to solve a product's environmental problems by performing toxicological studies.

Ethics

In any marketing situation, ***ethical behavior*** based on honest and proper conduct should be followed. Ethical issues can be divided into two categories: process-related and product-related. ***Process-related***

Ethical behavior **involves process-related and product-related issues. Ethical decisions should consider the consequences of actions, the public good, honesty, and humanity.**

ethical issues "involve the unethical use of marketing strategies or tactics."[9] Examples include bait-and-switch advertising, price fixing, selling products overseas that have been found unsafe in the U.S., and bribing purchasing agents of large customers.

Product-related ethical issues involve "the ethical appropriateness of marketing certain products."[10] For example, how should tobacco products, intimate personal hygiene items, sugar-coated cereals, political candidates, and nonprofit organizations be marketed? More specifically, should cigarettes be manufactured? Should there be restrictions on their sales? Should advertising for cigarettes be limited? Should taxes on cigarettes be raised to discourage usage? Should cigarette smoking be banned in offices, restaurants, and planes?

In general, these broad questions should be considered:

1. What are the probable consequences of alternative proposals?
2. Which policy will result in the greatest possible good for the greater number?
3. Is a practice right? Is it just? Is it honest?
4. Does the policy put people first?
5. Is humanity treated as an end and not merely as a means?
6. What will relieve the conflicts and tensions of the situation?
7. Does the proposed strategy or solution anticipate consequences in the larger environment as well as in the immediate situation?[11]

Benefits and Costs of Social Responsibility

Social responsibility has costs as well as benefits.

The performance of socially responsible actions has both benefits and costs. See Figure 18-4. Among the benefits are improved worker and public safety, as reflected in fewer and less severe accidents, longer life spans, and less disease; cleaner air; more efficient use of resources; economic growth; a better image for business; government cooperation; public education; an attractive and safe environment; and self-satisfaction for a firm. Many of these benefits cannot be quantified. Furthermore, although costs are borne by all, the benefits of worker safety programs and many industrial environmental programs are enjoyed primarily by workers and their families.

The costs of socially responsible actions vary. The cumulative costs of pollution control devices were estimated at $43 billion for the period from 1973 to 1982. Pollution control and worker safety programs account for 12.5 to 23.7 per cent of the capital budgets for chemical, petroleum, nonferrous metals, steel, and paper companies. Some environmentally questionable products that are efficient and innovative have been removed from the marketplace or greatly modified. Procter & Gamble spends more than one quarter of its research and product development budget in coping with the present and anticipated environmental and human-safety concerns of regulators. Cannon Mills spends about 25 per cent of its capital expenditures to ensure that it conforms to cotton dust standards set by the Occupational Safety and Health Administration.[12]

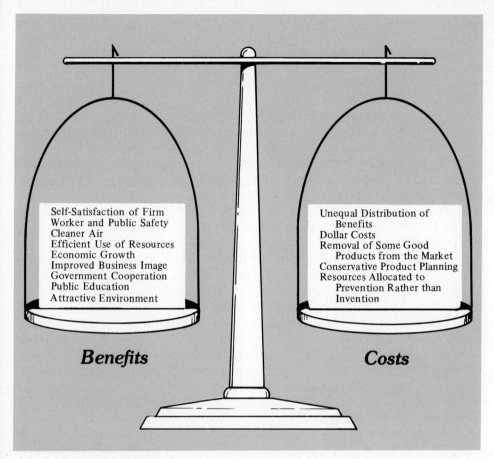

Figure 18-4
Benefits-Costs of Social Responsibility

Consumerism

Whereas social responsibility involves the interface of marketing with all of its publics, consumerism is limited to the relationship of marketing with its consumers. **Consumerism** can be defined as

> a social force within the environment designed to aid and protect the consumer by exerting legal, moral, and economic pressure on business.[13]

and

> the widening range of activities of government, business, and independent organizations that are designed to protect individuals from practices that infringe upon their rights as consumers.[14]

Consumerism has evolved through three distinct eras. The first era occurred in the early 1900s and concentrated on the need for a banking system, product purity, postal rates, antitrust, and product shortages. Emphasis was on business protection against unfair practices.

Consumerism protects consumers by placing legal, moral, and economic pressure on business.

There have been three major eras of consumerism. The present, third era began in the early 1960s.

President Kennedy stated a *consumer bill of rights:* information, safety, choice, and a voice in decision making.

The second era lasted from the 1930s to the 1950s. Important issues were product safety, bank failures, labeling, misrepresentation, performance standards, stock manipulation, deceptive advertising, credit, and consumer refunds. Consumer groups, such as Consumers Union and Consumers' Research, and government legislation grew. Issues were initiated but seldom resolved.

The third era began in the early 1960s and continues. It deals with all areas of marketing and has had a great impact on business. Two major events dominated the beginning of this era: President John Kennedy's announcement of a **consumer bill of rights** and publication of Ralph Nader's *Unsafe at Any Speed.* President Kennedy said that all consumers had four basic rights: information, safety, choice in product selection, and a voice in decision making. *Unsafe at Any Speed,* released in 1965, was a detailed examination and critique of the automobile industry.

Several other factors also contributed to the growth of the modern era. Birth defects related to the use of thalidomide by pregnant females occurred in the 1960s. A number of books, including the *Hidden Persuaders* by Vance Packard (about marketing's ability to influence people), *Silent Spring* by Rachel Carson (about marketing's contribution to a deteriorating environment), and *American Way of Death* by Jessica Mitford (about practices in the funeral industry) were published. Consumers became increasingly dissatisfied with product performance, processing of complaints, and deceptive or unsafe business practices. In addition, consumers became more sophisticated and skeptical, and they set higher, and perhaps unrealistic, expectations. Product scarcity increased. Self-service retailing and complex products caused uncertainty for some customers. The media began to publicize poor business practices more frequently. Government intervention heightened; in particular, the Federal Trade Commission expanded its activities in consumer issues.

In the following subsections, these key aspects of consumerism are examined: consumer information and education, consumer safety, consumer choice, consumers' right to be heard, responses of business to consumer issues, and the future of consumerism.

Consumer Information and Education

The right to be informed includes protection against fraudulent, deceitful, or grossly misleading information, advertising, labeling, pricing, packaging, or other practices. A number of federal and state laws have been enacted in this area.

A *warranty* assures consumers that a product will meet performance standards.

One example on the federal level is the Magnuson-Moss Consumer Product Warranty Act regarding warranties. A **warranty** is an assurance given to consumers that a product will meet certain performance standards. An express (stated) warranty is one that is explicitly provided to the consumer, such as the accuracy of a watch. An implied (implicit) warranty does not have to be stated to be in effect; it stipulates that a product is fit for use, packaged and labeled properly, and conforms to promises made on the label. For the most part, the terms warranty and guarantee are synonomous. The major distinction is that the term guarantee is used more frequently in promotion, such as satisfaction guaranteed or money-back guarantee. Specific guarantee provisions are regulated by the same laws as warranties.

Magnuson-Moss ensures that warranties are properly stated and enforced through several provisions. Warranties must be made available prior to purchases, so that consumers may read them in advance. The FTC is empowered to require product-accompanying information regarding the identity and location of the warrantor, exceptions in warranty coverage, and how consumers may complain. A full warranty must cover all parts and labor for a specified period of time. A limited warranty may contain stipulations and exceptions as well as a provision for labor charges. Implied warranties may not be disclaimed.

Individual states have regulations relating to information. As an illustration, cooling-off laws (allowing consumers to reconsider and, if they desire, cancel purchase commitments made in their homes with direct-to-home salespeople) are currently in force in about forty states. Unit-pricing legislation, aimed at enabling consumers to compare prices of products that come in many sizes (such as small, medium, large, family, and economy), is also on a state-by-state basis. Food stores are most affected by unit pricing and, in many cases, these stores must express price per unit of measure as well as total package price.

The existence of information does not mean that consumers will use it in their decision making. Studies have shown that consumer information is often ignored or misunderstood, especially by those who need it most (such as the poor). Accordingly, consumer education is necessary. *Consumer education* is defined as "a learning process whereby the consumer acquires the skills and knowledge to use his or her financial resources wisely in the marketplace."[15]

The great majority of state departments of education have consumer education staffs. Some states, such as Illinois, Oregon, Wisconsin, Florida, Kentucky, and Hawaii, require all students in public secondary schools to take a course in consumer education. Hundreds of consumer-education programs are conducted by federal, state, and local governments, as well as private profit and nonprofit institutions. These programs typically cover how to prudently purchase products and services, important features of credit agreements, contracts, and warranties, and consumer-protection laws.

Teaching consumers the wise use of financial resources in the marketplace is the goal of consumer education.

Consumer Safety

In large part the concern over consumer product safety arises from the fact that annually more than 20 million people are hurt, 110,000 disabled, and 30,000 killed in incidents involving products other than automobiles. The yearly cost of product-related injuries is several billion dollars. It has been estimated that up to 25 per cent of these injuries could be prevented if manufacturers produced safer, better-designed products. Table 18-2 contains a listing of the consumer products whose use results in the greatest number of injuries.

The Consumer Product Safety Commission (CPSC), established in 1972, is the federal agency with the major responsibility for product safety. It has jurisdiction over more than 11,000 products, such as aero-

Concern for product safety results from the more than 20 million people involved in accidents annually.

Table 18-2

Consumer Products Involved with the Greatest Numbers of Injuries	1. Stairs, ramps, landings (indoor, outdoor) 2. Bicycles and bicycle equipment 3. Baseball-related equipment and apparel 4. Football-related equipment and apparel 5. Basketball-related equipment and apparel 6. Skating-related equipment and apparel 7. Nails, carpet tacks, screws, thumb tacks 8. Chairs, sofas, and sofa beds 9. Tables (nonglass) 10. Architectural glass 11. Beds (including springs and frames) 12. Swings, slides, seesaws, and playground climbing apparatus 13. Cutlery and knives 14. Glass bottles and jars 15. Lumber 16. Swimming-related equipment 17. Desks, cabinets, shelves, bookcases, footlockers 18. Drinking glasses 19. Fences 20. Soccer-related equipment and apparel

Source: From data compiled by the Consumer Product Safety Commission, *1981 Annual Report: Fiscal Year 1980* (Washington, D.C.: Government Printing Office, 1981), pp. A2–A4.

The *Consumer Product Safety Commission (CPSC)* has a number of enforcement tools at its disposal, including *product recall*.

sol spray cans, television sets, bicycles, lamps, ranges and ovens, ladders, carbonated beverages, bottles, aluminum wiring, and lawn mowers. The CPSC also regulates structural items in homes such as stairs, retaining walls, and electrical wiring.

The only products over which the CPSC does not have jurisdiction are food, drugs, cosmetics, tobacco, automobiles, tires, firearms, boats, pesticides, and aircraft. Each of these products is regulated by other agencies. For example, the Environmental Protection Agency has the authority to recall cars not meeting emission standards. The Food and Drug Administration regulates drugs, medical devices, radiation emissions, and food.

The CPSC has extensive powers. It can

1. Require products to be marked with clear and adequate warnings and instructions.
2. Issue mandatory standards pertaining to performance, construction, and packaging that may have the effect of forcing companies to redesign their products completely.
3. Require manufacturers, private labelers, distributors, and retailers to notify the agency immediately whenever they discover that a product manufactured or sold by them contains a defect that would create a substantial risk of injury. This covers defects in design, manufacture, or assembly.
4. Require manufacturers to conduct reasonable testing programs to make sure their products conform to established safety standards. After testing, manufacturers must supply distributors or retailers with certificates stating that all applicable consumer protection safety standards have been met.

If after investigation the CPSC determines a product hazard exists, it can issue orders compelling a manufacturer to bring the product into conformity with the provisions of the applicable safety rule or repair the defect in the product, exchange the product for a like or equivalent item that complies with safety requirements, or refund the purchase price of the product less a reasonable allowance for use.

Firms found in violation of safety standards can be fined from $2,000 to $500,000 per violation; top executives can be fined up to $50,000 and imprisoned for up to one year. However, the primary enforcement tool used by the CPSC is ***product recall.***

For example, small appliances have incurred large recalls. In May 1979 the CPSC recalled about 12.5 million hair dryers because they contained asbestos. According to the CPSC, the dryers presented unreasonable cancer risks. The eleven affected manufacturers and retailers agreed to repair or replace the dryers or offer refunds if requested by consumers.

Since 1972, the CPSC has issued product recalls involving about ten million items (excluding automobiles) such as toys, electrical products, and flammable clothing. It also banned products such as flammable contact adhesives, easily overturned refuse bins, certain asbestos-treated products, and Tris (a flame retardant used in children's clothing that was linked to cancer).

The automobile industry, under the jurisdiction of the National Highway Traffic Safety Administration, has had a number of motor vehicles recalled. During one five-year period, 1976 to 1980, more than 35 million automobiles were recalled for a variety of safety reasons. In fact, in 1977, the number of vehicles recalled was roughly equal to the number of new cars that were manufactured that year.[16] Table 18-3 shows the recall record of General Motors' cars from their introduction through February 1983.

Between 1976 and 1980, more than 35 million automobiles were recalled.

In addition to these government activities, consumers have the right to sue the manufacturer or seller of an injurious product. A suit filed on behalf of many affected consumers is known as a ***class-action suit.***

A *class-action suit* involves many consumers.

Consumer Choice

The right to choose means that consumers have available several products and brands from which to select. In this regard the government has taken various actions. Exclusive patent rights are limited to seventeen years. After this period, all firms can utilize the patents. Noncompetitive business practices such as unfair price cutting are restricted. Firms with trademarks, such as Borden's Realemon, are encouraged to license their products to competitors.

When consumers have several alternatives available to them, they are given the right to choose.

The government examines the potential impact of company mergers on consumer choice. In some cases, it has stopped proposed mergers or forced firms to divest themselves of certain subsidiaries if the product and service offerings in an industry would be lessened. Likewise, franchise restrictions requiring franchisees to purchase all goods and services from their franchisors have been loosened.

Table 18-3	Date	Problem	Number of cars
X-Car Recalls*	September 1979	Deficiency in material of automatic transmission cooler hose—possible leak and fire hazard (1980 models)	225,000
		Fatigue cracks in steering gear mounting plates (1980 models)	160,000
	October 1979	Improper installation of turn flasher unit (1980 models)	236
	October 1980	Incorrect routing of power-steering hoses—possible fire hazard (1981 models)	25,400
	March 1981	Possible flaw in electrical ground cable (1981 models)	105,000
	August 1981	Possible rear-wheel lockup and loss of control (1981 models)	47,000
	March 1982	Faulty clamps on fuel-filler and vent-pipe hoses (1982 models)	150,000
		Possible scraping of clutch cable against left front brake line (1982 models)	5,000
	January 1983	Possible failure of brake hoses to meet standards (1982 models)	8,500
	February 1983	Possible rear-wheel lockup (1980 models)	240,000

*Excluding five recalls before introduction.
Source: Douglas R. Sease, "X-Cars, Once GM's Pride, Getting a Shoddy Reputation with Customers," *Wall Street Journal* (March 3, 1983), p. 27.

Retailers are encouraged to carry wide ranges of product categories and different brands within each category. The media are monitored to ensure that advertising space or time is made available to small as well as large firms. Imports are allowed to compete with American-made items. Information standards are enforced. A number of industries, such as banking, airline, and railroad, have been deregulated to foster price competition and encourage new firms to enter the market.

All of these activities are intended to increase competition and provide consumers with a number of alternatives when making purchases.

Consumers' Right to Be Heard

Although there is no general federal consumer agency, there are federal, state, and local agencies involved with consumers.

The right to be heard means that consumers have input into decisions affecting them. As of this date, no overall federal consumer agency exists to represent consumer interests, although several federal agencies regulate various business practices pertaining to consumers. The addresses and phone numbers of these agencies, as well as those of trade associations, are listed in the *Consumer's Resource Handbook*, published by the Office of Consumer Affairs. See Figure 18-5. Most states and municipalities have consumer affairs offices, as do many major corporations. Each encourages consumer input. During the last several years, these offices have been quite active.

In addition to government and industry consumer specialists, there are many consumer groups that have acted on behalf of the general public or specific consumer segments. These groups are quite motivated in their attempts to voice consumer complaints, represent consumers before government and industry hearings, and otherwise generate consumer input into the decision-making process of government and indus-

Figure 18-5
The Consumer's Resource Handbook

This book contains a complaint-handling discussion, sources of help for consumers, and a consumer assistance directory. Free single copies are provided to consumers upon request by writing to Handbook, Consumer Information Center, Pueblo, Colorado, 81009.

try. Because a single consumer rarely has a significant impact, consumer groups frequently become the individual's voice.

Responses of Business to Consumer Issues

Business responses to consumerism range from illegal acts to supportive behavior, as shown in Table 18-4. The remedial alternatives for protecting consumers against unfair or deceptive practices are explained in Table 18-5.

Over the past two decades, great advances have been made in the reactions of business to consumerism; today many firms have formal programs and real commitments to resolve consumer issues. Nonetheless, a number of companies have raised legitimate questions about the impact of consumerism on their operations. Following are some of these questions:

1. Why do different states and municipalities have dissimilar laws regarding business practices? How can a national company be expected to comply with each of these regulations?

Companies have become much more responsive to consumers; yet, questions remain about the effects of consumerism on firms.

Table 18-4	*Response*	*Characteristics*
Range of Business Responses to Consumer Issues	Illegal behavior	Business practices that violate government statutes, such as price fixing, deceptive advertising, and price discrimination
	Questionable behavior	Legal business practices that are highly criticized, such as advertising to children
	Opportunistic behavior	Practices with which a firm capitalizes on the difficulties of a competitor, such as publicizing a product recall
	Adaptive behavior (a) Cooperative (b) Noncooperative	Actions after new laws or court rulings (a) Complete compliance (b) Circumvention efforts, such as withdrawing rather than modifying popular, but dangerous, products
	Defensive behavior (a) Cooperative (b) Noncooperative	Self-protective actions prior to government mandates (a) Voluntary improvements, such as unit pricing and nutritional labeling (b) Increased conflict with government, such as attacks on federal agencies and lobbying
	Regulated behavior	Industries operating in heavily regulated environments, such as taxicabs, public utilities, and education
	Supportive behavior	Voluntary efforts to improve practices taken at the initiative of business, such as labeling toys by the age of children

Source: Adapted from Paul N. Bloom and Nikhilesh Dholakia, "Marketer Behavior and Public Policy: Some Unexplored Territory," *Journal of Marketing*, Vol. 37 (October 1973), pp. 63–77.

2. Do government rules cause unnecessary costs and time delays in the introduction of new products that outweigh the benefits of these rules?
3. Is it the responsibility of business to ensure that consumers obey laws (such as littering) and use products properly (such as seat belts)?
4. Is it the role of government or business to make sure that the marketplace is responsive to consumer needs? Is self-regulation preferred over government regulation?
5. Are multimillion dollar jury awards to injured consumers getting out of hand?

Selected responses to consumerism by manufacturers, retailers, and trade associations are discussed next.

Manufacturers A number of manufacturers have developed systematic programs to deal with consumer issues, as these examples show. In 1961, Maytag introduced Red Carpet Service to improve its appliance repair service. Zenith set up a customer relations department in 1968; Motorola created an Office of Consumer Affairs in 1970; and RCA implemented a consumer affairs office at the corporate level in 1972.

Today Whirlpool has more than 1,200 nationwide franchised repair and service outlets that employ only trained technicians. Frigidaire presents an Award of Merit for dealers and service units that meet rigid

Alternative	Methods of Implementation	Table 18-5
Prevention	Consumer abuses prevented through 1. Voluntary codes of conduct by firms or trade associations. 2. Laws mandating information disclosure, such as truth-in-packaging, truth-in-lending, and unit pricing. 3. Substantiation of advertising claims.	**Remedial Alternatives for Consumer Protection**
Restitution	Compensation to consumers for product- or service-related losses, damages, or injuries through 1. Affirmative disclosure, requiring the firm to disclose both negative and positive points in its advertising. 2. Corrective advertising, requiring the firm to devote a proportion of future advertising to dispel past doubtful claims. 3. Refunds or replacement products. 4. Limitations on contracts, such as cooling-off laws, which give buyers the right to rescind certain direct-to-home contracts (usually within a three-day period). 5. Arbitration.	
Punishment	Future misconduct deterred by inflicting losses on wrongdoers through 1. Fines. 2. Loss of profits. 3. Class-action suits on behalf of many consumers.	

Source: Dorothy Cohen, "Remedies for Consumer Protection: Prevention, Restitution, or Punishment," *Journal of Marketing*, Vol. 39 (October 1975), pp. 24–31.

service standards. RCA trains thousands of service personnel annually; during one five-year period, 158,000 independent service people were trained.

General Electric processes complaints promptly through a well-defined system, and Motorola answers most complaints within twenty-four hours. Probably the best-known complaint-handling service is Whirlpool's Cool-Line, created in 1967. Cool-Line provides a national, toll-free telephone service. It is open twenty-four hours a day, seven days per week, and is staffed by consumer consultants. More than 90 per cent of the questions are answered over the telephone. Remaining problems are investigated and resolved by a field staff.[17]

In the area of product recalls, manufacturers' actions have varied widely, as these two examples show:[18]

- When Rely-brand tampons were shown to have a possible link with toxic shock syndrome, they were quickly and voluntarily removed from retailers' shelves by Procter & Gamble. The company halted all production and offered to buy back unused packages. Ads were placed warning women not to use Rely. Procter & Gamble's image was relatively unaffected, because of its prompt actions.
- Firestone Tire & Rubber Company agreed to recall its Firestone 500 tires only after heavy pressure from the National Highway Traffic Safety Commission and others. Information showed that 41 deaths and 65 injuries might have been caused by blowouts or other failures of the Firestone 500. To make matters worse, Firestone did not release test data that showed potential defects in the tires. By delay-

ing the recall for so long, Firestone tarnished its image and ended up spending $135 million for the recall.

Now, more and more companies are employing voluntary recalls when they become aware of product defects or unsafe product features.[19]

Retailers

Various retailers have expressed a concern for consumer issues, some for more than fifty years. For example, J. C. Penney adopted a consumer philosophy, shown in Figure 18-6, in 1913: Macy's established a Bureau of Standards to test merchandise in 1927; and Abraham & Straus recognized the need for merchandise labeling in 1937.

More recently, Sears developed an extensive education program and related literature; Hess Department Stores became heavily involved in community affairs and in 1977 introduced a "Consumer Expo," which demonstrates new products; and Giant Food, a large supermarket chain, developed its own consumer bill of rights:

1. Right to safety: no phosphates, removal of certain pesticides, age-labeling of toys
2. Right to be informed: improved labeling, unit pricing, readable dating of perishable items, and nutritional labeling
3. Right to choose: continued sale of cigarettes and food with additives
4. Right to be heard: dialogue with reputable consumer groups, in-house consumer advocate
5. Right to redress: money-back guarantee on all products
6. Right to service: availability of store services[20]

With *item price removal,* prices are only displayed on shelves or signs. Retailers favor this practice; consumers oppose it.

In one key area, retailers and consumer groups have opposing views. This involves **item price removal,** whereby prices are marked only on store shelves or aisle signs and not on individual items. Many retailers, particularly supermarkets, want to employ item price removal, since computerized checkouts allow them to ring up prices through premarked codes on packages. Retailers state that this practice reduces labor costs significantly and that these reductions can be passed on to consumers. Consumer groups believe the practice is deceptive and will make it difficult for them to guard against misrings. Item price removal is banned in a number of states and local communities. Giant Food is one of the major users of item price removal; it passes cost savings along to consumers.[21]

Trade Associations

Trade associations are organizations that represent groups of individual companies. The associations have been responsive to consumerism through a variety of activities, such as coordinating and distributing research findings, developing consumer and company education programs, developing product standards, and handling complaints.

The Major Appliance Consumer Action Panel (MACAP) is an effective educational and complaint-resolution program sponsored by the Association of Home Appliance Manufacturers, the Gas Appliance Manufacturers Association, and the American Retail Federation. The

Figure 18-6
The J. C. Penney Philosophy

Every store has its rules, so do we.

We call it The Penney Idea.

Adopted 1913

To serve the public, as nearly as we can, to its complete satisfaction.

To expect for the service we render a fair renumeration and not all the profit the traffic will bear.

To do all in our power to pack the customer's dollar full of value, quality and satisfaction.

To continue to train ourselves and our associates so that the service we give will be more and more intelligently performed.

To improve constantly the human factor in our business.

To reward men and women in our organization through participation in what the business produces.

To test our every policy, method and act in this wise: "Does it square with what is right and just?"

75 years ago, we decided that the only way we'd run our business was by doing what's right. For our customers. And for the communities we live in. In our stores it means offering the best merchandise and services at the fairest possible prices. In our home towns, it means giving what we can, when we can, on both corporate and personal levels. Ever since the first JCPenney opened in 1902, we've believed that doing what's right is good business.

Source: Reprinted by permission of J. C. Penney.

Bank Marketing Association stresses a Financial Advertising Code of Ethics (FACE) for member firms; the Direct Mail/Marketing Institute sets industry guidelines and operates a consumer action line; and the National Retail Merchants Association has a Consumer Affairs Committee and provides information to the public.

The Better Business Bureau (BBB) is the largest and broadest business-operated trade association involved with consumer issues. The BBB publishes educational pamphlets and books, investigates complaints, supervises arbitration panels, has available a Consumer Affairs Audit, outlines ethical behavior, presents symposiums, publicizes unsatisfactory practices and names the firms involved, and has local offices throughout the country. It emphasizes self-regulation as an alternative to government legislation.

Sometimes, trade associations vigorously oppose potential government regulation. For example, the Consumer Product Safety Commission estimated that 123,000 injuries from chain saws required medical attention in 1981. As a result, the CPSC proposed mandatory safety standards for chain saws in 1982. However, the Chain Saw Manufacturers Association claimed that the accident figures were inflated and did not justify mandatory regulations. The Association published a 56-page report asserting, among other things, that a chair was more dangerous than a chain saw.[22]

Future of Consumerism

Consumerism is now entering a period of maturity.[23] The 1980s will see much less activism than the 1960s and 1970s. This is due to several factors: the current level and quality of self-regulation, the success of consumerism, the increased conservatism of Congress and the American people, and the importance of other issues.

As noted throughout the text, and particularly in this chapter, organizations are much more responsive to consumer complaints and environmental conditions today. Because more firms have consumer-affairs departments, employ voluntary product recalls, and conduct ongoing consumer surveys, there is less pressure for government agencies or consumer groups to intervene. Accordingly, there is a strong trend toward industry deregulation as a way of increasing competition, encouraging innovative marketing programs, and stimulating lower prices. Deregulation is resulting in greater flexibility for firms and a more uncertain environment for them.[24]

Future consumerism activity will be less necessary because of the successes of past actions. On the federal, state, and local levels, government protection for consumers has improved dramatically over the last twenty years. Class-action suits have won large settlements from firms, making it clear that unsafe practices will be financially costly. Consumer groups and independent media have publicized negative company practices, so that firms are aware that such activities will not go unnoticed. The major goal for consumerism during the 1980s will be to hold on to and consolidate the gains of the 1960s and 1970s.

Many members of Congress and sectors of the American public are now more conservative about the role of government in regulating busi-

In the 1980s, consumerism will be in a phase of maturity—consolidating past gains.

ness than in the 1960s and 1970s. They believe that government has become too big, impedes business practices, and causes unnecessary costs. As a result, government agency budgets have been closely monitored and their activities limited. For example, from fiscal 1980 to fiscal 1981, total federal government expenditures rose by 14 per cent. Over the same period, the FTC's budget grew by 2.3 per cent, less than the rate of inflation. Furthermore, Congress passed the FTC Improvement Act of 1980, which restricted the agency's powers. Under this act, Congress was given veto power over industrywide trade regulations approved by the FTC.[25]

The FTC Improvement Act of 1980 gave Congress the ability to veto FTC trade regulations.

Finally, consumerism issues will not be as important to people as a number of other factors in the 1980s. These include unemployment, interest rates, industrial productivity, the rate of inflation, and product and resource shortages.

Summary

Marketing interacts with the society it serves. It can have both positive and negative effects on such areas as the quality of life and consumer expectations.

Social responsibility involves business actions based on a sense of moral obligation. The socioecological view of marketing considers all stages of a product's life from raw materials to junkpile and includes the interests of consumers and nonconsumers.

To stem the depletion of natural resources, cooperative efforts among business, stockholders, government, employees, the general public, consumers, and others are needed. In response to excessive littering and abandoned cars, several states have enacted legislation. Various environmental pollutants such as fluorocarbon propellants and certain pesticides have also been removed from the market.

Ethical behavior, based on honest and proper conduct, can be divided into two categories: process-related and product-related. Ethical considerations include the consequences of actions, consumer happiness, honesty, fairness, concern for all people, and spin-off effects. Social responsibility has many benefits as well as a number of costs; the two need to be balanced.

Consumerism deals with the relationship of marketing and its consumers. It is defined as a social force within the environment designed to aid and protect the consumer by exerting legal, moral, and economic pressure on business. Consumerism has progressed through three eras: early 1900s, 1930s to 1950s, and 1960s to the present. The latter era has been the most important and began with President John F. Kennedy's announcement of a consumer bill of rights. The Federal Trade Commission is the major federal agency responsible for consumer protection.

The right to be informed includes protection against fraudulent, deceitful, or grossly misleading information, advertising, labeling, pricing, packaging, or other practices. Consumer education involves teaching consumers to use their financial resources wisely. The right to safety arises from the large numbers of people who are injured, disabled, or killed in accidents. The Consumer Product Safety Commission has the power to order product recalls or modifications. The right to choose stipulates that consumers have several products and brands from which to choose. The right to be heard is the consumer's right to a voice in business and government decision making. A number of consumer groups and government agencies provide this voice.

Many individual companies and trade associations are reacting positively to consumer issues. This group grows each year. A smaller number of organizations intentionally or unintentionally pursue unfair, misleading, or dangerous practices. There are remedies to correct these actions.

Consumerism is beginning a period of maturity. The 1980s will see less activism as a result of self-regulation, the past accomplishments of consumerism, the increased conservatism in the U.S., and the importance of other issues.

KEY TERMS

After reading this chapter, you should understand these key terms:

Social responsibility
Socioecological view of marketing
Ethical behavior
Process-related ethical issues
Product-related ethical issues
Consumerism
Consumer bill of rights

Warranty
Consumer education
Consumer Product Safety Commission (CPSC)
Product recall
Class-action suit
Item price removal

QUESTIONS FOR DISCUSSION

1. As a competitor of Tylenol, how would you have acted after the Chicago poisonings?
2. What current social issues does your community face?
3. Comment on the statement of a mouthwash executive who said: "If the ethics aren't embodied in the laws by the men who made them, you can't expect businessmen to fill the lack."
4. Why does social responsibility pose a dilemma for marketers?
5. Explain the social responsibility of marketing in relation to
   a. The general public.
   b. Employees.
   c. Channel members.
   d. Stockholders.
   e. Competitors.
6. How may the depletion of natural resources, marring of the landscape, and environmental pollution be curbed?
7. What is ethical behavior? Give examples of five unethical, but legal, practices.
8. Weigh the benefits and costs of social responsibility. How may a balance be struck between benefits and costs?
9. Explain the consumer bill of rights.

10. Should marketing play a role in educating consumers? Explain your answer.

11. Evaluate the use of product recall as a tool for regulating product safety.

12. Comment on the questions companies have raised regarding the effects of consumerism.

13. What is the range of business responses to consumer issues? Give a specific example of each.

14. Comment on the future of consumerism.

NOTES

1. Nancy Giges, "J&J Begins Its Drive to Keep Tylenol Alive," *Advertising Age* (October 11, 1982), pp. 1, 78; Michael Waldholz, "Tylenol Maker Mounting Campaign to Restore Trust of Doctors, Buyers," *Wall Street Journal* (October 29, 1982), p. 33; Nancy Giges, "New Tylenol Package in National Press Debut," *Advertising Age*, (November 15, 1982), pp. 2, 78; "Burke Reflects on Tylenol Woes," *Advertising Age* (November 22, 1982), p. 50; Thomas Moore, "The Fight to Save Tylenol," *Fortune* (November 29, 1982), pp. 44–49; Nancy Giges, "Tylenol Tablets Lead Rebound," *Advertising Age* (December 13, 1982), pp. 1, 55; and Michael Waldholz, "Speedy Recovery," *Wall Street Journal* (December 24, 1982), pp. 1, 19.

2. Dik Twedt, "Irate Buyer Needs Quick Reply," *Marketing News* (April 6, 1979), pp. 1, 5; Shelby D. Hunt and John R. Nevin, "Why Consumers Believe They Are Being Ripped Off," *Business Horizons*, Vol. 24 (May–June 1981), pp. 48–52; and Ralph L. Day, Klaus Grabicke, Thomas Schaetzle, and Fritz Staubach, "The Hidden Agenda of Consumer Complaining," *Journal of Retailing*, Vol. 57 (Fall 1981), pp. 86–106.

3. Robert C. Albrook, "Business Wrestles with Its Social Conscience," *Fortune* (August 1968), p. 90.

4. Etienne Cracco and Jacques Restenne, "The Socio-Ecological Product," *MSU Business Topics*, Vol. 19 (Summer 1971), pp. 27–34.

5. Stuart Diamond, "Garbage: Our Wasted Resource," *Newsday Long Island Magazine* (May 6, 1979), pp. 43–44.

6. Esther Peterson, "Consumerism as a Retailer's Asset," *Harvard Business Review*, Vol. 52 (May–June 1974), p. 95.

7. Lawrence A. Crosby and James R. Taylor, "Consumer Satisfaction with Michigan's Container Deposit Law—An Ecological Perspective," *Journal of Marketing*, Vol. 46 (Winter 1982), pp. 47–60; and Rick Brand, "Happy Returns on Mich. Law," *Newsday* (March 28, 1982), pp. 7, 25.

8. Jim Troedtman, "By-Products of Chemical Age Are Leaving Legacy of Danger," *Newsday* (April 29, 1979), p. 27.

9. Gene R. Laczniak, Robert F. Lusch, and William A. Strang, "Ethical Marketing: Perceptions of Economics Goods and Social Problems," *Journal of Macromarketing* , Vol. 1 (Spring 1981), p. 49.

10. Ibid.

11. Adapted from James M. Patterson, "What Are the Social and Ethical Responsibilities of Marketing Executives?" *Journal of Marketing*, Vol. 31 (July 1966), pp. 12–15. See also, Laura L. Nash, "Ethics Without the Sermon," *Harvard Business Review*, Vol. 59 (November–December 1981), pp. 78–79; and Kenneth E. Goodpaster and John B. Matthews, Jr., "Can a Corporation Have a Conscience?" *Harvard Business Review*, Vol. 60 (January–February 1982), pp. 132–141.

12. See "Government Intervention: The Surprisingly High Cost of a Safer Environment," *Business Week* (September 14, 1974), pp. 104–106; Edward G. Harness, *Views on Corporate Responsibility* (Cincinnati: Procter & Gamble), p. 9; and Barbara Ettore, "Cannon's Goal: New Ventures," *New York Times* (June 5, 1979), p. D14.

13. David W. Cravens and Gerald E. Hills, "Consumerism: A Perspective for Business," *Business Horizons*, Vol. 18 (August 1970), p. 21.

14. George S. Day and David A. Aaker, "A Guide to Consumerism," *Journal of Marketing*, Vol. 34 (July 1970), p. 12.

15. Paul N. Bloom and Mark J. Silver, "Consumer Education: Marketers Take Heed," *Harvard Business Review,* Vol. 54 (January–February 1976), p. 32.

16. Walter Guzzardi, Jr., "The Mindless Pursuit of Safety," *Fortune* (April 9, 1979), p. 56.

17. Kevin E. Dembinski, "Consumerism and the Appliance Industry," in Joel R. Evans (Editor), *Consumerism in the United States: An Inter-Industry Analysis* (New York: Praeger, 1980), pp. 29–32.

18. Elizabeth Gatewood and Archie B. Carroll, "The Anatomy of Corporate Social Response: The Rely, Firestone 500, and Pinto Cases," *Business Horizons,* Vol. 24 (September–October 1981), pp. 9–16; Mark N. Dodosh, "Big Firestone Recall Changes Used Tires into Collector's Items," *Wall Street Journal* (October 30, 1978), pp. 1, 22; and "Firestone Recall," *New York Times* (November 25, 1979), p. 49.

19. See Michael deCourcy Hinds, "Voluntary Recall of Products Is Increasing," *New York Times* (October 17, 1981), p. 9.

20. Peterson, "Consumerism as a Retailer's Asset."

21. Deborah A. Randolph, "Giant Food Faces Fight on Two Fronts Over Cuts in Prices and Price-Labeling," *Wall Street Journal* (April 14, 1981), p. 37.

22. Ray Vicker, "Rise in Chain-Saw Injuries Spurs Demand for Safety Standards, But Industry Resists," *Wall Street Journal* (August 23, 1982), p. 17.

23. See Paul N. Bloom and Stephen A. Greyser, "The Maturing of Consumerism," *Harvard Business Review,* Vol. 59 (November–December 1981), pp. 130–139.

24. Paul N. Bloom, "Deregulation's Challenges for Marketers," in Bruce J. Walker, et al. (Editors), *An Assessment of Marketing Thought & Practice* (Chicago: American Marketing Association, 1982), pp. 337–340.

25. See Dorothy Cohen, "Unfairness in Advertising Revisited," *Journal of Marketing,* Vol. 46 (Winter 1982), pp. 73–80.

CASES

1 MANVILLE CORPORATION: A PROFITABLE FIRM FILES FOR BANKRUPTCY TO STOP PRODUCT LIABILITY LAWSUITS*

On August 26, 1982, Manville Corporation (a large construction and forest-products manufacturer) asked for court protection under Chapter 11 of the federal bankruptcy code, despite a net worth of $1.1 billion. Chapter 11 status allows companies to continue their operations and reorganize debt, without interference from creditors or other outside parties.

When Manville voluntarily filed for court protection, it was a very profitable firm that had no intention of going out of business or changing the way in which it operated. Rather, Manville sought to halt the lawsuits brought against it by people suffering health problems caused by exposure to asbestos and products made with asbestos that were produced by Manville. By gaining bankruptcy status, all pending lawsuits against the company would be ruled on by a bankruptcy judge (rather than state and federal courts), legal proceedings would be delayed, and new lawsuits could not be brought. Manville planned to remove itself from bankruptcy standing after its legal problems were resolved.

Manville defended its application for Chapter 11 protection in full-page newspaper ads appearing on August 27, 1982. Manville offered these reasons for its actions:

---

*The data in this case are drawn from Neil Maxwell, "Manville Tries to Fight Wave of Problems, Including Costly Rise in Asbestos Lawsuits," *Wall Street Journal* (June 9, 1982), p. 31; Neil Maxwell, G. Christian Hill, and Raymond A. Joseph, "Radical Tactic," *Wall Street Journal* (August 27, 1982), pp. 1, 8; and "Despite Strong Business, Litigation Forces Manville to File for Reorganization," *Wall Street Journal* (August 27, 1982), p. 29.

1. 16,500 lawsuits were pending, with 500 new lawsuits being filed each month. It was estimated that 32,000 more lawsuits could be brought against the company. The total costs of settling 52,000 lawsuits at $40,000 per claim (Manville's average) would amount to more than $2 billion.
2. Asbestos-related health problems were not discovered until 1964. Up to then existing medical knowledge showed that Manville operated properly. The largest group of plaintiffs against the company was shipyard workers using asbestos insulation on ships built or modified during World War II, when asbestos was viewed as safe.
3. The U.S. government should be responsible for a compensation program for asbestos-related injuries. Furthermore, it was virtually impossible for the company to defend itself in every state, under different statutes.

Manville's critics believed the firm was not acting in a socially responsible manner and was misusing bankruptcy protection (which was intended for companies with severe financial, not legal, problems). These critics asserted that

1. Manville was trying to force the federal government to develop a bailout plan for the company.
2. By cutting off lawsuits, Manville was not allowing plaintiffs to exercise their legal rights.
3. Manville "fraudulently concealed" information about asbestos hazards. In 1980, the California Supreme Court ruled that plaintiffs were eligible for punitive damages because of this. These damages would not be covered by insurance, but by Manville itself.

QUESTIONS

1. Was Manville justified in applying for court protection? Explain your answer.
2. Should a company be liable for health hazards not discovered until years after a product is introduced? Why or why not?
3. How do you view the large settlements U.S. juries are awarding to plaintiffs in product liability trials? For example, a Texas woman was awarded $2 million by a jury ($1 million in punitive damages) for asbestos-related health problems of her deceased husband.
4. Will Manville's actions have a long-term impact on the company's image? Explain your answer from the perspective of both stockholders and consumers.

REGULATION VERSUS DEREGULATION IN THE U.S. AUTOMOBILE INDUSTRY† 2

Beginning in 1981, President Reagan and the U.S. Congress significantly altered an almost twenty-year trend toward increased consumer protection regulation. The very existence of major consumer protection agencies, such

†The data in this case are drawn from Henry Gilgoff, "An Agency Imperiled," *Newsday* (February 1, 1983), Part II, p. 3; John Holusha, "What Deregulation Means for G.M.," *New York Times* (November 1, 1981), Section 3, pp. 1, 26; and Richard I. Kirkland, Jr., "Hazardous Times for Product-Safety Czars," *Fortune* (June 15, 1981), pp. 126–134.

as the Federal Trade Commission (FTC) and the Consumer Product Safety Commission (CPSC) was challenged. Their budgets were severely curtailed (for example, the budget for the CPSC was reduced from $44 million in fiscal 1980 to under $34 million by fiscal 1983); and "antiregulation" heads were appointed for various agencies.

The automobile industry provides a good illustration of the ongoing struggle between business and consumer advocates, and the change in government actions. Automobile firms have been heavily regulated by a number of federal agencies since the mid-1960s. Among the areas in which federal regulations have been enacted are seat belts, antipollution devices, bumper guards, crash ratings, and fuel economy.

General Motors has estimated its costs of compliance with existing regulations to be over $2.2 billion annually. Meeting emission standards has raised the average price of a car by $725; and safety standards have added another $400 to selling price. Auto makers also claim that regulations have forced them to reduce the number of new models they can introduce.

While auto companies have lobbied for deregulation, consumer advocates continue to believe that the gains in clean air and auto safety have occurred only because of mandatory regulations. They want even tighter regulations. For example, one observer estimates that a passive restraint system (such as air bags), which does not rely on the consumer to fasten seat belts, could save the country $4.5 billion in medical costs, insurance costs, and lost wages due to deaths and injuries. Another proposal, to publish the ratings of cars in 35-mile-per-hour crash tests and to require bumpers that protect autos from damage at 5 miles per hour (instead of the current 2.5), would also save lives and costs.

During 1981, these forthcoming regulations were repealed: air bags and passive seat belts to be required by 1983, stickers with ratings of crash tests to be placed on the windows of new cars, gas mileage standards beyond 1985, tamper-proof odometers on new cars, and minimum windshield visibility requirements. Said the new head of the National Highway Traffic Safety Administration: "Many of these rules are trivial."

QUESTIONS

1. Evaluate the position of the auto makers.
2. Evaluate the position of the consumer advocates.
3. Can the controversy be settled to the satisfaction of both parties? Explain your answer.
4. Deregulation is predicted to continue for several years. What are the positive and negative implications for marketers?

Part
Eight

Marketing
Management

Introduction to Part Eight

In Part Eight the concepts introduced in Chapters 1 through 18 are integrated, and how to plan for the future is discussed. The first portion of the chapter explains how to develop, integrate, and analyze marketing plans. A five-step procedure for marketing planning is presented: identifying opportunities and potential problems, setting objectives, creating an appropriate strategy, implementing tactics, and monitoring results.

The second portion of the chapter shows the importance of anticipating and planning for the future. Consumer demographic and lifestyle trends and their implications for marketers are studied. A number of environmental trends and their significance for marketers also are examined: competition, government, the economy, technology, resource shortages, and global events. The chapter concludes with a discussion of marketing strategies for the 1980s.

Marketing Management and Future Planning

19

Chapter Objectives

1 To show the value of integrated marketing planning

2 To study the components of a marketing plan: identifying opportunities and potential problems, developing objectives, creating an appropriate strategy, implementing tactics, and monitoring results

3 To examine consumer and environmental trends in the 1980s and their marketing implications

4 To consider marketing strategies for the 1980s, with emphasis on product, distribution, promotion, and price planning

Steven Jobs and Stephen Wozniack, then in their very early 20s, founded the Apple Computer company in 1977. By 1982, the company had annual sales of almost $600 million; and a total of 700,000 Apple II personal computers had been sold between 1977 and the end of 1982.

Apple's success was due to several factors:

- It defined and developed the market for personal computers.
- It reduced the mystery of computers to consumers.
- Prices were relatively low.
- A solid distribution network was established.
- Independent programmers were encouraged to write programs. This led to a 16,000-program library.
- Young product designers were attracted to work for the company.

Apple has not been without its problems. The Apple II was its only major success from 1977 through 1982. The widely promoted Apple III had design problems, which caused it to be recalled shortly after introduction. An improved Apple III has not met company sales expectations. At the same time, intensive competition has kept profit margins low, brought out innovative products, and driven some firms from the market. Among the 150 companies now selling personal computers are IBM, Radio Shack, Atari, Commodore, Texas Instruments, Xerox, Exxon, Wang, Hewlett-Packard, NCR, Data General, Control Data, Digital Equipment, and Sperry.

In order to sustain its success in the long run, Apple recognizes that it must regularly develop and market new personal computer products. With this goal in mind, Apple introduced two new products in January 1983, Apple IIe and Lisa. Apple IIe is an "evolutionary" product that improves upon the features of the Apple II. It was first priced at under $1,400. Lisa is a "revolutionary" new computer that is very easy to learn and use; and it has a large storage capacity. Its initial price was $10,000. See Figure 19-1. Apple also planned to market the new Macintosh personal computer in late 1983. Macintosh is a scaled-down and less-expensive ($2,000) version of Lisa.[1]

Developing and Integrating the Marketing Plan

Throughout this text there has been a focus on systematic planning in each functional area of marketing (product, distribution, promotion, and pricing). In this section the development and integration of the entire marketing plan are discussed. In the second half of the chapter, planning for the future is examined.

For example, although a promotion plan primarily deals with one strategic element, it must also be integrated with other functional areas. Promotion planning includes decisions about the promotion budget, media, timing, message content, frequency, and the combination of advertising, personal selling, sales promotion, and publicity. To be effective, promotion must be coordinated with product, distribution, and pricing plans. It must reflect the proper image for the firm's products, foster channel cooperation, and demonstrate that the products are worth the prices set.

The total marketing effort of an organization can be integrated and coordinated through a ***marketing plan:*** the process for deciding what

A ***marketing plan*** outlines actions, why they are needed, responsibility, and where and how completed.

Figure 19-1
New Products from Apple

marketing actions to undertake, why those actions are necessary, who is responsible for carrying them out, where they will be accomplished, and how they will be completed.[2] A plan may be short run (one year), moderate in length (two to five years), or long run (five to ten or fifteen years).

The overall marketing plan has five elements: identifying opportunities and potential problems, developing objectives, creating an appropriate strategy, implementing tactics, and monitoring results. See Figure 19-2. These elements are discussed separately in the following subsections.

Identifying Marketing Opportunities and Potential Problems

In developing a marketing plan, a firm must first undertake a ***situation analysis,*** which identifies marketing opportunities and potential problems that face the company. Situation analysis seeks answers to two general questions: Where is the firm now? In what direction is the firm headed?

*A **situation analysis** determines the firm's current standing and future direction.*

Figure 19-2
**The Elements of a
Marketing Plan**

Identifying Marketing
Opportunities and
Potential Problems

Developing Objectives

Creating an
Appropriate Strategy

Implementing Tactics

Monitoring Results

The company's present position can be determined by studying its strengths and weaknesses, market share, sales by product, territory, and price, degree of plant utilization, image, and distribution channel. Its direction can be assessed by studying the trends in consumer markets and the environmental factors facing the organization and the industry and by forecasting sales, prices, costs, and return on investment.

Colgate-Palmolive provides a good illustration of how situation analysis can be used. In 1980, the firm announced plans to get rid of its processed meat, sports equipment, and restaurant businesses, as a result of a thorough situation analysis. Included were Hebrew National Kosher Food, Ram Golf, and Lum's restaurants. Helena Rubinstein was also placed on the market by Colgate-Palmolive.

Colgate had learned that successfully marketing toothpaste and laundry soap did not guarantee success for hot dogs, hockey sticks, and nail polish. Management attention was diverted from relevant product introductions and maintenance to unrelated businesses with which it had no experience.

Keith Crane, president and chief executive officer, reviewed Colgate's long-run objectives and concluded that:

> By planning to discontinue those operations which do not fulfill our objectives, we are freeing up financial and management resources to be put to better advantage elsewhere in the company.[3]

After responding to the results of its situation analysis, Colgate was able to raise profits by 21.5 per cent from 1980 to 1981. In addition, by better using resources, sales actually increased from 1980 to 1981, despite the elimination of the businesses noted previously.[4]

Developing Objectives

Next, both general and specific objectives are established. General objectives give direction to the firm and its marketing plan. Examples of general objectives are increased market share, decreased dependence on key customers, expanded distribution capabilities, increased brand awareness, and improved company image.

Specific objectives enable performance to be measured and corrective action to be taken if the objectives are not met. They also ensure a coordination of all marketing functions. A way to determine whether an objective is specific is to see if there are numbers within it. Examples of specific objectives are to reach a market share of 40 per cent, to have the largest five customers account for no more than 40 per cent of sales, to obtain distribution in 98 per cent of all supermarkets, and to attain brand awareness by 80 per cent of potential customers.

General objectives direct a firm's marketing plan; specific objectives set performance standards.

Creating an Appropriate Strategy

A *strategy* outlines the manner in which marketing is used to accomplish a firm's objectives. Often, a firm must select a strategy from among two or more possible alternatives. For example, a company that wants to achieve a market share of 40 per cent may accomplish this objective in several ways. It can improve product image through extensive advertising, adding salespeople, introducing a new product model, lowering prices, or selling through more retail outlets. Another option would be to combine these marketing elements in a well-coordinated way.

A strategy describes the marketing plan that will accomplish objectives.

Each alternative strategy emphasis has different ramifications for marketers. For instance, a price strategy may be very flexible, because a price can be raised or lowered more frequently than product modifications can be introduced. However, a strategy based solely on low price is the easiest to copy. In addition, a successful price strategy may lead to a price war, with disastrous effects on net profits. In contrast, a strategy based on locational advantages may be difficult to copy, because of long lease terms and the unavailability of appropriate sites for competitors. This strategy may be inflexible and adapt poorly to environmental changes.

The *product/market opportunity matrix* is one broad method for strategy planning. This approach offers four alternative strategies for

The product/market opportunity matrix distinguishes among market penetration, market development, product development, and diversification.

Figure 19-3
Product/Market Opportunity
Matrix

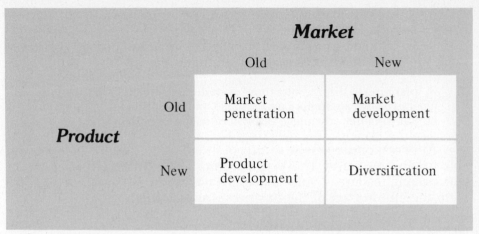

Source: H. Igor Ansoff, "Strategies for Diversification," *Harvard Business Review*, Vol. 35 (September–October 1957), pp. 113–124.

maintaining and/or increasing sales: market penetration, market development, product development, and diversification.[5]

In **market penetration,** a firm seeks to expand the sales of its present products in its present markets through more aggressive promotion and distribution. In **market development,** a firm seeks sales from new markets or new product uses. Existing products are involved. In **product development,** a firm develops new or modified products to appeal to present markets. In **diversification,** a firm develops new products for new markets. Figure 19-3 shows the product/market opportunity matrix. Table 19-1 applies this matrix to Coca-Cola, which uses each of these alternative strategies.

A second broad method for strategy planning is the **Boston Consulting Group matrix,** which enables a company to classify each of its products on the basis of the product's market share relative to the industry's leading brands and the annual growth rate of the product's industry. By using the matrix, the firm can determine which of its products are dominant compared to competitors and whether the industries in which it operates are growing, stable, or declining.[6]

The primary assumption of the Boston Consulting Group matrix is that the higher a firm's market share, the lower its per-unit costs and the higher its profitability. This is the result of economies of scale (larger firms can mechanize and automate production and distribution), the experience curve (as projects and operations are repeated, time requirements are reduced), and improved bargaining power.

This matrix identifies four types of products: star, cash cow, problem child (question mark), and dog, and suggests appropriate strategies for each. Figure 19-4 shows the Boston Consulting Group matrix.

A **star** is a leading product (high market share) in an expanding industry (high growth). It generates substantial profits but requires large amounts of resources to finance continued growth. Market share can be maintained or increased through price reductions, more advertising, product modifications, and/or greater distribution. As industry growth slows, a star becomes a cash cow.

The *Boston Consulting Group Matrix* classifies products as *stars, cash cows, problem children (question marks),* or *dogs.*

Table 19-1

**Product/Market
Opportunity Matrix
Applied to Coca-Cola**

I. Market Penetration: Increase Sales of Present Products in Present Markets

A. Use of "Coke Is It" campaign; more adults used in commercials
B. Sales to fast-food chains; use of dealer promotions, premium offers, and advertising programs
C. Continued domination of soda fountain market, which represents one third of current sales.
D. Greater promotion of nonCoke brands

II. Market Development: Increase Sales of Present Products by Entering New Markets

A. Coke's division of its world market into three parts, with an executive in charge of each: U.S., Central America, and South America; Europe, Africa, Southwest Asia, and Indian subcontinent; and Canada, Far East, and Pacific
B. Change of image from children's drink to family beverage

III. Product Development: Increase Sales by Developing New or Improved Products for Present Markets

A. Improvement of product quality
B. Addition of new flavors and brands (such as diet Coke)

IV. Diversification: Increase Sales by Developing New Products for New Markets

A. Production of juice, coffee, and tea
B. Manufacture of water treatment and conditioning equipment
C. Production of disposable plastic cutlery and straws for food-service chains and hospitals
D. Purchase of Columbia Pictures

A *cash cow* is a leading product (high market share) in a relatively mature or declining industry (low growth). It generates more cash than is required to retain its market share. Profits support the growth of other company products. The firm's strategy is oriented toward maintaining the product's strong position in the market.

A *problem child* or *question mark* is a product that has made little impact in the marketplace (low market share) in an expanding industry (high growth). It needs substantial cash to maintain or increase market share in the face of strong competition. The company must decide whether to market more intensively or remove this product from the market. The choice of strategy depends on whether the company believes the product can compete successfully with adequate support and what that support will cost.

A *dog* is a product with limited sales (low market share) in a mature or declining industry (low growth). A dog usually has cost disadvantages and few growth opportunities. A company with such a product can attempt to appeal to a specialized market, delete the product, or harvest profits by cutting support services to a minimum.

Scott Paper Co. is one of the many firms that currently follow the strategy principles suggested by the Boston Consulting Group matrix. Scott makes paper towels, bathroom tissues, disposable mats, baby wipes, tissues, napkins, and other products. The company hired the

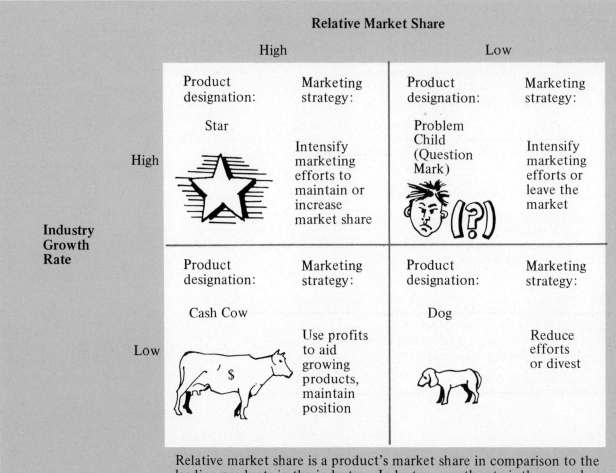

Relative market share is a product's market share in comparison to the leading products in the industry. Industry growth rate is the annual growth of all products in the market (such as sugarless gum).

Figure 19-4
Boston Consulting Group Matrix
Source: Adapted from Bruce D. Henderson, "The Experience Curve Reviewed: IV. The Growth Share Matrix of the Product Portfolio" (Boston: Boston Consulting Group, 1973), Perspectives No. 135.

Boston Consulting Group in 1980, after seeing its market share shrink and erratic earnings occur. These events were brought on by company complacency and inefficient, outdated equipment.

Now, Scott has developed the first overall strategic plan in its more than 100-year history. The strategy is straight-forward: to pour money into products that have realistic chances to be industry leaders and to provide less resources for other products. This approach is not as easy as it seems. As a Boston Consulting Group vice-president observed, "I think the hardest thing for every company in the world is knowing when to limit your activity and not to do everything you want."

Scott's new strategy means that some well-known brands will be relatively neglected over the next few years. Included are Cottonelle and Soft 'n' Pretty bathroom tissue, which were introduced in the 1970s to compete with Procter & Gamble's Charmin brand (the industry leader). Some of Scott's products will be "milked" for whatever cash they can produce. Others will be repositioned. Still others will probably be dropped.[7]

Because it is still evolving, the Boston Consulting Group matrix has been criticized by a variety of observers. For example, there is no conclusive research to show that the unit costs of large firms are lower than those of medium-sized firms. An analysis of 200 items at General Electric found no relationship between market share and rate of return. Another study found a group of companies with low market shares that consistently outperformed their larger rivals.[8]

Implementing Tactics

Tactics are specific actions undertaken to implement a given strategy. In the Coca-Cola example in Table 19-1, market penetration is one of the company's strategies. The enactment of a specific campaign, to promote nonCoke brands more extensively, involves tactics. Table 19-2 contains several examples of tactics based on well-defined strategies for a variety of companies.

Tactics are specific actions used to carry out a strategy.

Two important tactical decisions relate to expense levels and the timing of marketing actions. Marketing expenses can be classified as order processing and order generating. *Order-processing costs* such as warehousing and credit are similar to manufacturing overhead. The goal is to minimize those costs subject to obtaining a given level of service. *Order-generating costs,* such as advertising, packaging, and personal selling, are revenue producing. Reducing these costs may have a detrimental effect on a firm's sales and profits. With order-generating costs, the objective is to determine the optimal mix of marketing variables. Specifically, what combination of marketing expenditures will yield the highest level of profits?

Order-processing costs are similar to overhead. Order-generating costs are used to produce revenue.

Company	Strategy	Tactics	**Table 19-2**
ABC Television	Development and maintenance of situation comedies for the 18–35 audience	Airing of "Three's Company"	**Examples of Tactics**
American Express	Use of celebrities to promote American Express cards	Advertisements with Tom Landry (coach of the Dallas Cowboys) and Peter Benchley (author of *Jaws*)	
Heinz	Strong marketing support for well-established products	For Heinz Ketchup, 1981 advertising budget of $11 million, many consumer promotions, and introduction of a 44-ounce bottle	
IBM	Constant introduction of new computer equipment	Marketing the IBM Personal Computer in August 1981	
Kraft	Diversification of business	Merger with Dart Industries, maker of Tupperware	
McDonald's	To maintain a family-oriented image	Building McDonald's Playland facilities at many outlets	

The timing of marketing activities is important.

The second major tactical decision deals with the timing of marketing activities. Proper timing may mean being the first to introduce a product, bringing out a product when the market is most receptive to it, or quickly reacting to a competitor's strategy to catch him or her off guard. The company must balance its desire to be an industry leader with a clear-cut competitive advantage against its concern about the risk of innovative actions.

Monitoring Results

Monitoring results entails an analysis of performance for a given period of time.

Monitoring results involves the comparison of planned performance against actual performance for a specified period of time. Budgets, timetables, sales statistics, and cost analyses can be used to assess results. If actual performance lags behind plans, some corrective action should be taken after problem areas are highlighted.

In some cases, plans have to be revised because of the impact of uncontrollable variables on sales and costs. Many farsighted companies develop contingency plans that outline in advance their responses should unfavorable conditions arise.

The next two subsections discuss sales analysis and the marketing audit, and how they are used in monitoring a strategy.

Sales Analysis

With *sales analysis,* data are evaluated to determine the correctness of a marketing strategy.

Sales analysis is the detailed study of sales data for the purpose of appraising the appropriateness of a marketing strategy. Sales analysis enables plans to be set in terms of sales by product, product line, salesperson, region, customer type, time period, price line, or method of sale. It also compares actual sales against planned sales. Without adequate sales analysis, the importance of certain market segments and territories may be overlooked, sales effort may be poorly matched with market potential, fashion trends may be overlooked, or assistance for sales personnel may not be forthcoming. According to the latest survey by the American Marketing Association, 96 per cent of companies report that they use sales analysis.[9]

Levi Strauss is an example of a firm that applies sales analysis. It has a shipment analysis system that organizes invoices, customer credit approval information, and product descriptions into monthly sales summary profiles. These show specific product sales by units and dollars within each sales region. This information allows Levi Strauss to establish sales goals by garment and customer type and evaluate progress toward goals.[10]

A key principle in sales analysis is that summary data such as overall current sales or market share are usually insufficient to diagnose a firm's areas of strength and weakness. More intensive investigation is necessary. Two sales analysis techniques that offer in-depth probing are the 80–20 principle and sales exception reporting.

The *80–20 principle* notes that a large amount of sales (profit) often comes from few customers, products, or territories. Errors in analysis may be due to the *iceberg principle.*

The *80–20 principle* states that in many organizations a large proportion of total sales (profit) comes from a small proportion of customers, products, or territories. In order to function efficiently, firms should determine sales and profit by customer, product, or territory. Then resources would be allocated accordingly. Companies err when they examine only total sales (profit) rather than isolate and categorize data.

Through faulty reasoning, they would place equal effort into each sale instead of concentrating on larger accounts. These errors are due to a related concept known as the **iceberg principle,** which states that superficial data are insufficient to make sound evaluations.

Through in-depth analysis, the Firestone Tire & Rubber Company discovered that it was operating under the 80–20 principle and responded appropriately. Of the 7,289 different tire types it produced (counting all widths, styles, sizes, and in-house and private brands), the Firestone brand represented 65 per cent of sales but only 25 per cent of all items. The frequent changeovers in the factory caused by product proliferation led to higher down time, higher costs, and lower quality standards. Firestone eliminated 2,400 items while retaining those with the highest profit margins.[11]

Simple sales analysis also can be improved by using **sales exception reporting,** which lists situations where sales goals are not met or sales opportunities are present. A slow-selling item report lists items whose sales are below those forecasted. It suggests corrective actions such as price reductions, promotions, and sales incentives to increase unit sales. A fast-selling item report lists items whose sales exceed those forecasted. It points out sales opportunities and items that need more inventory on hand to prevent stockouts. Finally, sales exception reporting enables a firm to evaluate the validity of sales forecasts and make the proper modifications in them.

Sales exception reporting records cases where goals are unmet or further opportunities exist.

Marketing Audit

The **marketing audit** is defined as

> a systematic, critical, and unbiased review and appraisal of the basic objectives and policies of the marketing function, and of the organization, methods, procedures, and personnel employed to implement those policies and to achieve those objectives. Clearly, not every evaluation of marketing personnel, organizations, or methods is a marketing audit; at best, most such evaluations can be regarded as parts of the audit.[12]

A marketing audit examines a firm in a systematic, critical, and unbiased manner.

An audit includes an investigation of the firm's marketing objectives, strategy, implementation, and organization. An effective audit is conducted on a regular basis, comprehensive, systematic, and carried out in an independent manner.[13]

The marketing audit process consists of six steps:

1. Determination of who does the audit. An audit may be conducted by company specialists, company division or department managers, or outside specialists.
2. Determination of when and how often the audit is conducted. An audit may be undertaken at the end of a calendar year, at the end of a company's annual reporting year, or when undertaking a physical inventory. An audit should be performed at least annually, although some companies prefer more frequent analysis. The audit should be completed during the same time period each year to allow comparisons. In some cases, unannounced audits are useful to keep employees alert and ensure spontaneity of answers.

3. Determination of areas to be audited. A **horizontal audit** (often referred to as a marketing-mix audit) studies the overall marketing performance of the company with particular emphasis on the interrelationship of variables and their relative importance. A **vertical audit** is an in-depth analysis of one aspect of the firm's marketing strategy, such as product planning. The two audits should be used in conjunction with one another because the horizontal audit often reveals areas that need further investigation.

4. Developing audit forms. Audit forms list the areas to be examined and the exact information required to evaluate each area. The forms usually resemble questionnaires, and they are completed by the auditor. An illustration of an audit form is contained in Figure 19-5.

5. Conducting the audit. The decisions to be made at this stage involve the time duration of the audit, whether employees are to be aware of the audit, whether the audit is performed while the organization is open or closed, and how the final report is to be prepared.

6. Presenting the results to management. The last step in an audit is to present the findings and recommendations to management. However, the auditing process is complete only after appropriate responses are taken by management. It is the responsibility of management, not the auditor, to determine these responses.

The idea of using independent evaluation to review performance is not new. For example, the accounting profession audits financial records for accuracy and honesty; inventory levels are frequently audited; many firms analyze their organizational structures on a periodic basis; long-term manpower needs and resources are regularly audited; and recently, firms have begun to evaluate their social responsibility performance.

Despite the long-standing application of audits, many firms have not adopted a formal marketing audit. Three factors account for this. One, success or failure is difficult to establish in marketing. An organization may have poor performance despite the best planning if environmental factors intervene. On the other hand, good results may be based on the firm's being at the right place at the right time. Two, when marketing audits are completed by company personnel, they may not be comprehensive enough to be considered audits. Three, the pressures of other activities often mean that only a small part of the firm is audited or that the audit is done on a nonregular basis.

Anticipating and Planning for the Future

The decade of the 1980s promises to be a significant one for U.S. marketers as they try to anticipate trends and plan long-run strategies. On the positive side, the 1980s should see increasing consumer affluence, improvements in technological capabilities, expanding worldwide markets, greater deregulation of industry, and other opportunities. On the

Does your department, division, or firm . . .

Answer Yes or No to Each Question

Planning, Organization, and Control
1. Have specific objectives? _____
2. Study customer needs, attitudes, and behavior? _____
3. Organize marketing efforts in a systematic way? _____
4. Have a market planning process? _____
5. Engage in comprehensive sales forecasting? _____
6. Have strategy and tactics within the marketing plan? _____
7. Have clearly stated contingency plans? _____
8. Monitor environmental changes? _____
9. Control activities through marketing cost analysis, sales analysis, and the marketing audit? _____

Marketing Research
10. Utilize marketing research for planning as well as problem solving? _____
11. Have a marketing information system? _____
12. Have adequate communication between marketing research and line executives? _____

Product
13. Utilize a systematic product planning process? _____
14. Have a procedure for developing new products? _____
15. Monitor competitive developments in product planning? _____
16. Revise mature products? _____
17. Phase out weak products? _____

Distribution
18. Motivate channel members? _____
19. Periodically evaluate channel members? _____
20. Evaluate alternative shipping arrangements? _____
21. Compute economic order quantities? _____
22. Modify channel decisions as conditions warrant? _____

Promotion
23. Have an overall promotion plan? _____
24. Measure the effectiveness of advertising? _____
25. Seek out favorable publicity? _____
26. Have a procedure for recruiting and retaining sales personnel? _____
27. Moderate the use of sales promotions? _____

Price
28. Have a pricing strategy that is in compliance with government regulations? _____
29. Have a pricing strategy that satisfies channel members? _____
30. Estimate demand and cost factors before setting prices? _____
31. Plan for competitive developments? _____
32. Set prices that are consistent with image? _____

Figure 19-5 **A Horizontal Marketing Audit Form**

negative side, they may witness some raw material shortages, increasing competition from foreign companies, a relatively stagnant domestic market, and an uncertain economy among the potential problems.

Long-range plans must take into account both the external factors facing the firm and its capacity for change. Specifically, what factors will affect the firm? What trends are forecast for them? Is the firm able to respond to these trends (for example, does it have the necessary resources and lead time)? A company that does not anticipate and respond to future trends has a good possibility of falling into Levitt's marketing myopia trap and losing ground to more far-sighted competitors.[14]

As two recent observers noted:

> American management, especially in the two decades after World War II, was universally admired for its strikingly effective performance. But times change. An approach shaped and refined during stable decades may be ill suited to a world characterized by rapid and unpredictable change, scarce energy, global competition for markets, and a constant need for innovation. This is the world of the 1980s and, probably, the rest of this century.[15]

This part of the chapter focuses on marketing during the decade of the 1980s. First, consumers and environmental factors are analyzed. See Figure 19-6. Then each of the basic elements of marketing is examined.

Consumers in the 1980s

Although some population segments and characteristics will remain constant, others will change substantially.

In the 1980s there will be shifts in both the demographics and life-styles of consumers. These shifts will have a large impact on long-run marketing plans.

Demographic trends have important implications for marketers. For example, the rise in incomes will result in greater demand from some consumers for luxuries and high-quality, high-priced goods; working women will demand convenience goods and shopping services; and small households will demand individual servings of foods. Table 19-3 shows selected implications of demographic trends for marketers.

Many emerging trends in consumer life-styles are expected to continue in the 1980s. Four of these are voluntary simplicity, the me generation, the blurring of gender roles, and the poverty of time.

Voluntary simplicity is based on material simplicity and ecological awareness.

Voluntary simplicity is a life-style in which people seek material simplicity, have an ecological awareness, strive for self-determination, and purchase do-it-yourself products. It grew out of the 1960s and 1970s, when people first became aware that many natural resources were being depleted. This life-style is expected to remain and expand if Americans are faced with some shortages and rising prices.

The *me generation* stresses self-expression and self-improvement.

While voluntary simplicity and the conservation ethic will be increasing in the 1980s, there will also be advances in a more lavish life-style, that of the ***me generation.*** This life-style stresses "being good to myself," "improving myself," and "my life, my way."[16] Like voluntary simplicity, the me generation began in the 1960s and 1970s as free-expression and self-expression became more acceptable.

Figure 19-6
Factors Affecting Marketing in the 1980s

As greater numbers of women enter the labor force, more husbands will assume the traditional roles of their wives, thus **blurring gender roles.** These husbands will work in the home and share the tasks of managing a household and feeding the family. In 1967, 60 per cent of the adult women respondents to a survey agreed with the statement, "A woman's place is in the home." By 1975, only 26 per cent agreed with this statement and the majority favored a marriage in which the husband and wife shared homemaking and child-care responsibilities.[17] Today, even more women believe in their right to work and share responsibilities. Younger, better-educated, more-affluent women are most prone to favor sharing.

For many consumer households, the increase in working women, the long distances between home and work, and the rise in people working at second jobs contribute to less rather than more free time. The **poverty-of-time** concept states that for some consumers greater affluence will result in less free time because the alternatives competing for time will expand. As the prices of houses, automobiles, food, and other goods and services continue to go up in the future, more households will require two incomes and a second job for the main earner.

Blurring gender roles involves more men undertaking household duties.

Poverty of time exists when greater affluence results in less free time.

Table 19-3	*Trends*	*Implications*
Selected Marketing Implications of Demographic Trends	Stable U.S. population	Foreign markets may hold greater opportunities for growth.
	Increase in middle-aged and retired persons	There is potential for multiple-segmentation strategies. Wilson Sporting Goods plans to market golf clubs that assist golfers in getting the ball in flight more quickly. Levi Strauss has designed fuller-cut jeans. Proctor & Gamble is marketing disposable diapers for incontinent adults. Universities are expanding their programs for adults.
	Shift to southern and western regions	The northeast faces continued out-migration of population and industry. Brands distributed nationally will prosper as consumers move about.
	Rise in real income	There will be opportunities for discretionary goods and services, such as home computers and vacation travel.
	Increase in working women	These women have little time for shopping or preparation of foods. Faster checkouts, expanded evening hours, one-stop shopping, and convenience goods will be needed. Expenditures in business clothing, luggage, and airline travel will rise.
	Increase in education	Consumers will be more discerning and critical.
	Rise in white-collar jobs	Consumers will have more leisure time. There will be opportunities for entertainment forms.
	Growth of single-person households	Smaller homes and condominiums will be demanded, as will single-serving products.
	Changing home market	There will be demand for home-oriented goods and services. Luxury townhouses will be popular, especially those with large master bedrooms that make it easier for two working people to dress in the morning.

These life-style developments will have broad implications for marketing strategy, as shown in Figure 19-7.

Environmental Factors in the 1980s

During the 1980s a number of environmental factors will affect marketing. These include competition, government, the economy, technology, resource shortages, and global events. These factors are described in the following subsections.

Competition

Most domestic competition in the 1980s will remain at its current level, but the impact of foreign competition will grow.

Domestic competition will remain at approximately its current level because the number of U.S. firms in most industries will be relatively stable. In some cases, competition will increase as a result of government deregulation. Mass media, transportation, banking, and communication industries will all have far greater competition due to deregulation. The ongoing airfare wars are a specific example of this.

The impact of foreign competition will continue and grow. In the United States foreign manufacturers are now capturing large market shares—30 per cent of automobiles, 30 per cent of sport and athletic

Trend	Implications
Voluntary Simplicity 	Expansion will occur for do-it-yourself products such as repair kits and "knock-down" furniture. There will be consumer interest in quality, durability, and simplicity (rational goals). No-frills retailing will grow. Fuel-efficient cars, bicycles, and public transportation will be used more frequently. Ecologically benign products will be desired. These will include recycled paper, phosphate-free detergents, and biodegradable packages. Sales of insulation, solar energy, and energy-efficient products will grow rapidly.
Me generation $10,000	Individuality in purchase decisions will gain greater acceptance. Luxuries will be desired. Nutritional themes will be important in food purchases. The interest in physical fitness will expand sales for health spas, bicycles, and exercise equipment. Health and beauty-aid products and personal-care retailing will grow. The concern for self-improvement will lead to more continuing education programs and the enrollment of adults in colleges.
Blurring of gender roles 	Unisex products, services, and stores will be popular. Shopping conditions will be favorable to joint husband and wife purchase behavior. Advertising will feature couples. There will be demand for products and services that can be used jointly. Male and female stereotypes will no longer be applicable.
Poverty of time 	Catalog and mail-order sales will grow. Service providers will need to make and keep customer appointments. The sales of labor–saving devices will rise. One-stop shopping will be more important. Wardrobe consultants will save customers time. Well-known brands will ease shopping.

Figure 19-7 Selected Marketing Implications of Life-Style Trends

goods, 34 per cent of microwave ovens, 90 per cent of both CB radios and motorcycles, and almost 100 per cent of videocassette recorders. Also imported in large numbers are radial tires, calculators, food processors, premium beer, cameras, stereo components, digital watches, pianos, and outboard motors.[18] The success of foreign companies is based on their prowess for innovation, quality control, somewhat lower costs, good distribution, and promotion.

Competition in overseas markets will also be more intense for U.S. firms in the future. The greatest potential for increased exports will probably be in the computer technology field.

It is imperative for U.S. firms to seek out innovations, reduce the time necessary to respond to market conditions, and upgrade quality control. Before aggressively wooing foreign markets, firms must reestablish themselves among American consumers:

> On balance you might argue that American cars are now as good as the imports, but the public clearly doesn't think so. In a recent survey for the American Society for Quality Control, Americans panned U.S.-made autos. This judgment may be too harsh, or lag behind the facts, but perception can be as important as reality. It has the same effect in the marketplace.[19]

Government

Government regulation of business during the 1980s will be more limited than during the 1970s.

In the 1980s the most relevant government actions facing marketers are likely to involve deregulation, antitrust, and consumer protection.

The trend toward deregulation, noted in Chapter 18, will continue throughout the 1980s. For example, the Federal Communications Commission is in the process of deregulating FM radio stations. Banks will be fully deregulated by 1985; they will be able to provide a broader range of financial services and competitive rates for savings. Further deregulation is predicted for other industries. Overall, deregulation will induce greater price competition, encourage competitors to enter the marketplace, and offer consumers further choices. Success and failure will be more determined by marketing skills than government supports and restraints.

During the 1980s, the U.S. government will be less likely to seek to break up large firms (such as IBM) and more likely to approve mergers between leading companies (such as U.S. Steel and Marathon Oil). The government will also be more restrained in monitoring Robinson-Patman violations, full-line forcing, territorial restrictions, and dealer terminations.

Restricted powers for consumer protection agencies, such as the FTC (Federal Trade Commission) and CPSC (Consumer Product Safety Commission), will continue. These agencies will have less authority to investigate industries and impose trade rules. For example, the FTC has already been forced to cut back on actions directed at children's advertising, insurance, funeral homes, opticians, and other areas. Business self-regulation will gain in importance and companies will act more responsibly on their own initiative.

The Economy

Forecasting the U.S. economy is difficult because of the uncertainty of many factors, particularly inflation, unemployment, and such outside factors as OPEC (Organization of Petroleum Exporting Countries) prices.

To illustrate the complexity of predicting the economy, consider that during 1982 alone the inflation rate fell from 8.4 per cent to 4.0 per cent, the unemployment rate rose from 8.5 per cent to 10.8 per cent, and the price of a barrel of oil dropped about $4.

According to forecasters, such as Townsend-Greenspan (the economic consulting firm headed by Alan Greenspan, who was chairperson of the Council of Economic Advisors under President Ford), the highest projection for real economic growth in the United States through the 1980s is 3 to 4 per cent each year; and the rate could be much lower. During 1982, the U.S. economy was stagnant; there was no real economic growth.

After going through a sustained period of stagflation (stagnant economy and high inflation), the U.S. appears to now be in a period with much lower inflation, coupled with a slow-growth economy. To achieve the strongest possible U.S. economy, industry will need to accomplish several tasks. First, productivity must be improved. Second, wages and profits should be tied to better productivity and quality control. Third, companies should develop their own credit facilities to offer consumers reasonable terms for large-ticket purchases. Fourth, a high rate of employment must be maintained to assure consumer purchasing power. Fifth, nationalistic approaches ("Buy American") should receive more attention. Sixth, U.S. firms should learn from the successes of their foreign competitors.

Technology

Advances in computerization will offer great opportunities for new marketing techniques such as video-shopping services, electronic banking, and electronic mail. They will also enable firms to be more efficient in operations.

Video-shopping services will include electronic catalogs, telephone-oriented cable ordering systems, and interactive cable ordering systems.

The ***video-shopping services*** that are emerging can be divided into three categories: merchandise catalogs on videodiscs or videocassettes, telephone-oriented cable television ordering systems, and interactive cable television ordering systems. Traditional merchandise catalogs are being placed on videodiscs or videocassettes by retailers such as Sears. These catalogs are then by viewed in the store or in the consumer's home through a video player (an order would be placed by telephone). For example, Sears placed its 18,000-item summer 1981 catalog on a videodisc and experimented with the system in test markets.[20] See Figure 19-8.

Telephone-oriented cable television ordering systems rely on specialized "videoshopping programming." Products are displayed on programs and consumers order through special toll-free 800 telephone numbers. For example, "Shopping Channel" has over 150,000 subscribers in cities such as Hartford, Conn.; Louisville, Ken.; Springfield, Ill.; Midland, Tex.; and Newark, Oh. The programming is shown seven days per week, 16 hours each day, in half-hour segments. Each segment is repeated five times every month.[21]

Interactive cable television ordering systems also use specialized programming but they enable consumers to place orders directly through their home computers. The Comp-U-Star system, provided by Comp-U-Card, is the only such service that is available throughout the

Figure 19-8
Sears Video Catalog

In addition to its regular print format, the Sears Summer 1981 catalog was put on a videodisc and tested in Washington, D.C. and Cincinnati stores. Special equipment allowed shoppers in these stores to electronically view merchandise—complete with action and sound. The test was also conducted in 1,000 households across the U.S. Courtesy Sears, Roebuck and Co.

U.S. With Comp-U-Star, the consumer views a videoshopping program and then feeds information into his or her home computer (which is hooked into Comp-U-Card's main computer); the order is placed, billing completed, and delivery processed via the system.[22]

As of now, the use of these video-shopping services is very limited. From a manufacturer's or retailer's perspective, these systems are expensive, reach a limited audience, and require advanced technology. From a consumer's perspective, the systems do not replace seeing products in person, are costly to employ, and easily result in errors. Expansion of video shopping is forecast during the 1980s, as the problems noted are resolved and cable television is installed in more homes. By 1990, it is expected that 60 per cent of U.S. homes will have cable television, up from 34 per cent in 1982.

Electronic banking involves the utilization of automatic teller machines and instant processing of retail purchases. It provides centralized record keeping and enables customers to conduct transactions 24 hours a day, seven days a week at many bank and nonbank locations (such as supermarkets). Deposits, withdrawals, and other transactions can be completed.[23] See Figure 19-9.

In 1982, more than 26,000 automatic teller machines were operating in banks, shopping centers, airports, and other high-traffic sites. This figure is expected to triple by 1987. To allow customers to make financial transactions over wider geographic areas, a number of banks have formed regional automatic teller machine networks. For example, a consumer can complete transactions in six seconds at any one of 400 banks in Texas and Louisiana who belong to the PULSE network.[24]

As electronic banking spreads, more firms will employ a debit-only transfer system. In this arrangement, when a purchase is made, the amount is immediately charged against the buyer's account; no delayed billing is permitted without an interest charge. The debit-only plan is quite different from current credit-card policy whereby consumers are sent end-of-month bills and then remit payment. A debit card will receive wide acceptance as a substitute for checks. As of 1982, 4 million

Computerization will enable *electronic banking* to offer a wide variety of financial services and convenience.

Figure 19-9
Electronic Banking at Citibank

This is one of more than 220 electronic banking centers operated by Citibank. Reprinted by permission.

Visa and MasterCard debit cards and 50 million bank debit cards had been issued.[25]

Electronic mail **can transmit a letter coast-to-coast in less than one minute.**

GTE's Telenet Corporation introduced **electronic mail** in August 1980. Its system is able to transmit a letter from New York to San Francisco in less than one minute. In under one year, Telenet attracted eighty corporate clients. AT&T, IBM, Xerox, and others are also working on electronic mail plans. From a $70 million per year business in 1980, electronic mail is expected to become a $2 billion annual business by the late 1980s.[26]

Improved computer technology in the 1980s will enable small firms to purchase or lease equipment at substantially lower prices than were available during the 1970s. This will allow them to be more competitive with larger firms who have already installed computer machinery. Computerization will raise the efficiency of order processing, shipments, inventory control, and analysis of employee performance. It will further revolutionize real estate, insurance, and supermarket operations by coordinating information, evaluating opportunities, reducing service time, and minimizing employee errors.

Resource Shortages

Despite efforts at conservation, many raw materials, processed materials, and component parts may remain scarce in the 1980s. The effects of these shortages may be further aggravated by the political instability and/or rapid price increases of product-supplying countries. In recent years shortages have occurred for a variety of basic commodities such as home heating oil, other petroleum-based products, plastics, synthetic fibers, aluminum, chrome, silver, tungsten, nickel, steel, glass, grain, fertilizer, cotton, and wool.

Continued shortages may result in substitute materials, higher prices, and abandonment of some items.

Sustained shortages may result in three actions by companies. First, substitute materials will be used in constructing products. This will require intensified research and product testing. Second, prices will be raised for products that cannot incorporate substitute materials. Third, companies will abandon some products where resources are unavailable or used ineffectively and demarket others where demand is greater than it is able to supply. In general, firms will use existing resources much more efficiently in the 1980s.

For example, after acquiring the popular Duraflame fireplace logs in 1978, Clorox Co. quickly ran into trouble with the brand. The logs were made from petroleum derivatives which were in limited supply. This meant costs (and prices) escalated rapidly from 1978 to 1982, when Clorox had to drop the logs.[27]

Global Events

Worldwide events will have an impact on both domestic and multinational firms.

Global events in the 1980s will offer opportunities and risks. Population growth, rising worldwide per capita incomes, heightened literacy, and standardization in measures will all contribute to opportunities in foreign markets. Political disruptions, nationalism, improved capabilities of foreign companies, and countries' interest in self-sufficiency each pose risks for both domestic and multinational firms. They must plan accordingly.

Examples of global events which should be monitored during the 1980s are

- OPEC actions.
- Policies of economic communities (such as the European Community).
- Political unrest throughout the world.
- The rate of industrialization in foreign countries.
- Worldwide economic conditions.

Marketing in the 1980s

In order to succeed in the 1980s, marketers need to develop strategies that are responsive to consumer trends and the changes in the surrounding environment:

> The word that best summarizes recommended marketing in the eighties is *precision*. Inflated costs will necessitate tighter budgets, lower inventories, and more efficient use of the sales force. Riskier markets stocked with shrewder customers will require more effective segmentation schemes and more caution in new product introduction. Marketers will have to approach the future with the flexibility to abandon traditionally successful techniques and the innovativeness to replace them.[28]

The next subsections examine product (service), distribution, promotion, and price strategies for the 1980s.

Product or Service Strategy

The 1980s will see further use of formal, systematic product and service strategies. Through comprehensive analysis, companies will be able to position each of their offerings against competition, maintain a balanced product or service mix, identify areas of strength and weakness, monitor items over the product life cycle, and develop long-run plans. Computers will ease this analysis.

During the rest of the decade, there will be product categories in various phases of the product life cycle. Among the products forecast to grow rapidly are personal computers, videocassette recorders, videodisc players, and computer software.

Personal computer, videocassette recorder, videodisc player, and computer software sales should grow substantially throughout the 1980s.

- In 1982, personal computer sales were more than $6.1 billion worldwide; by 1986, they should reach $21 billion.[29]
- Between 1981 and 1982, annual sales of videocassette recorders rose from 1.3 to 2.0 million units. Sales are expected to rise sharply throughout the 1980s. By 1990, four times as many units will be owned by consumers.[30]
- During 1980, less than 100,000 videodisc players were sold. In 1982, 225,000 units were shipped. As a result of price decreases and improved quality, sales between now and 1990 are predicted to increase dramatically.[31]
- In 1983, about $1 billion in personal computer software was sold. Experts believe sales will reach $7 billion in 1988. As more small firms and final consumers purchase personal computers, their demand for word processings and financial programs, educational games, etc. will rise rapidly.[32]

While the sales of some mature products will be extended because of innovations, others will decline.

Some products will experience relatively little growth. For example, the markets for many household appliances are already saturated and leave little room for growth in the 1980s. At present, virtually all U.S. households have refrigerators and gas or electric ranges, 77 per cent have clothes washers, and 98 per cent have televisions. Each of these products has a long life and is replaced infrequently. Of the categories mentioned, only television sales are expected to increase as the number of multiple television households expands. Of the 16 million televisions sold in the U.S. each year, just one third are replacement purchases. By the late 1980s there will be one television for every man, woman, and child in the United States.[33]

Many mature products will have extended life cycles because of new technology. For example, telephones will incorporate programmed numbers, bathroom scales will have electronic readouts, and postage scales will calculate costs. Other products will decline significantly, as newer items make them obsolete. These include movie cameras, pinball machines, and traditional telegrams.

Product quality will have increased importance.

Consumer interest in improved product quality will continue in the 1980s. Research shows that every year a higher proportion of those surveyed say they would be willing to pay more for better quality in merchandise. This trend can be attributed to better consumer education, increased product complexity, growing servicing requirements, and greater expectations. Accordingly, firms will need better quality-control techniques, heightened input from control personnel, modular parts to simplify repairs, large-scale service organizations, and expanded product testing.[34]

Distribution Strategy

Distribution strategy in the 1980s will take into account rising costs, advances in technology, and the evolving nature of retailing.

High energy and capital costs, along with the widespread adoption of vendor marking systems (such as UPC and OCR-A), will result in greater uses of computer-based inventory systems. The inventory systems will help control stock on hand and provide more frequent sales and cost analyses by product item. Computer models will also be used to route trucks and sales personnel.

Product planning in the 1980s will respond to rising distribution costs.

Responses to rising distribution costs will frequently interrelate with product-planning decisions. For example, Sacramento Tomato Juice is now shipped as a concentrate to regional plants. At these plants, it is reconstituted by adding water and seasoning and canning operations are performed. As one brand manager noted:

> It costs about 18 cents to ship a 46-ounce can of juice across the country, and most of that weight is water. If we send the concentrate as a paste and it is reconstituted and shipped locally, that cost drops to 7 cents a can. . . . Any juice processor that does not go into concentrates will probably go out of business.[35]

Other products with high water contents that may require changed warehousing or product formulations to reduce transportation costs include soft drinks, beer, canned vegetables, canned food, and household bleach.

Two major trends in retailing in the 1980s will be the increases in discounting and nonstore retailing. Discount retailing will gain further importance in the 1980s because tight economic conditions will allow discount retailers to make economical purchases from manufacturers who have accumulated high inventory levels and cause consumers to be more value conscious. As described in Chapter 10, discount retailers include flea markets, factory outlet stores, and off-price chains.

The newest development in discounting is the **discount mall,** in which a variety of low-price retailers are located together. The mall arrangement saves gasoline, encourages one-stop shopping, and expands the trading area of each retailer. Among the sites of discount malls are Macon, Ga.; Utica, N.Y.; and Lakeland, Tenn. Off-Center Chicago is a six-level, 63,000-square-foot mall that specializes in discount merchandise.

A second retailing trend will be the continued growth of nonstore retailing. This growth will result from the high cost of transportation, working women being unable to shop during conventional hours, the desire for leisure time, the popularity of national brands, and the size of the senior citizen market. Technology will also contribute to nonstore sales: toll-free 800 numbers can be called at any time, catalogs are pinpointed at specific markets, and home video-shopping is emerging.

Discount retailing will grow as a result of tight economic conditions, with discount malls spreading.

Promotion Strategy

The advertising and personal selling aspects of promotion will undergo significant changes in the 1980s. Advertising will be influenced by new video tools and higher television rates. Personal selling will be affected by rising costs and computerization.

The largest shift in advertising strategy will be the result of the greater reliance on cable television, two-way interactive television, videocassettes, and videodiscs. For example, in 1982, cable advertising revenues were between $150 and $200 million; by 1990, these revenues are expected to near $2 billion.[36] A recent study showed that cable customers will accept further advertising if it is between programs and helps keep costs down.[37]

A major attraction of the new video tools is their ability to **narrowcast,** which is to present special programming to specific audiences. Narrowcasting makes cable television a natural for the advertising of local firms. It may also lead to coupons, premiums, and refund offers being presented on cable television. Specialty magazines and mail-order companies may be adversely affected if cable television provides better results.

Many advertisers are now experimenting with cable television. For example, Tender Chunks dog food sponsors an "All About Pets" information segment. General Foods, Anheuser-Busch, and Procter & Gamble are the leading advertisers on cable television.

Advertising strategy will be responsive to higher commercial television rates. These rates increased at nearly double the inflation rate during the 1970s and this is expected to continue in the 1980s.[38] It is forecast that **multiunit advertising,** whereby two or more products are included in a single ad, will rise substantially. In addition, other, less-expensive media will be used as substitutes for television.

Nonstore retailing will increase because of transportation costs, working women, and other factors.

A narrowcast is video programming for specific audiences.

More firms will use multiunit advertising, in which two or more products are placed in a single ad.

Efforts will be made to make selling more efficient.

Personal selling costs such as transportation, hotel, and compensation will rise throughout the 1980s. This will result in greater emphasis on effective routing of sales personnel to minimize travel time and expenses. Reduced attention will be given to small customers and orders. Telephone selling will be more frequently used, especially for smaller accounts. Many firms will specify minimum order sizes and require surcharges for lesser orders.

Computerization will improve the efficiency of the sales force by providing information and fast service, coordinating orders, and identifying the most lucrative prospects.

Price Strategy

Doubt about future material, labor, and capital costs will focus greater attention on cost-based pricing strategies.

The uncertainty with regard to future material, labor, and capital costs will focus further attention on cost-based pricing strategies. These include delay-quotation pricing in which prices are not confirmed until production is completed, raising across-the-board prices based on a firm's average costs, and reliance on escalator clauses. Higher costs and product shortages may also result in greater reliance on skimming prices for new products and salespeople having less flexibility to negotiate price.

High interest rates affect the credit policies of manufacturers and retailers. To complete sales they may have to arrange credit for customers, particularly when large-volume purchases are involved. For example, Xerox loans money to customers at low rates to encourage sales. XEEP (Xerox Equipment Equity Program) finances about half of the company's U.S. sales with corporate funds.[39] Xerox could earn higher rates on its loans, but it believes that sales volume more than offsets the low interest charges.

Unbundling prices will result in various services being optional and allow consumers to benefit.

Consumer reactions to prices will take various forms. They may hoard or stockpile goods whose prices they feel will increase or postpone purchases until they feel financially better prepared to buy. Marketers will respond by explaining the relationship of costs to prices, expanding the use of coupons and specials, and concentrating on sales to less price-sensitive market segments. Marketers may also **unbundle prices.** This policy breaks down prices by individual components such as gift wrapping, delivery, and installation and allows customers to purchase services on an optional basis. See Figure 19-10.

Summary

The total marketing effort of an organization can be integrated and coordinated through a marketing plan. The overall marketing plan consists of five steps. First, opportunities and problems are uncovered through a situation analysis, which determines where the firm is now and where it is headed. Second, general and specific objectives are set; these give direction to the plan. Third, an appropriate strategy is developed. The product/market opportunity matrix and the Boston Consulting Group matrix are two broad methods that aid in strategy planning. Fourth, tactics (specific actions to implement a strategy) are undertaken. Order-

Figure 19-10
Unbundling Prices

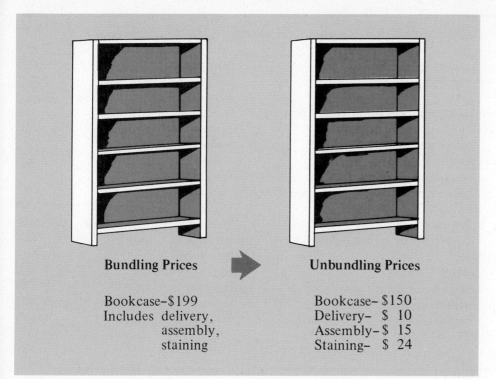

Bundling Prices → **Unbundling Prices**

Bookcase–$199
Includes delivery,
              assembly,
              staining

Bookcase– $150
Delivery– $ 10
Assembly– $ 15
Staining– $ 24

processing and order-generating costs are studied during this step. Fifth, results are monitored through sales analysis and a marketing audit. The 80–20 principle, the iceberg principle, sales exception reporting, and horizontal versus vertical audits must be considered.

Marketers need to anticipate and plan for the future. There will be many important demographic trends in the U.S., including low population growth, an older society, movement to southern and western regions, higher real income, more working women, and increases in education, white-collar jobs, and single-person households. Four newer life-style trends are developing: voluntary simplicity, the me generation, blurring gender roles, and the poverty of time. During the 1980s, a number of environmental factors will affect marketing. These include competition, government, the economy, technology, resource shortages, and global events.

In order to succeed in the 1980s, marketers must develop strategies that are responsive to consumer trends and the changes in the surrounding environment. Formal, systematic product and service strategies will be enacted more frequently. Companies need to identify growing, mature, and declining products and react accordingly. Distribution strategy will take into account rising costs, advances in technology, and the evolving nature of retailing. Advertising strategy will be influenced by new video tools and higher television rates. Personal selling strategy will be affected by rising costs and computerization. Prices in the 1980s will react to uncertain costs. Cost-based strategies will become more important.

KEY TERMS

After reading this chapter, you should understand these key terms:

Marketing plan	80–20 principle
Situation analysis	Iceberg principle
Strategy	Sales exception reporting
Product/market opportunity matrix	Marketing audit
Market penetration	Horizontal audit
Market development	Vertical audit
Product development	Voluntary simplicity
Diversification	Me generation
Boston Consulting Group matrix	Blurring gender roles
Star	Poverty of time
Cash cow	Video-shopping services
Problem child (question mark)	Electronic banking
Dog	Electronic mail
Tactics	Discount mall
Order-processing costs	Narrowcast
Order-generating costs	Multiunit advertising
Monitoring results	Unbundling prices
Sales analysis	

QUESTIONS FOR DISCUSSION

1. Must a marketing plan be in writing?
2. Develop one-year and five-year marketing plans for the Apple Computer company.
3. How do objectives aid the firm in establishing an integrated marketing plan?
4. What are the risks of Coca-Cola's diversification strategies?
5. Explain the 80–20 principle. Does it apply for all sales situations?
6. How could resistance to the marketing audit be overcome?
7. Develop a vertical audit to evaluate the promotional efforts of your university.
8. Comment on the statement, "The key to long-term success—even survival—in business is what it has always been: to invest, to innovate, to lead, to create value where none existed before."
9. How should McDonald's respond to the demographic trends of the 1980s?
10. Comment on the statement, "On balance, you might argue that American cars are now as good as imports, but the public clearly doesn't think so."
11. Name five global events that could affect marketing in a positive way.
12. How may firms improve product quality while keeping prices down?
13. How may traditional shopping centers compete with discount malls?
14. Give three examples of unbundling prices.

NOTES

1. Peter Nulty, "Apple's Bid to Stay in the Big Time," *Fortune* (February 7, 1983), pp. 36–41; "Apple Takes on Its Biggest Test Yet," *Business Week* (January 31, 1983), pp. 70–79; and Marilyn Chase, "Apple Computer Has a Lot Riding on 'Lisa,' Two Other New Models," *Wall Street Journal* (January 4, 1983), pp. 31, 37.

2. David W. Cravens, Gerald E. Hills, and Robert B. Woodruff, *Marketing Decision Making: Concepts and Strategy*, Revised Edition (Homewood, Ill.: Richard D. Irwin, 1980), pp. 448.

3. Barbara Ettore, "Colgate Cleans House Speedily," *New York Times* (April 12, 1980), pp. 31.

4. Ibid.; and Gail Bronson, "Back to Basics," *Wall Street Journal* (November 23, 1981), pp. 1, 8.

5. H. Igor Ansoff, "Strategies for Diversification," *Harvard Business Review*, Vol. 35 (September–October 1957), pp. 113–124.

6. See *Perspectives on Experience* (Boston: Boston Consulting Group, 1968); George S. Day, "Diagnosing the Product Portfolio," *Journal of Marketing*, Vol. 41 (April 1977), pp. 29–38; and Subhash C. Jain, *Marketing Planning & Strategy* (Cincinnati: South-Western, 1981), pp. 417–422.

7. Scott Paper Fights Back, At Last," *Business Week* (February 16, 1981), pp. 104, 106; and Bernard Wysocki, "Torn Up by Rivals, Scott Paper Draws Up a Long-Term Strategy to Regain Its Stature," *Wall Street Journal* (May 11, 1981), p. 29.

8. "Boston Consulting Group's Market Share—Experience 'Law'," *Marketing News* (December 15, 1978), p. 6; "Market Share—ROI Corporate Strategy Can Be Oversimplistic Snare," *Marketing News* (December 15, 1978), pp. 6–7; and R. G. Hamermesh, M. J. Anderson, Jr., and J. E. Harris, "Strategies for Low Market Share Businesses," *Harvard Business Review*, Vol. 56 (May–June 1978), p. 95. See also, Walter Kiechel III, "Corporate Strategists Under Fire," *Fortune* (December 27, 1982), pp. 34–39.

9. Dik Warren Twedt, *1978 Survey of Marketing Research* (Chicago: American Marketing Association, 1978), pp. 41–44.

10. "Levi Strauss Computers Find Consumer Preferences," *Marketing News* (September 5, 1980), p. 8.

11. Thomas O'Hanlon, "Less Means More at Firestone," *Fortune* (October 20, 1980), p. 119.

12. Adapted from Abraham Schuchman, "The Marketing Audit: Its Nature, Purpose, and Problems," *Analyzing and Improving Marketing Performance*, Report No. 32 (New York: American Management Association, 1959), p. 13; and Alfred R. Oxenfeldt, *Executive Action in Marketing* (Belmont, Calif.: Wadsworth Publishing, 1966), p. 746.

13. Philip Kotler, *Marketing Management: Analysis, Planning, and Control*, Fourth Edition (Englewood Cliffs, N.J.: Prentice-Hall, 1980), p. 650.

14. Theodore Levitt, "Marketing Myopia," *Harvard Business Review*, Vol. 53 (September–October 1975), pp. 26–44, 173–181.

15. Robert H. Hayes and William J. Abernathy, "Managing Our Way to Economic Decline," *Harvard Business Review*, Vol. 58 (July–August 1980), p. 68.

16. Roger D. Blackwell, "Successful Retailers of '80s Will Cater to Specific Lifestyle Segments," *Marketing News* (March 7, 1980), p. 3.

17. Fred D. Reynolds, Melvin R. Crask, and William D. Wells, "The Modern Feminine Life Style," *Journal of Marketing*, Vol. 41 (July 1977), p. 38.

18. Jeremy Main, "The Battle for Quality Begins," *Fortune* (December 29, 1980), pp. 28–29.

19. Ibid., pp. 29–30.

20. "At Sears, 'Thumbs Up' to the Video Catalog," *Business Week* (May 11, 1981), pp. 33–34.

21. John E. Cooney, "New Channels for Sales," *Wall Street Journal* (July 14, 1981), p. 52.

22. Andrew Pollack, "Introducing 'Tele-Shopping'," *New York Times* (December 24, 1981), pp. D1, D4. See also, Craig Reiss, "Qube at 5—Just Hitting Potential," *Advertising Age* (December 6, 1982), p. 75.

23. "Electronic Banking: Networks for Retail Banking Making Money from Transactions," *Business Week* (January 18, 1982), pp. 70–80.

24. Ibid., pp. 71, 76.

25. Ibid., p. 72.

26. Peter J. Schuyten, "G.T.E.: The Promise of Electronic Mail," *New York Times* (November 2, 1980), pp. F1, F22, F23; and "High-Speed Digital Facsimile Transceivers Reduce Phone Costs of Electronic Mail," *Marketing News* (November 26, 1982), Section 1, p. 21.

27. Jennifer Pendleton, "Clorox Hones Battle Plan, " *Advertising Age* (June 28, 1982), p. 92.

28. Alan J. Resnick, Harold E. Sand, and J. Barry Mason, "Marketing Dilemma: Change in the '80s,"

California Management Review, Vol. 24 (Fall 1981), p. 57. See also, Tom Richman, "Peering into Tomorrow," *Inc.* (October 1982), pp. 45–48.

29. "The Coming Shakeout in Personal Computers," *Business Week* (November 22, 1982), p. 72.

30. Laura Landro, "Home-Video Price Cutting Spurs Sales Boom but Eliminates Profit," *Wall Street Journal* (February 4, 1983), p. 27; and Thomas E. Caruso, "New TV Technologies to Be in 75% of U.S. Households by '90," *Marketing News* (February 4, 1983), p. 2.

31. Phil Mintz, "Videodiscs Overcome a Shaky Start," *Newsday* (January 30, 1983), p. 62.

32. "Mass Marketers Are Reprogramming the Software Business," *Business Week* (August 29, 1983), pp. 82–83, 86.

33. Walter Kiechel III, "Two-Income Families Will Reshape the Consumer Markets," *Fortune* (March 10, 1980), p. 117.

34. Bill Abrams, "Research Suggests Consumers Will Increasingly Seek Quality," *Wall Street Journal* (October 15, 1981), p. 31; Frank Allen, "Bosses Tout Quality of U.S. Goods, But Single Out Autos For Criticism," *Wall Street Journal* (October 12, 1981), pp. 29, 47; and "Quality: The U.S. Drives to Catch Up," *Business Week* (November 1, 1982), pp. 66–80.

35. Mimi Sheraton, "To Retailers' Dismay, A Supermarket Classic Changes," *New York Times* (January 3, 1981), p. L44.

36. Bill Abrams and Laura Landro, "Many Cable Services Facing Trouble as Ad Sales Fall Below Expectations," *Wall Street Journal* (November 11, 1982), p. 33; and Howard Polskin, "Casting for Cable Numbers," *Advertising Age* (May 24, 1982), p. M-29.

37. Philip H. Dougherty, "Advertisers Look Closer at Cable TV," *New York Times* (January 11, 1981), National Economic Survey, pp. 52–53.

38. Bill Abrams, "Advertisers Growing Restless over Rising Cost of TV Time," *Wall Street Journal* (January 27, 1983), p. 29.

39. Jeffrey A. Tannenbaum, "To Prop Sales, Xerox Gives Bargain Loans," *Wall Street Journal* (January 8, 1981), p. 21.

CASES

1 RECORD RETAILERS DIVERSIFY TO AVOID A SALES DECLINE*

The music industry is singing the blues. The economic recession, the in-home audiocassette taping that has cut so drastically into prerecorded music sales, record/tape counterfeiting, the aging of the population, diminishing the prime 15- to 34-year-old record consumer group—all have taken a toll.

In combination, these factors caused unit music sales (singles, albums, audiocassettes, and eight-track cartridges) to decline from the 1978 high of 726,000 units to 550,000 units in 1982. Further decreases are expected.

To combat the loss of music sales, a number of record retailers have begun diversifying their product mixes. They have added blank audio tapes (which were previously avoided), videogames, blank videocassettes, cleaning and storage accessory products, and prerecorded videocassettes and videodiscs.

The record retailers have reached these general conclusions about their expanded mixes:

1. Blank audio tapes cost the retailers about $1 billion in lost prerecorded music sales each year. This is balanced by the large volume of tapes that can be sold from a small display.

2. Videogames attract the retailers' main target market, 15- to 24-year-olds. New games often have high initial sales. Said one retailer, "It's a perfect

*The data in this case are drawn from Bob Marich, "Record Retailers Test Enemy Waters," *Advertising Age* (January 24, 1983), 44–45.

blend with records." While the profit margins are lower than for records, turnover is faster.

3. Videocassettes and videodiscs do not draw the retailers' prime target market, but instead appeal to older consumers. In addition, there are more rentals than outright sales.

The retailers are also interested in stimulating music sales, and have found two strategies successful: permanent price reductions for items maintained in inventory and tie-ins with cable television concerts and movie-soundtracks. Video music albums have solid long-run sales potential.

QUESTIONS

1. Evaluate the record retailers' new marketing approach.
2. Describe several general and specific objectives that record retailers could adopt.
3. How could these record retailers use the product/market opportunity matrix?
4. How would you measure the effectiveness of the retailers' new strategy?
5. Develop a five-year marketing plan for a record store located near your university.

IN-HOME BANKING: WILL IT CATCH ON?† 2

As part of their long-term marketing strategies, a small number of banks have begun offering in-home banking services linked to consumers' personal computers. During 1983, about 50 banks provided such services. These companies hope that in-home banking services will provide them with several benefits, such as: lower overhead costs, a specific and loyal consumer market, a larger geographic market, and a jump on more conservative competitors. Despite these goals, the banks recognize that it may take five to ten years to secure widespread consumer acceptance.

First Bank System of Minneapolis began a pilot program in May 1982 by marketing in-home banking services to 200 farmers in its area. The farmers were quickly attracted to the system, named FirstHand, which was created specifically for them by the bank. In addition to fund transfers, bill payments, and bill statements, FirstHand provided information on commodity prices, production, weather, and agricultural news.

First Bank System is one of the few firms that has developed its own in-home banking program. Most hook into programs established by computer-service companies such as CompuService. These "third-party" programs are very inexpensive to operate, $200 per month versus $100,000 and up in developmental costs to develop a unique program. However, they are not tailored to individual audience needs and may become more identified with the computer-service company (which may deal with several banks) than with the bank itself.

Since in-home banking is so new, programming and marketing errors are likely. For example, United American Bank of Memphis began using a third-

†The data in this case are drawn from Maria T. Padilla, "Home-Banking Tests Begin in a Few Places, But the New Systems May Be Slow to Spread," *Wall Street Journal* (January 17, 1983), p. 25.

party in-home banking program addressed to professionals such as physicians and lawyers, without realizing that these customers had little knowledge of personal computers. It had to revise the program's instruction to make them clearer. As a United American Bank official noted, "We weren't aware of how much time was needed to spend with customers explaining the system."

As the banks have discovered, there is an underlying consumer demand for good in-home services. Said one satisfied customer:

> I can control interaction with banks and merchants I pay bills to. The whole essence of the computer revolution is that you are in command.

QUESTIONS

1. Will in-home banking catch on? If so, how quickly? Explain your answer.
2. Which emerging consumer life-style(s) will be most attracted to in-home banking? Which will be least attracted? Why?
3. What environmental factors will have the greatest impact on the success or failure of in-home banking? Explain your answer.
4. Develop a plan to market in-home banking (include service, distribution, promotion, and price decisions).

Appendix A

Careers in Marketing

Career opportunites in marketing are quite extensive and diversified. Many marketing positions give a considerable amount of discretion to people early in their careers. For example, within six months to one year of being hired, assistant retail buyers are usually given budget authority for purchases involving hundreds of thousands of dollars. Beginning salespeople typically begin to call on accounts within several weeks of being hired. Marketing research personnel actually develop preliminary questionnaires, determine sampling procedures, and interpret study results within a short time after initial employment. A marketing career is excellent preparation for a path to top management positions in all types of organizations.

A number of marketing positions are highly visible. These include sales personnel, sales managers, retail buyers, brand managers, industrial traffic managers, credit managers, and advertising and public relations personnel. This allows effective persons to be recognized, promoted, and properly compensated. In fact, the compensation in sales positions is usually based on sales volume and/or profitability and is directly linked to the individual's own performance.

A marketing background can also train a person to operate his or her own business. Among the entrepreneurial opportunities available are careers as retail store owners, manufacturers' agents, wholesalers, insurance and real estate brokers, marketing consultants, marketing researchers, and free-lance advertising illustrators or copy writers.

Table 1 contains a detailed listing of job titles in marketing. Table 2 shows the types of firms that employ people in marketing positions. Table 3 outlines selected marketing career opportunities for the 1980s.

In the last century, jobs in marketing have grown at a much more rapid rate than those in production. For example, from 1870 to 1950, the number of people employed in retailing and wholesaling activities increased more than 1200 per cent. In the same period, the number of production workers increased by 300 per cent.[1] The growth of marketing jobs has continued strongly since 1950. Today, there are over twenty million people working in retailing and wholesaling activities, representing more than 22 per cent of all nonagricultural workers in the U.S. This does not include self-employed or unpaid family workers.[2]

A1

The need for marketing personnel reflects the expanded role of marketing, the larger demand for marketing services, an improved ability to mechanize and automate production but not marketing, the use of marketing by nonprofit institutions, political candidates, and other nontraditional institutions, and the changes in U.S. society (such as television, leisure time, and discretionary income).

The 1982 starting salaries for marketing personnel typically ranged from $8,000 to $14,000 for those with an associate's degree, $12,000 to $18,000 for those with a bachelor's degree, and $17,000 to $35,000 for those with a master of business administration degree. In addition to salary, many marketing positions provide a company car, bonus, and/or expense account that are not common to other professions. By 1990, entry-level marketing compensation is expected to rise significantly, much higher than the rate of inflation.

Table 4 outlines the compensation ranges for established personnel in selected marketing positions. Many of the positions have open-ended ranges, because commissions or bonuses depend on performance. The figures in Table 4 do not include expense accounts.

Table 1 **Selected Job Titles in Marketing**

Job Title	*Description*
Account executive	Liaison person between an advertising agency and its clients. The individual is employed by the agency to study the clients' promotional objectives and create promotional programs (including message, layout, media, and timing).
Advertising copywriter	Creator of headlines and content for advertisements.
Advertising layout person	Producer of illustrations or one who uses other artists' illustrations to formulate advertisements.
Advertising manager	Director of a firm's advertising program. He or she determines media, copy, size of budget, advertising frequency, and the choice of an advertising agency.
Advertising production manager	Person who arranges to have an advertisement filmed (for television), recorded (for radio), or printed (for newspaper, magazines, etc.).
Advertising research director	Person who researches markets, evaluates alternative advertisements, assesses media, and tests advertisements.
Agent (broker)	Wholesaler who works for a commission or fee.
Commercial artist	Creator of advertisements for television, print media, and product packaging. This artist selects photographs and drawings and determines the layout and type of print to be used in newspaper and magazine advertisements. Sample scenes of television commercials are sketched for clients.
Consumer affairs specialist (customer relations specialist)	Company contact with consumers. This person handles consumer complaints and attempts to change the firm's policies to reflect customer needs. Community programs, such as lectures on product safety, arise from the consumer affairs specialist.
Credit manager	Supervisor of the firm's credit process, including eligibility for credit, terms, late payments, consumer complaints, and control.
Direct-to-home salesperson	Person who sells products and services to consumers by personal contact at the consumers' homes.
Display worker	Person who designs and sets up retail store displays.

Table 1 **Selected Job Titles in Marketing (Contd.)**

Job Title	Description
Fashion designer	Designer of apparel, such as beachwear, hats, dresses, scarves, and shoes.
Franchisee	Person who leases or buys a business that has many outlets and a well-known name. The franchisee normally operates one outlet and participates in cooperative planning and advertising. The franchisor sets rules for operating all outlets.
Franchisor	Person who develops a company name and reputation and then leases or sells parts of the firm to independent businesspeople. The franchisor oversees the company, sets policy, and usually trains franchisees.
Freight forwarder	Wholesaler who consolidates small shipments from many companies.
Industrial designer	Designer who improves the appearance and function of machine-made products.
Industrial traffic manager	Arranger of transportation to and from firms and customers for raw materials, fabricated parts, finished goods, and equipment.
International marketer	Person who works overseas or in the international department of a domestic company and is involved with some aspect of marketing. International marketing positions are available in all areas of marketing.
Inventory manager	Person who controls the level and allocation of merchandise throughout the year. This manager evaluates and balances inventory amounts against the costs of holding merchandise.
Life insurance agent (broker)	Person who advises clients on life insurance policy types available relative to their needs. Policies provide life insurance and/or retirement income.
Manufacturers' representative	Salesperson who represents several, usually small, manufacturers that cannot afford their own sales force. The representative normally deals with wholesalers and retailers. He or she determines needs and then displays, demonstrates, and describes products and services, often at the customer's place of business.
Marketing manager (vice-president of marketing)	Executive who plans, directs, and controls the entire marketing functions of the company. The manager (vice-president) oversees all marketing decisions and personnel.
Marketing research project supervisor	Person who develops the research methodology, evaluates the accuracy of different sample sizes, analyzes data, and assesses statistical errors.
Media analyst	Person who evaluates the characteristics and costs of available media. The analyst examines audience size and traits, legal restrictions, types of messages used, and so on. The effectiveness of company messages is also measured.
Media director (space or time buyer)	Person who determine the day, time (for radio and television), media, location, and size of advertisements. The goal is to reach the largest desirable audience at the most efficient cost. The director (buyer) negotiates contracts for advertising space or air time.
Missionary salesperson	Support salesperson who provides information about new and existing products.
Packaging specialist	Person responsible for package design, durability, safety, appeal, size, and cost. This specialist must be familiar with all related legislation.
Pricing economist	Specialist who studies sources of supply, consumer demand, government restrictions, competition, and costs and then offers short-run and long-run pricing recommendations.
Product manager (brand manager)	Person who supervises the marketing of a product or brand category. In some firms there are product (brand) managers for existing items and new-product (brand) managers for new introductions. For a one-brand or one-product company, the product (brand) manager is actually the marketing manager.

Table 1 Selected Job Titles in Marketing (Contd.)

Job Title	Description
Property and casualty insurance agent (broker)	Person who evaluates client risks from such perils as fire, burglary, and accidents, assesses coverage needs, and sells policies to indemnify losses.
Public relations director	Manager of a company's efforts to keep the public aware of its accomplishments and benefits to society and minimize negative reactions to company policies and activities. The director constantly measures public attitudes and seeks to maintain a favorable public opinion of the firm.
Purchasing agent	Buyer for a manufacturer, wholesaler, or retailer. The agent purchases items necessary for the operation of the firm and usually buys in bulk, seeks reliable suppliers, and sets precise specifications.
Real estate agent (broker)	Liaison who brings together a buyer and seller, lessor and lessee, or landlord and tenant. This salesperson receives a commission.
Retail buyer	Person responsible for purchasing items for resale. The buyer generally concentrates on a product area and develops a plan for proper styles, assortments, sizes, and amounts of the product. The buyer analyzes vendors on the basis of quality, style, availability, fit, flexibility, reliability, and price.
Retail department manager	Supervisor of one retail department, often at a branch store. The manager usually works with the buyer and is responsible for displaying merchandise, counting it, and reordering it. Department manager is often the first position a college graduate assumes after the initial training program.
Retail merchandise manager	Supervisor of several buyers. This manager sets the retailer's direction in terms of styles, product lines, image, pricing, and so on and allocates budgets among buyers.
Retail trade salesperson	Salesperson for a retailer who deals with final consumers.
Retail store manager	Supervisor of the day-to-day activities of a store. All in-store personnel report to this manager.
Sales engineer	Support salesperson involved with technical products or services.
Sales manager	Supervisor of the sales force, responsible for recruitment, selection, training, motivation, evaluation, compensation, and control.
Salesperson	Company representative who interacts with consumers. A salesperson may require limited or extensive skills, deal with final or intermediate customers, work from an office or go out in the field, and be a career salesperson or progress in management.
Sales promotion director	Person involved with supplementary promotional activities, such as trading stamps, coupons, contests, giveaways, and free samples.
Securities salesperson	Salesperson involved with the buying and selling of stocks, bonds, government securities, mutual funds, and other securities.
Traffic manager	Supervisor of the purchase and use of alternate methods of transportation. This manager routes shipments and monitors performance.
Warehouser	Person responsible for storage and movement of goods within a company's warehouse facilities. The warehouser maintains inventory records and makes sure older items are shipped out before newer ones (rotating stock).
Wholesale trade salesperson	Salesperson representing a wholesaler to retailers and other firms.

Table 2

Selected Employers of Marketing Personnel

Advertising agencies	Marketing research firms
Agents or brokers	Marketing specialists
Common carriers	Media
Computer service bureaus	Nonprofit institutions
Consulting firms	Product testing laboratories
Credit bureaus	Public relations firms
Delivery firms	Raw material extractors
Entertainment firms	Real estate firms
Exporters	Retailers
Financial institutions	Self-employed
Franchisees	Service firms
Franchisors	Shopping centers
Government	Sports teams
Industrial firms	Transportation firms
International firms	Warehousers
Manufacturers	Wholesalers

Table 3

Outlook for Selected Marketing Careers During the 1980s

Job Classification	Employment Outlook
Advertising worker	Average
Credit manager	Slower than average
Display worker	Average
Industrial designer	Slower than average
Insurance agent (broker)	Average
Manufacturers' representative	Average
Marketing research worker	Faster than average
Public relations specialist	Faster than average
Purchasing agent	Average
Real estate agent (broker)	Faster than average
Retail trade salesperson	Average
Securities salesperson	Faster than average
Wholesale trade salesperson	Average

Source: *Occupational Outlook Handbook, 1982–1983 Edition* (Washington, D.C.: U.S. Government Printing Office, Bureau of Labor Statistics, April 1982).

Table 4

Annual Compensation for Established Personnel in Selected Marketing Positions*

Retailing Positions	Compensation
Downtown store manager	$17,000–$ 50,000
Buyer	$23,000–$ 50,000+
Divisional merchandise manager	$23,000–$ 80,000
General merchandise manager	$30,000–$100,000+

Sales Positions	Compensation
Real estate agent (broker)	$12,000–$100,000+
Insurance agent (broker)	$15,000–$100,000+
Manufacturers' representative	$16,000–$ 60,000+

Table 4	*Sales Positions*	*Compensation*
Annual Compensation for Established Personnel in Selected Marketing Positions* (Contd.)	Wholesale trade salesperson	$18,000–$ 50,000+
	Securities salesperson	$29,000–$100,000+
	Product Management Positions	*Compensation*
	Assistant product manager	$22,000–$40,000+
	Product manager	$40,000–$65,000+
	Group product manager	$60,000–$80,000+
	Advertising Positions	*Compensation*
	Assistant account executive	$18,000–$25,000
	Account executive	$25,000–$40,000+
	Vice-president/account supervisor	$45,000–$70,000+
	Miscellaneous Marketing Positions	*Compensation*
	Display worker	$15,000–$30,000+
	Industrial designer	$15,000–$30,000+
	Marketing research worker	$18,000–$35,000
	Public relations specialist	$22,000–$36,000
	Sales promotion director	$35,000–$50,000
	Distribution executive	$40,000–$60,000
	International general sales executive	$40,000–$75,000+
	Top Marketing Positions	*Compensation*
	Senior public relations executive	$40,000–$ 60,000+
	Senior international executive	$50,000–$100,000+
	Senior sales executive	$50,000–$100,000+
	Vice-president/management supervisor–advertising agency	$60,000–$ 80,000+
	Senior vice-president–advertising agency	$65,000–$115,000+
	Marketing director	$70,000–$110,000+
	Vice-president of marketing	$70,000–$700,000+

*Includes bonus.

Source: Updated from Harry Brown, Robert Bartlett, and Andrew Minstein, *Executive Compensation Survey of the Retail Industry* (New York: National Retail Merchants Association, Personnel Division, 1977), p. 12; *Occupational Outlook Handbook, 1982–83 Edition* (Washington, D.C.: U.S. Government Printing Office, Bureau of Labor Statistics, April 1982); Al Urbanski, "S&MM's Annual Survey of Executive Compensation," *Sales & Marketing Management* (October 11, 1982), pp. 56–60ff; Bill Abrams, "In Advertising It Pays to Go Corporate," *Wall Street Journal* (April 22, 1982), p. 31; and John A. Fischer, "The High Cost of Keeping Up," *Sales & Marketing Management* (November 17, 1980), pp. 54–55.

In the United States marketing executives are frequently chosen as the chief executive officers of major industrial and nonindustrial corporations. Table 5 shows some of the U.S. companies that had chief executives with marketing backgrounds during 1982. The executives listed in this table each earn at least several hundred thousand dollars per year plus bonuses. According to a recent study of corporate chief executive officers, about one seventh have had a career emphasis in some functional area of marketing.[3] In addition, the senior marketing executive is included in the top management teams (five to nine managers) of 50 per cent of all major U.S. companies.[4]

Table 5

		Selected Companies Whose Chief Executive Officers Had Marketing Backgrounds, 1982
American Brands	Hammermill Paper	
American Home Products	Hershey Foods	
American Stores	Honeywell	
Associated Dry Goods	IBM	
Automatic Data Processing	K mart	
Avco	Kellogg	
Avon Products	Eli Lilly	
Black & Decker	LTV	
Brown Forman Distillers	McDonald's	
Burlington Industries	MCI Communication	
Campbell Soup	Monsanto	
Caterpillar Tractor	NCR	
CBS	Owens Corning Fiberglas	
Chesebrough-Ponds	PepsiCo	
Colgate-Palmolive	Philip Morris	
Dayton Hudson	Quaker Oats	
Deere	R. J. Reynolds Industries	
Walt Disney	Richardson-Vicks	
Dun & Bradstreet	Sears Roebuck	
Firestone	J. P. Stevens	
General Foods	Uniroyal	
General Mills	U.S. Gypsum	
Goodyear	Warner Lambert	

Source: "Who Gets the Most Pay," *Forbes* (June 7, 1982), pp. 74–78ff.

Table 6 cites sources that may be contacted for additional marketing career information.

Career opportunity	Sources	*Table 6*
		Selected Sources of Additional Marketing Career Information
Advertising	American Advertising Federation 1225 Connecticut Avenue., N.W. Washington, D.C. 20036	
	American Association of Advertising Agencies 666 Third Avenue New York, NY 10017	
	Business Professional Advertising Association 205 East 42nd Street New York, NY 10017	
Buying	Association of Buying Offices 100 West 31st Street New York, NY 10001	
Commercial art	National Association of Schools of Art 11250 Roger Bacon Dr. No. 5 Reston, VA 22090	
Direct selling	Direct Selling Association 1730 M. Street, N.W., Suite 610 Washington, D.C. 20036	
Industrial design	Industrial Designers Society of America 6802 Poplar Place McLean, VA 22101	

Table 6	*Career opportunity*	*Sources*
Selected Sources of Additional Marketing Career Information (Contd.)	Life insurance sales	American Council of Life Insurance 1850 K Street NW Washington, D.C. 20006
		National Association of Life Underwriters 1922 F Street, N.W. Washington, D.C. 20006
	Manufacturers' representation	Sales & Marketing Executives, International 380 Lexington Avenue New York, NY 10168
	Marketing	American Marketing Association 250 S. Wacker Drive, Suite 200 Chicago, IL 60606
		College Placement Annual 62 Highland Avenue Bethlehem, PA 18017
	Property and casualty insurance	Insurance Information Institute 110 William Street New York, NY 10038
		Independent Insurance Agents of America 100 Church Street New York, N.Y. 10007
		Professional Insurance Agents 400 N. Washington Street Alexandria, VA 22314
	Public relations	Public Relations Society of America Inc. 845 Third Avenue New York, NY 10022
	Real estate sales	National Association of Realtors 430 N. Michigan Avenue Chicago, IL 60611
	Retailing	National Retail Merchants Association 100 West 31st Street New York, NY 10001
	Securities sales	Securities Industry Association 20 Broad Street New York, NY 10005
	Supermarket industry	Food Marketing Institute 1750 K Street, N.W. Suite 700 Washington, D.C. 20006
		National Association of Retail Grocers of the U.S. 1825 Samuel Morris Drive Reston, VA 22090
	Traffic management	American Society of Traffic and Transportation P.O. Box 33095 Louisville, KY 40232
	Wholesaling	National Association of Wholesaler-Distributors 1725 K Street, N.W. Washington, D.C. 20006

1. Harold Barger, *Distribution's Place in the American Economy Since 1869* (Princeton, N.J.: Princeton University Press, 1955), pp. 4–5.

2. *Statistical Abstract of the United States: 1982* (Washington, D.C.: U.S. Bureau of the Census, 1982).

3. James E. Piercy and J. Benjamin Forbes, "Industry Differences in Chief Executive Officers," *MSU Business Topics*, Vol. 29 (Winter 1981), p. 25.

4. *Who Is Top Management?* (New York: Conference Board, 1982).

NOTES

Marketing Arithmetic

In order to properly design, implement, and review marketing programs, it is necessary to understand basic business arithmetic from a marketing perspective. Accordingly, this appendix describes and illustrates the types of business arithmetic with which marketers should be most familiar.

The appendix is divided into three areas: the profit-and-loss statement, marketing performance ratios, and pricing.

The Profit-and-Loss Statement

The **profit-and-loss (income) statement** presents a summary of the revenues and costs for an organization over a specific period of time. Such a statement is generally developed on a monthly, quarterly, and yearly basis. The profit-and-loss statement enables a marketer to examine overall and specific revenues and costs over similar time periods (for example, January 1, 1984 to December 31, 1984 versus January 1, 1983 to December 31, 1983), and analyze the organization's profitability. Monthly and quarterly statements enable the firm to monitor progress toward goals and revise performance estimates.

The profit-and-loss statement consists of these major components:

Gross sales—The total revenues generated by the firm's products and services.

Net sales—The revenues received by the firm after subtracting returns and discounts (such as trade, quantity, cash, and special promotional allowances).

Cost of goods sold—The cost of merchandise sold by the manufacturer, wholesaler, or retailer.

Gross margin (profit)—The difference between sales and the cost of goods sold; consists of operating expenses plus net profit.

Operating expenses—The cost of running a business, including marketing.

Net profit before taxes—The profit earned after all costs have been deducted.

When examining a profit-and-loss statement, it is important to recognize one difference between manufacturers and retailers. For manufacturers, the cost of goods sold involves the cost of manufacturing products (raw materials, labor, and overhead). For retailers, the cost of goods sold involves the cost of merchandise purchased for resale (purchase price plus freight charges).

Table 1 shows an annual profit-and-loss statement for a manufacturer, the General Toy Company. From this table, these observations can be made:

- Total company sales for 1983 were $1,000,000. However, the firm gave refunds worth $20,000 for returned merchandise and allowances. In addition, discounts of $50,000 were provided. This left the company with actual (net) sales of $930,000.
- As a manufacturer, General Toy computed its cost of goods sold by adding the cost value of the beginning inventory on hand (items left in stock from the previous period) and the merchandise manufactured during the time period (costs included raw materials, labor, and overhead), and then subtracting the cost value of the inventory remaining at the end of the period. For General Toy this was $450,000 ($100,000 + $400,000 − $50,000).
- The gross margin was $480,000, calculated by subtracting the cost of goods sold from net sales. This sum was used for operating expenses, with the remainder accounting for net profit.

Table 1

General Toy Company, Profit-and-Loss Statement for the Year January 1, 1983 Through December 31, 1983

Gross sales		$1,000,000
Less: Returns and allowances	$ 20,000	
Discounts	50,000	
Total sales deductions		70,000
Net sales		$ 930,000
Less cost of goods sold:		
Beginning inventory (at cost)	$100,000	
New merchandise (at cost)*	400,000	
Merchandise available for sale	$500,000	
Ending inventory (at cost)	50,000	
Total cost of goods sold		450,000
Gross margin		$ 480,000
Less operating expenses:		
Sales force compensation	$150,000	
Advertising	75,000	
Administration	75,000	
Rent	30,000	
Office supplies	20,000	
Miscellaneous	20,000	
Total operating expenses		370,000
Net profit before taxes		$ 110,000

*For a manufacturer, new merchandise costs refer to the raw materials, labor, and overhead costs incurred in the production of items for resale. For a retailer, new merchandise costs refer to the purchase costs of items (including freight) bought for resale.

- Operating expenses involve all costs not considered in the cost of goods sold. Operating expenses for General Toy included sales force compensation, advertising, administration, rent, office supplies, and miscellaneous costs, a total of $370,000. Of this amount, $225,000 was directly allocated for marketing costs (advertising, sales force).
- General Toy's net profit before taxes was $110,000, computed by deducting operating expenses from gross margin. This amount would be used to cover federal and state taxes as well as owner profits.

Performance Ratios

Performance ratios are used to measure the actual performance of a firm against company goals or industry standards. Comparative data can be obtained from trade associations, Dun & Bradstreet, Robert Morris Associates, and other sources. Among the most valuable performance ratios for marketers are the following:

$$(1) \text{ Sales efficiency ratio (percentage)} = \frac{\text{Net sales}}{\text{Gross sales}}$$

The **sales efficiency ratio (percentage)** compares net sales against gross sales. The highest level of efficiency is 1.00; in that case, there would be no returns, allowances, or discounts. General Toy had a sales efficiency ratio of 93 per cent ($930,000/$1,000,000) in 1983. This is a very good ratio; anything less would mean General Toy was too conservative in making sales.

$$(2) \text{ Cost of goods sold ratio (percentage)} = \frac{\text{Cost of goods sold}}{\text{Net sales}}$$

The **cost of goods sold ratio (percentage)** indicates the portion of net sales that is used to manufacture or purchase the goods sold. When the ratio is high, the firm has little revenue left to use for operating expenses and net profit. This could mean costs are too high or selling price is too low. In 1983, General Toy had a cost of goods sold ratio of 48 per cent ($450,000/$930,000), a satisfactory figure.

$$(3) \text{ Gross margin ratio (percentage)} = \frac{\text{Gross margin}}{\text{Net sales}}$$

The **gross margin ratio (percentage)** shows the proportion of net sales that are allocated to operating expenses and net profit. When the ratio is high, the company has substantial revenue left for these items. During 1983, General Toy had a gross margin ratio of 52 per cent ($480,000/$930,000), a satisfactory figure.

$$(4) \text{ Operating expense ratio (percentage)} = \frac{\text{Operating expenses}}{\text{Net sales}}$$

The **operating expense ratio (percentage)** expresses these expenses in terms of net sales. When the ratio is high, the firm is spending a large amount on marketing and other operating costs. General Toy had an operating expense ratio of 40 per cent in 1983, which meant that forty cents of every sales dollar went for operations, a moderate amount.

$$(5) \text{ Net profit ratio (percentage)} = \frac{\text{Net profit before taxes}}{\text{Net sales}}$$

The **net profit ratio (percentage)** indicates the portion of each sales dollar that goes for profits (after all costs have been deducted). The net profit ratio varies drastically by industry. For example, in the supermarket industry, net profits are about 1 per cent of net sales; in the industrial chemical industry, net profits are about 6.5 per cent of net sales. The 1983 net profit for General Toy was 12 per cent of net sales ($110,000/$930,000), well above the industry average of 2.2 per cent.

$$(6) \text{ Stock turnover ratio} = \frac{\text{Net sales (in units)}}{\text{Average inventory (in units)}}$$

or

$$\frac{\text{Net sales (in sales dollars)}}{\text{Average inventory (in sales dollars)}}$$

or

$$\frac{\text{Cost of goods sold}}{\text{Average inventory (at cost)}}$$

The **stock turnover ratio** shows the number of times during a specified period, usually one year, that the average inventory on hand is sold. It can be calculated on the basis of units or dollars (in selling price or at cost). In the case of General Toy, the 1983 stock turnover ratio can be calculated on a cost basis. The cost of goods sold during 1983 was $450,000. Average inventory at cost = (Beginning inventory at cost + Ending inventory at cost)/2 = ($100,000 + $50,000)/2 = $75,000. The stock turnover ratio was ($450,000/75,000) = 6. This compared favorably with an industry average of 2.6 times. This meant General Toy sold its merchandise more than twice as quickly as competitors.

$$(7) \text{ Return on investment} = \frac{\text{Net sales}}{\text{Investment}} \times \frac{\text{Net profit}}{\text{Net sales}} = \frac{\text{Net profit}}{\text{Investment}}$$

The **return on investment** compares profitability with the investment necessary to manufacture or distribute merchandise. For a manufacturer, this investment includes land, plant, equipment, and inventory costs. For a retailer, it involves inventory, the costs of land, the store and its fixtures, and equipment. To determine the return on investment for General Toy, total investment costs would be determined from its **balance sheet,** which lists the assets and liabilities of a firm at a particular time. The management at General Toy calculated that an overall investment of $550,000 was necessary to yield 1983 sales of $930,000. Therefore, the firm's return on investment before taxes was 20 per cent ($110,000/$550,000). This was a little above the industry norm.

Pricing

The material in this section expands upon the discussion in Chapters 14 and 15. Four specific aspects of pricing are examined: price elasticity, fixed versus variable costs, markup, and markdown.

Price Elasticity

As defined in Chapter 14, **price elasticity** refers to the sensitivity of buyers to price changes in terms of the quantities they will purchase. It is expressed as the percentage change in quantity sold divided by the percentage change in price:

$$\text{Price elasticity} = \frac{\dfrac{\text{Quantity 1} - \text{Quantity 2}}{\text{Quantity 1} + \text{Quantity 2}}}{\dfrac{\text{Price 1} - \text{Price 2}}{\text{Price 1} + \text{Price 2}}}$$

For purposes of simplicity, price elasticity is often expressed as a positive number (as it will be here).

Table 2 shows a demand schedule for women's blouses at several different prices. When selling price is reduced by a small percentage from $40 to $35, the percentage change in quantity demanded rises significantly from 100 to 150 units. Demand is highly elastic (very price sensitive):

$$\text{Price elasticity} = \frac{\dfrac{100 - 150}{100 + 150}}{\dfrac{\$40 - \$35}{\$40 + \ \ 35}} = 3.0 \text{ (expressed as a positive number)}$$

As price is reduced, total revenues go up.

At a price of $25, the market becomes relatively saturated; the percentage change in price from $25 to $20 is directly offset by the percentage change in quantity demanded from 240 to 300 units:

$$\text{Price elasticity} = \frac{\dfrac{240 - 300}{240 + 300}}{\dfrac{\$25 - \$20}{\$25 + \ \ 20}} = 1.0 \text{ (expressed as a positive number)}$$

Selling Price	Quantity Demanded	Elasticity[1]	Total Revenue[2]	Table 2
$40	100		$4,000	**Maxine's Blouses,**
		3.0		**A Demand Schedule**
35	150		5,250	
		1.5		
30	190		5,700	
		1.3		
25	240		6,000 ← Maximum	
		1.0	total	
20	300		6,000 ← revenue	
		0.8		
15	375		5,625	
		0.7		
10	500		5,000	

[1]Expressed as positive numbers.
[2]Total revenue = Selling price × Quantity demanded.

Total revenues remain the same at a price of $25 or $20. This is known as **unitary demand,** whereby total revenues stay constant as price changes.

At a price of $20, the market becomes extremely saturated; and further price reductions have little impact on demand. A large percentage change in price from $20 to $15 results in a small percentage change in quantity demanded from 300 to 375 units. Demand is inelastic (insensitive to price changes):

$$\text{Price elasticity} = \frac{\dfrac{300 - 375}{300 + 375}}{\dfrac{\$20 - \$15}{\$20 + 15}} = 0.8 \text{ (expressed as a positive number)}$$

Notice that total revenue falls as demand changes from elastic to inelastic or inelastic to elastic.

Total revenue is maximized at the price levels where price and demand changes directly offset each other (in this example, $25 and $20). How does a firm choose between those prices? It depends on marketing philosophy. At a price of $25, profit will probably be higher because the firm needs to produce and sell fewer products, thus reducing costs. At a price of $20, more units are sold; this may increase the customer base for other products the firm offers and thereby raise overall company sales and profits.

It is important to remember that price elasticity refers to percentage changes, not to absolute changes. For example, a demand change from 100 to 150 units involves a greater percentage change than a demand change from 375 to 500 units.

Fixed Versus Variable Costs

When making pricing decisions, it is essential to distinguish between fixed and variable costs. **Fixed costs** are ongoing costs that are unrelated to production or sales volume; they are generally constant over a given range of output for a specific time period. In the short run, fixed costs cannot usually be changed. Examples of fixed costs are rent, full-time employee salaries, plant, equipment, real estate taxes, and insurance.

Variable costs are directly related to production or sales volume. As volume increases, total variable costs increase; as volume declines, total variable costs decline. Per-unit variable costs frequently remain constant over a given range of volume (e.g., total sales commission goes up as sales rise, while sales commission as a per cent of sales remains constant). Examples of variable costs are raw materials, sales commissions, parts, salaries of hourly employees, and product advertising.

Figure 1 graphically shows how fixed, variable, and total costs vary with production or sales volume for Eleanor's Cosmetics, a leased-department operator selling popular-priced cosmetics in a department store. In this figure, total fixed costs are $10,000. Variable costs are $5.00 per unit. Figure 1A depicts total costs: as volume increases, total fixed costs stay constant at $10,000, while total variable costs and total costs rise by $5.00 per unit. At 1,000 units, total fixed costs are $10,000, total variable costs are $5,000, and total costs are $15,000. At 5,000 units, total fixed costs are $10,000, total variable costs are $25,000, and total costs are $35,000.

Figure 1B depicts average costs: as volume increases, average fixed costs and average total costs decline (since fixed costs are spread over more units), while average variable costs remain the same. At 1,000 units, average fixed costs are $10.00, average variable costs are $5.00, and average total costs are $15.00. At 5,000 units, average fixed costs are $2.00 ($10,000/5,000 units), average variable costs are $5.00, and average total costs are $7.00.

By knowing the relationship between fixed and variable costs, marketers are better able to set prices. They recognize that average total costs usually decline as sale volume expands, which allows them to set skimming prices when volume is low and penetration prices when volume is high. They also realize that the firm can reduce its losses with a selling price that is lower than average total costs; as long as the price is above average variable costs, a transaction will contribute toward the payment of fixed costs. Finally, the break-even point can be shown on a total-cost curve graph. See Figure 2.

With a selling price of $10.00 per unit. Eleanor's Cosmetics would lose money unless 2,000 units could be sold. At that amount, the firm breaks even. For all sales volumes above 2,000 units, the company would earn a profit of $5.00 per unit, an amount equal to the difference between selling price and average variable costs (fixed costs are assumed to be "paid off" when sales reach 2,000 units). A sales volume of 5,000 units would return a profit of $15,000 (total revenues of $50,000 − total costs of $35,000).

Markup

Markup is the difference between merchandise cost and selling price for each channel member. Markup is usually expressed as a percentage:

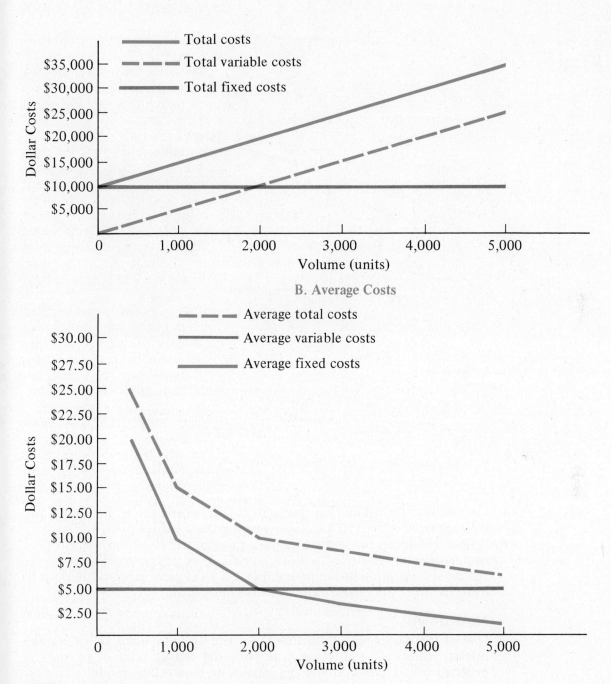

Figure 1
Fixed and Variable Costs for Eleanor's Cosmetics

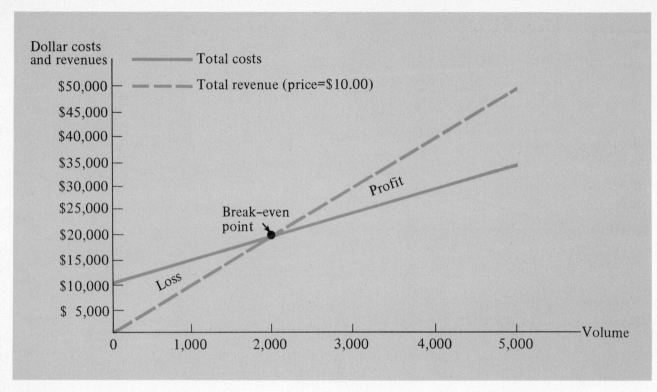

Figure 2
Break-Even Analysis for Eleanor's Cosmetics

$$\text{Markup percentage (on selling price)} = \frac{\text{Selling price} - \text{Merchandise cost}}{\text{Selling price}}$$

$$\text{Markup percentage (at cost)} = \frac{\text{Selling price} - \text{Merchandise cost}}{\text{Merchandise cost}}$$

Table 3 shows markup percentages on selling price and at cost for an item selling for $10.00 under varying costs. Since companies often consider markup percentage as the equivalent of the gross margin percentage discussed earlier in this appendix, they use the markup percentage on selling price in their planning. As with gross margin, markup is used to cover operating expenses and net profit.

Markdown

One of the major price adjustments made by most firms is the **markdown,** which is a reduction in the original selling price of an item in order to sell it. Markdowns are caused by slow sales, model changes, and other factors.

Markdown percentages can be computed in either of two ways:

$$\text{Markdown percentage (off-retail)} = \frac{\text{Original selling price} - \text{Reduced selling price}}{\text{Original selling price}}$$

Selling Price	Merchandise Cost	Markup (on selling price)	Markup (at cost)	*Table 3*
$10.00	$9.00	10%	11%	**Markups on Selling Price and at Cost**
10.00	8.00	20	25	
10.00	7.00	30	43	
10.00	6.00	40	67	
10.00	5.00	50	100	
10.00	4.00	60	150	
10.00	3.00	70	233	
10.00	2.00	80	400	
10.00	1.00	90	900	

Formulas to convert markup percentages:

$$\text{Markup percentage (on selling price)} = \frac{\text{Markup percentage (at cost)}}{100\% + \text{Markup percentage (at cost)}}$$

$$\text{Markup percentage (at cost)} = \frac{\text{Markup percentage (on selling price)}}{100\% - \text{Markup percentage (on selling price)}}$$

$$\frac{\text{Markdown percentage}}{\text{(off-sale)}} = \frac{\text{Original selling price} - \text{Reduced selling price}}{\text{Reduced selling price}}$$

For example, the off-retail markdown percentage for an item that originally sold for $20 and has been marked down to $15 is ($20 − $15)/$20 = 25. The off-sale markdown percentage is ($20 − $15)/$15 = 33. While the off-retail percentage is more accurate for price planning, the off-sale percentage indicates a larger price reduction to consumers and may generate increased volume.

QUESTIONS

1. What information can a marketer obtain from a profit-and-loss statement?
2. Develop a profit-and-loss statement for The Deluxe Phone Center, a retail store, based on the following:

Beginning inventory (at cost)	$ 200,000
New merchandise (at cost)	400,000
Ending inventory (at cost)	100,000
Gross sales	1,000,000
Returns and allowances	100,000
Marketing expenses	200,000
Administration, rent, supplies	150,000

3. Using the profit-and loss statement from Question 2, calculate:
   a. Return on investment.
   b. Stock turnover ratio.
   c. Net profit ratio (percentage).
   d. Operating expense ratio (percentage).
   e. Gross margin ratio (percentage).
   f. Cost-of-goods-sold ratio (percentage).
   g. Sales efficiency ratio (percentage).

4. How would The Deluxe Phone Center determine whether or not its perform-ance ratios are satisfactory?

5. A newspaper publisher has conducted research concerning its readers' sen-sitivity to price. These are the results:

Price	Estimate of Readership
$ .10	1,000,000
.25	600,000
.35	400,000

   a. Calculate price elasticity as price goes from $ .10 to $ .25 and from $ .25 to $ .35.
   b. At what price is total revenue maximized?
   c. What price should be set? Why?

6. A tire manufacturer has fixed costs of $1,000,000 and variable costs of $25.00 per tire.
   a. Calculate total costs for volumes of 10,000, 25,000, and 50,000 tires.
   b. Calculate average total, fixed, and variable costs for the same volumes.
   c. At a volume of 25,000 tires, would the firm make a profit or loss with a selling price of $75.00? What is the total profit or loss?

7. A shaving cream manufacturer sells medium-size containers for $.99; they cost $.40 to make. Large-size containers sell for $1.99; they cost $.95 to make.
   a. For each size container, determine the markup percentage on selling price and at cost.
   b. Why would the company use a different markup percentage for medium containers from that for large containers?

8. A glove retailer originally sold suede gloves for $30 per pair. An end-of-season sale has reduced the price of these gloves to $15.
   a. Compute the off-retail and off-sale markdown percentages.
   b. Why is there a difference in these calculations?

Appendix C

Glossary

Absolute Product Failure Occurs when a company is unable to recoup its production and marketing costs. The firm incurs a financial loss.

Accelerator Principle Final consumer demand affects several layers of organizational consumers.

Accessory Equipment Industrial capital items, which require a moderate amount of decision making, are less expensive than installations, last a number of years, and do not change in form or become part of the final product.

Adaptation Responses to the surrounding environment, including both opportunities and threats.

Additional Markup Used to raise regular retail prices because demand is unexpectedly high or costs are rising.

Administered Channel One in which the dominant firm in the distribution process plans the marketing program and itemizes responsibilities.

Adoption Process The procedure an individual goes through when learning about and purchasing a new product. The adoption process consists of six stages: awareness, interest, evaluation, trial, adoption, and confirmation.

Advertising Any paid form of nonpersonal presentation and promotion of ideas, goods, and services by an identified sponsor.

Advertising Agency An outside company that usually works with a firm in the development of its advertising plan.

Advertising Themes The overall appeals for a campaign. Themes can be product or service, consumer, or nonproduct and nonconsumer in orientation.

Agent A wholesaler compensated through payment of a commission or a fee. It may be a manufacturers' agent, selling agent, or commission (factor) merchant.

Airway The fastest, most expensive form of transportation.

All-You-Can-Afford Technique A means of developing a promotional budget in which the firm first allocates funds for every element of marketing except promotion. Whatever funds are left over are placed in a promotion budget.

Approaching Customers The stage in the selling process that consists of the preapproach and greeting.

Atmosphere The sum total of the physical characteristics of a retail store that are used to develop an image and draw customers.

Attitude (Opinion) A person's positive, neutral, or negative feelings about products, services, companies, issues, and institutions.

Audience The target of the message in a channel of communication.

Backward Invention An international product strategy in which a firm appeals to developing countries by making products that are less complex than the ones it sells in its domestic market.

Bait-and-Switch Advertising An illegal procedure whereby a retailer lures customers into a store by advertising items at exceptionally low prices and then telling customers that the items are out of stock or are of inferior quality. The retailer has no intention of selling the advertising items.

Balanced Product Portfolio Maintaining a combination of new, growing, and mature products.

Balanced Tenancy Relates the type and number of stores within any planned center to the overall needs of the surrounding population. To ensure balance a shopping center may limit the merchandise lines any store carries.

Battle of the Brands Manufacturer, dealer, and generic brands each attempting to increase their market share at the expense of the other. In particular, this is a battle between manufacturers and retailers.

Benefit Segmentation Uses the benefits people seek in consuming a given product as the means of segmenting markets.

Blurring Gender Roles Occurs when husbands assume a greater share of the traditional role of their wives.

Bonded Warehouse Used to store imported or taxable merchandise, which is released for sale only after appropriate taxes are paid.

Boston Consulting Group Matrix Enables a company to classify its products in terms of their market share relative to the industry's leading brands and the annual growth rate of the industry. The matrix identifies four types of products: star, cash cow, problem child (question mark), and dog, and suggests appropriate strategies for each.

Brand A name, design, or symbol (or combination of these) that identifies the products and services of a seller or group of sellers. There are four types of brand designation: brand name, brand mark, trade character, and trademark.

Brand Decision Process Consists of nonrecognition, recognition, preference, and insistence stges that consumers pass through.

Brand Extension A strategy applying an established brand name to new products.

Brand Loyalty The consistent repurchase of and preference for a brand. The consumer attempts to minimize risk, time, and thought.

Brand Mark A symbol, design, or distinctive coloring or lettering.

Brand Name A word, letter, or group of words or letters that can be spoken.

Break-Even Analysis. See *Traditional Break-Even Analysis* and *Modified Break-Even Analysis.*

Broad Price Policy Coordinates pricing decisions with the firm's target market, image, and marketing mix.

Broker A temporary wholesaler, paid by a commission or fee. The most common is a food broker, who introduces buyers and sellers and helps complete transactions.

Business Analysis Projects demand, costs, competition, investment requirements, and profits for new product ideas.

Buyer-Seller Dyad Two-way flow of communication between both parties.

Buying Structure of an Organization Depends on its size, resources, diversity, and level of specialization.

Canned-Sales Presentation A memorized, repetitive presentation given to all customers interested in a particular item. This approach does not adapt to customer needs or traits but presumes that a general presentation will appeal to all customers.

Cash-and-Carry Wholesaling Enables a small businessperson to drive to a wholesaler, order products, and take them back to the store or business.

Cash Cow A high market-share product in a low-growth industry. Cash cows generate more cash than required to maintain their market share.

Cease-and-Desist Order Requires a firm to discontinue deceptive practices and modify its promotion messages.

Chain-Markup Pricing A procedure in which final selling price is first determined, then markups for each channel member are examined, and the maximum acceptable costs to each member are computed. Chain-markup pricing extends demand-minus calculations from the retailer all the way back to the manufacturer.

Chain-Ratio Method A sales forecasting technique in which the firm starts with an overall forecast and ends with an estimate of the size of each market segment.

Chain Retailer Common ownership of multiple units.

Channel Functions The functions completed by some member of the channel: marketing research, buying, promotion, customer services, product planning, pricing, and distribution.

Channel Length Refers to the number of independent members along the channel.

Channel Member An organization or person in the distribution process.

Channel of Communication The mechanism through which a source sends a message to its audience. It consists of source, encoding, message, medium, decoding, audience, feedback, and noise.

Channel of Distribution All the organizations or people involved with the movement and exchange of products or services.

Channel Width Refers to the number of independent members at any stage of the distribution process.

Class-Action Suit A suit filed on behalf of many affected consumers.

Class Consciousness The extent to which social status is desired and pursued by a person.

Client The constituency for which a nonprofit organization offers membership, elected officials, locations, ideas, products, and services.

Closing the Sale The stage in the sales process that involves getting the customer to agree to a purchase. The salesperson must be sure that no major questions remain before attempting to close a sale.

Cognitive Dissonance Doubt that the correct purchase decision has been made. To overcome cognitive dissonance and dissatisfaction, the firm must realize that the purchase process does not end with the purchase.

Combination Compensation Plan Combines salary and commission plans to provide control, flexibility, and employee incentives.

Commercialization The final stage in new-product planning. The firm introduces the product to its full target market. This corresponds to the introductory stage of the product life cycle.

Commission (Factor) Merchant Agent who receives goods on consignment, accumulates them from local markets, and arranges for their sale in a central market location.

Common Carrier A transporter who must provide service between designated points on a fixed schedule. It cannot refuse to transport the goods of any shipper unless the carrier's rules are violated.

Company-Controlled Price Environment Characterized by a moderate level of competition, well-differentiated products and services, and strong control over price by individual firms.

Comparative Advantage Benefit to countries by trading goods in which they have relative production advantages for those in which they have relative disadvantages.

Competition-Based Pricing Prices set in accordance with competitors. Prices may be below the market, at the market, or above the market.

Competitive Bidding Sellers asked to submit independently price bids for specific products, projects, and/or services.

Competitive Parity Technique A method in which the company's promotional budget is raised or lowered according to the actions of competitors.

Component Material Semimanufactured industrial good that undergoes further changes in form. A component material is considered as an expense rather than a capital item.

Concept Testing Potential consumers asked to respond to a picture, written statement, or oral description of a new product, thus enabling the firm to determine attitudes prior to expensive, time-consuming prototype development.

Conclusive Research Structured data collection and analysis for the solution of a specific problem or objective.

Conflict Resolution Procedure in organizational buying for resolving disagreements in joint-decision-making situations. The alternatives are problem solving, persuasion, bargaining, and politicking.

Consistency of Product Mix The relationship among product lines in terms of their sharing a common end use, distribution outlets, consumer group(s), and price range.

Consumer Bill of Rights Stated by President Kennedy in 1962: information, safety, choice, and a voice in decision making.

Consumer Cooperative a retailer owned and operated by consumer members.

Consumer Demand Refers to the characteristics and needs of final consumers, industrial consumers, channel members, government institutions, international markets, and nonprofit institutions.

Consumer Demographics Easily identifiable and measurable statistics that are used to describe the population.

Consumer Education A learning process whereby the consumer acquires the skills and knowledge to use his or her financial resources wisely in the marketplace.

Consumer Price Index (CPI) Measures the monthly and yearly changes in the prices of selected consumer items in different product categories, expressing the changes in terms of a base year.

Consumer Product A good or service destined for the ultimate consumer's personal, family, or household use.

Consumer Product Safety Commission (CPSC) The major federal agency responsible for product safety. It has jurisdiction over more than 11,000 products.

Consumer Survey A method of sales forecasting that obtains information about purchase intentions, future expectations, rate of consumption, brand switching, time between purchases, and reasons for purchases.

Consumerism A social force within the environment designed to aid and protect the consumer by exerting legal, moral, and economic pressure on business.

Consumer's Decision Process Involves the steps a consumer goes through in purchasing a product or service: stimulus, problem awareness, information search, evaluation of alternatives, purchase, and postpurchase behavior. Demographics, social factors, and psychological factors affect the consumer's decision process.

Containerization Shipping innovation that allows goods to be placed in sturdy containers, which serve as mobile warehouses.

Continuous Monitoring The procedure by which the changing environment is regularly viewed.

Contract Carrier Provides one or a few shippers with transportation services based on individual agreements.

Contractual Arrangement Specifies in writing all the terms regarding distribution functions, prices, and other factors for each channel member in an indirect channel.

Control The monitoring and reviewing of overall and specific performance.

Controllable Factors Decision elements that are directed by the firm and its marketers. Included are the selection of a consumer market, marketing objectives, marketing organization, marketing plans, and control.

Convenience Good An item purchased with a minimum of effort, where the buyer has knowledge of product characteristics prior to shopping. Types are staples, impulse, and emergency goods.

Convenience Store A store featuring food items that is open long hours and carries a limited number of items. Consumers use a convenience store for fill-in merchandise, often at off hours.

Cooperative Advertising Allows expenses to be shared by channel members. It can be vertical or horizontal.

Corporate Symbols Firm's name, logo, and trade characters that play a significant role in the creation of an overall company image.

Corrective Advertising Requires a firm to run new advertisements to correct the false impressions made by previous ones.

Cost-Based Pricing Prices set by computing merchandise, service, and overhead costs and then adding the desired profit to these figures. Demand is not analyzed.

Cost-Plus Pricing Prices set by adding a predetermined

profit to costs. It is the simplest form of cost-based pricing:

$$\text{Price} = \frac{\text{Total costs} + \text{Projected profit}}{\text{Units produced}}$$

Culture A group of people sharing a distinctive heritage.

Currency Stability An economic factor that could affect sales and profits if a foreign country revalues its currency in relation to the company's home currency.

Customary Pricing Occurs when a channel member sets product or service prices and seeks to maintain them for an extended period of time.

Data Analysis The coding, tabulation, and analysis of marketing research data.

Data Storage Contains all the information previously collected through marketing research and continuous monitoring that is retained by the organization for future reference.

Dealer Brand An item that contains the name of the wholesaler or retailer. Dealers secure exclusive rights for their brands and are responsible for their distribution.

Decline Stage of the Product Life Cycle Period during which industry sales decline and many firms leave the market because customers are fewer and they have less income to spend.

Decoding The process in a channel of communication whereby the message sent by the source is interpreted by the audience.

Demand-Based Pricing Prices set after researching consumer desires and ascertaining the ranges of prices acceptable to the target market.

Demand-Minus Pricing Process whereby the firm ascertains the appropriate final selling price and works backward to compute costs. The formula used in demand-minus pricing is

Maximum merchandise cost =
          Price [(100 − Markup per cent)/100].

Demarketing A marketing strategy intended to reduce overall demand when an organization's offering is in short supply.

Department Store A large retailer, employing 25 + people and usually selling a general line of apparel for the family, household linens and dry goods, and furniture, home furnishings, appliances, radios, and televisions. It is organized into separate departments for purposes of buying, promotion, service, and control.

Depth of Product Mix The number of product items within each product line.

Derived Demand Bases the demand for industrial goods on consumer goods' demand. Manufacturers must be aware that they are selling through wholesalers and retailers and not to them.

Developing Country Has rising education level and technology, but a per capita income of only $1,500.

Differential Advantage The set of unique features in a company's marketing program that causes consumers to patronize the company and not its competitors.

Diffusion Process Describes the manner in which different members of the target market often accept and purchase a product. The process spans the time from product introduction until market saturation.

Diminishing Returns May occur if a firm attempts to attract nonconsumers when its market is relatively saturated.

Direct Channel of Distribution Involves the movement of goods and services from manufacturer to consumer without the use of middlemen.

Direct Ownership A form of international marketing organization that involves the full undertaking and control of all international operations.

Direct-to-Home Retailer Sells directly to consumers in their homes.

Discount A reduction from final selling price that is available to channel members and final consumers for performing certain functions, paying in cash, buying large quantities, purchasing in off-seasons, or enhancing promotions.

Discount Mall A shopping location in which a variety of low-price retailers are situated together.

Discretionary Income Earnings remaining for luxuries after necessities are bought.

Disposable Income Aftertax income to be used for spending and/or savings.

Distributed Promotion Communication efforts spread throughout the year.

Distribution Planning The systematic decision making pertaining to the physical movement and transfer of ownership of a product or service from producer to consumer. It includes transportation, storage, and customer transactions.

Distribution Standards Clear and measurable goals regarding customer service levels in physical distribution.

Diversification A product/market opportunity matrix strategy in which a firm develops new products for new markets.

Dog A low market-share product in a low-growth industry. A dog usually has cost disadvantages and few growth opportunities.

Donor The constituency from which a nonprofit organization receives resources.

Drop Shipper (Desk Jobber) A form of limited-service merchant wholesaler which purchases goods from manufacturers/suppliers and arranges for their shipment to retailers or industrial users.

Dual Channel of Distribution A strategy whereby the firm appeals to different market segments or diversifies its business by selling through two or more different channels.

Dumping Selling a product in a foreign country at a price lower than that prevailing in the exporter's home market or below the cost of production, or both.

Economic Order Quantity (EOQ) The order volume corresponding to the lowest sum of order processing and holding costs.

80-20 Principle States that in many organizations a large proportion of total sales (profit) comes from a small proportion of customers, products, or territories.

Elastic Demand Occurs if relatively small changes in price result in large changes in quantity demanded.

Elasticity of Demand Defines the sensitivity of buyers to price changes in terms of the quantities they will purchase. Price elasticity is computed by dividing the percentage change in quantity demanded by the percentage change in price charged.

Electronic Banking Enables all types of financial transactions to be completed through computerized systems, such as 24-hour automatic tellers.

Electronic Mail Enables a firm to transmit a letter from New York to San Francisco in less than one minute.

Embargo A form of trade restriction that prohibits specified products from entering a country.

Encoding The procedure in a channel of communication whereby a thought or idea is translated into a message by the source.

Escalator Clause Allows a firm to contractually raise the price of an item to reflect higher costs in the item's essential ingredients without changing printed list prices.

Ethical Behavior Based on honest and proper conduct.

European Community (EC) Also known as the Common Market. The EC calls for no tariffs among members and a uniform tariff with nonmember nations. In addition, there are common standards for food additives, labeling requirements, and package sizes.

Evaluation of Alternatives Stage in the consumer's decision process in which criteria for a decision are set and alternatives ranked.

Exchange The process by which consumers and publics give money, a promise to pay, or support the offering of a firm, person, place, or idea.

Exclusive Distribution A policy in which a firm severely limits the wholesalers and retailers it utilizes in a geographic area, perhaps employing only one or two retailers within a specific shopping district.

Exempt Carrier Has no economic regulations, only safety requirements. Some commodities moved by water, such as coal and most agricultural goods, are exempt from economic restriction.

Experiment A type of research whereby one or more factors are manipulated under controlled conditions. Experiments are able to show cause and effect.

Exploratory Research Used when the researcher is uncertain about the precise topic to be investigated. This technique develops a clear definition of the research problem by utilizing informal analysis.

Exporting When a company reaches international markets by selling directly through its own sales force or indirectly through foreign merchants or agents. An exporting structure requires minimal investment in foreign facilities.

Extended Consumer Decision Making Occurs when considerable time is spent on information search and the evaluation of alternatives before a purchase is made. Expensive, complex products or services with which the consumer has had little or no experience require this form of decision making.

Fabricated Part Used in industrial goods without further changes in form. A fabricated part is considered as an expense rather than a capital item.

Family A group of two or more persons residing together who are related by blood, marriage, or adoption.

Family Branding A strategy in which one name is used for several products. It may be applied to manufacturer and dealer brands.

Family Life Cycle Describes how a typical family evolves from bachelorhood to marriage to children to solitary retirement. At each stage in the cycle, needs, experience, income, and family composition change.

Federal Trade Commission (FTC) A federal regulatory agency formed to eliminate monopolies and restraint of trade and to enforce rules against unfair methods of competition.

Feedback Information about the uncontrollable environment, the organization's performance, and how well the marketing plan is received. Also, the audience's response to a message.

Field Warehousing Occurs when a receipt is issued by a public warehouse for goods stored in a private warehouse or in transit to consumers.

Final Consumer A family or person who buys a product or service for personal, family, or household use.

Fine Dollar penalty levied on a firm for a deceptive promotion or other practice.

Flexible Pricing Allows the marketer to adjust prices based on the consumer's ability to negotiate or the buying power of a large customer.

Food Broker Introduces buyers and sellers to one another and brings them together to complete a sale.

Forward Invention An international product strategy in which a company develops new products for its international markets.

Franchise Wholesaling Format whereby independent retailers affiliate with an existing wholesaler in order to use a standardized storefront design, business plan, name, and purchase system.

Franchising A contractual arrangement between a franchisor who may be a manufacturer, wholesaler, or service sponsor and a retail franchisee, which allows the franchisee to conduct a certain form of business under an established name and according to a specific set of rules.

Freight Forwarder Consolidates small shipments (usually less than 500 pounds each) from several companies, picks up merchandise at the shipper's place of business, and arranges for delivery at the buyer's door.

Frequency How often a medium can be used.

Full Disclosure Requires that all data necessary for a consumer to make a safe and informed decision be provided.

Full-Line Discount Store A retailer characterized by low prices, a broad merchandise assortment, low-rent location, self-service, brand-name merchandise, wide aisles, shopping carts, and most merchandise displayed on the selling floor.

Full-Service Merchant Wholesaler Assembles products, provides trade credit, stores and delivers merchandise, offers merchandise and promotion assistance, provides a personal sales force, offers research and planning support, makes information available, provides installation and repair services, and acts as the sales arm for its manufacturer.

General Agreement on Tariffs and Trade (GATT) A multilateral agreement that allows every nation covered to obtain the best contract terms received by a single nation. GATT members agree to meet every two years and to negotiate for tariff reductions.

General-Merchandise (Full-Line) Wholesaler Carries a wide assortment of products, nearly all the items needed by the retailer to which it caters.

Generic Brand An item that contains the name of the product itself and does not emphasize the manufacturer's or dealer's name.

Geographic Demographics The basic identifiable characteristics of towns, cities, states, and regions.

Geographic Pricing Outlines the responsibility for transportation charges. The basic forms of geographic pricing are FOB (free on board), uniform delivered price, zone pricing, and base-point pricing.

Government Consumer Uses products and services in the performance of its duties and responsibilities. There are 1 federal, 50 state, and 80,000 local governmental groups.

Government-Controlled Price Environment Characterized by prices set or directed by the government.

Government Stability Refers to the consistency of policies and the orderliness in installing leaders.

Gross National Product (GNP) The total value of goods and services produced in a country each year.

Growth Stage of the Product Life Cycle Period during which industry sales expand rapidly as a few more firms enter a highly profitable market that has substantial potential.

Hard Technology The way some services are industrialized by substituting machinery for people.

Heavy-Half The market segment that represents 50 per cent of consumers but accounts for as much as 80 to 90 per cent of sales.

Hidden Service Sector Causes service data to be under-

estimated because many firms that perform services are classified as manufacturers.

Hierarchy-of-Effects Model Outlines the intermediate and long-term promotional objectives the firm should pursue: awareness, knowledge, liking, preference, conviction, and purchase.

Horizontal Audit Studies the overall marketing performance of the company with particular emphasis on the interrelationship of variables and their relative importance.

Horizontal Price Fixing Agreements among manufacturers, among wholesalers, or among retailers to set prices. Such agreements are illegal according to the Sherman Antitrust Act and the Federal Trade Commission Act, regardless of how "reasonable" the prices are.

Household A housing unit with one or more people.

Hybrid Technology A technique for industrializing services that combines hard and soft technologies such as computer-based truck routing and specialized low-priced auto repair facilities.

Iceberg Principle States that superficial data are insufficent to make sound evaluations.

Idea Generation The continuous, systematic search for new-product opportunities. It involves a delineation of the sources of new ideas and methods for generating them.

Ideal Point Represents the attribute consumers would like to see a product possess.

Importance of a Purchase Has a major impact on the time and effort a consumer will spend shopping for a product or service, and on the amount of money allocated.

Incremental Technique A promotional budget method in which the company bases its new budget on previous expenditures. A percentage is either added to or subtracted from this year's budget in order to determine next year's.

Independent Retailer Operates only one outlet.

Indirect Channel of Distribution Involves the movement of goods and services from manufacturer to independent channel member to consumer.

Individual Branding See *Multiple Branding.*

Industrial Marketing Occurs when a firm deals with organizational consumers.

Industrial Product A good or service purchased for use in the production of other goods or services, in the operation of a business, or for resale to other consumers.

Industrial Services Maintenance and repair and business advisory services.

Industrial Supplies Convenience goods that are necessary for the daily operation of the firm.

Industrialization of Services Improves service efficiency by applying hard, soft, and hybrid technologies.

Industrialized Country Has high literacy, modern technology, and high per capita income.

Inelastic Demand Occurs when price changes have little impact on quantity demanded.

Information Search Stage in consumer's decision process that requires the assembly of a list of alternative products or services that will solve the problem at hand and a determination of the characteristics of each alternative. Information search may be either internal or external.

Inner-Directed Person One who is interested in pleasing him- or herself.

Innovativeness The willingness to try a new product or service that others perceive as having a high degree of risk.

Inseparability of Services Inability of many services to be separated from the service provider.

Installation An industrial good capital item used in the production process the does not become part of the final product.

Institutional Advertising Used to improve company image and not to sell products or services.

Intangibility of Services Inability of many services to be displayed, transported, stored, packaged, or inspected before buying.

Intensive Distribution A policy that places merchandise into as many outlets as possible in an area.

International Marketing Involves the marketing of goods and services outside the organization's home country.

Introduction Stage of the Product Life Cycle The period during which only one firm has entered the market and competition is limited. A consumer market must be developed.

Inventory Management Ensures a continuous flow of goods and matches quantity with sales demand.

Isolated Store A free-standing retail outlet located on either a highway or side street.

Item Price Removal Practice whereby prices are marked only on store shelves or aisle signs and not on individual items.

Joint Decision Making The process by which two or more consumers have input into purchases.

Joint Venture An agreement by which a firm combines some aspect of its manufacturing or marketing efforts with those of a foreign company in order to share expertise, costs, and connections with important persons.

Jury of Executive or Expert Opinion A sales forecasting method by which the management of a company or other well-informed persons meet, discuss the future, and set sales estimates based on experience and intuition.

Law of Demand States that consumers usually purchase more units at a low price than at a high price.

Lead Time The time required by the medium for placing an advertisement.

Leader Pricing Advertising and selling key items in the product assortment at less than their usual profit margins. The objective of leader pricing is to increase store traffic or to gain greater consumer interest in an overall product line.

Leased Department A department in a retail store (usually a department, discount, or specialty store) that is rented to an outside party.

Less-Developed Country Has low literacy, limited technology, and per capita income of less than $500.

Licensing Agreement Permits a company to use another firm's trademark by paying a fee.

Life-Style The pattern in which a person lives and spends time and money. The combination of personality and social values that has been internalized by an individual.

Limited Consumer Decision Making Occurs when a consumer uses each of the steps in the purchase process but does not need to spend a great deal of time in each of them. The consumer has some past experience with the product or service under consideration.

Limited-Service Merchant Wholesaler Buys and takes title to merchandise, but does not perform all of the functions of a full-service merchant wholesaler.

List Price A regularly quoted price provided to customers. It is preprinted on price tags, in catalogs, and in dealer purchase orders.

Loss Leader An item priced below cost that is restricted by unfair-sales acts in many states. Retailers use loss leaders, typically well-known and heavily advertised brands, to draw customer traffic into a store.

Mail Order Retailing Occurs when the seller seeks customers through television, radio, printed media, or the mail, receives orders through the mail or telephone, and ships merchandise to the customer's home.

Mail-Order Wholesaler Uses catalogs instead of a personal sales force.

Majority Fallacy Concept stating that companies sometimes fail when they go after the largest market segment because competition is intense. A potentially profitable market segment may be the one that is ignored by other firms.

Manufacturer A firm that produces products for resale to other consumers.

Manufacturer Brand An item that contains the name of the manufacturer. The major marketing focus on manufacturer brands is to attract and retain consumers who are loyal to a firm's offering and to control the marketing effort for the brands.

Manufacturer/Channel Member Contract A written agreement that focuses on price policy, conditions of sale, territorial rights, services/responsibility mix, and contract length and condition of termination.

Manufacturer Wholesaling Wholesaling facilities owned and operated by the manufacturer.

Manufacturers' Agent Middleman who works for several manufacturers and carries noncompetitive, complementary products in exclusive territories. A manufacturer may employ many agents, each with a unique product-territorial mix.

Markdown Reduction from the original retail price of an item.

Market Buildup Method A sales forecasting technique in which the firm gathers data from small, separate market segments and aggregates them.

Market-Controlled Price Environment Characterized by a high level of competition, similar products and services, and little control over price by individual companies.

Market Development A product/market opportunity matrix strategy in which a firm seeks sales from new markets or new product uses with existing products.

Market Penetration A product/market opportunity matrix strategy in which a firm seeks to expand the sales of its present products in its present markets through more aggressive promotion and distribution.

Market Segmentation An appeal to one, well-defined consumer group through one marketing plan.

Market Share Analysis A method of sales forecasting that is similar to simple trend analysis, except that the company bases its forecast on the assumption that its share of industry sales will remain constant.

Marketing The anticipation, management, and satisfaction of demand through the exchange process.

Marketing Audit A systematic, critical, and unbiased review and appraisal of the basic objectives of the marketing function and of the organization, methods, procedures, and personnel employed to implement these policies and to achieve these objectives.

Marketing Company Era Recognition of the central role of marketing. The marketing department becomes the equal of others in the company. Company efforts are integrated and frequently re-evaluated.

Marketing Concept A consumer-oriented, integrated, goal-oriented philosophy for a firm, institution, or person.

Marketing Department Era Stage during which the marketing department participates in company decisions but remains in a subordinate or conflicting position to the production, engineering, and sales departments.

Marketing Environment Consists of controllable and uncontrollable factors, the organization's level of success or failure in reaching objectives, feedback, and adaptation.

Marketing Functions These include customer analysis, buying, selling, product (service) planning, price planning, distribution, marketing research, opportunity analysis, and social responsibility.

Marketing Information System A set of procedures and methods designed to generate, store, analyze, and disseminate anticipated marketing decision information on a regular, continuous basis.

Marketing Intelligence Network The part of a marketing information system that consists of marketing research, continuous monitoring, and data storage.

Marketing-Manager System Format under which all the functional areas of marketing report to one manager. These areas include sales, advertising, sales promotion, and product planning.

Marketing Mix Describes the specific combination of marketing elements used to achieve objectives and satisfy the target market. The marketing mix consists of four major factors: product or service, distribution, promotion, and price.

Marketing Myopia A short-sighted, narrow-minded view of marketing and its environment.

Marketing Objectives More customer-oriented than the overall goals set by top management.

Marketing Organization The structural arrangement for directing marketing functions. The organization outlines authority, responsibility, and the tasks to be performed.

Marketing Performers Include manufacturers, wholesalers, retailers, marketing specialists, and final consumers.

Marketing Plan The process of deciding what marketing actions to undertake, why these actions are necessary, who is responsible for carrying them out, where they will be accomplished, and how they will be completed.

Marketing Research The systematic gathering, recording, and analyzing of data about problems relating to the marketing of goods and services.

Marketing Research Process Consists of a series of activities: definition of the problem or issue to be resolved, examination of secondary data, generation of primary data (if necessary), analysis of information, recommendations, and implementation of findings.

Markup Pricing Price set by calculating per unit merchandise costs and then determining the markup percentages that are needed to cover selling costs and profit. The formula for markup pricing is

$$\text{Price} = \frac{\text{Merchandise costs}}{(100 - \text{Markup per cent})/100}.$$

Mass Marketing An appeal to a broad range of consumers by utilizing a single basic marketing program.

Massed Promotion Communication concentrated in peak periods, like holidays.

Maturity Stage of the Product Life Cycle Period during which industry sales stabilize as the market becomes saturated and many firms enter to capitalize on the still sizable demand.

Me Generation A consumer life-style that stresses "being good to myself."

Medium The personal or nonpersonal tool in a channel of communication used to convey a message.

Merchant Wholesaler Buys, takes title, and takes possession of products for its own accounts. Merchant wholesalers may be full-service or limited-service.

Message The combination of words and symbols transmitted to the audience through a channel of communication.

Message Permanence Refers to the number of exposures one advertisement generates and how long it remains with the audience.

Middleman See *Channel Member.*

Minimum Price Laws See *Unfair-Sales Acts.*

Missionary Salesperson Type of sales support person used to distribute information about new products or services. This person does not sell, but describes the attributes of the new item, answers questions, and leaves written data.

Mixed Approach to International Marketing Combines standardized and nonstandardized efforts to enable a company to maximize production efficiencies, maintain a consistent image, exercise home-office control, and yet be sensitive and responsive to local needs.

Mixed-Brand Strategy Occurs when a combination of manufacturer and dealer brands (and sometimes generic brands) are sold by manufacturers and retailers.

Modified Break-Even Analysis Combines traditional break-even analysis with an evaluation of demand at various levels of price.

Modified Rebuy Purchase Process A moderate amount of decision making undertaken by organizational consumers in the purchase of medium-priced products that have been bought infrequently before.

Monitoring Results Involves the comparison of planned performance against actual performance for a specified period of time.

Monopolistic Competition A situation in which there are several competing firms, each trying to offer a unique marketing mix.

Monopoly A situation in which only one firm sells a particular product or service.

Most-Favored Nation Principle Allows every nation covered by the General Agreement on Tariffs and Trade to obtain the best contract terms received by any single nation.

Motivation The driving force within an individual that impels him or her to action.

Motive A reason for behavior.

Motor Truck Predominantly transports small shipments over short distances.

Multidimensional Scaling A survey research tool in which respondents' attitudes are ascertained for many product and company attributes. Then computer analysis enables the firm to develop a single product or company rating, rather than a profile of several individual characteristics.

Multinational Marketing Occurs when an organization is engaged in marketing operations in many foreign countries.

Multiple Branding Separate brands used for each item or product category sold by the firm.

Multiple-Buying Responsibility Results in joint decision making by organizational consumers.

Multiple Segmentation An appeal to two or more well-defined consumer groups through different marketing plans.

Multiple-Unit Pricing A practice by which a company offers final consumers discounts for buying in quantity.

Multistep Flow of Communication Adds to the two-step flow by suggesting that the target market also communicates back to opinion leaders.

Multiunit Advertising Two or more products included in a single ad to economize.

Narrowcast The presentation of specialized programming to a specific audience.

National Brand See *Manufacturer Brand.*

Nationalism Refers to a country's efforts to become self-reliant and raise its status in the eyes of the world community. Frequently nationalism leads to tight restrictions for foreign companies and fosters the development of domestic industry at their expense.

Need-Satisfaction Approach A sales presentation method based on the principle that each customer has different characteristics and wants. The sales presentation is adapted to each customer.

Negotiation Situation in which the buyer uses bargaining ability and order size to influence prices.

New Product An innovation or the modification of an existing product that the consumer perceives as substantive.

New-Product Manager System Utilizes a product manager for existing products and a new-product manager for new products. After a new product is introduced, it is managed by the product manager.

New-Product Planning Process Consists of seven basic steps: idea generation, product screening, concept testing, business analysis, product development, test marketing, and commercialization.

New-Task Purchase Process A large amount of decision making undertaken by organizational consumers in the purchase of expensive products that have not been bought before.

Noise Interference at any stage along the channel of communication.

Nongoods Service Provides personal service on the part of the seller. It does not involve a product.

Nonprice Competition Reduces the role of price as a factor in consumer demand. This is accomplished by the creation of a distinctive product or service as expressed through promotion, packaging, delivery, customer service, availability, and other factors.

Nonprofit Institution Involved with nonprofit marketing.

Nonprofit Marketing Conducted by organizations that operate in the public interest or to foster a cause and do not seek financial profits. Nonprofit marketing may involve organizations, people, places, and ideas as well as products and services.

Nonstore Retailing Includes vending machines, direct-to-home sales, and mail order.

Objective-and-Task Technique A promotional budget method in which the firm clearly outlines its promotional objectives and then establishes the appropriate budget.

Observation A research technique by which present behavior or the results of past behavior are observed and recorded. People are not questioned, and their cooperation is not necessary.

Odd-Pricing Strategy Used when final selling prices are set at levels below even dollar values.

Oligopoly Situation in which there are few firms, generally large, that comprise most of an industry's sales.

One-Price Policy The same price charged to all customers who seek to purchase a product or service under similar conditions.

Opinion Leader Person who influences the purchase behavior of other consumers through face-to-face interaction. An opinion leader normally has an impact over a narrow range of products.

Optical Character Recognition (OCR-A) Department store system for electronically coding information onto merchandise. OCR-A is readable by both machines and humans and can handle more information than the UPC.

Order Cycle The period of time from when the customer places an order until it is received.

Order-Generating Costs Costs that are revenue producing, such as advertising, packaging, and personal selling.

Order Getter Type of salesperson who is involved with generating customer leads, providing information, persuading customers, and closing sales.

Order-Processing Costs Costs associated with filling out order forms, computer time, and merchandise handling. Order processing costs per unit usually drop as order size increases.

Order Size Depends on the availability of quantity discounts, the resources of the firm, inventory turnover, the costs of processing each order, and the costs of maintaining goods in inventory.

Order Taker Type of salesperson who processes routine orders and reorders. The order taker usually handles products or services that are presold.

Organizational Buying Objectives Include the availability of items, reliability of sellers, consistency of quality, delivery, and price.

Organizational Consumer Formal entity that purchases products and services for further production, usage in operating the organization, or resale to other consumers.

Organizational Consumer's Decision Process Consists of expectations, the buying process, conflict resolution, and situational factors.

Outer-Directed Person One who is interested in pleasing the people around him or her.

Owned-Goods Service Involves an alteration or repair of a product owned by the consumer.

Package Consists of a product's physical container, label, and inserts.

Packaging Functions Consist of containment and protection, usage, communication, market segmentation, channel cooperation, and new-product planning.

Patent Awards exclusive selling rights for 17 years to the inventor of a useful product or process.

Penetration Price A low price intended to capture the mass market for a product or service.

Perceived Risk The degree of uncertainty perceived by the consumer as to the consequences or outcomes of a specific purchase decision. There are five types of perceived risk: functional, physical, financial, social, and psychological.

Percentage-of-Sales Technique A promotional budget technique in which a company ties the promotion budget to sales revenue.

Peripheral Service A complementary service needed to supplement the basic service offering.

Perishability of Services Occurs because many services cannot be shifted from one time period to another. They cannot be stored for future sale.

Personal Demographics The basic identifiable characteristics of individual people.

Personal Selling An oral presentation in a conversation with one or more prospective buyers for the purpose of making sales.

Personality The sum total of an individual's traits that make the individual unique.

Persuasive Impact The ability of a medium to stimulate consumers.

Physical Distribution The broad range of activities concerned with the efficient movement of finished goods from the end of the production line to the consumer. In some cases it includes the movement of raw materials from the source of supply to the beginning of the production line.

Physical Distribution Strategy Includes the transportation form or forms to be used, inventory levels and warehouse form(s), and the number and locations of plants, warehouses, and retail locations.

Physical Distribution System The coordination of a firm's transportation and inventory management strategies.

Pipeline Involves continuous movement, with no interruptions, inventories, and intermediate storage locations.

Planned Shopping Center A retail location that is centrally owned or managed, planned, and operated as an entity, surrounded by parking, and based on balanced tenancy. The types are regional, community, and neighborhood.

Postpurchase Behavior　Stage in the consumer's decision process when further purchases or reevaluation are undertaken.

Poverty of Time　A consumer life-style where greater affluence results in less free time because the alternatives competing for time rise significantly.

Predatory Pricing　Occurs when large firms attempt to drive small firms out of business by setting extremely low prices.

Prestige Pricing　Assumes that consumers do not buy products or services at prices that are considered too low.

Price　Represents the value of a product or service for both the seller and the buyer.

Price Competition　Demand influenced primarily through changes in price levels.

Price Discrimination　A demand-oriented pricing technique with which the firm sets two or more distinct prices for a product or service in order to appeal to different final consumer or organizational consumer market segments. Price discrimination may be customer, product version, time, or place based.

Price Elasticity of Demand　See *Elasticity of Demand.*

Price Guarantee　A manufacturer's assurance to wholesalers or retailers that the prices they pay are the lowest available. Any discount given to competitors will also be given to the original purchaser.

Price Leadership　Occurs when a dominant firm regularly takes the initiative in price changes.

Price Lining　Involves the sale of merchandise at a range of prices with each individual price representing a distinct level of quality.

Price Planning　The systematic decision making pertaining to all aspects of pricing by the organization.

Price-Quality Association　Concept stating that consumers believe high prices connote high quality and low prices connote low quality.

Price War　Situation in which various firms continually try to undercut each other's prices.

Primary Data　Collected to solve the specific problem or issue under investigation.

Primary Demand　Consumer demand for a product category. Important when the product or service is little known.

Private Brand　See *Dealer Brand.*

Private Carrier　A shipper possessing its own transportation facilities.

Problem Awareness　A stage in the consumer's decision-making process during which the consumer recognizes that the product or service under consideration may solve a problem of shortage or unfulfilled desire.

Problem Child　A low market-share product in a high-growth industry. A problem child requires substantial

cash to maintain or increase market share in the face of strong competition.

Problem Definition　A statement of the topic to be investigated in marketing research. It directs the research process toward the collection and analysis of specific information for the purpose of decision making.

Process-Related Ethical Issue　Involves the unethical use of a marketing strategy or tactic.

Product　A basic physical offering that is accompanied by a set of image and service features.

Product-Adaptation Strategy　An international product-planning strategy in which domestic products are modified to meet foreign conditions, taste preferences, electrical requirements, water conditions, or legal requirements.

Product Development　A product/market opportunity matrix strategy in which a firm develops new or modified products to appeal to present markets.

Product Development Stage of New-Product Planning　Converts a product idea into a physical form and identifies a basic marketing strategy.

Product Item　A specific model, brand, or size of a product that the company sells.

Product Life Cycle　A concept that attempts to describe a product's sales, profits, customers, competitors, and marketing emphasis from its inception until it is removed from the market. It is divided into introduction, growth, maturity, and decline stages.

Product Line　A group of closely related items.

Product-Manager System　Format under which a middle manager focuses on a single product or a small group of products. This manager handles new and existing products and is involved with everything from marketing research to package design to advertising.

Product/Market Opportunity Matrix　A method for strategy planning that suggests four alternative strategies for maintaining and/or increasing sales: market penetration, market development, product development, and diversification.

Product Mix　Consists of all the different product lines that a firm offers. See also *Consistency of Product Mix; Depth of Product Mix;* and *Width of Product Mix.*

Product Planning　The systematic decision making pertaining to all aspects of the development and management of a firm's products, including branding and packaging.

Product-Planning Committee　Staffed by executives from functional areas including marketing, production, engineering, finance, and research and development. It handles product approval, evaluation, and development on a part-time basis.

Product Positioning　Enables the firm to map its offerings in terms of consumer perceptions and desires, competition, other company products, and environmental changes.

Product Recall　The primary enforcement tool of the Consumer Product Safety Commission.

Product-Related Ethical Issue Involves the ethical appropriateness of marketing a certain product.

Product Screening Stage in new-product planning when poor, unsuitable, or otherwise unattractive ideas are weeded out from further consideration.

Product Specifications The minimum specifications set by organizational consumers. They deal with engineering and architectural guidelines, purity and grade standards, horsepower, voltage, type of construction, and materials employed in construction.

Production Era of Marketing Devotion to the physical distribution of goods and services due to high demand and low competition. Consumer research, product modifications, and adapting to consumer needs are unnecessary.

Profit-Based Objective Orients strategy toward some type of profit goal: profit maximization, return on investment, and/or early recovery of cash.

Promotion Any form of communication used by a firm to inform, persuade, or remind people about its products, services, image, ideas, community involvement, or impact on society.

Promotion Mix A combination of advertising, publicity, personal selling, and/or sales promotion.

Promotion Planning Systematic decision making pertaining to all aspects of the development and management of a firm's promotional effort.

Prospecting A procedure for generating a list of customer leads. Prospecting is common with outside selling.

Psychological Pricing Assumes consumers are perceptually sensitive to certain prices. Departures from these prices in either direction result in decreases in demand. Customary, odd, and prestige pricing are all forms of psychological pricing.

Public Relations Mass and personal communications that are image directed.

Publicity Nonpersonal stimulation of demand for a product, service, or business by placing commercially significant news about it in a published medium or obtaining favorable presentation upon radio, television, or stage that is not paid for by an identified sponsor.

Publicity Types Consist of news releases, business feature articles, service feature articles, finance releases, product releases, pictorial releases, background editorial material, and emergency publicity.

Publics' Demand Refers to the characteristics and needs of employees, unions, stockholders, consumer groups, the general public, government agencies, and other internal and external forces that affect company operations.

Pulling Strategy Demand first generated through direct advertising to customers, then dealer support is obtained.

Purchase Act An exchange of money or a promise to pay for the acquisition of a product or service.

Pure Competition Situation with many firms selling identical products or services.

Pure Nonstandardized Approach An international marketing strategy that assumes that each market is different and requires a distinct market plan.

Pure Standardized Approach An international marketing strategy that assumes that all markets are similar and a uniform plan can be used.

Pushing Strategy Dealer support and cooperation first attained; then advertising is addressed to customers.

Question Mark See *Problem Child*.

Rack Jobber A wholesaler that furnishes the racks or shelves on which merchandise is displayed. The rack jobber owns the merchandise on its racks, selling the items on a consignment basis.

Railroad Usually carries heavy, bulky items that are low in value (relative to their weight) over long distances.

Raw Material An unprocessed primary industrial material from extractive and agricultural industries. Raw material is considered as an expense rather than a capital item.

Reach Refers to the number of viewers or readers in the audience.

Real Income Income adjusted for inflation.

Rebate A cash refund given directly from the manufacturer to the consumer in order to stimulate consumption.

Reciprocity A procedure by which organizational consumers select suppliers who agree to purchase goods and services as well as sell them.

Reference Group A group that influences a person's thoughts or actions.

Relative Product Failure Occurs when the company is able to make a profit on an item but the product does not attain profit objectives and/or adversely affects image.

Rented-Goods Service Involves the leasing of a product for a specified period of time.

Reorder Point Establishes the stock level at which new orders should be placed. The reorder point depends on order lead time, usage rate, and safety stock. The reorder point formula is

Reorder point = (Order lead time × Usage Rate) + (Safety stock).

Research Design The specified framework for controlling data collection. A research design includes decisions relating to the person collecting data, data to be collected, group of people or objects studied, data-collection techniques employed, study costs, method of data collection, length of study period and time, and location of data collection.

Retail Catalog Showroom A warehouse-type outlet at which consumers select merchandise from a catalog.

Retail Cooperative A format that allows independent

Subliminal Advertising Controversial technique that does not enable a consumer to consciously decode a message.

Substantiation Requires that a firm be able to prove all promotion claims it makes. This means thorough testing and evidence of performance are needed prior to making claims.

Supermarket A departmentalized food store with minimum annual sales of $2 million.

Superstore A large food-based retailer that is much more diversified than a supermarket.

Surcharges Used when the firm seeks to alter the prices of a number of items by a given percentage.

Survey The systematic gathering of information concerning attitudes, past purchases, and consumer characteristics from respondents by communicating with them in person, over the telephone, or by mail.

Systems Selling A combination of goods and services sold by a single source. This enables the buyer to have single-source accountability, one firm with which to negotiate, and assurance of the compatibility of various parts and components.

Tactic Specific action undertaken to implement a given strategy.

Target Market The defined customer group to which a firm appeals.

Target Pricing A cost-based pricing method in which prices are set to provide a specified rate of return on investment for a standard volume of production. Mathematically it is

Target price =
[(Investment costs × Target return on investment %)/Standard volume] +
(Average total costs at standard volume)

Tariff The most common form of trade restriction in which a tax is placed on imported goods by a foreign government.

Technology Refers to the development and use of machinery, products, and processes.

Terms The provisions of price agreements, including discounts, timing of payments, and credit arrangements.

Test Marketing Involves placing a product for sale in one or more selected areas and observing its sales performance under the proposed marketing plan. The purpose of test marketing is to evaluate the product and pretest the firm's marketing plan prior to a full-scale introduction of the product.

Time Expenditures Involve the types of activities in which a person participates and the amount of time allocated to them.

Total-Cost Approach Determines the distribution service level with the lowest total costs, including freight, warehousing, and the cost of lost business. The ideal system seeks a balance between low distribution costs and high opportunities for sales.

Trade Character A brand mark that is personified.

Trade Deficit Occurs when the value of imports exceeds the value of exports.

Trade Quota A form of trade restriction in which limits are set on the amount of goods that may be imported into a country.

Trademark A brand name, brand mark, trade character, or combination thereof that is legally protected under the Lanham Act of 1946. Exclusive rights are retained as long as the trademark is used.

Traditional Break-Even Analysis Determines the sales quantity (in units or dollars) at which total costs equal total revenues for a chosen price:

$$\frac{\text{Break-even point}}{\text{(units)}} = \frac{\text{Total fixed costs}}{\text{Price} - \text{Variable costs per unit}}$$

$$\frac{\text{Break-even point}}{\text{(sales dollars)}} = \frac{\text{Total fixed costs}}{1 - \dfrac{\text{Variable costs per unit}}{\text{Price}}}$$

Transportation Service Company Handles the shipments of moderate-sized packages. The three kinds of companies are government parcel post, private parcel service, and express service.

Truck/Wagon Wholesaler Has a regular sales route, offers items from a truck or wagon, and delivers goods as they are sold.

Two-Step Flow of Communication Theory stating that a message goes from the company to opinion leaders and then to the target market.

Unbundling Prices A strategy that breaks down prices by individual components. This allows customers to purchase services on an optional basis.

Uncontrollable Factors Those elements affecting an organization's performance that cannot be directed by the organization and its marketers. These include consumers, competition, government, the economy, technology, and independent media.

Unfair-Sales Acts Legislation in several states preventing retailers from selling merchandise for less than the cost of the product plus a fixed percentage that covers overhead and profit.

Unit Pricing Prices expressed per unit of measure as well as by total value.

Universal Product Code (UPC) Industrywide electronic system for coding information onto food and related merchandise. The UPC requires manufacturers to premark items with a series of thick and thin vertical lines; price and inventory data are contained but are not readable by employees and customers.

Unplanned Business District Site at which a group of stores are located in close proximity to one another; but the combination of stores is not based on prior planning. There are four types of unplanned business districts: central business district, secondary business district, neighborhood business district, and string.

Value Analysis A comparison of the benefits of different materials, components, and manufacturing processes in order to improve products, lower costs, or both.

Variability of Service Quality Due to the difficulty of diagnosing a problem (for repairs), the inability of the customer to verbalize his or her service needs, and the lack of standardization and mass production for most services.

Variable Markup Policy Different percentage markups assigned to separate categories of goods and services in response to differences in selling costs.

Variable Pricing Prices modified to coincide with fluctuations in costs or consumer demand. The same product or service may be priced at two or more levels based on the customer's ability to pay, service location, or time.

Variety Store Sells a wide assortment of low- and popularly priced merchandise.

Vending Machine Involves coin-operated machinery, eliminates the use of sales personnel, allows around-the-clock sales, and can be placed outside rather than inside a store.

Vendor Analysis The rating of specific suppliers in terms of quality (such as the per cent of defective merchandise), service (such as delivery speed and reliability), and price (such as credit and transportation terms).

Venture Team A small, independent department consisting of a broad range of specialists who manage a new product from idea generation to market introduction. Team members work on a full-time basis and function as a separate unit within the company.

Vertical Audit An in-depth analysis of one aspect of the firm's marketing strategy.

Vertical Price Fixing Occurs when manufacturers or wholesalers control the retail prices of their products or services. This practice is sometimes illegal.

Video-Shopping Services Can take one of three forms: electronic catalog shown on a video player, cable television system with telephone ordering, or cable television system with ordering through a personal computer.

Voluntary Simplicity A consumer life-style in which people seek material simplicity, have an ecological awareness, strive for self-determination, and purchase do-it-yourself products.

Warehouse Used to receive, identify, and sort merchandise. Both private and public warehouses are utilized.

Warranty An assurance given to consumers that a product will meet certain performance standards.

Waste The portion of a medium's audience that is not in the firm's target market.

Waterway Transportation that involves the movement of goods on barges via inland rivers and on tankers and general merchandise freighters through the Great Lakes, incoastal shipping, and the St. Lawrence Seaway.

Wearout Rate The period of time it takes for a message to lose its effectiveness.

Wheel of Retailing A theory describing how low-end (discount) strategies can turn into high-end (high price) strategies, thus providing opportunities for new firms to enter as discounters.

Wholesale Cooperative Owned by member firms to economize functions and offer broad support. There are producer-owned and retailer-owned wholesale cooperatives.

Wholesaler An organization or individual involved with wholesaling.

Wholesaling Encompasses the buying and handling of merchandise and its resale to retailers, organizational users, and/or other wholesalers but not the sale of significant volume to final consumers.

Width of Product Mix The number of different product lines a company has.

Word-of-Mouth Communication The process by which people express their opinions and product-related experiences to one another.

Name Index

A37

Subject Index

Asterisks indicate terms defined in glossary